The Palgrave Mac

Series Editors: **Akira Iriye**, Professor of History at Harvard University, and **Rana Mitter**, Profesor of the History and Politics af Modern China at the University of Oxford.

This distinguished series seeks to: develop scholarship on the transnational connections of societies and peoples in the nineteenth and twentieth centuries; provide a forum in which work on transnational history from different periods, subjects, and regions of the world can be brought together in fruitful connection; and explore the theoretical and methodological links between transnational and other related approaches such as comparative history and world history.

Editorial Board: **Thomas Bender**, University Professor of the Humanities, Professor of History, and Director of the International Center for Advanced Studies, New York University; **Jane Carruthers**, Professor of History, University of South Africa; **Mariano Plotkin**, Professor, Universidad Nacional de Tres de Febrero, Buenos Aires, and member of the National Council of Scientific and Technological Research, Argentina; **Pierre-Yves Saunier**, Researcher at the Centre National de la Recherche Scientifique, France and Visiting Professor at the University of Montreal; **Ian Tyrrell**, Professor of History, University of New South Wales.

Titles include:

Gregor Benton and Edmund Terence Gomez
THE CHINESE IN BRITAIN, 1800–PRESENT
Economy, Transnationalism, Identity

Sugata Bose and Kris Manjapra (*editors*)
COSMOPOLITAN THOUGHT ZONES
South Asia and the Global Circulation of Ideas

Sebastian Conrad and Dominic Sachsenmaier (*editors*)
COMPETING VISIONS OF WORLD ORDER
Global Moments and Movements, 1880s–1930s

Martin Conway and Kiran Klaus Patel (*editors*)
EUROPEANIZATION IN THE TWENTIETH CENTURY
Historical Approaches

Joy Damousi, Mariano Ben Plotkin (*editors*)
THE TRANSNATIONAL UNCONSCIOUS
Essays in the History of Psychoanalysis and Transnationalism

Desley Deacon, Penny Russell and Angela Woollacott (*editors*)
TRANSNATIONAL LIVES
Biographies of Global Modernity, 1700–present

Jonathan Gantt
IRISH TERRORISM IN THE ATLANTIC COMMUNITY, 1865–1922

Eric Hotta
PAN-ASIANISM AND JAPAN'S WAR, 1931–45

Martin Klimbe and Joachim Scharloth (*editors*)
1968 IN EUROPE
A History of Protest and Activism, 1956–77

Erika Kuhlman
RECONSTRUCTING PATRIARCHY AFTER THE GREAT WAR
Women, Gender and Postwar Reconciliation between Nations

Deep Kanta Lahiri Choudhury
TELEGRAPHIC IMPERIALISM
Crisis and Panic in the Indian Empire, c. 1830–1920

Bruce Mazlish
THE IDEA OF HUMANITY IN THE GLOBAL ERA

Glenda Sluga
THE NATION, PSYCHOLOGY, AND INTERNATIONAL POLITICS, 1870–1919

Mark Tilse
TRANSNATIONALISM IN THE PRUSSIAN EAST
From National Conflict to Synthesis, 1871–1914

The Palgrave Macmillan Transnational History Series
Series Standing Order ISBN 978–0–230–50746–3 Hardback
978–0–230–50747–0 Paperback
(*outside North America only*)

You can receive future titles in this series as they are published by placing a standing order. Please contact your bookseller or, in case of difficulty, write to us at the address below with your name and address, the title of the series and the ISBN quoted above.

Customer Services Department, Macmillan Distribution Ltd, Houndmills, Basingstoke, Hampshire RG21 6XS, England

The Chinese in Britain, 1800–Present

Economy, Transnationalism, Identity

Gregor Benton

Emeritus Professor of History, School of History and Archaeology, Cardiff University, UK

and

Edmund Terence Gomez

Faculty of Economics and Administration, University of Malaya, Malaysia

palgrave
macmillan

First published in hardback 2008 and in paperback 2011 by
PALGRAVE MACMILLAN

Palgrave Macmillan in the UK is an imprint of Macmillan Publishers Limited, registered in England, company number 785998, of Houndmills, Basingstoke, Hampshire RG21 6XS.

Palgrave Macmillan in the US is a division of St Martin's Press LLC, 175 Fifth Avenue, New York, NY 10010.

Palgrave Macmillan is the global academic imprint of the above companies and has companies and representatives throughout the world.

Palgrave® and Macmillan® are registered trademarks in the United States, the United Kingdom, Europe and other countries.

ISBN 978–0–230–52229–9 hardback
ISBN 978–0–230–29641–1 paperback

For Shen Yuanfang and Sharmani Gabriel

Contents

List of Illustrations

List of Tables

Series Editors' Foreword

This book magnificently fills a puzzling gap: until now, there has been no full, historically grounded study of one of Britain's most important, if smaller, migrant communities: the Chinese. Covering the ground from 1800 to present day, the authors have combined historical research of great depth and rigour with an analysis that questions received wisdoms, and refuses to accept easy answers about the nature of an immigrant population's relationship with the country in which it settles.

This book is a welcome addition to our series in transnational history, for it has something powerful to say to both parts of the series description. For historians of Britain and China alike, there is plenty here to shatter assumptions about the history of either of those countries being enclosed within borders. How many readers will have known about the Chinese presence at the Normandy landings, the moment of Europe's deliverance from tyranny, for which the Chinese were praised at the time, only to be forgotten and discarded a few years later by racist British immigration law? How well known are the attempts by both the Nationalist and the Communist parties to place activists in groups not only in Britain but in a variety of other European countries in the 1920s and 1930s?

The book makes powerful and provocative challenges to the field of transnational studies. The authors stress the importance of historicizing our understanding of transnational phenomena, saying that 'a major shortcoming of transnational studies is their failure to work more consistently in historical depth, without which diasporic communities cannot be fully grasped'. The book questions the nature of ethnic identities proposed by more present-centred analyses of transnationalism among overseas Chinese communities. As it points out, there are clear cross-border influences that have shaped the Chinese community in Britain, such as information from the larger Chinese–American community, whose experiences were reported and transmitted to their British counterparts. However, other frameworks which undermine the idea of a monolithic national or ethnic identity, such as class or provincial differences, have also shaped the community in notable ways. Not all readers will agree completely with the arguments made here, but at the same time, they will undoubtedly have to engage with the depth and seriousness of the scholarship that underpins them. This series takes pride in taking transnational studies forward by publishing a work which questions key tenets of transnationalism as a framework: for as in other elements of the scholarly enterprise, it is only through such questioning that the sharpness and usefulness of such theoretical frameworks can be maintained, rather than simply becoming a new orthodoxy. Furthermore, we welcome this book as it takes its place as the state-of-the-art study of the Chinese experience in Britain.

Rana Mitter

Akira Iriye

Oxford, February 2007

Preface and Acknowledgements

This book is the outcome of nearly a decade of collaboration and friendship. The ideas that animate it can be traced back to 1996, when we won funding from the British Academy for a study on the Chinese economy in contemporary Britain (carried out by Gomez). Our primary interest was to find out whether or to what extent culture and shared identities determined the economic activities of ethnic communities, in this case Britain's Chinese community. This aim sprang from our concern that numerous theories based on essentialised patterns of enterprise development among minority Chinese communities in various national contexts were beginning to gain currency. These studies tended not only to homogenise the business styles of Chinese communities of the diaspora but brought into question their claim to national identity in their countries of residence. We felt that a corrective to these studies was needed, as they dangerously distorted the processes of identity formation, particularly the emergence of national affiliations and identification within immigrant groups and their descendants. Some of these ideas were first developed in Gomez's study on the economic history of the Chinese in Malaysia.

Our ideas on the links between culture, identity, economy, and transnationalism were broadened in 2000 when we began a comparative study on Chinese economy and society in Europe, Southeast Asia, and Australia, as part of the Transnational Communities programme run by the Economic and Social Research Council (ESRC Award No. L214252046). In 1999, Benton received funding (from the AHRC) for a study on the history of Chinese settlements in Western Europe that also tackled these issues. These projects have resulted in numerous publications, listed in the bibliography under Benton or Gomez or both.

While the ESRC and AHRC projects were underway, Benton proposed a book on the 200-year history of Chinese migrations to Britain to show that Chinese migrants to the United Kingdom had come from different regions in Asia, to capture identity shifts over time, and to trace how these different identities served to divide more than unify this community. Benton intended his research to encompass several related topics, including the early economy of these migrant communities, their social, cultural, and political institutions and transnational activities, the ethnic identifications of ethnic Chinese born and raised in Britain, and the causes and effects of British sinophobia. Our earlier research findings and writings helped clarify issues central to the present volume, enriched it factually and conceptually, and provided some illuminating comparative perspectives. We collaborated on the book's theoretical framework and on formulating its research questions and methods. Benton researched and produced Chapter 2, Chapters 4 to 7, and the historical section of Chapter 3, which deals with the economy in the period before Chinese immigrants and ethnic Chinese began joining the professions and the business mainstream in large numbers; and he collected the photographs. We jointly wrote those parts of Chapter 3 which deal with the contemporary non-catering sector, largely on the basis of Gomez's research. We also co-authored Chapters 1 and 8. Those chapters authored solely by Benton benefited from Gomez's commentary and input and drew on our earlier publications on ethnic and migrant Chinese in Britain and other countries. In that sense, the book is a collaborative undertaking throughout.

We would like to thank a number of people who helped us with this volume. The ideas for it were first formulated when we were both based at the Department of East Asian Studies in Leeds University. Flemming Christiansen helped prepare the proposal for the ESRC project and provided in-depth comments on the manuscript. We would also like to acknowledge the help and support of Don Rimmington, Delia Davin, Penelope Francks, and Tom Wingfield, all members of the Department of East Asian Studies when we first began formulating our ideas for this study, and of Steve Vertovec and Jeffrey Henderson, leaders of the Transnational Communities programme. The issues raised in the volume have been presented at numerous conferences and seminars over the past decade. We are grateful to colleagues at these meetings for helping us refine our arguments. The staff at Companies House were extremely helpful when Gomez sought their advice for his research on business enterprises in the United Kingdom owned by ethnic Chinese. We would also like to thank the businesspeople and members of the Chinese Chamber of Commerce in the United Kingdom who kindly consented to be interviewed. Deng Lilan of Nankai University spent some time at Cardiff University working with Benton on the history of Chinese transnationalism in Britain, and provided much useful data that Benton incorporated into the study. (Deng Lilan's stay in Britain was funded by the Sino-British Fellowship Trust and the K. C. Wong Fellowship scheme.) Benton also visited the Overseas Chinese Office in Tianmen, Hubei. Finally, Benton would like to acknowledge the support of his friends and colleagues in the School of History and Archaeology at Cardiff University, where much of the book was written.

The research was done at the libraries of the London School of Economics, the School of Oriental and African Studies, Leeds University, Liverpool University, and Manchester University; the archives sections of Bethnal Green Public Library, Liverpool Public Library, Manchester Central Library, and Cardiff Central Library; the Public Records Office and the British Library; the Tower Hamlets Local History Archive; the National Archives of Singapore; the Hong Kong Public Records Office; the National Library of Australia; the National Museum of Labour History, Manchester; the Modern Records Centre at Warwick University; the Working Class Movement Library at Salford; the Institute for Social History in Amsterdam; the Gemeentearchief in Amsterdam; the Centre de Recherches sur la Chine Moderne et Contemporaine, the EHESS Centre Chine, and the Bibliothèque Inter-universitaire des Langues Orientales in Paris; Prato's Centro di Ricerca, Documentazione, Servizi per la Comunità Cinese; Beijing Library and Shanghai Library; and the Free China Centre in London.

Other individuals who helped in various ways include Bobby Chan, Graham Chan, Thomas Chan, Chen Yandong, James Chin, Jenny Clegg, Charles Foley, Judith Gordon, Polly Green, Mary Heidhues, Jiang Guowei, Barbara King, Richard Kirby, Jabez Lam, Tony Lane, Kam Lee, Tong Soon Lee, Li Wei, Rubin Lien, Andrew Potter, Bill Shang, Shen Yuanfang, Wilfred Sng, Pamela So, Frank Soo, Dylan Sung, Kenny Tam, Harry Tharp, Geoff Wade, Wan Hong, Ian Welch, Wen Liangsheng, Ye Zhen, and Zhou Nanjing. To all of them, our grateful thanks.

We are grateful to Akira Iriye and Rana Mitter, editors of Palgrave's Transnational History series, for recommending this study for publication. We thank Michael Strang, History publisher at Palgrave, for submitting our manuscript to the series editors for review and Ruth Ireland for preparing it for publication. We are extremely indebted to Padma Narayanan, a most gracious Project Manager at Integra, who dealt patiently with our many questions and problems when the manuscript was being copyedited.

1
Introduction

This book traces successive waves of Chinese migration to Britain from the early nineteenth century through to the present and assesses the economic and social standing of Chinese in this country over the past two centuries and more. By the beginning of the twenty-first century, a new generation of British-born Chinese had emerged that can be classified as middle class in terms of educational qualifications and earning capacity, a development that reflects the community's greatly improved economic position.[1] The emergence of this new generation of British Chinese – together with similar developments in other ethnic minorities – has generated new debates about the implications for British society of 'identity change' among migrants and their descendants.[2]

In spite of their entry into mainstream society and economy, British-born Chinese are still commonly viewed by white British as 'outsiders', 'migrants', or members of a 'diaspora' who occupy 'spaces' in British society. This style of reasoning is strongly connected to studies that depict Chinese in Britain as a transnational community, constantly on the move across national borders, rather than as a constituent of the British nation.

The book presents a meta-narrative of the social and economic history of the Chinese in Britain. It strives to capture the past and present experiences of the community at the grassroots. Economic and social transitions and different waves of Chinese migration have contributed to the development of multiple and overlapping identities in the community. At first a largely disenfranchised group without much education or skills and employed primarily in catering and laundering, much of the community today is highly educated, socially mobile, and increasingly represented in the professions and the hi-tech sector. Transnational Chinese companies, predominantly from Asia, are prominent in various

1

sectors of the British economy, including manufacturing, port services, hotels, banking, and retailing.[3]

The different waves of Chinese migration over the past two centuries resulted in the arrival of different types of ethnic Chinese, in terms of place of origin and class background. What sectors did these migrants look for jobs in? What economic fields did the entrepreneurs among them venture into as they sought ways of surviving in an alien setting? What communal and political associations did they form? How far did such institutions adopt a transnational approach, so that they could maintain ties with the Chinese homeland and preserve their culture, language, and identity? How did institutions evolve and how far did they help reinforce ethnic-Chinese identity in the long term? To what extent have new generations of Chinese distinguished themselves in terms of ethnic and national identity from the migrant generation? In what ways have members of the migrant cohort become ethnically distinct from their kin in the homeland after a long period of settlement in Britain? Why do such differentiations happen? Has social mobility and generational change led to 'ethnic passing', that is, to the decline of a strong Chinese identity?

By asking these questions and focusing on the issues of migration, association-building, community-building, and enterprise development, we show that transnational politics, business, and social organisation happen at multiple levels. The Chinese in Britain are divided along numerous lines, including lines of class and sub-ethnic difference, evident in the intra-ethnic relations among Chinese in the labour market and in relevant economic sectors. These cleavages hinder attempts by Chinese to mobilise collectively against the discrimination and racism they have met in Britain.

A study of migration patterns and community formation among the Chinese and an analysis of their changing social and economic profile form the basis for our analysis of identity formation among members of this small yet diverse population. Their associations and economic activities show how they relate to British society and how the white population impinges on their world. This dual approach also yields insights into issues raised by transnational studies concerning the organisation of capital flows and identity formation among migrants and diasporic individuals.

Among the fundamental factors that determine the decision to migrate and shape identity among migrants and their descendants are state policies and socio-economic conditions. By looking at the state and its policies and at societal relations between native British and

Chinese migrants and their descendants, we identify key factors in identity formation or re-formation. While social and economic conditions persuaded ethnic Chinese from predominantly Asian countries to migrate to and settle in Britain, state policies have had a major impact on inter- and intra-ethnic relations and forms of identity. We use a structural and historical perspective to analyse Chinese social and transnational networks, including community associations, business tie-ups, ways in which these linkages have evolved, and the impact they have had on intra- and inter-ethnic relations. Concentrating on Chinese social and economic activities at the grassroots, both within and beyond Britain, permits us to take into account the specific historical circumstances that shaped the community's evolution and to assess the impact on it of state policies.[4] This mode of analysis brings into focus the rapid changes that Chinese societies in Britain are undergoing – changes to which the British state and white majority have so far failed to adapt.

Transnationalism, a concept much in vogue in studies on ethnic minorities, has given rise to scholarship that claims major theoretical insights into how common ethnicity helps engender global flows of capital and information through international business networks and influences enterprise development. Transnational studies on Chinese and Indians posit a pan-ethnic unity in these diasporas that promotes interlocking economic and social ties and facilitates the development of their enterprises around the globe. New means of communication have supposedly fortified these transnational networks, reputedly a key characteristic of 'ethnic capitalism'.[5]

While transnational studies assume a high degree of diasporic identity,[6] our historical perspective reveals profound differences in ethnic communities, both within and beyond national boundaries. We show how state policies and public discourses on ethnicity sustain, undermine, or re-invent notions of ethnic and national identity. Immigration laws, for example, have played a crucial role in influencing identity formation among British Chinese. British immigration legislation has transformed Chinese patterns of kinship and homeland ties. When migrants were allowed to import their families, they stopped returning to their places of origin and began to see Britain as their home.

By adopting the host country as 'home', migrants throw into question core arguments of transnational studies. Ethnic minorities that have lived in a country for more than one generation are even more resistant to the transnational label. To apply it indiscriminately can diminish the notion of national identity among people who do not continue to cross borders and reinforce stereotypes in the majority community about ethnic minorities' supposed lack of a sense of loyalty or belonging to the country they live in. In short, transnational theories have little to say about transformations of identity and the emergence of new forms of national identity.

To discover how Chinese define themselves and how others define them, we look at the links between members of the Chinese community in Britain and abroad. We contest transnational theories that homogenise migrants of the same ethnic background. Instead, we stress the differences among the Chinese, differences upon which new identities form and reform in a seemingly inexhaustible cycle. While they may all belong to the same ethnic group, Chinese do not have the uniform features ascribed to them by transnational theory.

In line with this observation, we note an absence of community among the Chinese in Britain of the sort bonded by ethnic identity. In so far as an ascriptive community exists, it is divided by class, language, place of origin, period of arrival, and reason for coming, as well as by physical segregation within Britain. Not all Chinese come from China, Hong Kong, or Taiwan. They lack common genealogies or symbols, boundary markers of an ethnic community with shared identities. They lack the bonds of a common religion, unlike South Asians of the Muslim and Hindu faiths. Instead, the community is heterogeneous and individual identities are increasingly hybridised.

Chinese migrants to Britain over the past 200 years have found different ways of coping with their new environment, depending on the overall context and the opportunities available at the point of migration. In view of their differences, they rarely aspire to congruence. The numerous social and economic institutions that represent their interests, few of which survive for more than a few months or years, are evidence of their collective incoherence. Most of their historic associations have been fraught with divisions and ceased to operate. However, this diversity has not, on the whole, been recognised, either by host institutions or social scientists.

Paradoxically, while the Chinese lack distinctiveness and communality, they are made to feel as if they were a unified whole by the way in which the white majority views them. State policies are another reason for this paradox. Governments have shown little understanding of the issue of generational change and social mobility among Chinese, whose largely uneducated parents have raised children whose educational achievements have allowed them to climb quickly up the class ladder. This mobility strongly influences identity formation among the new generation, whose self-view, in terms of national identity, differs strikingly from that of their migrant parents.

The problem with transnationalism

Transnationalism is an emergent, rather ill-defined field whose distinguishing features Alejandro Portes and others have tried to fix. Following Robert Merton's three conditions for 'establishing a phenomenon', they confine the term 'transnational' to activities that involve 'a significant proportion of persons in the relevant universe' (principally, immigrants and their hometown reciprocators), are stable and regular rather than fleeting or spasmodic, and differ in content from activities captured by existing concepts such as immigration (the transnational migrants' contacts across national borders were sustained and regular, those of the immigrants were erratic).[7]

The history of the transnational concept is relatively short. Writing about capitalism and transnationalism, Masao Miyoshi drew attention in 1993 to the evolution of 'multi*national*' corporations into '*trans*national' corporations, able through their international web of investment networks to operate across national borders. In drawing this distinction, Miyoshi argued that a TNC, unlike an MNC, 'might no longer be tied to its nation of origin but is adrift and mobile, ready to settle anywhere and to exploit any state including its own, as long as the affiliation serves its own interests'.[8] Manuel Castells, on the other hand, noted that MNCs 'down-size' by outsourcing jobs as a way of lowering production costs.[9] This outsourcing has led to the development of 'network enterprise' in which a densely interlocking group of firms engages in a range of industries and operates in different countries.

Castells' formulation of 'networks' is similar to Gary Gereffi's concept of 'global commodity chains', in which production networks connect a large number of different enterprises.[10] The networks are designed to cut costs, improve the quality of goods, and smoothe the way to innovation. Castells, however, places greater emphasis on the impact of new technologies and the rise of the 'informational society' as a driving force behind the development of these networks. In the case of Chinese firms, he makes the relatively nuanced argument that most such enterprises are family-owned and the production ties they engender are highly personalised, fluid, and mutable.[11] However, he exaggerates the extent to which companies owned by family members are represented in such networks. In reality, most include firms owned by people outside the family circle.

At around the same time, Linda Basch, Glick Schiller, and Blanc-Szanton (writing about Caribbean and Filipino migrants to the United States) pointed up the complexity of the concept of migrant 'belonging'. They argued that the term 'transnationalism' as previously employed by social scientists lacked specificity and failed to recognise that immigrants develop ideologies, lifestyles, and networks that span homeland and host society. Defining transnationalism as 'the processes by which immigrants forge and sustain multi-stranded social relations that link together their societies of origin and settlement', they maintained that immigrants tend to 'develop and maintain multiple relationships – familial, economic, social, organizational, religious, and political – that span borders'.[12] Basch and her colleagues concentrate on the rights of individuals within nation states in an age of growing cross-border movement by corporations and people, though their focus is on migrant communities rather than long-settled communities with several generations of descendants.

The several types and levels of transnational relationship, ranging from the informal and affective to the highly institutionalised, interact and overlap to the point where distinctions blur. Affective relationships with family or kin in the hometown or sending village can intersect with economic and political ties. Transnational cultural practices stretch from émigrés' private consumption of homeland cultural products and their public staging in exile of homeland cultural events to the activities of the transnational media. Politically, transnationals can engage from abroad in homeland affairs, but they can also recruit the ancestral state or other diasporic outposts into supporting their own expatriate interest against threats from the host state or society. In a few cases, transnational dissentients can try to win the support of the host state or society for political campaigns against the homeland state. As technology speeds the globalisation of politics, diasporas become politically more vocal, at either end of the migration process and in the globally dispersed interspaces. Economic transnationalism is mainly the province of big corporations, but members of ethnic groups are also players in the world economy, by virtue of their remittances to and investments in the homelands. Governments know the worth of this inward flow and play on the ethnic loyalty of 'nationals' abroad to gain access to their capital. Economic resources flow through diasporic networks as well as to the homeland. Homeland resources can also flow abroad with expatriate help.[13]

Much new scholarship sees transnational migration as the product of recent shifts in society, economy, and technology. For Portes et al., historical examples of economic transnationalism are rare and usually 'of an élite type'. They include trade diasporas (like the early Chinese cross-border traders in Southeast Asia) whose members 'self-consciously preserved their distinct identities' and the circular labour migrations of the nineteenth century (the workers stayed abroad only briefly and relied on home-country networks). Early political transnationalism (usually the championing of a nascent homeland state) is deemed rarer still. According to Portes et al., the preconditions for normative transnationalism – the rich countries' growing demand for migrant labour (a thing of the relatively recent past) and the rise of new forms of transport and space-compressing technologies that facilitate international communications (more recent still) – were not yet available to earlier immigrants. Transnational relations were exceptional because they were unsupported by the 'thick web of regular instantaneous communication and easy personal travel that we encounter today'.[14]

Today, processes such as globalisation, the technological revolution in the means of transport and communications, political changes in society as a result of decolonisation or the universalisation of human rights, and the spatial expansion of social networks 'from below', which aid cross-border migration and trade, are said to have transformed immigration to the point where immigration studies can be reconstituted as transnational studies. The growth in transport and communications allows family and kinship ties to move 'from a local to a global scale where they have been reproduced and extended'. The growth in the volume of remittances 'has now become so important that in many cases they determine the development prospects of villages, towns and entire regions'. As the kin-based economic transactions multiply, 'the "home" and "host" societies dissolve into one another'.[15]

Some studies use 'globalisation' and 'transnationalism' more or less interchangeably. In their book on Fujianese migrants, for example, Frank Pieke, Pál Nyíri, Mette Thunø, and Antonella Ceccagno adopt the term 'Chinese globalization' (although they title their volume *Transnational Chinese*). Defining 'Chinese globalization' as 'multiple, transnational social spaces straddling and embedded in diversifying smaller regional or national systems on the one hand, and, on the other hand, as a part of a unifying global system', they argue that due to China's growing presence in the global economy, even migrants with only a distant memory of the 'fatherland' or who would like to dissociate themselves from it find that China 'is rapidly integrating itself into the fabric of their daily life'. They therefore treat 'transnationalism' as an 'empirical issue' and try to trace Chinese globalisation 'by mapping the transnational social spaces opened up by mobility, work, settlement, and political involvement of a particular category of Chinese international migrants'.[16] This way of conceptualising Chinese globalisation has two drawbacks: it focuses on recent migrants, who by definition have strong ties with China; and it credits the Chinese state with an influence over migrants, both recent and long-established, that is probably exaggerated. Once having left their country of origin behind, few migrants are strongly influenced by the outlook and rhetoric of its authorities. State leaders have tried to influence the Chinese diaspora by helping to establish and support cultural and business associations in European and other countries, but these organisations hardly matter to most migrants, unless they derive some benefit from participating in them.

Since Pieke et al. understand the concept of Chinese globalisation primarily in relation to migration, the experience of migrants in a global environment, and the 'spaces' they create for themselves in order to cope with settling into a new country, they resort far too readily to the term 'transnationalism'. Transnational studies provide a clear definition of this term, which invites in-depth interrogation.

A transnational community is a social formation best exemplified by ethnic diasporas. It has three dimensions: its globally dispersed self, the states it inhabits, and its ancestral homeland.[17] Researchers claim that such networks work at the level of the diaspora as a whole as well as in its separate 'homelands' (ancestral and adopted), and that new technologies connect them 'with increasing speed and efficiency'.[18] Many assume that institutionalised ethnic networks permit diasporic co-ethnics to move capital across national boundaries. Examples can be found in the triumphalist discourses of Chinese capitalism, which maintain that the creation of intra-ethnic business networks based on a sense of group cohesion facilitates the movement of funds across borders and the mutually beneficial pooling of resources in enterprise development.[19]

Ludger Pries argues that Guarnizo and Smith provide two important insights into the nature of transnationalism. First, it is not a 'boundless or deterritorialized social phenomenon'. Second, its social practices are not merely transitory, like the 'ambiguous and contradictory social integration' of first-generation immigrants. The identity of transmigrants is not free-floating but an emergent 'embedding and disembedding in different social spaces'.[20]

Although studies are careful to avoid depicting transnational processes as wholly new and allow for earlier instances, they often magnify the element of novelty. Glick Schiller et al., in their seminal article, called for a 'new conceptualization' of this 'new field of social relations' and draw a sharp distinction between the earlier immigrant, who 'evokes images of permanent rupture', and the 'new migrant population'.[21] Others who allow that contemporary transnationalism may have precedents in the 'high' period of the nation state nevertheless emphasise the concept's emergent character.

Older scholarship, in contrast, holds that ties and identities of an essentially transnational character are not a late twentieth-century innovation but have regularly marked out the immigrant generation, after whose demise an assimilationist trend takes hold and transnationalism falls into disuse and eventual oblivion. Adam McKeown, while agreeing with many of the tenets of transnational studies, also questions the narrow time-frame within which they are usually confined and sets out to write a longer history of Chinese transnational practices. A major shortcoming of transnational studies is their failure to work more consistently in historical depth, without which diasporic communities cannot be fully grasped.

Other issues raised in theoretical writing about transnational communities include the medium through which ties are realised (the network, dynamised by new communication technologies) and the 'consciousness' they engender (one marked by multiple identifications, cultural fluidity, and creolisation or hybridity). We explore aspects of economic networking in the chapter on the British Chinese economy. In other chapters, we extend our analysis to non-economic practices. We also look at the role played by class and cultural difference in forming transnational communities (McKeown criticises transnational studies for homogenising migrants and emphasising the autonomy of global processes) and at the impact of transnationalism on consciousness and identifications.

The above theories and approaches provide a framework for distinguishing between different types of transnationalism, tracing its evolution through time, and measuring its past and present extent. The hypothesis that normative transnationalism depends on certain prerequisites (principally, the power of modern electronics) and the conflicting perspectives of transnationalists and assimilationists are matters that we also try to clarify.

A fundamental distinction is between grassroots and top-down transnationalism – what Luis Guarnizo calls transnationalism 'from below' and 'from above'.[22] Under grassroots transnationalism we count local-place ties (formal and informal), remigration across national borders, some forms of trade unionism and low-level political activity, and other sorts of initiatives taken by ordinary immigrants in league with their counterparts in the homeland or elsewhere overseas. Top-down transnationalism includes activities by embassies, states, churches, the press, and business corporations.

Between these two extremes of top and bottom lies a less clear-cut halfway field. Hometown associations, for example, sometimes start from a plebeian base but branch out into ever grander forms that are exploited by homeland states and political parties. In some cases, they are captured into larger bodies by the call of patriotism, or by personal or sub-ethnic ties transmuted into political loyalties. In other cases, the prospect of jobs and fame attracts self-promoting individuals who see Chinatown's status hierarchy as parochial and stunted and prefer to strut on wider political stages. Protest movements or political campaigns that emerge spontaneously in Chinatown sometimes join forces with home-land political parties or international parties (like the Comintern). Other movements were the product of such parties' agitation. The trade unions formed by migrant and transnational workers, especially seafarers, are also Janus-faced – they look inwards to local class-based communities and their issues, outwards to the global seaborne fellowship and its distant ports and hometowns.

These perspectives provide the framework for this study on the Chinese community in Britain. In their reader on diasporas and transna-tionalism, Vertovec and Cohen note that the 'lineaments and links' they make require elaboration and specificity: 'Which state and which transnational groups are we examining and over what period?'[23] In the following chapters, we try to meet this criterion of specificity. At the same time, like McKeown, we look into the longer history of Chinese transnationalism.

In so doing, we confront a popular narrative about Chinese business that has grown up in reciprocal interaction with transnational studies. According to the exponents of this narrative, contemporary Chinese capitalism has distinctive characteristics that facilitate its growth. Chinese culture and value systems determine decision-making among firms owned by Chinese, while intra-ethnic networks based on trust and kinship ties help reduce transaction costs and diminish risks.[24] These business networks are said to be tightly knit and embedded in inter-locking ownership and interlocking directorships with strong ethnic and solidaristic dimensions. A failing that many such studies share with transnational theories is that they treat Chinese as a homogenous and monolithic group.

While transnational studies assume a high degree of diasporic identity, an emergent body of literature argues that ethnic identity is of little importance in national and transnational business transactions.[25] True, ethnicity can be used by politicians to justify state policies and endeavours (at the national level) and to promote trade and business (at the international level). However, in neither case is there much evidence that common ethnicity helps unify a community or promotes economic pursuits, with or without state support. New migrants employ ethnic identity strategically in their host societies to get jobs in firms run by co-ethnics, establish businesses with other immigrants, or venture into economic sectors that provide goods or services of an 'ethnic' kind, for example, in the catering domain. However, these co-ethnic ties seldom survive once businesses begin to embed themselves in their new environment and new generations emerge.

Aihwa Ong 翁爱华 sets out in her work on transnationalism to 'reorient the study of Chinese subjects' by means of the concept of 'flexible citizenship'. She argues that 'global capitalism in Asia is linked to new cultural representations of "Chineseness" (rather than "Japaneseness") in relation to transnational Asian capitalism'. In her view, 'overseas Chinese' and mainland China are becoming ever more closely tied in production, trade, and finance 'circuits' that generate a form of 'fraternal network capitalism' or 'Chinese capitalism'. These ties are said to have 'induced long-assimilated Thai and Indonesian subjects to reclaim their "ethnic Chinese" status as they participate in regional business networks'.[26] But Ong fails to ask whether these long-assimilated Thais and Indonesians are not instead, as business investors, using their ethnic identity to facilitate investment in China. In our view, such investment does not result from an atavistic impulse but is usually made in response to political exhortation by state authorities. Ong's thesis, on the other hand, suggests that all ethnic Chinese in Southeast Asia, even the 'long-assimilated', celebrate as well as profit from the supposed rise of 'Chinese capitalism' in Asia.

This tripartite link between transnationalism, capital, and identity is explained most lucidly by Aihwa Ong and Donald Nonini in their *Ungrounded Empires: The Cultural Politics of Modern Chinese Transnationalism*.[27] Ong and Nonini argue that in the course of the transnational experience, Chinese migrants develop a 'third culture', defined as a 'modern Chinese transnationalism' that 'provides alternative visions in late capitalism to Western modernity and generates new and distinctive social arrangements, cultural discourses, practices, and subjectivities'. This culture includes the deployment of economic strategies such as the family firm and networks of social relations (or *guanxi* 关系) as a means of accumulating capital.[28]

Ong and Nonini point up the strength of the state in Asia and its capacity to control 'globalisation'. They make the case that much of the 'new capitalism of the Asia-Pacific is state-driven and state-sponsored'. However, their argument that 'modern Chinese transnationalism is expanding ever more rapidly across the Asia Pacific and indeed launching the capitalist development of China itself' is hard to sustain, for while Chinese-owned firms in East and Southeast Asia have invested in the mainland, it is an exaggeration to suggest they have generated China's economic expansion over the past decade.

Some of Ong and Nonini's other contentions are similarly dubious. These include their assertion that 'Chinese transnational capitalists act out flexible strategies of accumulation in networks that cut across political borders and are linked through second-tier global cities such as Shanghai, Guangzhou (Canton), Hong Kong, Taipei, Singapore, Bangkok, and Kuala Lumpur. These overlapping business, social, and kinship networks stitch together dynamic, productive, financial, and marketing regions that are not contained by a single-nation or subject to its influence'. In the same study, they suggest that 'diasporic capitalist interests can subvert state disciplining by transferring economic capital out of their host countries to overseas locations, and thus act to transform national economies under the rubric of "market forces"'.[29] On the one hand, they exaggerate the role played by Chinese-owned capital in driving the East Asian economic boom; on the other hand, they minimise the capacity of the state to discipline Chinese capitalists and exaggerate the capitalists' ability to transfer their assets across borders. Their claim that Chinese capitalists in the region act through tightly knit ethnic 'networks' as a dynamo for economic growth in Asia is wrong in two respects. By linking transnationalism, identity, and capitalism, it tends both to essentialise patterns of enterprise development among Chinese and to homogenise diasporic communities.

Theorising such a tripartite linkage essentialises capitalism and intra-ethnic business networks. Gordon Redding and Gary Hamilton[30] have been the most vocal proponents of the growing transnational impact of Chinese businesses and networks (though they do not write within the framework of transnational theory). Studies on ethnic enterprise, particularly the work of Ivan Light and Roger Waldinger, have taken the essentialising of Chinese-owned enterprises even further. Huntington's[31] theories about the 'clash of civilizations' and concepts like 'bamboo networks'[32] and the 'Chinese commonwealth'[33] are the most extreme examples of the homogenising of ethnic communities and culture.

The idea that Chinese diasporans have a strong collective identity that influences their business style and the development of their enterprises has given rise to a prodigious literature sometimes called the 'culturalist perspective'.[34] Its proponents, who favour an old-fashioned anthropological approach, argue that members of ethnic groups share patterns of values, behaviour, and cognition that distinguish them from other such communities. Anthropologists and economic geographers assume a typically Chinese pattern of enterprise development. Diasporic Chinese enterprise is, in essence, said everywhere to have the same 'ethnic style', namely family firms and intra-ethnic business networks. The family firm and intra-ethnic national and transnational social connections and networks play a crucial role in capital formation and accumulation. These two modes of business and social organisation are central to the 'Confucian ethic', a perennial theme and key explanatory tool for analysts of Chinese enterprise who think culture matters a lot.

Few scholars would disagree that family and kinship ties are a key constituent of Chinese enterprise.[35] It is commonly accepted that kinship ties are an important consideration in hiring staff and acquiring funds in the initial stages of enterprise formation. At the point of its creation, a firm is usually under the control of its founder and his close relatives, who play a crucial role in setting its style of management. (It should be added that this phenomenon is not uniquely Chinese.)[36]

The argument about 'networks' is more contentious. Redding, for example, maintains that Chinese networks in Taiwan and Hong Kong share commonalities that indicate 'cultural predispositions, most of which are traceable to Confucian values'.[37] Supporters of this view argue that Chinese enterprise is a form of 'network capitalism' or *'guanxi* capitalism'.[38] Networks are said to be a unique institutional feature of 'Asian capitalism', one that distinguishes it from the Western notion of bureaucratisation and efficiency.[39] This form of capitalism supposedly provides Chinese firms in Southeast Asia with major competitive advantages.[40]

Others go even further, and talk about 'Chinese diaspora capitalism'. Lever-Tracy and Tracy argue that this form of capitalism is based on personalised, long-term horizontal networks that bind together Chinese-owned family companies. These networks are 'embedded in relations of reciprocity' and rest on the principle of trust. This type of capitalism is said to pre-date 'modern capitalism' and to attach less weight than other forms of capitalism to corporate expansion and maximising profit.[41]

Few scholars would deny the existence of 'networks' created by Chinese-owned enterprises. The main problem for critics of the 'culturalist perspective' is not the idea of networks as such but the notion of 'Chineseness', which in the critics' opinion plays only a minor role in determining how Chinese businesspeople make decisions and develop their enterprises.[42] In the critics' view, culturalist analyses misrepresent the basis for and extent of business ties among Chinese firms. Networks do not form in a single dimension but primarily comprise chains of producers or sub-contractors that operate at multiple levels and whose membership changes over time. Co-ethnic cooperation for the benefit of the community, the basis according to the culturalist analysis on which such networks form, fails to explain these ties.

The history of ethnic-Chinese communities in Southeast Asia suggests that triadic-style definitions of transnationalism apply (if at all) only to migrants.[43] Even the identity and national allegiance of some longer-settled members of the migrant cohort undergo a profound reconfiguration. This transformation is evident in the rising number of immigrants that seek and secure political office in Australia, Canada, the United States, and Britain.[44] The Chinese communities in Southeast Asia provide the most interesting examples of the complexity of ethnic and national identity, its evolution over time, its reconfigurations in the context of political and economic change, and the erosion of migrant solidarity and cohesion.

Unlike Southeast Asia, Britain has been receiving ethnic-Chinese migrants more or less uninterruptedly since the nineteenth century. New arrivals constantly replenished the Chinese community, but added to its complexity and cleavages. The cleavages, based on place of origin, class difference, generational difference, and sub-ethnic difference, stand in the way of a pan-Chinese identity. Moreover, ethnic Chinese lack an equivalent of Islam, which helps to some extent to unify Muslim migrants of different ethnic backgrounds.

At the turn of the twentieth century, the number of Chinese in Britain was small. Most were seafarers who had deserted their ships or been abandoned by their employers after landing in British ports. In the 1880s, some Chinese migrants fled the United States during an anti-Chinese campaign and settled in Britain, where they started up businesses based on their experience in America. There is little evidence that these 'double migrants' established close ties with Britain's longer-standing Chinese community. By the middle of the twentieth century, the community was on the point of extinction, and would probably have melted into the larger community but for the arrival of tens of thousands of Hong Kong Chinese starting in the 1950s.

The diminished sense of ethnic cohesion among Chinese is evident from the manner in which ethnic-Chinese-owned firms have developed in Britain, where starting up businesses was one of the main ways in which Chinese coped with their limited ability to find employment in an essentially alien, English-speaking environment. They forged business partnerships to overcome the problem of limited funds and a limited supply of labour. As these businesses (usually in the catering sector) grew, so too did the demand for labour, which entrepreneurs met by exploiting kinship ties and importing family members into Britain. The partnerships broke up and evolved into family firms, thus reinforcing the trend away from community-based enterprise. Competition escalated, since most migrants were engaged in the same sector.

This competition necessitated the community's dispersal and further hindered attempts to struggle collectively for better protection by the authorities against the racism the immigrants encountered. The experience of racism forced them ever deeper into the 'ethnic niche', consisting mainly of restaurants and takeaways, thus heightening the competition and placing further limits on communal cooperation. Seafarers (in the first half of the twentieth century) and immigrants from Hong Kong (in the 1970s) were unable to cooperate with settled groups to challenge immigration and labour policies of the British Government that discriminated against them. Together with the generalised racism Chinese migrants encountered, these policies trapped Chinese in economic spheres where their links with the host population were curtailed and competition with whites was minimised. Competition also prevented Chinese caterers from uniting in the face of damaging new tax laws that came into force in the 1960s.

The situation was little different among large Chinese-owned transnational firms from Asia investing in the British economy. Such companies have rarely if ever cooperated and there is minimal evidence of interlocking ownership and directorate ties.[45] In a word, the disunity of ethnic-Chinese populations at all levels of British society and economy belies the widespread assumption of diasporic solidarity.

The emergence of new forms of identification among diasporic groups and their descendants raises important questions about the claim that ethnic Chinese (and other minorities) act as key players in the world economy by virtue of the flow of resources through ethnically based networks. It also casts doubt on another fashionable theory, that ethnic Chinese channel funds into China because of the 'pull of the homeland'.

These findings suggest that the normative definition of transnationalism fails to capture the identity transformations that occur as diasporic generations deepen. Writings extrapolate from the experience of the migrant cohort to the group as a whole, fail to incorporate the experience of the migrants who strike roots or (more importantly) of the locally born generations, neglect differences of class and sub-ethnic affiliation, ignore other differences that undermine group unity, generally exaggerate the coherence of diasporic groups, and elide the rich diversity and ambivalence as well as the divergent cultural histories of rooted diasporic communities.

We would therefore argue that transnational studies are of equivocal value. They make a major contribution to our understanding of identity by focusing on hybridity and pluralism, but they fall into the trap of essentialising ethnicity as soon as they venture into the domain of capitalism in its transnational mode. A fundamental problem of many such studies is the liberal and unquestioning use of the term 'network'. They suggest that ethnically based 'networks' are institutionalised and help diasporan co-ethnics mobilise capital and move it across national boundaries. Once transnational studies switch from politics, human rights, and the creation of an inclusive nation state to the domain of capitalism, they venture onto dangerous ground. It is true that members of ethnic minorities, particularly those born in their country of domicile, stress the multiplicity of identities and object to the dominant majority's questioning of their loyalty to the nation state. However, it does not follow that the dynamism and development of Chinese enterprises in Asia is due primarily to intra-ethnic business networks forged in opposition to an oppressive nation state and that Chinese enterprises thrive because such networks allow them to move funds across borders for the benefit of the ethnic community.

Transnational studies that posit an ethnic economic solidarity also fail to capture class dimensions of the issues they raise. Their primary interest is in people who can migrate with ease and rotate from country to country in pursuit of better returns on their investment. However, they appear to frame their conclusions in terms of all Chinese communities, including poor migrants who lack the capacity to invest in foreign countries and even the very means to engage in multiple migrations. Ong's multiple-passport holder may well be an apt description of the prosperous and well-travelled elite, but most Chinese and ethnic-Chinese migrants lack the skills and independent means of the 'progressive cosmopolitan intellectual', the 'astronaut' commuter, and the peripatetic multicultural manager with 'flexible capital' by the bagful.[46]

Since they deal mostly with migration, transnational studies inevitably concentrate on migrants who retain homeland ties and on those with the resources to migrate, a preoccupation perhaps inevitable in an age of transnational flows of capital and a burgeoning literature on the Chinese networks through which such funds are said to flow. This selective focus is a major shortcoming. By conceptualising migration and networks so narrowly, they create a false impression of how migrants view themselves in relation to other Chinese in the world and of how they develop their enterprise in local and foreign economies. Most studies on Chinese migration and enterprise development written from a transnational perspective fail to explore the implications of their generalisations for Chinese who do not cross borders, or for those born in their migrant parents' adopted country.[47] We would question the extent of the mobility not only of the offspring but also of the pioneers. The 'myth of return' is by now a cliché of migration studies. Migrants talk of home but rarely return, given their investment of capital and emotion overseas and their children's lack of ties to the ancestral homeland.

We identify two key problems in transnational studies. First, since they deal mainly with migration, they concentrate on migrants who retain homeland ties. Second, in an age in which flows of capital are increasingly transnational, they are chiefly interested in the networks that facilitate these flows and in the people who maintain the networks – in a word, in those with the resources to migrate not just once but repeatedly. This narrow conceptualisation of migration and networking creates a false picture of how Chinese migrants view themselves in relation to other Chinese in the world and of how they develop their enterprise in foreign settings.

The contention that ethnic identity serves as a basis for group and business formation is, as we go on to show, usually true only at a migrant's point of entry into the country of settlement. Transnational studies rarely explore the issue of how migrants' children view transnational migration and of their relationship to their place of birth or upbringing, where they are not usually subjected to factors of the sort that drove their parents to emigrate. We will also show that there is little likelihood of migrants' children, particularly those who have attained a high level of education, leaving for abroad. Our key finding and belief is that this span of a generation or more has a profound impact on identity, which is likely to hybridise. However, the British mainstream tends not to view migrants' descendants as British citizens with a strong national identity, stronger even than their ethnic identity.

Key themes

This volume has six chapters. The first chapter deals with patterns of Chinese migration to Britain, the second with the institutions migrants have formed, the third with changes in Chinese economic activity over time, and the fourth with transnationalism. The fifth and sixth chapters revert to an analysis of state and society. They explore government policy, anti-Chinese racism, changing patterns of identity, and the interaction among these three threads.

Common themes such as migration, racism, and intra-ethnic divisions inform the entire study. The Chinese who reached Britain in the late nineteenth and early twentieth centuries were chiefly seafarers and refugees with ties to the homeland and little intention of staying. Their sojourner mentality helps explain why few fared well in business. Among those who set up laundries in the ports, a prime aim was to maintain ties with compatriots abroad and keep abreast of events in China.

Early Chinese migrants to Britain belonged to several different sub-ethnic groups, including Siyinese, Hubeinese, and Hakkas. They were divided not only by language but also by reasons for migrating. Many Siyinese arrived as seafarers and acquired the funding to start up businesses only after their arrival in Britain. They imported prior divisions that inhibited unity abroad. A history of economic conflict in China or Hong Kong, for example, in the struggle for control of farming land, was hard to overcome, despite the shared experience in Britain of isolation, exploitation, and marginalisation.

Intra-ethnic divisions were everywhere rife because of the diversity of the Chinese population in Britain. Alongside the early seafarers from mainland China and the postwar migrants from Hong Kong were students from former British colonies and refugees from Vietnam. Although the community remained relatively small, its diverse geographic and class origins prevented any form of pan-ethnic association. A large number of poor Chinese migrants forced to work for other Chinese were so badly exploited that they left at the first opportunity to set up their own enterprises.

The role of the state is a theme present throughout this volume. Government policies heavily influence migration patterns and determine forms of enterprise development by ethnic minorities. As seafarers working for the British merchant marine, Chinese were fiercely exploited by employers acting with state approval and support. As a result of legislation, British shipping firms were allowed to pay their Asian crews far less than whites, an example of the institutionalisation of racism by state authorities acting on behalf of British economic interests. In the First World War, Chinese and other non-whites were recruited to replace seafarers deployed to the Royal Navy but were summarily repatriated at the war's end, once they had served their purpose. The British authorities tacitly approved the use of Chinese contractors and middlemen to recruit and manage Chinese crews, ostensibly as a means to handle an unruly workforce. The Chinese seafarers were, in effect, ghettoised by state measures aimed at ensuring their availability for the merchant marine sector.

Government policies have also borne centrally on the issues of integration, identity formation, citizenship, and rights. The Thatcher Government's strategy in the late 1970s and early 1980s of promoting small enterprises was conceived as a way of dealing with racism. The government concluded that immigrants preferred to concentrate in small business as a strategy for overcoming disadvantages experienced in Britain, principally language barriers and racial discrimination, which made it difficult for them to enter mainstream labour markets alongside native British.

States have also played a role at the transnational level. The governments of China, Taiwan, and Singapore have helped promote the rise of Chinese associations, both within Britain and globally. Chinese associations have been convening global meetings since the mid-1990s, with support from regional and national authorities in Asia. Such meetings are supposed to enable entrepreneurs to spin business ties and gain access to lucrative corporate ventures. In reality, they have failed in that objective. They also seem to have failed to unify Chinese, even those from the same country. The apparent futility of these meetings throws into question theories about the unifying role of ethnicity in transnational settings.

Generational change is another important theme. By 1991, the average Chinese in Britain was younger by nine years than the average white. Most Chinese were immigrants. Three-fifths were aged 20–40. Their high childbearing capacity implies the likelihood of a rapid rise in the British-born population. More than one-third of Chinese men were self-employed in 1991. Generational change has had an important bearing on changes in the form of enterprise development. For the migrant generation, enterprise usually served as a vehicle for social mobility and a means of dealing with isolation and alienation. However, large numbers of children of Chinese immigrants have excelled at school and university and are disproportionately represented in the professions and the hi-tech sector. Many scorn the idea of taking over their parents' businesses, especially small ones. The dreariness and drudgery of life in the takeaway has alienated an entire generation of well-educated Chinese from the niche formed by the migrant cohort. The rise of the British-born Chinese with their special view of national identity may eventually lead to a new set of problems, linked to issues of rights and belonging.

The findings of this study provide important insights into the debate about identity formation among migrant communities. The social and economic history of the Chinese in Britain is hard to reconcile with tenets of transnational studies, which look primarily at immigrants at the point of entry and their early experiences in the new setting. Our study shows that immigrants were highly exploited by the co-ethnics who facilitated their entry into Britain. Chinese businesses competed ferociously and distanced themselves from one another, a further obstacle in the way of ethnic solidarity. The trend towards ethnic competition and dispersal throws into question another dimension of transnational theory, in that long-term residents view migrants as a threat rather than as a means towards the communal pursuit of common economic interests.

Transnational theory damages ethnic relations in multi-racial societies by reinforcing the notion of 'host country' and implying that ethnic minorities feel a sense of loyalty and 'belonging' to the 'homeland'. Our study focuses attention on the formation and transformation of identity among longer-settled members of migrant communities and their descendants. The emergence of new forms of identification among diasporic groups undermines the claim that ethnic minorities function as cohesive units in economies or societies by combining to protect vested interests. Studies that adopt a transnational perspective seldom pay much attention to identity transformations in newer generations of diasporic communities. Instead, they repeat old discourses about the ties of provenance or ancestry assumed to bind such groups.

2
Migration and Settlement

The fashionable British view on the Chinese has, over the last 300 years, rung many changes on the bells marked vice to virtue, including (in roughly chronological order): philosopher, tyrant, Arcadian phalansterist, yellow peril, evil genius, opium-victim, drug-peddler, noble patriot, rabble-rouser, wartime ally, Red threat, frugal peasant, blue ant, seaman, landsman, washerman, laundry-lord, pauper-cook, get-rich-quick caterer, inscrutable outsider, benighted illiterate, academic whiz kid, likely member of the professions and salariat, and (most recently) illegal immigrant and exploited cockle-picker. Some of the images stem from racist imagining. Others reflect real transformations over time.

Not all the stereotypes rolled out over the years have been laid to rest. Old prejudices are held in reserve, to be dusted off and restored to currency as required. We subject these perceptions and preconceptions to closer review at relevant points. Here, we describe the main periods of Chinese immigration, its provenance in China, types of immigrant, the places and types of settlement, and basic demographics.

Today, most people of Chinese descent living outside China were not born in the mainland and are not China's citizens. However, only a minority of the Chinese living in Britain, and even fewer of those living in mainland Europe, were actually born in Europe, although most were born outside China (excluding Hong Kong and Taiwan) and are citizens of their countries of residence. The question of what to call people of Chinese descent living outside China has led to a debate in ethnic and China studies. 'Overseas Chinese', the usual term, is a standard rendering of the word *Huaqiao* 华侨, meaning a Chinese national residing, or sojourning, abroad. Its connotations are therefore inappropriate for people who, on the whole, are neither sojourners nor

Chinese settlers but of Chinese ancestry. Wang Gungwu 王赓武 has proposed the term 'Chinese overseas' as a compromise.[1]

In Southeast Asia, where most Chinese regard themselves as Thai, Indonesian, Malaysian, and so on, the term 'ethnic Chinese' has come into vogue, as a neutral descriptive term corresponding to the Chinese *Huaren* 华人. In Europe, where Chinese ethnic identification is more complex and varied, the term is not yet widely applicable, for the older generations, still in the majority, continue to adopt a Chinese identity. This ethnic affiliation is a result of the recency of Chinese settlement, combined with white racism and the de facto adoption of a multiculturalist ideology by the governments of some European countries.[2]

Since no existing term covers the range of Chinese identities in Britain and Europe, we follow an eclectic strategy. Sometimes we speak of European (or British, or French) Chinese, depending on the context. Where a general term is necessary, we use either overseas Chinese (in the sense of *Huaqiao*), the term favoured by most Chinese in Europe, or Chinese overseas, as Wang Gungwu advises.[3]

Earliest arrivals

In the early days of Sino-British contact, between the seventeenth and nineteenth centuries, a handful of Chinese arrived in Britain as individuals. Many studies document the early European presence in China, yet Europe's early Chinese visitors have been rendered largely invisible,[4] even though they embodied the spirit of intellectual exchange and mutual respect that typified Sino-European relations before the nineteenth century and strongly influenced some aspects of early modern European thought, particularly in the field of *scientia politicomoralis*. Chinese accounts give pride of place to these lonely pioneers. Like us, however, they do not have much to say about them.

We know little more about these early Chinese residents than their names and occupations. They were tiny in number, for whereas the early European traders, soldiers, missionaries, and adventurers flocked to China with the backing of their governments, the Qing court regarded going abroad without permission as a capital offence. This prohibition deterred many would-be emigrants.[5] Treaties signed between Britain and China in Nanjing in 1842 (after the first Opium War) and in Beijing in 1860 (after the second) allowed Chinese to 'ship themselves and their families' to British ports as emigrants, but they were more important for securing the 'security and protection' of the British in China than of the Chinese in Britain.[6]

Probably the first Chinese to reach Britain was Shen Fuzong 沈福宗 (also known as Michel Shen Fo Tsoung or Shen Fu-tsung), a native of Jiangxi and son of a prominent Christian physician. Like other early Chinese visitors, Shen was a Catholic. In 1683, he accompanied the Flemish Jesuit missionary Philippe Couplet on a 'propaganda tour' of Europe, to promote the interests of the Jesuits' China mission and demonstrate to Rome 'the excellent Chinese candidates available for the priesthood'. Shen's visit 'received great publicity in papal, royal, and intellectual circles'. In France in 1684, he was received by Louis XIV. After moving to England in 1687, he was received by James II, who commissioned Sir Godfrey Kneller to paint a portrait of the Chinese that later hung in the king's bedchamber. In Oxford, Shen was the guest of Thomas Hyde, a well-known Orientalist and librarian, with whom he corresponded in Latin. Shen also instructed Hyde on the nature of the Chinese language and started cataloguing the Bodleian Library's Chinese collection. In 1688, he left England for Lisbon.[7] In the late eighteenth century, a Chinese known variously as Chitqua 钱呱 and Tan-chet Gua worked in London as a modeller.[8] Other occasional visitors, including painters, were noted on rare occasions in writings of the period.[9]

Men like Shen and Chitqua played a part in propagating the idealised view of China that inspired European thinkers and writers. According to Couplet's biographer, Shen's visit to the courts 'sparked great interest ... [It] may well have been the final push to the establishment of a French Jesuit mission to China [whose] voluminous reports ... ignited eighteenth century interest in China as a model for Europe'.[10] Shen's presence and that of other Chinese scholars, artists, and diplomats helped pave the way for the Chinese craze, while Chitqua's visit coincided with its final stages.

With Shen and Chitqua, the list of pre-nineteenth century educated Chinese visitors to Britain is practically exhausted. The eclipse of rococo, *chinoiserie*, rhododendronomania, the Anglo-Chinese garden, and sinophilism after the French Revolution, when China came to be viewed as the land of oriental despotism and India took over as Britain's favourite exotic place, led to the burying in oblivion of other Chinese visitors. 'Because of the almost complete extinction of the cult of China after 1789 the great majority of European historians have failed to do justice to the influence of Chinese ideas in eighteenth-century Europe,' wrote Geoffrey Hudson in his survey of Sino-European contacts. His comment also applies to the treatment of those Chinese who helped to introduce Chinese art and moral philosophy to Europe. By 1842, wrote Chan Shau Yi, the English were 'perfectly disillusioned as to the once reputed wisdom and goodness of the Chinese'.[11]

None of these early visitors left an account of their experiences. All but one of the handful of Chinese descriptions of Europe that appeared in the eighteenth century were second-hand, based on information gained from Russians. Probably the earliest first-hand account was by the Cantonese Xie Qinggao 谢清高, a seafarer who went to sea at the age of eighteen in 1782 and spent 14 years sailing between the ports of Europe, America, and Asia aboard a foreign trading vessel. Xie was illiterate (and later lost his sight), so his reminiscences were written down on his behalf by a visitor. They described countries throughout the world, including England. The description of England, which extended to English customs and government, is a mixture of fact and fantasy. Unlike accounts of China by westerners, it abstains from moral judgement.[12]

Early Chinese mariners and the East India Company

The first evidence of plebeian Chinese reaching Britain dates from 1782, when Chinese seafarers were reported in East London. [13] By the turn of the century, Chinese seafarers were a familiar sight in the ports and in cartoons depicting 'low life' in the capital.[14]

At the time, the East India Company, a group of bankers and merchants protected by Royal Charter, exercised a monopoly over the India trade (which they retained until 1813) and the China trade (until 1833). In the Napoleonic Wars of 1799–1815, Lascars and Chinese seafarers were employed by the Company to replace Britons recruited into the Royal Navy.[15] Larger numbers of Chinese arrived in London, where their presence was noted in the *Times*.[16]

The crowded tenements of Poplar and Stepney (including Shadwell) had been home ever since the Elizabethan age to successive waves of foreign immigrants. They included Irish, Jews, Huguenots, Germans, and Scandinavians, as well as a native population of workers and paupers. By the end of the Napoleonic Wars, they had been joined by a new group of Asian residents. A Parliamentary Committee in 1817 revealed that foreign seafarers – 'Lascars, Chinese, Greeks and other filthy people of that description' – lived in barrack-style accommodation of the sort provided by the East India Company and in public houses; and 'that the women of the Town never cohabit with any other people than that description of people'.[17] This spilling over of

Chinese into the general population on streets like the Ratcliff Highway, 'a notorious London Rookery', and in the nearby Blue Gate Fields area created Britain's first permanent Chinese toehold.[18]

Most of the Chinese were seafarers who had deserted before the expiry of their contracts. However, quite a few were dumped in London by unscrupulous shipowners. In 1854, an American ship abandoned 44 Chinese in Shadwell, where they fell on hard times and searched in vain for a homebound vessel prepared to enlist them.[19] Other Chinese fled to Britain from the United States to escape the anti-Chinese movement that swept California after the depression of the 1870s.[20] This transnational connection introduced new business possibilities and contacts to the early Chinese community in Britain.

London's early Chinatown

The term Chinatown cannot properly be applied to the Chinese community in Britain, which is radically different in character from the Chinese settlements in San Francisco and New York for which the term was coined. Today, Chinese in Britain lack the residential density of the North American Chinatowns, where Chinese both live and work. The revamped and commoditised Chinatowns that adorn some British city centres have little in common with their transatlantic counterparts beyond a few external trappings. For the early community, however, the contrast fails to hold, for the Chinese were densely concentrated in just a few small streets where they resided, earned their living (in the case of non-seafarers), and took their leisure. The main difference was of extent, for the Chinese population was minute, a Chinatown in miniature.

Shadwell's incipient Chinatown also differed from Chinatowns elsewhere in the world in its lack of complexity and diversity. Chinese migration to Southeast Asia had its origin in the development of trade and industry by Chinese entrepreneurs and, at a later stage, in the demand for labour; in America, in the discovery of gold and transcontinental railroad-building. The economies and frontiers of both regions were, for a time, relatively open. Chinese who turned up in response to the demand for labour and the entrepreneurial opportunities aimed to better themselves and sometimes had the chance to do so. The Chinatowns in which they congregated evolved a dynamic commerce and civic organisation. By comparison, the Chinese streets of London started as inert outgrowths from the chief Chinese activity, seafaring. Most Chinese who settled in Britain in the early days seem to have ended up there by accident rather than as a result of long-term planning.

The prospect they faced was not boundless demand and lengthening horizons but how to scrape by in a hostile or indifferent environment, in the world's most industrialised country.

Although their settlements were shrunken replicas of the Chinatowns in other parts of the world, the Chinese in Britain insisted on using the term *Huabu* 华埠 ('Chinaport', a standard Cantonese word for Chinatown) to describe them. The same basic taxonomy was retained even after the spread of Chinese settlement to the smaller towns in the second half of the twentieth century, when the term *fauh jai* 埠仔 (little port) was applied.[21]

Chinaport suggests a world of seafarers, but the settlement stabilised only by turning its back on the sea. At first, the quayside community was highly mobile and formed little more than a pool of labour. In time, however, Chinese entrepreneurs arrived and some seafarers deserted or were laid off, giving rise to a more settled group. Even as late as 1901, 61 per cent of Britain's China-born residents were classed as seafarers. Yet as life ashore became more agreeable and the Chinaports swelled into real communities, more quit the sea. If three out of five of Britain's Chinese were seafarers in 1901, by 1911 less than two out of five were. Chinese switched to the land at a faster rate in London than in other British cities. By 1901, only 42 per cent were seafarers.[22]

The number of London's China-born residents grew steadily between 1851 (when they were first counted in the Census) and 1921, save for a dip in 1901. (See Table 2.2.) In the 1860s and the 1870s, the area around Blue Gate Fields in the East End was sometimes referred to as the 'Chinese Quarter' (although registered Chinese numbered fewer than twenty). Both Charles Dickens and the Prince of Wales visited opium-dens there.[23] By 1885, the centre of the community had shifted to the Limehouse district near the West India Docks. Chinese shops and cafes sprang up along two streets in particular, Limehouse Causeway and Pennyfields.[24]

In the First World War, thousands of Chinese joined the British merchant fleet and hundreds remained stranded in British ports in 1918. The armistice 'brought recession and a return to xenophobia', which culminated in race riots in 1919 and calls for the repatriation of non-whites. In 1918, the government tried to encourage voluntary repatriation of Chinese.[25] Government officials justified their attempts to get rid of the 3000 unemployed Chinese seafarers and labourers demobilised from construction sites by pointing to the 'very considerable feeling' among British seafarers. They threatened compulsion and tried to arrange the deportation of Chinese to France and Belgium, to take part in reclamation work.[26] In 1919, 800 Chinese labourers were picked up at Devonport and deported under the terms of the contract labour system.[27]

By late 1920, this combination of threats and encouragement had begun to produce results. The *Manchester Guardian* reported (somewhat exaggeratedly) on 13 December that 'Chinatown, in fact, had practically ceased to exist' in London. A sustained campaign by the press and the local police-court magistrate was said to have reduced the size of the Limehouse Chinatown from 4000 to just 300 in 1920.[28] The exodus probably had as much to do with economic changes as with government measures. The congestion of the ports as a result of the war-induced shipping crisis had ended, so jobs at sea were freed up for hundreds of Chinese.[29] Subsequently, the shipping slump of the 1920s and 1930s led many more Chinese to leave.[30]

The cumulative effect of official curbs and harassment and of changes in the general economic climate led to a big decline in Britain's Chinese population. Although the number of Chinese (excluding those from Hong Kong) nearly doubled between 1911 and 1921, it fell back by several hundred over the next decade. The figures for 1921 and 1931 included the British-born wives of Chinese nationals, deemed aliens under the provisions of the 1914 Act,[31] so the actual fall was even steeper. The decline was particularly steep in Liverpool, where the Chinese population, put at 502 in 1911, had grown by just 27 by 1930 (including local wives).

After crumbling away in the 1920s, Chinatown was finished off first by urban renewal and, finally, by German bombs. In 1934, Liverpool's Chinatown was torn down and its inhabitants were evicted without compensation.[32] As for Limehouse, its Chinese population had declined to just 100 in 1934. There was talk of building a new road through Pennyfields and removing the Chinese to Dagenham.[33]

Chinese contract labourers in the First World War

In the First World War, many tens of thousands of Chinese labourers (called Huagong 华工) were recruited by the British, French, and Russian Allies to work as battlefield ancillaries. Their jobs included digging trenches, transporting materials, and taking care of other logistical and supply problems at the front. The French are said by one source to have recruited 150,000 and the British 50,000, but other sources give different figures. Most of those recruited by France and Britain worked on the

Western Front, though some ended up in the Balkans. In France, nearly 10,000 Chinese are said to have lost their lives at the front.[34]

The great majority of Huagong returned to China after the war. However, 'no few later wandered about destitute in foreign countries, and came to constitute a part of the overseas Chinese', in the words of a Chinese study.[35] Chinese sources put the number that stayed on in Europe at 3000.[36] Most stayed in France, but quite a few moved to other parts of Europe.[37]

These workers were, by some accounts, the most mixed of Europe's early Chinese migrant groups. One source suggests that between 80 and 90 per cent originated in Shandong and the rest in other provinces, but this seems unlikely.[38] Nearly all were poor and uneducated. The literacy rate of the labourers in France was said to be only 20 per cent at the time of their recruitment. (It had apparently risen to 38 per cent by the end of 1920, as a result of classes organised by Chinese students.)[39]

Studies discount the Huagong as a source of Chinese immigration to Britain. According to one account, 'only the dead remained on British soil'.[40] (Some lie buried at Shorncliffe Military Cemetery near Folkestone, others at a cemetery in Plymouth.[41]) However, a few hundred Chinese were employed in Birmingham and other industrial towns under a separate agreement from those employed in France.[42] Some had factory jobs, others (at one point numbering more than seven hundred) were employed in building aerodromes or in catering.[43]

Many proved hard to remove at the war's end: some could not find a ship to employ them, others wanted a better pay-off, and still others had no intention of going back to China for the time being. Most of the discharged labourers who escaped repatriation gravitated to London and Liverpool, where they melted into the existing Chinese communities. Some of the Chinese factory workers and building workers may have been recruited from among Chinese already resident in Britain, or from among seafarers killing time ashore.[44]

These stayover Chinese became associated with crime and disorder in the eyes of the authorities, who predicted they would be a red rag to seafarers and troops returning from the war.[45] Most were removed, 'voluntarily' or by compulsion, but some acquired residence by marrying local women or slipped the net by diving underground. The immigrants settled down to a life of hard graft or crime and enlivened Chinatown with a new ingredient, formed by experiences quite different from those of its customary residents. The ties of some to Huagong on the Continent formed the basis for illegal networks in the postwar years.

The Chinese in Britain in the Second World War

On the eve of the Second World War, the Chinaports seemed destined for extinction. Their long-term survival was secured only in the 1950s and 1960s, when tens of thousands of Chinese immigrated from the New Territories of Hong Kong and revolutionised the community. In the meantime, the fortunes of the Liverpool Chinaport were temporarily revived by a wartime influx of up to 20,000 Chinese seafarers, recruited to keep Britain's western approaches open during the Battle of the Atlantic.

These men, who formed the Chinese Merchant Seamen's Pool, were recruited in London, Liverpool, Rotterdam, and ports in Asia.[46] Unlike earlier Chinese crews, most of whom were Cantonese, many of the new recruits were from east China. They were often referred to as Shanghainese, perhaps because they found it more convenient to give officials the name of their first port of embarkation (and regional big city), a name westerners could recognise and cope with, rather than descend into particulars. In reality, they came from all round the Yangtze Delta and beyond, as well as from south China.

Publicly lauded as 'plucky allies' by a flagwaving press that not so long before had called for Chinatown to be closed down, they were nevertheless scandalously exploited. The quayside hostels in which they lived during turn-round were so crowded and ill-provided that they shocked the photo journalist Bert Hardy, who went to Liverpool to record how they lived but decided his photos were 'too revealing to be used'.[47] A Chinese described the conditions:

> When we arrive in port after our long hazardous voyage, we are herded into boarding houses of the most scandalous kind specially provided for us Chinese. In these boarding houses often over 20 or 30 men are crowded in one room permanently blacked out with no ventilation at all. In houses with 60 or 80 inhabitants there is not a single bathroom, the only place for washing being the kitchens where only buckets are provided for our washing purposes. The various housing regulations of this country, much to the convenience of our employers, do not seem to apply to our case, with the probable implication that we Chinese are not worth bothering about.[48]

The wartime presence of up to 3000 Chinese seafarers at any given time rejuvenated Liverpool's Chinatown, where business boomed.[49] Some local Chinese made small fortunes.[50] The prosperity survived into the peace. Having practically died out by 1927,[51] the community was reintegrated in another part of the city after the war. Some residents were veterans of the early settlement; others were remnants of the wartime Pool who had married local women.[52] This rebirth was achieved only by a struggle against great odds, for the transition from war to peace in 1945 was, for the seafarers, a repeat performance of the events of 1919, when Chinese were subject to mass repatriation, 'voluntary' or not.[53]

Hundreds of Chinese fell prisoner or died in the Normandy landings or as a result of enemy action at sea. A few were decorated for courage.[54] In the eyes of senior policemen, civil servants, and members of Britain's postwar Labour Government, however, their usefulness ended with the war. In the familiar pattern of 'recruitment followed by repudiation',[55] officials turned their attention to the problem of how to get rid of the Chinese. They were particularly incensed by 150 seafarers said to have gone missing to try their luck ashore. Other issues that troubled relations between the authorities and the Chinese included equal pay under the peace. Not only did the wages of Chinese on British ships fall after the war, but allowances paid to British seafarers in Asia were withheld from them.[56]

During and after the war, the press was no longer as hostile as it had been after 1918. In 1946, the *News Chronicle* reported that a defence association had been formed to oppose compulsory repatriation and noted that the British wives of Chinese seafarers would be 'left destitute'.[57] In October 1947, when plans for a new Chinese Seamen's Welfare Centre were announced, the *Liverpool Daily Post* spoke of 'a welcome addition to the amenities available for a gallant body of men whose service to the Allied cause, through the Merchant Service, is greatly appreciated'.[58] This new tone of support and appreciation was not just a late echo of wartime alliances. It reflected a change in thinking about Chinese, based on new media images produced by western supporters of China's War against Japan.

Official papers do not reveal the exact number of Chinese deported in 1945 and 1946 and deny newspaper reports of the deporting of Chinese married to local women, except for 'one or two' cases. In any case, the wages of Chinese seafarers were so much lower than in the war that the seafarers were no longer able to maintain their families, so some agreed to leave. By March 1946, 800 had been repatriated and some 1900 remained, in Liverpool and Glasgow. The hunt for 'pool deserters' continued, and in December further 'bulk clearances' took place.[59]

Only a few hundred Chinese remained in Liverpool by the late 1940s, and the number of permanent residents was about 400 in the early

1950s.[60] The seafarers who had gained residence ashore by marrying did not entirely lose their tie to the sea, which was kept alive by others (estimated in 1957 at 2700) who continued to work from Liverpool[61] and by the shore-based residents' continuing ties to shipping firms.

In earlier years, Liverpool's Chinese population had always been smaller than London's.[62] In the postwar period, however, for a time it matched London's. (In the early 1950s, 45 per cent of Chinese lived in London's East End, 45 per cent in Liverpool, and 10 per cent in Manchester and elsewhere.[63]) During Liverpool's subsequent decline as a port and economic centre, Liverpool Chinese were part of the movement that planted new colonies in Manchester and other parts of northwest England.

During the war, many Chinese moved from Limehouse to Liverpool. The community in Pennyfields lingered on in the early 1940s, but the Chinese areas in both cities suffered major damage in the Blitz, followed after the war by a further round of demolition of Chinese streets as part of a general campaign to pull down ruins and clear the slums. In earlier years, the dockland Chinatowns had been constantly replenished by a trickle of seafarers who quit the sea for a life on land, but the arrivals ceased after the communists took power in China.[64]

Today, the parts of Limehouse that were once Chinatown are the site of postwar housing projects.[65] A minority of old-timers stayed on and continued to run Chinese restaurants and shops, but most left. All that remains are the Chinese street names. (By the mid-1980s, however, the Chinese population of Limehouse approached 3000 as a result of new immigration, a far higher figure than in the prewar days.[66]) In the meantime, a new Chinatown had grown up around Gerrard Street in London's West End.

These events marked the end of an era and cleared the way for the transformation of the Chinese community. The dispersal of veterans, either to the leafy suburbs or to the postwar tenements, led to the community's disintegration. It also led to a weakening of the tie between the two immigrant waves, in the first and second halves of the century, for there was no longer a strong focus for Chinese life. Instead, the newcomers were forced to start afresh.[67]

Early provenance

Chinese migration to Britain has always been predominantly Cantonese, except for a Fujianese presence in the very early years and in recent times. The only exceptions were the pools of seafarers formed in times of war, when the base of recruitment broadened. The Seamen's Pool set up in Liverpool in the Second World War was dominated by men from Jiangsu and Zhejiang. Those Chinese who settled down or spent some time in Britain during and immediately after the First World War also included many non-Cantonese.

The Chinese in the rest of Europe, at least until the 1970s, came from eastern and northern China. Most of the first Chinese to arrive in France, Germany, Austria, the Netherlands, Belgium, Spain, and Italy, often by way of Moscow, were Zhejiangese, together with a handful of Hubeinese, Shandongese, and other northerners. Other Zhejiangese sailed to Europe, as passengers rather than as crew. A few Cantonese worked their passage to Continental ports, but they and the Zhejiangese remained largely separate. Many of the Zhejiangese and the northerners arrived in western Europe either on foot or by rail, after the opening of the trans-Siberian route in 1904.[68] The Zhejiangese originated in the port of Wenzhou and in Qingtian, a then remote inland county upstream from Wenzhou, for whose migrants Europe was for a long time a main overseas destination.[69] This difference in provenance can be explained by geography and history. Britain was not directly open to the land-routes out of China, and most Chinese who reached Britain as crew were recruited in Britain's Asian colonies, where the majority of seafarers were Cantonese and Fujianese.[70]

The Siyinese

Siyi 四邑 ('four districts', variously transliterated as See Yip and Sze Yap) is the collective name of the four counties of Taishan 台山,[71] Xinhui 新会, Kaiping 开平, and Enping 恩平 in Guangdong's Pearl River Delta region, home to a cluster of communities that depend heavily on emigration. The Siyinese dialect[72] belongs to the Yue 粤 (or Cantonese) group of Chinese languages. In the 1990s, around 1.8 million people of Siyinese descent were said to live outside China, together with another 1.1 million in Taiwan, Hong Kong, and Macao. These figures compare with Siyi's population of 3.6 million. Siyi was the greatest single source of Chinese emigration to the English-speaking world in the nineteenth and early twentieth century. Taishan accounted for no less than 60 per cent of the early Chinese population of the United States, while the other three counties provided a further 20 per cent.

Around 35,000 people of Siyinese descent lived in Europe in the late 1990s.[73] Although this represents only a tiny proportion of Siyinese overseas, Siyi was the biggest single source of early Chinese emigration to

Britain.[74] In Liverpool, Siyinese were the main group until the Second World War; in Cardiff, until the start of the postwar catering boom. In London, they were always an important group, though shipping-masters from Bao'an 宝安 and Dongguan 东莞 (contiguous to Hong Kong) seem to have controlled the early Chinatown in the capital (and in some mainland ports).[75] Material evidence of the early Siyinese presence can be found on tombstones in the Chinese sections of cemeteries in Cardiff and Liverpool.[76]

Some Siyinese remigrated to Britain from the United States in the 1880s, at the time of the American anti-Chinese campaign. Many returned to China or resettled in Hong Kong, where they established a thriving business and banking community.[77] Those who came to Britain[78] seem to have applied business and survival strategies pioneered in California. This was not the only instance of Siyinese transnational remigration. A similar movement took place between California and Australia in the nineteenth century. Another instance of such links was people-smuggling by way of Britain to the United States and the Dominions in the late nineteenth and early twentieth centuries.

In Hong Kong and North America, the Siyinese were despised by many other Cantonese, particularly those from Sanyi 三邑 ('three districts', usually transliterated as Sam Yap, denoting Nanhai 南海, Panyu 番禺, and Shunde 顺德). Sanyi, the centre of Guangdong's silk production, was wealthier than Siyi, which the Sanyinese saw as inferior and backward. The Siyinese, initially marginalised in Hong Kong, including by the British authorities, identified with the Qing Dynasty's patriotic policies and, after 1911, with the Revolutionary Government in Guangdong. They accumulated a huge amount of political capital and maintained ethnic and kinship networks across the world, from California to Southeast Asia, before the collapse of their business empire in south China in the 1930s.[79]

Scholars who compare the Chinese in Britain in the nineteenth century with those in other parts of the world describe them as unprepared and aimless. A Chinese study comments that few went with formulated schemes and most arrived 'by accident'.[80] Another notes that 'unlike those who went to Australia to look for gold, or to South Africa to dig coal, or to Malaysia to mine tin, or to north America to build railways, or to Cuba to tend sugarcane, they had no specific purpose in coming'. The earliest arrivals were 'reluctant émigrés, poor, ill-educated, and easily exploited by their own countrymen and by foreigners alike'. As for the crews employed by the East India Company, many of them were 'poor and helpless'.[81] They had few of the resources and opportunities of the Chinese who spread across the Malay Archipelago as traders and cultivators.[82]

However, this distinction between the shiftless Chinese in Britain and their focused and entrepreneurial compatriots elsewhere is not wholly accurate. Migration was a way of life in Guangdong's Siyinese communities. For some Siyinese who ended up in Britain, signing up on a British vessel was more a means to an end than an end in itself. Working the sea-routes between China and the world was an act of business reconnaissance in which opportunities were spotted and contacts laid. Hu Zhiqiang 胡志强, for example, believes that although the Siyinese arrived as seafarers, the purpose of many was to get a foothold, form businesses, and import relatives.[83]

The Siyinese diaspora was a connective tissue that transported people, things, and ideas across the world, before shrinking into separate parts as the migrant generation died off. For some, the difference between ending up in North America or the British Dominions and in Britain was one less of motivation than of opportunity. The way into the United States was largely closed after 1882, when Australia and New Zealand also started passing anti-Chinese laws. In those years, some Cantonese chose to explore the British market from the bridgehead established in Britain in mid century. Over the decades, some prospered, whereas others returned home or headed off to new destinations. The diasporic tie gave Britain's Siyinese a more cosmopolitan identity than the Zhejiangese, who rarely ventured beyond mainland Europe.

Most of the tens of thousands of Taishanese and other Siyinese who flocked to California between the 1850s and the early 1880s were drawn by the discovery of gold.[84] Later, Siyinese in the United States worked in market-gardening and the laundry business,[85] and went on to pioneer the fast-food trade. Chinese have engaged in all three lines of business across the world. Siyinese themselves credit their stateside cousins with inventing the takeaway introduced into Britain in the 1960s.

Today, Siyinese successor generations continue to play a role in elite circles in the old Chinaports, particularly in Cardiff and northwest England. Around 1960, some moved from Liverpool (then in decay) to Manchester, where they planted a new colony.[86] In time, their influence began to wane, as Siyinese businesses met stiff competition from new Chinese immigrants and Siyinese identity gave way to a wider concept of Chineseness. In the 1980s and the 1990s, however, new developments in the political sphere started to counteract this decline.

Hong Kong's New Territories

The seafarers who set up Britain's early Chinaports were, for the most part, Chinese nationals. The community continued to consist chiefly of mainlanders until after 1945. However, many Chinese claimed Hong Kong provenance to gain the right of abode in Britain. In any case, the distinction between sojourner and resident was never hard and fast in Hong Kong, a Cantonese-speaking port city that attracted workers from across the whole of Guangdong. The mainland origin of the pioneering groups meant that the community was, for years, cut off from sources of replenishment when China went communist. Some relatives and fellow-villagers did manage to emigrate in periods of relaxation, but the community seemed, for a time, fated to die out.

After the war, large numbers of Hong Kong's local Cantonese began to move to Britain. Hong Kong Chinese first began to spread out across the world as seafarers and adventurers when the British colonised Hong Kong Island. In 1841, men from Lamma Island 南丫島 enlisted on British ships. In the first few decades of the twentieth century, young Hakkas 客家人 from Sai Kung 西贡, Hang Hau 坑口, and Sha Tau Kok 沙頭角 left for the West Indies, others from Lantau Island 大屿山 went to Britain and the United States, and men from San Tin 新田 and Lo Wu 罗湖 in the New Territories were already working in Chinese restaurants in European ports. According to the 1931 Census, 1.15 per cent of the registered population of the New Territories were born in Common-wealth countries outside Asia.[87] However, migration to Britain did not take off until the 1950s and the 1960s.

The two migrations – from the mainland up to 1950 and after that from the New Territories – were in many respects different. The two sorts of migrants reached Britain in different ways, with different expecta-tions, rights, and resources, and under different political circumstances. Moreover, the two groups had a history of mutual antagonism. Ethnic rivalries, some relatively ancient, others encouraged by colonial prac-tices in Hong Kong, crossed with the migrants into Britain.

The main ethnic distinction in Hong Kong was between Cantonese and 'Shanghailanders', a catch-all term covering Chinese from outside Guangdong. However, other rivalries divided the Cantonese from the Hakkas, the New Territories Hong Kong Cantonese from the urban Hong Kong Cantonese, and the Hong Kong Cantonese from outsider Cantonese groups like the Siyinese.[88] The persistence of such divisions prevented the newcomers and the old hands from making common cause.

The Siyinese and other mainland Cantonese had turned up in British ports as seafarers and had subsequently taken up land-based occupations. Their settlement in Britain was part of a wider journeying through established networks. They belonged to a true diaspora. They had recourse to a repertoire of skills, experiences, and worldwide contacts of the sort that went with a long history of emigration. The immigrants from the New Territories, on the other hand, had little history of moving between continents and fewer employable resources.

The circumstances under which New Territorians emigrated to Britain were also quite different. General studies explain early Chinese migrations as a result of economic instability and social disorder caused by foreign aggression and domestic troubles. Siyinese migration, for example, is explained by a local contest for control over resources between Siyinese, Hakkas, and other groups at a time when southern Guangdong was exposed to violent fluctuations in world trade.[89] By the 1860s, however, when sail gave way to steam on the world's sea-routes, leaving Siyi to seek a fortune abroad was not an impromptu decision but a strategy to deal with a crisis that had been dragging on for decades. Social and economic dislocation may have been the context in which Siyi's population spread across the world, but by the time the Siyinese reached Britain, emigration had become a way of life.

In the New Territories economic and social crisis was not the remote background explanation of the emigration but its trigger. Until the 1950s, farming thrived in the New Territories, where 'ancestral rights' were protected under the treaty of 1898 by which the region was leased to the British Crown. After 1949, large numbers of peasants fled to Hong Kong, where they leased or squatted on land and competed with the indigenous population.[90] In the 1950s, the New Territories came under pressure when the colonial government started importing cheap rice and encouraged farmers to switch to vegetable production to end the colony's dependence on China. This 'vegetable revolution' undermined the stability of the New Territories by enriching a minority of landlords and displacing poorer farmers. Hong Kong's rapid urbanisation eroded the amount of available farmland and drove up the price of farm labour, further undermining traditional agriculture. After the 1950s, paddy farming was virtually abandoned. The collapse was particularly severe in the marshlands around San Tin, where the paddies were single-crop and therefore even less lucrative. The presence of large numbers of refugees on the labour market made it difficult for farmers to switch to other occupations in the urban areas, and conservatism prevented poorer groups from competing with the immigrants in farming vegetables.[91]

Worst hit were the Hakkas, who tilled marginal land and were deemed inferior by the majority Cantonese Punti 本地, descendants of the first Han inhabitants of southern China, who consider themselves Hong Kong's true natives. However, even Punti villagers fell victim to the changes. The best example is San Tin's Man 文 lineage, whose brackish land is unsuited to growing vegetables or white rice.[92]

The colonial government responded by giving 'fullest encouragement' to emigration as a way of easing rural unemployment.[93] The Hakkas were probably the first to export their young men to Britain, closely followed by the poorer Punti lineages, including San Tin's Man lineage. 'It appears that those who responded earliest to the opportunity were those in greatest hardship,' concluded Hugh Baker, 'the men of the poorest villages who had had only marginal livelihoods before, with no ready-made diversity of income and no reserves of capital to fall back on. They were followed fairly quickly by members of the larger wealthier lineage villages as they too felt the pinch and came to realise the financial gains to be made by working in voluntary exile.'[94] Their arrival in Britain coincided with the start of a Chinese catering boom, as a result of a general boom in commercial catering and the British discovery of a taste for the exotic.

The transition from farming to emigration in rural Hong Kong in the 1950s was sudden rather than protracted, and the communities were short of practised travellers. Within a few years, chains formed between the new European bridgeheads and the villages, but the vanguard arrived without maps or contacts. Though 'colonial subjects', their knowledge of the British way of life and English was practically nil – even less than that of the seafarers, most of whom had picked up some pidgin English in the ports. They had no relatives abroad, except for a handful of villagers scattered across different parts of Europe. The few contacts they did establish were with other Chinese, in whose restaurants they went to work. Their tie to these people was fraught with tension and mutual resentment. Beyond catering, they had no relationship whatsoever to British life, against which they were cocooned by their choice of occupation.

Postwar immigration: the early days

Few who travelled to Britain from the New Territories in the 1950s and the 1960s arrived with more than a few pounds in their pockets,[95] so they were at first dependent on established Chinese restaurants for employment. Many owners were mainlanders cut off from China by the revolution. Unable to recruit staff from their own communities, they welcomed the influx from the New Territories, whose inhabitants enjoyed unrestricted access to Britain until 1962.

The migrants' relations with the owners were never likely to blossom, given the combination of ethnic and class hostility that divided them. All but a few took the earliest opportunity to set up their own businesses. Some went to work for fellow-villagers who had settled in Britain in the early days, alongside the Siyinese and northerners, but even they itched to go independent.

The postwar restaurant boom and the new appetite for foreign food put the dream of proprietorship within the grasp of immigrants prepared to take business risks and work all hours. Most who cut loose did so in partnerships, but these partnerships increasingly dissolved as their members withdrew to go it alone. As new firms hived off, new staff were recruited along migration chains. Kinship was the basis upon which most chains formed. Elsewhere in the world, Chinese networks tended to rest on ties of dialect or native place, but the relative small-ness of Chinese settlements in Britain ruled out more encompassing groups.

Even lineage-based chains were the exception, limited to a handful of powerful lineages. Most chains were based on the extended family, usually brothers and their sons. Watson noted that 'the closed nature of the migration chains has important implications for the character of the Chinese community in Britain'. One implication was that the community lacked the cohesion of its counterparts in Southeast Asia and North America.

Chinese migration across much of Asia and the New World was asso-ciated in the period of the coolie trade with contract labour and the credit-ticket system. The communities thus formed were rarely random conglomerations, for the crimps and brokers concentrated on places in coastal areas of Guangdong and Fujian. The migrants, having struck root, set up chains to their native places that confirmed the regional pattern of recruitment. Even so, communities formed by press-ganging and commercial recruitment came from a spread of villages and counties and tended towards segmentation and competition.

Chinese immigration to Britain was never on the same scale as inter-national labour migration from other parts of China. Immigration from the New Territories was organised not by intermediaries but from within. Moreover, its geographical origins were narrow by comparison. These differences help to explain why it never produced effective umbrella organisations of the sort that characterised bigger Chinatowns.

Studies assume that the immigrants from the New Territories were peasants, whose skills were limited mainly to rice cultivation.[96] However, the population of the New Territories is no more confined to peasants than that of any other rural Chinese community. Analyses of the occupations of first-generation immigrants from the region suggest a broader range of backgrounds. Miri Song's investigation into the previous employment of a sample of 25 immigrant couples working as caterers came up with only five farmers compared with seven factory workers, two tailors, three nurses, two teachers, a dock worker, a sailor, two chefs, a radiographer, and various other non-peasant occupations.[97] Yuet Ngor Mary Pang's 彭月娥 analysis of occupations in the country of birth likewise yields just five farmers out of a sample of 20.[98] Although not necessarily representative, these findings suggest that farmers were less likely to emigrate than other inhabitants of rural Hong Kong.

Given that the migrants came from all sorts of backgrounds and brought with them a whole range of skills and attainments, it is interesting to ask why all but a few ended up in catering, of which only a tiny minority had previous experience. The answer has several strands, including Chinese mariners' early experience of racist exclusion and their ways of coping, the landward translation of practices pursued on shipboard, and the transmission to Britain of entrepreneurial skills that had proved profitable in the United States and elsewhere. However, we should not ignore the role of Home Office strategists in actively channelling Hong Kong migrants away from jobs in mainstream industry, despite requests for the import of 'British subjects from Hong Kong' by British manufacturers in industries experiencing 'acute labour shortages'[99] – and, of course, the reluctance of native British to work in catering, a low-status occupation.

'Stateless' immigrants from Hong Kong

Changes in British nationality law between 1962 and 1981 more or less ended so-called primary immigration by Commonwealth non-whites. Although blacks and South Asians were their intended targets, the new laws radically affected the Chinese too. The main result was a temporary boom in so-called secondary immigration, by wives and other dependants of existing immigrants, a development that transformed Britain's Chinese community and economy.

The steep fall between 1962 and 1972 in the number of Commonwealth citizens admitted on employment vouchers created labour shortages in the Chinese economy in Britain. These shortages could only partly be made good by bringing in dependants. The restaurants (as opposed to the takeaways) were particularly vulnerable. Fortunately for the restaurant-owners, voucher-holders and dependants were not the only source of exportable labour in Hong Kong. The work-permit system, established in 1920 for aliens seeking work in the United Kingdom, continued to operate despite the new laws. Alien permit-holders were subject to internal controls and enjoyed far fewer rights than voucher-holders. They had no right to settle in the United Kingdom or bring over their dependants, they had to register with the police, and they could not change jobs without permission. Unlike the rights-conferring vouchers, work permits yielded a class of workers viewed by governments as malleable and disposable. They were a 'control in the context of the labour market' (in the words of a Home Office Minister), peculiarly responsive to seasonal fluctuations and business cycles.[100]

Unlike other British colonies, Hong Kong had a large number of 'stateless aliens', mostly people who had arrived after 1949. Many were Cantonese-speakers from counties on the nearby Chinese mainland. As holders of Hong Kong Certificates of Identity rather than British (Hong Kong) passports, they were exempt from the restrictions imposed on Commonwealth immigration in 1962 and 1968 and eligible for work permits.

The immigration from Hong Kong by China-born aliens was not just a strategy by Chinese employers to evade the restrictions imposed on Commonwealth immigration by taking advantage of a 'loophole' (as has been suggested).[101] The Government actively promoted the switch to alien immigration in the belief that it would cost less and be easier to master. In fact, immigration by Chinese aliens as opposed to 'British Chinese' predated the new restrictions. It was the subject of representations by the British catering trade as early as 1959, when the Government defended the 'steady flow' of 'a few Hong Kong Chinese... when we have no option but to accept large numbers of British Chinese'.[102]

These China-born aliens constituted a 'cheap pool on which the established restaurants would draw when necessary'. Between 1962 and 1973, around 10,000 such aliens were imported by Chinese caterers to meet the labour shortage caused by market growth and the defection of staff.[103] The number of permits rose from 356 in 1962 to around 1300 in 1970, after which it tapered off, to just 225 in 1972–1973.[104] At its peak, immigration from Hong Kong by aliens on work permits was several times higher than that by British citizens.[105] A large minority of these aliens steered clear of the caterers, who treated them as second class, and found jobs in the mainstream economy. In 1969, for example, 375 of the 1335 'stateless' Chinese immigrants went to work in hospitals and private industry.[106]

In 1973, when the Immigration Act of 1971 came into force, employment vouchers were abolished and Commonwealth citizens were subjected to the same work-permit system as aliens. As a result of this equalisation, and of a more general clamp-down on immigration, the influx of stateless Chinese largely ceased.[107] Between 1971 and 1981, holders of British (Hong Kong) passports admitted to Britain for employment slightly outnumbered holders of Hong Kong Certificates of Identity, by 2581 to 2235.[108]

The influx of Chinese aliens had a big impact on the Chinese community. Although work-permit holders lacked automatic right of settlement, they could apply annually for an extension of stay. The Government probably intended them to return to Hong Kong after a brief period of employment. In the event, however, most took advantage of the rule that the conditions on settlement by work-permit holders with a record of four years' approved employment are normally removed. In this way, they achieved settled status and became 'free in the country'.[109] At one point, they are thought to have formed as much as one-sixth or more of Britain's Chinese population.[110] Their recruitment created an underclass with few rights and resources. It deepened divisions and introduced yet more regional and occupational diversity into Britain's hitherto relatively uniform Chinese population.

Ethnic-Chinese migrants from countries outside China

Immigration into Europe by ethnic Chinese from outside China (including Hong Kong, Macao, and Taiwan) has been associated in recent times with the former European colonial powers, particularly countries (like Britain, France, Portugal, and the Netherlands) with colonies in Southeast Asia. All four countries imported Chinese into their colonies as indentured labour. Some of this migration was intercontinental, from China to Africa, the New World, Australasia, and Oceania. Even in colonial days, it led to Chinese migration from Southeast Asian to non-Asian colonies and from colonies to the metropolitan countries.

Small numbers of Chinese have moved to Britain over the last hundred years from India, Burma, Mauritius, Guyana, Jamaica, Nauru, and other former colonies.[111] Some came as students and failed to return home, others arrived under the British Nationality Act of 1948. In some cases, ethnic Chinese from outside Asia had a sub-ethnic tie to the Siyinese, for Siyi was a main source of provenance of Chinese migration to the

South Pacific and the Caribbean.[112] (The Chinese of India and Mauritius are predominantly Hakka.[113]) The largest source of Chinese migration to Britain from outside China, Hong Kong, and Taiwan is Southeast Asia, chiefly Malaysia and Singapore, where ethnic Chinese form around 29 and 78 per cent of the population. The Caribbean provided most of the rest. Around 18,000 Chinese arrived in the British Caribbean as indentured workers in the nineteenth century. In the second half of the twentieth century, many Chinese and their descendants joined in the Guyanese and Caribbean migration to Britain and North America.[114]

Chinese from Southeast Asia migrated to Britain in relatively large numbers towards the end of the twentieth century and now play a major part in the British Chinese economy. Many have professional and technical qualifications and the means to fund important business ventures. They are far more likely than British-born or Hong Kong-born Chinese to work or do business in the mainstream economy.[115]

Chinese immigrants from countries outside China are sometimes mistakenly referred to as twice migrants. Strictly speaking, twice migrants are people who, having migrated to one country and settled in it, then remigrate to another. The term can hardly apply to the ethnic Chinese of (say) Southeast Asia, the overwhelming majority of whom did not themselves emigrate from China but were born in Southeast Asia, to immigrants or the descendants of immigrants. Even so, ethnic Chinese from countries outside China do have some features in common with twice migrants properly understood.

The East African Asians are the best example in Britain of postcolonial remigration. In *Twice Migrants*, a study of Britain's East African Sikh community, Parminder Bhachu has developed a framework of analysis useful for understanding Chinese immigrants from outside Chinese-speaking countries.[116] The East African Sikhs left the Punjab in the early twentieth century as indentured labour and started remigrating to Britain in the 1960s. In some ways, they are unlike the Chinese from Southeast Asia. For example, they belong predominately to a single caste and maintained their community and perpetuated traditional values in Africa through endogamous arranged marriages and marriage alliances. Most were public-sector workers in Africa. Although they did not arrive in Britain as refugees, like the Asians expelled from Uganda in 1972, they were, as public-sector workers and civil servants, hard hit by the Africanisation of public life after independence.

Chinese migrants from Southeast Asia, on the other hand, belong to many different sub-ethnic groups and lack the traditional attachments, cultural cohesion, and community skills of the East African Sikhs. They are also far less likely to have a public-service background, so they were less affected by indigenisation measures after independence.

In other respects, however, Bhachu's analysis is relevant. Both the East African Sikhs and the Southeast Asian Chinese had previous experience of living as an ethnic minority. (Singapore, where Chinese are the majority, is of course different.) Both groups were urban in origin (mainly because of colonial policies restricting their access to farmland), were familiar with urban institutions, and knew English. Quite a few of the Chinese were skilled and prosperous, like the Sikhs. (The Chinese were usually proficient in business, the Sikhs in administration.) Very few Chinese and even fewer Sikhs had a 'home orientation' (towards China or Punjab) of the sort that shaped the attitudes of immigrants from China (including Hong Kong) or South Asia. (However, most Chinese from Southeast Asia are far less alienated from their homeland than Sikhs from Africa.) Finally, like the great majority of the Sikhs, more Chinese from outside China than of those from China and Hong Kong migrated in family units, an indication of their commitment to settling in Britain.

Many Chinese migrants and their locally born descendants in British colonies became traders, often because other occupations were closed to them by the colonial authorities, which sought to engineer class formation along ethnic lines. When power was transferred into the hands of indigenous elites, the ethnic minorities were scapegoated and harassed by some postcolonial governments and driven to seek refuge in the 'mother country'. The ethnic Chinese from Vietnam and those from Indonesia (a few of whom turned up in Britain) are good examples. Even ethnic-Chinese immigrants from Malaysia and the Caribbean countries sometimes complain of political and social discrimination in the country of origin.

Vietnamese Chinese

Vietnamese Chinese reached Britain as refugees under an international resettlement scheme in the years after the American defeat. Between 1978 and 1989, around one million fled Vietnam. Among them were some 700,000 ethnic Chinese who had suffered harassment and persecution by the Hanoi Government at a time of worsening relations between Hanoi and Beijing, culminating in 1979 in a short but bloody border war.

The Vietnam-born Chinese who sought safety abroad are sometimes lumped together with Britain's ethnic-Chinese immigrants from

Malaysia and Singapore as 'twice migrants'. However, they differ in most respects from the Chinese who reached Britain along the Commonwealth connection, not least in the manner of their migration. Their departure from Vietnam was sudden, traumatic, and unplanned. They were unfamiliar with the English language and British culture and had no prior connection to the UK, whose existing Chinese communities belonged to speech groups other than their own. They also differed in terms of their educational and class background. Probably the only important experience they had in common with the Chinese from maritime Southeast Asia was that they had lived as an ethnic minority before migrating.

In the late 1970s and early 1980s, nearly 20,000 Vietnamese refugees were admitted to Britain. By 1990, the figure had reached around 22,000. Of these, a good half were admitted under internationally agreed quotas, while the rest were 'boat people' rescued from the sea or people brought in to join their families.[117]

An estimated 70–85 per cent were ethnic Chinese from North Vietnam, while the rest were either ethnic Vietnamese or ethnic Chinese from South Vietnam.[118] Few were equipped to work in Britain's industrialised economy. In Vietnam, most were farmers or fishermen, with some craftsmen and hawkers and a handful of traders and professionals. Whereas the level of education of other Chinese groups in Britain is, on average, higher than that of the majority whites, most Vietnamese Chinese were far worse educated on arrival. Even refugees with qualifications found it hard to get them recognised.

The British Government spent £21 million on resettling the refugees. Initially, it dispersed them to reception centres, of which there were up to forty, chiefly in parts of the country with many empty houses but few jobs.[119] The authorities justified this scatter policy on two grounds: there were insufficient funds for centralised accommodation, and they were anxious to avoid creating ghettos that might hinder the refugees' integration.[120] During the period of reception, which lasted from three months to a year, they were expected to learn the 'British way of life' and prepare for settlement.[121]

The scatter policy copied measures applied to Ugandan Asian refugees in the early 1970s, when the United Kingdom was divided into 'red' zones said to have too many South Asians and 'green' zones with few or no South Asians, and therefore considered suitable for new settlement. The Ugandan Asians voted with their feet against this arrangement and moved of their own accord into 'red' zones, where they felt less isolated.[122] It is puzzling why the authorities thought that a policy that had failed the East African Asians would work for the Vietnamese – especially since most of the Asians knew English, whereas few Vietnamese did.

The decision to scatter the refugees thinly was soon recognised to be wrong. Refugee Action said the policy could 'be severely criticised from social and welfare perspectives'. 'There were Vietnamese families in Northern Ireland who wanted to move back to the British mainland,' noted one critic. 'There were people in Scotland who wanted to move to England, there were Vietnamese scattered in the rural areas who wished to move into the cities.' An officer of the settlement programme concluded: 'The mistaken thinking behind this [scatter policy] is that you can take people and shape them into any culture you want, as if they were made of clay.' Under the scheme, refugees sent to small rural communities were particularly neglected. Many were deprived of statutory services and specialist help. Isolated and traumatised, the refugees developed 'post-settlement depression'.[123]

Eventually, the refugees took affairs into their own hands and spontaneously regrouped in the cities.[124] Their principal target was London, which had a Vietnamese-Chinese population of around 4000 in 1985 and an overall Vietnamese population (including ethnic Chinese) of 14,000 in the early 1990s. Birmingham was the second main city of resettlement, followed by Manchester and Leeds. This remigration led to severe overcrowding. It helped overcome the loneliness and despair but laid the refugees open to racist abuse on inner-city housing estates.

The refugees were troubled from the start by internal divisions. Those from South Vietnam spoke better English and were better educated and better acquainted with Western culture than those from the north, and the ethnic Vietnamese were better organised and had a clearer political agenda than the ethnic Chinese.[125] Although many of the ethnic Chinese spoke Vietnamese, they were from a variety of Chinese speech groups, including Cantonese, Teochiu 潮州话, Hokkien 福建话, Hainanese 海南话, and Hakka 客家话.[126] Some were Catholics, others Buddhists. A minority from Cambodia and Laos complicated the picture even further.

Not until after the remigrations of the early 1980s did the refugees start to overcome their fragmentation and achieve some solidarity. More than forty self-help groups and associations sprang up in London in the 1980s and the early 1990s, including two housing associations and several employment projects, many of them funded by government grants.[127]

The refugees tended to gravitate to areas with a Chinese presence, where they could buy specialist foods and seek employment in a

Chinese-speaking environment. However, they were often on bad terms with the Hong Kong Chinese. Although they thought of themselves as Chinese and took pride in their heritage, many Hong Kong Chinese considered them culturally corrupted. Caterers saw them as a business threat, catering workers saw them as rivals on the labour market.

Some refugees took casual work in Chinese restaurants as kitchen helps, mainly in Soho's Chinatown, or found menial employment outside the ethnic enclave. A few set up takeaways or clothing work-shops.[128] However, 70 per cent remained unemployed in the mid-1980s. The 1991 Census ignored the distinction between Chinese born in Vietnam and in other parts of the world, so Census data fail to show how the situation subsequently evolved.

Refugee Action commented that the scatter policy 'clearly inhibited the development of viable Vietnamese communities which could have provided the refugees with the cultural, emotional and service support of their own people'.[129] Chinese activists pointed out that the policy was incompatible with the Home Affairs Committee's own report on Britain's wider Chinese community:

> [T]he problems faced by the refugees have been compounded by the government's policy of dispersal. The report notes the problems of dispersal of the UK Chinese community caused by the pressures of the catering trade. Yet it has nothing against the deliberate scattering of refugee families into remote parts of Britain, where they are totally isolated.[130]

Few of the refugees were equipped for employment in the main-stream. Most were of working-class origin and had little schooling.[131] In France, by contrast, the refugees showed an extraordinary capacity for self-improvement and transformed the face of Chinatown.[132] France had long been a destination for Vietnam-born Chinese of all social classes. In 1954, after the French defeat at Diên Biên Phu, a couple of thousand ethnic Chinese with French nationality were among several thousand refugees 'repatriated'. They were followed by further waves of refugees in 1957 and others who left in the 1960s. Some Vietnamese Chinese sent their children to study at French universities, often as a way of preparing for family migration at a later point. The refugees were able to join networks formed before the major exodus. Some had earlier exported assets to Europe, which they now invested in enterprises.[133]

In refugee eyes, France, the United States, and Australia were more favourable destinations than Britain. These countries therefore tended to attract a disproportionate number of resourceful and highly motivated settlers. Like France, the United States had a relatively prosperous Vietnamese-Chinese community to which newcomers could turn. In France, the United States, and Australia, the refugees gathered in far greater numbers than in Britain and settled more densely. France, for example, took up to 200,000. Tens of thousands congregated in Paris' 13th arrondissement.[134] By 1990, they accounted for 20.5 per cent of Chinese economic activity in Paris.[135]

Chinese students

Students have always formed a substantial minority of Britain's Chinese population. In principle, they are distinct from labour and business immigrants, for they are supposedly transients and most have a different regional and social background from conventional settlers. In practice, however, the distinction often fails. Chinese admitted to study often take up part-time jobs, usually in the ethnic enclave, and some settle. Conversely, children of Chinese who arrive as entrepreneurs or workers go on to study.

As an ex-imperial power, Britain has always attracted foreign students. The Chinese first started sending students abroad during the Self-Strengthening Movement 自强运动 of 1861–1895, a programme of military modernisation launched after China's defeat in the Opium Wars. In 1875, a small group of students went to France and Britain. They were followed in 1876 by a larger group, most of whom went to Britain, and by others in 1881, who studied naval and military science. A few self-supporting students also came.

At around the turn of the century, after China's defeat by Japan in 1895 and the start of the imperialist 'scramble for concessions', a second wave of students enrolled at British colleges and universities, as part of a new drive for modernisation. In 1900, around 35 students arrived to study engineering. The last big prewar enrolment started in 1908, when a special Chinese mission brought more than 140 state-sponsored students to London and sent others to mainland Europe. Between 1887 and 1902, larger numbers of ethnic Chinese, many of them Straits-born, took up places at universities all over Britain. By that time, Britain had more private Chinese students than the whole of the rest of Europe.[136]

On the eve of the First World War, more than 350 Chinese were studying in Britain. Three-quarters were self-financing, the rest were funded by the Chinese government.[137] London had the biggest number (116), followed by Edinburgh, Glasgow, and Birmingham. The students were spread evenly over medicine, law, economics, and engineering. They included a dozen or so women and girls.[138] In the war, the number fell beneath three hundred, but it continued to exceed that of Chinese students elsewhere in Europe.

Like Chinese students throughout the world, some of the prewar visitors took up the cudgels on behalf of Chinatown. This engagement probably started in 1914, when the Chinese Students' Christian Union set up classes for local Chinese.[139]

In the 1930s, the Chinese student population in Britain increased as a result of new schemes created under an inter-governmental agreement, including one to assist Chinese to study in engineering workshops. These schemes were funded by Britain's Universities' China Committee from reparations paid by China under the Boxer Protocol. By 1931, 450 Chinese students were studying in Britain, including 240 from China, 120 from Malaya, and 35 from Hong Kong. Half were in London, where the China House and the China Institute (founded by the Universities' China Committee) were set up to meet their needs.[140]

A comparison of Chinese students across western Europe in the first half of the twentieth century reveals differences and similarities between Britain and other countries. Most China-born students in Britain in the 1930s and the 1940s received scholarships. However, if one excludes beneficiaries of the Boxer Indemnity Fund, far fewer publicly funded students went to Britain than to France and Germany in the 1930s. Seen from another angle, far fewer self-financing Chinese students (who made up 90 per cent of the whole) studied in any of the three countries than elsewhere.[141] Britain also received large numbers of self-supporting ethnic-Chinese students from its colonies in Southeast Asia and elsewhere. These students had closer ties to Britain than those from China, were more likely to participate in British institutions, and were free to stay after graduating.

In this respect, Britain resembled France and the Netherlands, also destinations of ethnic-Chinese students from colonies in Southeast Asia and across the world.[142] Chinese students in Britain between the wars showed less interest in politics than those in France, Germany, and the Netherlands.[143] Chinese students in France had a radical tradition going back to 1919, when the first contingent of 2000 young Chinese reached France as part of a work-study movement set up in Paris by Chinese anarchist intellectuals.[144] Many who went to Germany were drawn by the association either with Karl Marx (in the 1920s) or with Nazism (after 1933).[145] In the Netherlands, where all but one or two of the students were Peranakan Chinese from the Dutch East Indies, the overwhelming majority joined the Chung Hwa Hui 中华会, an antico-lonial association.[146] Chinese students in Britain had a weaker political tradition and were more diverse, so no single interest predominated. Their intervention in the Chinese community was usually restricted to moral issues and general education.

After the Second World War, Hong Kong and Southeast Asia were, for many years, practically the sole source of Chinese student immigration to Britain. In the 1960s, their numbers grew rapidly (although the failure to record their ethnic as opposed to national origin makes it difficult to say by how many). Every year, several thousand students were admitted from Hong Kong. Table 2.1 shows the overseas student population in Britain in selected years up to 1998. (The figures indicate country of origin rather than ethnic group.) In the late 1970s, more than 70 per cent of Malaysian Chinese in the United Kingdom were of student age.[147]

The number of Taiwan students at British universities, second only to that in the United States, increased from 2739 in the first six months of 1994[148] to more than 11,000 in the late 1990s.[149] Thousands of students from mainland China have studied in Britain since the 1980s, accompanied in many cases by dependants.[150] During 1995–1996, 2746 Chinese were studying in Britain. By the late 1990s, their number had more than doubled, to 6094, possibly with an equal or greater number of dependants. By 2002, they were set to reach 20,000, an increase described by a minister as 'dramatic'.[151] According to a British Council forecast, they were expected to reach as high as 145,000 by 2020.[152]

The conditions and prospects of the three groups of students – ethnic Chinese from current or former British colonies, Taiwanese, and mainland Chinese – differ greatly. Most in the first two groups lead a relatively prosperous and carefree life. Before 1980, many stayed on after completing their courses. Some set up businesses, others provided services either within the Chinese community or in the general

Table 2.1 Commonwealth students in UK tertiary education, 1979–1998

	1979–1980	*1988–1988*	*1997–1998*
Hong Kong	6251	7386	5486
Malaysia	14,326	6517	15,712
Singapore	1787	2052	5120

Source: Times Higher Education Supplement, 30 June 2000, p. 13.

economy. Many mainland students, in contrast, live poorly in unsatisfactory and overcrowded accommodation. Student associations and the Chinese Embassy play an important part in organising their lives.[153] Those with inadequate funds or keen to save find work in Chinese restaurants, usually at sweat-shop rates. Students from all three groups joined in the protests against the crackdown on the student movement in China in 1989, as a result of which several hundred mainland students were allowed to stay in Britain. Since 1989, few students from any of the three groups have shown much interest in homeland politics.

Students from mainland China and their families are, in theory, transitory. In reality, however, many are here to stay. Nominally, they are *liu xuesheng* 留学生, 'students studying abroad', but many take up jobs in Britain after graduating and have no intention of returning to China to live, at least for the time being. In effect, they are part of a new wave of highly skilled migration into Britain, where they are viewed as an economic and easily assimilable asset. Even so, they (and their dependants) retain the *liu xuesheng* label, which has come to denote a fixed social identity separate from that of 'overseas Chinese', an identity they tend to look down on and reject.[154]

Chinese demographics

It is not easy to trace Chinese demographic development in Britain in all its phases, for censuses before 1991 recorded only country of birth and ignored ethnic origin. They therefore counted people of non-Chinese ethnic origin (including whites) among those born in China and East Asia and failed to count separately people of Chinese ethnic origin born in Britain to immigrants. They also excluded ethnic Chinese from British colonies. Tables 2.2 and 2.3 show the China-born population of England and Wales and in Scotland up to 1931.

The data for the postwar years up to 1981, summarised in Table 2.4, suffer from the same limitations as the earlier figures. They are based on place of birth rather than ethnic origin, so they include non-Chinese born in East Asia and do not include the British-born children of ethnic Chinese or Chinese immigrants born outside the Far East Commonwealth. They include temporary residents and visitors, especially educational transients. In 1971, for example, more than half the estimated 20,000 Chinese from Singapore and 8000 from Malaysia were reckoned to be nurses and students.

The 1991 Census gave the first estimate of the number of Chinese in Britain based on a direct counting of people considered by the Census

Table 2.2 The China-born population of England and Wales, 1851–1931

Year	Number
1851	78
1861	147
1871	202
1881	665
1891	582
1901	387
1911	1319
1921	2419
1931	1934

Source: Census Reports, cited in Ng 1968, p. 6.

Table 2.3 The China-born population of Scotland, 1901–1931

Year	Number
1901	38
1931	760

Source: Panayi 1994, p. 52.

Table 2.4 The Chinese population of Great Britain, 1951–1981

	China	Hong Kong	Singapore	Malaysia	Total
1951	1,763	3,459	3,255	4,046	12,523
1961	9,192	10,222	9,820	9,516	38,750
1971	13,495	29,520	27,335	25,680	96,030
1981	17,569	58,917	32,447	45,430	154,363

Source: Census, cited in Taylor 1987, p. 40. The figures for 1951 and 1961 cover England and Wales only.

form-filler to be Chinese and thus opened the way to the first detailed analysis of the group's demographics and social and economic characteristics. The Fourth National Survey of Ethnic Minorities, undertaken in 1994, used Census data to create nationally representative samples of the Caribbean, South Asian, and Chinese groups in England and

Wales.[155] The Census and the Survey provide a dependable basis for an analysis of the Chinese community in the early 1990s.

The 1991 Census counted 156,938 ethnic Chinese, representing 0.3 per cent of the British population. The Chinese were the smallest ethnic group identified, but the third largest if blacks and South Asians are grouped as global categories. (See Table 2.5.) One-third came from Hong Kong and more than one-quarter were born in Britain, followed by China, Malaysia, Vietnam, Singapore, Taiwan, and Mauritius.[156] The remaining 5 per cent came from a wide range of countries.[157] These residual groups are consigned in Table 2.6 to the category 'Other'.[158]

Informal Chinese estimates in the late 1980s put the size of the population much higher, at around 200,000.[159] Such estimates have become all but axiomatic in British ethnic-Chinese studies, but they are based on little more than guesswork. Even so, they serve to remind us that the Census figures are, in the Chinese perception, a probable underestimate.

The average Chinese in Britain in 1991 was younger by nine years than the average white.[160] Most ethnic Chinese were immigrants. Three-fifths were aged 20–40. This age group far exceeded in number the under twenties. Around 20 per cent of the population aged 16 and over were students, but this figure included an unquantifiable number of overseas students.[161] More than one-third of Chinese men were self-employed, nearly twice the rate for white men, as were 20 per cent of Chinese women, three times the rate for white women. Overwhelmingly, Chinese men (60.5 per cent) and women (50.9 per cent) worked in the distribution sector (which covers hotels, catering, and retailing). One-fifth of Chinese men were managers and proprietors and one-third

Table 2.5 Population of Britain by ethnic category, 1991

White	51,874,792
Black Caribbean	499,964
Black African	212,362
Black other	178,401
Indian	840,255
Pakistani	476,555
Bangladeshi	162,835
Chinese	156,938
Other Asian	197,534
Other groups	290,206

Source: Cheng 1996, p. 161.

Table 2.6 Chinese in Britain by country of origin, 1991

Country	Percentage
Britain	28
Hong Kong	34
China	12
Malaysia	10
Vietnam	6
Singapore	3
Taiwan	1
Mauritius	1
Other	5

Sources: Owen 1994, p. 2, and Chan and Chan 1997, p. 126.

worked in 'personal services', usually meaning catering and associated trades in both cases; the percentages for Chinese women were 15.3 and 21.5. The percentage of Chinese men employed as science and engineering professionals (7.3 per cent) and health professionals (4 per cent) was more than twice that of white men (3.7 and 0.8 per cent, respectively). The unemployment rate for Chinese men was marginally lower than for white men and lower than for any other listed ethnic minority. The unemployment rate for Chinese men in their forties was half that of white men.[162]

Since 1991, the Chinese population has increased steadily, as a result of natural growth, student immigration, 'illegal' immigration from the Chinese mainland, and immigration from Hong Kong under the terms of the British Nationality (Hong Kong) Act, 1990, introduced to give full British citizenship to 50,000 selected people and their dependants as part of the arrangements for Hong Kong's retrocession to China in 1997. Chinese observers around 1997 suggested that the Chinese population of Britain was 250,000,[163] making it either the largest Chinese community in Europe or one of the two largest, together with France.[164] This guesstimate is hard to square with the Census, for the possible sources of accrual could hardly account for an increase of 100,000 in just a few years, even assuming substantial undercounting in 1991. By 2002, one unofficial estimate had risen to 400,000.[165]

It is not known how many Hong Kong residents have resettled in Britain under the scheme introduced in 1990, for the destination of those leaving the territory is not recorded and people arriving in Britain under the scheme are treated as UK citizens and also not recorded.[166] However, observers dismiss as 'a sublime conceit' British predictions of a massive influx. They point out that for many, getting a British passport is an insurance policy rather than an indication of intent, and that Britain is the fifth favourite destination of Hong Kong emigrants after Canada, Australia, the United States, and Singapore. Others argue that would-be immigrants believe that Britain treats Chinese without warmth and is a country in decline. In any case, it is estimated that 10 per cent of those who leave Hong Kong under such schemes will eventually return, for business and financial reasons.[167]

The total of emigrants from Hong Kong in the late 1990s is probably indicative of trends in Hong Kong emigration to the United Kingdom. The number dropped from 40,300 in 1996 to 30,900 in 1997 to 19,300 in 1998.[168]

'Illegal' immigration

The term 'illegal immigrant' (first used of Jews entering Palestine without permission in the later years of the British mandate) refers to people whose entry into Britain is unlawful or who overstay or fail to observe a condition imposed on their leave to enter. Until the twentieth century, there was no statutory machinery for regulating immigration into Britain. The first systematic controls were introduced under the Aliens Act of 1905, by which time anti-foreign agitators had succeeded in lumping together in the popular imagination 'the criminal, the destitute, and the job-stealing alien'.[169] As a result of the Act, aliens thought likely to become a charge on public funds were earmarked for exclusion, together with criminals, anarchists, prostitutes, and other people of 'notoriously bad character'.[170]

Although framed largely with Jews in mind, the Act was also used to control illegal entry by Chinese. During the long years of Chinese exclusion from the United States and Australia, people-smuggling by way of Europe became a profitable business in parts of China. Most of the smuggling was to the British Dominions and the New World, but some stowaways stopped off in Europe.[171] It is not known how many Chinese were kept out or deported as 'undesirables' under the Aliens Act and associated legislation, but they were not the least of its targets.

Until 1962, Commonwealth Chinese had the right to settle in Britain but alien Chinese continued to be subject to controls. As we have seen, relatively large numbers of China-born aliens were admitted to Britain from Hong Kong in the 1960s and the early 1970s. In the 1980s and 1990s, when China reverted to its traditional status of a land of extensive out-migration, more mainland Chinese left for Europe than ever before in the history of Chinese migration. By that time, however, many legal avenues into Britain had been closed off, so proportionately fewer Chinese migrants ended up in Britain than on the western European mainland, which was easier to enter.[172]

As the mainland western European countries tightened their immigration policies in the late 1980s, syndicates of Chinese 'migration brokers' became more active in transporting people to a new life in Europe, where they claimed asylum or slipped underground. By 1996, the fee for smuggling someone into Europe could be as high as 200,000 RMB (Chinese yuan), a couple of hundred times what the average peasant earned in a year.[173] The usual way in was through Russia or an Eastern European country. Tougher immigration controls by the United States and Canada starting in the late 1990s helped make Europe a more attractive destination, accessible (unlike North America) by land as well as by sea and air.[174]

The extent of this immigration into the United Kingdom is unknowable, but the steep rise in the 1990s in the number of Chinese applying for political asylum indicates an upward trend, if one assumes that nearly all asylum applicants are driven by the same economic motives as the illegal immigrants. Many originate in the coastal provinces of Fujian, Guangdong, and Zhejiang, but illegal Chinese immigration into Europe is far more diverse in origin than into the United States.[175] Britain's National Criminal Intelligence Service and the Immigration and Nationality Directorate Investigation Service, which monitor irregular immigration, believe thousands of Chinese entered Britain in the period up to June 2000, when the tragic discovery of 58 dead Chinese stowaways in the back of a lorry on its way to Dover brought the issue of people-trafficking to international attention.[176] In subsequent years, the numbers of applications for asylum by Chinese continued to grow – from 2390 in 2001 to 3675 in 2002, when Chinese made 4 per cent of all applications.[177] (See Table 2.7.)

Most of the big changes in the Chinese community in Britain over the decades happened as a result of developments in immigration law. The clampdown on illegal entrants and asylum seekers in the late 1990s and the consequent switch to secret trafficking as the main form of Chinese immigration into Britain are also having a major impact on the

Table 2.7   Chinese applications for asylum
in the United Kingdom, 1992–1997

Year	Number
1992	330
1993	215
1994	425
1995	790
1996	820
1997	1945

Source: Nyíri and Van lokven 1999, p. 80.

community. One effect is to hammer a further nail into the coffin of community cohesion and control. Whereas most previous immigration was a group affair conducted along established chains, much of the new-style human traffic is diverse in origin, with individuals from all over China coming together only for the last stage of the journey into Britain.[178] The people-traffickers recruit their customers wherever they can find them. Unlike earlier migrant cohorts, the illegal entrants are unlikely to have many points of contact in the established Chinese community. Instead, they cause the community to ravel out, just like the influx of Chinese aliens in the 1960s and the early 1970s frayed the community of caterers.

The presence of large numbers of illegal immigrants may also lead to a rise in Chinese crime. The theory that Chinese crime in Europe is on the increase is based largely on intuition and extrapolation from past experience rather than on hard data. Analysts work on the assumption that the growth of illegal immigration creates the conditions for a rise in crime. The exclusion of illegal immigrants from social rights and the difficulty that undocumented workers encounter in finding work is an incentive to commit crimes in order to secure a living. Many illegal immigrants are heavily in debt to the traffickers, another incentive to turn to crime.[179]

A rise in crime threatens the Chinese in two ways. It lays their community open to attack from within, for Chinese criminals and racketeers abroad usually target their compatriots or co-ethnics; and from without, for it helps to promote or revive ancient stereotypes of the Chinese, as disreputable and dishonest. It therefore increases strains and tensions both within the Chinese community and between it and the majority population.

'New migrants'

Illegal Chinese immigrants and mainland Chinese student immigrants, together with immigrants of various sorts who have succeeded since the late 1970s in establishing their presence in Britain and elsewhere on a legal footing, are part of the worldwide phenomenon known in China as 'new migrants' 新移民, to distinguish them from the old-style 'overseas Chinese'. While some higher-level Chinese state officials balk at the indiscipline, lawlessness, and absence of scruple with which some new migrants are associated, both at home and overseas, other officials, from centre down to county, view them as a potential economic asset and conduit into China for new investment. The new migrants are thus given the mission of speeding China's transformation 'old migrants' seem incapable of delivering. At local level, some officials actively promote and broker this emigration.[180]

In the past, Chinese communist authorities did everything in their power to prevent students and scholars from settling overseas. In the 1990s, however, Beijing started to adopt a more pragmatic approach, as the inevitability of the brain drain became apparent. Students who opt to stay abroad are now free to visit China and to leave again, a transition signalled by the official switch in motto from *huiguo fuwu* 回国服务 (return to serve the country) to *weiguo fuwu* 为国服务 (serve the country). The new policy is primarily designed to win the support of the highly educated group for Beijing's modernisation programme. It also has a foreign-policy rationale: to rally new migrants behind Beijing's global campaign for a united front of Chinese patriots, a campaign to which most old migrants are indifferent or hostile.[181]

Many students and scholars who have gone abroad in recent years have become permanent residents of the host countries. On the whole, such people represent a new kind of immigrant, but quite a few are connected to other groups, including migrant entrepreneurs who find purchasing a university education for their offspring (or for themselves) the easiest way to get an entry visa. Many students take on paid jobs abroad. Some abandon their studies and join the ranks of migrant labour, thus blurring class lines even further.

Among the new migrants are quite a few from Fujian, a maritime province on China's southeastern coast. Historically, Fujian is second only to Guangdong as a source of emigration. Fujianese crewed some of the vessels that plied between Asia and Britain in the days of the East India Company, but for most of the time they were never a major component of Chinese communities anywhere in Europe. Even today the United States and Japan are their preferred destinations overseas, but as the barriers around those countries grew in the late twentieth century, more and more Fujianese headed for Europe, often by way of Moscow. Criminal gangs known as 'snakeheads' broker much of this migration.

At least one county government in Fujian at one time supported this trade in labour, to generate an inflow of foreign currency. Other authorities – local and national – have encouraged the founding of native-place associations among migrants in Europe. Counties that encourage new emigration may lack an existing population base overseas.

An unprecedentedly large number of Fujianese (around ten thousand) came to live in Britain, Italy, Germany, the Netherlands, and France in the late 1990s and early 2000s. According to research by Pál Nyíri, tiny groups of Fujianese seafarers who had settled in European ports in the 1940s formed the bridgehead on which the newcomers gathered.[182] Later, the snakeheads took over. Of the various Fujianese destinations in Europe, Britain is currently the preferred one. The British Chinese community's old sending places are by now too prosperous to provide sufficient fresh supplies of cheap unskilled labour, while the Zhejiangese who staff the Chinese kitchens and workshops of mainland Europe have not so far penetrated the British market. The Fujianese therefore see Britain as their best bet in Europe. Their arrival helped relieve the labour shortage in Chinese restaurants and drove down wages. According to the authors of a recent report on 'the Fuzhou diaspora in Europe', the Fujianese are simultaneously among the most disadvantaged and the most mobile transnational groups. As illegal immigrants, they are particularly vulnerable to exploitation, by both the snakeheads and the Chinatown caterers. For the same reason, they are least likely to integrate into the host society, and therefore most likely to seek support in the diaspora.[183] According to this same research, they 'remain very much in control of their own destiny'.[184]

In their book on new Fujianese migration, Pieke, Nyíri, Thunø, and Ceccagno argue that it

> consists of separate migration configurations, each with its own unique history and institutional arrangements. Each configuration, moreover, encompasses individual experiences and practices, which together render Chinese migration extraordinarily complex, resilient, and variegated. We found that the new migration often fans out to entirely new destinations before falling into the more familiar and conventional pattern of chain migration. One key feature of the

Chinese migration is its combination of pioneering exploration of unknown and even unlikely destinations with later mass migration to specific areas.[185]

They also note that the children of migrants born or raised in Europe, specifically in Hungary and Britain, are 'generally upwardly mobile and lost to the family business, and this corresponds to the wishes of the parents'.[186]

We are persuaded in part by this definition of new Chinese migration, given the heterogeneous character of the Chinese and Fujianese population in Britain and Europe. Our research confirms that the second generation, through education, succeeds in climbing some way up the British class ladder. However, we question the extent to which new Chinese migrants might engage in 'pioneering' exploration of new territories before settling into areas occupied by earlier migrants. Our research suggests that Chinese migrants lacking education, skills, and extensive experience of moving across territories tend to work in enterprises owned by co-ethnics before venturing into new places, mainly in order to avoid competition. Migrants with class resources, on the other hand, tend to work alone: on the rare occasions they do form partnerships, it is out of necessity and seldom with co-ethnics.[187]

Our research confirms that many of the new Chinese migrants to Britain are from major urban centres in Asia and highly educated, though not necessarily well connected. Given their high levels of education and access to funding, they have been able to move into a variety of businesses and industries, including upmarket restaurants, hi-tech ventures, electronic and electrical manufacture, and professional services. However, we found most of them were from Taiwan, Hong Kong, and Southeast Asia. There is little evidence of mainland Chinese investing in the United Kingdom and starting up small enterprises.

Men and women from urban areas in northeastern China, including Shenyang, formed a separate stream of immigration into Britain and Europe. Many such immigrants were former workers who lost their jobs as a result of the post-Mao industrial reforms. They differ in character and behaviour from the Fujianese, who are mainly rural. They are mostly older than the Fujianese, in their late thirties and early forties, and better educated. Some arrived on official passports, perhaps ostensibly on official business, and then disappeared from official view. They were generally less open and less likely to congregate than the Fujianese, who had their teashops in the Chinatowns. They have tended to leave

London and seek work in the provinces. Since they arrived independently, they lacked ties to the snakeheads and were not burdened by debt in the same way as the Fujianese. They had less entrepreneurial drive than Chinese from other provinces and were more likely to view themselves as sojourners than as settlers.[188]

Nyíri argues that migrants from Fujian travel to Europe along many different routes and by different means, and that the visas and documents they use are obtained in several different ways, both legal and illegal. In his view, however, it is often unhelpful to distinguish between these different modes of migration, since in practice they merge and converge. According to him, it is ultimately immaterial whether visas are obtained from individual migration brokers, licensed agencies, or snakehead gangs.[189] We question this conflation of illegal migrants and people with class resources in the 'new wave' of Chinese migration. We agree that class resources serve legal migrants well in foreign settings, but we would propose a clearer distinction between legal and illegal migrants and analyse each group separately. Our research suggests that Chinese illegal migrants in Europe bring few skills with them, suffer on account of their illegal status, and work mainly outside the mainstream (usually for other ethnic Chinese who migrated earlier).

We also doubt whether such migrants are as highly mobile as Nyíri and others claim. According to our informants, most Fujianese either remain in the United Kingdom or go to the Irish Republic. Nor do they return frequently to China, if only because resettlement in a new environment is time-consuming and expensive. While it would be wrong to depict such migrants solely as the 'hapless victims' of circumstance or criminal gangs, to portray them as 'new cosmopolitans' who 'never reach a final destination but can always move on if the conditions are right' runs the risk of romanticising them.[190] Chinese volunteers who work with Britain's Fujianese note a high incidence of mental troubles and a frantic chasing after work and reacting to rumours of immigration amnesties, often spread by snakehead brokers for business reasons.[191]

As Nyíri himself points out, class differences have begun to eclipse sub-ethnic differences among Chinese migrants. According to him, the only unifying force that survives among Chinese migrants of the 'new wave' is therefore a pan-Chinese identity based on the mainland government's state ideology. However, we find little evidence of such a unifying ideology, at least among the new Chinese in Britain. Where new Chinese migrants do identify with the Chinese regime, the identification is often superficial. We question the prediction that 'deterritorialised nationalism' will, as a result of new migration, prevail over integration even among these relatively settled and rooted groups.

Conclusions

Over the past two centuries, different groups of Chinese have reached Britain along different paths, by different means, and with different projects. At one time, right up to the 1970s, they could be said to constitute a community of sorts, despite lacking a centralised authority and concentrated settlement. By 2000, however, when the catering niche had ceased to exhaust their 'effective social universe', interrelations among Chinese groups and individuals were based less and less on an expectation of reciprocity and more and more on calculations of separate self-interest.

From the point of view of the authorities, the Chinese have often seemed intractable and anarchic, chiefly because they have organised their own affairs in their own ways, often with barely a nod to the rules. A striving for independence and self-sufficiency was the hallmark of the pioneers, ever since they first spilled over from the Shadwell barracks into the London rookeries and planted the Chinatown tradition. Even the original barracks community, nominally under the control of the East India Company, was unruly and unmanageable.

Gradually, as the community became more rooted, it began to run its own recruitment, from the point of emigration to the point of settlement, a development consummated in the postwar emigration from rural Hong Kong, which was Chinese-managed. In that sense, the Chinese differed from most of postwar Britain's immigrant minorities, many of whose members were signed up and shipped in by the British. The Chinese organised not only their own passage into Britain but their own employment, again unlike most other non-white immigrants.[192]

Ethnic Chinese from Malaysia, Singapore, and former British colonies throughout the world and urban Chinese from Hong Kong and Taiwan came either as students or as entrepreneurs. Those who settled used their qualifications and resources to enter the professions and the mainstream economy. Their ties to the caterers have been quite slender, as were the ties of earlier generations of Chinese students to the seafarers. The refugees from Vietnam included a majority of ethnic Chinese who failed at first to replicate the business success of Britain's other Chinese and ethnic-Chinese immigrants. This failure was due both to a lack of skills and resources and to deficiencies in the programme set up to induct them. For a while, many remained jobless and demoralised. Some hung around Chinatown, on the margins of the Hong Kong Chinese community. Recent immigration from China, starting in the 1980s, has produced the most variegated group, ranging from political refugees to scholars, well-connected business people, and an underworld.

The experience of the Chinese community in Britain differs in important ways from that in other European countries. Britain's relationship to China was, at one time, uniquely close (and uniquely tortured) because of the exceptional extent and duration of the British interest in China and the Hong Kong connection. No other country except Portugal had a colony in China, and Macao was nowhere near as important for Portugal as Hong Kong was for Britain. As for the French and the Dutch, their experience in Southeast Asia was diluted across cultures and peoples, of which the ethnic Chinese were just one. In the mid-twentieth century, the community was also distinguished from others outside Europe by its narrow provenance. Between the late 1950s and the early 1970s, nearly all Chinese in Britain had a personal or ancestral tie to one tiny region, the New Territories of Hong Kong. For a time, the Chinese community in Britain was therefore more uniform and stable than in many other countries – qualities likelier to produce conformity than Southeast Asian-style tycoons. Not until the last quarter of the twentieth century was it rendered diverse by new immigration.

3
The Chinese Economy in Britain

Chinese first arrived in Britain in large numbers as seafarers rather than (like the Irish and the Jews) as settlers. Their presence increased as a result of the growth of the entrepôt trade in Southeast Asia, the opening of the Treaty Ports in China, and the opening of the Suez Canal. They were, at least initially, transnational workers and passage migrants rather than would-be sojourners or immigrants. However, their turn-round in the ports was not instantaneous, so a certain infrastructure, including board and lodgings, was needed to look after them. Some seafarers took advantage of their time ashore to spy out the chances for business activity and lay contacts, for many came from communities with a tradition of emigration and had a good idea of what to look for. Their transit facilities served as a base from which to reconnoitre the environs. A tiny Chinatown was born, with an economy to match.

By comparison with other parts of the world, however, the opportunities to work or trade were sparse. Although 'not negligible as a goal of immigration' in the late nineteenth century, Britain was more a place of emigration and transmigration.[1] Union rules impeded entry into skilled trades and there was no shortage of native unskilled labour. 'In the eyes of people from Wuyi 五邑,' according to a study by scholars from Wuyi (roughly equivalent to Siyi 四邑), 'wages in Europe were low and life was hard, so few chose to go there'.[2]

Foreigners found it hard to get employment in the factories that had replaced much of the workshop system. The main immigrant trade was clothing, supplemented by boot and shoe-making, cap-making, cabinet-making, slipper-making, and furriery. The Jews, many of them tailors by profession, settled down in these sectors and some prospered. Nearly all Britain's white immigrants in the late nineteenth and early twentieth century were townspeople who felt at home in and around London, where 60 per cent of them lived and worked.[3] Similar employment opportunities were rarely if ever open to Chinese. In the case of Chinese from a rural background, this was probably because their customary occupations were not relevant to British needs. Even those with skills and competencies suited to the mainstream economy were hindered by racist hostility and their own lack of English.

They were, moreover, alone in a strange land. Jewish and Catholic refugees could seek assistance from an existing range of institutions set up by British Jews and Catholics to minister to their coreligionists, institutions that cemented the communities. Their skins were white; they were perceived as culturally less distant, despite suffering religious discrimination; and they had less difficulty than the Chinese in learning English. They formed communities of tens of thousands, able to sustain relatively large numbers of ethnic shops and services. Like the refugees, the Chinese also needed shops and services, but their community was too small and precarious to support an economy capable of branching out more widely.

A distinction can be drawn between the early Chinese in Britain and those in the United States and Australia. In the United States in 1880, only 23 per cent of Chinese lived in urban areas. (The percentage rose to 66 in 1920 and 94 in 1950. The American Chinese were driven into urban ghettos after the 1880s by mob violence during the anti-Chinese campaigns.[4]) In Australia, only 32 per cent lived in metropolitan areas in 1911 (compared with 37.5 in 1921, 41.4 in 1933, and 58.9 in 1947, when the percentage exceeded that of whites for the first time).[5] In Britain, where agriculture was in swift decline as a proportion of the overall economy, Chinese settlement was exclusively urban. In this sense, the pioneering generation of Chinese in the United States and Australia had the advantage over their compatriots in Britain. They could compete on a more equal basis with local whites and sometimes even had the upper hand. From their rural bases, they could urbanise in a more diversified and successful way, with fewer penalties and handi-caps. The rural sojourn served as a decompression chamber through which those who had been peasants could manage the transition to urbanism.

Britain and the other European countries were also far smaller and more crowded than the United States and Australia and British society was less open, for although Americans and Australians followed the same racist dogmas as the British, they lacked a strict class hierarchy.[6] The early Chinese in North America and Australia therefore found a wider range of outlets for their talents.

Studies picture the early Chinese in northern Australia as coolies recruited to work in the mines and build railways. In fact, many were skilled tradesmen. They included bricklayers, stone masons, carpenters, cabinet-makers, and boiler-makers. By the early twentieth century, the range of jobs and trades open to them – as craftsmen, market gardeners, laundrymen, shopworkers, boarding-masters, timber-men, shepherds, and so on – made them more mobile, self-sufficient, and independent than generally supposed.

The variety of Chinese occupations in America was even wider until the anti-Chinese strikes and riots, the sinophobic legislation, and the campaign of 'occupational eviction' in the four decades after 1870 resulted in their expulsion from the labour market:

> Not only did Chinese work in abandoned goldfields, build railroads, and wash clothes in America, but they also labored in many areas of mineral extraction; several kinds of fishery and cannery work; a number of different types of construction; the cigar, woolen, shoe, boot, and slipper industries; and garment manufacture. Chinese workers were employed in making bags, brooms, cordage, matches, candles, soap, bottles, pottery, and whips. A considerable amount of the reclamation work in the early West was done by Chinese. In the rural areas of California and other western states Chinese were employed in digging irrigation ditches, underground wine cellars, and reservoirs; in picking grapes, apples, peaches, cherries, pears, and olives; in growing cabbages, pumpkins, celery, and asparagus; and in building stone bridges, rock walls, and paved roads. A Chinese brought fellow Chinese workers to Monterey to pick wild mustard. Others discovered artificial methods of egg hatching, while still other Chinese developed the extensive truck-gardening and flower growing industries of the West. In the towns and cities Chinese restauranteurs [*sic*] provided a menu of exotic cuisine..., artisans from Canton carved jade, and Chinese adolescents and old men worked as waiters, busboys, butlers, and domestics.[7]

In Britain, by contrast, laundering is the only ethnically nonspecific trade in which land-based Chinese have ever engaged in large numbers. Most Chinese remained confined to tiny ethnically based enterprises. Even when Chinese business did get going, towards the end of the nineteenth century, it remained marginal and introverted for most of the next century and failed to shake off its introverted character even after the Second World War. It has remained overwhelmingly small in scale, except for a handful of businesses formed by ethnic Chinese from Southeast Asia.[8]

Seafaring

Britain's early Chinese visitors made the journey on all but one occasion aboard a non-Chinese vessel. The only Chinese ship to enter British waters before the twentieth century was the Keying 耆英, an 800-ton Guangzhou-based junk manned by 30 Chinese and 12 British. The junk touched shore in Liverpool in 1847 after a perilous voyage round the Cape of Good Hope and a detour by way of New York after running short of water and provisions. It sailed on to Gravesend, after which it was exhibited as a curiosity at the International Fair in 1854.[9] Its appearance was a freak event. Decades passed before the next Chinese ship arrived.

Chinese seafarers started to enlist on British ships (of the East India Company) in the late eighteenth century, when London monopolised Britain's Asia trade and Britain was on the point of becoming the world's leading manufacturer. However, they were not, at first, particularly numerous. Lascar crews had been recruited a couple of centuries earlier, though not in any great numbers.

British employment of Lascars and Chinese increased after 1813, when the East India Company lost its monopoly in India, and 1833, when the China trade was thrown open to private shipowners and free competition. In 1834, the Duchess of Clarence was the first Liverpool ship to arrive home on the River Mersey with a tea cargo and a Chinese crew. In the same year, the Symmetry, which sailed from Liverpool to Guangzhou and returned with an assorted cargo, was the first to make the return journey. These sailings marked the start of a commercial revolution.[10] In 1850, the Navigation Laws, which ruled that the merchant marine must be crewed by at least 75 per cent British, were repealed.[11] That and the proliferation of new 'arteries of Empire' under the Red and the White Ensign as a result of steam navigation made Asian crews a familiar sight on British ships.

Initially, Chinese and Lascars were put ashore in the London docks area to await the start of the return voyage and to 'drink, debauch, and contract the attendant diseases'.[12] The company's treatment of them was, said the *Times*, 'shameful'. They were housed in bare rooms and left penniless until the next sailing, their illnesses untreated.[13] Public criticism embarrassed the East India Company into providing barracks at Shadwell, one for Lascars and another for Chinese, an improvement on the previous neglect. This arrangement allowed for the segregation of the Chinese community in London, a first step on the road to Chinatown.

The corralling of the seafarers increased the controls on them but failed to resolve the tensions of shoreside living. In 1813, 'dangerous riots' broke out in Shadwell in which at least three Chinese died and some 17 were wounded. Two armed sects, the 'Chenies' and the 'Chin-choo', entered 'a state of entire hostility' and fought each other with knives the size of cutlasses.[14] It is hard to say who the 'Chenies' and the 'Chin-choo' were. One possible explanation is that they were Cantonese and Fujianese. The Cantonese may have been Siyinese, for the men from Siyi were strongly oriented to seafarers' work and willing emigrants. Chin-choo may be a corrupted form of Quanzhou 泉州 or Zhangzhou 漳州, famous seaports of Fujian, or of Chaozhou 潮州, home of a Fujianese dialect spoken by one of the first groups to get into 'British' business.[15]

The Shadwell riots showed how slight was the Company's hold on the seafarers. Within the barracks, they were organised independently, by provenance. Chinese seafarers plying British trade routes and early Chinese immigrants always demonstrated a relatively high degree of self-organisation (although they were sometimes at each other's throats). This quality of self-reliance, an enduring theme of Chinese migration, has tended to set the Chinese apart from other migrants and expatriates, who are more likely to succumb to controls. Its causes, and some of its consequences, are dealt with later.

Not long after the riots of 1813, an Act of Parliament was passed requiring the Company to provide for its Asian seafarers' needs. A Parliamentary Committee that investigated conditions in the Shadwell barracks noted in its report (submitted in 1815) that the accommodation at Shadwell was too cramped and 'totally wanting' from the point of view of health and hygiene, with 'no regular hospital, nor any sufficient means of separating the diseased from those in health'. The Committee concluded that the Chinese 'appeared well and contented'.[16] However, the medical attendant to the barracks told the Company that 31 Chinese (and 91 Lascars) had died in the barracks between May 1813 and April 1814. A humanitarian society noted that Asians in the barracks were starved and beaten.[17]

The Company imported a Chinese administrator to oversee the mariners. Renamed John Anthony, he was the first Chinese to be naturalised in Britain.[18] He had accumulated a great fortune by the time of his death in 1805, at the age of 39. After his death, having 'abjured Paganism and embraced Christianity', he was borne from his country house at Hallowall-down in Essex to his other residence in Shadwell in the East End, followed by 'all the Chinese in town'. (A figure of 'above 2000 [mourners] of the neighbouring poor and other persons' is mentioned in his obituary: it is not clear whether they were all Chinese.)[19]

John Anthony's presence confirms that the Company was not in control of its Chinese crews and needed a middleman, who took a big cut from the funds it made available for 'the care of the Chinese and Lascars employed in navigating their shipping to and from China'. His role presaged that of the boarding-masters who accommodated Chinese seafarers in British ports in the late nineteenth and early twentieth centuries, the main difference being that he was employed by a bureaucratic monopoly and able to enrich himself to a degree that his successors could only have dreamed of.

The East India Company justified using Asian crews as an emergency wartime measure and promised to stop once Napoleon was defeated. In 1823, however, eight years after the peace, it shipped a further 1336 Asians to England. The Company lost its commercial monopoly at Guangzhou in 1833, when other shipping companies entered the China trade. These events, together with China's cession of Hong Kong to Britain and the opening of five Treaty Ports to British trade at the end of the Opium War in 1842, brought about an increase in shipping on the China routes that led to the employment of even more Chinese crews in ports throughout East Asia.[20]

The Asian crews were paid far less than whites, a practice enshrined in legislation by the Merchant Shipping Acts of 1894 and 1906; and their discharge in Britain was forbidden in 1823, even where they were Britain's 'imperial subjects'.[21] They were deemed by employers to be more docile than white seafarers, partly because they were less addicted to strong liquor. Usually, they were more amenable to discipline on shore and shipboard as a result of self-policing by the Lascar serangs and Chinese gangers, the system of 'number ones' that made trade-union activity so difficult among Asian crews. They were an isolated and vulnerable group, subject to discrimination and extreme exploitation by the shipping companies and despised by white seafarers.

In the late nineteenth and early twentieth centuries, Chinese seafarers were perceived as cheap, biddable labour and potential strike-breakers by white trade unionists and socialists, a subject we shall return to in our discussion of the racialisation of Chinese workers over the centuries. The threat they were said to present was out of all proportion to the actual scale of their employment. Lascar seafarers far outnumbered the

Table 3.1 Census of foreign seafarers (excluding Lascars), 1911

Total foreign seafarers	29,628
Norwegians	2598
Swedes	2091
Germans	1986
Danes	1259
Chinese	1136
Russian (excluding Russian Poland)	1124
Spanish	1098

Source: May 1973, p. 36.

Chinese, who were among the smallest of the main groups of foreign seafarers in 1911, a not untypical year (See Table 3.1).[22]

Seafarers' leaders said as many as 48,000 Chinese were serving in the British merchant marine in 1911, but this figure conflates Lascars (who numbered nearly 43,000) and Chinese. The actual number of Chinese was probably less than one-tenth of that claimed, even when 'British' Chinese (from Hong Kong and other colonies) are included.[23] However, Chinese were a greater object than Lascars of white seafarers' venom.

During the First World War, the number of non-white seafarers on British ships increased greatly, to replace the 8000 merchant seafarers redeployed into the Royal Navy and the 9000 'enemy aliens' sacked from the fleet.[24] Before the war, the National Union of Seamen and two racist organisations (the Navy League and the British Brothers League) associated with the union had agitated against the employment of Asian seafarers, either by demanding their exclusion or by hypocritically calling for equal pay and conditions for them, in the knowledge that such parity would reduce their numbers. In 1914, however, the agitation was suspended. In 1916, the new Ministry of Shipping announced national wage rates, but 'Chinese, Asiatics and Coloured ratings' who had previously worked below the standard rate were excluded. Many Lascar and Chinese seafarers deserted to take advantage of the labour shortage caused by the war.[25]

After the war, thousands of Chinese seafarers were repatriated, partly because of British seafarers' antipathy. However, Government ministers were less firmly opposed than the unions to employing Chinese crews in 1919, for they privately believed that they could not allow concessions to the popular mood to damage shipping interests, already threatened by the prospect of future labour shortages.[26]

Table 3.2   Chinese and 'colonial' Chinese seafarers, 1908–1911

	1908	1909	1910	1911
Chinese	4695	5797	5954	4595
British	417,681	415,690	437,534	n. a.

Source: May 1973, pp. 36–37.

Table 3.2 shows the number of Chinese and 'colonial seamen of Chinese race' (mainly Chinese whose birthplace was recorded as Hong Kong or the Straits Settlement) on British foreign-going ships. The percentage of Chinese according to these criteria rises somewhat, but not by much. (The figures include repeated engagements of the same men.)

Chinese ratings on British ships received not only far less pay than whites but fewer and smaller benefits. At the start of the twentieth century, those who signed on in Asian ports got between one-fifth and one-third of the white wage. In port, they were denied the extra payments towards the cost of board and lodgings made on discharge to British seafarers.[27]

The internal structure of the Chinese seafaring community in Europe in the nineteenth and early twentieth centuries, and of its economy, was dominated by two key figures: the Chinese shipping-master, who superintended the signing-on and discharging of seafarers, and the boarding-master, who kept the boarding houses in which they lodged between ships.[28] At first, Chinese seafarers in Britain lodged in non-Chinese boarding houses, but at some point in the first years of the twentieth century Chinese settlers started to provide lodgings.[29] Thereafter, shipping-master (or crimp) and boarding-master were usually one and the same person. (Boarding houses were also known as crimping houses, in confirmation of the fact.) Many boarding-masters kept more than one boarding house.[30]

The shipping-master or crimping system was generally abolished in Europe in the course of the nineteenth century, after public criticism by seafarers, journalists, and social reformers. In his history of shipping employment, Jonathan Kitchen describes the crimps' role in British ports before their abolition:

'Crimps' were usually proprietors of ale-houses or lodging-houses in seaports offering cheap accommodation to seafarers and ostensible havens for deserters. Their aim was to make the seafarer part with his money so that he could be sold on to a merchant vessel under threat. Once he had been induced into debt the seaman would be taken by the crimp to a ship where he would be signed on and be given an advance of wages. The crimp would then discount the note for the advance at a ridiculously low rate of exchange having first deducted his debts. Although seamen were invariably duped in this way they were generally in an extremely disadvantaged position and the crimps gave seamen little chance to escape.[31]

The crimp was just one of a class of waterfront predators. According to Herman Melville, they included a

variety of land-sharks, land-rats, and other vermin, which make the hapless mariner their prey. In the shape of landlords, bar-keepers, clothiers, crimps and boarding-house loungers, the land-sharks devour him limb by limb; while the land-rats and mice constantly nibble at his purse.[32]

Legislation passed by Parliament in 1845 'for the Protection of Seamen entering on board Merchant Ships' introduced a system of licences for people wishing to provide seafarers for merchant ships and forbade the overcharging of seafarers for their lodgings and the making of payments to anyone but the seaman. These measures were not entirely effective, so a new Act was passed in 1850. In 1894, Sections 111 and 112 of the Merchant Shipping Act were also passed 'to prevent crimping'. The campaign to stamp it out was reinforced by the efforts of enlightened shipowners and voluntary organisations to provide clubs and hostels in the ports and thus keep the seafarers out of disreputable hands.[33]

Despite the legislation, however, the crimping system was kept in being to recruit and accommodate Chinese seafarers passing through European ports. The anti-crimping law depended for its effect on the seafarers' cooperation, but few Chinese spoke English well enough to act for themselves in dealing with employers. Moreover, their welfare in port was not served by the same set of institutions as those available to European seafarers, so they were in no position to dispense with crimps. Seafarers' boarding houses in Britain had usually been run along ethnic lines.[34] Those run by and for Chinese continued to act in the old way, even after crimping had ceased to be an important issue for other seafarers.

In 1908, at a time of anti-Chinese agitation by white seafarers, Winston Churchill told the House of Commons that 'Chinese boarding-house keepers were not, and would not be, allowed access to the Board of Trade premises for the purpose of supplying crews of Chinamen' and crimps who did try to supply crews would be liable to prosecution under the Act of 1894.[35] But the fact that Churchill was speaking 14 years after Parliament had supposedly banned the system shows how ineffective such laws were in the Chinese case. Crimping, though illegal, was carried out quite openly by Chinese boarding-masters in Liverpool, Belfast, and other ports.[36] As late as 1919, authorities distributed a proportion of the sum (varying from £7 to £10) used to pay off Chinese labour employed in the war years to the boarding masters, as a form of compulsory debt-repayment.[37]

Although the British authorities tried to preserve the appearance of even-handedness, in reality they were in no hurry to dispense with the role of contractors and intermediaries in recruiting and managing Chinese crews worldwide, although they were ashamed to be seen to approve it. Sng Choon Yee, Chinese Assistant to the Secretary for Chinese Affairs in Malaya, revealed in an interview in Singapore in 1981 that the British privately communicated to him their insistence that no measures be taken against the system of contractors, which they felt gave employers a useful handle on otherwise unruly Chinese crews. Sng was forced to give up his attempt to put an end to the practice, though he personally considered it to be discriminatory and exploitative.[38]

So the ghettoisation of the Chinese seafarers cannot be ascribed solely to Chinese particularism, as is sometimes done. The ethnic organisations that Chinese recruits to the British fleet joined were, like the Chinatowns into which they were ghettoed in the ports, as much a product of British laws and practices as of Chinese exclusiveness.[39]

On the whole, Chinese ratings lacked the support structures – international solidarity, strike funds, official representatives, and so on – necessary for supporting industrial action. However, where they did get the chance to sign up to class-based organisations, they joined. In 1918, for example, Chinese who had spent the war years working ashore were far less tractable than before and no longer automatically did the boarding masters' bidding. In London's Poplar district, Chinese crews formed a Chinese Labour and Seamen's Union that set itself up in competition with the boarding masters by recruiting workers for shore jobs.[40] During the Second World War, Chinese crews on British ships supported the Chinese Seamen's Union, as did those in Australia, actively encouraged by the Australian Seamen's Union.

A good contemporary description of the system of Chinese shipping-masters and boarding houses in Europe is by Henk Wubben, a Dutch seafarer turned anthropologist. Wubben's study, in Dutch, is on the Chinese seafaring community in Rotterdam and Amsterdam, but it applies in most respects to British ports, if only because the shipping companies – and the Chinese – were transnationally organised.[41]

The Chinese shipping-master received a commission of 5 per cent of each recruit's monthly wage from the shipping company. He took another cut from the seafarer himself, who had to pay even more if he wanted a better job on board. The greater part of the shipping-master's profit came from accommodating and victualling the seafarers. The actual cost of providing quarters was minimal, for large numbers of seafarers were packed into sparsely furnished dormitories.[42] The facilities usually included a shop, a gambling den, and an opium den, where the seafarers ran up further debts while awaiting ship.

These debts were usually settled from the advance-note given to the seafarer by the company when he signed on. The shipping-master often cashed this note (which promised the future payment of money on account of wages to be earned at sea) on the seafarer's behalf, while deducting yet more commission and the debt accumulated by the seafarer in port.

The methods employed by the shipping-masters and the companies they worked for had much in common with the coolie trade in China and Hong Kong, where local crimps recruited or entrapped coolies on behalf of Chinese brokers or foreign agents. The brokers and agents held them in crimping houses or barracoons before sending them overseas on coolie ships. Most coolies sailed under the credit-ticket system or signed up to some form of indenture contract. After arriving overseas, they had to repay the credit (with interest) or serve out the terms of the indenture.

Unlike white workers, very few Chinese seafarers found employment on European ships as free-standing individuals. Most Chinese were recruited in gangs as part of a package deal, by Chinese shipping-masters who controlled the entire process of recruitment, including negotiating the seafarers' wages. They took all the usual commissions, including a month's wages to 'cover costs'.

On shipboard, the gang was in the hands of the Chinese number one, appointed to this post by the shipping-master (at a price). (The relationship between number one and shipping-master was roughly analogous to that between serang and ghaut serang among Lascars.[43]) The number one was responsible for distributing tasks among the Chinese crew, who paid him to get the least unattractive assignments in what was generally a hell-hole. In this way, he recouped his own payment to the shipping-master at the gang's expense, while at the same time accumulating a tidy additional sum on his own behalf.

The Chinese ratings were chiefly employed as stokers and firemen, feeding and trimming the fires for the boilers of the ship's steam-engines. A smaller number worked as carpenters, a less demanding occupation said at one time to be specially associated with Chinese.[44] The qualities that recommended Chinese workers above their European colleagues for this employment were summed up in 1911 by a Dutch socialist politician, writing in the seafarers' journal: the Chinese coolie was 'class-unconscious, stone-cold sober, highly adaptable, climate-proof, a willing worker, a non-striker, and highly frugal'.[45] Tending the furnace was punishing work, particularly in the tropics, where the temper-ature in the stokehold could reach 55 degrees Celsius. Other Chinese worked as trimmers. The job of the trimmer, who received less pay than the stokers and the firemen, was to shovel and fetch coals from the bunkers, on wheelbarrows. At sea, his journey to the stoke-hold steadily lengthened, as the nearer piles of coal in the unventilated bunker were consumed.

The Chinese who worked for British, French, American, and other shipping companies in the nineteenth and the early twentieth century were not tied to one port, even within Europe, but switched from place to place at the convenience of the companies. In 1911, Blue Funnel ships of Rotterdam's Stoomvaart Maatschappij Oceaan, part of the Liverpool-based Holt fleet, imported Chinese stokers and trimmers from London's East End to break a seafarers' strike.[46] During the First World War, in a remarkable (but, from the Chinese seafarers' point of view, politic-ally insignificant) act of flag-switching between the Central Powers and the Entente, several hundred Chinese changed berth from Hamburg to London by way of neutral Rotterdam, where a London-based Chinese broker recruited them to the British fleet. (After the armistice, the labour flow reversed, from Britain back to Germany.)[47]

Feeding and trimming the furnaces and bringing in the coal were jobs suitable only for relatively young men. By the age of 35, most stokers, firemen, and trimmers were no longer up to such work and tried to transfer to less back-breaking engine-room occupations. The jobs most sought after by older Chinese seafarers were those of the greaser, who cleaned and lubricated the machinery, and the donkey-man, who tended the smaller and less demanding donkey-engines that fed the boilers of the propelling engines.

One way out of the oceangoing misery was to jump ship and seek work ashore. Among the Chinese who deserted and sought a living in British ports were no few burnt-out seafarers, together with younger men who could not tolerate the abuses and cupidity that Chinese seafarers experienced on all sides, not least from their compatriots. Even ashore, the shipping-master's power was unrelenting. The boarding-masters were not just crew-contractors and shopkeepers but de facto rulers of the land-based community, in nearly all respects.[48] The seafarers' poor English combined with the racist practices of local trade unions and employers to rule out the prospect of a job in the main economy. The boarding houses and the incipient Chinatowns offered some scope for employment – as managers, accountants, cooks, washermen, and sundry drudges – but such jobs usually went to the shipping-master's relatives.

Other Chinese ratings unhappy with their inferior status and pay also deserted, not to seek work ashore but to improve their conditions of employment, since re-registering for work in British ports entitled them to greater parity with white seafarers.[49] These deserters travelled from their original ports of discharge to new ports, to 'ship on other vessels ... at slightly less than the rate of wages payable to British seafarers, which is considerably in advance of that paid to them when they sign on at Hong Kong for the round voyage'.[50]

It seems that more Chinese were contracted in British ports than Lascars, who tended to be both engaged and paid off in India. This ship-switching suggests that the Chinese were better able to assert their own self-interest than the Indians. The number of Chinese who signed articles at British docks rose from 1872 in 1905 to 4384 in 1907 and 5600 in 1908.[51] By 1912, however, the number had fallen back to just 3000, probably as a result of protests by white interests.[52] To transfer to another berth after reaching Europe was a leap in the dark, for although life as part of a gang had drawbacks, it also conferred strength in numbers and relieved gang members of the need to treat independently with the shipping-offices. Chinese freelancers, on the other hand, were vulnerable to attack or exploitation on all sides: by white ratings, the shipping companies, and the Chinatown potentates. Even those who did manage to sign on articles in British ports were not guaranteed equal pay or treatment (for example, regarding shipboard food and accommodation).[53]

The number of Chinese who jumped ship in Britain fluctuated from year to year. In the first three months of 1907, a commission established that 1.5 per cent of Chinese seafarers passing through Liverpool deserted, representing 'an accession of 84 Chinamen yearly from this source alone'.[54] The percentage of absconders grew along with the

Chinese settlement in Britain, for a denser population offered more opportunities to duck from sight and find work and lodgings. In the depression years after 1929, the number of deserters dwindled, but it rose again after 1939, both in Britain and, in far greater numbers, among Chinese crews on British ships docked in New York.

The shipping-masters ran their dockside empires by wielding ties of kinship or provenance, usually coinciding with dialect. The Ng 吳 brothers controlled Europe's two principal Chinese settlements, in Limehouse and Rotterdam. The London branch, headed by Ng Ah Fook, acted as agent for four British shipping companies, including Anglo-Saxon Petroleum, and one of the big Norwegian companies. If Dutch police files are to be believed, Ng Ah Fook was a member of the police athletics association in London and had a weapons permit.

The Ng lineage's ancestral home was in Bao'an 宝安, to the east of Siyi in Guangdong's Pearl River Delta region. The Ng empire was transnational in the early twentieth century, with additional branches in Singapore, Marseilles, Amsterdam, and Willemstad in Curaçao. Ng strongmen controlled a Bao'an association that stretched across the European ports. Membership conferred various privileges, including a reduction in the amount paid in commission to the shipping-master.[55]

On the eve of the Second World War, quite a few more foreigners were employed on British merchant ships than on the eve of the earlier war. As a proportion of the workforce, the increase was even greater, for many British seafarers had lost their jobs in the interwar years. In 1938, 50,700 out of a total workforce of 192,375 were Indians or Chinese, representing 27 per cent of those engaged on foreign-going vessels. A further 5 per cent were Indians, Chinese, and other non-whites domiciled in British ports. In all, non-white seafarers made up nearly one-third of the workforce, a proportion that grew as a result of the recruitment of Chinese and other non-white crews after the start of the war. In 1939, around 5000 Chinese seafarers were employed on British-registered ships, rising to between 10,000 and 20,000 in the war. The three main employers were Blue Funnel, Ben Line, and Shell (that is, Anglo-Saxon Oil). Most members of the wartime Chinese pool were recruited after the outbreak of the Pacific War in December 1941.[56] A Dutch pool of Chinese seafarers also operated in Britain, independently of the British pool.[57]

In some ways, the manner of their recruitment resembled the earlier method, before and after the First World War, but the seafarers were freer. In port, they were mainly accommodated either in company hostels (set up to replace the boarding houses destroyed in the Merseyside Blitz of May 1940) or on shipboard.[58] The accommodation was the target of much criticism by the seafarers,[59] but they were less prey to the boarding-masters than in the past.[60] They were also liberated from the shipping-masters, for they were committed for the duration of the war to a British employer and registered in British ports, an arrangement that made the old-style intermediaries redundant.

In the war, they were supported by new forms of representation. The communist-influenced Chinese Seamen's Union, fortified by the restoration of the united front between Chiang Kai-shek and the Chinese communists in 1937, agitated among the crews. The British shipowners and the Ministry of War Transport refused to recognise the union, but its existence strengthened the seafarers' hand. The employers and the Ministry tried to deal with Chinese crews by talking with officials of the Chinese Embassy and its consulates, who in turn asked the advice of the International Transportworkers' Federation.[61] Although such negotiations delivered relatively few benefits, they were an improvement on the old system, under which the shipping companies dealt with the Chinatown elite behind the seafarers' backs and against their interests.

China's Guomindang Government declared war on Germany, Italy, and Japan on 9 December 1941, two days after Pearl Harbor, thus becoming an ally of the Americans and British. As for the Indians and the Chinese from colonial Hong Kong and Southeast Asia, they were theoretically at war from the very start, as 'men of Empire origin'. However, the idea of a united front of the antifascist peoples of the world or (as Tony Lane has shown) of a colonial marine cemented to the mother country by filial loyalty in a 'people's war' was fraudulent. The war led at best to a partial rejumbling of the shipboard ethnic hierarchy. In other respects, it heightened ethnic grievances and tensions.

The war resulted in an increase in Asian seafarers' wages but not to white rates. Here, however, the Chinese had a remedy. Unlike the Indians, who could be sent home if they started to cause trouble, they were stranded by the fighting and no longer in danger (while it lasted) of repatriation, whether by shipping bosses or the British Government.[62] (The promotion of industrial unrest by aliens had been made a criminal offence under the 1919 anti-alien law, although this clause was never used.[63]) They were therefore in a better position than the Indians to make a firm stand.

Non-white seafarers' two main grievances were inequalities in wage levels and the war-risk bonus. The pay of Chinese seafarers engaged in Hong Kong or Shanghai in September 1939 was set at one-fifth of the British rate, rising to just over half in May 1942. War-risk bonuses were not paid automatically or at a uniform rate, as they were to British seafarers. 'Not only are our wages the lowest among all allied seamen,' wrote one pool member in 1942, 'but in matters of compensation for loss of life and for mutilation, we are put under different schemes which are invariably much less favourable as compared with the corresponding schemes for British or even Indian seamen'.[64] Both issues led to peaceful protests, which some shipowners tried to settle by force, and to occasional riots. The Chinese seafarers fought back in 1942 by refusing to re-engage. A settlement guaranteeing 'equality of treatment' was reached with the help of Chinese diplomats, but Chinese basic wages remained up to 30 per cent lower than white basic wages despite the agreement. According to Lane, this differential, 'accompanied by unrelenting British intransigence and heavy-handed behaviour by everyone from ship's officers, through senior civil servants, senior partners in shipowning firms to diplomats, produced unending conflicts with Chinese seamen'.

Officials of the Chinese Seamen's Union and of the Chinese Embassy and British backbench politicians of all parties protested at the shipowners' failure to pay Chinese seafarers the same as British seafarers for facing the same risks. The Union pointed out in October 1940 that around 100 Chinese had been killed on British ships since the start of the war, a figure that had risen to 831 by March 1943. (Some of the dead are commemorated on the monument at Liverpool's Pier Head.) Another 254 had been reported missing and 268 had been notified as prisoners of war. During the Normandy landings, up to 700 Chinese are said to have died.[65]

In the Holt fleet, the very first wartime killings were of eight Chinese ratings, in February 1940. But, as Lane notes, accounts of Chinese (and Lascar) crew behaviour under fire veer between portrayals of stoic loyalty on the one hand and cold feet on the other, in an unconscious alternation between old stereotypes and new. A good example is Captain Roskill's war history of the Holt fleet, which contains an equal number of accounts of Chinese 'calm' and Chinese 'panic'. Only a tiny handful of the hundreds of wartime honours and awards made to the men of Alfred Holt & Co. went to its Chinese employees (who numbered in their thousands).[66]

Needless to say, the Chinese were no less brave (and no less cowardly) than their British shipmates in face of danger. If there was a difference in attitude, it was that Chinese mariners did not identify with the British cause in the European war. They were more likely to identify against than with the caste of white British shipmasters and officers, many of whom behaved like colonial satraps.[67] To the extent that the Chinese did risk their lives to succour endangered shipmates, their motive was human solidarity.

A wartime issue even more explosive than unequal remuneration was the ill-treatment of Chinese seafarers by British officers. The most notorious incident was the shooting dead of a dissident Chinese seaman in New York in April 1942 by a British tanker master. The master was arrested but released, whereas the Chinese crew was held in detention on Ellis Island.

After the incident, large numbers of Chinese – sometimes as many as three-quarters of a ship's crew – deserted when British vessels docked in New York. Chinese jumping ship in United States ports was nothing new – it was a favoured method of evading the provisions of the exclusion acts of the late nineteenth century.[68] During the war, however, the practice became rampant. In 1943, one in four of all Chinese seafarers given shore leave in New York deserted. The trigger was racist arrogance, but the opportunity was afforded by New York's Chinatown, another advantage that Chinese crews had over the Indians, who lacked a comparable safe haven. The ethnic-Chinese economy in the United States was desperately short of labour in the war, when large numbers of local Chinese found employment in factories and skilled occupations vacated by whites sent off to the front.[69] Chinatown employers snapped up the deserters. The overwhelming majority of Chinese in New York were from Taishan in Siyi, as were many of the Chinese on the ships.[70] Some seafarers tracked down relatives and fellow-villagers. Whether from Siyi or elsewhere, they absconded in such large numbers that they were rarely at a loss for contacts and support.

The Chinese fought their corner in the war far more effectively than other non-whites employed by the shipping lines. However, their reputation for aggressive self-confidence and self-reliance was not born in 1939 but was practically as old as their presence on British ships. The special circumstances under which they were employed in the war added to the credence of the legend. Chinese crews were far less likely than other non-white groups (excluding Lascars) to be mixed with other non-whites and were therefore far more likely to maintain a collective identity. As already mentioned, they could not be sent home if they stepped out of line, and they had the option of jumping ship in New York. These advantages gave them the edge over the Lascars, who were employed in far greater numbers (there were 40,000 Lascar ratings on British ships in 1939) but lacked the clout of the Chinese, who easily out-earned them.[71]

Chinese seafarers continued to serve on British ships even after the war. Although formally recognised as 'British' (by virtue of the 'nationality' of the ship), they continued to be exploited as cheap labour, at an average rate of pay two-thirds that of their UK shipmates, a form of inequality sanctioned by the Race Relations Act of 1976. Even so, they still managed to command higher wages than other less assertive and worse organised non-white seafarers employed by British shipping companies. Their numbers fell by around 20 per cent in the 1960s, to just under 9000. Other Chinese serving on British-owned ships sailing under flags of convenience received far less pay.[72] Chinese merchant seafarers were among those killed on British ships in the Falklands War.[73]

The Blue Funnel Line

As we have seen, the first Chinese seafarers to reach Britain sailed on ships of the East India Company. After China's violent opening to foreign trade by the Opium Wars, European shipping lines took on Chinese crews in Asian ports. The employers most closely associated with early Chinese crews were Liverpool's Alfred and Philip Holt, who registered the Ocean Steam Ship Company (which set up the Blue Funnel Line) in 1865. The Holts' role in the Chinese community in Britain and other European ports was central and warrants a separate discussion, as a case study for the more general relationship between Chinese seafarers and British shipping companies.

In 1866, the Holt brothers started the first direct steamship service from Europe to China, a venture aided by the opening of the Suez Canal a year later. By 1898, their fleet had more than trebled in tonnage and complement, to 49 ships. Some studies suggest that the first generation of Chinese reached Liverpool aboard Blue Funnel vessels, but it was not until 1893 that the company employed a large Chinese crew (whereas both Liverpool and London had a tiny but settled Chinese community as early as the mid-eighteenth century).[74] By the twentieth century, however, most of the company's ordinary deck ratings and all its engine-room ratings were Chinese. The Chinese community in Liverpool in its first full bloom was chiefly associated with Blue Funnel.[75]

In its peacetime heyday, Blue Funnel employed Asian crews numbering around 3000.[76] In the Second World War, when it administered its liner section for the Ministry of War Transport as part of the Chinese Seamen's Reserve Pool, it employed even greater numbers of Chinese recruited in ports around the world, including Calcutta and

Bombay. At any given time, it maintained a wartime pool of 2000–3000 Chinese in Liverpool.[77] During the war, it promoted some Chinese to the rank of skilled fitters or repairers and even had a handful of Chinese Third Officers and Engineers.[78]

After the war, Alfred Holt & Co. continued to employ 2700 Chinese domiciled in Liverpool, by arrangement with the British Shipping Federation and the National Union of Seamen. Around 2400 were employed as regular seafarers (mainly stokers, firemen, greasers, cooks, laundrymen, bosuns, and stewards), while a further 300 shoremen worked in the shipyards (as fitters, carpenters, unskilled labourers, foremen, clerks, and administrators) or served on ships sailing in UK and home-trade waters.[79] The Blue Funnel pool of former deep-sea Chinese seafarers and their Liverpool-born sons remained in existence until 1972, when Liverpool's demotion from the first rank of ports led to the pool's disbandment.[80]

The company maintained close contact with the Chinese community over the decades. According to an early study, it did so 'partly because of the paternalistic benevolence which has inspired its policy towards its employees, and also because it is legally responsible to ensure that alien seafarers... leave the United Kingdom before the expiry of the limited period – usually a month – stated in their conditions of landing'.[81] So benign was its regime said to be that in 1911 the Chief Constable of Liverpool claimed its altruism was probably the main reason why relatively few Chinese deserted in Liverpool, compared with London and Cardiff.[82]

In many respects, however, Alfred Holt & Co. treated their Chinese crews with the same mixture of exploitation and manipulation as other bosses. The Blue Funnel Line's Chinese crews were originally recruited in Hong Kong by way of a comprador, who was paid indirectly by Hong Kong's Butterfield and Swire. The deck crews and engine crews were recruited from different sub-ethnic communities, to stop them 'ganging up' and to facilitate the company's control. Although enlisted in Hong Kong, many were mainland Cantonese, while others signed on in Singapore or Liverpool. Wherever they joined up, they were paid a lot less than whites, though it is not known by how much, since the comprador took a cut of an undisclosed size. In 1936, a Chinese crew received £710 a voyage, a little more than one-third of the £2038 paid to a European crew. Even in 1961, individual Chinese continued to receive half the standard white wage (£32 as opposed to £62 a month). And the Chinese shipboard quarters were less comfortable and capacious.

In the early days, Blue Funnel, like other shipping companies plying the East Asian trade routes, delegated the recruitment and control of Chinese crews to Chinese middlemen, but after the Second World War it incorporated a Chinese system of management into its procedures. It continued to segregate Chinese crews from European crews, but it employed a handful of Asian clerical workers and administrators – house compradors, so to speak – to handle the Asians (most of whom were Chinese).[83]

The postwar Chinese seafarers and shoremen were integrated into the structure of the company, where they could hope for promotion from manual grades to steward's or white-collar grades. Around one-third of the shoremen were permanently employed at fixed monthly rates, but most preferred to sign on for temporary spells of employment in the shore gangs, only some of which were at work in the docks and shipyards at any given time.[84] 'Northerners' and 'southerners' – presumably, Chinese from around Shanghai and Cantonese – operated in separate groups, at their own insistence. A Chinese foreman was responsible for selecting the duty group.

Many of the Chinese shoreworkers employed on a semi-casual basis spent their free time running businesses in and around Chinatown. They invested their savings – and, at a later point, their redundancy pay – in cafes, restaurants, and laundries, the same lines of work some pursued at sea. Their reluctance to rely solely on Alfred Holt & Co. for a livelihood and their determination to diversify into other fields proved farsighted when the pool was terminated in the 1970s.

In the postwar years, the company treated its Chinese employees more solicitously than it did its other non-white workers. It 'raised their status above that of Negroes and Moslems in the town' by granting them security of employment, sickness benefits, and pension rights. Until 1969, it maintained two boarding houses and a social centre for them. Other Asian and black workers, in contrast, got the lowliest jobs and enjoyed little or no security. The Chinese seem to have valued their association with the company and are said to have shown no inclination after the war to join a trade union.[85]

However, numerous episodes in the company's history demonstrate the limits of its paternalism. In the mid-1920s, Blue Funnel joined with shipping-masters and the Home Office in a campaign to prevent its 'own' Chinese from 'deserting' to other firms (and thus improving their terms of engagement).[86] Shortly after the Second World War, it sought to discourage smaller companies from granting national maritime rates of pay to Chinese based in British ports, for fear of jeopardising its own source of cheap labour. At more or less the same time, it requested (and received) government help to force 'recalcitrant' Chinese to board a vessel whose description as a 'hell-ship' was deemed even by government officials to be an understatement.[87] While prepared to countenance a measure of autonomy for its Chinese crews where it suited its purposes (for example, when taking advantage of Chinese ganging arrangements as a means of enforcing discipline), it opposed the crews' unionisation and operated a postwar black list against suspected left-wing Chinese labour agitators when urged to do so by the British authorities.[88]

It is interesting to consider why Alfred Holt & Co. favoured its Chinese employees domiciled in Liverpool over its other non-white workers. After all, Chinese crews were commonly perceived to be more combative, assertive, and given to solidarity – in short, more trouble – than other non-Europeans.[89] In one sense, the Chinese were beneficiaries of circumstance, for they managed to evade repatriation in Liverpool at the end of both world wars in roughly the right numbers for them to form a workforce compact and minimally viable but not big enough to provoke a hue-and-cry. To avoid deportation, they made use of their relatively effective ethnic organisational resources, which few other non-white seafarers could match, or they married local women. The Blue Funnel managers were familiar with Chinese crews and knew how to handle them. That the company preferred them over the other groups probably had much to do with their reputation for self-reliance, dependability, and hard work. However, one should not minimise as part of the explanation for their elite status among non-whites their ability to organise on their own behalf and press for a square deal.

The Chinese connection with Blue Funnel is interesting in several ways. The company's early management of its Chinese workforce was typical of the deals Western employers struck with Chinese compradors and other intermediaries to squeeze crews to the limit to the mutual benefit of capitalist and broker-crimp. The crewmen, for their part, strove to turn the relationship to their own advantage, particularly in times of war or labour shortage, when they were on vantage ground. In the end, they managed to wrench a better deal.

The Blue Funnel Line's Chinese pool is unique in the history of the Chinese in Britain, in that its members ended up as part of the Liverpool proletariat. Their experience exposes as a platitude the notion that Chinese immigrants are predestined either to form an ethnic niche or to join the middle classes. The decision of some to invest their savings in small ethnic enterprises can be understood as a preparation of lines of retreat to be used in the event of unforeseen difficulties and as a manifestation of the entrepreneurial spirit common in the immigrant generation. The far bigger Chinese proletariat in France, which at one point numbered several thousand in the 1920s, also switched to petty trading at the start of the economic depression, after being among the first to get laid off.[90]

The land-based economy

In parts of Southeast Asia, the Americas, and the British Dominions, Chinese settlements were sufficiently extensive, even in the nineteenth century, to support thriving and diverse ethnic economies. Britain's Chinese economy was, by comparison, primitive, and stayed so right through until the late twentieth century. Its institutions were, in part, a side-effect of the boarding houses. However, they also drew inspiration from the Chinese experience in other places, in particular the United States, where fellow Cantonese had discovered which trades and occupations a group like themselves, with little or no capital and few relevant skills, could best ply in a strong capitalist economy.

The land-based economy of London's early Chinatown was geared to servicing the domestic needs of a transient all-male community that lacked the benefits of family support. While ashore awaiting turn-round, the seafarers needed somewhere to eat, sleep, have their washing done, and kill time. At sea, cooking and laundering was the domain of a specialist Chinese crew, while accommodation was automatic and recreation looked after itself. (The most common Chinese ratings after stoker and fireman on British ships were steward and cook.) Ashore, the boarding-masters provided the accommodation and Chinese who had picked up the necessary skills at sea cooked and washed for their compatriots.

It was only a matter of time before Chinese cafes and laundries sprang up around the docks as a spin-off. Though their original purpose, as part of an inchoate household-style economy, was to serve Chinese seafarers, at a certain point they differentiated into institutions with a wider clientele. The entrepreneurs who wrought this transformation took their lead from the Chinese in America, who in the mid-nineteenth century set up eating houses and hand laundries to serve the Chinese labourers who built the Transcontinental Railroad, worked in the mines, and cleared the farmlands on the western frontiers. After the completion of the railroad, restaurants and laundry businesses came to provide the basis for a Chinese economic niche in the United States.[91] Since the conditions of Chinese labourers on either side of the Atlantic were in some ways not dissimilar, it is quite likely that the American experience was copied by the Chinese in Europe. However, the copying could not extend to other aspects of America's more powerful and complex Chinese economy. For example, the early experiments in industrial, financial, and agricultural enterprise and the system of chambers of commerce and civic organisations were not replicated.

Up to now, we have emphasised the part played by deserting seafarers in creating the Chinaports. Yet the seafarers' role in the dockland communities was subordinate to that of a more enterprising class of Chinese immigrants who settled in Britain not on impulse but by design. The first to come were crew contractors, who exercised a stranglehold over the fledgling Chinese economy. After anti-Chinese feeling in the United States and Australia deepened in the late nineteenth century, other would-be Chinese entrepreneurs not connected with the shipping industry turned their sights on Britain, France, and other parts of Europe.

Such people were more likely to reach Britain as steerage passengers, a status that guaranteed their right to land under the provisions of the Aliens Act of 1905. Even some apparent Chinese seafarers had in fact paid for their passage but were put on the articles as crew members, to avoid dues chargeable to passengers on entering the Suez Canal.

According to Maria Lin Wong 王林, the great majority of the Chinese who settled in Liverpool were literate and resourceful. Many were businessmen and professionals. Their mission was little different from that of Chinese emigrants the world over: to found an enterprise and raise their social standing.[92] The *Weekly Courier* of 1 December 1906 reported that most Chinese

> are of CANTON COOLIE CLASS...but the men serving as marine stewards, interpreters and coolies, and residing in Liverpool as laundry men, restaurateurs, shopkeepers, boarding masters and in other capacities are of a distinctly higher class. They are the true intellectuals and progressives of their country.[93]

Interviews with descendants of Liverpool's China-born failed to turn up a single illiterate among their immigrant forebears (although illiteracy was widespread in China).[94] In Cardiff, too, few if any of the first generation of Chinese launderers were uneducated seafarers.[95] Later, Chinese with fewer skills and assets – including former seafarers – joined the laundry trade, but they built their enterprises in niches carved out by the business pioneers.

Recreation in Britain's Chinese quarters often took the form of opium-smoking and gambling, either in the boarding houses (which doubled as social centres) or on premises designed for catering or laundering, or in clubs set up for the purpose. The clubs, like the cafes, eventually began to attract white customers. Thus were laid the four main strands of the early Chinatown economy – laundering, catering, drug-selling, and gambling. In time, a fifth was added: people-smuggling, into Britain and across Britain to other continents.

The 1905 Aliens Act, which permitted the removal or exclusion of aliens deemed unable to support themselves and their families 'decently', and legislation passed after the war that established the work-permit system helped shape the British Chinese economy's structural features. Apart from the war years, when able-bodied British men went off to fight, the Chinese had little or no chance of a job in industry or on the docks, overwhelmingly white preserves. The Act made prior appointment to a job a condition for landing. An ethnic enclave based on patronage was therefore inescapable.

Chinese seafarers played roughly the same role throughout northern Europe, where dockland communities formed in Germany, the Netherlands, Belgium, and France. However, the Chinese land-based economy was different in Britain from in mainland Europe. In Continental countries, Chinese peddlers hawked their goods around the towns and villages, where they became a familiar sight. Fixed businesses (particularly laundries) run by Chinese were less common, except in France. In Britain, on the other hand, fixed businesses were the rule.

Part of the explanation for the absence of Chinese hawkers and peddlers from British towns and cities may be that street-selling had become highly competitive by the turn of the nineteenth century, particularly in London, where Russians and Poles vied for trade with a native costermongerdom increasingly hostile to its foreign rivals.[96] However, the chief reason was probably that former seafarers lacked supply networks and capital with which to acquire stock and in any case had no experience of huckstering or stall-holding, even had they spotted the market opportunity. Unlike the Jews, they also lacked a community of sufficient size to provide a protected base from which to cross over into the wider market.

Continental Europe, on the other hand, was mainly 'colonised' not by Cantonese seafarers but by Zhejiangese traders, who specialised in hawking goods from door to door and street to street and who expanded across the Continent by importing relatives, either by land (through Russia) or by sea. These Zhejiangese confined their activities to mainland countries and rarely if ever seem to have reached British shores. They formed the basis for relatively large Zhejiangese immigrant communities in France, the Netherlands, Italy, Spain, and elsewhere in the 1990s, after the post-Mao relaxing of emigration controls.[97]

The early Chinese community in France was different in two important ways from that in Britain. It was socially diverse; and for a while (between the wars) some of its members joined the land-based industrial proletariat – far more than the postwar Chinese shoremen in Liverpool. Chinese sources claim that Chinese traders turned up in France as early as the mid-eighteenth century and that when the first Chinese migrants officially recorded by Chinese authorities reached mainland Europe in 1866, they encountered Chinese running laundries and restaurants in Paris.[98] In 1878, Xie Daming 谢大铭 accompanied the Qing minister Zeng Jize 曾纪泽 to France and settled down to trade in antiques. In 1900, the Zhejiangese Luo Qinzhai 罗芹斋 went to Paris to work in the tearooms at the Universal Exhibition and stayed on after the exhibition closed. In 1902 or 1903, Li Shizeng 李石曾 and Zhang Jingjiang 张静江 (later to become famous as anarchists and then as members of the Guomindang) turned up in the French capital with Sun Baoqi 孙宝琦, head of the Chinese Legation in France, and took up residence in France. Zhang opened an antique shop and a teahouse, whereas Li left a more indelible stamp on the history of the Chinese community in France. When Dai Hongci 戴鸿慈, President of the Chinese Board of Rites, visited England at the start of the twentieth century, he noted that 'there are still no Chinese traders in this place', unlike on the Continent, where he recorded a Chinese business presence.[99]

Li Shizeng was an energetic and creative man who founded projects that drew quite a few young Chinese to France. After settling down in Paris, he dedicated himself for a while to studying chemistry and biology. Later, he published a thesis on soya's potential for reforming the world food system. In 1909, he returned to China to recruit 30 young Chinese to work in a soy-bean factory, La Caséo-Sojaïne.[100] Other groups of Chinese students (totalling more than 2100, mainly southerners) made their way to France as part of the Work-Study Movement 勤工俭学 (also known as the Society for Frugal Study by Means of Labour), founded by Li Shizeng and his fellow anarchist Wu Zhihui 吴稚晖.[101] This society helped Chinese to enter France, find work, find a school, and use their earnings to subsidise their studies. Most of its recruits returned to China, where several (notably Chen Yi 陈毅, Li

Lisan 李立三, and Deng Xiaoping 邓小平) played important roles in the communist revolution.[102]

On the eve of the First World War, the Chinese in France included an unusually varied range of social types. Live Yu-Sion lists them: 'Students, anarchist intellectuals, journalists, diplomatic representatives of Imperial China, traders in Chinese art objects, a few restaurateurs, some chiropodists, and around fifteen workers in an artificial silk factory in Dieppe and a soya factory near Paris'. Not only did their origins and their reasons for migrating differ from one to the next, so too did the varieties of Chinese they spoke. In this sense, they were quite different from the Chinese in Britain, who spoke Cantonese and were nearly all seafarers.

The Huagong 华工 who served at the front in France in the First World War formed the main component of the French Chinese community. Most Huagong returned to China soon after the 1918 armistice, either as part of the organised general repatriation or in a steady trickle, but some 3000 stayed behind. A few made their way to nearby countries (including Belgium and the Netherlands), but most took up labouring and other jobs in France. Some had worked in factories in the war years. The rest had been disciplined and regimented at the front, in ways that translated with relative ease to the factory floor. Many went to work in the car factories (including Citroën and Renault) in Greater Paris. Quite a few stayed in industrial areas like Lyon. Some 1850 skilled workers went to work in the metallurgical, chemical, and other industries. Around 300 worked in the mines. The great majority of the Chinese residents of Greater Paris in 1931 were said to be either general labourers (55 per cent) or specialised workers (37 per cent). Only a handful (4.2 per cent) were petty traders; an even smaller number (3.8 per cent) were classed as 'students, hairdressers, and hoteliers'.[103]

Later, however, this proletarian group largely dissolved, after the start of the economic crisis of the 1930s. It is hard to say whether the Chinese willed this change, or whether it was forced upon them by circumstance. However, it is a fact that the depression affected immigrant groups more severely than French workers.

In the 1970s and the 1980s, a new wave of Chinese immigrants from Indochina went to work for Citroën and Renault, following in the footsteps of the Huagong. But most soon left to seek a better living in the ethnic enclave. So the trajectory of the Chinese community in France was quite different from that of Chinese communities in Britain and throughout most of the world.

The laundries

Hand laundries and eating houses, initially joined to the boarding houses and then in the form of separate enterprises, were a necessary feature of the Chinatown economy, and began to make marginal inroads into the host economy as businesses in their own right. The transition 'from salt to soap' marked the end of the Chinese confinement to dockland occupations serving a seagoing community and the start of a wider social embeddedness.[104] The second transition, from soap to soy, later opened another tiny pathway to economic desegregation. Together, these two conversions paved the way for the passage from migrant to immigrant.

Chinese laundries spread quickly through some British ports, so much so that one newspaper was moved to comment in 1892 that 'the great Chinese national industry is laundrying'.[105] In the ensuing years, before and after the First World War, Chinese launderers fanned out across a number of inland towns and cities. In 1901, no more than 12 per cent of Chinese in Britain were employed in laundries. By 1911, the absolute number of Chinese laundrymen had more than quadrupled, to 26 per cent of the total. Ten years later, laundering had overtaken seafaring as the chief occupation.[106]

In her study on English laundresses between 1850 and 1930, Patricia Malcolmson says that Chinese hand laundries 'constituted an insignificant portion of the industry' in Britain, unlike in parts of North America.[107] This statement is true for the country as a whole, where the industry employed more than 200,000 people at its peak at the turn of the nineteenth century, compared with just a few hundred Chinese. At the time, the British laughed at what they saw as the American hysteria about the 'threat' allegedly posed by Chinese laundries.[108]

In several British ports, however, Chinese inroads into the trade were not negligible. In Liverpool and Birkenhead, which had 600 laundries of all sizes in the early twentieth century, the number of Chinese laundries grew from just one in 1890 to 63 in 1906 and to more than 100 in 1907, a big proportion.[109] Cardiff had around 30 Chinese laundries in 1911 (serving a much smaller population than Liverpool's, of just 182,000). By 1931, there were between 500 and 800 Chinese laundries in Britain as a whole.[110]

The switch to laundering represented the first step away from the quayside and into the wider community. Maria Lin Wong notes that 'outside of Liverpool 1 [near the docks], laundry work was the only form of employment in which Chinese labour became visible'.[111]

In Cardiff and London, the laundries were 'quite well dispersed throughout the city' – a necessary arrangement, given the nature of the market.[112]

The laundry craze was partly a matter of opportunity. The Chinese were excluded from the main land-based occupations by discrimination and their ignorance of English. Although there were no laws to forbid employing Chinese, unlike in the United States, the informal barriers – backed by the hobnailed boots of organised white labour – were scarcely less effective. At the century's turn, laundries were the main breach in the racist wall of closure.

The British laundry industry was in the throes of modernisation around 1900. The disarrangement laid it open to penetration. 'Formerly a purely domestic industry, organized upon the economic principle of one woman one wash-tub,' wrote a Fabian pamphleteer,

> it is now a typical, modern, machine 'business', characterized by aggregation of workers in one building under one head, subdivision of labor and the use of labor-saving machinery. All over the country...there has been a rapid multiplication of large laundry companies and syndicates.[113]

In 1900, the Chief Inspector of Factories described the impact of these changes:

> [Some syndicates] own as many as a dozen or more fine, well equipped steam-laundries, filled with the latest ingenious inventions in labor-saving machinery.... In place of the elderly married woman or widow 'washer', we find skilled engineers in charge of a shedful of machinery still called the wash-house, while scores of girls and young women from thirteen upwards 'tend' the various kinds of ironing machines with exactly the same precision and routine as those in any other factory.[114]

However, this mechanisation, although extensive, came relatively late and was not completed until after the Second World War, when independent washerwomen were finally eliminated.[115] The lingering moment of transition gave the Chinese their chance. The competitive pressure on the hand laundries opened the door to the Chinese, whose special advantages enabled them to survive in an industry increasingly under siege.

It is not unusual for workshop industries in decline to fall into the hands of ethnic newcomers better able, by virtue of their more effective human resources and capacity for spartan living, to compete with the forces of mechanisation and modernisation. A case in point is the Chinese leatherwear and garment industry in Tuscany, which grew up in a region whose local population had been active in the same field. Like the Chinese who supplanted them, the native Tuscans had organised their businesses along family lines and by way of business networks. In the 1980s, Italy's 'Tuscan model' entered into crisis. The Tuscan family was changing and big firms were becoming more flexible, heralding the beginning of the end for the traditional small firm. The Chinese, for their part, 'adapted to the new situation by recuperating...the original characteristics of the Tuscan region'. They reproduced Tuscan manufacturing practices and made use of preexisting channels of raw-material provisioning and sales. They did not produce the Tuscan crisis, though they are often accused of having done so. Instead, their presence in Tuscany was a product of the crisis.[116]

The Chinese capture of part of the domestic laundry industry in some British ports was an example of the same process of displacement at a time of radical change. Unlike most native washers, the Chinese 'sweater' was in a position to take on the new steam laundries and beat them on the grounds of price and service. His main strengths were a determination to become his own boss, entrepreneurial resourcefulness, a willingness to work all hours, the ability to endure extreme misery and privation if necessary, and reliance on family labour, hallmarks of ethnic-Chinese business nearly everywhere in the migrant generation.

Hand-laundries required little capital outlay. The only equipment needed was a washtub, a washing dolly, a scrubbing board, a mangle, and an ironing board. The main running costs were for soap, starch, and heating fuel. Most of the laundries were set up in old cheap-to-rent terraced houses roughly adapted to the purpose. Few of the laundrymen spoke much English and most relied on their local wives or helpers to talk to customers. In any case, keeping such businesses required little ability to communicate, for laundry methods were still primitive and treatments were uniform and rarely required negotiation. The washroom was often housed in tin-roofed extensions in the yard. The drying was done in the downstairs back room. The front room served as the shop, where the laundry was received and the ironing done. These houses were like Southeast Asian shophouses in that the upstairs floor usually served as the proprietor's place of residence.[117]

Native-run hand laundries in early twentieth-century Britain were notoriously insanitary. Most of the workers and owners were women. The floors were usually wet or flooded and the washing was done standing up. The laundress worked bathed in steam and up to her feet in water, rendering her 'especially liable to pulmonary complaints, varicose veins and ulcerated legs'. While the modern laundries were subject to the 1901 Factory Act, which set limits to the rate of exploitation and minimum conditions of health and safety, the laundry workshops were (until 1907) covered by the far less exacting 1895 Act, which did little more than prohibit excessive hours.[118]

The Chinese laundrymen were not bound by the provisions of either of these Acts, which (with the exception of the Sunday observance ordinances) applied solely to women and children.[119] Even so, their laundries impressed the Medical Inspector of Health in Liverpool in 1906, who said they 'compare favourably with the ordinary English laundries'.[120] In Cardiff, an official report noted that 'the Chinese employed in [the] laundries are for the most part well conducted, clean, industrious and temperate people'.[121]

The Chinese encountered opposition from vested interests in Britain whichever line of work or business they set their hand to. In that respect, Britain was no different from most other countries, and the laundry industry was no different from any other industry. At the end of the nineteenth century and the start of the twentieth, Chinese laundries were the object of white wrath in Australia, where a long-running boycott was organised; in California, where white-labour laundries were set up to compete with the Chinese laundry workers, whose numbers in San Francisco were cut by one-third; and in other places.[122]

In Britain, Chinese laundries met with opposition from organised labour and street mobs, as well as from sections of the press. Trade unionists in Liverpool, where Britain's first Chinese laundry was set up (in 1886), protested in 1891 against the influx of 'pauper immigrants' (mainly Jews) and of the Chinese 'bob-tailed people', who were 'competing against the laundrywomen, and were springing up like mushrooms in this land [and should be] put a stop to'.[123] The first Chinese laundry to be set up in London's Poplar district (in 1901) was stoned by a mob.[124] In 1906, Liverpool's Head Constable noted in a report that 'the competition of the Chinese with the laundries and boarding house keepers' lay at the bottom of the anti-Chinese outcry in the city.[125] The worst violence was in Cardiff in 1911, when rioters wrecked up to 30 Chinese laundries during a seafarers' strike.[126]

However, hand laundries differed in important respects from industries that the Chinese did not seek to enter. The industry was in the throes of change, as we have seen, and vulnerable to aggressive competition. Laundering was stigmatised and unattractive, but one remove from housework, and – for the same reason – women's work. (The proportion of women and girls in the industry ranged from 99 per cent in 1861 to 93 per cent in 1911.)

The industry's female character did not prevent labour protests against the 'alien invasion'. Trade unionists had supported the laundresses' struggle for shorter hours and better conditions and helped them set up a laundresses' union in Liverpool in 1891.[127] However, organised labour was, at the time, largely male and more likely to champion male interests. Its support was usually restricted to the factory laundries. It showed less concern for the laundry workshops.

The owners of the British power laundries were opposed to the independent washerwomen, whom they viewed as competitors. According to Arwen Mohun's study of steam laundries in Britain and the United States, '[t]rade journal rhetoric [in Britain] about these women echoed the bombast of the American laundry journals'.[128] This view was not without its supporters among laundry employees.

Englishwomen, wrote Beatrice Potter Webb in 1887, were 'the Chinamen of this class [of native workers]: they accept any work at any wage. They grasp after the leavings of the Jew in the coat trade'.[129] Webb's thesis, that women and Chinese occupied the same rung on the labour ladder and competed on the labour market even more unfairly than the Jew, is one of several parallels and ties that commentators established between British women and Chinese immigrants from the 1880s to the 1920s. While Webb's point is phrased in terms redolent of the anti-semitism and sinophobia that pervaded the labour movement, from the fellow-travelling snobocracy down to the shopfloor, it is aptly raised. In fact, female workers were, for a long time, practically the only group Chinese could risk confronting.

Laundering was strategically targeted as a niche occupation by Chinese in many countries, but only in Britain was it practically their sole land-based occupation. In the United States, Chinese who moved into the cities set up all sorts of small enterprises, from laundries and grocery stores to restaurants and coffee shops, while others ran market gardens and industrial businesses.[130] In Australia, they worked not only as laundrymen but as cabinetmakers, market gardeners, urban labourers, and businessmen after the exhaustion of the gold-fields.[131] Their failure to branch out similarly in Britain can be explained by Britain's abundance of labour, the strength of the trade-union movement, and competition from other groups like the Russian and Polish Jews, who filled niches Chinese might otherwise have tried to enter.

Neither the male trade unionists nor the middle-class tradespeople who ran civic institutions and represented 'public opinion' cared much about the needy widows who ran small hand laundries, or about the wives of labourers or invalided husbands who took in washing. The Chinese seafarers could be confined to below decks and excluded from mainstream occupations by the threat of strikes. However, the laundresses and their supporters lacked the menfolk's economic muscle to deal with Chinese competitors. The anti-Chinese agitators must have viewed with satisfaction the 'laundry riots' that hit Poplar in 1901 and Cardiff in 1911.

J. P. May's study on the 1911 British seafarers' strike includes a detailed account of the Cardiff riots. Although some rioters were seafarers, large numbers were women, girls, and local men without any direct link to the sea. May himself concludes that 'British workers' opposed the Chinese laundrymen because they saw them as 'a symbol of all those forces of capitalism which were felt to be working against the aspirations of the working-class', in the context of class polarisation in the aftermath of the Boer War.[132] But this analysis ignores the more obvious explanation – that the community as a whole was concerned at the threat to a familiar institution by the foreign interloper, and that the main casualties were women.

Although the Chinese hand laundries drove some British wives and widows to the wall, women nevertheless played a vital part in them. Local women were employed in some Chinese wash-houses, just as they were in the new steam laundries. Their presence was in part responsible for the allegations, investigated by the Liverpool authorities in 1906, that Chinese laundries were 'nothing less than brothels'. In fact, some women helpers ended up marrying their Chinese bosses.[133]

Just as the British washerwomen got their husbands and children to help out in the business, so most of those working in the Chinese laundries were members (of all ages) of the proprietor's family. Others were from the broader Chinese or British-Chinese community. (Some of the latter saw the relationship as exploitative.) The number of people employed in the Chinese laundries was therefore far higher than suggested in the reports, which counted only men.

The various tasks – washing, mangling, starching, ironing, folding, airing, and taking orders – were organised according to a gendered division of labour. The wives and the half-Chinese children did the lighter jobs, including light ironing and dealing with the customers in the shop section, while the men did the washing, applied the heavier irons, and specialised in ironing awkwardly shaped items like collars, which required a strong wrist.[134] (This division of labour mirrored that in the power laundries, where washing was the only task done by men and boys.[135]) Once the laundries were up and running, some proprietors arranged permits for their kinsmen to join them in Britain, to increase the workforce and expand.[136]

This family labour was highly flexible, instantly available at all times, and usually unpaid. The service provided was therefore cheap, reliable, and sensitive to customer demand. Laundry work was seasonal, with major troughs (for example, when the gasworkers were laid off in the summer and the building workers in the winter), and highly vulnerable to fashion changes (for example, from starched cotton to synthetics).[137] The Chinese laundries' elasticity helps explain their runaway success.[138] Their adaptability and competitiveness allowed them not only to outclass the traditional domestic laundries but to hold their own against some of the new steam laundries, while taking in their stride a torrent of racist vilification from critics and opponents.[139]

They could also provide quality service. In some cases, they were criticised for cleaning their customers' laundry too abrasively. On the whole, however, they avoided the shredding and tearing with which the power laundries became associated in the public mind.[140]

For the white laundresses, prosperity and success were usually elusive. On top of the industry's volatility and price-sensitivity came the need to juggle laundering with domestic tasks, ranging from childcare to household chores. Getting customers to pay for work done was sometimes difficult. Then, there was the hard drinking of some laundresses, a self-imposed obstacle to saving. The Chinese laundryman had fewer handicaps. Childcare and household tasks were not his business. As a community outsider, he was less likely to be troubled by defaulters. And he was usually abstemious and frugal.

The Chinese laundryman also benefited, perversely, from racial exclusion by the Trade Board inspectors, who well into the 1930s continued to view Chinese laundries as beyond their sphere of responsibility and subject to discretionary exemption from acts of parliament. 'For many inspectors,' wrote Arwen Mohun, 'the Chinese did not belong to the political community with which the law was an agreement, and they were generally thought to be incapable of understanding or agreeing to the intentions of the acts'. British launderers, on the other hand, 'found it more and more difficult to conduct their business beyond the reach of the state'.

The laundries were the only Chinese institution besides the shops and boarding houses, which they far outnumbered, so it is not surprising that a lot more than mere washing happened on laundry premises. The seasonal nature of the business made additional income-generating strategies necessary throughout the industry,[141] and Chinese laundries were no exception. The proprietors' options were numerous, as a result of their seagoing connections, and included smuggling.

Some laundries acted as distribution points for opium,[142] and some laundries served as clearing houses for immigrants. These new arrivals – legal or illegal – were probably relatives of the proprietors recruited to staff the old laundries or start new ones. A historian of the community points out that 'these family businesses were natural places for newcomers to get employment'.[143]

Probably the most persistent charge was that Chinese laundries doubled as brothels and gambling dens. The commission of inquiry appointed by the Liverpool City Council in 1906 noted that 'the evidence [regarding brothels] has been of a conflicting character', adding that there was no room for doubt 'that frequent immorality has taken place on some of the premises'.[144] But the conventional British view of interactions between Chinese and local women was strongly coloured by mixophobia, as we show in a later chapter.

In our attempt to explain the Chinese association with laundries, we have looked so far at opportunity and resources. It remains to explore diffusion as a factor in the spread to Britain of the Chinese laundry business. Arwen Mohun has shown how, in the white mainstream, 'people and ideas slipped back and forth' between Britain and the United States from the very start of the steam laundry industry, with mutual visits and an active copying on each side of the Atlantic, especially the British, of methods of management and laundering developed on the other.[145] We should therefore not be surprised to learn that the Chinese too were participants – albeit invisible – in this transnational exchange, importing into Britain ideas and techniques first developed by Chinese in the United States. One might almost say that the Chinese laundry was a transatlantic import.

Hostile British journalists and officials alleged that the Chinese were strangers to the laundry business before coming to Britain. They 'first learned the work from poor laundrywomen and then discharged them' according to one report, which described the alleged practice as 'pernicious'.[146] But such charges fail to explain why Chinese became a byword for laundering in much of the English-speaking world.

The Siyinese connection seems to have been the foundation on which Chinese laundries spread. America was the origin of the Siyinese association with the laundry trade. In California, the Siyinese were employed throughout the economy in the mid- to late-nineteenth century, but they were especially linked with two main occupations, washing and market-gardening.[147] In New York, the association with washing was far closer and more exclusive, for whereas the Chinese in California worked in a wide range of jobs and industries, not all that different from the occupational profile of other immigrant groups, in New York they were concentrated to a far greater degree in this one trade. In Australia, too, the Chinese worked in a variety of fields. However, Chinese laundries appeared in far greater numbers in the 1890s in Melbourne, where the Siyinese preponderated, than in Sydney, which had a more diverse Chinese population.[148] A similar pattern holds in Britain, where the two main centres of the Chinese laundry business at the start of the twentieth century were Liverpool and Cardiff, Siyinese strongholds. In London, on the other hand, which had a more mixed Chinese population, Chinese laundries started later and there were fewer of them in the early twentieth century[149] (just 30, compared with more than twice that number on Merseyside[150]). However, the situation was not entirely comparable, for French and Italian launderers had already set up in business in the capital,[151] which also had the biggest concentration of power laundries.[152] Both factors narrowed the scope for new competition.

The contrast between California and Australia on the one hand and New York and Britain on the other suggests a typology of Chinese immigration to the English-speaking countries. In territories still under settlement, where Chinese immigration was sometimes encouraged, the range of Chinese occupations was, for a while, not much narrower than that of the generality of immigrants. In settled and highly urbanised locations like the American east coast and Britain, a different pattern obtained. Here, Chinese employment was directed into niches. In New York, the Chinese association with laundering probably had its origin in the importation of 150 Chinese from California in the early 1870s to replace militant Irish laundresses. (In the event, the Chinese turned out to be no less militant.)[153] In Britain, the Chinese were admitted to just one trade, seafaring, and spread to just one other, laundering, by virtue of the American connection and the nature of the Chinatown economy, geared to servicing the needs of transients.

The connection between laundering and Siyinese migration remained a hunch until we read the file on Ng Seng Mun, a second-generation

Singaporean laundry manager, in the oral history section of Singapore's National Archives. Ng, a native of the Siyinese county of Enping, explains that nearly all Singapore's professional laundry workers in the previous generation had been either Siyinese from North America or their kin. Ng recites the Hong Kong film scene that inspired the Siyinese 'washermen' (an American term imported to Singapore with the trade): 'Uncle, what are you doing in America?' 'I am a washerman. I wash the one million dollar fortune. I wash out the one million dollar fortune. I made a million dollars out of it'.[154]

More recently, the exact circumstances of the transport of the laundry tradition from the United States to Britain were explained in a publication that drew on the memoirs of local Taishanese migrants. Sometime around the turn of the nineteenth century, a Taishanese called Mei Xuanli 梅轩利 moved from the United States to Liverpool, where he used knowledge gained in the United States to set up a laundry. Once his business took off, he imported relatives from Taishan. As a result, 'Taishanese became the lingua franca of the [Chinese] laundries in Britain'.[155]

The Siyinese connection was central to the creep of Chinese laundries across Britain. Yorkshire, for example, had a Chinese population of 265 in 1921, most of them in the laundry business. York, 100 miles from the nearest Chinaport, had a Siyinese-run laundry as early as 1910 and 18 Siyinese residents by 1921. In 1919, this business was sold on to another Siyinese, Fung Foo (born 1882), whose offspring in York numbered more than 20 by 1975 and whose relatives and fellow-villagers were running seven laundries in the city by 1938. Only in 1958 did the Siyinese stranglehold on York end, when the Siyinese owner of the city's first Chinese restaurant was forced to recruit Chinese from the New Territories to staff it. (Within no time, the newcomers had reduced the old hands to a minority.)[156]

There is strong evidence that clan and lineage was the chief tie along which Chinese laundries spread across Britain, starting in the ports. In both London and Cardiff, the trade was dominated by the Lee clan. In the case of Cardiff, Lees were not active in any of the other known forms of Chinese enterprise, keeping shops and lodging houses. In Liverpool, a quarter of all laundry-owners were called Lee.[157] In short, the Chinese laundry industry in Britain was a creation not just of Siyinese but of the Lees.

This new perspective on the trade throws into question Paul Siu's well-known thesis about the Chinese laundry industry in the United States. According to Siu, the concentration of Chinese in laundries showed that the sojourner mentality was 'largely conditioned by the persistent exclusionary and discriminatory policies of the host society'.[158] Without wanting to belittle American sinophobia in the early years of Chinese settlement, we would point out that the Chinese resisted the role of victim to which white America and Britain wished to consign them, and that their inroads into the laundry industry in both countries can be better understood as the mobilisation of transnational experience and resources than as a result of ethnic persecution.

In Europe, only in Britain did laundries become inextricably associated with Chinese. Chinese laundries sprang up in a few other European countries, including France, Belgium, Germany, and Russia, but nowhere to the same extent. The Netherlands had just one or two and Denmark, Spain, and Italy apparently had none.[159] France, Belgium, and Germany had shipping links with Asia and were urbanised and industrialised, so they had both a supply of potential Chinese laundrymen (in the ports) and a strong urban market for the trade.[160] However, Chinese laundries failed to boom there. Most Chinese on the European mainland were not Cantonese seafarers, as in Britain, but Zhejiangese peddlers, who preferred selling goods to services. This sub-ethnic difference perhaps helps explain the cross-Channel difference in Chinese business culture.

The Chinese laundry trade experienced one final upsurge in the Second World War, before dying away after the war. 'For laundry workers', noted a historian of the industry, 'wartime was a boon'. A new market was created by the billeting of hundreds of thousands of troops across the country,[161] a bonanza in which Chinese laundries shared.[162] However, war also led to the industry's accelerated mechanisation and its concentration in ever fewer hands, a process the Chinese were unable to keep pace with. The finishing blow was delivered in the 1950s and the 1960s, by the laundromat and the self-service launderette.

By the 1970s, there were just two Chinese laundries left in Liverpool, and proportionately even fewer in the rest of Britain.[163] A handful of businesses continued in the 1960s and 1970s to do labour-intensive starch work (on collars, cuffs, aprons, and the like), which the industrial laundries could no longer undertake because of postwar labour shortages. Others withdrew from active trade but stayed open for a while as receiving offices, from which they sent customers' laundry to the big firms in return for an agent's discount.[164] However, such businesses eventually closed.

Yet the demise of the Chinese laundry trade was not inevitable. Chinese laundries in the United States found it extremely hard to compete with power laundries and the big laundry companies after the Second World War, and with the invention of the domestic washing machine.[165] Even so, around 1000 Chinese laundries survived there into the 1980s by reorganising as launderettes or as distribution stations for washing and drying plants. More recently, Chinese in France have started investing in the modern laundry business.[166] In Britain, some laundries with a family trade have successfully accommodated to the new age of launderettes, dry cleaning, contract laundering, and linen rental,[167] but they include few if any Chinese.

Why did the Chinese fail to adapt to the new conditions in the industry? There are several explanations, ranging from inertia and lack of vision on the part of the founders to a loathing of the trade by their sons and daughters. Renqiu Yu 于仁秋 reported in his study on New York's Chinese Hand Laundry Alliance 纽约洗衣馆联合会 that such was the shame felt by Chinese in New York that they disguised their association with laundering in correspondence with their families, who were led to believe that their prosperous sons ran not laundries but 'clothes shops'.[168] The stigma attached to washing other people's soiled linen was reason enough for many second-generation Chinese in Britain to turn their backs on it.

An analysis of the records of Chinese-owned companies incorporated in the United Kingdom turned up none that had at any point been connected with the laundry industry. Even though the Chinese had a large presence in the laundry sector long before its mechanisation and modernisation, none managed to build on their experience in the business. This failure was probably due in part to an inability to raise the capital required to upgrade facilities. It would therefore seem right to conclude that the laundry business, like the takeaways of the postwar period, was for many Chinese migrants less an entrepreneurial venture than a means of survival.

Harry Tharp, who ran a laundry in Leicester up until retirement, suggests a further explanation for the failure of Chinese firms to make the transition to mechanisation:

The laundry premises would spread, sometimes to occupy whole blocks [of terraced houses]. These businesses, as they grew, could finance the purchase of machinery to take advantage of the latest technology. In this development, the native English businesses would merge to grow under the most effective management, but the Chinese would strive to exist independently rather than amalgamate with a rival.[169]

Only at sea did the Chinese continue to launder for the British. Starting in the Second World War, thousands of Hong Kong Chinese were recruited as laundrymen by the Royal Navy, under the same 'number one boy' system as in the merchant navy in the old days, with each ship served by a single kinship group. (Some Chinese laundrymen died in action, including two in the Falklands.) The arrangement continued until 1998, when they were replaced by a British company.[170] Thus ended the Chinese connection with British laundering.

By the 1960s at the latest, the Chinese laundry was a closed chapter and had given way to catering, the other great Chinese industry in twentieth-century Britain. The two trades were different, yet the one was in many respects a dress rehearsal for the other. The links and likenesses are worth exploring. Now that Chinese catering is negotiating the transition between generations and showing signs of a looming crisis of confidence and succession, what lessons does the laundry experience hold for it?

Chinese enterprise in European countries in the past has tended to be based on a single idea exported from its point of origin, in the ports, to the hinterland, often by the pioneers' kinsmen or sub-ethnic associates. This method of cellular expansion was characteristic (for example) of the laundry trade in Britain, the soapstone-statuette trade in France and elsewhere, the *pindakoekjes* 花生糖 (peanut-cake) trade in the Netherlands, and – most spectacularly of all – the catering trade. Each time, the trade spread outwards – in the case of catering, from bases in Britain to the whole of Europe.

This bandwagoning is well known in China, where it goes under the name of *re* 热, literally 'heat', that is, fad or craze. Not all such crazes catch on, but when they do, they have obvious benefits. The franchisee (so to speak) gets trained by relatives or friends and can consult them and use their networks. He or she also profits from their reputation. The ultimate cause of this wave-like proliferation of an identical trade or occupation lies in the structure of the migrant group (which depends on networks for intelligence and employment) and the nature of the resources available to the migrants (resources natural to a community of mariners and sojourners, stranded in a society with few uses for them other than manning ships or practising unpopular land-based occupations on its margins). Beyond these factors internal to the Chinese group, exclusionary practices by British workers, bosses, and officials work to consolidate its economic ghettoisation.

This mode of economic growth has drawbacks. In the case of the laundries, a sudden proliferation of Chinese wash-houses in one place, as in Cardiff in 1911, attracted the mob. Chinese caterers do not seem to have suffered attacks of this sort, but they have experienced related problems, including market saturation. Cellular reproduction can also lead to a suicidal aversion to fresh ways of doing business.

The Chinese laundryman's failure to adopt new techniques after 1945 is a case in point. A similar disinclination to leave the beaten track undermined the vitality of the Chinese catering industry in the 1980s. That the two industries seem to have followed the same pattern is hardly surprising, given that those engaged in them have a similar class and educational background. In the case of the laundries, the failure to innovate led to extinction.

In sum, the idea of running laundries did not originate with the Chinese in Britain but was a borrowing from California and New York. Chinese who had worked as washmen and cooks on British ships were familiar with the tricks of the trade (which were, in any case, quite rudimentary). For the Chinese laundryman, business tended to be family-based. The laundry (like the later takeaway) functioned as a shophouse to accommodate the family and newcomers from China, depended on family labour, and operated according to a division of labour based on age and gender and organised along similar spatial lines, with the washerman in the back room and the wife and kids in front, at the counter. For a business of this sort to hold together across the generations, the children must identify with it. But whereas identification with the family as a collective unit was strong, identification with the business as such was not. The hours were unsocial and long and the work was often experienced as shameful, for it amounted to a commercialised form of domestic service in a most intimate domain, washing. The work was hard and boring. A main attraction from the pioneers' point of view was that little capital was required and labour-intensive methods could be applied. From the children's point of view, however, these methods of work were repulsive. What was true in the early part of the twentieth century of Chinese laundries was, in part, also true of takeaways in later years.

The Chinese and opium

Opium was introduced to China from the Middle East sometime in the Tang Dynasty (618–907), on a relatively small scale. In the late eighteenth century, the East India Company started to export huge quantities of the drug to China from Bengal, where it held a monopoly on its processing. To disguise its role, the Company left the trade to the so-called 'country ships', which sailed under its licence. After the company's withdrawal from China in 1834, the trade was taken over by other British companies. The Qing Court tried to suppress it, but to little effect, particularly after China's defeats in the Opium Wars. British merchants and Chinese criminal gangs made vast fortunes out of opium, which was traded at one point on a scale greater than any other international commodity. In 1894, opium made up 14 per cent of China's imports, on top of large quantities of the drug processed domestically. In 1900, 27 per cent of Chinese men were to some degree addicted. The Chinese balance of trade was reversed by the traffic, from a huge surplus at the start of the nineteenth century to a huge deficit at the end of it, and Chinese society was ravaged by the consequences.

The stereotype of the 'opium-addled Chinese' originated in China in the nineteenth century and emigrated to wherever the Chinese settled. The opium trade, and the stereotype, flourished among Chinese in the United States in the railroad-building years and in Australia during the goldrushes.[171] However, the Chinese use of opium was for a long time seen throughout the world, including in Britain, as unexceptionable, the Chinese equivalent of smoking tobacco or drinking alcohol. Nor was the opium habit by any means confined to the Chinese. In the nineteenth century, opium was legally tolerated and universally obtainable at low cost in many countries. It was widely employed as a painkiller in home remedies and patent medicines and as a stimulant or source of pleasure.

In Britain, opium was openly on sale until the Pharmacy Act of 1868, which theoretically brought its supply under pharmaceutical control. It was available, wrote Barry Milligan in his book on opium and British culture in the nineteenth century, 'to any retailer who cared to buy and resell it, including not only chemists and druggists but also grocers, bakers, tailors, publicans and street vendors.... Britons could buy opium in pills, powders, and plasters, liniments, lozenges, and laudanum, syrups, suppositories, and seed capsules straight off the poppy stalk. And it was relatively cheap – in fact it was cheaper than liquor'.[172] It was even cultivated in some parts of England, notably the Fens.[173] Even after 1868, opium continued to be freely available from pharmacists, for the new statute was more concerned with regulating it (and other substances) as a poison, of potential use to homicides, than as a cause of addiction. The pharmacists themselves protested strongly against including opium in the act. Laudanum (opium in alcohol) was the favoured drug of the British lower classes, especially in the Midland manufacturing towns, and morphine was fashionable among the upper classes. As Matthew

Sweet joked in *Inventing the Victorians*, 'For the Victorians, opium was the opium of the people'.[174] In such a climate, the pipe habit of the self-contained Chinese communities in London and Liverpool aroused little comment.

In the 1870s and 1880s, British social and medical attitudes to opium began to change, partly because of the damage the drug was seen to have done in China, where its ravages were found indefensible by increasing numbers of Christians and politicians. (The Society for the Suppression of the Opium Trade was founded in Britain in 1874.) In the early twentieth century, a series of international conferences resolved to tighten controls on opiates and other drugs. The meeting of the Shanghai Opium Commission of Control in 1909 denounced the non-medical use of opium. Opium Conventions followed in the Hague in 1912 and Geneva in 1924.

In 1908, the Poisons and Pharmacy Act restricted the sale of opium in Britain to persons known by the pharmacist. In 1912, Britain signed the Hague Convention, which called for state control of the production of and trade in opiates. However, the government took no real steps to impose controls until midway through the First World War, in response to an increase in cocaine addiction among members of the armed forces and civilians and the smuggling of opium into the United States on British ships. In July 1916, the Home Office made it an offence (by Regulation 40B under the Defence of the Realm Act 1914) to possess either drug without a doctor's prescription.

The Dangerous Drugs Act 1920 codified the wartime regulations by creating various new offences, ranging from the import of raw opium to manufacturing, dealing in, or possessing prepared opium without authority or allowing premises to be used for such purposes. In 1923, the maximum penalties were increased from £500 or two years' to £1000 or ten years' imprisonment. As a result, a small black market began to develop. After 1925, however, drug abuse declined and practically ceased in the United Kingdom until the 1960s, when it again started to become widespread.[175]

The Chinese opium dens in Britain originated in the Chinese boarding houses, which provided facilities for gambling and smoking opium. In time, the dens developed into separate businesses, particularly after the 1894 Merchant Shipping Act allowed local councils to withdraw licences from boarding houses that encouraged such activities.[176] A visitor described the early dens as 'poorly fitted social clubs, and certainly free from anything [as] visibly objectionable as, to say the least of it, public houses of the same class'.[177] As many as 20 or 30 men and women would sit or lie on shipbunk-style shelves in various stages of stupefaction, behind tightly drawn curtains. The smoker's outfit consisted of a pipe and bowl, a small lamp, and two steel needles on which to spit the opium and cook it in the lamp's flame, before placing it in the pipe.[178]

At first, the clientele was exclusively Chinese, but it was not long before local customers began to frequent the dens. Some were down-at-heel addicts, others romantics, bohemians, or upper-class slummers attracted by curiosity or fashion, including 'men with names well-known in various walks of life'.[179] In the early days, these British users took their opium with the Chinese. By the century's turn, a minority of dens – perhaps two out of a total of six in London – had begun to cater exclusively for the expensive non-Chinese market. In 1907, a reporter described what 'the man of means' would get for 20 or 30 shillings (compared with a charge of between half-a-crown and five shillings in a low-class den):

> The soft light of shaded lamps...discloses a spacious hall. The feet sink in the rich, heavy carpet as the visitor passes on to the next floor, where there is an excellent restaurant.... Its patrons sometimes include Society women seeking a new sensation. But only privileged visitors have access to the rooms above, where the opium smoker may surrender himself in retirement to the enjoyment of the pipe.... There are a number of apartments in the upper stories set apart for this purpose. Each contains a couch upon which the drug victim reclines. The mattress and the cushions are of silk. An attendant noiselessly enters the room bearing the necessary utensils.[180]

The legislation passed before the First World War did little to inhibit the sale and smoking of opium by Chinese in Britain. The 1908 Poisons and Pharmacy Act led to some prosecutions, but the trade persisted.[181] In the wake of the act, the London County Council passed a by-law aimed at abolishing the dens by tightening up the licensing of boarding houses.[182] However, the by-law had the opposite effect. It spread the habit over an even greater number of premises, by driving it from the Chinese boarding houses into private homes where it was harder to control.[183]

Not until after the start of the war did government anti-drugs legislation begin to bite. Under the new wartime law, a number of Chinese were arrested in 1916 with a view to deportation without trial and their furnaces and equipment were destroyed. These measures were said to have created a mood of 'general consternation...among the Chinese resident community'.[184] The government represented its actions as a moral crusade. However, its sense of outrage did not extend to banning the export of morphine to Japan (from where it was sold on to China), a policy that would have risked alienating a wartime ally. (In public, though, it pretended to have gone for the virtuous option.)

Home Office officials took sadistic delight in the 'general fear' that the raids created in the tiny Chinese population in the seaports.[185] British trade unionists joined in the sinophobic outcry. Their proclamations provoked a scornful riposte by a small group of Chinese trade unionists in Liverpool, who claimed that opium smoking by Chinese had 'entirely stopped' in Britain and pointed out that the traffic had originally been forced on China by the British.[186] Chinese residents also protested to their Embassy and gained support from Guomindang activists in Britain.[187]

The wartime measures were a foretaste of the postwar crackdown on the Chinese opium trade, underpinned by a joint demonisation of dope and Chinese in the British press. Arrests and deportations continued throughout the 1920s, while other Chinese left Britain of their own accord. The new legislation passed in the 1920s, in particular the stiffer penalties introduced in 1923, seems to have had the effect intended, by clearing away the dens and pushers. A few Chinese were arrested on opium charges in the 1930s, but nothing like the same number as in the 1920s, when a steady stream of Chinese appeared before the courts. By 1934, the police knew of only two remaining opium-smokers in Limehouse and maintained that younger Chinese did not touch the drug.[188] Not until after the start of the Second World War, when a new generation of Chinese seafarers entered Britain, did the Chinese traffic in opium revive.[189] Ten years after the war, in 1955, drug addiction 'among seamen of Asiatic origin' in British ports seemed to have died out altogether, according to a report by the British delegate to the United Nations Narcotics Commission.[190]

Not until the late 1960s or the early 1970s was significant narcotics smuggling once again reported in the Chinatowns of Amsterdam and London. The new traffic was in heroin, produced in Thai laboratories and smuggled into Europe through Schiphol and other airports. Chinese Triads from Malaysia and Singapore were said to control this trade, which in London at first catered to Chinese restaurant workers but later spread to the wider population.[191]

Opium dealing, like laundering, started out as one element in a diffuse household-style economy designed to meet the everyday needs of Chinese seafarers during their time ashore. It briefly developed as a branch of business in its own right, but was driven back into concealment by its criminalisation between 1908 and 1916. Opium was subsequently traded under cover of more respectable occupations such as catering and laundering. Once declared illegal, dealing became linked to other criminal or disreputable activities.

Smuggling – of guns and people as well as opium – was an obvious choice for a small minority of members of a community so closely tied to the docklands and the sea. The likely networks and supply lines along which the Chinese drug trade flowed after the war stretched from Turkey by way of Marseilles (where the drug was probably prepared) to ports in Belgium and the Netherlands, whence it was distributed across Europe and into Britain. Onward routes extended from British ports to the United States. Most of the opium was smuggled across the Channel in the bilges and engine rooms of cargo ships; smaller quantities were hidden in folds and seams of the seafarers' clothing. Within the United Kingdom, Chinese dealers used ships crewed by Chinese to supply outlets in the major ports, including London, Liverpool, Glasgow, and Cardiff. In London, British women in the dealers' pay were said to have helped extend the market for opium 'from the East [End] to the West End'.[192]

Studies on the Chinese in Britain (most of them written by ethnic Chinese) tend to ignore, play down, or deny their historical connection with crime. This approach, which echoes that of Chinatown veterans who indignantly deny the community's lawlessness and shipboard origins, stems from an honourable impulse, to combat the stereotypes that attached to Chinese immigrants in the early days and continue to rankle and resurface. However, there is ample evidence from police records and court cases that some early Chinatown strongmen got rich by running rackets. Annie Lai, herself an addict and a prostitute in the 1920s, has provided a frank account of the activities of the small-time Chinese underworld in the East End of London, which revolved around drugs, gambling, prostitution, and illegal immigration. According to her, the ostensibly respectable Siyinese-based Chee Kung Tong 致公堂 was behind the Chinatown-based rackets.[193] In that respect, however, the Chinese in Britain are no different from immigrants of all nationalities throughout the world, a few of whose aspiring entrepreneurs are sometimes diverted by exclusion from the mainstream business into trying their hand at crime.[194]

Even so, it is important to avoid tarring the entire community with the same brush. The popular press wrote as if all Chinese smoked opium. 'Limehouse knows...that nearly every Celestial more or less likes to smoke opium', claimed an article titled 'The Cockney John Chinaman', published in *The English Illustrated Magazine* in 1900. In fact, the habit was far less widespread than made out. The Liverpool commission of inquiry reported in 1907 that 'it is principally among the Chinese seamen that the habit prevails, as distinguished from the resident Chinamen', and that 'no crimes due to the use of the drug have come to the knowledge of the Head Constable'.[195] In London, the settled Chinese had a good reputation, particularly in prewar days. 'Limehouse', continued *The English Illustrated Magazine*, in the article already cited,

> knows...that 'people who live in glass-houses should not throw stones'; and while there are so many drinking-shops in the district where it can find English men and women lying dead drunk outside the doors, it does not see any particular vice in the inhabitants of Limehouse Causeway having his pipe of opium where he does not make an open spectacle of himself to all the world.... Taken altogether,...the Chinaman in Limehouse is a most peaceable, inoffensive, harmless character. He is on good terms with his neighbours, most of whom speak well of him. He is picturesque in a region where it is sadly needed.[196]

In 1925, Chinese shipping-masters in the Netherlands questioned by the Dutch police gave different estimates of the number of Chinese seafarers who used opium, ranging from one-third to 70 cent. Since they had no reason to exaggerate and good reason to minimise the extent of the practice (one of the two crimps questioned had himself been found guilty on opium charges), we can conclude that probably a majority of Chinese seafarers smoked the drug.[197]

Resident Chinese who did not use or deal in opium deplored the boom in opium smoking and gaming in Chinatown after the First World War, which they blamed on 'the incursion of new elements'.[198] These respectable residents – called 'the better class of Chinaman' – were aware of the damage that drug-trafficking did to their legitimate businesses. Some opposed opium smoking for the same reason as reformists and revolutionaries in China – it dishonoured the nation and corrupted the people.

The Chinese association with opium and other drugs became automatic in the early twentieth century and has remained so, on and off, ever since, due to the anchoring of the stereotype in the press, the cinema, and popular literature. In the first half of the twentieth century, drug use in Britain was largely confined to the Chinese community, even at the height of the British opium scare. The hue-and-cry had far less to do with an actual threat to society than with a xenophobic urge to scapegoat Chinese. It was also due, in part, to the shaping of British perceptions of Chinese by developments overseas (a phenomenon we will return to in the discussion of anti-Chinese racism in Chapter 6). The decline in the number of Chinese and non-Chinese opium-smokers in mid-century relegated the stereotype from the headlines but not from the popular psyche. Then, in the 1970s, the 'Chinese connection' shot back onto the front pages as a result of the explosive growth of the heroin trade.

Blaming the Chinese for Britain's drug trade is not only unfair but richly ironic. Opium was sold in Britain long before the Chinese arrived. The Chinese responsible for importing opium and heroin into Britain were not representative of the wider Chinese community: on the contrary, they preyed on its shopkeepers and caterers. The British export of opium to China, on the other hand, marked the start of widespread Chinese addiction. The British traders were not some secretive criminal gang operating on the fringes of society but government-sponsored godfearing merchants backed first by diplomatic missions and (when the missions failed) expeditionary armies, which imposed opium on China at gunpoint.

The Chinese catering trade

The origins and early history of Chinese catering in Britain mimic those of its older brother, the laundry trade. Like washing clothes, cooking, and serving food started as a function of the boarding house but branched out as an enterprise in its own right. Chinese caterers, like the launderers, spread outwards from the ports along more or less the same routes, on the same principle of 'saturation and dispersal'.[199] Once it had proved successful in one place, the catering formula was copied by kith and kin in another, just like the laundry formula before it. In time, the caterer became an indelible part of the Chinese racial stereotype, even more so than the washerman.

Chinese catering businesses also resembled the laundries in that they were versatile and multifaceted, especially in the early years. Their products were not just confined to meals but often included garments, home-sewn by wives and mothers for wholesalers in the rag trade on a piece-work basis, alongside or instead of helping out in the kitchen. 'Their living rooms', noted one author, 'were not only a play-area for the children, but also a bustling clothing workshop'.[200] This sort of doubling-up is typical of ethnic-Chinese enterprise in its early phase. In Italy today, Chinese leather workshops and restaurants are often joined under one roof, with several families active in both trades plied from the same residential base.[201]

By the late twentieth century, the role played by Chinese cuisine as a global culture and identity marker connecting Chinese communities across continents was proverbial, but its early diffusion along transnational migration chains is less widely known, perhaps because its migrations were obscured by catering's transparently functional origins in the boarding-house system. Although in one sense an outgrowth of the Chinese domestic economy in the ports, catering as both an institution and a cooking style was (again like laundering) pioneered in North America, largely by Siyinese, whose relatives and fellow-villagers imported it to Britain.[202] The food, as Hugh Baker has pointed out, 'owed more to the California gold rush of a century earlier than it did to native Chinese cuisine'.[203] The very term 'chop suey' was an American invention.[204] Wrongly believed to be the name of a great Chinese national dish, it was in fact a generic name for makeshift meals, a corruption of the Cantonese *jaap sui* 杂碎, 'mixed bits'.[205]

Writing about Chinese cuisine in Papua New Guinea, Hawaii, and Taiwan, David Y. H. Wu 吴燕和 has argued that its globalisation did not follow the rules suggested by current general theories, which are based on Western capitalist practices. Rather than spread as 'a direct flow of cultural traditions from the centre to the periphery [or as] the diffusion of capitalized cooking industry pushed from the Chinese homeland by professional chefs and restaurateurs', it was invented or recreated abroad by self-taught cooks, as an indigenised version of Cantonese peasant food, and was subsequently standardised.[206] Chinese culinary culture in Britain and the United States was also an overseas invention, but not necessarily a creolism. Instead, it grew beyond its local contexts on foreign land and radiated as world food along the international sealanes, on orbits coterminous with the Siyinese diaspora.

All Britain's early Chinese communities had cafes where Chinese immigrants and transients could meet to eat and socialise. One of the first such cafes (actually, a coffee shop that doubled as a chop-suey house) was set up in London in 1886 by Zhang Quan 张权 and Zhang Shou 张寿, brothers who had previously worked as ship's cooks for the Blue Funnel Line. Later, the Zhang brothers (Cheung in Cantonese) set up two more restaurants in the same vicinity, one of which was still in existence in the 1980s (though the business had by then passed out of

Zhang hands).[207] The brothers were the founders of the Cheung dynasty of restaurant proprietors, which dominated Chinese catering in London right through until the 1960s.

In London, five early restaurants catered largely to British diners. However, the general run of Chinese cafes rarely served non-Chinese customers, save for the occasional local resident who might pop in for a chicken wing or a jug of chop suey (an early form of takeaway).

By the mid-1920s, many of London's restaurants were in the hands of the Cheungs, who had moved some of their businesses from the East End to the West End, to catch the theatre trade. In the 1930s, Britain's tiny Chinese catering industry fell on hard times. Most of its remaining customers were Chinese students and – in the docklands – 'members of the lower working class'. Yet the Cheungs clung on to their niche and formed the nucleus of the Chinese business community in Soho's Gerrard Street in the 1970s.[208]

The best-known of the prewar restaurants, Maxim's, was set up in Wardour Street by Chang Choy. A onetime Embassy chef, he built on his success in London by setting up a chain of restaurants in Paris, Berlin, Geneva, Vienna, and Hamburg, after which he returned to China as a millionaire. During the anti-Japanese boycott of 1937–1938, his restaurants banned Japanese diplomats and businessmen.[209]

After the Second World War, when steam laundries went out of fashion, the business focus of the Chinese community switched wholesale to catering. The move was timely. Profound social and economic changes had set the scene for a revolution in British eating habits that the Chinese, with their entrepreneurial flare and culinary traditions, were well placed to exploit.

The best study on the context within which Chinese catering developed after 1945 is by Susan Chui Chi Baxter.[210] Baxter maps the transition from prewar British catering, mainly in the form of domestic service and craft-style production, to the postwar boom in commercial catering, the basis for which was laid in the war by the introduction of factory canteens and state restaurants. She concludes with a review of the fast-food revolution starting in the 1970s, when the arrival in Britain of multinational format chains undermined the ethnic sector, including the chop-suey houses, and led to a restructuring of Chinese catering that ended with the takeaway.

Baxter attributes the growth of industrial catering to two main factors, the undermining of domestic catering by the re-entry of married women into the labour force and the fall in the cost of eating out relative to eating in, as a result of technological change. The war was pivotal to both processes, for it released women workers from the home and led to a massive investment of resources in catering technology. Wartime legislation required factory owners to set up canteens, while other workers ate in the so-called British Restaurants, set up and subsidised by the state. The wartime expansion of communal and commercial catering required the recruitment of large numbers of migrant workers, chiefly refugees and Irish, a prefiguration of postwar developments in this industry.[211] The impact of the changes in catering management on the British public's eating habits was deep and lasting.

After the war, the state gave up its direct role in communal catering, which was hived off to commercial entrepreneurs. Again, many were migrants and refugees. In the 1950s, women once more entered the paid labour force in strength, leading to a rise in household spending power, a resurgence in the market for ready meals and eating out, and the start of a new fast-food boom.[212]

Chinese caterers rushed to turn the new trend to account. They were doubly favoured, for while they profited like the rest of the food industry from the postwar upturn in commercial catering, they also reaped the benefits of new cultural attitudes generated by the war and its aftermath. The stunted restaurant culture of the egalitarian wartime years and of the postwar era of food rationing had, as Jack Goody points out, started to die out, under pressure not only of economic growth but of 'boredom with uniformity'. The end of scarcity marked the start of prosperity for Chinese and other foreign restaurateurs.[213]

British consumers in the late 1940s and the 1950s not only ate out more often but became more adventurous and knowledgeable about food. British and American servicemen newly returned from duty tours in Asia had acquired a taste for 'exotic' cooking. Others had repatriated after working in the colonial administration or in business in East and Southeast Asia. In the new food-catholic era, Chinese restaurants became fashionable. They were more affordable than other restaurants, whose ingredients and labour tended to be dearer. Chinese cafe owners and restaurateurs who had previously catered to Chinese adapted their dishes to the wider public. With the end of rationing in 1954 and a further increase in the 1950s in family spending, the catering boom accelerated.

In his study on the Chinese community in Britain, Hu Zhiqiang 胡志强 calls the 1950s the period of economic 'growing to maturity'.[214] In London, veteran restaurateurs with prewar experience in the trade expanded their operations, sometimes in the form of tiny chains. Where possible, they went upmarket, to cater to the middle classes.[215] Newcomers of different ethnic and geographic origins – former staff of the old Chinese Embassy (most of them northerners), ethnic Chinese from Malaya and Singapore, immigrants from Hong Kong's New Territories, and non-Chinese proprietors – also joined the field.[216]

The ethnic-Chinese proprietors from different parts of Asia proved unable to get along. Their inability to protect their common interests and sustain a working relationship set a pattern for the trade that subsequent generations of Chinese caterers failed to break. Former Nationalist bureaucrats and diplomats ran luxury restaurants, in some cases backed by non-Chinese capital. However, their cooks and waiters were mostly Cantonese-speakers recruited in Hong Kong, who communicated in pidgin English with their Mandarin-speaking bosses. The 'class contradiction' between capital and labour was thus reinforced by a powerful sub-ethnic difference. Very soon, these restaurants were submerged by a less exclusive style of business oriented to mass consumption.[217]

Before the war, Chinese restaurants serving the general public were most associated with London's West End, but after 1945 Chinese cafes and eating houses in other parts of the capital and the country began throwing their doors open to non-Chinese. The Chinese restaurants in London's East India Dock Road continued serving English workers. In Liverpool, where Chinese cafes had sprung up during the war, some demobilised members of the Chinese Merchant Seamen's Pool invested their savings in new catering ventures and targeted a non-Chinese clientele. By 1951, 7.8 per cent of Chinese businesses in Liverpool were in catering, compared with less than 2 per cent at the start of the war; by 1956, the proportion had risen to 18.4 per cent.[218]

'Overseas Chinese' are by now associated with catering in nearly all countries in which Chinese communities have formed, but the notion that the Chinese were 'born cooks' is as laughable as the stereotype that they were born laundrymen. Very few of Britain's Chinese caterers had any previous experience of the trade. All but a handful learned their culinary skills 'on the job', in Britain.[219] A Chinese essayist describes their lightning apprenticeship: 'Apparently the great Chinese chefs of those days graduated into their profession after half an hour's training. The key to their success was a cauldron-scraper, a bottle of soya-bean oil, and a bag or two of bean-sprouts'.[220]

In Britain as in France, the proportion of Chinese engaged in catering is often greatly exaggerated, as part of a general stereotyping.[221] In the mid-to late 1990s, Chinese sources claimed that the trade accounted for around 90 per cent of Chinese employment in Britain, the same figure as that suggested (a decade earlier) by the Home Affairs Committee report on the Chinese community.[222] However, Yuan Cheng's analysis of data from the Labour Force Surveys between 1983 and 1989 found just 57 per cent of Chinese in 'distribution, catering, hotel and repairs', while a 10 per cent sample of the 1991 Census yielded just 36 per cent.[223]

The rate of catering employment is not uniform across different subgroups of the ethnic-Chinese population. Nearly one-third as many Hong Kong Chinese as Chinese of other ethnic or geographic origins worked in the industry in 1991. The comparison between Hong Kong Chinese and Chinese from Southeast Asia was starker: for each Chinese caterer from Southeast Asia there were nearly six from Hong Kong.[224]

The business activities of ethnic Chinese worldwide are potentially no less varied than those of any other ethnic and immigrant minority. Within the limits set by exclusion and chain migration, Chinese business in Britain can be grasped as a creative adaptation to circumstance, and as a series of stages each of which is viewed as one moment within a strategic plan. In terms of catering, several such moments can be identified, including endgame, when the successful entrepreneur bows out of the ethnic enclave and either expands into the mainstream economy or plants members of the successor generation in a profession. The propensity of Chinese entrepreneurs to follow in each other's footsteps can be explained by the host society's exclusionary practices and by Chinese employers' habit of importing recruits along migration chains, which predisposes them to conform.

The paths along which immigrant strategists set out are far from uniform. In some cases, the initial transition was from boarding house to shop or cafe, followed by a further switch from cafe to restaurant. The transition from laundry to restaurant was another route many followed. Neighbourhood fish-and-chip shops have also figured as bases from which Chinese immigrants have embarked on more ambitious catering careers.

Over the years, the 'Chinese chippy' has become a familiar institution, no more so than in Liverpool in the 1950s, where youngsters were at one time tempted to believe that the chip shop was a Chinese invention.[225] That the switch to fish and chips happened first in Liverpool should come as no surprise, for the city was perhaps the nearest that Britain got in the early years of immigration to a melting pot in which stranded Chinese seafarers developed friendships and family ties with local people. Without the local knowledge, confidence, and connections gained through such relationships, the idea of the Chinese chippy would hardly have been conceivable. In Manchester, 'colonised' by Chinese from Liverpool after the port's decline in the 1960s, a clear majority of takeaways were founded on English fish-and-chip shops. Elsewhere in the northwest, the north, and the Midlands, a similar pattern was repeated, as a second wave of Chinese entered the fish-and-chip trade.[226]

An indigenous form of fast food, distinguished from the fast-food chains by its relative lack of capitalisation, fish and chips are sold across the counter to be eaten elsewhere. Studies on Britain's Chinese catering economy often assume that the takeaway developed from the restaurant in the late 1960s and the 1970s, as a result of changes in the British fiscal system and the demographic composition of the Chinese population. This is only partly true. In many cases, it grew out of British-style fish-and-chip shops, whose original menus it supplemented (or, less commonly, supplanted) with Chinese dishes. In some cases, restaurants grew out of takeaways, again contrary to the usual theory.

The chip shop was an ideal investment for the would-be takeaway owner or restaurateur and remained a target of Chinese immigrants for the rest of the century. It cost relatively little to buy or convert, and it inherited a ready-made customer base. Fish and chips, said the President of Manchester's Fish Fryers' Society in 1976, 'slide down the menu and finish at the end of the line when a Chinese frier takes over'.[227] By promoting a wider range of dishes, the new proprietor upped his sales and profits and headed, hopefully, down the path to exit from the trade or to expansion.

Unlike the takeaways, most Chinese restaurants in Britain started from scratch, rather than on the ruins of a failing British business. In Manchester, for example, only one in ten Chinese restaurants was found to have directly replaced a British restaurant. Nearly three-quarters of Chinese restaurants in Manchester were newly opened; the rest replaced existing Chinese restaurants.[228]

Forms of ownership have varied. Restaurants founded between the wars and in the first years of the peace were run as sole-proprietor enterprises with relatively high levels of capitalisation, in some cases as chains. The owners, mostly urban and educated, were prosperous, well connected, and at home with British business methods. Such restaurants were more capacious and professional than in Paris, where the food was said to be worse. They also had a higher capital value. 'Sources agree,' wrote Monica Taylor, 'that these early restaurateurs displayed particular enterprise, industry and astuteness and were generally the wealthiest Chinese in their localities'.[229]

Some of the restaurants run by former employees of Chiang Kai-shek's London Embassy, on the other hand, were derided by their Chinese competitors as amateurs. Managers were usually employed to look after such businesses. The owners, lacking in experience of or aptitude for commercial catering, were incapable of mucking in, for example, if the cooks and waiters staged walk-outs.

At the start of the 1950s, there were just 36 Chinese restaurants in Britain, according to the Census. Throughout the rest of the decade, however, their numbers rose steadily. They finally achieved take-off in the mid-1960s, when there were up to 200 in London alone.[230] The restaurants of this second wave were organised and financed quite differently from those of the first. Most of the old-style restaurateurs were well-heeled individualists with ample access to investment funds, either their own accumulated savings or credit provided by a bank. The newcomers, on the other hand, were neither affluent nor creditworthy and lacked the collateral usually necessary for securing bank loans. Most of the newcomers were said to have arrived in Britain with no more than a five-pound note in their pockets, to spend on necessities.[231] However, many had access to funds entrusted to them by family members in Hong Kong, to be invested on the family's behalf in a restaurant partnership.

Such partnerships, usually formed among kin or fellow villagers, were typical of the pioneering and boom phases of postwar Chinese catering. By ganging up and sheltering behind them, new arrivals were able to gate-crash the industry and cushion themselves against the risk of failure.

The partners not only pooled their capital; most also worked in the restaurants as cooks and waiters, under a senior manager who usually held the biggest stake. Only in a small minority of cases did the investors include 'sleeping partners'. James Watson explained the system: 'The usual arrangement was for the ownership to be divided among the workers and the resident manager. For example, a cook might own two shares, a young waiter one, and the manager four – there may be a dozen shares in even the smallest restaurant'.[232] This set-up made financial sense and also solved a second problem, the immigrants' lack of English. In the mid-1960s, fewer than one in five staff members could hold even a simple conversation in English. But in a business owned in partnership, only the restaurant manager and the senior waiters needed to communicate with customers and officialdom. The kitchen staff could live their lives for much of the time as if they were still in Hong Kong.[233]

Most small- and medium-sized restaurants set up in the early postwar period began as partnerships. After a few years, however, they converted to individual ownership, with the help of bank loans and personal savings. (Three out of four of the restaurants studied by Yi Liao in Manchester were funded in this way.)[234] The partnerships were as if built to fail. Nearly all the partners saw the arrangement as temporary and aspired in the long run to run businesses of their own. Some partnerships disbanded amicably and according to plan, others broke up as a result of strains and tensions.

The misgivings and resentments inherent in restaurant partnerships, including living under one roof, often erupted into conflict. Even where relations remained equable, trying to keep more than one family (either back in Hong Kong or in Britain or in both places simultaneously) on the basis of one enterprise was unrealistic. The period of partnership was one of learning the ropes and accumulating enough capital to cover that part of starting-up costs not met by bank loans and loans from family and friends.[235]

Even those who started out not as part-owners but as cooks and waiters in the bigger restaurants aimed to branch out on their own. Those employed in the high-class restaurants run by wealthy northerners were doubly motivated to leave, for friction was rife as a result of the ethnic divide.[236] However, even those employed by relatives and fellow Cantonese itched to go independent.[237]

Once employed in Britain, villagers from the New Territories broke loose from the control and patronage of the veteran restaurateurs and set up new businesses, which they staffed by importing relatives and neighbours. The population base they drew on was, of course, tiny compared to Siyi and the counties of southern Guangdong that delivered most of Britain's prewar Chinese immigrants.

The fate of the Siyinese community in York, transplanted from Chinatown in the first decade of the twentieth century, illustrates the mainlanders' eclipse by immigrants from the New Territories. Before 1958, York was a 'colony' of the Siyinese, but their recruitment of a dozen workers from Sha Kok Mei 沙角尾 in Hong Kong's Sai Kung 西贡 to staff a new restaurant marked the beginning of the end of their preponderance. Very soon, they were reduced to a minority by the newcomers, who founded their own restaurants and takeaways.[238] The same happened to ethnic-Chinese restaurateurs from elsewhere in mainland China and from Southeast Asia who hired staff from the New Territories.

The chains along which New Territories emigrants reached Britain to join the catering boom were based largely on the extended family and the lineage and only marginally on shared dialect or place of provenance. In this respect, postwar Chinese immigration into Britain differed from Chinese immigration at other times and to other places. Only in periods of extreme labour shortage did the average degree of relationship between immigrant and employer widen. Emigration agencies in Hong Kong, in some cases organised by lineages, found would-be emigrants jobs in Britain and arranged travel (usually paid for by the prospective employer, as an advance on wages) and accommodation on arrival. The Commonwealth Immigration Act of 1962 temporarily reinforced these chains and the Chinese concentration in the catering niche by introducing a voucher system that made new immigrants dependent on the patronage of established immigrants, who were required to apply for vouchers on behalf of prospective employees.[239]

The Chinese catering economy in Britain has never seen protracted social conflict between owners and employees. Class conflicts do occur, but they are nearly always resolved by means other than collective bargaining or confrontation. One reason for this class peace is the recruitment system. Where relations between restaurant workers and bosses are founded in ethnicity or kinship, organisation along lines of social class is difficult.[240]

Conversely, where the class and ethnic divides coincide, each distinction deepens the other and conflict is practically inevitable. Such was the case in the late 1940s and the early 1950s, when northern Chinese, Siyinese, ethnic Chinese from Southeast Asia, and non-Chinese staffed their restaurants from the small first wave of immigrants from the New Territories. The workers had scant respect for their employers' entrepreneurial and management skills, and thought they could do better. The two sides spoke mutually unintelligible forms of Chinese. Workers in these ethnically divided businesses had no sense of a common identity with their employers and few qualms about acting on their grievances, even to the point of staging walk-outs.[241] However, desertion and defection were commoner than resistance. In the postwar ethnic catering boom, the more dynamic and resourceful newcomers withdrew from waged employment to set up their own enterprises, either as partners or as individuals.

In the case of partnerships, class distinctions were less relevant. Even in new restaurants under single ownership, bosses and workers usually came not only from the same district but from the same village or lineage or even family. However, this system of sponsorship bore little resemblance to the credit-ticket traffic in coolies in the nineteenth century, a byword for rapacious abuse, for the process of recruitment was informal and the connection often close enough to prevent extreme exploitation.

In restaurants where the relationship is one of employer and employee, wages and conditions have usually been determined by fluctuations in the labour market. Up to 1965, the inflow of labour from

Hong Kong favoured the employer, whereas the subsequent decline in immigration and the rise of the takeaway lent clout to the employee. In the 'day of the employer', before 1965, restaurant managers acted arbitrarily and dictatorially. The hours of work were long and hard (stretching in some cases from 8 am to midnight), conditions were poor by British standards, duties were elastically interpreted to the employee's disadvantage, there was little or no talk of days off or sickness pay, statutory entitlements were practically unknown, and accommodation was tied to employment and overcrowded. The comment by one study that chain migration and the voucher system led to 'total reliance on Chinese employment channels [that] put workers completely at the mercy of their employers' was, under such conditions, hardly exaggerated. After 1965, however, when the 'day of the employee' dawned, wages rose and conditions became a matter of negotiation, particularly for skilled and experienced workers, who could pick and choose where to work.[242]

Some staff benefited less than others when the balance of opportunity tipped in favour of the workers. In nearly all catering establishments, labour was arranged in hierarchies based on skills and status that determined levels of reward. In the bigger restaurants, such hierarchies were strict and fairly complex. The chef ruled the kitchen, assisted by the second chef. Kitchen-helps kept the kitchen clean and supplied the chefs with materials. The pantry worker fetched and carried. The waiters served at table. The managers took orders.[243] Between chef and pantry worker, the pay differential was wide. Out front, a similar distinction applied among waiters, a good half of whose income was from service tips that were shared according to seniority and rank.[244]

There have been attempts at various times to organise Chinese restaurant workers in trade unions, but never to any lasting effect. In 1968, when officials of the Hong Kong Government Office (HKGO) in London set up a Chinese Chamber of Commerce 英国华商总会 in an attempt to influence Chinese traders in the United Kingdom, they also mooted a parallel organisation for restaurant employees, but nothing came of the scheme.[245] In the 1970s, some restaurant staff – mainly the China-born, who were treated harshly by their Chinatown employers – talked of setting up a union, and other sporadic attempts to unionise this or that Chinese restaurant followed in later years.

However, it has proved hard to persuade Chinese workers in catering to join unions. Union officials who try to break through into the trade come up against the language barrier. Even in restaurants where workers have no direct stake in the business, staff are rarely numerous enough to foster a strong feeling of 'them and us'. In the 1980s, most restaurants employed fewer than fifteen workers. In the West Midlands, less than one-third of all Chinese catering firms employed workers; of those that did, most averaged ten to twenty waged employees.[246] Most small caterers rely on friends and relatives to staff their businesses and strike informal deals on pay. The Chinese habit of underdeclaring wage levels to evade taxes is also a powerful deterrent to protest, for it inhibits workers from appearing in public before tribunals. Workers who speak no English rely for employment on the catering niche, a small community that can easily blacklist 'troublemakers'. Given the racist nature of the wider job market, such ostracism can lead to permanent loss of employment.

In the 1980s, radical activists set up a Chinese Workers' Union 华人工会, which gained recognition as a section of the Transport and General Workers' Union (TGWU). The union lasted for four years and led a strike against white employers in Brighton. The strikers won compensation but failed to get their jobs back, and the TGWU was criticised for its ineffectiveness. The Chinese community supported the strike because the employers were white, but it gives little backing to strikes by Chinese against Chinese. As a result of the apathy, the Chinese Workers' Union folded in 1987.[247]

Only a handful of restaurateurs in some of the bigger cities went against the general trend and set up large-scale restaurants and catering chains. These business leaders included some who had arrived from Hong Kong in the early 1960s.[248] By the end of the century, some of the biggest Chinese restaurants employed up to several dozen workers.[249]

This sketch of the social and economic structure of Chinese catering suggests that class relations are less antagonistic in businesses not divided along ethnic lines. In this light, it is worth remembering that not all Chinese immigrants to Britain in the second half of the twentieth century originated in the New Territories. As we have already shown, Britain received approximately 10,000 of urban Hong Kong's China-born residents between 1963 and 1973, most of whom found jobs in catering. So did quite a few Vietnamese Chinese refugees in the late 1970s and early 1980s. More recently, several thousand undocumented immigrants from Fujian and elsewhere in China have joined the underground workforce in Britain's Chinatowns. All three groups have laboured under various disadvantages.

The first China-born group, who gained entry to Britain on the basis of work-permits, had fewer resources and rights than Chinese born in the New Territories, who had British citizenship under the terms of the Nationality Act and looked down on the outsiders. Those admitted on such permits were required, at least in theory, to stick to a particular job with a named employer, a condition that robbed them of bargaining power. According to Watson, they had 'few friends and even fewer relatives already established in Britain, so they do not have a protective network of personal contacts'.[250] The Vietnamese Chinese lacked not only resources and connections but cohesion. Some found work in Chinatown, but usually of a menial nature. In the eyes of many Chinese in Britain, even their claim to Chineseness was questionable.[251] As for the second China-born group, most of whom arrived at around the turn of the twenty-first century, their illegal status renders them more vulnerable to mistreatment, by both employers and criminal gangs.

The degree of exploitation of restaurant employees differs from case to case, depending on factors such as staff size, the state of the labour market, the ethnic relationship between staff and owner, and the workers' immigration status. However, the tensions that perceived injustice generates rarely reach breaking point, for exit options are open to the more aggressive and assertive workers, who in other circumstances might lead revolts.

One option is to get a job in another restaurant, and thus a rise in pay (in recognition of previous experience). In the 1970s, a study revealed that more than half of all employees changed jobs at least once a year.[252] The more popular option in the 1970s was to cut loose. Those with sufficient resources, pooled or private, and confidence in their own managerial abilities set up a restaurant. The great majority, however, invested their savings in a takeaway. Junior shareholders in catering partnerships also tended to follow this path, after selling out to the senior shareholder.[253] Some immigrants made the transition to independent entrepreneurship within just two or three years of reaching Britain.[254]

In 1971, the number of Chinese takeaways in Britain was said to be growing at the rate of three a week.[255] In the 1970s, takeaways became part of the street scene in every suburb and small town. The term takeaway, which may (like chop suey) have originated in the United States, was quickly nativised and even took local forms, such as 'packed meal' (in South Wales) and 'carry-out' (in Scotland).[256]

The switch to takeaways happened when developments in the general catering economy and the British fiscal system knocked the bottom out of the plans of many would-be restaurateurs. At the same time, demographic changes in the Chinese population favoured takeaways. The makeshift living arrangements associated with the early restaurants may have suited a community of men, but they were no longer adequate once Chinese families began to form or reunite in Britain.

The takeaways grew up during the fast-food revolution that started in the late 1960s. The term fast food refers to standardised meals produced at high speed for immediate consumption on or off the premises. At one end of the fast-food scale are the multinationally owned chain outlets like McDonalds and KFC, which depend on massive capital investment in labour-saving technology, the deskilling and cheapening of the labour that is retained, and 'scientific' management and marketing techniques. At the other end is the chip shop and the takeaway.

The invasion of Britain in the 1970s by American fast-food companies employing cost-cutting management techniques and production technologies drove down prices and put a tight squeeze on the profits of domestic caterers, whether native British or ethnic, who continued to operate almost without exception on a labour-intensive basis. Restaurants catering for the mass market found themselves increasingly unable to compete, despite a big growth in the market for catered food. The old-style chop-suey houses, unable to match the economies of scale achieved by the big chains, were among the first casualties of the fast-food onslaught. The government clampdown on immigration and the reduction in the number of work permits issued also drove down restaurant profitability, by making labour dearer.

Ethnic-Chinese restaurant groups have tried to take on the fast-food giants at their own game, but such ventures remain exceptional and tend to get their capital from Hong Kong and Southeast Asia. Few had much impact. Other Chinese restaurants have tried to go upmarket, by adjusting their cuisine and management style. As customers became more experienced and discriminating, restaurateurs took care to choose ingredients that were fresh, appropriate, 'authentic', and (where necessary) imported. Some restaurants of the old chop-suey genre started to specialise in haute cuisine or regional traditions of Chinese cooking and to import well-known chefs. However, the market for such ventures is limited.

By far the most successful way of surviving the fast-food revolution was to join it: to fight for a share of the fast-food market by substituting cost-cutting family labour for costly labour-saving technology. Hence the rise of the Chinese family takeaway, which superseded the Chinese restaurant in the 1970s.

The introduction of new taxes contributed to the sudden popularity of the takeaway. Selective employment tax (SET, introduced in 1966 as a levy on the payroll) and value-added tax (VAT, which replaced SET in 1973 and was levied on the difference between the cost of materials and the selling price of a commodity or service) diminished the profitability of the entire catering trade but had a particularly adverse effect on restaurants. The rise of the takeaway compounded the crisis in the restaurants, by robbing them of customers and reducing the labour pool.

Such were the external, economic constraints within which the takeaway strategy took shape. However, the strategy might have failed to capture the imagination of Chinese investors but for radical changes in the structure of Britain's Chinese population, starting in the mid-to late 1960s. The most important development was the wave of Chinese family unions and reunions, in response to British restrictions on primary immigration. This process, which peaked in the 1970s, ended the old all-male community. The community that emerged was as if tailored to the takeaway economy, and vice versa.

As we have seen, most shareholders in Chinese catering partnerships and many Chinese workers in waged employment aimed sooner or later to break free and set up their own businesses. The rise of the takeaway at the expense of the restaurant speeded up this process of business fragmentation by making independent proprietorship easier to realise, for takeaways were far cheaper to found and run than restaurants.

A takeaway requires no prime location in the city centre or on a busy shopping street, and suitable premises can be purchased or rented far more cheaply than for restaurants. Lower rates, land values, and property prices are usually a critical element in a takeaway owner's choice of site. A converted house or fish-and-chip shop provides space enough, for the food is quickly cooked from prepared ingredients and quickly served, so long queues rarely form. Chairs, tables, tableware, and expensive décor are unnecessary.

A takeaway can be opened for around one-third the price of a restaurant. A takeaway run from rented premises in the West Midlands in the mid-1980s cost between £10,000 and £15,000 to start up, whereas one run from bought premises cost up to £50,000. A restaurant, by comparison, cost between £70,000 and (where premises required conversion) well over £100,000. Personal savings have usually formed a major part of starting-up costs. A study of Chinese catering in Manchester in the early 1990s calculated that one-third of owners relied solely on personal savings, whereas the remaining two-thirds used a combination of personal savings and bank loans. None of the takeaways studied was based on a partnership.[257]

Businesses that rely on family labour have competitive advantages over non-family firms. Authority is usually automatic and most family members are loyal, honest, flexible, and prepared to adjust their working time to business needs. Chinese food requires intensive preparation but relatively little cooking, a feature that recommends it to the takeaway trade, which depends on swiftness of delivery from kitchen to counter. The work of cutting up vegetables and meat and preparing sauces is rarely mechanised in takeaways and ideally suited to family labour.[258]

Takeaway opening hours require flexibility on the part of family members. The degree of self-exploitation to which takeaway families subject themselves can be gauged by a comparison with the British fish-and-chip shop. Whereas most fish-and-chip shops open on average no more than five days and around 20 hours a week, excluding public holidays, most Chinese takeaways open nine or ten hours a day six days a week, including most public holidays. (Takeaways normally close on Sundays.)

A typical working day might lasts as many as 16 hours. Between 5 and 7 o'clock in the morning, the owner visits the wholesale market to buy meat and vegetables. The hours between 7 and 10 are devoted to sleep or rest. Between 10 o'clock and midday, vegetables and meat are prepared for cooking and the rice is boiled. Daytime shop hours extend from midday to 6, with a break from 2 to 4 for lunch and cleaning up. The hours from 6 to 8 are spent preparing for the evening shift, which might extend from 8 to one o'clock in the morning.

Most takeaways were initially formed by husband-and-wife teams, usually after a couple of years in which the newly imported wife worked alongside her husband in a restaurant, driving up the rate of saving. Although labour-intensive, takeaways dispense with many of the tasks of restaurants. There are no dishes to wash and no tables to be waited on. A chef and a counter assistant are, in theory, the minimum personnel required. However, the importation (or growing up) of sons and daughters increases the labour available and reduces the pressure on the two adults. Only a small minority of takeaways hire part-time workers. Recurrent costs – rent, rates, light, and heating – can also be kept low.

This self-reliance saves on wages and allows takeaway owners to get by without recourse to the social capital and connections vital to staffing restaurants. In his study on the Chinese economy in York in the 1970s, William Cheung 张传馨 argued that restaurants were an ideal investment for villagers who lacked the skills necessary for interacting with urban people (let alone urban foreigners) and participating in urban economic life.[259] This point is doubly relevant to the takeaway, where ethnic interaction is even more restricted.

Some academic researchers and concerned observers have portrayed life in the takeaway as a trap leading to intense self-exploitation and oppression, both of the family and within the family, where women and children bear the brunt of suffering. However, if joining the catering economy is viewed processually, the picture changes. When Chinese women and children first began to arrive in Britain in large numbers, many went to live with the father in tied restaurant accommodation. Their presence was regarded by restaurant owners as a further opportunity for exploitation, with free accommodation as the pretext. The women were underpaid for working as kitchen helps or cleaners and the children were often unpaid.

The tied lodgings, designed for bachelors, were usually provided free of charge, to lure workers out of London and into the provinces. In the late 1960s, three out of four workers lived in such places, which in the case of the bigger restaurants consisted of dormitories, usually above the place of work. They were ill equipped to accommodate families. Even where single rooms were available, they were often squalid. Some families shared rented flats and houses with friends or relatives. Such multi-occupational arrangements fostered a spirit of ethnic camaraderie and spartan making-do, but grim conditions, overcrowding, and a shortage of amenities led to unhappiness and discord.

For such families, the takeaway represented deliverance from a life of misery and a solution to the problem of family living. It was 'a welcome opportunity to resume some semblance of family life, seriously eroded by dormitory restaurant work and hampered by the statutory requirement to demonstrate that incoming dependants could be accommodated and maintained by their sponsor'.[260] It also had a powerful economic rationale, for it saved not only on accommodation costs but on travel and it allowed couples with young children to continue working. Even as late as the 1990s, when most takeaways were into their third decade, four out of five families lived 'over the shop'. In contrast, only one restaurant owner in ten did so.

Estimates of the profitability of Chinese takeaways vary widely, perhaps as a result of underreporting by some owners. In the 1980s, around half of takeaways in Birmingham were said by accountants to yield a net profit of less than £10,000 a year. The average turnover was put at between £1000 and £1500 a week, and one in three families struggled to remain solvent. In Manchester in the early 1990s, on the other hand, an average takeaway could apparently expect to make a profit of £4000–£5200 a month, still no fortune but more than enough to validate a strategy of family self-reliance and guarantee financial security, and far more than most paid jobs would have yielded.

The Chinese attachment to owning takeaways should therefore not be mistaken for economic irrationality or the lack of entrepreneurial drive. The takeaway strategy allows optimal use of the limited human resources of the immigrant family while simultaneously resolving problems of a social character, including residence. At the same time, it is one stage on a predeliberated journey into the wider society and economy and an enterprise to be relinquished when the time is right, for Chinese families that invest in takeaways evince a high degree of economic mobility – sideways, within the takeaway trade, and upwards, into other forms of livelihood.

A majority of the 25 families studied by Miri Song had run more than one takeaway, and four had run more than two. According to Song, families are able to sell up in this way because of their cellular autonomy and lack of dependence on a chain of producers.[261] Susan Baxter also found that takeaways change hands frequently, usually within five years. 'These take-away businesses are not meant to be permanent,' an accountant told her. 'If people are successful, they try to get rid of them and make some money. If not, they cut their losses and get out'.[262] The mobility was not just between businesses but across borders. Chinese caterers who had learned the ropes and accumulated capital in Britain spread the restaurant and takeaway phenomenon to Ireland and mainland Europe, where they sought fresh markets in response to the crisis in Chinese catering in Britain in the 1980s.[263]

Upward mobility has taken two main forms, both of which will be examined in a more detail later. Younger Chinese of the second or third generation tend to opt out of catering and make career choices in the professions.[264] The relatively untaught generation of caterers pursued a strategy, phenomenally successful, of targeting education as a means of pushing children born or raised in Britain up the social ladder. For the migrant cohort, entrepreneurship seems to have been framed primarily as a launch pad for the second generation rather than as a means of achievement in itself. This exit into the professions facilitated a wider process of diversification in the ethnic-Chinese economy, which started mainly as a result of catering saturation. Some Chinese entrepreneurs have used the catering surplus to invest in new forms of business, including supermarkets, property, and modernised trading sectors.[265]

Some commentators believe that the catering enclave provides a sure means to upward mobility, a view that would support the theory that enclave economies bring more or less the same returns to human capital as the wider labour market.[266] However, in her study on the Chinese enclave economy in Britain, Yuan Cheng shows that 'Chinese working outside the catering trade have an advantage over Chinese working inside the enclave in reaching the service class' (that is, the class of employers, managers, and professionals). Chinese parents' rejection of the enclave as a path to the good life for their children in favour of the children's participation in the wider labour market would therefore seem to be based on a rational calculation of comparative advantage.[267]

The success of the takeaway experiment in terms of capital accumulation and the upward propulsion of the second generation can only be fully appreciated when one allows for the constraints within which it was achieved. The initial shortage of capital and human capital – including industrial skills and a knowledge of English – was one constraint. Often overlooked is the context of racist exclusion, perhaps the main obstacle to Chinese admission to the general economy and its workforce. We will return to the subject of anti-Chinese racism in a later chapter, but it is important to note that Chinese were singled out by British racists as the object of intense attention well in advance of other 'coloured' minorities. The exclusionary practices to which British trade unionists subjected Chinese workers in the early twentieth century had, for the most part, petered out by the 1960s, but such abuses lived on in the collective memory.

Unlike other groups of workers from the New Commonwealth, the Chinese were not recruited by the British Government to specific industries and services and few were bold enough to try to join the main jobs market independently. Their concentration in commercial catering was hardly of their own free choosing. The catering trade has long been a preserve of migrant or immigrant labour, like domestic service in the nineteenth century. White workers turned their backs on an industry associated with low pay, long hours, poor working conditions, insecurity, and low social status. Chinese immigrants converged on catering in the early postwar years because they felt they were not welcome in the wider labour market and had better seek work in a trade where they would not have to compete with the natives.[268] (Their main competitors in the corner-cafe trade were the Italians, whom they largely ousted.[269]) The food industry was a place of quarantine or refuge for the Chinese rather than a fairway to the mainstream.

Once entered, the catering niche became a new arena for racial stereo-typing and abuse. Although it shielded Chinese immigrants from some manifestations of racist hostility, it could also lead in other situations to the reinforcement of existing prejudices and stereotypes, so that the Chinese were 'further marginalised and devalued'.[270] The ethnic-food enclave is peculiarly vulnerable to 'eat-and-run' customers, who pick on Chinese and other Asian caterers because of their often smaller build and because they continue working after the pubs close, when drunks descend on the restaurants and takeaways.[271]

The spatial requirements of the catering economy make the Chinese one of Britain's most dispersed ethnic minorities, with no ghettos to speak of. A study of the Chinese community in Manchester in the early 1990s confirmed that takeaways cater for an essentially local market and are scattered relatively uniformly across Greater Manchester as a whole, rising to at least one takeaway to each square kilometre in high-density areas of the city. Takeaways are most likely to proliferate in areas where there are more single households, a relatively big popula-tion, more students, more professionals, and more unskilled workers (in that order of importance). Tourist resorts also serve as magnets.[272] On the whole, most takeaways are, of necessity, out of one another's reach.

For the first generation, the catering existence was conceived in terms of a culture of positive isolation from British society, a regime of 'self-imposed psychological quarantine' and of 'short-term misery in the hope of eventual long-term joy back in the village'.[273] The perpetuation of two forms of seclusion – from other Chinese and from the white majority – laid the caterers, especially those running takeaways, even more open to discrimination and attack.

The long-term phasing out of catering, including the takeaway, as the leading weapon in the Chinese business armoury in Britain has two main explanations, one economic and the other generational. The economic explanation is that Chinese catering entered into a trading and management crisis in the late twentieth century from which it never fully recovered. The generational explanation has to do with the feelings and aspirations of British-born Chinese, who view catering differently from their parents.

In the early years, Chinese catering was a runaway success with British diners. In 1974, Chinese meals accounted for 9 per cent of the total spent on eating out. Two million Chinese meals were sold each week, ten times the number sold by South Asian caterers and almost three times that sold by Italians.[274] In the mid-1970s, however, sections of the Chinese catering industry entered into crisis. Among the causes were incipient market saturation and over-capacity, as more and more businesses competed.[275] The old-style chop-suey houses were particularly affected by the American format chains' invasion of the British market.[276]

The effects on Britain of the world recession of the 1970s and 1980s led to a further decline in the restaurant industry. Chinese takeaways managed for a while to sustain their market share, regardless of these developments. However, the adverse effects of the economic cycle on the performance of catering enterprises were partly offset by Government measures in the Thatcher years, particularly in the early 1980s, when policies were introduced aimed at producing a more entrepreneurial culture. This strategy had a major impact on Britain's small ethnic entrepreneurs, who were well represented among the nearly one million people who joined the ranks of the self-employed in the 1980s.[277] Incentives were provided to establish enterprises, leading to a marked rise in the number of ethnic firms, including – in the early to mid-1980s – some leading firms in the catering industry.

In the 1990s, as the general economy recovered, the demand for ethnic and Chinese food again increased. At the start of the decade, Chinese accounted for as much as one-sixth of the annual turnover of the takeaway and fast-food sector. Some ethnic-Chinese entrepreneurs set up their own format chains that boosted the Chinese share. These new, larger, more sophisticated food-retailers were professionals without ties to the takeaways, whose interests they endangered – a case of intra-ethnic competition. The growth in supermarket sales of ready-made 'ethnic' food and ethnic-food products (especially Chinese and Indian) for home cooking, together with the rise of the microwave, further undermined the takeaways. While companies like Singapore Sam pushed up the sales figures for Chinese food, the takeaways went into decline, unable to compete with the supermarkets and the food-chains. They were not structured to deal with such competition, nor did their owners show much interest in adapting their business style to the new circumstances. They were unable to grow in the new 'rationalised' food age.

Chinese commentators point to Britain's severe tax regime and its immigration laws as principal factors in the long-term catering crisis, for they increased the burden on restaurant owners and led to a shortage of waiters and trained cooks. As a consequence, staff costs in non-family businesses rose steeply. Commentators also note that restaurateurs were complacent about their market position and lacked specialist training in advertising and modern management, at a time when new styles of ethnic catering threatened the Chinese market share. The penalisation of a few restaurants by health inspectors as a result of infringements of hygiene laws created a negative image that alienated potential customers.

Despite the crisis, Chinese restaurants and takeaways still accounted for one in every four catering businesses in Britain in the early 1990s. Chinese sources estimated the number of restaurants (some of which double as takeaways) in the mid-1990s at more than 1500 and of takeaways at around 4000. In 1998, the number of businesses was said to have risen to 7600, including some 5000 takeaways. In 2002, sources claimed 9500 takeaways and 1500 restaurants. This density of Chinese catering establishments was among the greatest in Europe and either matched or exceeded that in France (although estimates in both countries are open to challenge).

However, the Chinese market share continued to come under heavy pressure. Excessive supply was exacerbated by stagnating demand in the 1990s, as the general economy remained weak. At the same time, a new wave of modernised, aggressive, and modestly priced Indian and Pakistani restaurants targeted Chinese caterers as their main competitors. By mid-decade, Chinese cuisine was only marginally more popular in Britain than South Asian cuisine according to *Sing Tao Daily* 星岛日报, which reported that 18.6 per cent of Britons preferred British, 15.8 per cent Chinese, and 12.5 per cent South Asian food. Other polls suggested that Indian curry was the most popular British dish.[278]

The other main factor in the protracted crisis of Chinese catering has been the response to the trade of younger Chinese, who have a far wider range of options than their parents. This issue is treated in Chapter 7, along with other transformations in the cultural and ethnic identity of the British-born generation.

The decline of Chinese catering, in the form first of the chop-suey house and then of the takeaway, does not spell its imminent demise. New labour migrants from mainland China who began turning up in Chinatown in London and the provinces in the 1990s, thus giving a new lease of life to restaurants and takeaways hit by labour shortages, will probably break away to set up small businesses of their own and revive the cycle of development.[279] At the top end of the trade, the big Chinese chains' strategic infiltration of the fast-food market on the high street and in the shopping malls will help to restore the appeal of Chinese food, which for a while fell out of fashion. The emergence of a highly educated generation of Chinese entrepreneurs and professionals will also have its effect on the style and structure of Chinese enterprise, including catering.

Other Chinese occupations

Shops

Chinese entrepreneurs in Britain specialised first in laundering and then in catering. The retail sale of other goods and services, from shops, along the wayside, or from door to door, was less prevalent among Chinese in Britain than on the European mainland, particularly in France and the Netherlands, where traders set up curio shops and retail businesses and Zhejiangese hawkers peddled soapstone carvings, foodstuffs, trinkets, and other articles.[280]

Chinese shops in Britain aimed to supply seafarers and other residents of the Chinatowns. Only a handful of tobacconists or curio vendors catered for the wider market.[281] For the local white community in the early twentieth century, a main function of Chinese shops was as distribution centres for pakapoo 白鴿票 (that is, lottery) slips, a craze that hit Pennyfields around 1920.[282]

The earliest Chinese shops in Britain seem to have grown out of the boarding houses. Boarding masters, shipping agents, and shopowners were often one and the same. In some cases, the shops were attached to restaurants. They sold groceries and other daily necessities, as well as ingredients for Chinese cooking. The shipping agents-cum-merchants who owned the shops formed the Chinatown elite. They also played the role of community financiers; some shops doubled as collecting places for Chinese banks. Their business interests were not confined to Britain but extended in some cases to mainland Europe.[283]

At the start of the twentieth century, some laundrymen also ran grocer's shops, funded by laundry profits. Shop-ownership conferred greater status than laundering. Merchandising brought the shop-owner into contact with importers across the Channel. The Chinatown merchant, wrote Susan Craggs, 'was in a position to act as employment agent, financier, [and] ambassador to the community and to keep in contact with political affairs in China'.[284]

In Liverpool, where Chinese immigrants were less segregated from the working class than in other places, business interactions with local people at street-level were more routine. Chinese vendors hawked roasted peanuts and toffee apples round the streets or sold 'Chinese' snacks – notably, fish-cakes with chilli sauce – round the pubs.[285]

However, peddling never assumed the same importance as it did on the European mainland.[286]

After the Second World War, the relationship between the Chinese shopkeeper and the broader Chinese community changed, as a result of the community's growing complexity. At one level, it became more homogenous, as immigrants from the New Territories, a relatively small and uniform sending area in migration terms, followed one another along chains. However, the Chinatown establishment was, for the most part, at first monopolised by Chinese of urban, Siyinese, or northern provenance. These people looked down on the new arrivals and felt little solidarity with them. There was far less social interaction between the settled merchants and the Chinese 'new chums' than in Britain in the past or in other countries. Chinese shopowners in London in the 1960s came from urban Hong Kong, unlike the other immigrants. Whereas Chinese storekeepers in New York or Sydney acted in various ways on behalf of fellow-exiles from the same clan or district (for example, by acting as holding centres for their mail), those in London maintained a purely business relationship with their customers, who shopped where prices were cheapest, regardless of ethnicity.[287]

Smuggling

Given the community's maritime origins and its continuing link to the sea, it is not surprising that smuggling has figured as a Chinese enterprise – major in profit terms, marginal in the degree of community involvement. Chinese seafarers working the international shipping lanes often trade in objects from one port to the next, for example, in specialist foodstuffs destined for Chinese kitchens. This symbiotic or shadow trade can be overt and permitted by the captain or the shipping companies or covert and illicit. It deals in things (in particular, drugs and firearms) that could not be legally imported without a licence and in people (to evade the bans imposed on Chinese immigration).

The Chinese association with illegal immigration started as a result of the 1905 Aliens Act. According to rumours and anonymous tip-offs to the police (usually by other Chinese), the Chinese laundries served as clearing houses for smuggled immigrants, including some brought in through Marseilles and other Mediterranean ports. Many laundries suspected of running immigration rackets were in fact reception centres and halfway houses for the sons, brothers, and cousins of established immigrants, who were legally entitled to import their relatives.[288] Merchants and shopkeepers were particularly suspect from a police point of view, on account of their links to Chinese importers in mainland Europe, and were often kept under close watch.[289]

After the First World War, stories about the large-scale smuggling of Chinese into Britain by emigration syndicates featured in police reports and the press.[290] The Home Office raided laundries, shops, and boarding houses after persistent reports of people-smuggling, where necessary bending police rules to achieve results.[291]

Chinese trafficking in illegal migrants was organised on a European basis in the 1920s, by shipping agents and criminal gangs operating out of Genoa, Marseilles, and Rotterdam, the main collecting point, in collaboration with gangs in China, Hong Kong, and Singapore. Police reported finding forged passports and lists of contact names in France. The end-destinations of the traffic were not necessarily within Europe. The European ports were used as staging posts for migration to destinations in the United States and Australia. These countries had closed their doors to the Chinese but were less likely to detect immigrants who arrived by indirect routes rather than directly from China. Would-be emigrants were secreted in groups around the ship's hold, as stowaways.

Some smuggling before and after the First World War, including of drugs, was from Britain and Europe into China. Consignments of morphine were smuggled east, as were pistols and other goods. The Chinese crime syndicates behind this traffic were pan-European in scope, with bases in London, Hamburg, Rotterdam, Antwerp, and other ports, as well as in the United States and China itself. Secret official reports suggested that smugglers worked hand in glove with ship captains and corrupt officials.[292]

Gambling

Gambling has always been a mainstay of Chinese life and economy in Britain. Hostile observers stereotype the Chinese as inveterate gamblers by 'racial' nature and media reports described gambling as one of 'the two great vices of the Chinaman' (the other being opium). However, a more informed view is that gambling is most prevalent among older and less educated Chinese workers and young bachelors.[293]

Chinese criminals in Britain have always run illegal gambling schemes (alongside drug-pushing and people-smuggling). In her memoirs, Annie Lai – a self-described British opium-dealer – attributes the leadership of these three branches of business in the early years of the twentieth century to the '[Chee Kung] Tong'.[294] Chinese gambling masters took the bets of white as well as Chinese gamblers after the First World War.

They were so successful that they made inroads into the profits of the big East End bookmakers, who complained to the press that 'the Chinese have had much of the money that used to be laid on horse-racing'.[295]

In the early years, pakapoo was the best-known game in non-Chinese circles, played mainly by women and children.[296] Fantan 番攤 (a form of roulette, played with beans or buttons) was the Chinese game of choice, played in tiny dens hidden in the back of shops and other premises.[297] Despite the seamy venues, huge bets were sometimes laid. The Chinese bookmakers were backed by ample funds and prided themselves on paying out wins however massive.[298]

Today, among family and friends, mahjong and poker are favourite Chinese pastimes. Chinese punters also bet on horses, dogs, soccer, the lottery, the casino, and other typical arenas of host-society gambling.[299] In Chinatown, some clubs and associations provide facilities for gambling; others specialise in it. The illegal gambling houses are popular and crowded venues, where card and tile games are played for high stakes. Fortunes have been made and lost over the years during the afternoon catering break, to the scandal (in the early days) of the village establishments in Hong Kong.[300] Exclusively for Chinese, the gambling houses double as centres of social life (with meals provided) and as unofficial employment exchanges.[301] In the early 1970s, before the days of family reunion, even small towns had their Chinese gambling joints-cum-social clubs.[302] However, the arrival of Chinese women and children led to a reduction in gambling, as the men gained new responsibilities.[303]

The commonest forms of commercial gambling in more recent times have been paigau 牌九 (a form of dominoes not unlike pontoon) and fantan, both banker games in which winnings are subject to a levy and therefore illegal under the Gaming Act (except on controlled premises). Pakapoo, mahjong, and various card games continue to be played. Though it is in principle illegal, police attitudes towards this gambling vary. Often a blind eye is turned.[304]

Chinese self-employment and unemployment

Self-employment and independent entrepreneurship have always been goals of the Chinese immigrant generations. Britain's Chinese are far less likely to be employees than whites and members of other ethnic groups and two to three times more likely to be self-employed. Chinese self-employed are far more likely to be entrepreneurs than whites or other self-employed, more likely than white self-employed to be in self-control and fully independent rather than part of a particular employer's work-force, and far more likely than whites to work from separate business premises (indicating a more substantial investment).[305]

If the analysis is confined to Chinese born in Hong Kong, the contrast is starker. Yuan Cheng found that such people are 5.7 times more likely to belong to the petty bourgeoisie (employers in small establishments and own-account workers other than professionals) than whites of the same age and qualifications. Most other groups of Chinese were also more likely to belong to the petty bourgeoisie, although to a lesser extent. Chinese from Southeast Asia, however, had the same propensity as comparable whites to join this class in the early 1990s.[306]

The main explanation for this high level of self-employment lies in the nature of early Chinese immigration (along chains) and the exceptional levels of education and resourcefulness of recent Chinese and ethnic-Chinese immigrants. Unlike other non-white immigrants, few ethnic-Chinese men were directly recruited by Government agencies to work as wage-labourers in British factories or public services, and many if not most (excluding the great majority of seafarers) arrived with the firm intention of founding businesses as soon as possible.

It is in the nature of chain migration that the vanguard leads the mass, especially in an economy (like the British) whose main sectors are often closed to ethnic outsiders save on terms set by the majority. The pioneers' adaptation to life on Britain's margins set a pattern that aftercomers followed. Racist legislation starting in 1905 and continuing, on and off, for the rest of the century reinforced this trend by requiring immigrants to be self-supporting and limiting their activities, thus driving many into the ethnic enclave.[307]

Chinese laundry workers in Britain were usually recruited along lines of kinship or provenance. Most entrepreneurs were Siyinese. Once established, some fetched over relatives to staff existing businesses or branch out into other suburbs or towns. However, the migration chain was weak and discontinuous, given the poor communications and China's instability. Large numbers of early immigrants were seafarers who quit the sea and sought a living ashore. Although also Siyinese in many cases, their ties with the established community did not necessarily extend beyond a speech-form. So although recruitment was ideally narrow, in practice it was often broad. Even so, the bandwagon rolled. The same happened with the postwar arrivals from Hong Kong's New Territories, whose exceptional homogeneity was reflected in an unusually high degree of occupational convergence – at a time when the British economy was more open (mainly as a result of the postwar boom) than it had ever been.

It is ironic, in the light of studies that predicate Chinese business success on ethnic networks and ethnic solidarity, that achieving security through family self-reliance and self-sufficiency has been the leading item on the agenda of Britain's Chinese, whose overriding goal is to throw off the shackles of waged labour and seek salvation in self-employment. Chinese opted for self-employment in the takeaway trade for several reasons, only one of which was its relative profitability. Perhaps the foremost motive was dread of unemployment, which most saw as a real danger as long as they depended on others for work. Another was the nature of waged labour in Chinese eyes. In Chinatown, waged labour is oppressive, gruelling, poorly rewarded, and held in low esteem. In the broader economy, it is rarely an option for the first generation, due to racism or the Chinese perception and expectation of racism as a result of affronts visited on previous generations and their own lack of human capital.

Miri Song's study of takeaways in Britain explains why shop ownership was, for a time, the 'only viable and conceivable' livelihood option. Not only was it

> more profitable than waged work, such as in restaurants and in clothing manufacturing, but the control [that Chinese families] were able to exercise, by virtue of self-employment, was seen as invaluable. Such control and autonomy was especially important in a larger social context in which they were relatively disenfranchized, by virtue of their often limited English language knowledge and experiences of racist hostility and discrimination.

The sense of security and well-being extended to feelings about food, whose abundance and availability many Chinese identified as a main benefit of running a takeaway.[308]

Normally, Chinese immigrants' resort to ethnic-sector enterprise and self-employment is explained in negative terms, by their lack of English, their reliance on kinship ties, and their exclusion from the main jobs market. However, studies show that many early caterers saw it positively, as a way of fulfilling their wish to own a business and do 'Chinese work'.[309] It brought them status in the Chinese community and allowed them to practise thrift and enterprise.

Self-employment was more remunerative for Chinese (and most other ethnic minorities) than employment. Whereas white men earned more from employment than from self-employment in the 1990s, self-employed minority-ethnic men earned more than self-employed white men and than minority-ethnic employees. Chinese men not only earned the same as white men from employment but earned far more than white men and more than other minority-ethnic men from self-employment.[310]

Beyond the takeaway, a number of developments in Britain in the 1980s led to a growth in self-employment in the ethnic (and Chinese) business sector despite an overall economic climate of recession, unemployment, restructuring, and (partly as a result of the contraction in the labour market) racist discrimination in the primary sector of the wider economy. These included government interventions to strengthen small business (of which ethnic business was a major beneficiary), thus reversing the strategy of successive governments in the 1960s and the 1970s. Another was the widespread switch on the part of big firms to decentralised production and subcontracting, a practice that creates opportunities for small (and thus ethnic) firms.[311]

By espousing the enterprise culture, Thatcher aimed to promote entrepreneurship as a means to capital accumulation and social mobility. Other aims included a growth in employment and self-employment and, as a result, a dampening of the ethnic unrest that spread across Britain in the early 1980s. Many new firms were founded, with the assistance of official schemes. A new generation of Chinese entrepreneurs who (at the time) no longer saw a future for themselves in Hong Kong spotted the opportunity and emerged as Britain's biggest-earning business community (in proportional terms). They were also the community least dependent on state aid.

Levels of Chinese unemployment in Britain are closely related to the pattern of self-employment. The overall unemployment rate among ethnic Chinese in the 1990s was 9 per cent for men and 6 for women, compared with 15 and 9 per cent for whites (the rates for most ethnic minorities other than Chinese are far higher).[312] However, this rate varied greatly between different groups of Chinese. According to an analysis of the 1991 census returns, for example, a white man was twice as likely as a Chinese man born in Hong Kong (and a white woman 1.3 times more likely than a Chinese woman born in Hong Kong) to be jobless, but an ethnic Chinese born in Vietnam ran a far higher risk of unemployment.

Ethnic Chinese in some occupations ran a greater risk of unemployment in 1991 than those in others. For example, Chinese men were more likely to be unemployed than white men in senior white-collar and managerial or professional occupations, but less likely than white men in unskilled or semi-skilled manual occupations (including catering).

The ethnic-Chinese unemployment rate (like the general minority-ethnic unemployment rate) also varied from generation to generation. Around 21 per cent of men aged 16–24 and 11.4 per cent of men aged 25–39 were unemployed, rates marginally higher than for whites but 7 or 8 per cent lower than those for other ethnic minorities. Among Chinese men in their forties, however, unemployment was only 3.3 per cent, less than half that of comparable whites.

Older Hong Kong Chinese immigrants were (and usually still are) insured against unemployment by the family enterprise, a safety net that permits involutionary job-sharing in hard times, 'even when it is sometimes not economically viable to do so'. On the other hand, ethnic Chinese from places other than Hong Kong, proportionately fewer of whom are self-employed or run family businesses, were twice as likely as whites to be unemployed in 1991.[313] Similarly, younger Chinese high-flyers competing with whites in the professions were at a disadvantage. These comparisons help to explain why the Chinese have, over the last 100 years, opted for self-employment in the ethnic sphere rather than enter the general labour market on unfavourable terms.

Economic and occupational diversification

The range of Chinese occupations in Britain until the late twentieth century was narrower even than in North America and Australia, where the pioneers similarly lacked the capital and skills necessary to compete in developed capitalist economies. Chinese immigrants in Britain were for many years confined to one or two niches and to manual labour, nearly always at sea. Towards the end of the century, however, ethnic Chinese began to diversify into new fields.

The saturation of Chinese catering and its crisis of management and image at a time of growing competition from big business and other ethnic foods are one explanation of this switch to new spheres. Another, as we have seen, is the second generation's upward mobility. Two factors we have not discussed are the growth of investment in Britain by ethnic Chinese from Hong Kong, Taiwan, and Southeast Asia; and the effect on the community of an increase in immigration from Hong Kong as a result of Hong Kong's retrocession to China in 1997.

Many British-born and new immigrant Chinese entered white-collar jobs and middle-class professions, including law, accountancy, banking, insurance, finance, computing, medicine, education, architecture, engineering, real estate, and leisure. (By the late 1980s, up to 2 per cent of Chinese were accountants; proportionately more worked in banks than any other ethnic group, including twice as many as majority whites.) Those who set up businesses other than catering are proportionately overrepresented in consultancies and the technology-based and computer sectors.

In the mid-1990s, Chinese ran several dozen law firms, a dozen Chinese-Western pharmacies, and numerous other service firms, ranging from print shops to cold-storage plants. Four per cent of Chinese men worked in the National Health Service, nearly six times the rate for white men (but one-third of that for Chinese women).[314] (This health focus suggests an analogy with Britain's early Chinatown, when vulnerable Chinese immigrants strategically targeted female jobs – first washing, then cooking, now nursing.) Others have diversified out of restaurant or takeaway catering into related fields. A handful have started farming, mainly vegetables and flowers. At one point in the early 1990s, four Chinese farmers were raising 25,000 ducks a month for Chinese restaurants in Paris.[315]

The desegregation of Chinese employment was speeded by a change in the nature of Chinese immigration. The 60,000 people who left Hong Kong for Britain and other destinations in 1991 included 21,000 in 'professional, technical, administrative, and managerial occupations'.[316]

Some observers analyse the diversification of Chinese business and employment in terms of the coming to maturity of the settled group, founded by immigrants from the New Territories, but this analysis is simplistic. True, a few caterers have invested the surplus from catering in more diversified forms of business, including the modernised trading sectors and supermarkets.[317] However, much of the new diversity is a result less of the maturation and differentiation of the existing community than of the accretion of new layers of well-funded and highly resourceful migrants and transnational businesspeople from East and Southeast Asia.[318]

Most new migrants have a middle-class background and originally came to the United Kingdom to study. Some gained professional qualifications before entering business, including catering. Among the most prominent ethnic-Chinese catering enterprises in the 1990s were companies like Singapore Sam plc, Colonial Catering Co Ltd, and the Oriental Restaurant Group plc, all owned by Chinese from Southeast Asia. Singapore Sam, for example, was founded by a dentist, while the Oriental Group is managed by an accountant.

Unlike other prominent catering firms owned by ethnic Chinese, these three companies were set up between the mid-1980s and the early 1990s. They were professionally managed and led by people with a strong entrepreneurial drive, who saw openings in the market, moved in to capture them, expanded rapidly, and now control food chains across London and the counties. They run a new type of ethnic-food enterprise that forms a major threat to the older, more established Chinese caterers. Managed by educated professionals, they have ready access to bank loans, one reason they have grown so quickly.

The immigrants from rural Hong Kong, on the other hand, had little or no access to bank loans when starting up or developing their businesses. Even so, a small number of the caterers who set up shop in the 1960s and early 1970s went on to prosper, not as restaurateurs but as suppliers of food products, primarily to the ethnic sector. In terms of turnover, the largest firms on our list of Chinese companies are owned by Hong Kong migrants who started out as caterers but later ventured into wholesaling and retailing ethnic food. They include W. Wing Yip plc 荣业行, See Woo Holdings Ltd 泗和行, and Loon Fung Ltd 龙凤行. Food wholesaling and retailing by ethnic Chinese is highly competitive, and some have had to seek new markets outside the United Kingdom.

The educated, highly professional newcomers and the catering veterans, together with their educated offspring, sometimes interact, but the trend would seem to be towards an assimilation of the second generation to the British career structure and the simultaneous emergence of a separate world of 'new' Chinese entrepreneurs beyond the ethnic enclave. Taiwan sources claim that the flow into Britain of Chinese capital from Hong Kong, Taiwan, Singapore, and other places in the 1980s and 1990s and its investment in import–export firms, manufacturing, the finance industry, and real estate has had an impact on the British Chinese, widening their horizons, giving them an 'arbitrating role' (not unlike that played by compradors in the old Chinese Treaty Ports), 'dragging them out of catering', and drawing them into the economic mainstream. However, the evidence does not support this view, which Taiwanese studies describe more as an aspiration than a *fait accompli*.[319]

In or around 1995, more than 190 Chinese firms were trading in Britain, often as agents for exporters in Taiwan, Hong Kong, Singapore, and elsewhere. These firms dealt chiefly in sports equipment, leisure goods, and other plastic, rubber, and chemical-fibre products. They also imported specialist ingredients to sell to restaurants and individuals, a new growth market.

Chinese firms keen to sell and invest in Europe are said to seek out ethnic Chinese as 'ideal partners in such cooperative ventures', a form of interaction that has allegedly helped promote British Chinese interest in trading. Similarly, the branches of Chinese-controlled East Asian banks and finance companies set up in London in the 1980s and 1990s are said to have helped British Chinese found finance and insurance companies.[320]

However, our own research suggests that Britain's largest Asian Chinese investors are, at most, lukewarm about pursuing intra-ethnic ties. East Asian banks have so far been unable to create a niche for themselves among Chinese firms operating in the United Kingdom.[321] We found little evidence that Chinese firms from Asia link up with British Chinese companies when setting up businesses. Even though some decide to invest in Britain after attending British-sponsored 'business conferences' designed in part to bring Chinese entrepreneurs together, none seems to have formed joint ventures with such firms or to use them as sub-contractors or suppliers.[322]

Such companies pick their partners strategically; most seem to prefer to work with non-Chinese firms to gain entry to the UK market. Their investment is more likely to be in response to an initiative by the British Government, networking on their behalf, than a result of intra-ethnic cooperation. Some Taiwanese companies form partnerships and set up collaborative research centres in Britain to learn about hi-tech and 'acquire the science and technology [their] country needs', a precondition that would rule out most British Chinese as useful partners. There is little evidence that investment in Britain by big East and Southeast Asian capitalists, which has boomed since the early 1990s, leads them to cooperate or to unite as an interest group. We turned up only one case of interlocking stock-ownership ties among foreign Chinese investors (between the Indonesian Chinese Oei Hong Leong 黄鸿年 and Hong Kong's Li Ka-shing 李嘉诚).

Competition among Chinese firms from the same country is apparently the norm. Taiwanese investors in the United Kingdom compete with each other in the manufacturing and distribution of computer products, while rival firms from Malaysia, Singapore, and Hong Kong have a major presence in hotels, upmarket retailing, and the property sector. Most businesses we studied borrowed primarily from British banks (in particular Barclays) rather than from East or Southeast Asian banks with British branches. None claimed to have secured loans on more favourable terms from such 'ethnic' banks.[323]

An interesting example is Daloon 大龙, a Chinese food-processing company in Denmark with interests in Britain and one of only a handful of European Chinese companies that invests outside its country of registration.[324] Daloon makes its business decisions independently of ethnic considerations. To the extent that it buys raw materials from British Chinese companies, it is because such companies produce Chinese food.

Intra-ethnic ties seem strongest between wholesalers and retailers. Chinese business in Britain still has a far stronger ethnic specialist dimension, that is, a far greater dependence on the provision of ethnic goods or services (chiefly in the catering sphere), than other ethnic groups.[325] Most Chinese wholesalers supply Chinese retailers, and both sectors focus on Chinese restaurants and takeaways. However, such transactions aim at maximising profits rather than at facilitating the development of each other's business operations.

Ethnic considerations have little evident effect on Chinese firms' employment strategies. Like some British Chinese companies, foreign Chinese investors often start by employing ethnic Chinese. Once their businesses take off, however, most employ non-Chinese. Elsewhere in Europe, many foreign Chinese companies also employ young European Chinese for their local knowledge and language and professional skills, at least initially. But such strategies can be explained as a rational exploitation of special skills rather than as ethnic networking.

In short, there is little substance in the view that intra-ethnic networking has underpinned the development of Chinese enterprise in Britain. Instead, a combination of factors has contributed to its growth. They include a productive use of experience gained in an industry before venturing into business, the entrepreneurial deployment of resources generated by the initial investment, and a focused approach to business. 'Class resources' and entrepreneurial traits (in particular, the ability to predict market trends and take risks by investing in potentially lucrative ventures) are more important than ethnic resources for explaining Chinese business success in Britain.[326]

'Ethnic style'

Studies argue that immigrant businesses display an 'ethnic style' characterised by intra-ethnic business transactions (both in the host state and with the 'homeland'), family firms, trade guilds, and rotating credit associations. To examine the assumptions that underlie such studies, we conclude by looking further at the role played by ethnic networks and family firms in British Chinese business. These two modes of business and social organisation are central to the 'Confucian ethic', a perennial theme in culturalist explanations of Chinese business success.

The role of networks in ethnic-Chinese business became a major topic of debate in the early 1990s, when academic and popular studies claimed that diasporic Chinese throughout the world, but principally in Southeast Asia, were collaborating through ethnically based business ties on ventures responsible for huge investments in China. Scholars coined terms such as 'global tribe' to describe this alleged 'network of entrepreneurial relationships' based on individual enterprises that 'share a common culture' and are tightly bound by interlocking business links.

Yet the notion of a proliferation of powerful Chinese networks seems to have scant basis in fact.[327] There is ample evidence in many countries of business networks defined as the pooling of resources in the form of one-off, short-term projects connecting ethnic-Chinese companies (both to each other and to non-Chinese businesses). However, there is little sign that big ethnic-Chinese companies anywhere in the world, including Britain, are joined by interlocking stock ownership and directorate links to other Chinese-owned companies, either domestically or across borders. Many Chinese who dabble in joint ownership end up at loggerheads. Most Chinese owners of large companies are loath to merge with other Chinese firms, for to do so would mean sharing control of the enlarged enterprise. (Some successful Chinese capitalists avoid not just mergers but any collective endeavour, including participation in Chinese Chambers of Commerce.)

The term 'network', the premise on which ethnic groups supposedly emerge as key players in the world economy, is used excessively and uncritically in some of the new literature on ethnic business and transnationalism,[328] which assumes that institutionalised ethnic networks permit diasporic co-ethnics to move capital across national boundaries. This attribution of the dynamism of enterprises owned by ethnic minorities in Asia and Europe to intra-ethnic business networks rests on a false understanding of the history of Chinese-owned enterprise. One observer, in zoomorphic idiom, even suggested that Chinese networks lie dormant, 'as *sleepers*, for a generation or longer'.[329]

To what extent do networks and other attributes of ethnic style inform ethnic-Chinese business in Britain, and how has their role changed over time? Chinese laundries, restaurants, and takeaways spread across Britain along ties of kinship. In the early twentieth century, Siyinese and other kinship networks were at the heart of Britain's Chinese economy. In the 1950s and 1960s, relatives or friends pooled their resources in business partnerships or acquired funds from their families in Hong Kong or Britain. However, there is little evidence of ethnic networking on a wider scale.

The sources of ethnic-Chinese capital in Britain before the 1980s tended to be personal or family savings, which explains why most early Chinese businesses had a meagre capital investment. Few business partnerships lasted: most served as springboards to individual ownership.[330] Strong networks and associations sometimes grow from migrant chains, but such a development was, in the British Chinese case, precluded by the buoyancy first of laundering and then of catering in the heyday of community formation, when sponsored immigrants could start up their own businesses with relative ease and cast off the shackles of clientship and exploitation.[331]

Particularly striking is the irrelevance to the Chinese economy in Britain of rotating credit clubs, the so-called tontines or *hui* 会. Such clubs, a business practice based on particularistic ties, are a traditional way of lending whereby petty entrepreneurs pool funds that one member claims each month at nominal or no interest. Often regarded as Chinese, they are in fact practised by many peoples.[332] In the past, smaller Chinese businesses in Southeast Asia and North America raised starting capital either from family, lineage, or clan sources or by means of tontines. The larger firms tended to fund their activities from retained earnings, to avoid indebtedness and possible surrender of control.

The tontine's popularity (along with that of ethnic guilds) has, in recent times, diminished among ethnic Chinese in Southeast Asia and the United States. Studies on mainland European Chinese business report a higher incidence of such 'ethnic' traits than in Britain, but the field is still relatively unexplored. In France, Thierry Pairault used the fate of the tontine as a chief test of the culturalist thesis about Chinese business. He asked whether 'Chinese forms of communitarian self-financing [such as tontines] . . . suffice to authorise a culturalist response' to questions about the nature of the Chinese business ethic in France. His answer: they do not. Pairault's research suggests that Chinese small entrepreneurs in France are several times more likely to finance their initial investment with personal savings or a bank loan than by tontines. Community sources of finance come a poor second in all respects to extra-community sources, for the entrepreneurs tend to approach French rather than Chinese banks for their loans. It seems they are better adapted to French norms and integrated into French institutions than is often thought.[333]

The British Chinese community's failure to use tontines was probably due to the role played in it by family ties, together with the relatively benign conditions in which postwar Chinese immigrants entered Britain (as Commonwealth citizens, at the height of the postwar boom).

However, the failure to establish credit associations may explain why many Chinese migrants were unable to develop their enterprises beyond the initial stage.

New laws restricting immigration weakened the migration chain. In time, obligations to the homeland community were seen as irksome and widely abandoned, except by a few old-style sojourners who invested in property in the New Territories and continued to help finance communal projects.[334] However, there is evidence that in the 1980s some entrepreneurs obtained funds to set up firms from family and friends in Hong Kong, worried about the colony's impending retrocession.

Even early studies noted far less social interaction and business cooperation among Chinese in Britain than in other countries. Rather than cooperate and exchange information, they behaved secretively. Chinese who branched out into more substantial ventures sometimes networked with co-ethnics in the start-up period, but rarely for long. Those partnerships that have endured are primarily with non-Chinese, mainly because most were formed (usually by British-born Chinese) on the basis of common or complementary expertise. The owners are more likely to use sophisticated financial and market techniques to develop their enterprises and more likely to be publicly listed.

Chinese entrepreneurs draw far less on community resources than British Asians, who use ethnic and family networks to hold down costs and get access to markets. This difference can be explained partly by cultural and historical factors, but the main explanation lies in conditions of residence and work. Many British South Asian businesses arose in the 1980s recession, when immigrant workers switched to petty retailing, trading, and manufacturing, often staking their redundancy pay to do so. By the early 1990s, as many as one-fifth of economically active British South Asians were employers or self-employed. They live in compact settlements that provide a niche market and a source of cheap ethnic labour and businesses networks. The Chinese, in contrast, arrived in Britain as petty entrepreneurs. Far from suffering unemployment, they suffered labour shortages. As isolated caterers, they lacked strong communities and the resources for network recruiting. Their businesses depended on special knowledge rather than on ethnic ties.

Some British South Asians had a business background before reaching Britain, for immigration from ex-colonial to metropolitan countries tends to bring a spread of classes rather than (as, say, in postwar Germany) just one stratum, usually workers. These traders had a ready-made ethnic market among workers' families,[335] for the British South Asian population is far bigger than the Chinese and British South Asians in many cities still live in enclaves. The Chinese also came to Britain to set up businesses, but formed just one narrow stratum. Save for that handful of restaurateurs who catered to Chinese in London's Gerrard Street and its provincial equivalents, they lacked an ethnic market and community networks comparable to the British South Asian ones.

Britain's ethnic Chinese from Southeast Asia resemble the ethnic Indians from Africa (and differ from the Hong Kong Chinese caterers) in that most have educational qualifications, financial resources, and experience of both trading and living as a minority. (In respect of resources, the uneducated and impoverished ethnic Chinese from Vietnam formed an exception.) They have the capacity to source funds in more sophisticated ways than immigrants from the New Territories, by borrowing from banks or setting up public companies. Their behaviour suggests a parallel with Chinese in France.[336]

Most of the new ethnic-Chinese companies were established after the 1980s and are family-owned. They do little intra-ethnic networking and lack a common identity as an 'interest group'. Few of the new breed of entrepreneurs see any need for Chinese Chambers of Commerce. More and more work with non-Chinese, thus transcending the ethnic factor, and some bigger companies induct non-Chinese managers. Profit, not ethnicity, determines decision-making. 'Class resources' and entrepreneurial traits, not ethnicity, are the crucial factor in their growth.

Another feature of ethnic style said to strengthen Chinese business is family enterprise. The family firm is seen by some business-school writers as an essential part of a wider culture of networks, one of a number of ethnic-Chinese institutions and practices said to facilitate the growth of enterprises and the emergence of business networks based on trust and kinship. These networks supposedly cut transaction costs, increase coordination, and lessen business risks.[337]

However, the best-known study on Chinese family firms, by Wong Siu-lun,[338] notes that they tend to go through set phases that end in disintegration, because of the problem of succession. Chinese family enterprise in Britain is likewise strongest at the point of founding and erodes or fractures with each new generation. The children of Chinese entrepreneurs, especially those in food-based businesses, show little interest in taking over from their parents, as we have seen. Some larger family firms professionalise management by appointing non-Chinese to senior positions. Ownership of such firms, however, remains with the family, as does decision-making about new ventures.

Few British Chinese investors are powerful enough to act as serious players in the global economy, so the question of transnational networks reaching to other countries, including China, is not relevant in the way it is often said to be for the Chinese in Southeast Asia. However, overseas remittances by British Chinese and, more recently, investment in Britain by ethnic-Chinese entrepreneurs from Malaysia, Singapore, Taiwan, and Hong Kong provide alternative measures of the extent of cross-border ties. Most remittances by Chinese in Britain are to relatives and most networks are family-based. Money is usually remitted from Britain to the New Territories, but it sometimes travels in the reverse direction. Many Chinese start their businesses with money sent by relatives in Hong Kong. Although remittances to Hong Kong were substantial in the early years of postwar immigration and rose steeply in the 1950s and 1960s, they nose-dived once immigrants started forming families.[339]

Conclusions

This chapter traces the historical evolution of the Chinese economy in Britain from seafaring to laundering to catering and describes the commonalities that bind its different phases. It analyses the sources of the successive booms and crises of the early one-track, introverted modes of Chinese economy in Britain, which spread by cell division, but notes the emergence in more recent years of a new style of Chinese business and a new breed of Chinese entrepreneur that has transcended the ethnic enclave and overcome the long-standing exclusion of Chinese traders from the mainstream.

Since the 1970s, Britain's ethnic-Chinese community has become increasingly diverse. The Chinese from Southeast Asia and Taiwan and the more recent migrants from Hong Kong have 'class resources' that early migrants lacked. Apart from being more educated and middle-class, they can fall back if necessary on the financial support of family and friends in the 'home country' to bolster their enterprises. Few have ties with the older wave of migrants. Many are in direct competition with them.

Divisions of class and provenance explain the differences in the ways in which Chinese business has evolved in Britain and Europe. While the early Chinese migrants on the European mainland were traders, those in Britain were seafarers who lacked the funds and know-how with which to develop market niches. Some migrants from Hong Kong with more entrepreneurial flare than the rest were able to switch from the restaurant trade to wholesaling ethnic-type food, like the Birmingham-based Wing Yip plc and the Glasgow-based Chan's Ltd. Other enterprises, for example, Singapore Sam and the Oriental Restaurant Group, have emerged far more quickly as major catering operations because they are led by Chinese professionals from Southeast Asia.

Structural factors help to explain Chinese migrants' ability to run small-scale businesses that thrived but nevertheless failed to grow in scale. The ubiquitous Chinese presence in the laundry and catering sectors was due to their willingness to take over and operate at a lower cost industries that were in decline or did not attract British whites. By using family labour, Chinese were able to offer their services at a cheaper rate and take over parts of the laundry industry in British ports. The presence of large numbers of women in the labour force after the Second World War and the cheap cost of eating out helped the Chinese develop a presence in the food industry. In both industries, however, few Chinese showed much desire to invest further in their enterprises or to innovate in order to reduce costs even further or make new products. Most Chinese caterers offered essentially the same menu, while the more ambitious moved up the ladder by switching from takeaway to restaurant. The Chinese presence in both industries therefore declined.

Generally speaking, extreme intra-ethnic competition prevented Chinese from working together to build on the opportunities that opened up in the laundry and catering sectors. Partnerships formed, but were seldom sustained and in nearly all cases evolved into family enterprises, especially when the entrepreneurs found they could source funds from British banks. The primary interest of most Chinese was to go it alone as soon as possible.

While the takeaways set up by poor Hong Kong migrants might have only a limited future, the businesses formed by the new arrivals from East and Southeast Asia, whose products range from food to hi-tech, are far more dynamic, innovative, and entrepreneurial. In other words, the community has not only produced a new British-born generation but acquired a greater depth and complexity as a result of new immigration. This diversity is the main key to understanding the likely future of Britain's ethnic-Chinese economy.

This new generation of British Chinese and the new-style migrants with skills and funding are more interested than the old-timers in creating inter-ethnic business links, when it serves their interests to do so. Where partnerships are forged, the partners are picked strategically, usually because they have a similar class background and resources to contribute to the new enterprise. The development of these new forms of inter-ethnic ties is a reflection of the identity transformations that have taken place over the last two to three decades among British-born

Chinese. It suggests that Chinese will continue to maintain a presence in the British economy, but probably not in sectors with which they have traditionally been identified.

There is little evidence in this chapter to support the argument advanced by transnational theorists that business ties are cultivated on the basis of common ethnic identity or that intra-ethnic networking has underpinned the development of Chinese enterprise in Britain. 'Ethnic style' in the sense of Confucian business networks and family enterprise sustained across the generations is largely irrelevant. The intense competition among Chinese undermines the idea that the dynamism of Chinese business derives from intra-ethnic cooperation. Although family enterprise is a prominent feature of the migrant generation, as a style of business it has little or nothing to do with Chinese culture. Instead, it emerged in Britain as a solution to the problems migrants faced in securing start-up capital and hiring labour. Ethnic identity is central only at the point of migration, when migrants use it to adjust to the new environment or search out business opportunities.

4
Institutions and Divisions

Chinese commentators identify voluntary associations, newspapers, and schools as the backbone institutions of ethnic-Chinese society. In the conventional and official view, they are the 'three pillars that support Chinese communities in alien settings', their 'core and epitome', the secret of their strength and unity, the bridge by which they engage in cultural exchange with their non-Chinese hosts, the repository and transmitter of 'traditional Chinese culture', and the 'emissaries promoting friendship and peace between the ancestral country and the government and people of the countries in which [ethnic Chinese] reside'.[1] This chapter analyses the role played by these institutions in the United Kingdom. It also looks at community divisions and the changing face of Britain's Chinatown over the years.

The chapter depends on a rough distinction between Chinese institutions designed to cope with the pressures of living and settling in Britain and those that look predominantly 'homewards'. Many communities formed by international migration are transnational in that they keep up close links (ranging from the affective and the primordial to the highly formalised) with the hometowns and the homelands, as well as with co-ethnics in the diaspora.[2] Political associations in the immigrant generation are particularly liable to focus on homeland issues, or to try to tackle political problems encountered overseas (in particular, racist exclusion) by appealing to homeland governments for support. A fuller discussion of the transnational dimension of Chinese life in Britain – the community's emotional, cultural, social, economic, and political ties, informal and institutional, with the sending community and its other foreign outposts – follows in the next chapter. However, the distinction between organisations fashioned to 'support Chinese communities in alien settings' and others created to maintain international networks is not hard and fast, so the transnational discussion is of necessity anticipated from time to time in the present chapter.

Associations

Ethnic associations, the primary Chinese pillar 'in alien settings', range in nature from tiny, loose, marginal, single-issue, and ephemeral to large, elaborate, multi-faceted, and permanent. Two circumstances shape them: those who form them live (except in Singapore) as ethnic minorities; and they are nearly always city-dwellers. In the first half of the twentieth century, membership in most countries was more or less obligatory for immigrants determined to survive in an often hostile setting. After 1945, however, membership was usually voluntary.

Ethnic-Chinese associations can be classified according to two main principles, ascription and function. The ascriptive associations most closely allied to the immigrant generation are based on kinship (fictive or real, incorporated in clan, lineage, or shared surname), provenance (the overlapping ties of native place and dialect), or sworn brotherhood. Functionally defined associations include guilds based on trade, profession, and occupation and clubs devoted to 'traditional' leisure pursuits like painting and poetry.

Pioneers also established organisations with a modern form and focus. These included trade unions and political organisations concerned with homeland issues, particularly China's defence against foreign aggression and the politics of the place of settlement. (It is well known that Sun Yat-sen, father of modern Chinese nationalism, called the overseas Chinese 'the mother of the revolution'.)

Other forms of association that grew up among the settled and foreign-born groups included Western-style commercial and professional bodies, churches, and charities. Like the 'new associations' Bernard Wong identified in New York in the 1970s and 1980s, they have a modern agenda and a broader social and regional base than the old associations. In recent years, the organisational style and internal structure of Chinese associations throughout the world has become even more diverse. Members of the second and later generations have begun to form associations openly oriented to and rooted in the host society. They include social-service providers and usually have ties with institutions of the larger society, for example, trade unions and government agencies.

This bifurcation leads to a second distinction, between traditionalist (or China-related) and modernist associations. Most traditionalist associations are led by successful businessmen (who strive on their own behalf to convert the symbolic power of the associations into social and economic capital). The modernist associations, on the other hand, are led by social workers, politicians, and professionals. In more mature communities, generational differences between old and new leaders can end in conflict and the supercession of the old elite.[3]

However, the distinction between new and old is not always useful in analysing leadership styles, for even in China many supposedly 'traditional' organisations had begun by the late nineteenth and early twentieth centuries to take up modern political issues and adopt modern forms. They included native-place associations and secret societies like the Triads, which spearheaded the early opposition to imperialism, particularly in the Treaty Ports.

The activities of today's Chinese associations can be analysed according to three criteria. Where the focus is on the immigrants themselves, activities include 'heritage' maintenance, leisure, campaigns for welfare rights, the promotion of local integration, and community defence. Where it is on the ancestral homeland, they include receiving official visitors, donating money to homeland causes, organising 'return' visits, and promoting business exchanges. Where it is on the receiving society, they include organising public displays of Chinese culture and promoting social welfare and dialogue with host-society institutions.[4]

Worldwide, the more important associations are said to have grown from 7687 in 1965 to more than 10,000 in the mid-1990s. Also in the 1990s, ethnic Chinese set up more than 100 international associations, with the help of newly available space-compressing communications and technologies.[5] Both these developments – the multiplication of ethnic-Chinese associations and their partial globalisation – were reflected in the British Chinese community in the late twentieth century.[6]

Despite their ubiquity and their centrality to the Chinese migrant experience, little has been written in English about these associations.[7] Most of the studies that have appeared focus on the larger communities in Southeast Asia and North America before the Second World War. Even studies in Chinese are rare, except for lists and descriptive works published by ethnic Chinese in this or that individual country. Only in the 1990s was this gap partly remedied by the publication in China of new reference works, in response to the worldwide revival of associations in the post-Mao age.[8] The only book in any language focusing principally on Chinese associations in a European country is Li Minghuan's 李明欢 Netherlands-based study.[9]

Chinese associations in Europe

In 1999, the *Encyclopaedia of Overseas and Ethnic Chinese* 华侨华人百科全书 listed around 4400 of the world's more than 10,000 local, national, and international ethnic-Chinese associations. Although associations everywhere have multiplied rapidly over the past half century, Europe has registered the biggest rise, scarcely smaller than that of Asia, America, Oceania, and Africa put together, and now has the third largest number of associations after Asia and America, if the *Encyclopaedia* is right.[10]

Chinese associations in European countries with relatively big Chinese populations like Britain, France, and the Netherlands have undergone a similar historical evolution, with only minor differences of emphasis. This evolution has some features in common with that of ethnic-Chinese associations throughout the world, whose transitions it replicates in miniature.

Between the 1900s and the 1920s, Chinese boarding-house keepers in British and Dutch ports formed native-place gangs and associations that policed and exploited seafarers of their own dialect group, provided help for Chinese in need, and acted as intermediaries between the community and the police. From the seafarers' point of view, the associations were a main form of protection against a hostile and unfamiliar world in which they lived as a marginal but highly visible minority. Also in those years, radical activists and community leaders in several European countries set up political associations dedicated to helping the destitute and protecting China's national interests.

In the 1930s, old associations based on native-place ties continued to promote the interests of the community elite and to help members in need of jobs or welfare. At the same time, some associations across the Continent joined hands with new organisations formed by Chinese radical students and political agitators to oppose the Japanese invasion of China, a subject discussed in the following chapter.[11]

The third quarter of the twentieth century was a period of relative dormancy. Old associations lapsed into inactivity, either to avoid the tensions that the political battles between Beijing and Taibei might engender or because their memberships had aged or started to die off and the survivors had become quietly prosperous and therefore less interested in community politics.[12] New associations failed to form or catch on in significant numbers.

Starting in the mid-to late 1960s and the 1970s, a fresh wave of associations arose. New immigrants from Hong Kong, China, and Southeast Asia produced larger and more complex communities, locally born generations reached maturity, China opened up to the world after Mao's death in 1976, and developments in broadcasting and communications led to new forms of ethnic organisation and awareness.[13] All these changes had their repercussions in ethnic-Chinese institutions, including in Europe. Protecting Chinese cultural and ethnic identity in the face of assimilatory influences was one reason for the drive to organise. In several European countries, including Britain, France, and the Netherlands, new government policies on immigration and multiculturalism promoted the formation of 'modernist' associations.[14]

Some associations have formed in response to initiatives by Beijing and Taibei, whose political leaders are keen to promote nationalist identifications in Chinese communities overseas. Although both governments have an economic motive for promoting associations, each does so in its own way. Beijing's main agenda is to exploit Chinese ethnic identity to persuade ethnic Chinese in Europe to invest in China. Taibei, on the other hand, has tended to use such associations to set up its own links with European governments and business groups, to facilitate Taiwanese investment. These associations are an important point of entry into Europe for Taiwanese firms. Some mainland authorities have used state-owned enterprises to invest in the United Kingdom, but they tend to depend less on European Chinese institutions to create or strengthen economic ties with European governments. In some cases, local mainland authorities at the county or regional level have sought to mobilise localist sentiments among their 'sons and daughters' in Europe (and elsewhere) as a means of creating or strengthening economic ties with foreign countries. In the European case, the best examples are the diplomatic offensives waged among Chinese overseas in recent years by local authorities in Qingtian and Siyi. Again, discussion of these transnationally inspired projects is kept for the next chapter.

The number of Chinese associations in Europe rocketed in the second half of the twentieth century. According to Taibei sources, there were only 22 associations in the whole of Europe in 1950 and around 100 in 1975. By the 1990s, however, the number had grown to around 520, according to Li Minghuan.[15] This rise coincided with an increase in investment in Europe by Asian companies.

Chinese associations in Britain

Early associations

Before the Second World War, Chinese associations in Britain were weak and few in number. Those that did form were distinguished from most of their postwar counterparts in two main ways. They were, for the most part, rooted in native-place attachments; and they tended to have a strong political focus, expressed in opposition to discrimination and abuse in Britain and support for political movements in China.

The homeland orientation was due to the migrants' transient status and sojourner outlook. As new immigrants, they maintained strong ties with their ancestral towns and villages, mainly in Guangdong's Siyi region, to which they intended – almost to a man – to return after making fortunes. (The return ideology usually became a return myth as original intentions were thwarted by war in China or business failure.) The global network of Siyinese provided for the interchange of ideas, people, and resources across the English-speaking world. These two connections, to the homeland and Siyinese outposts everywhere, nurtured ascriptive identity in a world in which southern Chinese cultures were not yet infiltrated (as they now are) by a national Chinese or pan-Cantonese identity.

The pioneers' political awareness can be explained partly by their experience of racism, both as seafarers and as laundrymen. Later generations of Chinese migrants were less vulnerable and therefore less vocal on this issue, for as ethnic caterers they occupied an enclave that exempted them from the need to compete with whites.[16]

Early Chinese associations in Britain were opaque by nature and hostile to outside scrutiny, like the secret societies upon which some were modelled. A few overlapped or interlocked with one another, or operated as controlling cells within bigger bodies (much like the Chinese communists, who applied similar tactics within their united fronts before 1949). Associations in fact based on native-place ties adopted names that suggested broader affiliations, in an attempt to widen their social base at the expense of rivals or gain credence with the shipowners or authorities. A final impediment to clarity is the variety of spellings used to transcribe the organisations' Cantonese names.

Native-place associations took formal shape in Britain at the start of the twentieth century, probably on the basis of earlier informal bodies set up by boarding masters and crew contractors.[17] In aims and nature, they resembled their counterparts across the world. Even in the 1970s and the 1980s, their basic functions remained those of ethnic-Chinese associations everywhere: to receive new immigrants and give members a 'social life, companionship and emergency aid'.[18] Only in two respects did they depart from the general model: they had fewer members and resources; and only in the case of the early seafarers do they appear to have made a habit of policing and lubricating the gate to ethnic employment or business.

In 1906 or 1907, the Hui Tong (or Oi T'ung) 惠东 Association[19] was set up in Poplar in London's East End, with another branch in Liverpool. It probably drew its members from *Hui*yang 惠阳, *Dong*guan 东莞, and Bao'an 宝安, counties just to the north of Hong Kong that include the ancestral home of the Ng 吴 shipping-masters, who once controlled part of the Chinese settlement in Limehouse.[20] Its stated aims were to organise mutual aid, improve Chinese living standards in Britain, fight discrimination, overcome disunity, and adjudicate in disputes between members (for example, over contracts and rents).

The Association originally consisted mainly of seafarers. However, it later opened its doors to shopkeepers and merchants, who paid a monthly subscription of two shillings as against the workers' sixpence. It looked after members in sickness and old age, donated money to the Sailors' Hospital and other charities, provided a grant of £15 to enable those aged 60 or more to return to China, and repatriated the remains of those who died. This society was just one of several set up in Britain at around this time. By the 1960s, it was little more than a recreational and gambling club for workers in the Chinese restaurants in the West India Dock Road and some Chinese seafarers, although it continued to organise visits to the graves of seafarers in the Chinese cemetery. At least until recently, it continued to carry out these and a few other activities. Although by origin a native-place association, it later adopted the title Chun Yee 正义 (Justice) Society, perhaps to broaden its constituency at a time of growing competition from other organisations.[21]

The Hui Tong Association's principal rival was Chee Kung Tong 致公堂, an offshoot of the Hongmen 洪门 Society. Probably Europe's oldest Chinese organisation, Chee Kung Tong was active in Liverpool as early as the 1880s, chiefly among seafarers. It was dominated by immigrants from Siyi. Sometime in the early twentieth century, it established a presence in London's East End.[22] Its first president was Liu Jue 刘爵, a Siyinese.[23]

The activities of organisations like the Hongmen Society in foreign lands were an extension of their role in China, where they served as support networks for peripatetics and migrants, especially the poor and the déclassé. Within China, they expanded along established inter-provincial migration routes.[24] From the southern coastal provinces, they accompanied emigrants overseas, where they performed the same role in the Chinatowns.

Chee Kung Tong performed ritual functions, adjudicated in China-town disputes, arranged jobs, ran mutual-aid schemes, organised funerals in the Chinese sections of British cemeteries (particularly Liver-pool's Anfield and Everton), and provided a safe meeting place for its members, like the Hui Tong Association.[25] According to a self-description, 'overseas brothers come to the Tong 堂 when there are disputes and businesses, and Tong members have priority when jobs become available'.[26]

In her study of the Tiandihui 天地会, a close relative of the Hongmen, Dian Murray points out that just as 'protection frequently shaded off into predation' in China, so 'elements of extortion, racketeering, or "criminal entrepreneurship"' often characterised organisations like the Tiandihui.[27] 'The Tong', as it became known in the British ports, also engaged in criminal activities.[28]

Britain's early Chinese came mostly from Guangdong's Pearl River Delta, a distinction they shared with the Chinese in Australia. As Cai Shaoqing 蔡少卿 has pointed out, the relative homogeneity of the Chinese in Australia precluded clan wars of the sort that rent ethnic-Chinese communities of more varied provenance.[29] The relative absence of factional strife, in Britain as in Australia, led in the early years to a comparatively centralised form of organisation that sought to unify the community.

Chee Kung Tong continued to play a part in Britain's Chinatowns until the late 1940s, when its authority was ignored or rejected by newer generations. By that time, its role had narrowed while its member-ship had widened, to embrace local whites with a connection to the Chinese.[30] (Fifty years later, its president expressed a readiness to accept black members.[31]) This development mirrored the retreat from transna-tionalism and the trend towards cross-cultural and transethnic interac-tion that often seems to mark the later stages of an ethnic minority's cultural and economic integration. In the early 1950s, one observer described Chee Kung Tong as 'innocuous' and 'moribund'. By the 1980s, it was little more than a hostel for elderly Chinese bachelors, although it continues to exist even now.[32]

In 1906, the Siyinese leaders of Chee Kung Tong in Liverpool set up an explicitly native-place association, the See Yip Chinese Association in England 英伦四邑总会馆, to represent the Siyinese and enable them to retain control of the more broadly based organisation, which included non-Siyinese. The new association had similar aims to the Hui Tong Association.[33] In later years, as we shall see, the See Yip Association declined, only to revive under the impact of developments in China in the 1980s.

Least known of all Britain's early Chinese associations is the fellow-countrypersons' association founded in London in 1909 by Yi Fucheng 易富成, a migrant from Tianmen 天门 in Hubei province. The Tianme-nese, whose transnational and British migrations are described in the next chapter, made contact through this organisation with progressive Chinese students in London and supported them financially.[34]

The classic distinction in 'overseas-Chinese' studies between tradi-tionalist and modernist organisation breaks down in practice. In the case of the Hui Tong Association, the See Yip Chinese Association, and the Tianmenese fellow-countrypersons' association, native-place ties were allied to more broadly based and directly political clubs, which grandees of the native-place societies used as fronts to spread their influence.

Another early association was the Chinese Mutual Aid Workers' Club 伦敦华侨互助工团 (also called the Chung Sam Workers' Club), founded in Liverpool in 1916 by seafarers to promote 'mutual aid and solid-arity' and transplanted to London in the early 1920s. The Workers' Club had more or less the same aims as Hui Tong and was financed by members' subscriptions, gambling levies, and donations.[35] Said to have been formed after the arrest of a Chinese under martial law imposed at the time of the Irish independence struggle, its aims were to represent the workers and no other class; and to provide a place where workers could meet safely, free of ridicule and molestation. It was founded by a committee member of London's Guomindang branch (whose officials addressed members' meetings).[36]

Chinese associations after the Second World War

During the Second World War, the united front between commun-ists and Nationalists in China created conditions for a unified polit-ical movement overseas, including in Britain, as we show in the next chapter. However, this movement disappeared after 1945, when the civil war resumed in China and many Chinese outside China turned their backs on homeland politics. Most seafarers returned from Britain to Asian ports, thus removing the main constituent of Britain's rejuvenated wartime Chinatowns.

In prewar days, Chinese associations had never flourished in Britain or in Europe to the same extent as elsewhere, where they dominated most aspects of community life. By 1950, they had virtually ceased to exist, except as relics with a greatly reduced membership and range of functions (principally as recreation centres and – in time – homes for the elderly). China's closure in the 1960s completed the severing of home-ties to Siyi and other mainland sending regions.[37]

In the 1950s, Xu Bin 徐斌 found a very low level of organisation among Britain's Chinese, which he explained partly by the crisis in mutual trust engendered by the change of regime in China in 1949 and of China's diplomatic representation in London in 1950. Even before 1949, the Chinese in Britain lacked 'economic associations'.

Some pro-Guomindang political organisations active in Britain in the postwar years did not survive Chiang Kai-shek's defeat on the Chinese mainland. The Guomindang Branch in Britain 国民党住英支部 was active until 1949, when it closed, allegedly under British pressure. Communist 'professional' students infiltrated two Nationalist student organisations, although apparently to no lasting effect.[38]

The start of immigration into Britain from Hong Kong's New Territories in the 1950s did little to save Britain's Chinese associations from the doldrums. At first, the associations helped provide some newcomers with jobs in Chinese enterprises and accommodation.[39] However, once they had settled down, the newcomers were less inclined than the old-timers to support these associations, for they were less interested in Chinese politics (only marginally relevant at home) and less beleaguered by racists than the pioneers. Those who did see the need for associations were more likely to set up their own than join an old one.[40] In 1968, Ng Kwee Choo 吴贵竹 wrote (wrongly, as it happens, but only just) that Chee Kung Tong was 'no longer in existence', that the Hui Tong Association had 'more or less vanished with the disintegration of Chinatown and the wide dispersal of Chinese immigrants', and that the Workers' Club was plagued by apathy and a dying membership (though it did have the largest number of members – around 250).[41]

New immigrants and associations since the 1960s

The dearth of associations was relieved in the decade of large-scale immigration from the New Territories that started around 1963. Some associations that emerged in those years were based on surname, dialect, or place of provenance.[42] Others were economic or professional. Still others played social and welfare roles – social in the early years of male sojourner immigration, welfare in the days of family formation and reunion. Some new associations were ostensibly political, in that they leaned to Beijing or Taibei, but they also provided recreational and welfare facilities. Others were religious, tied in some cases to churches of the host society. Umbrella groups formed, either at the national or (especially in later years) pan-European level. Clans and other ascriptively based groups set up transnational federations. As the community matured and aged, the range of associations expanded still further to include Chinese branches of mainstream charities, women's groups, activist organisations, Chinese sections of mainstream British political parties, and state-subsidised community centres.

Yet the extent to which British and European Chinese societies were organised into voluntary associations continued to lag behind other continents. Even though their numbers shot up in the 1980s and the 1990s, most associations were fairly inactive, especially outside the big cities. Some were one-off bodies put together in response to an incident or crisis. Few played more than a marginal role in members' lives.[43]

Within Europe, the United Kingdom has far more Chinese associations than any other country. However, unlike those in other European countries with big Chinese communities, the UK associations tend to draw their members from this or that town or region in the United Kingdom rather than from the country as a whole. Of the 134 associations in Britain listed by the *Encyclopaedia of Overseas and Ethnic Chinese* fewer than half are explicitly 'English' (usually meaning British or UK) in scope, whereas only four of the 85 associations listed for France are other than explicitly 'French'. (Three of the exceptions are Paris-based, one is Marseilles-based.)[44] In the Netherlands, two-thirds of the associations listed by Li Minghuan are nationwide in scope.[45]

This difference helps to explain the greater number of Chinese associations in the United Kingdom, where there are fewer higher-level bodies. The difference results from several factors: a contrast in provenance – urbanised, cosmopolitan, and highly organised in the French case (as a result of the immigrants' prior experience in Indochina), rural and parochial in that of Britain's immigrants from Hong Kong's New Territories; the contrast between the highly centralised French state, which promotes organisations formed in its own image, and its looser British counterpart; a contrast in the pattern of settlement – concentrated in France, where as many as three-fifths of Chinese live in Greater Paris, and dispersed in Britain, where just 30 per cent live in Greater London;[46] and the greater age of relatively large-scale Chinese settlement in Britain, which promotes accommodating to local circumstance. The centralist French political culture was for a long time reflected in discriminatory legislation that affected foreigners' right to associate. When associations did eventually form on a wider scale in France, it was under the impact of the wholesale importation of Chinese societies from Indochina in the 1970s and 1980s. The greater age and lesser concentration of the British Chinese population is particularly relevant to the rise of the Chinese Community Centres, discussed at the end of this section.

(a) Clan organisations

Probably the first Chinese clan organisation set up in postwar Britain was the Cheungs' Clansmen Charity Association (Europe) 欧洲张氏宗亲福利会, founded in 1965 in London to provide 'mutual aid', with members from both Hong Kong and Guangdong. The association was, from the outset, open to non-Cheungs.[47] The Cheungs' head start on other clans and lineages can be explained by their domination of London's Chinese restaurant sector, starting in the 1920s, and their deep roots in Britain, stretching back to the 1880s. In the 1970s, the Cheungs pioneered the colonising of Soho's Gerrard Street, today's Chinatown.[48]

Britain's two other well-known clan organisations are the Overseas Pang's Clansmen Association, England 英国海外彭氏宗亲会, formed in London in 1968,[49] and the bigger Man's Clansmen Association, UK 旅欧文氏宗亲会, formed (like the Cheungs' Association) with the whole of Europe in mind.[50] The Pang association draws support from the World Pang's Clan Association 世界彭氏宗亲联谊会 formed in Singapore in 1992, which keeps in touch with its namesakes in Britain and throughout the world by means of the *Shi Peng huixun* 世彭会讯 (World Pang association bulletin). As for the Man, they are Britain's most-studied Chinese lineage and the subject of James Watson's seminal work, *Emigration and the Chinese Lineage*.

Europe's early Man sojourners were noted for their cohesion. One explanation is that San Tin 新田, their native village in Hong Kong's New Territories, is a large single-lineage settlement, wielding far greater power than the smaller, multilineage communities that provided most of Britain's Chinese emigrants. The ethnic-Chinese status hierarchy was far less developed in Britain in the 1960s and early 1970s than in the New Territories, which therefore remained the focus of the Man community overseas. When Watson made his London study, in 1970, the Mans' identification with San Tin was so overwhelming that a formal lineage organisation in Britain was deemed unnecessary.[51] By 1976, however, San Tin had lost not only most of its young men but also many of their dependants, so a clan association was finally set up in London. In the early 1980s, it had around 1500 members across Europe (mainly in Britain and the Netherlands). Among its activities is an annual charter flight to Hong Kong, to coincide with the Chongyang 重阳 Festival, when homage is traditionally paid to ancestors.[52]

Clan associations like the Man 文, Pang 彭, Cheung 张, and Tang 邓 own freehold property in London, acquired in earlier years. In London as in Singapore and other areas of ethnic-Chinese population, clan-owned property lends power and influence to bodies that might otherwise have weakened. Land ownership in the New Territories also lends the clans strength. However, young people identify less with these organisations, and those that show an interest in changing them along modern lines are often deflected by the obstructive attitudes of the pioneers, who hold the reins of power.

Ascriptive associations of this sort have always been far rarer and smaller in Europe and Britain than in North America and Southeast Asia. They were also far rarer, in postwar Britain, than social and benevolent societies and are easily outnumbered today by Chinese organisations formed on the basis of a British suburb, town, or region. Moreover, their influence was fading rapidly until the recent attempt to create or revive clan ties worldwide (analysed below).[53] Most of the large number of Chinese villages, lineages, and surnames represented in Britain have never had a separate association. This lack of clan associations can be explained partly by the postwar economic environment, in which jobs and business opportunities were plentiful. Other factors include the extreme dispersal of the community and the strong role played in business by family and close kin as opposed to lineage and clan. According to Anthony Shang, 'Unlike in the United States and South East Asia, the economic gap that Chinese workers filled in Britain was not controlled by any specific association'.[54]

(b) Native-place associations

There are three main sorts of native-place associations in Britain: those descended from the Cantonese associations set up at around the turn of the nineteenth century; those set up by migrants from Hong Kong; and those set up by recent migrants from central and northern China.

The See Yip Chinese Association 四邑总会, founded in Liverpool in 1906, still has branches in northwest England and South Wales. Southern England is covered by the newer and related Ng Yip (five counties) Association 旅英五邑联谊会, founded in 1995.[55] Each branch acts, for the most part, independently, although the Ng Yip Association leaders envisage an association to cover the United Kingdom. A grand gathering takes place at Chinese New Year and the Mid-Autumn Festival. The associations have been replenished in recent years by new immigration from mainland China and from Hong Kong, where there is a strong Siyinese community. The leadership cultivates its relations with the Wuyi counties. Because they form a majority of the established Chinese community with mainland connections, they get support from the Embassy and are prominent at its gatherings.[56]

The old functions of immigrant mutual aid are no longer as important as they were. As early as the 1960s, associations that had once flourished were in decline, partly because of the drop in anti-Chinese feeling and the availability to the settled generation of universal government benefits. Also in the 1960s, the problem of succession became acute in some long-established associations. Today, banquets, shopping trips, and outings are the main activity of most. Like their counterparts throughout the world, they no longer find it easy to attract young Chinese, who are considered too westernised and individualistic.[57]

(c) Trade associations

In a community devoted to enterprise, one might expect trade associations to predominate. However, ethnic-Chinese trade and business associations in Britain have rarely prospered.

As far as we know, the Chinese laundries had no trade association.[58] The forms of association employed by Chinese laundrymen in Britain were apparently confined to family and kinship. The laundrymen waged patch wars. Some anonymously denounced their rivals to the authorities for allegedly peddling drugs and harbouring 'stowaways'. Unlike Chinese laundrymen in the United States, however, they stopped short of bombing and murder.[59]

An Association of Chinese Restaurateurs was set up in 1961, at a meeting of restaurateurs from all over Britain. Its goal was to 'unite in protecting our ever-expanding business... [and] the good reputation of all Chinese restaurants in the country'. It was dominated by the owners of big, established restaurants and headed by a member of the powerful Cheung clan. Like the Cheungs' Clansmen Charity Association, it recruited members among Chinese across Western Europe. Although it claimed to champion trade solidarity, an unstated aim was to protect the interests of the old-timers against the new migrants moving in on catering.

Not surprisingly, small restaurateurs were unenthusiastic, and even many bigger members were indifferent. Some caterers in the Netherlands and Belgium dropped out for want of any tangible benefits. The Association was probably the first attempt by members of the older generation to unite behind common interests. It fell apart for two main reasons: the elite restaurateurs' failure to take to heart the interests of the small proprietors, including of chip-shops, laundries, and allied businesses; and the rivalry between different factions of old-timers. By the late 1960s, the Association existed in name only.[60] A similar thing happened, though for different reasons, in Scotland in 1971, when a trade association collapsed within six months.[61]

In the decades since the 1960s, old associations have revived and new ones formed but none has flourished.[62] A vocal new arrival is the Chinese Takeaway Association 全英华人外卖公会,[63] formed in November 1992 in London, with committees in each London borough. This association was run at first by professionals, though a handful of takeaway owners were later recruited into its leadership. The professionals have good contacts in government and recruited Clare Short as their president. In 2001, the association claimed up to 400 members but its membership fluctuates, rising in times of crisis (for example, when foot-and-mouth was blamed on Chinese caterers) and falling when things get back to normal.[64] Despite its flair for self-promotion, it is not well rooted.

Trade bodies set up by other ethnic-Chinese communities in Europe usually meet the same fate as in Britain. Although catering has ruled the Chinese enclave throughout Western Europe for many years, early efforts to establish associations came to nothing. In the Netherlands, associations have come and gone. In Denmark, where Chinese also established a strong presence in catering, their grill-bars and restaurants never formed a business association.[65]

The exception is France, where the transplantation of subethnic organisations from Indochina has resulted in a different culture. The Chaozhounese 潮州人, who went to France as refugees from Cambodia and Laos, are France's largest Chinese group (with an estimated population of 66,000 in the early 1990s). Tightly structured and culturally hegemonic, they are more likely than other Chinese to live in Chinese parts of Paris.[66] In Southeast Asia, they are highly organised and widely spread. Their commercial base there has helped them dominate the Chinese economy in France. Hokkien 福建 Chinese also maintain ties to their several million co-ethnics in Southeast Asia, while at the same time engaging in commercial dealings with France's Chaozhounese majority.[67]

By the mid-1990s, several major new organisations had emerged whose goals included ensuring internal 'cooperation and solidarity' among ethnic-Chinese entrepreneurs and representing Chinese interests to the French authorities.[68] Even so, in other respects the French Chinese are poorly organised and most Chinese entrepreneurs are much better adapted to French norms and institutions than is often thought.[69]

(d) Front organisations

At the start of the twentieth century, organisations based on native-place ties (like the Hui Tong Association and the See Yip Association) used broader bodies to extend their influence over Chinese from other places. Other groups have done the same in more recent times. The Cheungs' role in the Association of Chinese Restaurateurs in the early 1960s is a case in point. The Association was set up mainly to control the activities of other Chinese businesses rather than to enhance the Cheung clan's own ties. The Man lineage pursued a similar strategy. To the extent that the Mans formally associated in the 1960s, it was by breathing new life into the Workers' Club, which other New Territories immigrants also joined. In the 1960s, nearly half the Club's 250 members were Mans from San Tin. By saving it from expiry, the Mans created a base for themselves that they continue to occupy.[70]

(e) From recreation to welfare

The Workers' Club is a good example of the switch in the 1970s from a recreational role, tailored to a community of male sojourners, to a family welfare role. In the early 1960s, the Club was best known for its gambling facilities and its first-floor dormitory (where new immigrants could sleep for ten shillings a week). With the commission earned from gambling, it bought a new premises and invited Chinese from all over Britain and Europe to the opening. In 1962, it donated a large sum to the Rural Consultative Council 乡议局 (Heung Yee Kuk) in the New Territories in support of flood relief, an example of its homeland orientation at the time. It was known in the 1960s as pro-Beijing – perhaps a relic of the radical ideology of its founders. As the bachelors acquired wives and children, the Club began to pay more attention to social welfare in Britain itself, including the need for Chinese-language classes for the second generation.[71] Other organisations that assumed a family welfare role in the 1960s include the pro-Beijing Kung Ho Association of London 伦敦共和协会, founded in 1947 by Sam Chen 陈天声, the communist seafarers' leader. Between 1966 and 1968, it set up a women's section and a thriving Chinese-language class.[72]

(f) The Chinese Chamber of Commerce

Britain's Chinese Chamber of Commerce 英国华商总会 (also known as the Chamber of Chinese Traders), was set up in London in 1968, on the initiative of the London-based Hong Kong Government Office (HKGO). A feeble contrivance, by mid-1970 its membership was acknowledged by its colonial creators to have fallen 'to a very low level'.[73] In an attempt to make belonging more attractive, in 1973 the HKGO sent a ten-person delegation to Hong Kong, where they were received in Government House.[74] Even so, it continued in a rather weakly state.

Despite its failings, it has represented Chinese business interests with more success than the Association of Chinese Restaurateurs. Its aims are to lobby the British government, provide welfare services, support Chinese trade and industry, unify the community, and fight for Chinese legal rights. At first, it concentrated on helping traders and restaurateurs register their businesses. Later, it branched out into culture and education. In the 1970s, it helped thwart plans by the City of Westminster to demolish Chinatown in Gerrard Street.[75] In 1980, as we shall see in the next chapter, it set up the Federation of Chinese Associations, UK.

Observers note that the Chamber of Commerce is poorly rooted in the community, especially outside London. It lacks an ear in high places and cannot claim to speak on the community's behalf.[76] Chinese wholesalers said in interviews that the Chamber was of little relevance.[77] Most had arrived in the 1960s and built up their enterprises by first moving into catering.

The Chamber was taken over in the 1980s by a more recent group, professionals and well-educated immigrants from Taiwan who used it to promote their business interests, giving it a new vitality. Its most influential leaders in the recent past have included Jason Tsai 蔡吉春, a Taiwanese engineer who established a thriving electronics company in Telford, and his ally Wilfred Sng, a Singaporean who at some point became a Taiwan national. Sng, an accountant by training and a long-term UK resident with experience of working in top auditing and consultancy firms, had influence with some politicians, whom he used to facilitate ethnic-Chinese investment in the United Kingdom. It is no accident that many investments by leading Taiwanese firms in the United Kingdom have been in Telford (like Jason Tsai). These companies are mainly in electronics (also like Tsai). Tsai stepped down as the Chamber's president in the late 1990s, while his enterprise has emerged as a major firm.

(g) Associational diversification

Towards the end of the twentieth century, the ageing of the Chinese community and its dilution by new immigrants led to a diversification of the ethnic-Chinese economy and society. Among associations reflecting this trend are the Chinese Lions' Clubs 华埠狮子会 set up in London, Birmingham, Manchester, and other cities (as branches of an international charity), the Hong Kong Overseas Professionals Association 英国香港海外专业协会 (founded in 1971), the UK Chinese Women's Association 英国华侨妇女 (founded in 1981), the British Association of Writers in the Chinese Language 英国华文作家协会 (founded in 1988), the Chinese Arts Association, UK 英国中华艺术协会 (founded in 1988), the Chinese Cultural Centre 英国中华文化中心 (founded in 1988), the Chinese Engineers' Study Society, UK 旅英中国土木工程学会 (founded in 1992), and the Association of Traditional Chinese Medicine, UK 英国中医药学会 (founded in 1995). Indicative of Chinese joining the mainstream was the establishment of the London Chinatown Conservative Association 伦敦华埠保守党协会 in 1988 and, at around the same time, of the Chinese for Labour group 英国华人工党.[78]

New immigration from places other than the traditional sending areas in southern China has also given rise to new associations. In the early 1980s, after an initial period of dispersal and social isolation, ethnic-Chinese refugees from Indochina set up more than 40 self-help groups and organisations (mainly in London).[79] The Taiwan Chinese, though few in number, are also well organised. In 1960, they set up the Overseas Chinese Association 华侨协会, which had more than 200 members in the early 1990s and uses Mandarin. There were ten Taiwan-linked associations in the late 1980s, some of them political.[80]

(h) Chinese Community Centres

In recent years, ethnic-Chinese associations in Britain have begun to push into new fields. Some have begun to campaign more forcefully for political and social rights and to represent the community to the authorities at local and national level.[81] In the late 1970s and the early 1980s, others won financial support from local authorities to set up Chinese Community Centres (CCCs), which marked a radical break with practice. By the early 1990s, there were 15 CCCs in different parts of the country.[82] This development is part of what some Chinese call 'fusion with local society' or 'localisation'.[83]

The CCCs emerged in response to changes in the demographic composition of Britain's ethnic-Chinese community and a new approach to ethnic minorities on the part of the British Government, including a perception that Chinese needed help to gain proper access to social services. The centres provide a range of assistance in housing, health, education, Chinese-language courses, employment, immigration, welfare entitlement, general welfare, and interpreting.[84] The gradual withdrawal from community affairs by the HKGO (introduced in detail in the following chapter) in the late 1980s and the 1990s and the closure of its offices outside London played a role in promoting bodies like the CCCs, which took over some of the HKGO's functions.

The CCCs are a stage between the old ideal of community self-sufficiency and the integrationist project of a new breed of community activists. Some CCCs were set up on the basis of existing associations, by modernisers keen to enter the mainstream or get a state subvention; others were founded by local social services or were independently organised.[85] In 1980, for example, the London Chinatown Chinese Association won an Urban Aid grant to set up a CCC that dispensed free advice about welfare and other issues.[86] In Liverpool, the Merseyside Chinese Community Services, founded in 1977 with a Manpower Services Commission grant, set up the Pagoda Centre 寺塔中心 in 1982, with a capital grant from the central government and local authority.[87]

Initially, many Chinese saw the new bodies as alien. 'It is no secret', explained a Chinese leader in Liverpool, speaking of the local CCC, 'that the centre was imposed on the community with little consultation with existing organisation.... It has meant that the Pagoda has had to work hard to establish credibility'.[88] In time, however, the CCCs established their usefulness and became accepted.

The impetus for CCCs came from within the Chinese community, but they received strong support in the mid-1980s in a report on the Chinese community by the House of Commons' Home Affairs Committee. The Committee identified four functions of CCCs: to act as an advice service for those in need; to provide mother-tongue and English-language classes; to create a space for 'recreational, cultural and social activities, such as lion dancing, martial arts, day nurseries, activities for old people, Chinese crafts, youth clubs and so on'; and to serve as 'a bridge between the Chinese and the rest of society', so that Chinese would become better-informed about British society and outside organisations could make themselves known to the Chinese. This bridge function was, in Government eyes, the CCC's chief rationale: to assist Chinese people's 'integration into British society'.[89]

CCC-style 'localisation' reflects the increasing marginality of old forms of self-sufficiency as well as an awareness of the politics of race relations and the availability of multicultural funding.[90] When the first centre was set up on the Merseyside in 1977, the *Guardian* hailed it as lifting a 'two-hundred-year-old barrier'[91] and the *Liverpool Echo* as a break with the tradition of self-reliance.[92] Like other bodies that seek to bridge Chinese and local society, the CCCs are staffed mainly by professionals and British-born or university-educated Chinese volunteers and social workers, who play an ever-increasing role in community affairs.[93]

For most Chinese, however, even the CCCs are an irrelevance. According to a study in the late 1990s of social contact and social support among ethnic Chinese, CCCs play little or no role in the lives of 77 per cent of Chinese people; even two-thirds of those with a CCC in their local area never visited it. People above the age of 50 were far more likely than young people to visit CCCs, and those born in Hong Kong or China were far more likely than those born in the United Kingdom to do so, whereas four out of five of those aged 16–29 never did. The alternative to attending a CCC is anomie. Ethnic Chinese were found by researchers to be more than two and a half times as likely as the general population to be categorised as having a low level of social support. (This was true even of those who visited a CCC at least once a week.)[94] It would seem that ethnic Chinese have discarded old forms of voluntary association but show little interest in new alternatives.

A rope of sand

Sun Yat-sen had great faith in the Chinese overseas as an antidote to the Chinese at home, whom he thought of as a rope of sand, fissionable and hard to rouse. His trust was repaid, in material and political support for the Republican cause. However, Chinese overseas were not equally well organised everywhere and always. In Southeast Asia, Australasia, and the New World, they cocooned themselves against local society in a world of clans and native-place guilds. In Britain and in Europe, on the other hand, they formed far fewer such bodies. European Chinese communities were, on the whole, poorly articulated. They, too, were ropes of sand.

(a) Dispersal

Why are the Chinese in Britain and Europe so disunited? One reason is they lack critical mass, never until recently having formed even half of 1 per cent of the population of any European country. In Britain, the ghetto inhabited by most first-generation Chinese immigrants was virtual. Cut off by invisible walls from British society, most Chinese also lived cut off from one another, in a scatter dictated by economics. This dispersal inhibited association. Where associations did form, they ignored the needs of the majority, who lived far from the city-centre Chinatowns.[95]

The Chinese in Britain have a far wider geographic distribution than most ethnic minorities. They are not only dispersed more evenly but form fewer concentrations. Although the Chinese have congregated in disproportionate numbers in Greater London, they are less likely than most other ethnic minorities to live there or in any other metropolitan area or conurbation, and are more likely than other ethnic minorities in southeast England to live outside London. They are overwhelmingly more likely than other ethnic minorities to live in local authority wards where only around 1 per cent of the population are drawn from their own ethnic group. (Nine out of ten Chinese live in such wards, compared with 21 per cent of Caribbeans, 18 per cent of Indians or African Asians, 14 per cent of Pakistanis, and 30 per cent of Bangladeshis.)[96]

The main exceptions to the pattern of even dispersal are Greater London, Merseyside, Greater Manchester, and Tyne and Wear. However, only in Greater London are the Chinese over-represented compared with the white population (by 51–30 per cent in 1991). Even in the Northwest, the proportion of Chinese is lower than that of whites.[97] Chinese comprise a uniform 0.2 per cent of the population in ten out of 17 'standard regions' (including Wales and Scotland) and metropolitan counties, a uniformity matched by no other ethnic minority.

Although London and Liverpool have more Chinese than other British cities, they are scattered rather evenly across many boroughs and far less concentrated than (say) the Chinese in Paris. In 1991, they formed no less than 1.5 and no more than 2 per cent of the population in ten London boroughs and in Liverpool's Riverside, their largest local concentrations.[98]

This pattern of relative dispersal characterised the Chinese population throughout most of the twentieth century. Both the laundry trade and the catering economy required an even spatial distribution, the first steps towards which were taken before the First World War. William Cheung 张传馨 noted in 1975 that the proportion of Chinese living in a given standard region was, with the exception of Merseyside and London, practically the same as that of the local population.[99] In 1975, it was practically impossible to find a town of 5000 in England without a Chinese restaurant or takeaway.[100]

Not all groups of Chinese display the same pattern of distribution. Although 51 per cent of Chinese live in the southeast, this figure disguises important differences between Chinese of different provenance. Forty six per cent of Hong Kong Chinese (the group most likely to be caterers) live in the southeast, compared with 66 per cent of Chinese from Southeast Asia and 56 per cent from elsewhere in the world (principally China and Vietnam). This difference can be explained by the employment profile of Chinese from China and Southeast Asia (many of whom have professional and technical qualifications) and by the Vietnamese flight from quarantine in the late 1970s and 1980s.[101]

The extreme dispersal of the Chinese population has had an enormous impact on its welfare and identity. Because of their dispersal, wrote Ann Dummett and Jenny Lo in 1986, 'they and their problems are nobody's priority: indeed their existence may scarcely be noticed'.[102] It was once thought that Chinese who lived above their shops and worked all hours in isolation from society would be rendered 'invisible' and therefore spared racist abuse, a compensation for the loneliness.[103] There is evidence, however, that dispersal leads not to invisibility but to vulnerability, especially for the second generation, which has no choice other than to cross the counter.

(b) Intra-ethnic competition

Another reason for Chinese disunity in Britain is intra-ethnic competition, a theme that pervades the entire history of the Chinese presence, starting with the Shadwell riots of 1813. More recently, in the catering sector, this competition has resulted from successive waves of Chinese immigration. Normally, continuing immigration helps sustain ethnic enterprise and generate ethnic enclaves, but in the United Kingdom it has twice practically torn the heart out of the ethnic-Chinese economy. In London in the 1960s, the rivalry between old-timers from China and newcomers from Hong Kong was intense. The Hong Kong immigrants, in their turn, faced strong competition from ethnic Chinese from Southeast Asia, whose market share of the restaurant sector shot up in the late 1980s and the 1990s. While the Hong Kongers cornered the takeaways, Southeast Asian Chinese emerged in the 1980s as big players in the Chinese restaurant and fast-food sector. In the 1990s, their fast-food companies challenged the takeaways on price, just as the takeaways had challenged the restaurants in the 1970s with a cheaper menu.

The takeaway owners were capable of undermining the early restaurateurs but not of overcoming their own incoherence. Intra-ethnic rivalry in the takeaway trade was the main reason for the wide dispersal of

Chinese across the British Isles, which in its turn precluded the emergence of ethnic-Chinese enclaves and effective associations. Spurred on by resentment at exploitation by established immigrants and a burning wish to succeed, Hong Kong immigrants from the New Territories threw themselves single-mindedly into accumulating capital, in an entrepreneurial free-for-all.

The Southeast Asian Chinese who arrived in the 1980s also failed to create a strong sense of community. Endowed with sufficient 'class resources' to develop their sophisticated food-based enterprises under their own steam, few had any incentive to seek strength in numbers. Nearly all such enterprises were sole proprietorships. Given their resources, most Southeast Asian Chinese have tended to work alone (or with immediate family members) or with non-Chinese British collaborators when establishing their new enterprises (which usually function as private companies).

The Southeast Asian Chinese are a special case, for they match British entrepreneurs in education and capital-raising ability. The petty caterers of the early postwar years, on the other hand, would on the face of it have benefited by joining forces. They were poor, uneducated, monolingual, and at home with the village forms said to engender urban associations. Even so, they rarely made common cause.

The atomisation of their trade was only one reason for their failure to stand together. Opportunity and insecurity (as a result of working in an alien environment) drove them to operate as family enterprises. Membership of a clan or native-place association was not a prerequisite for starting up in business. As Watson noted in the 1970s, 'for most migrants it is the tie of kinship – either family or lineage – that opens the door to a job in the Chinese restaurant trade. Even the clan association...does not act as a monopoly agency; the bond of common surname is not enough to ensure advantage in Britain'.[104] The family – in Britain and (in the early days) Hong Kong – supplied most of the necessary resources, human and financial. Beyond the family, the British state provided welfare and education, benefits that enabled Chinese parents to realise their main goal – catapulting their British-raised children into the professions – without co-ethnic help.

A deficiency of leadership further explains the failure to associate. William Cheung's study of the 200-strong York Chinese community in the mid-1970s provides a good example. When asked to nominate three Chinese to represent the community, most informants refused, on the grounds that there weren't three who were both selfless and competent in English. Of the dozen names nominated, none received more than three votes.[105]

The caterers have also been generally largely ignored by Chinese intellectuals, who might otherwise have represented them. In European terms, the British Chinese used to occupy a middle rung on the literacy ladder. They included proportionately more intellectuals than the Chinese in the Netherlands (excluding the Peranakan Chinese from the Dutch East Indies, who don't usually speak Chinese) but fewer than the French Chinese. The Chinese community in France was formed on the basis of a greater range of social classes, including a relatively strong and socially involved elite. Britain's Chinese intellectuals, by contrast, have tended to stand aside from the launderers and caterers, whose grievances and aspirations they failed to articulate, at least until recently.

Britain's postwar community of caterers was relatively undifferentiated, both culturally and socially.[106] Alongside but almost entirely separate from the community of seafarers, caterers, and launderers in the 1950s lived a tiny number of educated Chinese. They included a dozen journalists (some employed by the Chinese section of the BBC, others by the Taibei media), three or four artists, and a handful of wealthy exiles, including a few former government officials.[107] In the 1960s and the 1970s, the thin layer of professionals continued to keep its distance from the Chinese community at large, to which few had linguistic, affinal, economic, or political ties. If they did engage with community affairs – say, by helping caterers' children prepare for school examinations – it was an act more of charity than of solidarity.[108] The caterers lacked the resources and institutions to rope the professionals in as 'organic intellectuals'. The French Chinese refugee communities, on the other hand, range from peasants to poets and from shopkeepers to politicians, and live in compact, densely populated urban enclaves. Like the affluent and sophisticated ethnic-Chinese business communities of Southeast Asia from which they derive, they support a panoply of religious leaders, spokespeople, and savants.

Britain's younger educated generation of Chinese is mostly homegrown, but it has been enriched, especially in the late twentieth century, by admixtures of students from British colonies or former colonies and, more recently, from China and Taiwan. Both these groups, the homegrown and the acquired, have provided spokespersons for a community whose voice was once seldom heard. A few have joined old associations and breathed new life into them, others have formed new ones. However, many of those with a sense of social responsibility have been attracted to the newer forms of organisation, including the CCCs.

The diverse origins of the Chinese in Britain

'Chopstick culture' theories of the sort popular in the 1990s fail to distinguish between different groups of Chinese and assume that Chinese communities are knit together by affectivity and networking. However, the Chinese in Britain (and not just in Britain) are best understood as a community not of interest but of nativity or attribution, for they fall into sub-groups that are mostly indifferent to each other or in conflict. These groups form on the basis of generation, provenance, language, kinship, education, social class, nationality, politics, and other factors. No one group is even in a relative majority. Even within groups, social ties fray: in the wider community, they rarely even start to figure.

In the early 1970s, James Watson found that the Chinese caterers did conceive of themselves as a community, in the sense that their boundary against the outside world was stronger than their internal differences.[109] Later researchers, however, have argued that Watson's conclusions were probably influenced by the fact that his study was chiefly about the Man lineage, an unusually coherent group, and that much of the community organisation that emerged in the 1980s was created by non-caterers.[110]

Divisions were present right from the early days, particularly in the first couple of decades after the Second World War. In the early 1950s, Maurice Broady identified five mutually exclusive and segregated Chinese groups in Liverpool: the laundrymen in the suburbs; the shopkeepers in Chinatown; the on-shore workers who lived in tenements in the Pitt Street area; the married seafarers, who lived in the Canning Street area; and the wealthy restaurateurs and boarding masters, who lived in the middle-class districts.[111]

Also in the early 1950s, five groups of people set up restaurants: Chinatown veterans, many from Siyi and elsewhere in Guangdong; northerners, including former staff of the old Nationalist Embassy; Chinese from Malaya and Singapore; non-Chinese; and the first wave of Hong Kong Chinese. Inter-group relations were characterised by 'dislike and rivalry'. The old-timers from the southern mainland viewed the 'new boys' from Hong Kong as rude and arrogant carpetbaggers, bereft of community feeling.[112] The newcomers scorned the veterans as old-fashioned.[113] No less jumbled in the 1950s were the students. A Singaporean touring Europe reported that whereas the great majority of

Chinese students in Paris spoke Chinese among themselves, those in London either couldn't or wouldn't.[114]

A principal division among the postwar caterers was between the Punti 本地 ('natives', the majority group in Guangdong and Hong Kong) and the Hakkas 客家 ('guest people'), who speak mutually unintelligible forms of Chinese. The distinction is of class, too, for Hakkas are of lower status and usually till marginal land in China and Hong Kong.[115] In Britain, Hakkas formed around one-quarter of the Chinese population in the 1970s and are concentrated in the midlands and the north, where they at one point are said to have predominated.[116] The distinction between Hakka and Punti has acquired a political dimension in some places, for Hakkas formed the majority in London's leftwing Tai Ping Club.[117]

Although Hakka identity was important in the migrant generation, it has become far less so over time. Hakka cultural identity in Britain is in imminent danger of submersion by standard Cantonese and the commercialised products of the Hong Kong media industry. Hakka solidarity, once famed in China and among Chinese overseas, no longer plays a prominent role in Hakka business operations. An example: in terms of turnover, the largest Chinese food wholesaler and retailer in Britain, W. Wing Yip plc 荣业行, is owned by a Hakka, W. W. Yip, once a penniless migrant from Hong Kong, while the largest food catering enterprise, Singapore Sam plc, is owned C. L. Wong (a dentist by profession), also a Hakka, from Malaysia. According to Yip, the two men are distantly related. Even so, there are no business links between them.

Even the Cantonese Punti are far from uniform. Not all Punti in Britain are from the New Territories, and even New Territories Punti are divided not only by lineage but by type of lineage. In the 1970s, only one-third belonged to the powerful elite lineages (whose hold on lineage exiles subsequently weakened).[118] Most Punti come from multi-lineage villages, where lineage resources and identifications count for less.

Between 1963 and 1973, the Hong Kong group was further modified, as we have seen, by the arrival of some 10,000 'stateless' China-born residents of the territory. These people, mainly Cantonese Punti, were brought over by Chinese already in Britain. The newcomers were treated as second class by their employers, who paid them badly and gave them the worst jobs.[119]

The Vietnamese who started coming to Britain in the late 1970s added yet another ingredient to the ethnic-Chinese mix. Their relations with the Hong Kong Chinese were hostile or ambivalent. Some Hong Kongers employed them, mainly in menial tasks; many despised them as 'coarse and unruly'.[120] The Vietnam Chinese were divided among themselves, between southerners (who tend to be better educated) and the majority northerners.[121]

By the 1990s, the composition of the Chinese community had become even more diverse as a result of ageing and further influxes. Evidence of this demographic change can be found in a study on the Chinese in England published in 1999 by the Health Education Authority.[122] It reported a far smaller proportion of British-born Chinese than the Census: 19 per cent born in the United Kingdom (compared with 28 per cent according to the Census), 41 per cent born in Hong Kong (compared with 34 per cent), and 22 per cent born in China or Vietnam (compared with 18 per cent).[123] The British-born Chinese, the fastest-growing group according to the Census, have a different linguistic, educational, and employment profile from their parents and a different cultural identity (discussed in a later chapter). Recent research showed that only 77 per cent of Chinese in Britain speak a Chinese language.[124]

Immigrants from the New Territories are fast being outstripped by Chinese from other places. Though one-third of Chinese in Britain were born in Hong Kong, the rest include Chinese and ethnic-Chinese immigrants from across the world. The roughly 2000 people of Chinese ethnic origin in the Labour Force Survey sample analysed by Yuan Cheng came from no fewer than 36 different countries.[125] Many originated in former British colonies in Southeast Asia or in Africa or the West Indies.[126]

Urban Hong Kong is a main source of current immigration. The urban migrants, chiefly professionals and capitalists, are far richer and better educated than their rural predecessors. If 130,000 come, as allowed under arrangements made in the run-up to Hong Kong's retrocession, the changes of recent years will quicken greatly.[127] So, too, will the caterers' isolation.

Other Chinese who have entered Britain in significant numbers include so-called illegal immigrants, mainland Chinese student immigrants, and mainland Chinese immigrants of various other classes who have succeeded since the late 1970s in establishing their presence on a legal footing. These are China's 'new migrants', as distinct from the old-style 'overseas Chinese'.

The Chinese in Britain are divided not only by provenance, ethnicity, and generation but also by social and economic class, distinctions that have deepened over time. The relatively egalitarian early Chinaport separated into haves and have-nots. Poor immigrants from the New Territories took advantage of the postwar boom to shake off their obligations to the grandees who dominated Chinatown, creating a new division between petty caterers and big restaurateurs. The arrival in the 1980s and 1990s of wealthy and resourceful Chinese from urban Hong Kong and Southeast Asia, destitute Vietnam Chinese, and displaced intellectuals and *sans-papiers* from all over China has yielded an even greater tangle that falls not far short of the social diversity of the host society.

Little attention has been paid to the class divisions among ethnic Chinese in Britain, whose differences are obscured by approaches that either reduce all immigrants to a 'uniform, faceless mass of new proletarians' or analyse the Chinese in particular as a 'community of mutual interests [whose] divisions are not as strong as the perceived difference between Chinese and non-Chinese'.[128] However, some studies indicate a large degree of class polarisation.

Within the catering enclave, the cleavages are between capital and labour and among different categories of labour (ranging from chef to pantry worker).[129] Class also divides the wider Chinese community. Although more than twice as likely as the general population to be in social class I (10 per cent as compared with 4 per cent), ethnic Chinese are also far less likely to be in social class II (18 and 27 per cent, respectively). This polarisation has strong sub-ethnic and generational dimensions. Chinese born in the United Kingdom are half as likely as those born in other countries (for example, in Southeast Asia) to be in social class I (9 and 16 per cent, respectively). Merchants and restaurant workers are unlikely to come from the same places. Immigrants who have been in the United Kingdom for ten years or more are more likely to be in social classes I or II (31 and 19 per cent, respectively).[130]

Chinatown

In the previous chapter, we questioned analysing ethnic-Chinese business as the translation to new settings of culture made in China. Ethnic-Chinese social and political institutions are also often explained as transplants from the Chinese context. According to the *Encyclopaedia of Overseas and Ethnic Chinese*, for example, ethnic-Chinese associations replicate the 'secret societies and native-place guilds of the Ming and Qing era'.[131] In a more nuanced formulation, Lynn Pan calls them a 'reconstitution on new soil of older patterns...adumbrated in the Chinese homeland'.[132]

A classic statement of this translation thesis is Lawrence W. Crissman's essay on the origins of Chinatown, the compact urban settlements in which Chinese emigrants and their descendants tended in the past to reside, work, and trade.[133] Crissman compounded his ideal-type China-town from studies on Chinese societies in Southeast Asia and North America. Although his model is often criticised, even scholars who adopt contrary approaches take their bearings by it.

According to Crissman, the same segmentary organisation underlies the 'superficially different characteristics' of Chinatowns everywhere. The prime division is into speech groups, nearly all of which correspond to discrete localities in China and therefore allow an expression of sub-ethnic distinctions in geographic (or native-place) terms. Each speech community segments into sub-communities based on counties or villages. Surnames (of which China has relatively few in widespread use) are the basis for a further division. These two principles of segment-ation, locality (or speech group) and surname, create a set of overlapping sub-communities. Communities of people from the same village are the basic unit. They spiral upwards into ever larger communities with their associated organisations, 'until the level of speech communities and the total Chinese community is reached'. The leaders of the 'total' community, usually organised in a Benevolent Association or Chamber of Commerce, settle disputes among Chinatowners, conduct China-town's affairs, promote welfare and public services, mediate between Chinatown and the indigenous authority, 'and even have what amounts to foreign relations with the government of China'.

How to account for Chinatown's apparent worldwide 'structural uniformity'? According to Crissman, Chinatown mirrors China, where the rural and the urban are closely interknit and the principles of 'descent, locality and occupation' that order rural life are mobilised by rural migrants to cope with living in the cities. The same happens when villagers go abroad. Chinatown results from their projection onto alien settings of China's 'traditional urban forms', which derive from rural prototypes.[134]

Conceiving Chinatown as an extension of homeland practices was, for a time, quite commonplace. In the 1950s, G. William Skinner and others studied Chinese societies overseas as a substitute for China, rendered inaccessible by the revolution, and used them to explain Chinese society itself.[135] Stanford M. Lyman, writing about the United States, noted that Chinese social organisation 'was transplanted overseas'.[136] Bernard P. Wong traced the associations of America's Chinatown back 'to tradi-tional principles of social organization ... in the home communities of the early Chinese immigrants'.[137]

The idea that Chinatown copies structures that rural sojourners export to urban China is neat and architectonically elegant but deceptive.

Migrants of many different national and cultural backgrounds form compact, seemingly atavistic settlements abroad, either because they like to live among 'their own sort' or because government policy or racial discrimination drives them into enclaves. Conversely, not all Chinese migrants set up Chinatowns.

Chinatowns are no pre-programmed propensity, like spider-webbing, but the product of complex interactions with host societies. They arise where there is a felt need, where space obtains, and where Chinese occupational patterns permit concentrated residence. Where circumstance requires and allows Chinatowns, migrants might bring familiar principles into play. However, resort to them is a matter of choice and calculation, made according to expediency and need. Moreover, homeland forms are not mimicked in every detail. They undergo changes – sometimes shallow, often deep – in adapting to new environments and start to die out with the migrant generation. As they die, new forms arise to replace them.

This section explores Chinatown's changing functions and status in Britain over the past century and more. The word Chinatown is used in two different ways in this and other studies: metaphorically, of Britain's ethnic-Chinese society as a whole, as distinct from Britain's other ethnic groups, including its white majority; and literally, of streets and quarters with a strong Chinese presence. Here, our focus is on the literal rather than the metaphoric Chinatown.

Chinatown figures in British history as a protean site whose shapes and roles have varied over the years with Chinatowners' occupations and its own cultural and economic construction by local whites. The term is of American origin, first reported in 1857. The Chinese quarters of San Francisco and New York – like those formed by other low-status ethnic groups in American cities – were the product of two things: the racial segregation of residence, business, and employment and the ethnic resort to self-help and mutual aid in the absence of universal welfare provision and access to host-society institutions. It was probably first used in 1902 in a British context, by the investigative journalist George Sims (to describe Limehouse).[138]

Studies of the British Chinatown stress the differences between it and its North American and Southeast Asian namesakes. They point out that it has always been far smaller (consisting of just a street or two) and far less densely organised and tightly controlled; and that although Chinese work, shop, and have fun in it, few live in it. Size apart, its poor organisation and lack of a residential core are its main structural differences from better-known Chinatowns.[139] However, the picture changes if we distinguish between different phases of Chinatown, which as a focus of Chinese life in Britain has undergone razings, relocations, and metamorphoses. In the process, it has proved remarkably flexible and adaptive.

The earliest recorded Chinese habitation, in Shadwell at the start of the nineteenth century, was exclusively residential. The early Chinese settlements near the London, Liverpool, and Cardiff docks were geared to servicing the needs of Chinese crews and were under the thumb of the Chinese boarding house masters, crew contractors, and shopkeepers, who presided over their gradual transformation into more solidly based Chinatowns.[140]

All three of Britain's main Chinatowns began to crumble in the interwar years, as a result of the shipping slump, slum clearance, and the Blitz, followed by the postwar demolition of Chinese streets and buildings on Merseyside and in London. The move from Limehouse to Gerrard Street in London and from Pitt Street to Nelson Street in Liverpool marked the end of an era and weakened the tie between the two immigrant waves in the first and second halves of the century.[141]

Subsequently, the British Chinatown nearly everywhere lost its residential character and became commercial, emblematic, and a place for Chinese days-out. The one in Liverpool was a partial exception, in that it remained more residential, but it too served in the postwar years as a 'jumping-off point' for Chinese immigrants who scattered elsewhere and as a meeting point for Chinese from all over the north, until Manchester emerged as a new northern destination for Chinese Sunday visitors in the 1970s.[142]

The sinification of Gerrard Street in Soho in London's West End started in the 1960s.[143] Gerrard Street was seedy and dilapidated, an anomaly in an otherwise prosperous, booming location that included Shaftesbury Avenue, Oxford Street, and Piccadilly Circus. Property rents were low, a main attraction in the eyes of Chinese investors. Even in those days, however, residential accommodation in the West End was way beyond the pocket of even the best-paid waiter. In the early years, many staff members were transported between dormitory and restaurant by their bosses.[144]

But although large-scale Chinese residence along the street was ruled out, the area acquired many Chinatown features. Some restaurants – especially those serving real Chinese food rather than the adapted variety – discouraged non-Chinese customers. The larger restaurants, wrote Watson, took on the function of the traditional 'teahouses' which are found in all important market towns and cities in South China. In rural Hong Kong, teahouses are multi-storied restaurants that serve drinks, meals, and snacks; as in London, these establishments are the arenas for social exchange between widely scattered people and groups.

Gerrard Street was a place not just for swapping news and laying contacts but for visiting gambling houses, cinemas, stores, book shops, legal centres, accountants' offices, barber shops, travel agencies, Chinese clinics, taxi firms, and so forth. Visitors could do their banking at a nearby branch of the Bank of China or the Hong Kong and Shanghai Banking Corporation. Chinese from all over Britain drove long distances to spend their free time in Chinatown – some even crossed the Channel.[145] Gerrard Street was at the top of the British hierarchy of Chinese places, a status signalled by its name, *wohng sing* 皇城 ('imperial city').[146]

In the 1980s and 1990s, Gerrard Street lost some of its allure in the provinces and on the mainland, as potential visitors were drawn towards the new or renovated Chinatowns in Paris, Amsterdam, Manchester, Liverpool, and Florence and to Chinese streets in other parts of London like Bayswater, Victoria, and Hendon, which had clusters of high-class Chinese restaurants.[147]

Throughout, Gerrard Street remained a service centre rather than a place of Chinese residence. At most, it was an 'imaginary ghetto' – a public space where Chinese identity could be celebrated on special occasions, a place of fanciful belonging in which to renew one's sense of community and culture or to voice poltical sentiments (for example, after the Beijing massacre of 4 June 1989).[148]

In the naïve and romantic view, Chinatowns are autonomous worlds sealed against interlopers by a carapace of race and culture. In reality, Chinatowns everywhere are arenas in which shifting alliances of land speculators, urban planners, city governments, neighbourhood committees, ethnic activists, Chinatown business leaders, and Chinatown politicians lock horns over competing interests. The British Chinatowns are more vulnerable than many to outside pressures, for they moved from their original locations in the mid-twentieth century and lack the organic quality of the older Chinatowns of Southeast Asia and North America, where communities draw strength from extensive property ownership and roots that stretch over generations.

The worldwide struggle to defend Chinatown against the developers' bulldozers has helped to revive a sense of Chinese community and identity in many places. In Soho, a similar battle was fought and won in the early 1970s, when ethnic-Chinese business leaders defeated a City of Westminster proposal to redevelop Chinatown and managed to get it declared a preservation area.[149] However, Chinatown lacks a solid base in property and its future is largely in the hands of the non-Chinese investors who own the leaseholds on Gerrard Street and the surrounding area. The idea that it is self-directing does not bear scrutiny. Actually, it is 'shaped, owned and controlled in a complex interaction between Chinese entrepreneurs, non-Chinese investors and city councils, which through various forms of bargaining and contracts balance their different interests and power'.[150]

The main landowner in London's Chinatown is the non-Chinese Shaftesbury plc. In 2001, this company owned nearly 80 properties in Chinatown, up from just over a dozen at the time of its founding, and was worth more than ten times its initial value of £26.4 million, in 1987. The original development of Chinatown was essentially a joint venture by Chinese interests and Westminster City Council. Only later did the company recognise Chinatown as a flagship project with a special image that the company was keen to develop.

Chinatown leaders criticise the landlords' greed and point out that the area, now counted among London's top ten tourist attractions, owes its success to initiatives by Chinese entrepreneurs rather than by the property people.[151] However, although the interests of landlords and entrepreneurs conflict, the latter have found it hard to present a united front. Instead, they wheel and deal at each other's expense, for example, when rents come up for renegotiation.[152] Partly as a result of this disunity, Chinatown rents sky-rocketed by up to 300 per cent in the 1990s. In 2004, the area again came under threat when a property magnate announced plans to redevelop it and served tenants with notices to quit, a project that civil-rights activists in Chinatown predicted would lead to disaster.[153] In 2005, the developer Rosewheel said it wanted to 'regenerate' part of the area with 'a correct mix of east and west' businesses and reportedly aimed to raise rents from £1.6 million to £4.5 million.[154]

The regeneration of Liverpool's Chinatown, too, was engineered by an alliance of interests spearheaded by city planners and related agencies and local Chinese entrepreneurs and associations. The Liverpool Chamber of Commerce's twinning with its Shanghai counterpart in 1993 paved the way for a municipal twinning in 1999, which put the spotlight on the Chinese community. The City Council's decision to regenerate and redevelop the city centre with European Union funding and to promote tourism and inward investment in the Rope Walks area (which includes Chinatown) helped to publicise the community and led to the refurbishment of Chinese streets along 'Chinese' lines.[155]

In 2004, the London mayor Ken Livingstone announced similar plans to construct a second London Chinatown in the area to the north of the capital's Billingsgate fish market. Chinatown representatives welcomed the proposal, as a way of creating basic services and a social infrastructure and pool of housing of the sort lacking in the Soho Chinatown. Livingstone's strategy is an even more ambitious version of Liverpool's twinning tactic. 'We want to tap into the Chinese economy...', he explained. 'We want London to be the Chinese economy's gateway into Europe'.[156]

Chinatown worldwide has always been a site of cultural construction by outsiders, a screen upon which non-Chinese project their Oriental fantasies. On the screen, Chinatown enacts itself as a 'living tableau of queerness'.[157] In the early twentieth century, the narrative rules that governed Chinatown's representation by the British derived from popular books and films, which promoted the stereotype of a community of villains living in perpetual darkness.[158] This discursive equation of Chineseness and criminality, perpetuated by the yellow press, was translated at street level into the reality of racist controls and sinophobic outbursts.

In more recent times, Chinatown's cultural construction has taken other forms, due to the new complicity in it of business interests hoping to cash in on the commercial potential of the Chinatown 'mystique'. Chinese in Manchester and Liverpool (using local authority money, for the most part) vied to build Britain's widest *pailou* 牌楼 (archway) and to decorate their streets with 'scenic beauties' of the sort that adorn London's Chinatown: the 'wayside pavilion' (donated by the Chinatown Chinese Association 伦敦华埠街坊会), the stone lions at the Macclesfield Entrance (donated by the Chinese Embassy), the red-gold bollards, the 'Oriental' lamp posts, and the 'Chinese' phone boxes. The purpose, according to one British Chinese leader, was to 'give Chinatown an even more Chinese flavour' so that it appeared 'more ancient'.[159] According to David Parker 蒋大卫, a British scholar of Chinese descent, the aim is to show that the Chinese 'are somehow unknowable' and to make this mystery 'known and available' at a price, a process he calls commodification.[160]

In other areas, Chinatowns have sprung up in places with no strong Chinese connection. Birmingham's Arcadian Centre, built by Wing Yip and marketed as a 'mini-Chinatown', is one example. Designed to flaunt Chinese 'tradition', it also makes commercial sense, by putting Chinese business in the spotlight, and is a property investment useful (among other things) as collateral for securing bank loans.[161] Another example is the Chinatown commercial centre built on a seven-acre site in London's docklands in the late 1980s, at a cost of £80 million.[162]

In some places, Chinese residents create local Chinatowns that serve no other purpose (initially at least) than the Chinese population's own social and recreational needs. Such Chinatowns evolve as central places in regional market areas, providing goods and services to Chinese consumers within range. An example is Leeds, whose catchment area in the early 1970s covered much of Yorkshire and north Lincolnshire, except where consumers found it easier to use the adjacent Chinatowns in Manchester and Sheffield.[163]

Local authorities use the new Chinatowns to promote tourism and to strengthen civic and economic ties with China. In Liverpool and Manchester, the redevelopment of Chinatown was part of a broader scheme to regenerate inner-city areas that had fallen derelict in the postwar years and to attract investment.[164] The Chinatown elite can only benefit: the market for its products widens, its ties to local political and business leaders grow, and it edges closer to social acceptance after generations of racist disparagement. The Duke of Gloucester's presence at the opening of the pedestrianised Gerrard Street in 1985 signalled royal approval for the makeover. 'Not only did the official opening of Chinatown give us recognition and public attention', said a leader of the Chinatown Chinese Association, 'but we have become a tourist mecca. Thousands of people come here, even Chinese tourists! Decorating our streets has given real character to this area and stamped it with our distinctive character. This has been good for our businesses'.[165]

Hu Zhiqiang 胡志强 playfully traced Gerrard Street's climb up the market hierarchy by listing its supposed Cantonese names, variants on a Chinese phonetic rendering (done here in Mandarin) of the word Gerrard. In the early days, when Chinatown was 'cold, cheerless, out-of-the-way, garbage-strewn, and chaotic', it was called 'sow street' (*zhuna jie* 猪嫲街). Later, when the restaurant trade picked up, it was known as 'drunken-and-peppery street' (*zuila jie* 醉辣街). Finally, after businesses other than catering began to open, producing the effect of a full-blown Chinatown, it became 'the street of nobility and emolument' (*juelu jie* 爵禄街).[166]

That 'localisation' and 'commodification' arrived hand in hand is no accident.[167] As the real community faded into its surroundings, a theme-park Chinatown arose to replace it. The reinvention of Chinatown as an ethnic symbol and tourist attraction and its decking out by town planners and commercial consortia with exotica is an old idea whose day has come.[168] In 1944, a young Chinese architect 'envisaged a Chinatown for Liverpool which would be not merely a showplace but would give a true interpretation of Chinese life' to combat its 'insulting' Hollywood version.[169] (The plan, costed at £500,000, was not realised.)

Such schemes anticipate the end of Chinese identity as routine living and its postmodernist rejiggering as 'heritage'. Yet it would be wrong to jump to conclusions, for human spirit is resilient. While some Chinese denounced the new Chinatown as a 'picture-postcard, souvenir culture' that makes Chinese youth look like 'curious, exotic aliens' on a set built for a Peter Sellars film,[170] others praised it as a meeting place for Chinese, 'like English people have got everywhere'.[171] This comment reminds us that the role of such developments in identity formation cannot be reduced to their intended uses.

Chinese schools

Reputedly the first Chinese school outside China was the Mingcheng Academy 巴城明诚书院, founded in Batavia in the Netherlands East Indies in 1690.[172] In the late nineteenth and early twentieth centuries, the Qing court actively promoted Chinese education in Southeast Asia, North America, Japan, and elsewhere as part of a desperate attempt to stave off its own demise by reforming itself and rallying new forces behind patriotic goals. When the Qing fell in 1911, there were more than 100 Chinese schools outside China, and by 1937 there were around 2000.[173] However, the schools movement declined after 1945, as more and more ethnic Chinese renounced Chinese nationality and some post-colonial regimes in Southeast Asia placed restrictions on Chinese schools and even banned them. Since the 1980s, China's opening to the world, its booming economy, and the resumption of large-scale Chinese emigration has led to an international reflowering of Chinese education. There are now several thousand Chinese schools – the most ever – outside China, a vindication of their description as a pillar of overseas and ethnic-Chinese society.

The role of Chinese schools differs from place to place and has changed greatly over time. In the nineteenth century, an education in Chinese writing and the appropriate dialect was considered indispensable in parts of Southeast Asia and elsewhere for maintaining China-dependent businesses. In the first three to four decades of the twentieth century, when Chinese sojourners abroad were a mainstay of the Republic, schools set up with the help of emissaries from China strengthened the nationalist identification of the sojourners' offspring and even led to the partial 'resinification' of some ethnic Chinese. These trends were especially marked after 1927, when Nanjing's Overseas Chinese Affairs Commission (founded in 1926) made preparing young Chinese abroad to serve the new China a top priority. Chinese education expanded not just for patriotic reasons but because jobs outside the ethnic enclave were hard to get in many countries, so knowing Chinese could be a ticket to employment. In the postwar years, Chiang Kai-shek's expulsion from the mainland and Beijing's recommendation that Chinese overseas adopt the host country's nationality, intermarry with local people, and refrain from sending their children to school in China led to 'the transformation of overseas-Chinese education into Chinese-language education'[174] and the severing of its China link. In the 1950s, Chinese schools in the English-speaking world started to decline. The hard times lasted until the 1980s and 1990s, when local-born Chinese in North America, Australia, and parts of Europe who spoke little or no Chinese were exposed to a new wave of immigrants from China, Hong Kong, Taiwan, and Southeast Asia. Many of the newcomers were highly educated and culturally self-confident. They had a big impact on some local-born, who began rethinking their attitudes and values. This process, together with the new ideology of multiculturalism and China's now open door, created an interest in Chinese language and culture among ethnic Chinese for whom it was in many ways foreign.[175]

In Britain and Europe, Chinese settlement is relatively sparse and recent. Until the 1960s and the 1970s, there were few children and no substantial class of educated Chinese to provide teachers. Hardly any early immigrants depended on the China trade and their identification with the ancestral homeland yielded just two or three small schools. Britain's own education system, in any case, was compulsory, reliable, and free. Unlike in parts of Southeast Asia, where Chinese schools funded and managed by the community have striven to provide an entire primary and in some cases secondary education through the medium of Chinese, Chinese schools in Britain supplement the state system and teach little more than basic Chinese language and culture. They aim to pass on the rudiments of a Chinese heritage and ethical orientation to close the gap that has opened up between parents and children by socialising the children in Chinese values. In that sense, they are like the Chinese schools in North America and Australia and unlike those in (say) Malaysia. However, Britain's Chinese population boomed 20 years ahead of North America and Australia, where it did not take off until the 1980s, so Britain's schools also boomed earlier.[176]

Schools and voluntary associations are inextricably intertwined in Chinese communities overseas. Association is a mechanism to protect Chinese interests and identity; education, the means by which Chinese cultural identity is transmitted. Associations not only promote education but are, in some cases, formed to set up Chinese-language schools. Organisations that play a role in providing education include clan associations, political groups, churches, Chinese students' unions, and community centres.

Chinese-language education for Chinese children in Britain dates back at least to 1914, when the Chinese Students' Christian Union started organising classes in Chinatown. The classes covered English, Chinese, hygiene, and politics, including subjects such as 'the government of China and the meaning of the war' and criticism of the 'worldwide discrimination' against Chinese people.[177] In 1920, a second school was founded in Limehouse, with the support of the Chinese Consul and three Chinatown worthies and the 'practical aid of learned graduates, who can teach their own tongue as it is spoken by the more educated classes, and of ladies and gentlemen who have lived in China to give instruction in English'. Forty Anglo-Chinese children and 50 Chinese adults enrolled.[178]

These two schools differed in character from those in the 1960s, and also from each other. Both were founded by the educated elite intervening from on high, but each had a different political agenda. The 1914 school was inspired by the radical ideals of young Chinese students acting out their self-appointed role as political educators. The 1920 school was conservative in orientation, as the role played in it by the Consul (an appointee of the corrupt warlord regime in Beijing) shows. The two schools represented in miniature the battle for influence between left and right that raged in Chinese schools across the world in the first half of the twentieth century.

In 1928, the Chung Hwa School 伦敦中文学校, Britain's best-known early Chinese-language school, was set up above a restaurant in Penny-fields by Irene Ho 何艾伦, with a donation of £500 from Sir Robert Ho Tung 何东爵士, a wealthy benefactor and the founder's father. The school finally got going in 1933, and was opened on new premises by the Chinese Minister to the Court of St James, Quo Tai-chi 郭泰祺, in 1935.[179] Despite its tiny enrolment, of just 20 children, a teacher was specially recruited from China. From time to time, the Chinese Students' Union lent practical support.

Attempts to restart Chinese schools after the war failed, mainly because Chinatown had by then partly disintegrated.[180]A school set up in Chinatown in Liverpool closed for lack of support, partly because it taught Mandarin in a community where Cantonese or other Chinese languages were the norm.[181] Not until more than 20 years later did the tradition of Chinese schooling resume.

Like the two earlier schools, Chung Hwa illustrated themes of ethnic-Chinese schooling in many places. A charitable venture, it was consolidated by Nanjing's readiness to provide resources. It was then caught in a Lilliputian version of the battle for influence between Nationalists and communists that raged in ethnic-Chinese schools across the world in the first half of the twentieth century. Just before the war, its teacher was accused of communist sympathies and sent home, whereupon the school closed.[182] China then entered a crisis whose resolution in 1949 in favour of the communists left many Chinese in Britain stranded. The educational ideal persisted throughout the dark years of the war. The plan for a new Liverpool Chinatown put forward by a young Chinese architect in 1944 proposed not only a Chinese garden, a pagoda, restaurants, a museum, and a cinema but a school (with others to follow in London, Cardiff, and New York).[183]

In the 1960s, in the early days of Chinese family reunion, the movement to set up classes revived in London and Liverpool, where Chinese associations and churches founded schools. These schools were usually quite primitive, unless they were fortunate enough to get rich backing. Some occupied just one room of a damp cellar. However, a handful of the wealthiest schools had up to 20 classrooms.[184] Not all the early classes were successful. One set up by an organisation called the Overseas Chinese Service in 1963 enrolled just half a dozen pupils. English classes organised for restaurant staff in the 1960s and the 1970s also failed, because the workers were tired by overwork and the classes were in English.[185]

Chinese-language education did not become a major issue in Britain until the 1970s, when a successor generation appeared and the need for schooling became urgent. Some classes were held in state schools made available at no cost after the end of the school day, others in church halls and private houses.[186] The 1980s was a decade of dramatic growth. By 1984, there were 83 classes with nearly 9000 pupils – nearly one in three of Britain's school-age Chinese children.[187]

Two things were important in the schools boom. One was the failure of local education authorities to provide mother-tongue classes for Chinese in state schools. Chinese have fared worse in this regard than speakers of other languages, mainly because of their extreme dispersal, the divisions caused by 'dialects', and parents' failure to campaign. The other was the abandonment after the 1960s of 'granny socialisation' – the caterers' habit of leaving children in the care of paternal grandmothers in Hong Kong until adolescence, to ensure language retention and free both parents to work round the clock in Britain. This custom can be understood as a poor person's variant of the early habit of wealthy Chinese in Southeast Asia of sending their children to private schools in China or Hong Kong, where they received a 'native education' and a grounding in English.[188] The grandparents' later emigration to Britain and the parents' realisation of the harm done by family separation eventually put an end to this practice, for which the Chinese schools became a substitute.[189]

In the early years, Chinese schools suffered from a shortage of qualified teachers, equipment, and resources. This problem was partly solved by employing Chinese students enrolled at British universities. But although dedicated and enthusiastic, most lacked experience of teaching and few stayed for more than a year or two.

Originally, the schools were financed by benefactors or voluntary associations. In the early 1980s, however, the establishment of CCCs freed many schools from dependence on local authorities for premises. This eased the funding problem.

The availability of local authority support in the form of Urban Aid grants spurred on the ethnic-schools movement, although the resources on offer were limited and competition was fierce. The Inner London Education Authority (ILEA) helped in the 1980s by training minority-ethnic teachers, including around 15 Chinese, but the team disbanded in 1989 when the ILEA was closed down. Chinese-language classes featured centrally in Chinese evidence to the 1985 parliamentary inquiry on the Chinese community. Its report recommended help for Chinese teaching, but this recommendation was not taken up in the 1990 White Paper on education.

Chinese-language classes in Britain continue to cast about for an appropriate model. The best-known school is that run by the Chinese Chamber of Commerce in Frith Street in Soho. Set up in 1968 with just 20 pupils, divided into children and adults, in 1987 it developed a new teaching structure consisting of an infants' class, a primary class, and a middle-school class, while expanding its enrolment to nearly 1200. It runs a well-equipped library. Qualified teachers give classes from five to seven on weekday evenings and all day at weekends. It is better off than most Chinese schools. At one point, it received a weekly subsidy from the HKGO and donations from benefactors in Britain, mainland Europe, and Hong Kong, while also charging tuition fees. It is the largest Chinese school in Europe, with 1600 pupils in 1995. Other schools strive to follow its example, but most lack the necessary funds and quite a few employ unqualified teachers.

The administration of Chinese schools was regularised in the 1980s. In the early years, teachers acted as unpaid volunteers and had to meet their own travel expenses. In the 1980s and the 1990s, however, most such costs were reimbursed from parental contributions. Some teachers were paid, usually from funds provided by local authorities.

The great majority of schools teach Cantonese and unsimplified characters of the sort used in Hong Kong and Taiwan, although a handful teach Mandarin and mainland-style simplified characters. The teaching materials originate in Hong Kong, Taiwan, China, Singapore, or Malaysia. In the 1990s, more and more schools started producing their own teaching materials.

In the early 1970s, the HKGO began providing free textbooks. Teachers complained that the books, designed for use in Hong Kong (usually by younger children), were inappropriate, but used them for want of better. In 1994, the HKGO stopped providing help and in 1995 its education department was wound up, in preparation for Hong Kong's retrocession to China in 1997.[190]

Schools and classes vary greatly in size, from a dozen to more than one thousand pupils. Some open for just an hour a week, others for longer. Their terms and school years coincide with those of the state schools. Most pupils are 5–14, though some are as young as three and as old as 18.[191] Their main purpose is to teach Chinese, but the curriculum can also include general knowledge, art, calligraphy, music, and dancing.[192] In language teaching, the emphasis is often on oracy rather than literacy.[193]

In 1980, a group of young Taiwanese professionals set up a Mandarin school in London, with teaching materials provided by Taibei's Overseas Chinese Affairs Commission 中华民国侨务委员会. The school attracted pupils from the Singaporean and Malaysian Chinese communities, as well as some from Hong Kong.[194] In the 1970s and 1980s, ethnic-Chinese refugees from Indochina set up a dozen or so schools in parts of London and Birmingham to teach Mandarin.[195]

Towards the end of the twentieth century, Chinese education throughout the United Kingdom was flourishing as never before. In the mid-1980s, one in three Chinese children was thought to attend a class, on average for 5.4 years. Probably a similar proportion attended in the

Table 4.1 Chinese schools and pupils, selected European countries

	Number of schools/ classes	Number of pupils
United Kingdom	160	15,000
France	20	1,500
Netherlands	40	3,000
Germany	20	1,000

Source: Li Minghuan 1998, p. 37*.
* The relevant entries in Jiaoyu keji suggest that Li Minghuan's figures for France may be underestimates.

1990s.[196] In the late 1980s and the early 1990s, there were between 75 and 100 Chinese schools, with 7000–10,000 pupils.[197] Towards the end of the decade, there were around 160 classes and 15,000 pupils. (These figures fluctuate, as classes shut or split in two.)[198] (See Table 4.1.) Such is parents' enthusiasm for Chinese education that nearly half are prepared to spend at least an hour in getting their children to the nearest class. Some claimed in the 1980s to drive up to 100 miles to do so.[199]

Within Europe, the United Kingdom has more Chinese classes and pupils than any other country, absolutely and probably proportionately. (See Table 4.1). In the late 1980s, there were only a dozen or so after-school Chinese classes in France with an enrolment of nearly 1000 pupils (and more than 30 Chinese classes run during the summer holidays), far fewer than in Britain.[200]

There are several possible explanations for this difference. First, the Chinese community in Britain is older than in France (although close to it in size) and already well along the road from Chinese to English, so Chinese parents react by promoting language classes. This moment of transition has not yet been reached in France. Second, the British Chinese population is less compact than the French, whose pattern of residence corresponds more to that of the traditional Chinatown, a factor that favours language retention and lessens the need for classes. Third, there are differences in political culture between Britain and France that affect minority-ethnic social organisation. (We have already mentioned the French law restricting foreigners' right to associate, not revoked until 1981.[201]) The Chinese community in the Netherlands, on the other hand, whose schools movement is second only to the United Kingdom's in proportionate size, is more like the UK Chinese community in terms of its dispersed settlement and the political culture of its host society, which promotes self-help through association.

The HKGO played a big role in getting the schools movement on its feet and in creating a schools culture that survived the HKGO's own demise. At one point, the overwhelming majority of Chinese classes were HKGO-supported (56 out of 60 in 1982, 83 out of 84 in 1984). The HKGO helped export the schools movement to Ireland and mainland Europe. In the 1980s, it oversaw three schools in the Netherlands with 591 pupils, one in Denmark with 125, and one in Dublin with 17.[202] The HKGO had little lasting impact outside Britain, but its intervention in the Netherlands may help to explain the vitality of the Dutch Chinese-schools movement. (The ties between the Chinese communities in Britain and the Netherlands are not restricted to the activities of the HKGO but extend to kinship and business.)

Another reason why France's schools are less effective lies in the nature of its Chinese population, which is more mixed than in other European countries. In Britain, teaching is in Cantonese or Mandarin, depending on parental wishes. In France, where the range of Chinese languages is greater, Mandarin is adopted as the lingua franca through which to teach Chinese. However, its use remains largely restricted to the classroom.[203]

In recent years, more and more Chinese overseas have come to see Mandarin, China's national language, as more important and prestigious than Cantonese, as a result of China's rise in world standing and Hong Kong's retrocession. In mainland Europe, the demand for Chinese-language classes has risen steeply among new Chinese migrants, for whom Mandarin is usually the natural choice as a lingua franca alongside their provincial and regional dialects and local European languages. In the European context, English is less useful as a lingua franca among Chinese than in the United States, so Mandarin and Cantonese gain added currency. The change in attitude to Mandarin has also begun to affect Britain, both because of changed perceptions of China's status and changes in the provenance of Chinese immigration to Britain.[204]

Newspapers and the media

To modify Benedict Anderson's formulation, newspapers and the broadcasting media enable the community to imagine at the local, diasporic, and transnational level the 'deep horizontal comradeship' at the heart of ethnic identity.[205] Between 1815, when a Chinese newspaper is said to have appeared for the first time outside China (in Malacca), and 1996, at least 4000 Chinese periodicals were published in Chinese or in Chinese and other languages in 52 countries and territories, alongside at least another 200 published by Chinese in languages other than Chinese. The press was joined by radio in the 1930s, TV in the 1960s, and electronic media in the 1990s.[206]

Chinese newspapers in migrant and ethnic communities specialise in many subjects but fall into two basic types, those that preserve a transnational orientation (to the homeland, the diaspora, or both) and those that articulate a localised identity. The transnational press, whether in China or abroad, keeps would-be emigrants abreast of dangers and opportunities in potential destinations, keeps Chinese already abroad informed about the homeland, and keeps expatriates in touch with home by way of advertisements, columns, and news. Those – most typically in Southeast Asia and North America – serving a localised community document Chinatown's changing attitudes, mirror its debates about change and preservation, and help construct its identities.[207] This process reflects the broader evolution from overseas Chinese to ethnic Chinese. The break is rarely sudden and is often accomplished within the same covers, under the same title.[208]

The Chinese media in Britain differ in several respects from those in places of extensive or long-standing Chinese immigration. The main difference is in the size of the readership. For a long time, Britain's Chinese population was too small and poorly educated to support a voluminous press. Many laundrymen and caterers were semiliterate or illiterate. The professionals and intellectuals were too few to provide a big market.

In these respects, the Chinese community in Britain is outshone by that in France, with its bigger, more socially engaged intelligentsia. The difference is reflected in the greater number of Chinese-language periodicals recorded in France over the years: 57 compared with 34 in Britain.[209]

Chinese in Britain began to integrate and acculturate more quickly than in regions of large-scale immigration, so fewer read Chinese periodicals. Chinese communities in Southeast Asia and North America are far larger and more socially diverse than in Europe and tended in the past to form ghettos. (The Chinese in France are also more likely than in Britain to live in Chinese neighbourhoods.) Ghettos preserve language and throw up issues that need discussing at ethnic forums. British-style dispersal, on the other hand, accelerates language loss, as does subjection to an English-language formal education.

The first mention of a Chinese newspaper in Britain was in 1868, when Zhang Deyi, a student of Beijing's Interpreters College 同文馆, arrived in London with the Burlingame Mission. Zhang came across a Chinese newspaper called *Flying Dragon* 飞龙报, which he described as 'well printed but poorly written'.[210] Founded in San Francisco in 1867, *Flying Dragon* appeared mainly in English. Only parts of the title page and some business advertisements and recruitment notices were in Chinese. Aimed at promoting trade between the United States and East Asia, it published market and financial intelligence.[211] That it reached London suggests Britain's tiny group of Chinese traders maintained transatlantic ties.

Among Chinese periodicals published in Britain that have been preserved, probably the earliest is *Shangqun* 尚群 (For the masses), published by students in London in 1916. Its title suggests a radical standpoint.[212] In 1920, Chinatown was kept informed by a newspaper in the form of 'a written bill, stuck up on the street walls', about which we know only that it existed.[213] In 1927, students in London began publishing a literary biannual, *The Journal of the Chinese Students' Union in Great Britain* 留英学报, among whose editors were Zhu Guangqian 朱光潜 (1897–1986) and Lao She 老舍 (1899–1966).[214] In the early 1930s, the pro-communist *Jiefang* 解放 (Liberation) appeared in London, with articles criticising the Nanjing Government and items about Chinese students in the United Kingdom.[215] All these publications were transnational: they served sojourners and focused on homeland issues.

In the Second World War, Chinese in Liverpool launched *Chung Hwa Chou Pao* 中华周报 (*China News Weekly*),[216] another transnational publication that survived until 1949 and initially sold 2000 copies, including 500 in Chongqing (China's wartime capital), 400 in the United States, 1000 on Merseyside, and 400 in the rest of the United Kingdom.[217] Also during the war, the radical patriot Yang Xianyi 杨宪益 published resistance journals.[218]

After the war, several communist publications appeared. *Jiefang* continued to be published. In London, *Minzhu zhenxian* 民主阵线 (Democratic front) appeared from 1944 to 1949, in 19 issues, and *Jianguo zhoukan* 建国周刊 (National reconstruction weekly) was founded in Liverpool in 1946, with a focus on Chinese politics and trade unions. *Zhongguo xinwen* 中国新闻 (Chinese news, 1958) carried mainland news. *Ziyou Zhongguo xinwen* 自由中国新闻 (Free China news), a weekly, focused on Hong Kong and Taiwan.[219] All these publications served transnational agendas.

In the 1960s, at the beginning of the postwar Chinese influx, the United Kingdom saw an undeclared press war between the communists, organised by the Chinese Embassy, and Hong Kong-based newspapers like *Wah Kiu Yat Po* 华侨日报 (Overseas Chinese daily) and *Sing Tao Jih Pao* 星岛日报 (*Sing Tao daily*), each of which devoted a page to news about the New Territories and its overseas workers in the United Kingdom. *Wah Kiu Yat Po* also published workers' letters to their families back home.[220]

In the 1970s and the 1980s, Chinese-language dailies established outlets and editorial offices in London to cater to Britain's (and mainland Europe's) Chinese. The first to publish in London was *Sing Tao Jih Pao*, which today outsells the United Kingdom's other Chinese newspapers. In the early 1960s, *Sing Tao* had given as its goal the 'internationalisation of the Chinese-language press'. In the course of establishing a global Chinese publishing empire, it began printing in London in 1975 and founded a European edition in 1981. It carries news about China, the world, and the Chinese in Europe. *Sing Tao's* European edition is one of a number of regional editions. Its reporting has a European slant, including pages tailor-made for Chinese in different European countries and columns by their leaders. It claims sales of 50,000, from Moscow to French Polynesia. In 1981, the leftwing Hong Kong-based *Wen Wei Po* 文汇报 began publishing a European edition in London, with outlets in several European countries. In 1995, it had a circulation of around a 1000, chiefly in the United Kingdom. In 1985, *People's Daily* 人民日报 also started an overseas edition, distributed in Europe and throughout the world.[221]

Two rival dailies published in France but sold in the United Kingdom and throughout Europe are the pro-Taiwan *Europe-journal* 欧洲日报 (European Daily), founded in 1982 as a branch of Taibei's *Lianhe bao* 联合报, and the pro-Beijing *Nouvelles d'Europe* 欧洲时报 (European Times), founded in 1983 by a Cambodian Chinese but taken over by a Beijing-financed company in 1984. Both carry news about France, Europe, and the world.[222]

Britain's other significant Chinese periodicals have been published by the Hong Kong Government Office (*Hong Kong News Digest*), the Chinese Embassy, or pro-Taibei bodies such as the Free China Centre. Their focus is in part transnational.[223] Also transnational in its intent is the London-based bimonthly *Worldwide Chinese* 天下华人, whose mission is to 'unite ethnic Chinese worldwide, promote the Chinese cultural tradition, and foster mutual exchange and understanding between Chinese people and Western society'. Its circulation (of 1000) is confined mainly to Britain, but its purview is global (though its actual impact is limited).[224]

The main exception to this transnational focus is *Siyu* 丝语 (Threads of speech), a free bilingual monthly published from 1984 to 1996 in

Manchester by Simon Jones. Financed by adverts and subsidies, in its heyday *Siyu* had a print-run of 30,000. It carried information about welfare services, business, and Chinese associations. At one point, it received an official subsidy. It is perhaps the nearest British Chinese publishing has come to a nationwide periodical devoted to local issues.[225] For several years, the bilingual *Brushstrokes* appeared in Liverpool, initially as an occasional publication of the City Council's Writing Liaison Office serving local Chinese. It tried to be a forum for Chinese everywhere 'to discuss and reflect on their life experience'. Its print-run was 400, nearly all of which were distributed free. Despite targeting younger British Chinese, it failed to take off. Its poor circulation was an indication of the limited relevance of the community-based press to young Chinese.

The readers of Britain's Chinese press come from all walks, but educated professionals tend to read British newspapers. Most Chinese newspapers are sold from shops rather than by postal subscription and tend not to circulate outside the minority who live within easy reach of city centres. They are also unread by all but a few younger adults. Table 4.2 shows the rapid decline through the age-bands in Chinese newspaper reading.

Chinese-language broadcasting started in Britain in 1983, when Radio Merseyside put out a weekly news broadcast and Radio Manchester produced a monthly half-hour programme that was 40 per cent Chinese and 60 per cent English.[226] In 1990, the BBC began broadcasting its London Spectrum Radio Service, for one hour five days a week, in Cantonese. In the early 1990s, Chinese radio was eclipsed by the advent of satellite and cable TV – Chinese News and Entertainment 欧洲东方中文电视 (CNE), Europe's first Chinese satellite station, in 1993; and the Chinese Channel 无线卫星台, founded by the Shaw Media, in 1994. In 1995, CNE broadcast four hours a day, 60 per cent in Cantonese, 30 per cent in Mandarin, and 10 per cent in English. It

Table 4.2   Chinese use of English and Chinese media

Age group	16–29	30–49	50–74	All
Chinese newspapers	12	23	37	22
English newspapers	46	42	26	40
No newspaper	43	35	37	38
Chinese TV	52	44	53	48
Chinese radio				23

Source: Pitson 1999a, pp. 3–4 and 22.

imports most of its programmes from Hong Kong and China, supplemented by a few items of British Chinese news. The Chinese Channel broadcast 12 hours a day in 1996, also mainly in Cantonese.[227]

Table 4.2 illustrates the popularity of Chinese TV throughout the age groups. In the 1970s and the early 1980s, Chinese films were the main family entertainment. Late-night screenings took place most weekends, initially in restaurants and then in high-street cinemas. By the late 1980s, Cantonese videos imported from Hong Kong had taken over. As David Parker has shown, Hong Kong popular culture became a part of Chinese family life in Britain and videos and cassettes played a crucial role in the identity formation of young Chinese. Although less than one in five of Parker's informants could read and write much Chinese and most found spoken Cantonese difficult, 60 per cent of families watched videos at least once a week.[228]

The arrival of Chinese TV in Britain in 1993 (20 years after the United States[229]) helped arrest the decline of Chinese, promoted Cantonese at the expense of other dialects, and modified Chinese identities, a subject we return to in a later chapter. Even so, Chinese TV is not as popular or influential among young viewers as British TV – a further indication of the limited importance of Chinese media to young British Chinese.

The emergence of the Internet in the 1990s changed the nature of communication and community. Ethnic Chinese everywhere are increasingly 'wired'. The idea of the 'virtual community' is popular, but online communities have been described as 'nonetheless real'. Despite grand claims about a new democratic era and cyber-citizenship, however, life online is best enjoyed by the few in minority-ethnic communities. Some causes of exclusion – the cost of going online, semiotic illiteracy, the hierarchical ordering of cyberspace by netiquette, and the 'wizards' who hold programming power – are universal. Others are peculiar to the Chinese, whose immigrant community is more likely to be polarised into the wired and the great unwired by the primacy of English in cyberspace.[230] So changes in the ways in which Chinese inform and amuse themselves are not necessarily for the better, from the point of view of community solidarity. However, these assertions can only be tentative and provisional or may already be outdated.

Some cultural theorists criticise diasporic Chinese cybercommunities for constructing a reified identity out of 'national imaginings' hinged on an essentialised China. In their view, the 'Chinese digital diaspora' risks submerging the real differences between and within communities in an imagined global community. However, not all Chinese websites in Britain and elsewhere fall foul of resurgent nationalism. As Loong Wong points out, websites like dimsum.org.uk act to 'draw together very specific notions of community' whose interests they defend, rather than as transmission belts for a 'Chinese nation' project.[231]

What does this sketch of the Chinese media in Britain tell us about Chinese community? Community hinges on communication, and different forms of communication shape communities differently. In the early twentieth century, residents of the Chinaports met face to face in clubs and cafes. The literate frequented the club reading rooms, passing on what they read to their illiterate comrades. Almost all their reading was imported from China. In the postwar years, when the community broadened and dispersed, people bought their own newspapers and read them in their homes. Technological change in the media industry has also weakened physical interaction. The late-night film clubs of the 1960s closed down in the 1980s when videos took over. In the 1990s, when Chinese TV arrived, consumers no longer depended on the video outlets run by the Hong Kong TV stations in British cities – one less reason to visit Chinatown.

Unlike in Southeast Asia, North America, and Australia, Britain's 'local' Chinese newspapers are editions of parent newspapers in Hong Kong or China. They feature British and European news alongside articles reprinted from their parent editions. Although they do report briefly on the community in Britain, they do not contribute systematically (like the Chinese press elsewhere) to constructing local identities.

In the late twentieth century, the delivery of public and commercial TV stations by satellite made country-of-origin programmes available to diasporic communities. The effect of this development on the relationship of immigrant and ethnic minorities to the majority group is the subject of debate in migration studies. In what ways does the impact of diasporic TV on older generations of immigrants differ from that on younger generations? How does it affect members of ethnic minorities born in the 'host' country? Does it create new forms of transnational identity within the diaspora, by constructing a common frame of experience at a deterritorialised level? To what extent do 'local places and people' temper the transnational media's global dynamic? Are the different needs and interests of groups in different settings, and of the 'homeland' and the diasporic audience, acknowledged and respected? What role do diasporic media play in migrants' and ethnic minorities' negotiation of their social relations and of everyday life in the host society?[232]

The same questions apply to the newly globalised Chinese TV channels. These channels provide a mixture of Hong Kong pop and soap to British Chinese audiences. Nearly all the programmes are imported from abroad and relate to settings that are in reality foreign. They usually lack emotional depth and intellectual engagement. Can a diet of the slick, the bland, the trite, the shallow, and the exotic strengthen community cohesion and identity? Some Chinese criticise the channels' impact as 'schizophrenic'. For programmes more relevant to their lives, it would seem that young Chinese turn to British TV.

Few publications concentrate on Chinese community issues in a British context. Although Chinese newspapers are recognised as an important medium, there are no associations dedicated to supporting them. Two sets of readers coexist: one served by a Chinese press that deals only marginally with European Chinese concerns, and another whose reading habits are practically indistinguishable from other people's in Britain. Language loss partly explains why Britain's Chinese press has skipped the stage of localisation. But the dearth of locally focused publications results not merely from linguistic changes. In other parts of the world, such writing happens in languages other than Chinese. In Britain, community publications do appear in English, especially on the Internet, but to a far lesser extent than in countries where Chinese identity is more robust.

Conclusions

This chapter uses the pillars metaphor as a framework to analyse ethnic-Chinese society in Britain. It looks at ways in which the associations, supplementary schools, media, and churches that serve the community have changed over time and at their correspondences to and departures from the conventional norm of such institutions.

The Chinese community in Britain has always been less well organised than communities in the world's main places of Chinese immigration. The reasons lie in its small size, its extreme dispersal, its heterogeneity, and the nature of its economy, which has developed along more individualistic lines than in other countries. Institutions at the national level have usually remained weak and ineffectual. Neither culture-bearing nor trade-based associations show much resilience. Although joined by a common linguistic and cultural heritage and a shared set of moral values, in most other respects the Chinese in Britain lack the attributes held to signify community. These include territorial closeness, sympathetic association, and the will to pursue collective interests. The Chinese therefore suffer a 'double social exclusion' – not just from mainstream society, which treats them 'more as a commodity than as a citizen', but from each other.[233]

On paper, most associations were or are managed along modern lines by a general assembly of members and a board of directors. In practice, however, management tends to be along traditional lines, with decisions taken by a charismatic leader. Beyond the formal president or chairperson, large numbers of honorary presidents or chairpersons are drawn from the ranks of people from the same village, town, or county. Internal power struggles rather than outside pressures explain their decay and disappearance. Some powerful associations transfer their leadership to new migrants rather than to the British-born descendants of the old leaders, making it hard to maintain continuity. These constitutional flaws diminish the associations' influence both in Chinatown and in the homeland and hometown.

The economic and trade-based associations formed over the years were based not on mutually advantageous ties of cooperation, as writing about ethnic-Chinese business might lead one to expect, but on competition and with the clear aim of undermining Chinese business rivals. Attempts to unite restaurant-owners in associations came to grief as a result of internal conflicts, often because they were aimed at promoting vested interests.

Trade-based associations in the takeaway industry have also failed to thrive. The main reason is probably that many Chinese takeaway operators see their businesses as a means to employment and survival in a foreign environment rather than a long-term investment. Their children rarely show much interest in taking over. Many dislike the trade and strive for social mobility through education rather than through business.

Chinese clan associations today struggle to survive in a society in which many of their social-security functions have been taken over by the family, the state, and the CCCs. Even community centres controlled by Chinese associations are run by officially appointed professionals. Most associations (apart from a lucky few that live off rents received on property handed down by the pioneers) depend financially on the support of one or two wealthy patrons. Some procure 'ethnic' funding from local authorities, but the community's factional divisions and widespread ignorance of funding procedures often rule that out. Even though the associations linger on thanks to benefactors, the younger generation's lack of interest and commitment imperils the succession.[234]

In comparing the British Chinese experience with other parts of the world, it is important to distinguish between state discrimination and discrimination by society. In Britain, the state has rarely done anything to prevent Chinese from forming associations, promoting language classes, and publishing Chinese-language media. Chinese residents therefore feel less need to form associations to voice political grievances or mobilise behind their rights to language and culture. Ethnic minorities that see themselves as targets of institutional discrimination tend to transcend internal divisions – a process that reinforces overarching ethnic identities. In Britain, however, where the state has often been accommodating, the fight to establish Chinese schools and associations has had no comparable outcome.

The British Chinese community is poorly organised by comparison not only with its historical counterparts in Southeast Asia and North America but also with other ethnic communities in Britain. Religion provides Britain's Muslims and Hindus with a unifying focus that transcends intracommunal cleavages of class, nationality, and sub-ethnicity. However, religion and Chinese ethnicity are not closely linked and no major Chinese association is founded in religion. Anti-Islamic sentiment in the United Kingdom has further helped to galvanise the Muslims. The mosque and the temple have proved better able to unite migrants than secular associations of the sort Chinese form. Many ethnic Chinese are Christians, and therefore spared the religious anathematisation sometimes aimed at Britain's South Asians.

Social organisations that help pattern or reinforce a way of life are also relatively unimportant. The lack of interest in such organisations is evidence of a deep change in cultural identity from one generation to the next, thus confirming that cultural identity is not fixed but in permanent transition, where received identities are contested and remoulded.

All the pillars of the British Chinese community have a transnational dimension. Transnational ties at the primordial and associational level are analysed in the next chapter, but here we note that Chinese schools are almost by definition transnational, in that their purpose is to preserve Chinese language and culture. The role played throughout the twentieth century by Chinese expatriates and governments in Beijing, Nanjing, Taibei, and Hong Kong in promoting them proves this point.

5
Transnationalism

This chapter looks at the British Chinese community's ties to people and institutions beyond Britain, in the light of theories of transnationalism. It examines three main sorts of tie: with community members' hometowns or ancestral places; with homeland states (chiefly mainland China, Taiwan, and Hong Kong) or homeland political parties; and with diasporic Chinese communities in other countries. Some ties remain informal, others are formally incorporated into associations. A further distinction is between initiatives by ordinary immigrants and hometowners and those that are the top-down product of actions by states, big business, and other institutions.[1] Official bodies in the host society also sometimes play a role in creating and sustaining transnational ties.

Transnationalism and the founding of Britain's Chinese communities

Britain's Chinatowns are perhaps unique in that international wars played the chief role in their founding and refounding. Some of the earliest Chinese workers to reach Britain were recruited to replace seafarers sent off to fight the Napoleonic Wars. In the First World War, several hundred came ashore to work in factories. Chinese joined the British fleet in both world wars, at the end of which hundreds stayed behind. A further wave arrived at the end of the Vietnam War.

A technological precondition for Chinatown was the displacement of sailing ships by steamships. Steam, an agent of imperialist globalisation, gave rise to its reverse in miniature, the colonising of the Chinaports. 'The same advance in technology that had brought the English to the Orient', wrote Barry Milligan, 'was now bringing Orientals en masse to England'.[2]

Unlike the founders of the busy chains that connected Chinese in other places, few seafarers and refugees went to Britain harbouring grand plans. The early seafarers were migrant labourers, tied to their homeland and to hometown networks in a circular flow punctuated by brief sojourns in British ports. The small minority that stayed to form bridgeheads remained tied to the sea, at least for a while. Although their desertion was opportunistic and unplanned, organising further immigration developed into a business strategy. Newcomers enlisted by old hands kept coming, either as passengers or as ratings with no intention of working the return.

The sub-ethnic character of the community was determined by a combination of two factors: the provenance of the pioneers and the methods of British employers and authorities. The pioneers imported people – chiefly family members or lineage-mates – from their own hometown or dialect group. The shipping companies also recruited their Chinese employees from fairly constant sources, through local agents, so crews were often of the same extraction as the pioneers. The coolies recruited by the army in the First World War and the seafarers who ended up in Liverpool in the Second World War were mixed in provenance, but even they were not picked at random and had a potential for sub-ethnic organisation.[3]

The postwar immigration from Hong Kong can be explained by colonial rule and the immigrants' British nationality, as well as the colonial government's encouragement of emigration to ease rural unemployment. Prewar bridgeheads played a role. Hakka and Punti residents of Lantau Island 大嶼山, San Tin 新田, Lo Wu 罗湖, and other parts of the New Territories had begun working for the British merchant fleet in the nineteenth century and founded tiny colonies in Europe and America.[4] These early bases exercised a pull in the 1950s.[5]

Even the inflow of ethnic Chinese from Vietnam resulted from self-organisation as well as external management. The initial transplantation was arranged from above. The first arrivals had no ethnic base and only the refugee agencies to turn to. After a few months, however, they started regrouping and lobbied for the right of relatives to join them. Thus, yet more chains formed.

Only the most recent waves of immigration from urban Hong Kong, Malaysia, Singapore, and China depart from this pattern of sponsorship or recruitment by states and employers. The wealthier and better educated immigrants are more attuned to city life and have an individualistic outlook. They do not depend on co-ethnic ties and try to go it alone. The 'illegal' immigrants from rural China sometimes form sub-ethnic clusters tied to their hometowns by snakehead chains, but a stable flow of immigration is prevented by British restrictions and the immigrants' illegal status.

Transnational legends

The origins of Europe's Chinese trading communities are recited as legend in Chinese histories. Chroniclers nominate Chen Yuanfeng 陈元丰, from Qingtian 青田 in the coastal province of Zhejiang, and Yi Chenglin 易成林, from Tianmen 天门 in Hubei, deep in the Chinese interior, as founding fathers, sometime in the late nineteenth century. The Qingtianese, who peddled soapstone carvings and trinketry, spread across nearly all of Europe and were the biggest Chinese group until after the Second World War – they continue to form a thriving community, replenished by new migrants.[6] The story of their migrations, at least in latter times, is by now fairly well known to scholars in overseas-Chinese studies. The Hubeinese, on the other hand, are a far from familiar migrant group.[7]

Tianmen is a typical Chinese country. As in all Chinese counties of extensive outmigration, signs of the overseas connection are not hard to find. A main thoroughfare is named Overseas Chinese Road and there is an Overseas Chinese Bureau that chronicles the migration and maintains relations with emigrants and their relatives back home. However, Tianmen lacks the vibrancy and prosperity of its counterparts in the coastal provinces of Guangdong and Fujian. Whereas emigration has helped transform the coastal areas and fuel a boom, Tianmen languishes in relative neglect.

According to one account, Yi Chenglin set out from Tianmen in 1900 and headed for northeastern China, from where he crossed the border into Chita in Siberia. There, he set up as a tooth-puller. He also 'healed' teeth, by appearing to extract flesh-coloured 'tooth-worms'. These tiny 'worms' were in fact a sort of catkin, which he kept in a jar he had brought with him from Hubei. (This 'dentistry', a Tianmenese institution, is nowadays condemned by local officials as a 'backward tradition...with a mystical flavour'.) In a stroke of good fortune, Yi cured a Russian army commander's son of toothache, after which his business boomed. In a letter home, he summoned friends and relatives. A group of young adventurers from Tianmen teamed up with him in Siberia. Together they walked to Moscow, along the track (not yet opened to rail traffic) of the Trans-Siberian Railway. Known in China as jugglers and acrobats, the Tianmenese earned their living while marching across Russia by making papercuts, pulling and 'healing' teeth, and staging circus acts and performances of the flower-drum opera popular in Hubei. From Moscow, they walked on to Germany and Austria, from where they fanned out across the whole of Europe. Some ended up in France, Italy, Portugal, and Spain, where they sold paper flowers and juggled for the crowds. Others crossed the Channel and melted into the British China-towns. Far larger settlements formed in Southeast Asia, Korea, Japan, and India.[8]

Nearly all early Chinese emigrants were male sojourners bound to their villages by ties of kinship, but many Tianmen people migrated as young married couples. Along the route, they picked up smatterings of the languages of the countries they traversed. Some women had bound feet in childhood. Though the bindings were later cut away, their feet still showed signs of deformity and some found walking hard. One or two who gave birth on the march west left their babies in the care of local people. (The same story is told of the Chinese communists' legendary Long March.) Perhaps because they migrated in family groups, they seem to have formed fewer mutual-aid societies than other Chinese overseas.

Tianmen was, for a long time, the Chinese interior's most important region of overseas migration. By the late 1980s, nearly 60,000 local people and their descendants lived abroad, compared with Tianmen's population of 1.38 million. The county's history of floods and agricul-tural catastrophes is given as the cause of this outmigration, but Pam So, an ethnic-Chinese Scottish artist of Hubeinese ancestry, says the migrants claimed to have made up their minds to travel 'not because of poverty but out of a spirit of adventure'.

By the 1990s, there were around 280,000 Tianmenese in 40 coun-tries.[9] These 'overseas Tianmenese' include several well-known scient-ists and big entrepreneurs. Yet proportionately far fewer have main-tained ties to Tianmen than in other parts of China with a tradi-tion of emigration. Local leaders say Tianmen has given much to the world but received little in return. This haemorrhaging has two causes – the tradition of family migration, which favours striking roots in foreign land, and Tianmen's relative remoteness. The ances-tral county benefited from the emigration mainly through its schools, which received funding and inspiration from overseas. In the late 1980s, Tianmen had the highest rate of university entrance in China.[10]

Tianmen's northerly position may explain its inhabitants' choice of Europe as a destination, at a time when the sea-routes were monopolised by migrants from provinces on the littoral. Like the Qingtianese, the Tianmenese seeded Europe with settlers and sent people on to the United

States. A plan by one group to resettle in Australia came to nothing. Those who crossed over into Britain scattered to London, Liverpool, Cardiff, Bristol, and Newcastle, existing centres of Cantonese immigration. From Britain, some sailed to Ireland. While the imperialists in China were scrambling for concessions and pondering how to 'slice up the China melon', the Hubeinese jobbers, hawkers, and performers were slicing up the Europe pumpkin into tiny 'spheres of influence'. In Britain, some went to work in laundries set up by ex-seafarers from Siyi.[11]

The Hubeinese stayed in touch with one another by post, across seas and oceans. They exchanged photographs and visited one another's homes. A few went back and forth between Europe and Tianmen. They were not Europe's first Chinese transnationals, a title that belongs to the seafarers. However, while the Siyinese went west aboard British ships, the landlocked Hubeinese (like the Qingtianese, who arrived at roughly the same time) took an independent route to Europe, which they colonised more extensively than the Siyinese (though with fewer people).[12]

Informal hometown and diasporic ties

Britain's early Chinese communities – those originating in Guangdong, eastern China, and Hong Kong – established channels right at the start to maintain home contact. These channels were used not just to stay in touch but to send remittances and import immigrants. The migration chains were unintentionally fortified in the 1960s and the 1970s by immigration laws and the introduction of a system of vouchers and work-permit quotas. These measures strengthened the kinship groups and helped channel the immigrants into catering.

The ties that bound the Siyinese to their sending places were perfected by practice over decades, after the start of Cantonese emigration to California in the mid-nineteenth century and the decision by other Siyi settlers to move to Hong Kong in the 1880s when the United States introduced restrictions on Chinese immigration.[13] The Siyinese established their dominance in Britain's Chinese community by importing kinsmen and using them to extend the business frontier inland. In 1906, the commission set up to inquire into Liverpool's Chinese settlement noted 'the tendency on the part of a Chinaman, who is commercially successful in Liverpool, ... to send for his relatives and friends from China to share in his good fortune'.[14] Some Siyinese from poor families were 'sold' to compatriots in Britain, a term suggesting indenture.[15] The pauper Mao Wuguang 毛无光 (1860–1924), for example, was 'sold' to a Chinese in Britain in 1878, aged 18. (He wrote a narrative poem about his experiences.)[16]

Siyi's economy and society were strongly influenced by emigration. Remittances from across the world led to a building boom. Since many Siyinese migrated to English-speaking countries, young boys were taught English in towns and villages by returned relatives or sent to special schools where they received an education in both Chinese and English and in subjects such as bookkeeping.[17]

Once abroad, the migrants stayed in touch, both among themselves and with their families, by 'making liberal use of telegraphs, mail, railways, and shipping lines'. Letters travelled from and to the sending villages and towns, either by post or stuffed in the pockets of new migrants bound for foreign lands or of migrants on home visits.[18] Newspapers circulated not just out of China but within the diaspora, creating the sinews of a new transnational identity. A film made in Hong Kong in the 1930s about Chinese washermen in the United States was said to have helped inspire the Siyinese laundry boom in Singapore.[19] This was a world of transnational villages and families and of transnational overseas communities, tied into migration networks across the globe.

Many of the sons (especially the first-born) of Siyinese men and their British wives were sent to China to live for a year or two with the paternal grandparents and learn Chinese (a practice followed by Chinese worldwide), or to find a bride. The immigrants remitted money to support parents and relatives.[20] Such remittances transformed the home communities, which came to depend on them. It is not known how much was sent and for how long, but the remittances probably dried up when Guangdong was cut off from the West, either at the time of the Japanese occupation or after 1949.

In an earlier chapter, we noted that the enterprises – laundries and cafes – with which Britain's Chinese immigrants were associated were modelled on the Siyinese experience in America. Such ideas and tactics were perhaps imported to Britain by Chinese 'fleeing American persecution, as they were driven in their thousands from their homes in California' in the 1870s and 1880s and by other remigrations, as well as by the dissemination of news about new overseas entrepreneurial fashions in letters.[21]

Intra-diasporic migration by Siyinese was cross-Channel as well as transatlantic. Not just seafarers crossed into Britain to resettle. At the end of the First World War, hundreds if not thousands of the tens of the thousands of Chinese labourers recruited by the Allies to work on the

Western Front fanned out across Europe in search of work. This postwar migration was a key event in the founding of Chinese communities in northern Europe.[22] Most labourers stayed in France, but some slipped into Britain.[23] They included at least one Taishanese who somehow ended up in Liverpool after catching a boat to the US.[24]

The progression from laundries to shops also strengthened the Chinese pan-European network. Chinese newssheets carried advertisements placed by Chinese importers on the Continent. The tie was not just economic. Merchants who developed contacts with compatriots across the Channel were more likely to stay abreast of Chinese politics than laundrymen. A good example is Way Soo Hoo, who had business interests in both Liverpool and Marseilles and whose business partner Wong Kau 黃球 was a Republican leader in Liverpool.[25]

The next wave of Chinese immigrants to Britain was the 'Shanghainese', actually seafarers from Jiangsu, Zhejiang, Guangdong, and elsewhere based in Liverpool in the Second World War. A small minority stayed behind after the peace as employees of the Blue Funnel seafarers' pool. The Blue Funnel connection helped not only to unify the Chinese but to preserve their homeland ties. Chinese domiciled in Liverpool remained in touch with native places through seafarers who carried back remittances for them. In rare cases, the shipping lines acted as chains for new immigrants. Even some who left the sea retained a tie to the seagoing community, by working as interpreters, boarding-house managers, and intermediaries between crews and companies.[26] This tie was weakened by the decline in visits by Chinese ships and the Blue Funnel pool's demise.[27]

Up to one-third of the Shanghainese hired as shore-gang workers by Alfred Holt & Co. made remittances averaging 20 per cent of wages, with company help. Although the remitters had Liverpool wives, the recipients included first wives in China.[28] Only 8 per cent of Holt employees from Hong Kong remitted money in this way. Maurice Broady, who studied the seafarers in the 1950s, suggests two reasons: either they sent back money through relatives, or they had been in Britain longer than the Shanghai men and their family ties had broken.

Poverty ruled out return visits for most seafarers, allied to the effects of the Sino-Japanese War, the Chinese Civil War, and the Cold War. Remittances dwindled in the 1950s, especially after the birth of children to Liverpool wives. Most seafarers died in exile. Only towards the end of their lives did a few manage the return trip.[29]

Although less connected with their hometowns than the Siyinese, mainly because wars and crises left them stranded, the Shanghainese developed links with Chinese outside Asia. Their ties in New York were so extensive that great numbers of them vanished into Chinatown after crossing the Atlantic – to the point where the shipping lines replaced them with Indians on the transatlantic route.[30] They were also tied fraternally with Chinese trade unionists in ports in Asia and Australia.[31] Some who continued to work at sea after the war used their transnational voyaging for trading purposes – to import Chinese foodstuffs from Asia, which they sold on to restaurants in Britain.[32] (This practice was common among Chinese seafarers in the Pacific.)

In the postwar years, the Chinese ceased to see themselves as sojourners and came to terms with the permanency of their settlement. However, the different groups continued to form separate enclaves with strong ethnic identities. Although Britain was now home, they were unable to transcend the sub-ethnic cleavages that divided them. Some older Siyinese responded positively in the post-Mao period to the overtures of authorities in the mainland, who were keen to build bridges to their overseas compatriots. Although there was no longer much chain migration to reinforce their cohesion, they tended towards territorial concentration, notably in Liverpool and Cardiff, and their cultural and socioeconomic boundaries coincided.

The informal hometown ties of the immigrants from Hong Kong's New Territories were of the same general character as those of the mainlanders but more intensive, at least in the early days. After the war, travel and communication became cheaper and easier. Unlike their predecessors, the new immigrants enjoyed the same formal rights as native British and were free to come and go, without the red-tapery that afflicted other Chinese. They arrived amid an economic boom, and they were better represented by homeland authorities. Whereas Chiang Kai-shek's government had left the old Chinese community mostly to its own devices, the Hong Kong colonial government sometimes acted after the late 1960s in support of its overseas residents.

Britain's early Chinese communities were made up largely of onetime seafarers. The immigration from Hong Kong, on the other hand, was self-initiated and self-organised. In that sense, it differed not only from earlier Chinese immigration to Britain but also from that to other destinations, which were supplied initially with labour imported under the coolie-trade system. This independence also distinguished the Hong Kong Chinese from Britain's other non-white immigrants, thousands of whom were recruited to work in the health service or channelled by market forces into public transport and manufacturing,[33] a process mainly beyond their control. This difference helps explain the special intensity of the Hong Kong immigrants' hometown ties.

Landownership tied emigrants from the New Territories to their native villages more strongly than many of the earlier Chinese. Short of fertile and arable land, the Siyinese were despised as paupers.[34] The wartime seafarers were probably less likely to own land.[35] Some migrants from the New Territories, on the other hand, retained land in their ancestral villages, which they either rented out to incomers from south China or left untended. When property boomed in the 1970s, this land provided the chance of windfall earnings. By the 1980s, many Chinese who had got rich in Britain saw trading in land and buildings in the New Territories as a business opportunity.[36] This tie was formalised through the activities of the Heung Yee Kuk 乡议局, an organisation whose role in supporting emigrant transnationalism is analysed later in this chapter.[37]

The best-known migration chain between Britain and the New Territories is run by the Man 文 lineage, the subject of James Watson's 1975 book. Watson found that San Tin 新田, the Man lineage village, had become an 'emigrant community' dependent on overseas remittances from its males, 85–90 per cent of whom were in Europe. He estimated there were around 30 such communities (defined as 'any village, hamlet, or town that depends upon regular [international] remittances for 50 per cent or more of its income') in the New Territories, around 5 per cent of all villages. San Tin migrants used lineage ties to get jobs, passports, entry certificates, passage money (as an advance on wages), flights (arranged by a Man-owned charter service), and work permits. 'The lineage', wrote Watson, 'is so well suited to the requirements of chain migration that it has been converted into a sort of "emigration agency" '.

The Man lineage is one of the New Territories' five elite lineages and San Tin is a single-lineage settlement, so it is untypical of the region's 600 villages. The 'critical links' of most Hong Kong migration chains were extended families, sets of brothers and their sons, who rarely cooperated with non-kinsmen.[38]

Throughout the twentieth century, but especially between the 1950s and the 1970s, remittances, investments, and public donations flowed into the New Territories. In the 1930s, remittances by kinsmen abroad or in urban Hong Kong were a 'significant item'. Between 1958 and 1963, remittances by restaurant workers (mostly in the United Kingdom) in the form of postal and money orders grew from 1.2 million to 29 million Hong Kong dollars. In the mid-1960s, remittances through the Post

Office averaged more than £2 million a year over a period of five years. In the 1970s, the remittances kept pace with inflation, fluctuating between 50 and 100 million dollars. Most workers remitted between one-fifth and two-fifths of their earnings.[39]

The remittances transformed living standards. Contrary to the predictions of some sociologists, however, they did little to promote modern change. Instead, they 'allowed the villagers to maintain a traditional style of life' that had fallen into disuse elsewhere in the New Territories. They fuelled a boom in 'sterling houses', reserved for the owner's use after retirement (and named after the British currency). Donations funded schools and temples. Before 1960, most migrants waited until retirement before undertaking the sea journey to Hong Kong, but in the 1960s, after the start of cheap charter flights, they returned on average once every three or four years. Some returned more than once a year. In the villages, they caught up with local news and helped make family decisions. Younger men who might previously have acquired a bride by 'mail order' now returned to find one.

Like some of the Siyinese fathers in the 1930s and 1940s, many migrants in the early years of family reunion sent their British-born children to be reared by their paternal grandmothers. From the children's point of view the most consequential of the transnational ties, its purpose was for them to be brought up speaking Cantonese and knowing Chinese culture – and, from the grandparents' point of view, to serve as hostages for the absent fathers. In the late 1960s, two-thirds of Man children fathered in Europe were sent to San Tin. At the other end of the life-cycle, the remains of deceased immigrants were also flown home.

In the 1960s, researchers agreed that the Chinese were the least assimilated of Britain's immigrant minorities. They had little interest in British society and minimal contact with it. The restaurants were islands from which they could 'interact with the outside world on their own terms'. Most had just a smattering of English. Many Chinese cooks spent years in Britain without ever exchanging a word with a local. Life in Britain was, for them, a prelude to retirement, to be spent in a sterling house.

The end of the 1960s and the start of the 1970s, however, marked a turning point. Legislation undermined and destroyed the sojourner ideal by necessitating family reunion. The repercussions of the Cultural Revolution caused many restaurant workers to think twice about going 'home' for good. In the 1980s, when the issue of Hong Kong's retrocession to China arose, the prospect of going back looked even less appealing. Some who did go changed their minds and returned to Britain to rejoin their children. In the meantime, some New Territories villages had emptied and seemed unlikely to be repopulated, while other areas were spoiled by urban sprawl.[40]

Towards the end of the twentieth century, migration chains, remittances, and return visits became less prominent in the lives of Britain's Hong Kong Chinese. Grandparent socialisation stopped, partly because the grandparents had themselves emigrated to rejoin their families. The parents were appalled to see their children fall behind at school in Britain after deferring their migration until their teens, or dismayed to discover that the children could not compete in the labour market with those raised in Britain. The migration chain was damaged not only by new immigration controls but by a drying up at the source. Parts of some villages had become disused – the New Territories were far less populated than the villages of Guangdong and Fujian, with their inexhaustible reserves. Besides, other career possibilities opened to young villagers, as the Hong Kong economy surged.

Remittances shrank as wives and children joined their menfolk and gave them a more immediate affective focus and financial commitment. After peaking in 1968, they levelled off and then declined. Today, Chinese in Britain most often remit money on 'special occasions', a pattern probably established in the mid-1960s, when the level of remittances (and return visits) rose at Chinese New Year and the August Moon Festival. They are less likely to remit regularly than almost any other ethnic group in Britain, even though they are exceptionally prosperous,[41] but more likely than any other ethnic group to have visited their family's place of origin. They are also more likely than Britain's South Asians to stay in touch by phone with parents living abroad (though less likely to do so by letter). These differences can be explained by their higher incomes and phone use rather than by closer ties.[42]

The informal hometown ties of Britain's Chinese communities remained robust for years and even decades. Indeed, it is hard to see why they should ever have frayed. The seafarers, washermen, and caterers were locked into niches. They lacked alternative choices and opportunities of the sort that promote assimilation. There were few of the 'sizeable back-and-forth movements and regular exchanges of tangible and intangible goods between places of origin and destination' that Portes et al. say create binational fields and encourage the preservation of original languages and cultures,[43] yet transnational practices were normative and routine. The line to Europe from Siyi looped into a worldwide mesh.

Even many ex-seafarers from communities without a tradition of emigration were bound to their hometowns and homeports by workmate ties. The transnational focus of the Hong Kong caterers, far less cosmopolitan in outlook than the older groups, lay in the sending society, where land and family awaited their return. Unlike the laundrymen and seafarers, who could communicate in pidgin or passable English, they were implacable monoglots.[44]

Even so, all Britain's early Chinese communities at some point made the transition to settling. Culturalist explanations imply that ethnic boundaries erode steadily over time as a result of cultural loss, leading to a long-term, imperceptible wearing away of home links. In the British Chinese case, however, the passage to settlement was not slow and prolonged but set in motion by sudden external causes.

Many studies note how wars, revolutions, and upheavals in the ancestral country can awaken national feeling in ethnic communities. Less noted is their potential for diminishing homeland identification and transnational ties, by closing off routes or splitting communities in half and thus contributing to their eventual depoliticisation.[45] The history of the Chinese in Britain shows how contact between places of origin and destination was curtailed by traumatic political events or, in the case of the New Territorians, by a combination of social unrest in China and Hong Kong, British immigration laws, and immigrants' loss of confidence in the colony. It also shows that the switch to settling was no destiny unconsciously realised but a strategic choice in response to political changes.

Today, the remittance habit survives among some of the new Chinese immigrant communities, particularly those from Fujian, whose members have their own ways of sending money home. Just as in the New Territories in the 1960s and the 1970s, this money is used in China to support immigrants' families and, in the case of the more successful immigrants, to build modern houses.

Formal hometown and intra-diasporic ties

The ties between Britain and China usually started out as loose and relatively casual (unless they were extensions of ready-made links, as in the Siyinese case). Later, they became more elaborate, as immigrants formalised their relations with the sending region. Some linked up with diasporic associations with global pretensions, especially towards the end of the twentieth century. We have looked at these associations in their British context. Here, we explore their hometown and diasporic dimensions.

Associations formed abroad on the basis of local provenance or dialect tend to preserve links to the hometown, at least for as long as the immigrants remain separated from their families. So too do trade unions, political parties, trade associations, and churches. Ostensibly, such organisations recruit their members on non-ascriptive grounds, but in practice provenance sometimes plays a role, especially where migration chains link the hometowns with economic enclaves overseas or where sub-ethnic loyalties are mobilised to wider ends.

Some immigrants remain so deeply embedded in the sending community that they treat life in exile as an extension of it. An example is the Man lineage, whose expatriate leaders in the 1960s and the early 1970s paid little attention to associational life abroad and instead looked forward to obtaining leadership positions in San Tin on retirement.[46] In time, however, the locus of power switched from San Tin to the new generation of informal leaders in Europe, entrepreneurs whose influence spread back to the ancestral village.[47]

Chinese native-place associations in Britain differ from those in most parts of the world. Native-place associations in Southeast Asia, North America, and Australia form a hierarchy that parallels the homeland hierarchy of places, starting in the village and rising through township, county, and city to province or region. These associations provide mutual help and protection in the absence of family or lineage ties. France too has a pronounced hierarchy of Chinese native-place associations – the *Encyclopaedia of Overseas and Ethnic Chinese* lists ten provincial associations (and others covering Shanghai and Beijing). These divisions derive in part from the Chinese experience in Southeast Asia, where Chinese make up much of the urban population. Most Chinese native-place associations in Britain have fewer degrees, ranging from village to county.

The reason is that most Chinese in Britain are from a single province, Guangdong (of which Hong Kong is part), so there is little basis for the provincial cleavages that segment more complex communities. In the case of immigrants from Hong Kong, there is no basis even for differentiation by county, for Hong Kong itself is less than a county. (Originally, it was part of the county of Xin'an 新安, today's Shenzhen 深圳.) As a result, practically Britain's only county-style Chinese associations are those based on Siyi 四邑, Wuyi 五邑, and other county-clusters in Guangdong. (New associations based on counties in other provinces – for example, the Yangzhou Chinese Association 英国扬州同乡会 – are less important.[48])

Britain has far fewer kinship associations than most Chinese communities overseas. Where such organisations form in Britain, they tend to cover all Europe, to make up for their small numbers. They draw their members from the villages of the New Territories, thus combining features of a surname group and a native-place association. They play only a small role in members' lives, and their impact is more affective than social and economic. According to Li Minghuan 李明欢, 'apart from organising annual dinners, they normally do not engage in much social activity. The main activity is sending delegations back to their ancestral places annually or once every several years at the time of large-scale ancestor worship, when they participate in honouring their ancestors'.[49]

Britain's main village-based native-place associations include the Dapeng Association Europe 旅欧大鹏同乡会, the Kat O Village Benevolent Society 格拉斯哥吉澳渔联会, the Kut O Benevolent Society 旅欧吉澳同乡回, and the Lam Chuen Overseas Chinese Community Europe 旅欧林村同乡会. The Kat O and Kut O societies are from a single village, the former composed of the families of onetime farmers and the latter of onetime fishermen. All four associations recruit their members from all of Europe, although their headquarters are in Britain.[50]

Generally speaking, the scope of native-place associations formed by people from Hong Kong in Britain is extremely narrow. They cannot provide the same range of connections as more broadly based associations in France and in other continents. For British-based associations closer to the general run of Chinese organisations overseas, one must look to the communities that originate in mainland China.

Siyinese migration chains stretched not just back to Guangdong but across the world. The American Chinese exercised a strong influence on the British Chinese community in the late nineteenth and early twentieth centuries, both politically and economically. The American Chinese (principally Siyinese) probably conducted their relations with Chinese communities in British colonies and the Dominions with the help of the British Siyinese, who had a hand in smuggling migrants across Europe and the English-speaking world.

This strong transnational dimension of Britain's Chinatowns dropped from sight for most of the rest of the twentieth century, but it re-emerged after new developments on a European and world scale. These included new migration, business globalisation, European unification, China's economic opening, and the communications revolution. Ethnically based institutions became progressively less important until developments in the global arena led to the establishment of new associations. These new associations were usually not a British Chinese initiative.

Today, transnational associations are organised at the European and the world level. Since the 1970s, at least 30 Chinese clans, native-place associations, business groups, and other bodies have established federations at the European level and several score have done so at the world level. The two are often linked, with the European federations serving as continental branches of the world federations. The reasons for the emergence of these associations in Europe include instigation by Chinese or Taiwan authorities acting in their own interests and action by existing international associations.[51]

In the Chinese perception, Europe, though thick with boundaries, is in many ways a single entity. For some seafaring pioneers, this perception was reinforced by plying among European ports. The labourers recruited by the British Army in the First World War were treated as a Europe-wide detachment, and those who stayed behind at the war's end flitted from country to country in search of a livelihood. The Zhejiangese peddlers who came to Europe in the early twentieth century paid little attention to borders and maintained continental networks, from Portugal to Czechoslovakia and from Italy to Scandinavia. The tiny group of Hubeinese explorers spread out across Europe and the world. The Siyinese who set up Britain's first Chinese laundries and restaurants had clansmen in several mainland European ports. The Chinese who joined the seafarers' pool in the Second World War were recruited from ports across the world, including on the European mainland. The Hong Kong caterers continued and intensified this pan-European tradition, a defining characteristic of Chinese immigration into Britain.

The Hong Kong caterers' cross-Channel migrations were an extension of their movement from London to the provinces and from England to Wales, Scotland, and Ireland. As island destinations 'filled', the movement spilled over onto the mainland. According to Watson, sons and nephews of immigrants branched out into the Netherlands as early as 1960, after which others founded outposts in Belgium, Germany, and Scandinavia, then 'the new frontiers for Chinese restaurant development'.[52] Some remigrants set up their own enterprises. Others started out by running restaurants on behalf of wealthy owners who controlled catering chains spanning the Channel.[53]

The Cheungs' Clansmen Charity Association (Europe) 欧洲张氏宗亲福利会 was founded in 1965. It was joined a decade later by the Man's Clansmen Association, UK 旅欧文氏宗亲会. However, these two bodies were created for practical reasons (the trickle of Cheung and Man caterers across Europe) rather than because of new ideological developments or changes in world business and communications, like their more recent counterparts. Clan associations organised at the European level since the late 1970s include the Lung Kung Federation of Europe (1978) 欧洲龙冈亲义总会, open to bearers of the surnames Liu 刘, Guan 关, Zhang 张, and Zhao 赵; and the Federation of Tsung Tsin Associations in Europe (1990) 欧洲崇正总 会联合会, formed to represent European Hakkas.[54] Other European Chinese associations are based on geographic provenance, religion, ideology, profession, sport, literature, culture, and learning.

In the 1990s, the Man lineage abroad entered a new and unexpected phase. By this time, the lineage had four thousand people in more than 20 countries and at least a score of multimillionaires. Members of its third and fourth generations 'overseas' were more comfortable in English, Dutch, or German than in Cantonese. The sterling houses in San Tin had been relegated to holiday homes. However, lineage members used air travel and electronic communications to set up a 'wired diaspora', while other lineages unravelled. Watson traces the Man revival to opportunities opened up to inhabitants of San Tin and their descendants by Hong Kong's retrocession to China in 1997. Man diasporans took over a Hong Kong Clan Association founded earlier by Man from other parts of China and transformed it into a channel for investing in the mainland. At the same time, they recruited patrilineal kin in the Shenzhen Special Economic Zone, including communist party cadres, as cross-border business partners. Why did they begin acting in the 1990s like 'an organized diaspora'? Because San Tin's thousand acres 'sit, quite literally, in the shadow of Shenzhen's high-rise office buildings' and offer the prospect of further enrichment to the lineage's descendants.[55]

In mainland Europe, the new migrants from China, whose homeland tie is recent and in some cases well organised, have provided fresh grounds for transnational identification. The associations formed by immigrants from Qingtian, a once impoverished county in Zhejiang, are a good example of the revival of an old community by new blood. The Qingtianese pioneered Chinese settlement of Europe, where they set up small trading communities. (Elsewhere in the world, and in Britain, they are relatively few in number.) In the 1980s, when a second wave of immigration from Qingtian reached Europe, new organisations arose to serve the community. Veterans in Spain set up the Asociación de Chinos en España 西班牙华侨华人协会 (Association of Chinese in Spain); their comrades in Denmark and the Netherlands formed similar bodies.[56] In 1992, the Spanish Qingtianese took the lead in founding a Friendship Association of Famous Overseas Chinese Personalities 浙江省海外侨团 知名人士联谊会, to represent Zhejiangese worldwide and strengthen their homeland ties.[57] The Association had the support of the Zhejiang authorities, eager to use the new body to counter Taibei's influence on Europe's older generation of Qingtianese.[58] In March 1996, the Friendship Association set up yet another tier of organisation, the European Qingtian Association 欧洲青田同乡会. At around the same time, Qingtianese associations emerged in France (1994), Italy (1995), Belgium (1997), and Germany (1998).[59] In August 1996, a Spanish Qingtian Association 西班牙青田同乡会 was set up, at the request of the European Association, to function as an explicitly Qingtianese body alongside the more inclusive Asociación de Chinos en España. Subsequently, these associations were used as models to export Qingtianese organisation in Hungary. In 2001, plans were announced in Beijing for the launching of an international association of Qingtianese.[60]

This dialectical interplay between Qingtian and Europe and among the three tiers of Qingtianese diaspora (at world, continental, and nation-state level) looks at first sight like a powerful realisation of theories of transnationalism. However, the Qingtianese border-crossing networks are relatively new. Their true extent, intensity, and durability remain to be measured. Whether they will strike root or stay as half-realised semi-bureaucratic blueprints is a question that will be decided by the Qingtianese community as a whole, rather than by overseas notables and Qingtian committee chiefs.

A British parallel is the Siyinese group, until recently semi-moribund as a result of China's closure and the postwar overrunning of Britain's Siyinese strongholds by new immigrants. In the 1980s and 1990s, the 'ethnicisation' of local politics in Britain and the revival of Siyi's links to the outside world created a generation of activists keen to revive this remnant of the early Chinatown. The availability of ethnic grants played a role. So did the community leaders' contacts with ambitious notables in Jiangmen 江门, focal point of Wuyi (incorporating Siyi). The arrival of new immigrants from Wuyi and of new Wuyinese immigrants from Hong Kong and Southeast Asia reinforced this tie.[61]

These and other developments helped revive Siyinese organisation throughout Britain. In 1994, a South Wales See Yip Association 南威尔士四邑同乡会分会 with a largish body of officials arose in Cardiff, once a Siyinese-controlled Chinaport, after official visits to the city by a delegation from 'the councils in See Yip'.[62] This Welsh group worked together with the bigger and older See Yip Chinese Association, based in northwest England, and with the related but smaller Ng Yip Association 旅英五邑联谊会, founded in 1985.[63] But such revivals are unlikely to halt the long-term decline of the Siyinese community. Siyi's Taishan dialect, heard throughout the early Chinatowns, is dying in the face of competition from English, standard Cantonese, and Mandarin. Even the President of Britain's Ng Yip Association apparently speaks no Taishanese.[64]

The Hakkas' Tsung Tsin Association, UK 英国崇正总会 is another example of the transnationalisation of parts of Europe's Chinese community. A similarly named association active in Liverpool in the interwar years ceased to exist after 1945, as a result of the wartime scattering of its members.[65] In 1987, it was revived at a London meeting as part of a campaign by the World Hakka Association 世界客属总会 (organised in 1971) to extend its influence beyond Asia. (The French equivalent, the Association Hakka Tsung Chinh en France 旅法崇正总会, was founded in 1984.) In 1990, British Hakkas helped found the European Tsung Tsin Federation 欧洲崇正总会联合会 under the honorary presidency of Huang Shihua, the Hong Kong Hakka leader, another example of the intermeshing of different levels of organisation worldwide. They also helped found the Tsung Tsin association in Benelux 荷比卢崇正总会 (in 1989). In 1991, the association's British-based president led a delegation of more than 220 Hakkas from seven European countries to 'visit the ancestors' in Henan.[66] Transnational ties are not the sole reason for the revival. Hundreds if not thousands of Hakkas have come to Britain since the crackdown in China in 1989 and now seek strength in numbers.[67]

The new global associations of the 1980s and the 1990s were formed on the basis of ancestral hometown, dialect, or surname, mainly by enthusiasts in Southeast Asia and elsewhere using the new electronic technologies. Many scholars claim a link between these organisations and the globalisation of Chinese capital and argue that they play a central part in promoting investment in China by manipulating ties of place and kinship. However, when such investment happens, it is the result of political exhortation by state authorities rather than the 'pull of the ancestral homeland' and is usually directed towards the economic powerhouses of central-eastern China with no tradition of outward migration rather than to the ancestral places.

The global associations are rarely used for serious business networking. Most have a 'no politics' rule that distinguishes the new-style bodies from the anti-Japanese federations set up by Chinese throughout the world in the 1930s, whose very reason for existence was homeland politics. (See below.) They have few functions other than facilitating 'root-seeking' and organising annual gatherings for entertainment, social hobnobbing, and moral exhortation at which senior high-fliers generation can raise their social standing.[68] Despite the appearance of extensive branching, their roots are shallow.

Intra-diasporic migration by ethnic-Chinese students and political activists

Intra-diasporic Chinese migrants to Britain have included both China-born remigrants and ethnic Chinese born outside China (usually in British colonies or former colonies). Even some of those born outside China were drawn to Britain in part by a diasporic tie to fellow-Cantonese.

Many early Chinese students in Britain from Southeast Asia identified with China and played an active role in the late-Qing reform movement. Wu Tingfang 伍廷芳, an ethnic Cantonese whose ancestral home was in Xinhui 新会 in Siyi, visited the new Chinese Embassy the day after the first diplomats arrived. Born in Singapore, Wu read law at Lincoln's Inn. He declined Guo Songtao's 郭嵩焘 invitation to work as an Embassy translator in London and Chen Lanbin's 陈兰彬 invitation to head a consulate in the United States. After serving as a judge in Hong Kong, he was appointed in 1896 as the Qing court's Foreign Minister in the United States, Spain, and Peru. He played a big part in the late-Qing reforms. After 1911, the Republican Government regarded him as a comrade. His brother-in-law He Qi 何啟, whose father was a missionary in Malacca and Hong Kong, also went to England, to study medicine, and also played a role in the Qing reforms.[69]

Two other twentieth-century Cantonese-descended leaders in Britain were born in Jamaica. Chen Tiansheng 陈天声, also known as Samuel Chinque (1908–2004), became a seafarer and went to Liverpool in 1929, where (as Sam Chen) he became a labour leader and supporter of the radical movement (see below). (His daughter Anna is a British Chinese artist, broadcaster, and writer.) Liu Xitang 刘锡棠 (born 1939) left Jamaica for Hong Kong in 1949 but remigrated to Britain, where he became an academic.[70] Many other Chinese migrated within the British Empire or Commonwealth.

Britain's best-known Caribbean Chinese remigrant was Eugene Chen 陈友仁 (1878–1944), the Trinidad-born son of Hakka immigrants who became China's foreign minister in the 1920s. Chen, one of Trinidad's first Chinese solicitors, moved in his mid-thirties to London, where he was at the centre of a circle of Chinese nationalists and radical students from Africa and the Americas and developed an interest in revolutionary Chinese politics. In 1912, he left London and went to China. There he met Sun Yat-sen. He became Sun's close associate and represented him at the Paris Peace Conference in 1918. His son Jack Chen 陈依范, a painter and author, spent many years in China and England and was a sympathiser of the communists.[71]

Other diasporan remigrants, chiefly students from Southeast Asia, lacked the strong patriotic feelings of their mainland counterparts. They tended to speak good English and poor Chinese and were less likely to take China's side. The Qing Government offered financial support to those who agreed to study subjects China needed and to live in China after graduating, and sent people to teach them Chinese. However, the gap between them and 'real Chinese' remained. 'Overseas students criticised mainland student as extremists', said a contemporary report, 'while those from the mainland called the students from overseas *yangnu* 洋奴 (foreign slaves)'.[72]

Chinese students, Chinatown, and the homeland polity

After the late-Qing educational reforms, a new generation of students and intellectuals assumed a leading role in China's cultural and political revolution. Overseas study was prized in the new climate of regard for Western learning. Chinese students in Britain lacked the political weight of those in Japan or the academic influence of those in the United States. Their influence on the British Chinese community was also comparatively weak. Even so, they were more active on political issues than any other Chinese group in Britain.

By the late nineteenth century, educated Chinese everywhere were waking to the foreign threat. Nationalist feeling deepened among those abroad, angered by the indignities to which China and they were subjected. In October 1916, Chinese students in Britain held a meeting to commemorate the Republican martyrs Huang Xing 黄兴 (1874–1916) and Cai E 蔡锷 (1882–1916). In 1917, when Zhang Xun 张勋 tried to restore the deposed emperor, the students issued a statement that 'Chinese students in England stand firmly by the parliament and urge the whole nation to organise a common government and forces to punish the unscrupulous rebels'.[73]

Students continued to stir up the community for the rest of the century. Students from China and Southeast Asia who visited Britain before the Second World War went seeking ways to save the ancestral country by 'making an England in China', whereas ordinary Chinese went to earn a living and 'make a China in England'. State-sponsored intellectuals had few contacts with Chinatown, but some did their best to bridge the gap. Their ideas and sentiments were crucial to the emergence of diasporic nationalism.

However, homeland politics were naturally more attractive to them than the small-time politics of Chinatown. To many student expatriates, warlordism in China represented a failure to copy Western politics and realise a Chinese England. Others who had studied in Britain ended up working for the northern warlord government. In 1916, 112 students returned to Beijing, of whom 71 served under warlords. Among those who returned was the onetime revolutionary Zhang Shizhao 章士钊, a student at Edinburgh University between 1908 and 1911. After founding a radical magazine in Beijing, Zhang went back to Britain, where he met Harold J. Laski, H. G. Wells, G. D. H. Cole, and other leftwing thinkers. In the mid-1920s, as Minister of Education under the warlord Duan Qirui 段祺瑞, Zhang promoted classical Chinese language and learning, which radicals of the New Culture Movement had exposed as reactionary and obscurantist. Other well-known returners were Ding Wenjiang 丁文江 and Luo Wengan 罗文干, who published the weekly *Nuli* 努力 (Endeavour). Luo worked as Finance Minister, while Wang Chonghui 王宠惠 became Prime Minister. In 1917, Li Jiannong 李剑农 and Yang Duanliu 杨端六 set up the liberal journal *Taiping yang* 太平洋 (Pacific Ocean), to which other British Chinese students were the main contributors. Wang Shijie 王世杰 and Chen Yuan 陈垣, members of the Chinese Students' Union in Britain, published the well-known journal *Xiandai pinglun* 现代评论 (Modern review) after their return to China.[74]

Some Chinese students from Britain opposed Chiang Kai-shek after 1927. Between the 1910s and the 1930s, several subsequently well-known Chinese intellectuals studied at the London School of Economics and Political Science (LSE), a centre of socialist thinking founded by the Fabians Sidney and Beatrice Webb. Zhang Junmai 张君劢 (Carson Chang) visited England in 1915–1916 and translated the *Grammar of Politics* (1925) by Harold Laski, a lecturer at LSE. Luo Longji 罗隆基, Wang Zaoshi 王造时, and Chu Anping 储安平 all studied in London and were deeply influenced by the Fabians. Zhang, Luo, and Chu took part in the struggle against Chiang Kai-shek's authoritarian regime.[75]

Although students played a big part in Chinese transnational politics in Britain, their fixation on the homeland and their transient status ruled them out as a long-term influence. For such people, China's interests absolutely outweighed those of Chinese communities abroad. They judged their actions on behalf of the Chinese in Britain less by their intrinsic worth than by the extent to which they contributed to resolving China's crisis of sovereignty. Even their commitment to bringing literacy and hygiene to Chinatown was inspired mainly by a wish to stop British people looking down on the Chinese.

Transnationalism from the top down: organisations and activities sponsored by homeland representatives

Chinese political parties, homeland governments and their consular officials, the government and local authorities in Britain, and multilateral institutions formed at the European and the world level have all had a hand in promoting Chinese transnational ties in Britain. Here, we look at party or state-sponsored projects aimed at the 'transnational reincorporation'[76] of Chinese migrants and their descendants and the effects of British and European policies, as a manifestation of transnationalism 'from the top down'.

In the closing years of the Qing, the imperial court and its diplomats worked hard to influence Chinese overseas, as part of a global campaign to harness their resources and loyalties and to undermine support for the reformist Kang Youwei 康有为 and for Sun Yat-sen. The Chinese in Britain and Europe were not the main subjects of this competition for support, yet they did receive visits from Sun and Kang, who met Chinese radicals and encouraged them to engage in politics. Later, Chinese seafarers in British ports developed ties with labour-movement bodies and Comintern supporters. Between the wars, both the Guomindang and the Chinese Communist Party (CCP) ran branches in Europe. After the 1927 split in China, many of the Guomindang's functions were taken over by the Chinese Embassy, while the communists stayed underground.

In the Second World War, radicals created a patriotic movement among Chinese students in Britain and in Chinatown that resonated with British antifascism. The CCP-influenced Chinese Seamen's Union 中华海员工业联合总会 sought to influence Chinese crews and to win members to the party's British-based branch. Associations sponsored by Nanjing's representatives also appeared.

Not all transnational influences are tied to state or political institutions. Churches have helped cement ethnic-Chinese identities and link Chinese to their compatriots and co-ethnics in other places. Dissident campaigns that start in China but gain bases in the diaspora also try to influence Chinese residents and students and gain credibility through the global human-rights discourse.

(i) Early Chinese political parties and state-sponsored associations

The overseas-Chinese identity, constructed starting in 1880, was used first by imperial representatives and then by radical nationalists to agitate among Chinese in Southeast Asia and other places. Until the mid-nineteenth century, the imperial court viewed emigrants as renegades. By the 1880s, however, it had come to value its overseas 'compatriots' as a potential source of capital and skills and tried to develop ways of influencing and resinicising them. In 1901, it transformed the Zongli Yamen 总理衙门 (the General Office for the Affairs of Various Countries, established in 1861 to deal with foreign powers) into a Foreign Ministry that conducted diplomatic relations and administered labour migration, overseas study, and overseas-Chinese associations. In 1903, the Board of Trade in Beijing required Chinese traders overseas to set up Chinese Chambers of Commerce to be supervised by members of the diplomatic staff.[77]

At around the turn of the century, Kang and Sun competed for support among Chinese overseas. Their campaigns to spread political transnationalism and the idea of the expatriate sojourner were highly successful. The Revive China Society 兴中会, formed by Sun Yat-sen in 1894 to overthrow the Qing, recruited up to 80 per cent of its 300 members from among Chinese overseas.[78] The imperial court tried to counteract them by sponsoring yet more associations.

This strategy resulted in what was probably Britain's earliest pan-Chinese association, the Chinese Guild 中华会馆, a non-commercial body set up at the start of the twentieth century, perhaps in 1905, and mentioned by Dai Hongci 戴鸿慈 in his travel diary. It received its finances from Wang Daxie 汪大燮, the Chinese Minister in London (who awarded it an annual grant of £600), and from student contributions. One of quite a few such bodies founded across the world in the dynasty's dying years, it survived into the 1950s.[79] These organisations are the earliest example of attempts at the transnational engineering of ethnic identity by a Chinese government.

Ethnic Chinese who had suffered discrimination welcomed Kang's and Sun's campaign to support their rights and elevate China's status. However, Sun's agents encountered obstacles, two of which had to do with a deficit of Chineseness. Some Chinese identified not with China but with their 'overseas' place of residence, others less with China than with their ancestral place in China.[80]

Up until a couple of years before 1911, few Chinese in Southeast Asia supported Sun and far more followed Kang, who favoured a constitutional monarchy based on Confucian values and modern education. Sun and Kang were bitter rivals: their supporters sometimes clashed violently.[81] Subsequently, most Southeast Asian Chinese switched their allegiance to Sun and supported the Republic.

The most important early Chinese organisation in Britain was Chee Kung Tong 致公堂, set up by immigrants from Siyi.[82] We have looked at Chee Kung Tong's grassroots role. Here, we examine its elite connections.

Chee Kung Tong was also known, in English, as the Chinese Masonic Hall, a name that intimated its role in support of revolutionary movements, in the tradition of organisations like the Hongmen Society 洪门社. Equating Chinese secret societies with Masonry was the work of European Freemasons keen (at a time when Masonry was under political suspicion) to demonstrate that theirs 'was an honorable order that had originated in antiquity' and 'the Chinese and Masonic orders were descendants of a common mystic ancestor'. Organisations like Chee Kung Tong took advantage of the Masonic claim to adopt the name 'Chinese Freemasons' (although all they had in common were surface similarities).[83] Seen from another angle, use of the term suggests some Chinese wanted to advertise their modernising goals to the British public.[84]

Fraternities like the Hongmen Society lived on the underside of Chinese society, where they bonded worker to employer by swearing brotherhood and acted as criminal gangs and mutual-aid groups. At times, they rose up against the Chinese state, fomenting rebellion 'when ameliorative mechanisms fell short'. Most adopted a Ming-restorationist ideology and later linked up with Chinese political groups, in China and abroad.[85] When their attempts to overthrow the 'foreign' (that is, non-Han) Qing and restore the Ming dynasty failed, many leaders fled overseas. This political emigration helps to explain why groups like the Hongmen Society were so active among Chinese overseas.

Sun Yat-sen first came into contact with the Hongmen Society in 1886 in Guangzhou. In 1904, Chee Kung Tong in Hawaii admitted him as a member. Sun admired Hongmen's worldwide connections, which he hoped to harness for his revolution. He noted that it 'has long extended to [China's] eighteen provinces and to the countries of the five continents'. However, its disorganisation dismayed him, so he proposed reforms and tried to reorganise Chee Kung Tong's finances and constitution before heading for London.[86]

Chee Kung Tong in Britain was, as we have seen, controlled by Siyinese, who ran it alongside their See Yip Association. The circumstances of its founding in Liverpool are not known, but it was probably masterminded from San Francisco, where a forerunner had been set up by Siyinese in 1852.[87] Organisations of the same name and with a common ritual, ideology, and programme grew up across the world, as part of the milieu in which Chinese republicanism took shape.

The Siyinese lodge of Hongmen in San Francisco, known as the Lide tang 立德堂 (Society for Establishing Virtue), was said to have more than 100,000 members in the United States in the late nineteenth century, organised in semi-autonomous branches. In 1862, Chee Kung Tong came into being in San Francisco, also as a lodge of Hongmen. It spread rapidly across America by championing republicanism and campaigning against 'bullying and humiliation by hooligans, policemen, and immigration officers'.

The leaders of San Francisco's Chee Kung Tong campaigned to win support for their political goals in countries throughout the world, mainly among fellow Siyinese. A Cuban branch was set up in 1902 and an Australian branch in 1919, at their direct instigation, on the basis of fraternities established in earlier years under other names.[88] They directly influenced the course of the Jamaican Chee Kung Tong and probably had a hand in founding its South African and New Zealand lodges.[89]

In Southeast Asia, Hongmen was active more than 100 years earlier than in North America. Later, Chee Kung Tong joined the armed resistance to the British in Malaya.[90] It is not clear what role Southeast Asian lodges played in spreading the organisation,[91] but we do know Hongmen was exported to the Philippines in the late nineteenth century by Cantonese remigrants from the United States.[92]

This transnationalisation and modernisation of Chee Kung Tong, a society of arcane origins, was crowned in 1925 by the San Francisco society's decision to organise a political party, the China Chee Kung Party 中国致公党. Supporters tried to form such a party in China in 1912, but their efforts were blocked by Hu Hanmin 胡汉民 (1878–1936),

Sun Yat-sen's secretary at the time. Its supporters' sense of disappointment and betrayal led them to choose Chen Jiongming 陈炯明 as their first president in 1925, at a time when Chen was at war with Sun.[93] The new party established its headquarters in Hong Kong in 1931. In 1933, it claimed a membership outside China and in southern China of more than 400,000 (probably an exaggeration). After the start of the Sino-Japanese War in 1937, it collected money for the resistance. In 1946, it came under the influence of the CCP, which had a better understanding of how to handle such groups than Hu Hanmin and his colleagues. After 1949, it was incorporated as one of Beijing's 'patriotic and democratic' parties (in effect, ornaments on the regime).

Most overseas delegates at the China Chee Kung Party's interwar congresses, held in Hong Kong in 1925 and 1931, were from America, Oceania, and Southeast Asia. No one from Britain or Europe seems to have attended, and there is no apparent record of the British Chee Kung Tong ever joining. The party was a bureaucratic structure with no real power over its claimed sections. 'Hongmen associations overseas still had a large degree of independence and initiative,' according to a study. 'The resolution taken at the First Congress to become a party could not be widely implemented.' In 1932, its members in the United States received publicity for supporting the Nineteenth Route Army's anti-Japanese campaign in Shanghai, but in Britain there seems to have been no such action. Only later, during the Japanese War of 1937–1945, did Chee Kung Tong in Britain act simultaneously with its counterparts in North and South America in support of the resistance.[94]

In 1950, the China Chee Kung Party held its Fourth Congress under the new communist regime.[95] After that, it ceased its overseas activities and concentrated on organising 'returned Overseas Chinese' and 'relatives of Overseas Chinese' in China. (This switch coincided with Beijing's decision to abandon dual nationality and promote free choice of citizenship, to protect its foreign relations in Southeast Asia.) Towards the end of the century, the China Chee Kung Party had a membership of just 8463 and served the regime by doing 'friendship work' among Chinese overseas.[96] So Chee Kung Tong's transnational heyday came in the first half of the twentieth century, after which its horizons shrank dramatically under a supposedly internationalist but actually chauvinistic government in Beijing.

In Britain, Chee Kung Tong more or less stagnated after 1911. Its leaders continued to stay in touch with their counterparts in the United States, Canada, and Australia, but most such contacts were personal rather than official. Unlike Chee Kung Tong organisations in North

America, which were part of a broader network that spanned the continent, the British lodge was a lone outpost, without equivalents in Europe. Nevertheless, the Guomindang continued to take advantage of Chee Kung Tong's influence in Liverpool. In 1946, with elections planned in China, Chinese residents were encouraged to register at the Consulate, the local Guomindang branch, or Chee Kung Tong. Chee Kung Tong also collected money to relieve floods in Guangdong in 1948.[97] By that time, however, its political role was all but finished.

Chee Kung Tong failed to transform itself into an independent political party among Chinese overseas and to influence politics in China. After reuniting the country in the late 1920s, the Chiang Kai-shek regime went to great lengths to set up branches of the Guomindang in Chinese communities throughout the world. However, the Guomindang was no more prepared in the 1930s and the 1940s than the communists in the 1950s to share the stage with another party. The Liverpool Chee Kung Tong was to the Guomindang's exact taste – a non-political association dedicated to providing welfare.

Both Sun Yat-sen and Kang Youwei visited Britain and influenced Chinese radicals in organisations like Chee Kung Tong. First to arrive was Sun, who sailed into Liverpool in September 1896 and left London in July 1897.[98] Sun turned up in London again in the spring of 1905, when he told Chee Kung Tong supporters about his programme to reform the organisation and its finances.[99] In London, he met Yan Fu 严复, an educational administrator and prolific translator of Western works, who was then studying in Britain. Yan Fu was interested in politics and had earlier accompanied Guo Songtao to Parliament, but his and Sun's views proved to be irreconcilable.[100]

During his second visit to Europe, at the invitation of a group of students, Sun set up branches of the Revive China Society in Brussels, Berlin, Paris, and London. His European Chinese supporters paid his onward fare to Japan and pledged 20 per cent of their income to his movement.[101] In the same year, in Tokyo, he founded the Revolutionary League 革命同盟会 (reformed in 1911 as the Guomindang) by amalgamating several revolutionary groups. He then drew his European supporters into the new party, which had branches in British colonies throughout Southeast Asia and elsewhere as well as in Britain and mainland Europe. Members in Britain who had previously lived in Japan included Wu Zhihui 吴稚晖, a leader of the Chinese anarchists; Yang Changji 杨昌济, Mao Zedong's teacher in Hunan; and Zhang Shizhao.[102] One supporter, the student Yang Dusheng 杨笃生, was provoked by the failure of the anti-Qing rebellions to commit suicide by throwing himself into the sea at Liverpool, an incident commemorated at a memorial meeting by other Chinese.[103]

Sun visited Britain for the last time in November 1911, when he spent a few days in London and Paris before returning to China after the fall of the Qing. In London, his supporters got him to sketch a design for a new national flag, which they strung across a street in Chinatown.[104]

Despite his visits to Britain's Chee Kung Tong,[105] Sun expressed disappointment with the Chinese in Britain. 'In Europe now there are no Chinese students or new Chinese immigrants', he wrote (inaccurately) in his diary. 'Although my intention is to promote revolution, there's no point [in doing so in Europe]. Since my whole life is dedicated exclusively to making revolution, I won't stay long in Europe'.[106]

Kang was apparently even less enthusiastic about his British and European contacts. He visited Britain no fewer than eight times between 1899 and 1907, always as part of a wider tour.[107] However, he left only a fragmentary record of his stay. He does not refer to his meetings with Chinese immigrants, although he does mention talking with two Chinese women students in Edinburgh.[108]

The Siyinese in Britain, like those in other parts of the English-speaking world, gave Sun their support, perhaps because of his prior contacts with Siyinese in North America. Like Chee Kung Tong, the See Yip Association in Britain also backed China's republicans. However, the Association at first appears to have made little distinction between the revolutionary Sun and the reformist Kang. Today, it continues to treasure an inscription written by Kang while staying on its premises.[109]

Whereas parts of the Chinese community in Southeast Asia were long established and locally embedded by the early twentieth century, nearly all the Chinese in Britain were immigrants. In Southeast Asia, localist attachments (in China or in Southeast Asia itself) were an obstacle to identifying with the radical or reformist cause. In the English-speaking world, regional and political loyalties partly coincided: both Sun and Kang were Cantonese, like the great majority of Chinese in Britain and North America.

So it is not surprising that many Chinese in Britain responded enthusiastically to the overtures of China's émigré leaders. They closely followed the events of 1913, when Yuan Shikai 袁世凱 carried out a reactionary coup against a Guomindang-inspired rebellion (the so-called Second Revolution). 'Political feeling has run high during the recent events, in which the members of the [East End Chinese] colony have taken an absorbed and curiously simple and uncomprehending interest', wrote a patronising *Times* reporter. The report continued: 'With the most imperfect knowledge and childlike views of public affairs, the majority profess themselves admirers of Dr. Sun Yat-sen, who is generally believed, in some vague way, to have done much for China, and as Cantonese, they are for the south, and against north, to a man.'[110]

However, their response was less intense than in Southeast Asia, where Chinese communities were hundreds of times larger and more varied in composition. Although the early Chinese in Britain made a contribution to homeland politics in the early twentieth century, it could not match that of Chinese in other continents, who were among Sun's most dependable supports.

In the first decade of the twentieth century, Sun's influence gradually came to eclipse Kang's worldwide. Chinese political and native-place associations in Britain incorporated radical goals into their charters. The associations gave more or less equal weight to the interests of emigrants and the struggle in China.

Some Chinese leaders in the British ports saw their personal futures in terms of Chinese politics. Just after the Republican Revolution of 1911, Wong Kau 黃球,[111] vice-president of 'the Chinese Republican Society', left Liverpool in the hope (not realised) of taking up a post in China's new government.[112] Fong On, a merchant like Wong Kau, was a leader of the same group. 'Liverpool has never been a backwater in Chinese affairs', concluded Susan Craggs, on the basis of her study of them.[113]

Wong Kau's activities attest to his high political connections. He was not alone in failing to gain an official appointment under the Republic. Chee Kung Tong leaders in other countries were also disappointed and accused Sun of reneging on promises to reward them.[114] Many who had purchased bonds before the revolution were unable to cash them in. Others who wanted Chee Kung Tong to play a formal role in the new Republic under a new name[115] were (as we have seen) refused permission to register it as a political party. In other respects, however, Sun's Guomindang kept faith with its overseas supporters. It provided services for them and promulgated a nationality code in 1929 based on the principle of *jus sanguinis*.[116]

Although the British Chinatown's Cantonese origins predisposed it to support Sun, a politics based on regional connections can misfire if regional rivalries emerge or doctrine takes precedence. When Sun urged members of his Revolutionary League to join Chee Kung Tong in San Francisco in 1910, some younger supporters refused, on the grounds that it was backward and superstitious. In Britain, there is no record of League members joining Chee Kung Tong. The Tong in Liverpool lacked the full Republican ardour of its counterparts in the United States, where branches sold their premises to support Sun's cause. There is perhaps also an ethnic reason for its relative inertia. Whereas Chee Kung Tong was Cantonese, leaders of the Revolutionary League in Britain like Zhang Shizhao, Yang Dusheng, and Yang Changji were Hunanese. They scorned Chee Kung Tong's 'feudalism' and provincialism. Their regional origins and modern politics ruled out a close relationship with Chee Kung Tong. As for Wu Zhihui, he was an anarchist, despite his friendship with Sun, and had a doctrinal difference with the Sun-ites.[117]

Both before and during the First World War, the Guomindang ran a branch in London.[118] Another Chinese organisation with revolutionary connections was Liverpool's Progress Club 共进会, founded by the Singaporean Chinese Yeung (known as James Henry Young). Yeung's biography, like that of other Chinatown leaders, disproves the theory that Britain's Chinese community was no more than a collection of drifters, adventurers, and deserting seafarers. Yeung, a prosperous wine merchant's son, had studied law at Raffles College and qualified as an accountant before sailing to Britain as a Blue Funnel steward. His Progress Club was so close to the Guomindang that it lost many of its functions after the collapse of Chiang Kai-shek's regime in 1949 and the Chinese Consul's departure.[119]

Chee Kung Tong also continued to play a role in the interwar years. In 1920, a British journalist reported that Chinese in London's East End 'will faithfully obey any law their Consul lays down. Otherwise they are hauled before the "Chee Kung Tong", the influential body of Chinese gentlemen who hold judicial court in a building in High-street, Pennyfields, to inquire into grievances and wrongdoings of their fellow-countrymen'.[120]

Beyond these Chinese groups, individual Chinese socialists and radicals played a role in British organisations. The Chinese Lee Foo, identified as 'local secretary of the Chinese Seamen's Union', was a member before the First World War of Liverpool's International Club, an anarcho-syndicalist organisation associated with Jim Larkin, the Liverpool Irish workers' leader.[121] In London, Fung Saw was chosen as Labour's prospective parliamentary candidate in Holborn in 1927.[122] Other Chinese were active in leftwing parties and the trade unions, where they tried to represent Chinese and ethnic-Chinese interests and learned how to organise and agitate.

(ii) The British Chinatown and Japanese expansionism, 1919–1921

During the First World War, in 1915, the Chinese warlord government in Beijing secretly agreed under pressure to transfer German privileges in Shandong to Japan, in return for a loan.[123] To improve its international standing, the warlord government in Beijing sent labourers to work for the Allies as battlefield ancillaries. In 1919, it sent representatives to the Paris Peace Conference that ended the war. For China, the main issue was whether to validate the Shandong transfer. Many Chinese believed the Conference would deny Japan its Chinese gains, given President Woodrow Wilson's commitment to self-determination and world democracy. The decision in Japan's favour outraged Chinese patriots and led to mass demonstrations, the political culmination of an intellectual revolution that had started several years earlier. The militancy infected Chinese in Britain, who started a campaign of protest against the Versailles Treaty.

In February 1919, the Cambridge Anglo-Chinese Society passed a resolution expressing 'its deep sympathy and unreserved support for China's legitimate and just claim to rid herself of the suicidal obligations extorted from her by force and intimidation during the last four years in the form of treaties, conventions or agreements, secret or published, treaties purporting to impair China's sovereignty and integrity, contrary to the public law and morality of the family of nations and contrary to the new order of things under a League of Nations'.[124] In Paris, students and other Chinese gathered outside the delegation's residence and the conference hall and urged delegates not to sign the Treaty.

Two years later, sovereignty was still a burning issue for Chinese radicals, including in Britain. Between November 1921 and February 1922, the Powers met in Washington to work out new security arrangements in the Pacific region. The agenda included the need to reconstruct the Powers' relations with China and curb Japanese ambitions. Chinese throughout the world saw the Washington Conference as a chance to redress wrongs. In Britain, Chee Kung Tong and the Guomindang ran campaigns and a meeting of 150 Chinese set up a joint Committee of Workers, Merchants, and Students 工商学联合委员会. The meeting called on the Chinese delegation to fight for China's territorial integrity and political independence and to denounce secret deals. They condemned the Anglo-Japanese Alliance and demanded that the Shandong and Jiaoji Railways be returned to China, that Japan's demands be denied, and that the Powers give up their concessions and settlements and award China tariff autonomy.[125]

On September 4, at another meeting in London's East End, a merchant called Jiang 蒋 explained the iniquities of the Anglo-Japanese Alliance to an audience that included Chinese workers. The meeting cabled Sun Yat-sen to tell him to stand firm against the foreigners and form a joint delegation with the Beijing warlord government to send to Washington. In Liverpool, a 'Peace Conference' chaired by Luo Tan 骆潭 and Wong Kau heard speeches about the importance of the Washington Conference and about Chinese activities in London. An organisation known as the General Investigation Association of Workers, Merchants, and Students in Europe 旅欧工商学检查总会 pledged to contact Chinese overseas and monitor Chinese foreign policy. (Its president was the liberal intellectual Chen Yuan 陈垣.) One member was sent to the United States to visit compatriots and monitor the diplomats, while a merchant was sent to the Netherlands to found a branch there.[126] On 21 October, a banquet was held for Wellington Koo 顾维钧, en route to Washington. On 26 November, a special meeting cabled the Chinese delegates to say: 'Your ten points and strong stand against international control fully express sentiment Chinese people and have our unyielding support[. W]ithdraw from conference rather than submit'.[127] In 1922, Wong Kau hosted delegates returning to China from Washington by way of Liverpool.[128]

The Conference satisfied some Chinese demands, at least in part. It resolved to recognise Chinese sovereignty, independence, and territorial integrity and, in the longer term, to abolish extraterritoriality. Japan, for its part, agreed to relinquish some privileges in Shandong. But the meeting failed to assuage radicals in China, who launched a boycott of foreign goods. Before long, a mass movement against imperialism was taking shape that came to a head in new revolutionary upheavals.

The meetings in London and Liverpool in 1921 and the political ferment caused by the Washington Conference were unprecedented in the history of Britain's Chinese community. For the first time, students and ordinary Chinese united in a single association. They adopted a position independent of the Chinese Government and parties and told Sun to overcome his differences with the warlords and put on a display of unity in Washington, but they showed little trust in Beijing and monitored its diplomats. By sending representatives to the United States and the Netherlands, they demonstrated their transnational affiliations. Modern nationalism had taken root among Britain's Chinese. The Association of Workers, Merchants, and Students 工商学共进会 set up in 1921 to lead the patriotic movement lasted for several years.[129]

(iii) Chinese political parties and state-sponsored associations in the interwar years

(a) The Guomindang

The Guomindang continued to run branches in Europe between the wars, when the CCP also became active. The transition towards the First United Front between communists and Nationalists in China in 1923 was a crucial episode in the preparation of the Chinese Revolution. The main steps were taken in China, but the alliance first took shape – in the form of a fusion of members of both parties in a single body – in Europe. In November 1922, Wang Jingqi 王京岐 began preparing a Guomindang organisation in France. In Lyons in November 1923, he and Zhou Enlai 周恩来 and others set up the European Branch of the Guomindang 中国国民党旅欧支部. No one from Britain attended its founding conference – most of the 92 delegates were from Germany, Belgium, and France.[130] Subsequently, the German Branch of the Guomindang 中国国民党住德支部, founded in Berlin in 1925, became its strongest European section.

Before 1927, during the First United Front in China, the distinction between the two Chinese parties remained vague. In November 1923, Zhou Enlai and others set up the European Branch of the Guomindang 中国国民党旅欧支部 in Lyons.[131] Also in 1923, a London branch was set up by Qiu Zhusan and Zhang Daofan 张道藩. The European branch controlled cells in France, Belgium, Germany, and elsewhere and had some 200 members. The British and Russian branches were not included in the general branch, whose name changed to the French General Branch of the Chinese Guomindang 中国国民党驻法总支部.[132]

In 1923, the Guomindang in Guangzhou set up an Overseas Chinese Affairs Bureau 侨务局, transformed in 1932 into an Overseas Chinese Commission 侨务委员会 under the jurisdiction of the Administrative Yuan 行政院. The two-way traffic between Chinese overseas and China intensified, especially after 1935, when the Guomindang reformed its overseas organisation and called on Chinese overseas to increase their support for China.[133]

After the Guomindang split in 1927, some factions established bases abroad, including in Britain. One example is the Cantonese faction under Hu Hanmin. Hu's opposition to Chiang's constitution led to his arrest in 1931, sparking a revolt that forced Chiang to free him. Given the Cantonese provenance of the Chinese in Britain, Hu Hanmin sent the student Hu Lifeng to London to set up a new Chinese party (in June 1934).[134]

Once the Guomindang had formed its Government in 1927, many of its functions overseas were taken over by diplomats. The Embassy in London held meetings for Chinese residents at New Year and on important political anniversaries. On Mondays, it held a Sun Yat-sen memorial service, at which political issues were also discussed.[135]

In the 1930s, the Embassy directly supervised resident Chinese and kept an indirect eye on students through the Chinese Institute. This institute was founded in 1932 by the British Universities' China Committee as a centre for Sino-British cultural activities. Most members were students funded by Nanjing. The two other groups – the self-supporting offspring of rich families and those admitted on scholarships awarded from the Boxer Indemnity Fund – were less amenable to control and denounced the first group as 'Blueshirts 蓝衣社' (that is, fascists) and government informers.[136]

(b) The CCP

The early Chinese communists made no secret of their belief in the revolutionary potential of Chinese overseas. In 1927, Xiao Chunü 肖楚女 wrote that more than four out of five Chinese overseas were 'coolies', well placed to build an international front against imperialism.[137] Chinese labour in Europe was particularly amenable to radical influence given its role in shipping, an industry in which party organisers in south China had achieved their best results.

In the 1920s, France was the main European centre of Chinese radicalism. As Europe's first and, for a while, only country of extensive transoceanic immigration, France recruited large numbers of foreigners to work in industry, among them several hundred Chinese. Other Chinese, the Huagong, arrived in the war itself; several thousand stayed on after the armistice. Between 1919 and 1922, 2000 Chinese youngsters sailed to France to study and work, under a scheme organised by Li Shizeng 李石曾, a Chinese anarchist entrepreneur in Paris. In Paris, they founded the Chinese Communist Youth Party 少年共产党, which merged with the Chinese communists in Moscow and China.[138]

Chinese in Britain in the 1910s and the 1920s had fewer dealings with internationalist labour-movement bodies than their counterparts in France, Germany, and Belgium. In mainland Europe, Comintern supporters among the Chinese émigrés could make use of the networks and resources of local communist parties, which were bigger and better organised than Britain's. The founding of the precursor of the European Branch of the CCP 中国共产党旅欧支部 in Berlin in the autumn of

1922 benefited from Comintern and German communist resources. The founding of the Chinese Communist Youth Party in Paris happened independently of the Comintern but reflected the strength of Marxist ideas in France. Members of the European Branch were also active in Belgium and Russia. The Huagong provided a proletarian constituency for it to agitate among. In Britain, there were neither Huagong nor Chinese communists in any numbers.[139]

The European Branch confined its activities to mainland Europe, particularly France, where it recruited several dozen students and some labourers.[140] There is no evidence of any effort in the early days to spread communist organisation to the Chinese in Britain. The European Branch had sub-branches in France, Germany, and Belgium, but probably no more than about eight members in Germany, fewer still in Belgium, and none in Britain. In 1921, Zhou Enlai spent several months in Britain, where he made contact with Chinese, but his reports focused on world politics and British labour.[141]

The Chinese communists' omission of Britain from their European plan is hard to explain. Britain's role in China should have made it a prime target, while the pool of Chinese workers created by the shipping companies cried out for a party of the proletariat. However, the seafarers were polarised in the 1920s into mutually hostile groups and fought pitched battles on the streets. In the eyes of Lao She 老舍 and other Chinese observers, they were divided into the villains, who brought shame on China, and the patriots – 'hard-working, upright, illiterate workers who spoke no English, had no special skills, but who nevertheless had a deep sense of patriotism, and would rather starve to death than take part in anything that could possibly bring dishonor to China'.[142]

The most likely reason for the Comintern's failure to plant a Chinese cell in Britain in the 1920s lay in a lack of opportunity and resources. In France, the work-study project and the Huagong presence had created a community ripe for radical politics. As for Germany, Zhou Enlai was resident in Berlin, where the Soviets had diplomatic representation (unlike in Britain and France before 1924) and the Comintern could provide direction and assistance.[143] The Chinese communists in Germany were aided by the powerful German Communist Party (KPD) and hundreds of Chinese students.[144]

Chinese anarchists were also active in Chinese workers' organisations across Europe and sent a representative, Ou Shengbai 区声白, to Britain 'to confer with the labour movement'.[145] However, we have no further knowledge of Ou's British mission.

The anti-imperialist upsurge in Shanghai in 1925 in the wake of the May Thirtieth Incident (when British police shot dead demonstrators) was greeted with impassioned demonstrations by Chinese and others in France and Germany.[146] In Britain, the protests were mainly confined to solidarity actions by the local labour movement, except for a rally by the Guomindang's London branch and the publication by the Union of Chinese Associations in Great Britain 旅英华人各界代表联合会 of an anti-imperialist pamphlet.[147]

In 1925, Chinese in Moscow organised a congress attended by delegates from communist parties in 39 countries, to denounce military intervention in China. The Congress had an electrifying effect on Chinese in mainland Europe, especially France, where 28 associations organised an anti-imperialist committee that set up ties with Chinese and non-Chinese opponents of foreign intervention in China in several European countries, including Britain. The Chinese Workers' Federation 中国工人联合会 joined with the London Guomindang in the spring of 1926 to rally the British labour movement in support of workers in Hong Kong and Guangzhou.[148]

The victories of the Northern Expedition, launched by the Guomindang in 1926 in alliance with the communists, were greeted with rallies in Paris and Berlin. In London, the Guomindang held a meeting in Albert Hall attended by Labour Party and trade-union representatives and threw a banquet for more than 300 Chinese and British guests. Throughout 1926, Chinese in Belgium, France, Germany, and the Netherlands campaigned against an unequal treaty signed between Belgium and China in 1865. This treaty became a big issue for Chinese throughout mainland Europe, but not in Britain. Even in mainland Europe the united front of Chinese radicals collapsed in 1927, when the Guomindang in China turned on the communists.[149]

(c) Towards an anti-Japanese United Front

Political activity in the Chinese community in Britain died down briefly after 1927, but the crisis in Sino-Japanese relations in the late 1920s and the 1930s led to its revival. In May 1928, Chinese in London held a meeting to protest against a Japanese attack on the Northern Expedition in Jinan. The names of the organisations that sprang up show that they reached out to the settled community of entrepreneurs and laundrymen as well as to students. In late 1931 or 1932, a group of 'Chinese workers and merchants' in London set up an anti-Japanese alliance 抗日同盟会, followed in 1933 by a Chinese Students' National Salvation Association 旅英中华学生救国会 founded by Chinese from

Southeast Asia and China. In 1934, a London branch of the Chinese People's Armed Self-Defence Association 中华民族武装自卫团伦敦分会 was set up, in response to a worldwide appeal by Song Qingling 宋庆龄, Sun Yat-sen's widow. Similar movements started up in Liverpool, where more than 500 Chinese joined a National Salvation Association, and in Edinburgh, where a Patriotic Workers and Merchants' Association 爱丁堡华侨爱国工商会 was formed. In 1936, these organisations united in an all-British Overseas Chinese Anti-Japanese National Salvation Association 旅英华侨抗日救国会, which planned to send people back to China to join the resistance.

This upsurge was part of a Europe-wide political offensive directed from Moscow. In 1935, the Comintern sent a group of Chinese under Wu Yuzhang 吴玉章 to Paris, where they published *Jiuguo shibao* 救国时报 (National salvation times), an influential party journal at the time.[150] The Paris bureau coordinated Chinese radical movements throughout the world, including in Britain and Europe. The journal claimed a circulation of 20,000, half of which were distributed to Chinese in 43 countries. In early 1936, Wu Yuzhang urged Chinese communists all over Europe to form national-salvation associations on the basis of student unions. In August, Wu's team announced a Pan-European Overseas Chinese Anti-Japanese Congress 全欧华侨抗日大会.[151]

Hu Qiuyuan 胡秋原, a British-based Chinese (but not a communist), was secretary of the preparatory committee.[152] He also presided over the Congress itself, which took place in Paris in September 1936 with more than 450 delegates from Britain, France, Germany, Switzerland, and Holland. Hu, Wu Yuzhang, and the educationalist Tao Xingzhi 陶行知 set up a Pan-European Overseas Chinese Federation to Resist Japanese Aggression and Save the Nation 全欧华侨抗日救国联合会.[153] The federation published a fortnightly journal in English, French, and German. It also organised seminars on China attended by western sympathisers and Sinologists, wrote letters to the press, and circulated bulletins. Chinese businesspeople in Europe were asked to stop selling Japanese goods and a volunteer corps 回国参战服务团 was sent to China.[154]

The Federation called upon Chinese in America and Southeast Asia to follow its example and sent people to help them do so. In August 1937, one year after the founding of the European Federation, an association was set up to cover North America, with 47 branches. A year after that, in October 1938, a Southeast Asian association formed, and soon claimed more than 1000 branches. These wartime federations ran worldwide campaigns, exchanged personnel, and were linked by important political leaders like Song Qingling in Hong Kong. The communists were their mainstay, but they also found favour with non-communists. Even publications of Taibei's Overseas Chinese Commission praise the Congress as 'the greatest merger ever in the history of the overseas Chinese in Europe'.[155]

These events in Britain and Europe were a reverberation of the turbulence in China, where student demonstrations on 9 December 1935 touched off a year-long protest against Japanese aggression and Chiang Kai-shek's failure to resist it. The China protests helped pave the way for the Second United Front in 1937. The rousing of Chinese in Britain and Europe behind the CCP's programme also played a part in this, by encouraging the protest movement back in China, supporting the campaign for a unified resistance, and focusing liberal and radical Europeans on China.

The patriotic movement won widespread support among Chinese in Britain, but not to the same extent as in mainland Europe. In Berlin in the early 1930s, the KPD threw its weight behind the anti-Japanese movement led by Chinese students and a galaxy of communists and fellow-travellers including Deng Yanda 邓演达, Song Qingling, Wang Bingnan 王炳南, and Cheng Fangwu 成仿吾.[156] In Paris, the centre of Chinese communist work in Europe after the Nazi takeover in Germany, the movement benefited from a strong communist party and a Chinese radical tradition.

In the mid-1930s, support for the CCP in China began to revive, at the same time as the Comintern abandoned its extreme leftism and began wooing the bourgeois democracies as a counterweight to Hitler. In the new climate, the CCP set up its own direct links to Chinese overseas. In 1936, it sent Deng Fa 邓发[157] to Britain to lecture on party policy. In Britain, Deng became a friend of Sam Chen. After a few years back in China, he returned to Britain in late 1945 by way of Paris. In London and Liverpool, he restored ties to his old comrades and introduced British communists to Mao's concept of New Democracy, before dying in 1946 in a plane crash on his way to Chongqing.[158]

Yang Xianyi 杨宪益 (1914–), one of China's foremost translators, wrote an account of the campaign in Britain for a united resistance to Japan.[159] Yang, about to study at Oxford and Chairman of the Chinese Students' Union in London, often visited the Hampstead home of Professor Shelley Wang 王礼锡 in 1935, where he discussed politics with other exiles. Wang, a onetime member of the radical Fujian Government set up in 1934 by the Chinese Nineteenth Route Army, shared his house with other Chinese intellectuals, one of whom, S. I. Hsiung 熊式一, was the author of *Lady Precious Stream*, a well-known play written in English.[160] Wang created a lively circle of political debate. Wang, Hsiung, and the youthful Yang all played a part in organising an anti-Japanese movement, not only in Chinatown but among the wider British population. Nearly all Wang's circle returned to China in the late 1930s. In Oxford, Yang boosted support for the China Society (with a mainly British membership) from around 100 to more than 1000, by appealing to popular sympathy for China at a time of mounting Japanese aggression. He also brought out three issues of an English-language magazine, *Resurgence*, consisting of his own articles denouncing Japan.

During the Japanese War, Chiang Kai-shek saw Chinese overseas as a major source of support. An Overseas Chinese Anti-Japanese Mobilisation Association 华侨抗敌动员总会 set up in Guangzhou sent propaganda groups across the world and passed resolutions calling for an army of overseas-Chinese volunteers 华侨救国义勇军 and a campaign to boost overseas remittances.[161] The Chinese Government set up a propaganda office in London under Dr George Yeh 叶公超 and a branch of the Central News Agency under H. D. Liem.[162] These measures helped reinforce the patriotic movement among Chinese in Britain.

(iv) Chinese political activities in Britain in the Second World War

The Civil War that started in China in 1927 deterred many Chinese from expressing their political views. The start of the anti-Japanese agitation in China in the mid-1930s had a big effect on Chinese students in Europe but not, at first, on workers and entrepreneurs. However, the restoration of the united front in China in 1937 paved the way to the repoliticisation of Chinese communities everywhere, including Britain. After Chiang Kai-shek's declaration of war on the Axis in December 1941, Chinese seafarers, launderers, and caterers in Britain stood shoulder to shoulder with the students, until the resumption of the Civil War and the start of the Cold War drove them back into isolation.

In Liverpool, Britain's main centre of Chinese population in the war, the Consul encouraged the organisation of Chinese associations, which grew in number 'and extended their activities and influence from the confines of their ethnic group to the wider British society'.[163] The opening of a branch of the Bank of China in Liverpool in 1942 enabled the seafarers to transfer their earnings into Chinese currency.

Wellington Koo turned up in January 1941 to serve as Chinese Minister to the Court of St James, a post he had already occupied in 1920. Dr Koo, previously accredited as Minister to Washington and Paris, raised spirits by negotiating an end to extraterritoriality and helped weld the community to Chinese issues.[164]

In Liverpool, Chee Kung Tong and the Progress Club served as rallying points, service-centres for the wartime pool of seafarers, and a channel of communication between Chinese and British. The Progress Club was closely associated with the local Chinese Institute, run by agencies of the Chinese Government, and had the use of official staff and buildings.[165] Also in Liverpool, *Ju Ri xunkan* 拒日旬刊 (Anti-Japanese ten-day journal) began appearing in 1938. Liverpool Chinese staged gong-and-drum performances in Chinatown and played football matches against local teams, while Siyinese entrepreneurs withdrew their savings to buy war bonds.[166] Starting in 1942, National Savings Certificates worth £40,000 were sold to Chinese in the United Kingdom.[167] Articles in *Chung Hwa Chou Pao* 中华周报 (*China News Weekly*), the successor to *Ju Ri xunkan*, brimmed with patriotic sentiment.[168]

The old See Yip Association, moribund between the wars, was revived in 1941 under an affiliation with the Guomindang that continued until the Guomindang's expulsion from the Chinese mainland in 1949 and the exit of its consul from Liverpool.[169] It too collected money to support the war.[170] In London, the Workers' Club raised £7000 (a huge sum at the time) in support of the Chinese Government.[171]

Between 1937 and 1940, Britain's Chinese residents contributed a proportionately far greater amount to China's war effort than almost any other Chinese community overseas, as Table 5.1 shows. It would have been greater still had it included the contributions of the seafarers, who gave even more lavishly than the land community.

Welfare centres and associations affiliated to the Guomindang were founded to provide amenities for seafarers on shore leave. In 1944, a social club opened in Liverpool with the backing of the Merchant Navy Welfare Board and the Blue Funnel Line. Its aim, according to its Chinese warden, was to encourage seafarers to give up gambling and to 'listen to record recitals of Chinese opera and folk songs, watch TV, read Chinese newspapers and books, and join coach tours of English beauty spots'.

The stationing of thousands of Chinese seafarers in the city reversed the community's prewar decline. It also opened the way to the rebirth of the previously suppressed Chinese Seamen's Union. Homelessness caused by the aerial bombing of Chinese streets in Liverpool and London created another focus for community organisation.

The Chinese who sailed from Liverpool to keep the western approaches open helped to transform British perceptions, at least for the duration of the war and its ideology of antifascist inclusiveness.

Table 5.1   Contributions of Chinese overseas to China's war effort, 1937–1940

Place	Total donated (in Chinese dollars)	Chinese population, 1934	Average donated per month per person
Singapore/Malaya	125,768,003	1,709,392	1.89
Dutch East Indies	37,569,755	1,232,650	0.78
United States	50,979,103	74,954	17.44
Philippines	26,584,357	110,500	6.17
Hong Kong	11,842,119	825,645	0.37
Thailand	10,429,091	2,500,000	0.11
India and Burma	9,885,248	208,598	1.22
Vietnam	7,390,871	381,417	0.50
Australia	7,606,580	15,500	12.58
United Kingdom	5,366,707	8,000	17.20
Macao	257,770	119,875	0.06
Others	716,755	–	–
Total	294,396,358	4,059,035	1.86

Source: Liu Weisen 1999, p. 201.

Commentators admired their pluck and self-confidence, which they saw as a reflection of change in China. This report is typical:

> The Chinese seaman of today is very different from his predecessor of a generation ago. He is a child of the revolution and a soldier of China. Often as an engineer, fitter, joiner, repairer, he is doing highly skilled work he never did before and doing it well. He contributes without question – and sometimes without discretion – to the war funds of the Chinese Government. I was told of seamen who, returning from a long trip, subscribe the whole six months' earnings at one bang. The Chinese War Victims' Fund receives from Liverpool about £1,000 a month, most of it contributed by seamen.... The Chinese community in Liverpool today – the largest in Britain – is far removed from the fragment of Old Cathay, which the name of 'Chinatown' used to denote. New Chinatown is a microcosm of New China and in both, for the first time in the history of their race, all classes are welded into the common pool of emergent nationhood.[172]

Students continued in the first couple of years of the war to work for organisations like the communist-influenced Overseas Chinese Anti-Japanese National Salvation Association, until its disbanding in the late

1930s.[173] In 1937, Chinese communist officials in Paris began to draw British-based Chinese into their work. In July and August, Chinese delegates (including some from Britain) attended a communist-backed World Peace Conference in Brussels and a World Youth Congress in Geneva. In September, a second meeting followed.[174]

After the start of the Sino-Japanese War in July 1937, Yang Xianyi and other Chinese (including Shelley Wang) made propaganda for the resistance among the 800 Chinese restaurant and laundry workers in London's East End. They brought out *Resistance News*, a mimeographed daily consisting of translations of war news from the English press. The newspaper continued to appear until the winter of 1938.[175] In 1944, *Minzhu zhenxian* 民主阵线 (Democratic front) appeared in London, initially under Yang's editorship, and continued until September 1949.[176] At the end of the war, Chinese crowds in London, Amsterdam, and Paris took to the streets with dragon dances and banners as part of the victory celebrations.[177]

(v) Postwar political associations

(a) The Guomindang and the Taiwan connection

In the immediate postwar years, Chinese in Britain shared the mood of national optimism and euphoria in China. Gradually, however, their support for Chiang Kai-shek began to falter. The loss of faith can be traced through the pages of the last few issues of Liverpool's *Chung Hwa Chou Pao* (*China News Weekly*). In January 1948, an editorial urged readers to donate money to support the Nanjing Government.[178] Several months later, the same journal reprinted articles from liberal Chinese publications (*Dagong bao* 大公报 and *Guancha* 观察) criticising Guomindang corruption. An issue of particular concern was the war bonds. When peace returned in China, bondholders overseas expected their money back, but only the seafarers were refunded. 'If the government fails to understand the difficulties of people overseas or to carry out its legal obligation to protect the overseas Chinese', warned an editorial, 'it will forfeit their patriotism and support'.[179] At the very least and whatever its difficulties, the Government 'should pay back the overseas poor who have no means of livelihood'.[180]

After 1949, Beijing and Taibei began competing for the loyalty of Chinese abroad and for control of schools and associations. Despite their defeat and removal to Taiwan, the Nationalists continued to see themselves as China's sole government and protector of Chinese overseas and to favour them with laws and policies the communists abandoned. They profited from the Cultural Revolution of 1966–1976, when mainland leaders questioned the loyalty of Chinese with foreign ties and persecuted repatriates and relatives of Chinese abroad. They also benefited from China's general isolation in the Cold War years, when Beijing disregarded the interests of Chinese abroad. The rivalry resumed after Mao's death in 1976, when Beijing dropped its hostility to overseas 'compatriots'.

After the mainland fell to the communists and Britain recognised the new regime, Guomindang officials stranded in London were left to fend for themselves. Many formed the backbone of various pro-Taiwan associations. These included the Overseas Chinese Association 英国华侨协会, the Sun Yat-sen Society in the United Kingdom 英国中山协会, the Association of Chinese Culture 中华文化协会, the Chinese Chamber of Commerce 英国华商总会, and the Chinese Academic and Professionals Association in Britain 英国中华学术专业协会.

After the establishment of the Chinese Republic in 1912, the view that Chinese overseas should participate in homeland politics had become a Nationalist article of faith.[181] For most of the time, the Guomindang did nothing to fulfil its promise of a move towards democracy. In 1946, however, a National Conference met in Nanjing and Chinese abroad were permitted to take part in electing its committees.[182]

The European region elected Liu Ruxin as its representative. The election office was run from Paris; Chinese in Britain were urged to register at the Consulate or at the local offices of the Guomindang or Chee Kung Tong.[183] After returning from China, Liu Ruxin hosted celebrations in Paris, London, and Liverpool, where Chinese attributed the policy of 'assisting and protecting the economic development of overseas Chinese' adopted at the National Conference to his efforts.[184] The Guomindang preserved its policy of overseas representation even after its removal to Taiwan, but the overseas right to vote was both contentious and difficult to use. Flying to Taiwan was costly and dual nationals were disfranchised, while some Taiwanese questioned the legitimacy of suffrage that extended to non-tax payers. All in all, the policy was largely ineffective.[185]

In the 1950s and the 1960s, the Guomindang continued to run branches in several European countries including Britain, alongside organisations committed to 'anti-communist national salvation' and Sun Yat-sen's Three People's Principles. These organisations weakened when the European countries established diplomatic relations with Beijing. In later years, Taibei's focus changed to setting up Chinese cultural bodies and Free China Centres (formerly Free China Information Centres), which fought propaganda wars with the Chinese Embassy and pro-Beijing associations. Chinese scholars abroad continued to be invited to conferences in Taiwan. In 1981, the Guomindang sponsored the founding in London of *Ya Ou pinglun* 亚欧评论 (Asian European review), to promote its views and undermine the pro-independence propaganda of Taiwan's Democratic Progressive Party民主进步党 (DPP). Today, the handful of pro-Taibei associations tend to confine their activities to immigrants and sojourners from Taiwan rather than intervene in the broader Chinese community.[186]

The Taiwan-born leaders of the DPP that defeated the Guomindang in Taiwan's 2000 elections were less committed to supporting Chinese overseas than the old generation of mainland-born politicians, but the DPP preserved some of the institutions serving Chinese overseas. At the same time, it called on Chinese overseas to be 'not only mother of the revolution' (Sun's slogan) but 'father of democracy'.

(b) The Beijing connection

In the postwar liberation struggles in Southeast Asia, ethnic Chinese were portrayed by some indigenous leaders as a pro-Beijing fifth column. In the early 1950s, newly independent governments felt threatened by Beijing's calls on overseas Chinese to 'unite in a great patriotic alliance around China'. To protect its foreign relations and appease potential allies, Beijing subordinated its treatment of ethnic Chinese in the mid-1950s to its diplomatic relationships. It renounced the principle of *jus sanguinis*, gave up its policy of dual nationality, and promoted free choice of citizenship, while advising overseas Chinese to adopt the nationality of the host countries, intermarry with the local population, stop sending their children to school in China, and demonstrate allegiance to local governments. Most Chinese sought an accommodation with the new indigenous elites and played down their own ethnicity, for fear of being thought disloyal. Since the 1950s, only those people of Chinese descent who have not assumed foreign nationality count in Beijing's eyes as overseas Chinese, whereas the rest are ethnic Chinese.

Britain's recognition of Beijing in January 1950 resulted in a loosening of ties by Chinese in Britain. Nationalist historians claim that the arrival of Beijing's representatives in London led some entrepreneurs to scale down their business activities and step back from the limelight, to avoid attracting the Embassy's attention. This retreat is said to have 'directly or indirectly influenced the development of [Chinese] commerce and other aspects [of community life in Britain]'.[187] At the same time, clubs funded by the Nationalist Consul in the 1940s declined.[188]

Up until the late 1980s and the 1990s, the Chinese Embassy had little contact with the Chinese community. Most Chinese in the 1960s and the 1970s were immigrants from Hong Kong who enjoyed civic rights in Britain, did not require Chinese passports, and avoided homeland issues, unlike the pre-1927 pioneers.

However, organisations like the Kung Ho Association (founded by the communist labour leader Sam Chen in 1947) leaned towards Beijing after 1949. The older Workers' Club adopted a pro-communist stance in the early 1960s and raised China's Five-Starred Red Flag over its headquarters.[189] It displayed Maoist propaganda and was known locally as the 'Communist Club', although its members later denied that it was political.[190]

Two other leftist organisations are the Tai Ping Club, founded in 1948, and Liverpool's Wah-Shing 华声 (Voice of China).[191] In the 1960s, both organisations explicitly supported Beijing. Like the Workers' Club, the Tai Ping Club banned gambling and screened Chinese propaganda films. Also like the Workers' Club, it had an ascriptive as well as a political function – most members were Hakkas from Tai Po 大埔.[192] Before Beijing's adoption of an Open Door policy in 1978, the Workers' Club and the Kung Ho Association acted as unofficial links to China. In the absence of an adequate diplomatic service, they also received and entertained artists and athletes.[193]

In later years, the Kung Ho Association lost some of its political colouring and switched its focus to language teaching and sports. However, the Workers' Club identified even more strongly with Beijing after China's emergence from isolation and its economic and diplomatic advances. In 1984, its president Wen Liangsheng 文良生 was invited to celebrate National Day in Beijing, where he shook hands with Zhao Ziyang 赵紫阳.[194] In the 1990s, the Workers' Club sponsored some pro-Beijing associations, including the UK Chinese Activities Fund 全英华人华侨活动基金管理委员会 and the Society for the Promotion of Chinese Reunification 全英华人华侨中国统一促进会.[195]

Although Beijing has formally renounced the principle of dual nationality, mainland authorities continue to perceive ethnic Chinese as 'relatives and friends' and to adopt policies designed to win hearts and minds. One way in which they secure the allegiance of Chinese abroad is by rewarding individual supporters with political patronage, usually in the form of honorary appointments to official bodies and invitations to visit China. Chinese embassies and consulates are not without influence in associations representing mainland immigrants in Britain and Europe, which have access to a more effective propaganda machine than those associated with Taibei.[196]

Even in the early years of the People's Republic, veteran Chinatowners took pride in Beijing's achievements and perceived Taibei to be toothless and unreliable.[197] By the end of the twentieth century, the battle for the broad allegiance of Chinese in Europe with a patriotic outlook had been largely won by Beijing. Even so, those who closely follow Chinese politics are a small minority, and those who strongly identify with Beijing are a minority within the minority.

Clubs and societies formed by earlier generations of immigrants restored their ties to Guangdong in the 1980s and the 1990s, although their members are old and dwindling in number. In the Liverpool See Yip Association, Sun Yat-sen's portrait is exhibited alongside flags and pennants donated by mainland visitors. One leader reported donating £1000 to help build a road to his ancestral village.[198] The Chun Yee Society exhibits books from China, but an association leader admits that 'nobody reads them. They just speak Cantonese, they can hardly read or write Mandarin or English. The association has become a workers' club for old men. Politics is remote from them'.[199]

The main exception to the community's political reserve was the response to Beijing's crackdown on the student movement in June 1989, which brought hundreds of angry Chinese and British Chinese protestors onto the streets. The crisis even roused quite a few older immigrants, who saw the repression as writing on the wall for Hong Kong. The events continued to reverberate in the community in later years, but on nowhere near the same scale as in Hong Kong, and the initial ferment produced no political bodies with a broad base.[200] Nato's bombing of the Chinese Embassy in Belgrade in 1999 triggered a smaller demonstration in London as part of a worldwide chain, but most taking part were students mobilised by Embassy staff. Generally speaking, Chinese cannot match the political activism of other ethnic minorities.[201]

Chinatown UK v. colonial Hong Kong, 1967–1969

During China's Cultural Revolution of the late 1960s, Britain's Hong Kong community, usually thought of as apolitical and devoted overwhelmingly to the pursuit of money, appeared for a while in an unexpected light when some restaurant workers took to the streets to protest against imperialism.[202] As a result of the unrest, which was sparked by agitation in Hong Kong, the colonial authorities were pressured into inventing a commitment to migrant welfare that was less than heartfelt, though in the end it was more or less put into practice.

The Hong Kong Government Office (HKGO) in London

For a long time, the Hong Kong Government had no independent office in London, but one was eventually brought into being in the last year of the Pacific War, as a 'Rear Link' to help supply goods and services necessary for the colony's postwar rehabilitation.[203] Later, its role changed to promoting trade and providing information about Hong Kong. In time, several offices were set up across the world, but the London office (or KHKGO) differed in that Hong Kong was a British dependent territory until 1997. Its officials therefore discussed inter-governmental matters with Whitehall and promoted Hong Kong in ways other than just economic, including lobbying MPs and the press. Also unlike the other offices, it carried out consular and representative functions on behalf of Hong Kong residents in Britain. In the 1970s, it had a staff of 120 and offices in Liverpool and Edinburgh.[204]

Up until the late 1960s, the idea that the Hong Kong authorities represented the interests of ordinary Chinese residents, at home or abroad, would have met with derision in the colony. Practically to the end, the colonial government wielded almost absolute executive powers and its structure remained virtually the same as it had been at the start, in 1843. Its highest councils had no elected members and the councils' powers were advisory. It lacked political mechanisms capable of integrating the population and mediating social conflict. There was next to no organised political life until the 1980s and little sense of social anchorage or identification with the regime.

The Hong Kong Government's indifference was, for a long time, reciprocated by the emigrants. Its majority, from the New Territories, had experienced government in Hong Kong largely as a distant menace, to be blamed for importing cheap foodstuffs from China and driving farmers from the land. Officials of the colonial regime in London barely impinged on the lives of Hong Kongers overseas, who followed a policy of self-help.

Chinatown and the Cultural Revolution

In the late 1960s, the Hong Kong Government's behaviour changed. This change was prompted by the Maoist agitation that shook first Macao and then Hong Kong in 1966 and 1967, a repercussion of China's Cultural Revolution. In Macao, protestors forced the Portuguese to 'surrender unconditionally' after the shooting dead of eight Chinese. In Hong Kong, Maoist agitators tried to create their own 'Macao incident' by strikes and acts of terror. The colonial government refused to back down and defeated the campaign.[205] However, faced with an overwhelming preponderance of Chinese in Hong Kong and the nearby presence of a potentially hostile state inhabited by their compatriots, it privately conceded a more conciliatory approach was needed.[206] In an attempt to head off further unrest, it introduced reforms and granted workers new rights. This change in attitude was exported to Britain, where the HKGO began an unprecedented courting of the expatriate population.

The HKGO started providing consular-style care for Britain's Hong Kong residents in the early 1960s, when its student section extended its activities to helping workers and appointed a liaison officer.[207] However, the function was created in part due to the fortuitous presence of a Chinese on the staff of the Students' Office.[208] A more methodical and committed approach came only after the confrontations in the colony in 1967 forced a rethink.

The disturbances in Hong Kong and China had a big impact on Chinese in the United Kingdom. In London, members of the Kung Ho Association took to the streets to protest against 'British imperialism' and several were arrested. Mao Zedong's portrait was displayed prominently in the association building, together with his maxim that 'The East Wind prevails over the West Wind'. An association memoir described this as the 'period of political struggle'.[209] Members of the Workers' Club learned revolutionary songs and quotations from Chairman Mao and organised a 'propaganda team' to stage a 'model opera' of the sort promoted in China by Mao's wife Jiang Qing (an event that activists recalled with pride 30 years later).[210] The team took the revolutionary message to their compatriots in Liverpool and Manchester and in Ireland and showed films to midnight audiences across the United Kingdom. In a proclamation, the Workers' Club banned mahjong.[211]

Actions by Chinese diplomats in London, who scuffled with police and staged demonstrations, had a hand in stirring up the community, although there is no evidence of direct Embassy intervention. The main impetus was provided by the dramatic events in Hong Kong. Just as the Cultural Revolution in China owed its energy as much to social injustice as to Maoist instigation, so the inequalities of Chinatown and the indignities of a life spent waiting on the British were fertile ground for Red Guard-style sentiments.

Lurking in the background was a factor that has aroused little or no comment: the legacy in the New Territories of radical nationalism, imported into postwar Britain along with the cooks and waiters. In the Pacific War, Red guerrillas of the East River Detachment 东江支队 formed a Hong Kong-Kowloon Brigade that struck roots among the villagers and fishermen of the New Territories and took over some village governments. Children known as 'little devils' like their counterparts throughout China in the guerrilla years were its runners, look-outs, and helpers. Best known in the West for rescuing Allied POWs and downed airmen, guerrilla supporters infiltrated the Japanese administration and the Kowloon Dockyard, where they carried out sabotage. In March 1945, the Americans consulted them as part of the preparations for an Allied landing. At the end of the war, the British asked them to remain in the New Territories for a while to help maintain order. In June 1946, most guerrillas marched north to Shandong to join up with the communist regulars, but they left behind a thick tail of support.[212]

Some residents of the New Territories who joined the guerrillas later ended up in Britain. They included Li Zhizhang 李志章, a leader of the London community who had been a 'little devil' at the age of twelve.[213] Many immigrants bankrupted by economic changes in the New Territories regarded themselves as victims of British colonial policy. To such people, to campaign against imperialism made sense.[214]

Another radical influence on Chinatown was the tradition represented in the New Territories by the Farmers' Union 侨港种植总公会[215] – set up in the 1930s, restored in 1946 by anti-communists, but brought under communist control around 1950, after which it enjoyed the support of former members of the East River Detachment. At its peak, it had more than 7000 members. In the late 1960s, radicals helped set up a women's association, some of whose members were the mothers, wives, and daughters of men who had gone to work in Britain. They spearheaded campaigns against the policies of the colonial regime and set a further example to their menfolk overseas.[216]

The combination of Red Guard politics, demonstrations by Embassy staff, and the presence of leftwing veterans of the East River Detachment was a heady mixture that brought a radical mood to parts of Chinatown, especially its younger workers. Leftists collected money for the Struggle Committee 斗争委员会 in Hong Kong and embraced Beijing's propaganda.

The HKGO probably overestimated the links in Hong Kong of Britain's leftist Chinatowners. According to some officials, some riots in the New Territories were instigated by 'extremely left-wing Chinese people' who had returned home from the United Kingdom.[217] However, such reports lacked hard evidence. A source claims that migrants who did return were intimidated by the repression and 'quietly returned to England'.[218]

The distinction between immigrants from mainland China and Hong Kong helps throw light on this episode. In its radical phases, the Mao regime alienated potential supporters overseas by stigmatising their relatives and repatriates. For mainland immigrants, the Cultural Revolution was another chapter in the story of discrimination to which the authorities subjected those with overseas connections. Members of the See Yip Association in Liverpool, for example, showed no enthusiasm for the radical revival, having witnessed the devastating effects of earlier campaigns.[219] However, the great majority of Britain's Chinese residents were from the New Territories, where Mao's excesses probably caused less indignation than colonial neglect. So it is unsurprising that a vocal minority sided with the struggle faction.[220]

The HKGO's new leaf

Off the record, some HKGO officials decided that Chinatown's radicalisation was due in part to the Embassy. They privately conceded that the Embassy showed a greater readiness than the HKGO to help immigrants and that its propaganda was more effective, especially among young people.[221] Years later, a Chinatown leader confirmed that when restaurant staff ended up under arrest after fights with drunks or customers who refused to pay, only the Embassy acted to secure their release.[222]

The HKGO drew up a three-point plan to counter the agitation. It would set up a new team to protect and assist Hong Kong residents in Britain, join battle with the Embassy on the media front, and breathe new life into immigrants' home ties, especially those with 'traditional' forms of local government or 'clansman' organisations in the New Territories, whose hold on their people overseas was slackening.

This strategy was not without risk. Britain had been prepared to recognise Beijing in 1950 partly in exchange for its tacit acceptance of the status quo in Hong Kong, at a time when People's Liberation Army units were lined up along the border of the colony. Officials feared wooing Chinatown too vigorously might offend the Embassy and spark a reaction. A less urgent consideration was to avoid harming vested interests by rendering forms of assistance already provided commercially (for example, by lawyers and travel agents).[223] However, not to try to 'influence and unify' the community and isolate its troublemakers was, so it seemed, no option. In an official announcement, Governor Sir David Trench told Chinese traders in Britain the HKGO needed to step up its support for Britain's Hong Kong people.[224]

Under the new plan, the functions of the old Liaison Office were overhauled. Whereas it had previously aimed merely to give assistance, its new goals were broader and more explicit: '(1) to organise the Chinese in Britain so that the Liaison Office can be more effective in rendering service to the Chinese and in counter-acting communist influence…and (2) to project the image of the Hong Kong Government; to set it in its right perspective and to impress upon the Chinese population in Britain that the Hong Kong Government remains interested in their continuing well-being'. To improve other services, it laid plans for a community centre in London, offices in Liverpool and Edinburgh, community surveys, and an amenities fund. Staffing was to be increased to five and the liaison officer was to be 'Chinese and truly bilingual' – a put-down for the white expatriate-repatriates, who had up to then practically monopolised the HKGO. In short, an expanded agency would 'establish close contacts with the Hong Kong people working in Britain to minimise the opportunity for communist indoctrination'.[225]

Leftist firebrands among visiting Chinese seafarers were identified as another potential cause of trouble. Officials noted that 'the crews of ships calling regularly at Chinese ports are still being subjected to propaganda' and that this 'obviously has a depressive effect on crew morale'. They added that 'officers and crews who have not visited China in the recent past should beware of being disturbed or provoked by shore officers'.[226] To hit back against seaborne incitement, they mobilised ship-owners, agents, and crew suppliers to distribute HKGO propaganda.

Over the next few years, the HKGO met most of its objectives. In fulfilment of the promise to liaise with UK authorities on Chinese needs, officials went to Whitehall 'to supplement Hong Kong's representations on the immigration controls proposed [in 1971]'.[227] (How hard they pressed their case is another matter. In previous years, the Hong Kong authorities had on occasions put obstacles in the way of immigration to Britain.[228]) They loaned gramophone recordings of English lessons to meet a further need.[229] Other services included advice on immigration, help with applications for work permits, the provision of interpreting facilities, renewing passports, and mediating disputes. Officials also sometimes helped to sort out disputes and problems regarding land ownership in the New Territories.

The media were the second theatre in the HKGO's undeclared struggle against the Embassy. HKGO officials complained in 1967 that the

Embassy-supported press circulated much more widely than the 'feeble' *Wah Kiu Yat Po* 华侨日报, a Hong Kong-based daily.[230] In response, the *Hong Kong News Digest* was founded in 1968, freighted in by air, and distributed free to 19,000 subscribers. Several hundred copies were mailed to Hong Kong Chinese in mainland Europe and a further several hundred to seafarers. The Liaison Office used the publication to answer immigrants' questions and feed them the colonial viewpoint, as an antidote to communist propaganda.[231] Film shows were another site of feuding. Anti-communist film clubs had come under attack in the late 1960s and been forced to close down by strong-arm measures against these 'running dogs of the Hong Kong Government'. Commercial as well as political interests were at stake in this battle of the projectors. Eventually, the HKGO secured film venues for its supporters. In 1970, they showed 262 films with an average audience of 40 in restaurants and 400 in hired halls.[232]

After staying aloof for more than 20 years, the HKGO's reconstructed satraps started cultivating the community's senior members and putting perks and privileges their way. Plans were laid for an Advisory Committee of Chinatown grandees to meet twice-yearly with HKGO officials. In 1970, 150 community contacts were invited to a gathering in Hong Kong House and a meeting was arranged for the Chinese Chamber of Commerce to discuss problems and grievances with a senior policeman. Residents returning to Hong Kong were given tours of the New Territories to 'see recent developments' and immigrants' cooperation was sought for the colonial government's plans to redevelop the New Territories. HKGO officials visited the communities in Britain and mainland Europe.[233]

At the same time as trying to make themselves liked and useful in public, members of the Liaison Office waged war on another, secret front. They met several times with officials of the Ministry of Defence and Special Branch officers in provincial police forces to assess communist influence in Chinatown and swap intelligence. A measure of British concern is a letter from the Secretary of State to the Hong Kong Governor in early 1969 informing him of a demonstration in London by just 30 'Friends of China', protesting against 'Hong Kong police brutality'.[234]

The great majority of caterers belonged to Hong Kong's 'indigenous' population, descended from the original inhabitants of the New Territories. In the words of a Chinese observer, 'the native residents of the New Territories, cold-shouldered in the 1950s, became the darlings of the 1970s and the 1980s'. However, the HKGO failed to convince all Britain's Hong Kong residents of its good faith and approachability. In the early 1960s, immigrants had little choice other than to seek help from commercial organisations like the Overseas Chinese Service. However, many continued to look to such agencies even after the HKGO's change of policy.[235] For such people, the habits of independence and avoidance of authority were too ingrained. Despite its change of tack, the HKGO can hardly claim to have won all hearts and minds.

From the community's point of view, one of the HKGO's most important initiatives was its support for Chinese schools, a central pillar in preserving a Chinese identity. By providing textbooks designed for Cantonese speakers, the HKGO not only catered to the community's specific language needs (in a way that neither Beijing's nor Taibei's representatives would have done) but perpetuated a Cantonese identity.[236]

In the early 1980s, the previously forgotten issue of Hong Kong's relationship with China suddenly became urgent, as 1997 (and retrocession) pressed ever closer. Emboldened by victory in the Falklands, for a while Margaret Thatcher made great play of opinion polls showing an overwhelming majority in favour of the status quo and interpreted them to mean the people of the colony were 'pro-British'.[237] Hoping for a referendum on the retrocession in which overseas residents would also have the vote, the Hong Kong authorities acted as midwife to a series of new associations in the United Kingdom.[238]

In 1990, in the run-up to retrocession, the HKGO attempted to mobilise Hong Kong Chinese in Britain to act as 'mini-ambassadors' for the territory. Governor Sir David Wilson called on Chinese professionals and executives in the United Kingdom to contribute to the territory's success.[239] By this time, the British Government had abandoned its campaign to whip up a pro-British mood in Hong Kong and agreed to cede sovereignty, yet it still planned to leave under the best terms possible. This last-gasp campaign to rouse the émigré community failed to take off, not least because ordinary Hong Kongers felt excluded from the negotiations with Beijing, which were conducted in secret.

The HKGO continued to play a role in the affairs of the community until the 1990s. In the meantime, other forms of organisation – in particular, the Chinese Community Centres – had begun to take over some of its functions.[240] In July 1997, it changed its name to the Hong Kong Economic and Trade Office, one of ten such offices throughout the world in charge of promoting Hong Kong's economic and trade interests.[241] It dropped its consular functions and its official support for the Chinese community (though it still has informal ties).

Today, the interests of the UK's Hong Kong residents are officially represented by the Chinese Embassy, which deals with passports and plays a minor role in the community's social affairs. Radical actions of the sort Embassy staff helped stimulate in the late 1960s are unlikely to be repeated, because Chinese politics have swung to the right and the community itself has changed. To the extent that the HKGO managed to cultivate a relationship with the community, it took more than 20 years. The Embassy will find it hard to replicate that success, especially as the immigrant generation yields to its British-born offspring.

The Heung Yee Kuk and Hong Kong emigration

The Guangzhou-Hong Kong strike of 1925–1926 was the colony's first and last democratic movement until the 1980s. After the strike's defeat in 1926, the resurgent regime of colonial racism and expatriate rule banished the hope of participatory politics until the last 15 years of the colonial era. The sole exception to the inhibition on formal political participation was the Rural Consultation Office (the Heung Yee Kuk 乡议局, or Kuk for short). The Kuk, set up in 1926 to defend the 'traditional' local government of the New Territories' indigenous inhabitants, gained recognition as representative of the villages. It had three layers – village heads, rural committees, and the Kuk itself.[242] Although it claimed to stand for tradition, in reality it was influenced by British manipulations. For most of the next 70 years, it acted as an advisory body to the government on New Territories affairs and as a forum for opinion.

The Kuk's relationship with the colonial authorities went through several changes in their years of coexistence. They sometimes clashed, but they also formed alliances in which each manoeuvred to use the other. The Kuk was born of a clash of interests with the authorities that subsequently evolved into an alliance. In 1957, the authorities withdrew recognition for two years, after a confrontation.[243] In 1959, however, it became a statutory body on the enactment of the Kuk Ordinance, amended in 1988 to facilitate the participation of non-indigenous inhabitants. The alliance deepened in the late 1960s, when the Kuk and the British, deeming the stability of the Chinese community in Britain to be at risk, joined hands to shore it up. The Kuk had always maintained a strong interest in the emigrants. In 1967, when the turmoil in China spilled over into Hong Kong and the British were jolted into giving a new priority to securing emigrants' goodwill, the strategies of colonial officials and the Kuk converged and the two sides worked out a joint approach to Chinatown issues.

The proposal for a united front probably originated with the Kuk. Colonial officials gave it a cautious welcome. The Kuk suggested setting up a committee to assist the Chinese in Britain and their Hong Kong relatives and founding a government-funded magazine for distribution in the colony and Britain. The idea of using the Kuk's and the clans' 'traditional' authority to sideline troublemakers in the United Kingdom may have seemed a long shot to many; some feared the Kuk itself might redden. However, the plan received the support of the New Territories' District Commissioner, whose enthusiasm for reinforcing the emigrants' homeland tie was motivated not least by the more than £2 million they remitted annually through the Post Office.[244] The District Commissioner recommended funding a Kuk delegation to London and the establishment of 'clansman-type committees' and a 'sort of modified Kai Fong [街坊] Association' in Britain, to curb subversion.[245] In the 1970s, Kuk delegations visited the United Kingdom and the HKGO's Liaison Officer visited the New Territories, where he discussed the problems of the Chinese community in Europe.[246]

The relationship between the Kuk and the Hong Kong Government continued to become strained whenever their interests diverged. These conflicts sometimes drew in emigrants. In 1990, for example, the Kuk sent a delegation to London to lobby Parliament against a bill that would require landowners to get permission for any change in land use. The delegation solicited the support of 'indigenous clansmen' in Britain. Later, the Kuk appointed a couple of dozen 'overseas advisors' to support its stand.[247] Even today, land ownership and rural issues are a focus of interest for some New Territorians in Britain.

Anthropologists find the relationship between sending and receiving places in the migration process to be far more complicated than a theory of retrograde modernisation would suggest. Migration can reinforce or revive 'traditional' features of the 'native place' just as it can lead to a 'retraditionalisation' of cultural practices in the place of settlement.[248] The part played by the Hong Kong administration and the HKGO in reinforcing the connection between the Kuk and the emigrants adds yet another level of complexity to the idea of conservative restorationism. The Kuk itself was a product of colonial meddling as well as a 'traditional' relic of pre-colonial life. The British attempt to export it overseas to help tame rebellious workers doubly illustrates the constructed quality of diasporic traditionalism. In the event, the Kuk largely failed to restore its authority. The Red tide in Chinatown subsided, but it would have done so anyway, with or without the Kuk.

The transnational interactions of Chinese leftists in Britain in the late 1960s happened simultaneously from above and from below, and came to involve two state organisations (the Embassy and the HKGO) and three grassroots movements (the pro-communist Chinatown associations, the Struggle Committee, and the Kuk). In response to the unrest, the HKGO strove to counteract the emigrants' tie with homeland rebels and with the Chinese Embassy by mobilising its own resources and the Kuk's. The pressures it acted under were political (the need to preserve stability in Hong Kong and Chinatown) and economic (the desire to preserve remittances). In the run-up to 1997, the HKGO again tried to play on migrants' ties to the New Territories and foster their 'Hong Kong identity', but to even less avail.

These events are an example of working-class transnationalism, fanned into flames by Beijing's leftism and its effect on Hong Kong. Communist diplomats in London, members of the Struggle Committee in the colony, and Chinatown veterans of the Japanese War and their young supporters simultaneously confronted the British Government and the colonial authorities. Under different circumstances, the crisis might have at least jolted Whitehall's compromise with Beijing on the future of Hong Kong. The Hong Kong rebels provided the emigrants with arguments and an example; the emigrants responded with money and volunteers. The rebellion forced the colonial authorities to refashion their relations with Britain's Hong Kong residents and to care for their needs – a strategy that to some extent succeeded. In so doing, they did not extinguish the transnational moment in Chinatown but diverted it along new lines and thus helped to prolong Chinatown's diasporic connections, however briefly.

Chinese state-sponsored umbrella organisations

In Southeast Asia and North America, umbrella organisations mediated between rival Chinese associations. They also represented the community to the host and home authorities, keen to identify an overarching power in Chinatown with which to negotiate. The first federated organisation to emerge was usually a Benevolent Association, joined later by a Chamber of Commerce.[249] Similar bodies have arisen in postwar Britain, but they lack the representativity of their counterparts elsewhere. Two federated associations compete to represent the ethnic-Chinese community. (Similar competition is encountered in many countries.)

The Confederation of Chinese Associations, UK 英国华人社团联合总会, founded in 1960, at first enrolled just six associations (and three film clubs), but by 1993 its affiliates exceeded 40, most of them with Hong Kong connections. It receives delegations from mainland China and works to 'strengthen Sino-British friendship'.

The Federation of Chinese Associations, UK 英国侨团联合总会 was set up by the Chinese Chamber of Commerce in 1980. The Federation had just seven or eight affiliates in the mid-1990s. These included the Overseas Chinese Association, UK 英国华侨协会, founded in 1960 by Taiwan Chinese, with nearly 400 members. Though supported by Taibei's representatives, the Federation's agenda is less cultural and political than that its competitor's. Its main activities are representing ethnic-Chinese interests to the British Government and the Hong Kong authorities, supporting the Chinese Community Centres, and promoting mother-tongue education. It also organises summer visits to Hong Kong by Chinese youngsters. Neither the Federation nor the Confederation can claim to represent more than a small fraction of Britain's ethnic-Chinese associations.[250]

The Chinese Chamber of Commerce nominally steers clear of politics, but in reality it has Taibei's support. Its tie to Taiwan is more relevant than ethnic networks, business or cultural, to its ability to play an active role in the ethnic-Chinese economy. Taiwanese investors have received help from the Chamber when setting up enterprises in the United Kingdom. At a time when the British Government was keen to attract foreign investments, the Chamber drew its attention to Taiwanese investors' needs.

Bodies like the Chamber of Commerce thrive either because they enjoy state support or because they are managed by individuals who benefit. Since much of the new transnational literature propagates the idea that these Chambers are the site of important business networking, investors are drawn to them (though they also tap other sources to develop their enterprises). International meetings organised by pro-Taiwan Chambers of Commerce at which networking is supposed to take place have been funded by Taibei. These meetings are also a way for Taiwanese to meet ethnic Chinese who run ventures in Europe. The Taibei authorities hope the contacts established will enable Taiwanese companies to find opportunities to invest abroad, particularly in the hi-tech sector.[251]

Each federation has its counterpart at the European level. The Union of Chinese Associations in Europe (also known as the Conference of the Overseas Chinese Federations in Europe 旅欧华侨团体联合会议）was founded in 1975 under the sponsorship of Taibei's Overseas Chinese Affairs Commission. It spawned other pro-Taibei organisations at the European level and was used as a model for unions in Asia, Oceania, Africa, and America. Taibei representatives in Europe dominate its annual meetings. In 1983, the first steps were taken in Paris towards the formation of the pro-Beijing European Federation of Chinese Organizations (EFCO) 欧洲华侨华人社团联合会. The project dropped from sight for a while but was realised in 1992. Its emergence was intertwined with the process of European integration.[252]

'People to people' diplomacy

Throughout most of the twentieth century, Chinese and British people have come together in 'friendship associations' designed to support Chinese national interests. These associations, set up with the encouragement of leftwing parties, practise 'people to people' diplomacy 民间外交, a special case of top-down political transnationalism.[253] 'Friendship' associations exist in many countries, but until the 1960s those in Britain were considered especially important because of British economic and strategic interests in Asia, seen as inimical to China.

Until Chiang Kai-shek came to power in 1927, such organisations did not openly distinguish between Nationalists and communists but supported both parties against attempts by foreign powers to pull strings in China. Their members included trade unionists, peace activists, church representatives, and academics. Most were either communists or fellow travellers. After 1927, the noisiest campaigns were run by leftwingers, who stood up for their Chinese comrades against Chiang Kai-shek. In the Second World War, the pro-China campaign ostensibly backed the entire resistance, regardless of party, but in effect it chimed with the aims of the communists and their armies.

In the mid-1920s, the Hands Off China campaign opposed Britain's intervention against China's rising nationalist movement, while the Labour Council for Chinese Freedom (chaired by George Hicks, a prominent trade-union leader) organised hundreds of local groups to promote 'Peace with China'. After 1927, the Comintern's League against Imperialism opposed Britain's support for Chiang and its cooperation with Japan, provided news about the Chinese communists, and demonstrated against trade with Japan.

In the 1920s and the 1930s, the international peace movement campaigned among Chinese in Britain. A major figure was Lord Robert Cecil, an architect of the League of Nations Covenant in 1919 and winner of the Nobel Peace Prize in 1937. Organisations Cecil helped found in London, like the League of Nations Union (1915) and the International Peace Campaign (1936), formed Chinese branches that received support from across the political spectrum, from conservatives to communists.

Although a racist who favoured a world order led by white nations, Cecil was on excellent terms with Chinese leaders and intellectuals. His correspondents included the diplomats Quo Tai-chi 郭泰祺, Chai Feng-yang 翟凤阳, and Wellington Koo as well as Chiang Kai-shek and Song Qingling. Organisations that sought his support included the China Campaign Committee, the Chinese People's Foreign Relations Association, the London Chinese Association, the Chinese League of Nations Union, the China branch of the International Peace Campaign, the All-China Comforting Association, and the People's Political Council.[254]

Chinese students under Cecil's influence took word of the international pacifist movement back to China, where they formed branches. Han Li-wu, a returned student and official of the Guomindang, represented the Chinese League of Nations Union. Y. C. Hsu and others transplanted the International Peace Committee (IPC) to China.[255] Shelly Wang told Cecil that he had 'been asked for [sic] setting up IPC branches in the provinces and districts behind the Japanese line in order to show to the world that the land and people in the Japanese occupied areas are still under our control'.[256] Wang Ching-Chun published a book titled *Japan's Continental Adventure*, with a preface by Lord Cecil.[257]

Of all the pro-China organisations formed before 1949, the most successful was the China Campaign Committee, which succeeded in stopping some shipments of arms to Japan and raised medical funds for the communists.[258] The Committee emerged in 1937 from the Friends of the Chinese People, an organisation set up in 1936 by the then moribund League against Imperialism and founded in September at a meeting of British leftists and Chinese students. The Earl of Listowel and Victor Gollancz, founder of the Left Book Club, were its President and Chairman. Its objectives were 'to finance the collection of medical supplies and gifts in kind for China; [and] to arrange meetings and conferences independently or through other organisations in order to consolidate the feelings in the country to a moral protest strong enough to inspire a public and private boycott of Japanese trade'.[259] Meetings, study groups, and sponsored books and pamphlets brought the essentials of China's history, culture, revolution, and war to the British public and called on Britain to lead an international boycott of Japanese goods.

This appeal for a boycott was implemented to sensational effect by British dockers, who blacked Japanese cargoes in several ports.[260] The solidarity actions spread to France and Australia, where dockers also carried out embargoes.[261] The boycott campaign continued until 1938, when Munich came to obscure all other issues.

The Committee, led by Arthur Clegg, a communist student at LSE, continued in existence until 1949.[262] It had the support of prominent members of the Chinese community in London, including refugees like Professor Shelley Wang and Pat Koo, daughter of Wellington Koo. Chinese artists, actors, dancers, and writers joined the movement, among them Jack Chen and S. I. Hsiung. Its honorary treasurers included Dr C. C. Wang. Chinese speakers addressed meetings in towns and cities throughout the country.[263]

The China Campaign Committee set up branches throughout Britain and also had an impact on Chinese seafarers and the Chinese business community. The London Chinese Association gave the campaign generous monthly donations. Chinese restaurateurs helped by hosting Bowl of Rice Dinners to fund its hospital scheme, while community leaders' wives ran bazaars. At the height of the united front in China, Embassy staff sat on the committee. In 1941, Wellington Koo addressed a campaign dinner attended by the Soviet and American Ambassadors.

The Committee was affiliated to Lord Cecil's International Peace Campaign. In February 1937, these two organisations organised an 'International People's Assembly on China' in London, attended by representatives of 19 countries and international organisations.[264] John Dewey, Albert Einstein, Bertrand Russell, and Romain Rolland supported the Japanese boycott and the Chinese war of self-defence.[265] When the Committee was temporarily closed down by the British Government in 1940, one million people are said to have signed petitions calling for its reinstatement.

The China Campaign Committee won support in the labour movement and the political elite and had an international impact. Chinese leftwing organisers exploited these resources to reach out into the Chinese community. The Committee was created by a nucleus of British communists who broadened their influence, financial base, and social respectability by recruiting fellow travellers (a familiar tactic of the period). Clegg and his comrades pursued policies that reflected the Comintern's strategy, to build a transclass antifascist and anti-Japanese campaign and to organise Chinese workers along class lines. Although their chief aim was to win support for China in the British labour movement and among British parties, they also influenced the Chinese community by visiting Chinatown leaders and holding demonstrations in towns with Chinese populations.

After 1949, the British-China Friendship Association took over from the China Campaign Committee.[266] It campaigned to lift the trade embargo on China and made propaganda on Beijing's behalf. Its members included prominent academics like Joseph Needham and Joan Robinson. It was succeeded in 1965 by the Society for Anglo-Chinese Understanding (SACU), which had the support of scores of public figures until the Cultural Revolution. Like the Friendship Association, SACU was originally known for its uncritical support for whatever faction held power in Beijing, but it protested against the suppression of the student revolt in China in June 1989. Unlike the China Campaign Committee, it had a negligible impact on the Chinese community, which largely turned its back on Chinese politics after the outbreak of the Civil War in 1946. In any case, by the 1960s the community was made up chiefly of Hong Kong immigrants hostile or indifferent to the regime SACU supported.

Trade unions

Most Chinatown organisations before the First World War recruited their members on the basis of provenance. The slogans of those of a political colouring were transclass and nationalist rather than socialist. Even so, the community was mainly proletarian. Immigrants aspiring to a social status higher than that of seafarer, laundryman, or cafe-owner had little chance to realise their dream, and the community did not differentiate in social-class terms to the same extent as Chinese communities outside Europe. Its petty proprietors seldom united, as we have seen, but the seafarers set up labour gangs. The gangs, like most Chinese associations in Britain, were founded on native-place ties that slotted into the base of the Chinatown hierarchy.

Work on Chinese diasporic communities pays little attention to seafarers' role in shaping them, probably because seafarers are mostly transients. However, seafarers often influence migrant communities, and their history should not be artificially separated from that of Chinese on land. In some industrialised countries like Britain, deserting seafarers founded the communities, replenished them, and kept them in touch with their native places and the ancestral homeland. In times of war, foreign ports became a substitute for the Asian home ports under enemy occupation. As individuals, the seafarers formed relationships with their land-based co-ethnics and compatriots. In the collective, as members of gangs or unions, they sometimes exercised a strong pull.

Ships and seafarers played a momentous role in the Chinese Revolution in the 1920s, not unlike the 'seeding machine' to which Mao Zedong compared the Long March. Sun Yat-sen described their contribution: 'Wherever they touched port, they spread the news to resident overseas Chinese, propagated our proposals, collected funds, and performed meritorious deeds never to be obliterated.' The biographer of Liao Chengzhi 廖承志, who worked for the CCP among seafarers in Europe, explained further uses:

> The decisions and directives of the Comintern were brought [to Berlin] by passenger vessel. Letters to Comintern Executive member Qu Qiubai 瞿秋白 and reports to the Comintern and to the [Chinese] Party centre drafted for the Chinese-language section [of the German Communist Party] by Qu ... were also distributed across the world by oceangoing vessels sailing out of Hamburg. There were communist parties in many countries, but most were underground. Whether you compare them to scattered islands, unyielding fortresses, or foundation stones in the mansion of communism, the progressive seafarers who plied the world's ports were their steel bridge, constructed from their faith and their flesh and blood. Like the human nervous system, they punctually relayed commands; like the system of veins and arteries, they transmitted vital forces and nutrients to the cells and organs.[267]

Trade unions played an important role in shaping the Chinese community, nurturing its political consciousness, and sharpening its focus on China, the diaspora, and Chinese migrant labour worldwide. The link between the seafarers' unions and other Chinese overseas is exemplified by Liao Chengzhi, who worked with both the land-based and the sea-based communities. The son of Liao Zhongkai 廖仲愷, a leftwing Guomindang leader assassinated in 1925 because of his support for the Hong Kong-Guangzhou workers' strike, he was a leading figure in the Chinese seafarers' movement in Europe in the interwar years and a lifelong torchbearer for the interests of Chinese overseas.[268]

Trade-union activity by Chinese seafarers in British ports was first mentioned in November 1906, in a report in the *Liverpool Courier*.[269] This activity echoed that in southern Chinese ports, where in February of the same year Sun Yat-sen directed his followers to agitate for labour unity and to range workers behind his Revolutionary League. That the trade-union idea spread to Britain at such speed shows the galvanic power of Sun's seaborne networks. The early labour movement in China and the Chinese labour movement abroad developed in close step and mutual interaction. In the late nineteenth century, seafarers who had worked for foreign shipping companies started going home to take up jobs in China's fledgling industries. Some had joined Chee Kung Tong and absorbed its policies. With their patriotic enthusiasm and knowledge of Western trade-union practices, they formed a natural labour constituency for Sun Yat-sen's party, a development that helped mark the beginnings of the Chinese workers' movement.

In 1906, such people were in the van of Sun's trade-union project. They also served as crack units in the armed risings staged by his supporters. Some died as martyrs. In 1911, Chinese seafarers who had returned from abroad played a key role in preparing the Xinhai Revolution that brought in the Republic. In response to a call for help from Wuhan, where a rising was imminent, a couple of dozen Cantonese who had worked for years on British warships hurried north and regrouped in the city as part of the Cantonese Overseas Chinese Dare-to-Die Corps 华侨敢死队.[270]

In May 1912, in the first year of the Republic, riots broke out in London's East End between groups of Chinese seafarers wielding iron bars. The seafarers were said to belong to two rival associations, the Nautical Progress Society and the White Lily Society. Press reports failed to mention the issues at stake, but the names of the two societies suggest a clash between a modern-style workers' union and an old-style secret society.[271]

In Liverpool and London during the war and postwar years, Chinese seafarers engaged in class-based activities to match the revolutionary mood of the times. In 1911, Chinese in Liverpool 'organized themselves to cope with the antagonism of the British sailors'.[272] The Chinese Seamen's and Firemen's Association came to public notice in Liverpool in 1916.[273] The Chinese Labour and Seamen's Union was active in London in the spring of 1918, when it tried to break the boarding-masters' monopoly on recruiting labour. It was still around in 1919, when a Home Office report mentioned a union campaign for demobilised Chinese labourers to be allowed either to stay in Britain, perhaps as farm workers, or to work their passage home.[274] These two organisations, which may have been one and the same, were probably a continuation of the union founded in 1906 by the syndicalist Lee Foo. They may have been connected with the party branch Sun Yat-sen is said to have established among Chinese seafarers on foreign ships in 1914 (to help carry messages overseas) or with the Seamen's Mutual Benefit Society (later renamed the Chinese Seamen's Philanthropic Society) that he sponsored at around the same time.[275] Both organisations seem to have been short-lived, probably because of the economic hard times that followed the war and the expulsion of large numbers of Chinese from the British merchant fleet.[276]

The Chinese Seamen's and Firemen's Association was probably set up with the help of British radicals. Its letter published in the *Liverpool Courier* on 19 September 1916 – the only evidence we have of its existence – was written by someone, presumably a native, at home in British political rhetoric and trade-union matters. Many Liverpool socialists believed in internationalism and saw foreign seafarers as targets and potential allies, at a time when internationalists throughout Europe were locked in struggle with the jingo faction. Internationalists everywhere worked hard to influence foreign crews as a way both of overcoming 'racial' conflict among workers in shipping and influencing the crews' home ports. In Liverpool, contacts between Chinese workers and native leftists were probably formed in the International Club.

The early Soviet Union provides the best example of the postwar radicalisation of Chinese workers by non-Chinese political activists. In the First World War, the Tsarist Government contracted tens of thousands of Huagong to maintain communications and help the war effort. After the peace, some 60,000 were recruited by the pro-communist Federation of Huagong Sojourning in Russia 旅俄华工联合会. Huagong organisations established ties to China and received visits from Chinese revolutionaries eager to learn about their movement. Thus they played a role in the unfolding of the Chinese Revolution.[277]

The interaction between British radicals and Chinese workers in Liverpool was an obscure antecedent of this, with only minor political consequences. However, such contacts were part of the yeast in the postwar ferment in Chinatown, including the movement represented in London by the Chinese Labour and Seamen's Union.

For a while, the Labour and Seamen's Union had a real base in Limehouse, where its supporters, armed with 'hatchets, hammers, knives, and bars of iron', attacked Chinese non-unionists over several days. Its emergence echoed the unrest in China, where dozens of unions formed in

Guangzhou and Hong Kong. Chinese seafarers organised in benevolent institutions and boarding houses were in transition to full unionisation, under the leadership of Sun Yat-sen's followers.[278] It is unlikely that the union formed spontaneously in London, where Chinese seafarers were still under the control of the boarding and shipping-masters. The germs of modern unionisation must have been imported along the sea lanes, by activists who sped news of the events in Guangzhou and Hong Kong across the world.

A united Chinese Seamen's Union 中华海员工业联合总会 was eventually founded in Hong Kong in March 1921, with more than 2000 members.[279] Communists like Su Zhaozheng 苏兆徵 were prominent in its leadership. In the mid-1920s, Chinese communists sought the support of Chinese seafarers in European ports for strikes in Guangzhou and Hong Kong. In May 1927, after the collapse of the united front, the CSU was suppressed. Its Guangzhou branch was closed down and its headquarters were moved to Shanghai, where it came under the control of the new Guomindang authorities.[280] However, a rebel faction continued to exist in secret, claiming 300–400 members in 1933.[281] Throughout the 1920s and the early 1930s, the union tried hard to recruit seafarers working for European companies, but never to much effect. The communists were harassed by the boarding-masters and the shipping-masters and given a hard time by the European police.

Chinese agitators got the backing of officials of European communist parties and the Comintern's Red Trade Union International, which set up a Seamen's International and formed Chinese bureaus in Hong Kong, Singapore, and Hamburg after the purges in China of 1927. This organisation, directly subordinate to the Comintern, concentrated on developing 'an alliance of workers of the imperialist countries and their colonial brothers', particularly Chinese, who were a big part of the labour force and received less than half the white wage. It set up a Chinese Section and a Western European Branch of the CSU to cover the 30,000 Chinese shipping out of European ports. The Hamburg office coordinated work throughout Europe.[282] It was led by Liao Chengzhi 廖承志, who went to Germany on a Chinese Government scholarship in 1928, ostensibly to study political economy. In Berlin, Liao edited two seafarers' journals, *Chiguang* 赤光 (Red ray) and *Haiyuan banyue kan* 海员半月刊 (Seafarers' fortnightly). A year later, the Party sent him to Hamburg, where most of his organisers were students rather than seafarers. As a Cantonese, he found it easy to gain acceptance among the overwhelmingly Cantonese crews. In 1931, he was forced by police pressure to move to Rotterdam, where he set up a Chinese workers' school attended by 90 seafarers and created a cadre of activists before his arrest and deportation. He also took charge of the Western European Branch, which had nearly 100 members.[283]

To get access to the seafarers, Liao's student militants took jobs as stokers. They found conditions at sea hard to endure and made little headway. However, Liao did achieve one or two small victories. In September 1931, he led a Chinese strike on two British ships, whose crews joined the Western European Branch. As a result, he was arrested and expelled to Moscow. The Comintern's Hamburg bureau did not survive the Nazi takeover in 1933 and the union's European campaign faded out for a while.[284]

In Hong Kong, a local branch of the Chinese Seamen's Union was allowed to restart activities in 1937, under a communist chairman and a slightly different name from the old union.[285] In 1940 or thereabouts, a similarly named organisation spread to Liverpool, partly through the intervention of the China Campaign Committee.

One of the seafarers' leaders in Britain, Sam Chen, settled down in Liverpool and joined the CPGB in 1935 and at some point joined its International Committee. (He founded the Xinhua News Agency's 新华通讯社 London branch in 1947 and continued to supervise its operations until his retirement in 1982.) Chen played an important role in spreading the Help China movement to the docks. He and other British-based Chinese and British leftists influenced Chu Hsueh-fan 朱学范, head of the Chinese Workers' Delegation to the ILO in the late 1930s.[286] Chinese labour was also drawn into the boycott movement. With the help of a leftwing Chinese cafe owner in the East End, Sam Chen and Arthur Clegg met community leaders in Pennyfields and got them to dissuade unemployed Chinese from signing on a blacked Japanese vessel (and thus undermining the British dockers' boycott).

By helping to spread the Chinese Seamen's Union to Britain in 1940, Chen and his comrades realised a dream long cherished by the communists. He and other committee members organised anti-Japanese boycotts by Chinese seafarers and gave parties for ratings who had survived the sinking of their ships and for Chinese families bombed out of Chinatown. As a result of his work, Sam Chen was made honorary secretary of the union branch. Union members in Liverpool stayed in touch with Arthur Clegg throughout the war and paid him regular visits in London.[287] Some joined the Chinese Communist Party.

The union branch, established by Chu Hsueh-fan in June 1942, fought for equal pay, compensation for war loss of effects, and compensation for disablement and death due to war injury. It also represented workers' interests on the Boarding-Houses Committee and helped to administer the Seamen's Reserve Pool. The crews' mixed provenance probably made them easier to recruit. Previous crews had tended to come from Siyi and other parts of southern Guangdong and to stick together along sub-ethnic lines. During the war, social class was a more likely denominator. However, sub-ethnic divisions among seafarers from Guangdong, Fujian, Ningbo, and elsewhere could cramp recruitment. The Embassy's insistence 'upon the right to approve (if not to appoint) its officials and review its decisions', as in China, was an additional constraint.[288]

The Hong Kong Chinese Seamen's Union maintained ties of solidarity (at least until the start of the Pacific War in December 1941) with like-minded organisations elsewhere, particularly in the Chinese pools created in Britain and Australia by the wartime stranding of Chinese seafarers. Liverpool's Chinese Seamen's Union also had ties to the Australian Chinese Seamen's Union. 'We worked together internationally', said Arthur Lock Chang 郑嘉乐, the Chinese seafarers' leader in Australia.[289] Thus class-based internationalism, promoted by veterans of the one-time Seamen's International, was an important factor in keeping the Chinese community focused on China in the war.[290]

After the war, trade unions no longer played a conspicuous role among Chinese seafarers working from British ports. Most Chinese working for the Blue Funnel Line did not join trade unions – some say because the Holt fleet operated a system of paternalism, others that its employees were afraid of being blacklisted.[291] Members of the Hong Kong Seamen's Union 香港海员工会 tried to bring British ships to a stop in 1967, at the height of the Cultural Revolution in China and of politically-inspired unrest in Hong Kong. However, Blue Funnel ships sailed on time, despite some signs of militancy.[292]

The influence of the British authorities and the EU

Actions by indigenous institutions, whether benign or hostile, can fortify the immigrant community's homeland and diasporic ties. Governments sometimes use ethnic minorities to promote their own economic or foreign-policy initiatives in the immigrants' sending places. By strengthening the minorities' home ties, they hope to penetrate new markets.

In Singapore and Malaysia in the 1990s, government leaders used ethnic-Chinese capitalists to enable indigenous capitalists to tap into the China market.[293] In Singapore, the state used companies under its ownership and control to encourage investment in China, given that most privately owned Singaporean firms, chiefly small- and medium-scale enterprises (SMEs), were reluctant to do so because of the perceived risk. A further example is the economic boom experienced by the Chinese community in Italy as a result of the Italian-Chinese Treaty of January 1985. The treaty (which came into effect in 1987) agreed on the 'promotion and mutual protection of investments' and encouraged trade and the establishment of Chinese enterprises in Italy. Together with the *sanatorie* (amnesties) for 'illegal' immigrants in 1986–1987 and 1990, it helped to legitimise Chinese economic activity in Italy, previously perceived by Italians as semi-legal or illegal.[294]

The Chinese in Britain have rarely been the object of state measures aimed at their communal advancement. Measures dealing with Chinese migrants in the early years were reactive or punitive rather than supportive. Even in the 1960s and the 1970s, the Chinese barely figured in discussions on race relations or in studies. The situation did not begin to change until 1983, when the British Parliament launched an inquiry into the community and issued a report. The parliamentary committee met community leaders in five cities and received 90 submissions from organisations and individuals.[295] Subsequently, British state and local authorities took steps to encourage Chinese integration, ranging from awarding knighthoods and other honours to funding mother-tongue education, Chinese libraries, Chinese Community Centres, and the like. This encouragement of Chinese social and cultural activity as part of a broader multicultural strategy legitimised Chinese ethnic distinctiveness. Joined to strategies of co-optation employed by China, in some cases it strengthened immigrants' nationalist and transnational ties.

However, many Chinese immigrants continued to avoid or ignore British authorities.[296] Commentators noted the absence of organisations to match the highly politicised Indian Workers' Association or its Pakistani and West Indian equivalents.[297] The usual reasons given for this reticence are the aims of Chinese immigrants (to make money), the fact that they were both more encapsulated and more dispersed than most other ethnic minorities, the lack of political movements in Hong Kong, the lack of support in the community for Beijing, and the effects of Britain's early withdrawal of recognition from Taiwan.[298] Those few Chinese who have developed an interest in politics tend to act as individuals and through British domestic parties rather than focus on the fate of their own community (let alone China's fate).

The British Government's (and the European Community's) active support for the development of SMEs in the 1980s benefited many Chinese entrepreneurs, but only as part of a general promotion of minority business.[299] There is no evidence that these benefits resulted in the consolidation of the community as such (as opposed to its individual enterprises) or that it fostered the community's transnational relations.

Liverpool, Manchester, and Cardiff – three British cities with historic Chinatowns – have set up twinning agreements with Shanghai, Wuhan, and Xiamen respectively. Such agreements are designed mainly to foster business ties with China and pave the way for British SMEs to enter the China market. In planning them, city authorities try to use Chinese residents as political mediators. Projects to regenerate inner-city Chinatowns as tourist attractions are sometimes tied to such arrangements. In Liverpool, for example, a Chinese arch was built in Shanghai and reassembled in Chinatown by imported Chinese workers, a symbol of the twinning. The theme of friendship between Liverpool and Shanghai is used to boost the role of Chinatown's leaders and institutions.

These schemes breathe new life into the communities, but the campaigns to promote ties between local Chinese and China are artificial and unlikely to get far. Where such communities do keep up ties to China, it is to their ancestral or sending counties in Guangdong. Even Liverpool's Shanghai tie is only marginally relevant, for the wartime seafarers' Shanghainese designation was a blanket label and essentially misleading – in reality, the seafarers came from all over east-central China and beyond, and most Liverpudlian Chinese are of Cantonese descent.

European integration has opened up new avenues of transnational communication for Chinese businesses and associations. Chinese groups with pan-European ties generated from below (in voluntary associations) or by Beijing or Taibei were well placed in the 1990s to use new structures created by the European Union (EU).

Growing economic integration under the EU opened up opportunities that Chinese are more likely to use than native Europeans. Some Chinese in Britain showed a keen interest in the economic advantages to be gained, notably the free flow of goods, capital, and people across member states. As a result of the Union, they can remedy labour shortages in one country by recruiting from another. The existence of the single market has made it easier for British Chinese to escape the British catering market, after its saturation. It has also promoted a trend towards Chinese remigrations, from Britain to the European mainland or Ireland and from southern to northern Europe.

From a political point of view, Chinese observers believe Chinese ethnic and cultural rights were more likely to be guaranteed under the EU than under an uninhibited British authority and that development funds might become available for ethnic schemes. To some, the European project – including institutions like the Migrants' Forum, formed to give voice to non-nationals resident in the EU and an inducement to ethnic self-organisation – suggested the time had come to speak out more loudly on social issues.[300]

In the 1980s, European integration was a factor in the decision by a group of first-generation immigrants to found the pro-Beijing European Federation of Chinese Organizations 欧洲华侨华人社团联合会 (EFCO). After getting the blessing (in 1990) of the Overseas Affairs Office of China's State Council 国务院侨务办公室, the initiators went ahead with their preparations, which culminated with EFCO's establishment in 1992. The group's aim was to gain European recognition as the sole representative of Chinese in Europe. In the late 1990s, a delegation presented a report on the community to the European Commission (EC) and asked that 'relevant bodies' draw up policies to deal with Chinese problems (principally, the funding of mother-tongue teaching and the plight of the aged). The report's themes echoed EC concerns about minority rights. EFCO interpreted the meeting as a sign that the EC had recognised their organisation 'as the general representative of the Chinese immigrant community in Europe'.

How this interaction between European and Chinese transnationalism evolves remains to be seen. The enthusiasts in such ventures are nearly always immigrants, whereas a good third of Chinese in the United Kingdom until the recent influxes were born in Europe. Sceptics wonder whether EFCO (or its pro-Taibei equivalent) would exist without the home government's support. British-born Chinese have attitudes and lifestyles that call into question the idea of the community as a 'single field' and are founding new-style associations not embedded in a pan-European Chinese discourse. While EFCO claims to represent Europe's one million Chinese, the mechanisms of this representation are open to question.[301]

Religious organisations

In considering the transnational role of Chinese religion, one must distinguish between popular religion and the canonical religions, like Buddhism and Christianity. Many Buddhist and Christian organisations have copious funds and personnel and a powerful international infrastructure through which to channel their efforts, while Taoist groups and folk cults lack institutional resources and a tradition of proselytising.

Canonical religions and folk religions play their transnational roles in different ways. The big institutions usually connect with Chinese overseas from above and from outside, in the foreign setting, or they migrate abroad with individual immigrants. Only in exceptional cases do they translate with whole communities. Folk gods, on the other hand, migrate both with individual immigrants and with whole immigrant groups, as their supporting frame. Such cults are unlikely to acquire new followings by recruiting in Europe, where the canonical religions predominate among Chinese.

The majority (58 per cent) of Chinese in Britain today claim no religion, a greater percentage than of any other ethnic group, including the white majority. Among believers, Christianity predominates over Buddhism and indigenous Chinese faiths (by 23–19 per cent) and transmits more robustly across the generations.[302] Christianity's following among Chinese in Britain is proportionately greater than in Hong Kong, where there are about 300,000 Protestants and 240,000 Catholics, less than 10 per cent of the population.[303] It is also greater than it was in Britain 30 years ago, when missionaries estimated that only 3 per cent of Chinese were Christian (compared with 37 per cent 'secular' and 60 per cent with 'traditional beliefs').[304] The fact that it apparently has a greater following than in the past, than in Hong Kong, and than Buddhism and is more likely to survive among young people than Buddhism can be partly explained by the strength of Christian missionary work and the British Christian context.

The Christian influence in China before 1949 was out of all proportion to the size of China's Christian congregations. Christian Chinese students played an important role in reforming social relations in China and tried to influence communities abroad, including in Britain. Among Britain's early Chinese Christians was Pao Swen Tseng 曾宝荪, the great granddaughter of the Confucian military leader and administrator Zeng Guofan 曾国藩 (1811–1872), who took part in the Student Volunteer Movement during her stay in London in the early 1910s. For many years, the Chinese Students' Christian Union in the United Kingdom organised students' social activities.[305] The Chinese Christians had their own publications, *The East in the West* (a biannual) and *Ch'uen Tao* 纯道 (a monthly), and helped East End Chinese set up community organisations.[306]

Christian organisations were active among Chinese in Britain throughout the nineteenth and twentieth centuries. They included the British and Foreign Bible Society (1804), the Young Men's Christian Association (YMCA, 1844), the Young Women's Christian Association (1855), and the Christian Union. At first, they targeted students.

In 1914, the Chinese Students' Christian Union in London sent people to Chinatown to teach seafarers politics and hygiene.[307] In or around 1916, a Workers and Merchants' Union 工商工会 was initiated by the Christian Pan Shaotang, a Cantonese self-supporting student who lived in the East End among the seafarers and labourers. The Workers and Merchants' Union was set up to help Chinese find jobs and to put an end to gambling, fighting, and smoking opium in Chinatown. The students wrote to the Chinese Minister Shi Zhaoji 施肇基 asking him to repatriate opium traders. The Workers and Merchants' Union also tried to stop the trade. Some traders wanted to assassinate the Union's secretary, but the students intervened and persuaded the two sides to make peace 'for the sake of the mother country'.[308]

Independent Christian churches were driven from mainland China after the victory of the communist revolution. For many Chinese whose ties to the mainland loosened after 1949, Christianity became a substitute for politics in the Chinese community, including in Britain. Stephen Wang 王又得, a graduate of Beijing University unable to return to his missionary school in China, decided to work as a missionary in London. As a result, the Chinese Church 中华基督教会 and the Overseas Christian Mission 基督教华侨布道会 arose in the United Kingdom in 1950, from where they spread across Western Europe.[309] In the early days, members of the China Inland Mission 中国内地会 stranded outside China joined the Chinese Church and the Chinese Overseas Christian Mission, a substitute for evangelism in China. Most Church members were students, articled clerks, nurses, or graduates, aged 19–25. Most older members were semi-permanent residents of Britain employed in the professions or restaurants. The Chinese Church provided money for missionary work in Britain and Europe. For many years, the Church and the Overseas Christian Mission operated more or less as one body under Pastor Wang's leadership, until the Church registered separately in 1977. By 1980, the Mission had helped to set up 50 fellowships with at least one in every British city with a Chinese presence, compared with just a handful in the entire country in the 1950s.[310] Among its branches was Liverpool's Chinese Gospel Mission 利物浦华人福音教会, founded in 1953 by a missionary returned from China, and the Chinese Centre of the Missions to Seamen, founded in London's East End in 1958.[311]

The great majority of Chinese Christians in Europe are Protestants, as in China. Protestant evangelists are usually more successful than Catholics in recruiting Chinese immigrants. Their churches are active in parts of Zhejiang and other areas with a tradition of migrating to Europe. Even in Catholic countries like Italy and Spain, large numbers of Chinese join evangelical movements.[312] In southern Europe, the Catholic Church's importation of hundreds of Chinese priests and seminarians has resulted over the years in a large community of Chinese clergy and believers, including monks and nuns.[313] Such is not the case in Britain, where the Chinese Catholic Centre in Soho Square is alone among dozens of Chinese Protestant churches and fellowships.[314]

The main Chinese Buddhist organisation active in Britain and Europe is the Buddha's Light International Association 国际佛光会, a global body with headquarters in Taiwan and branches in every European country. It sends teachers (mainly nuns) to Europe to take care of local Buddha Light Associations and preach.[315] In the early period of immigration from the New Territories, Britain had no Buddhist temples and believers had to wait for a return trip to Hong Kong to worship their deities.[316] Today, there are shrines in several places. The Buddha Light Association runs a temple in London and a meditation centre in Manchester. Other groups manage temples in London and other cities and invite senior priests from Hong Kong, China, and Thailand.[317]

These churches are run by professional outsiders. Other churches migrate as part of a group cemented by religious faith. Over the ages, there have been many such migrations, usually caused by religious oppression. The combination of oppression and collective deliverance is a powerful unifier. Although there are no known instances of immigration to Britain by Chinese communities fleeing religious persecution, religion as a community resource can help immigrants cope with social exclusion and the danger of atomisation.

The True Jesus Church 真耶稣教会 is a nondenominational group that originated in Beijing in 1917 and is now run from Taiwan. Its Chinese founders set out to follow their own interpretation of the Bible rather than that of the Western denominations they broke from and to teach 'the restored truth that started from Beijing'. In 1967, the church set up an International Association 真耶稣教会各国联合总会 to stage world conferences. More recently, it claims 419 churches and 88,381 members worldwide, as well as one million in China. In the United Kingdom, where its main centres are in Scotland and northeast England, it had 1656 members, 44 deacons and deaconesses, and three preachers in the early 2000s, scattered over eight churches and a house of prayer.

The True Jesus Church spread to the United Kingdom in the early 1960s, as a result of immigration by students and workers from Malaysia and by fishermen from Ap Chau Island 鸭洲 in Hong Kong, a church stronghold. The islanders followed the usual pattern of New Territories immigration. They were single men, widely scattered across Britain.

Their presence came to the notice of a church member from Taiwan living in Germany, who helped to gather them in a community of faith.[318] Garland Liu 廖静玫, who has made a study of the True Jesus Church in Scotland, concludes that 'the social colony of the Ap Chau Chinese did not develop to the fullest extent until their religious faith, which was an integral part of life in their originating society, had been rekindled'.

The church was assisted by its Taiwan headquarters, which sent preachers and helped set up Chinese schools. In Elgin, both parents and children spent most of their spare time in the church. The community's spiritual solidarity is bolstered by a system of endogamy. Being so tightly knit, Ap Chau islanders preserve their cultural identity and their children preserve their linguistic competence far better than most Chinese in Britain. The children of Ap Chau immigrants are more likely than others to speak good Chinese, code-switch between Chinese and English, and value Chinese culture.[319]

The revival of the True Jesus Church among the Ap Chau islanders arrested the pioneers' dispersal and loss of community. Their regained sense of solidarity contrasts with the incoherence of most Chinese communities in Britain. Even so, tensions threaten this cohesion. The main threat is from members' business activities, which set priorities that challenge religious unity. Island life on Ap Chau created a cooperative ethos and a mutuality of interests. In the United Kingdom, islanders work in catering. Whereas fishing reinforced the spirit of mutuality, catering undermines it, for each immigrant wants his own shop and must compete with fellow-churchmen or move away.[320]

In the ethnic-Chinese communities of Southeast Asia, early immigrants set up temples in which they worshipped gods and spirits associated with their clans and native places and synthesised regional varieties of folk religion. Tan Chee-Beng 陈志明 has called this process 'interculturation' or the 'localization of Chinese religious traditions'. This local development of religious traditions is usually complemented by transnational contacts between worshippers in different countries, a little-studied aspect of Chinese religious practice. Up until the late 1970s, most such contacts emanated from Taiwan or Southeast Asia, but since Mao's death the circuit of connections has broadened to include China.[321]

Taoist and folk deities figure in Chinese religious practice in Europe, but rarely on an institutional basis.[322] Generally speaking, Chinese immigrants to Britain leave the hometown's folk gods and spirits in the safe keeping of the sending community, where both they and the immigrants are deemed to belong. Their failure to perpetuate the rich religious traditions of the New Territories by importing them to Britain is another illustration of the pioneers' commitment to the ancestral villages and rejection of the idea of permanent foreign settlement.[323] Folk gods and ghosts are rarely worshipped publicly in Europe, unlike in Southeast Asia, where Chinese temples are widely found.

An exception is the Kut O Association 旅欧吉澳同乡会, which (like the True Jesus Church) caters to people from a fishing village in the New Territories and their British-born descendants. This association follows the cult of Mazu 妈祖, also called Tianhou 天后, the goddess of seafarers. With its European headquarters in Glasgow, it is the best example of Chinese folk-religious transnationalism in Britain.[324]

Mazu is a popular transnational deity whose cult started in Fujian in the tenth century. Today, it claims 100 million adherents in China (principally Fujian), Taiwan, and Hong Kong and among Chinese in Southeast Asia. The cult's export started in the early-seventeenth century. By the twentieth century, it had spread across Southeast Asia. Around the world, more than 1500 temples are dedicated to Mazu. Most are in China and Taiwan, but there are several dozen in Hong Kong and Malaysia and one each in France, Norway, and Denmark. Chinese scholars conclude that without this transnationalisation, Mazu would not have become such an important deity. For centuries, the cult has played a part in promoting transnational contact between Chinese in different countries and across the Taiwan Strait. In Europe, the cult acts as a transnational focus. The sacrificial ceremony held each year in Europe on the 23rd day of the second lunar month (the goddess' birthday) attracts thousands of members of the Kut O group from all over the Continent.[325] The British-based Kut O Fishermen's Cooperative 吉澳区渔村侨民互助社 (later renamed the Kut O Buddhist Association 旅欧吉澳渔联会[326]) hosts the annual Tin Hau Festival 天后节.[327]

The major institutional religions and folk cults in Britain thus play a transnational role. Not all the Chinese churches and Buddhist centres use only Chinese in their services and rituals, but most do, and nearly all cherish links to Chinese culture. They tend to focus on Chinese issues and to push diasporic awareness – religious practice and patriotism are no less compatible now than at the start of the twentieth century. The transnational cults are even more closely wedded to a global Chinese culture. Churches, temples, and cults reconstitute a Chinese civil society overseas, with a full spread of social classes and age-groups and a complex status hierarchy to satisfy the ambitious.

Conclusions

In this chapter, we identified as deep transnationals the seafarers and (to a lesser extent) the postwar caterers. The seafarers, organised in native-place gangs, were connected by capitalism across vast spaces, to each other and their sending communities. They were the global equivalent afloat of the railway workers who knitted together China's early labour movement. In Britain, some fell under nationalist sway. Many were alienated by British racism. However, their movement calmed down after its initial surge in the early 1940s, and those who remained in Britain after the war did not stay in close enough touch with China to keep their transnational identifications. The caterers, for their part, were tied to their sending villages by kinship practices; the collective memory of racist exclusion before and between the wars; the private agencies, post-offices, and banks through which they remitted money; and – but only at a later date – the start of cheap flights and communications and the activities of the HKGO. Yet even before planes, phones, and bureaucrats made their translocal practices *physically* regular, the caterers habitually *imagined* their tenure abroad to be temporary and lived Chinese lives.

Transnational practices and institutions pervaded the community in its immigrant phases, both from below and from above, and are as old as Chinese immigration to Britain. As the community ages and the immigrants die out, transnational ties to the sending towns and villages fray and break. Yet political transnationalism of the sort promoted by Chinese state institutions and political parties can sometimes interrupt and temporarily reverse their decline and patch broken connections.

Transnationalism as a product of the interaction of imperialist globalisation and Chinese state-formation arose in the nineteenth century. Its technological preconditions, ranging from steam and the telegraph to electronics, can be cancelled by sudden or evolutionary changes affecting the ethnic community. Transnational sentiments and organisation cannot be artificially drummed into being. Political transnationalism lives on in the ethnic community only insofar as it coincides with community needs and feelings.

Working typologies of transnationalism distinguish between 'transnational activities initiated and conducted by powerful institutional actors' (including states and political parties) and 'grass-roots initiatives by immigrants and their home country counterparts'.[328] In the case of Chinese in Britain, however, the two types often intersect. Elite influences (emanating from the Embassy, political parties, and other institutions) can be detected in many of the Chinese voluntary associations established in Britain over the last 150 years. Practically the sole exceptions are those formed by immigrants from the New Territories. Even associations seemingly based in kinship and provenance were tied to Chinese political movements led by people like Kang Youwei and Sun Yat-sen. Like Kang and Sun, nearly all Chinese in the English-speaking countries were Cantonese. Communists like Liao Chengzhi and Sam Chen also infiltrated the communities along Cantonese connections.

The Chinese body politic has repeatedly campaigned to co-opt sections of the British Chinese community into its projects (ranging from the struggle for the Republic at the start of the twentieth century to that for the Third United Front at the end of it). However, states are an unreliable base for transnational identifications. The role of motherland governments in Chinatown politics is double-edged. They help to improve organisation and management, but they reduce democracy and independence. Their political enthusiasm is fitful: one moment it wells up, the next it fizzles out. After whipping up support in Britain for his party in 1904, Sun Yat-sen went on to dash his British-based supporters' dreams of government posts. For a while after 1927, the Guomindang neglected the communities abroad that had willed it into power. In the 1950s and the 1960s, Beijing turned its back on Chinese overseas. In 2000, political developments in Taiwan dented Taibei's patriotic credentials as their steadfast supporter. Two factors that have contributed to the shrivelling of the British Chinese community's transnational links to homeland states over the years are its small size and relative prosperity. In the United States, the Chinese community has long been sufficiently populous to feature at times in the diplomatic equation, whereas Britain's Chinese residents have always been too few to weigh much in Sino-British relations. The Chinese in Britain have also tended to thrive, and have therefore neither sought nor attracted much homeland attention. The expatriate perception that political home ties are based on state self-interest and can be loosened and tightened at will has, over the decades, dispelled much of the transnational magic.

The Chinese community in Britain is extremely diverse and originates largely outside mainland China. For most of the time, this diversity has reinforced its apolitical character. Immigrants are often fixated on events in the ancestral homeland. Since 1927, however, the rivalry between communists and Nationalists in China, and then between Beijing and Taibei, has stunted expatriate Chinese politics, including in Britain. Chinese professionals and intellectuals have usually steered clear of political commitment (except in the war and during other abnormal interludes) and older immigrants have kept their own counsel, while most caterers are indifferent to Chinese politics, given their Hong Kong background.[329]

The British Chinese community's diversity and self-sufficiency has therefore hampered homeland representatives' efforts to focus it on Chinese affairs. The Chinese in France, on the other hand, whether from China or Southeast Asia, have been less inhibited about taking sides, given the mainland origins of the older group of Zhejiangese and the organisational tradition of the refugee groups from Indochina and the political context in which they reached France.

Host states and organisations, British or European, are also an unreliable support. Although committed in theory to respecting non-nationals' human rights, their policies are not secure against domestic racism. State-inspired transnationalism is fragile, used self-interestedly and to different ends by different groups and institutions.

Religious faith plays a robust part in preserving transnational identities. Chinese in Britain follow several faiths affiliated to world movements with their headquarters in Asia, but most of the Chinese have no religion. Religion's effect on Chinese transnational ties is therefore weaker than on other groups, especially the South Asians, three-quarters of whom are devout believers, and even more so the Muslims, driven together by Islamophobia.

Transnational connections to other parts of the diaspora are also as old as Chinese settlement overseas. The Siyinese in North America took the lead in politicising communities formed by their fellow-Siyinese in the English-speaking world and launched culinary and entrepreneurial fashions that spread everywhere. In the Second World War, thousands of British-based seafarers went to ground in New York's Chinatown after crossing the Atlantic. Within Europe, diasporic Chinese networks predated by decades Europe's formal integration.

The transnational world of the Chinese in Britain has several intersecting layers, corresponding to subethnic, political, and class divisions. Scholars have paid class identity less attention in this context than other identities, but it can play an important role. Campaigns to recruit Chinese seafarers in Britain into Sun Yat-sen's labour alliance and, in the early 1940s, into a proletarian world front created a movement that connected not only with Chinese seafarers throughout the world but with white trade unions. Red organisers of Chinese in Europe in the 1920s and the 1930s were most active on the European mainland, where the Chinese communists had their earliest base and the Comintern and its national sections supported them politically and logistically. When the mainland fell to the Nazis, the seafarers and their movement retreated to Britain, their sole remaining refuge.

It is a conventional wisdom of writing about China that Chinese migrants bring into play in their new settings (both in China and abroad) habits of association-forming imported from the ancestral counties: that they carry the memory of village forms of organisation into the cities, where they use it to build associations. Even within China this translation theory is dubious. Following Siu and Faure, we can better understand clan and native-place associations as a product of interaction between local communities and the encompassing Chinese state rather than as an atavistic reflex born of 'static sets of traits within an all-encompassing cultural tradition... [and of] neatly bounded social units frozen in time and space'.[330] While this theory does not rule out the export of Chinese forms, it should alert us to the activities of the home and host polity in shaping migrant institutions. In communities both in China and overseas, association-forming is a complex process in which states and political elites can play a decisive role.

In this chapter, we have explored the extent to which the home and host polity have influenced the Chinese community. Associations formed by the Chinese in Britain and Europe have interacted much less with Chinese or foreign state authorities than in other continents. In Southeast Asia and North America in the last years of the Qing and the early years of the Republic, the imperial court in Beijing and successive generations of constitutionalists, nationalists, and communists competed to woo the Chinese overseas. More recently, in postcolonial times, indigenous regimes in Southeast Asia have tried to undermine or co-opt Chinese organisations. Perversely, the associations can even be said to have benefited from repression, which generated a culture of resistance. In Britain and Europe, on the other hand, the patronage Chinese associations have received from the ancestral and the host state is marginal. The relative absence of state intervention in Chinese associations helps explain their weakness.

In the 1990s, the China link and advances in European integration sped the birth of pan-European Chinese associations. Chinese and Taiwanese authorities favoured their formation and competed to sponsor them. Community leaders tried to contrive a public opinion to support this movement. In 1996, for example, the author of a handbook on the Chinese in Europe urged his co-ethnics to overcome problems of language, culture, and race by uniting: 'Whether you are a French

Chinese, a German Chinese, or a British Chinese, you can still feel that your hearts beat in step.'[331] But such sentiments are rarely translated into practice.

The social and political impact of the new transnational associations is far less than their leaders would have us think. The federations serve the interests of their self-appointed officials more than of an active membership. A Chinese study lists some other defects:

> They use their transnational links to gain publicity, but they cannot help their members to solve practical problems. They can establish and strengthen transnational networks for their members, but they are too poor to meet more than once a year. Stating one's purposes on paper is one thing, fulfilling them in real life is another. It should come as no surprise that many transnational Chinese associations exist more in name then in reality.[332]

Both the Europe-wide bodies and the global associations they are linked to function largely as vehicles for achieving status.[333] To ethnic Chinese seeking fame beyond the narrow caterers' society, the European and world stage now beckons. Yet despite the associations' manufactured nature, some leaders are well known in Chinese circles and influential. The rediscovery of the uses of transnationalism by homeland communities since the 1980s has strengthened the leaders' hand and played a role in promoting transnational ties in Europe.

Members of the early native-place associations were tied to compatriots in China, the English-speaking world, and the European mainland. The pioneers gained access to Britain with the help of an external agency, commercial or governmental, and got a foothold. They then established their own route to the sending place, independent of any host. At a later stage, the immigrant community became sufficiently established to fan out and establish new bridgeheads and diasporic nodes. By this time, its transnational contacts to the hometown were usually institutionalised in associations. Sooner or later, its homeland ties and its diasporic ties were similarly institutionalised.

Since the late 1970s, the governments of China, Hong Kong, Taiwan, and the Chinese home regions have all played a part in creating and sustaining associations. So have native-place, clan, and dialect associations organised at the international level. However, these recent ties lack the resonance and organicity of those that linked the pioneers. The umbrella organisations set up at the instigation of Beijing and Taibei to unite Britain's ethnic-Chinese associations cover only a small minority – a failure that can be explained partly by political rivalry between different federations, which alienates potential members, and the perception by many that they are superfluous. As in their constituent associations, a big problem is ensuring the succession.

So a hardwiring of the transnational circuits is unlikely. Chief among its counteractants are identity changes among immigrants and especially their descendants. Wars, political crises, revolutions, and other developments can play a role in inhibiting transnationalism. So can the British Chinese perception that transnational associations are founded in the narrow interests of this or that state, political clique, or business group. Even where transnational connections do persist, they are not made to last.

We have identified four main propositions of transnational studies that our work does not bear out: transnationalism is the novel product of recent shifts in the global order; its necessary 'technological' precondition is easy air-transport and electronic communication; historical examples of transnationalism, in the few places where they obtain, are more likely to be economic than political; and early transnationalism was usually a preserve of the élite. A fifth hypothesis – that the more distant the origin, the less vibrant the transnationalism[334] – would also seem invalid, given that Britain's Chinese came further than almost anyone yet engaged more than most in transnationalism.

The technological argument is restrictive and deterministic. Even in pre-electronic days Chinese transnational ties with the homeland and the diaspora were sustained to the dizzy limit by letter, telegraph, and visits back and forth by ship and rail. The ethnic press created the ligaments of community, among as well as within diasporic communities. Changes in the nature of sea transport – the introduction of steam propulsion and oil-burning boilers – shrank distances hardly less spectacularly in their day than did planes and electronics in the late twentieth century. Chinese migrants signed on with the shipping lines as crew or passengers and sailed to destinations in America, Southeast Asia, Australia, and Europe. The hometown counties in mainland Guangdong in the early twentieth century and in Hong Kong's New Territories in the 1960s looked much like the migration counties of contemporary Fujian: foreign-style buildings proliferated, the men were abroad, the post-offices and the remittance agencies were never empty, and a migration culture ruled, with language schools for migrants' sons and films about life in the diaspora. Business ideas (ranging from laundries to chop-suey houses) steamed across the Atlantic from America to Liverpool and across the Pacific to Singapore and Australia and back again, as did Chinese political activists and ethnic newspapers.

Associations and ethnic networks are immigrant institutions and an everyday feature of the Chinese immigrant experience. As the community ages, they give way to new institutions and identities. Transnationalism is also an immigrant activity but less commonplace, for it requires special facilitating circumstances. The difference between Chinese transnationalism at the turn of the twentieth century and of the twenty-first is of degree rather than of quality. Early Cantonese migrants to the English-speaking countries were at bottom not much less transnational than today's Fujianese and were served by similar institutions, ranging from people-smugglers to false papers and crooked lawyers. Time must pass, says Robin Cohen, before we can conclude that this or that group of migrants will form a diaspora rather than 'merge into the crowd, lose their prior identity and achieve individualised forms of social mobility'.[335] If our findings are a guide, merging with the crowd is the more likely outcome.

Chinese migration to Britain, North America, and the Dominions in the nineteenth century was overwhelmingly proletarian but nonetheless transnational, in that it was stable and regular and involved large numbers of immigrants and their hometown reciprocators. Though basically economic, the transnational communities were political. Capturing a mass base among Chinese overseas was a central strategy of late-Qing dissidents. In overseas contexts, the divide between rich and poor came second to the ethnic difference. Crucially, China's early radicals shared a Cantonese sub-ethnicity with their compatriots in North America, Britain, Australia, and much of Southeast Asia. These findings challenge transnational theories, which stress contemporaneity, economics, and elites.

6
British Racism and the Shaping of the Chinese Community

Political and scholarly discourse on race began in Britain and the West in the mid-eighteenth century and went through numerous evolutions and mutations over the next 250 years. According to the dominant early theory, the number of racial types was fixed, the differences between them were permanent, and they were arranged in a mental and cultural hierarchy that had whites at the top, blacks at the bottom, and yellows somewhere in between. Despite the Darwinian theory of evolution, which argued the impermanence of species, this ideology of racial determinism kept going well into the twentieth century.[1]

Michael Banton traced the origin of the theory of racial types to early thinking on the prehistory of the world and the origin of species, coloured by Europeans' imperfect knowledge of non-European peoples in the eighteenth and early nineteenth centuries. He doubted a strong causal connection between imperialism and racial doctrine, which he saw mainly as the product of internal developments in scientific thinking. However, he did allow that the popularity of racial typologies and the increase in racial prejudice in nineteenth-century Britain were stimulated by contemporary events in China, India, and elsewhere abroad and that British and others viewed race in the context of an imperial relationship 'with backward races overseas'.

Race-thinking was nurtured by the rise of Social Darwinism, an application (not rooted in actual Darwinism) of the concept of evolution to the development of human societies that caused 'an immense thrill of enlightenment'.[2] Proponents of the theory, which rationalised conservative and imperialist viewpoints, foresaw the extinction of inferior races in a struggle for the survival of the fittest.[3] In the nineteenth century, racist imagery and doctrines from before high imperialism were available for appropriation by new-style colonial ideologists.

Between the world wars, 'scientific' racism continued to keep a hold over parts of the British anthropological community. In the 1930s, however, when social anthropology came to the fore, racist theories began to drop away. The defeat of Nazism led to the discrediting of racism as a political and academic doctrine.[4]

'Scientific' racist doctrines were just one source among several of the belief in white superiority. Racist thinking was powerfully shaped by the negative accounts of merchants, colonists, missionaries, and other travellers dating back to the sixteenth century.[5] Christianity also contributed to the racialising of 'coloured' peoples. The Christian doctrine of equality before God and universal brotherhood served at one point as a barrier to the polygenist belief 'that not all human tribes were the offspring of the same act of creation'.[6] In the late nineteenth century, however, ideas about the pastoral duties of the 'white race' and missionary reports about the depraved character of black and yellow peoples encouraged racist views. For many, British economic prosperity and Britain's unequalled military power justified the idea of Anglo-Saxon superiority. 'Penny papers' and mass-produced fiction popularised notions of racial superiority among urban workers, who came to share some beliefs of the merchants and industrialists.[7]

Pre-nineteenth-century British writers' views on the Chinese

Perhaps the earliest English reference to China (as Cathay) was in *Voiage and Travail* by Sir John Mandeville. The book appeared in or around 1375 and remained abidingly popular. Written to entertain and borrowing heavily from encyclopaedias and travel stories, it gave a fantastical and idealising view of China. China then seems to vanish from English writings for the next couple of centuries.

Shakespeare referred just twice to the 'Cataian', as a byword for dishonesty and chicanery ('I will not beleeue such a Cataian, though the Priest o' th' Towne commended him for a true man', *Merry Wives of Windsor*; 'My Lady's a Catayan', *Twelfth Night*). At around the same time, Sir Francis Drake came across a Chinese aristocrat in the East Indies who pleaded to be taken back to England, but Drake 'could not on such perswasions be induced'. Several English writers at the end of the sixteenth century and the start of the seventeenth described China in positive terms. Richard Hakluyt wrote a picturesque account in his

Principall Nauigations (1598). Samuel Purchas, in 1625, described China 'as a land in which marvels and profits abound'. Also in 1625, Peter Heylin described the Chinese as a race 'ingenuous and politicke' and the historian John Speed lauded Chinese culture. In 1668, John Webb said China was a place of perfect morality and Chinese were 'of the City of God'. Such writings show not all early authors spoke slightingly of China, contrary to Edward Said's Orientalist theory.[8]

The sinophilic fashion in Britain, which peaked in the seventeenth century, coincided with a campaign to discover new routes to the East. However, it was thrown into the shade by the China mania in the Catholic countries, sparked by trade and missionary activity. Whereas numerous informed publications on China appeared in mainland Europe in that period, the first systematic account in English (*The Chinese*, by John Francis Davis) was not published until 1835. Most English writings drew heavily on French authors.

'No writer of the period', noted Chan Shau Yi, speaking of eighteenth-century England, '...was a profound admirer, or a persistent critic, of Chinese culture'. True, Daniel Defoe denounced the Chinese as a 'haughty, imperious, insolent people in the midst of the grossest simplicity and ignorance', while Dr Johnson decried them as 'barbarians' and said he did not wish to be 'numbered among the exaggerators of Chinese excellence'. Most, however, were mildly favourable (like Pope and Addison) or equanimous (like Goldsmith).

Intellectuals and literati in mainland Europe derived most of their knowledge of China from the writings of Jesuit missionaries. Such people were sympathetic to Chinese culture, which they studied at close hand. Some described the Chinese as descendants of Noah, who was said to have prepared them for Christianity by passing on to them the principles of natural religion. Other Europeans whose travels were to China's south and east, away from the 'civilised' courtly centre, wrote books reviling the Chinese. A British example was Anson's *A Voyage Round the World in the Years 1740–4*, based on ten months spent in southern Chinese waters, which contributed to the spread of a hostile view.[9]

On the whole, British knowledge about Chinese was sketchy before the nineteenth century. Opinion was likelier to be adverse than complimentary and was far removed from that of France's *philosophes* and physiocrats, many of whom preached the politically inspired notion that China was ruled by benevolent philosophers. Even so, serenity and exoticism were likelier attributes of China as portrayed by the British than of the non-Chinese Orient, associated in popular tales of medieval and early modern times with sorcery, sadism, and demonism.[10]

Early 'scientific' views on racial types

A starting point for the debate on human racial types is the Swedish naturalist Carolus Linnaeus, active in the early-eighteenth century. Linnaeus devised a classification of humans and described their variations in his *Systema Naturae* (1735), which influenced British scholars. He rejected the idea of human equality, stigmatising the Asian as 'yellowish, melancholy, endowed with black hair and brown eyes,...severe, conceited, and stingy. He puts on loose clothing. He is governed by opinion'. The white European, in contrast, 'is changeable, clever, and inventive. He puts on tight clothing. He is governed by laws'.[11]

Other eighteenth-century thinkers, Britons among them, tackled the causes of human difference, including the supposed tendency of Asian societies to 'stagnate'. Environmentalists attributed diversity to the effects of climate, while the polygenists suggested that human groups were variously descended from independent pairs of ancestors. The German scholar Johann Friedrich Blumenbach proposed a classification into five great families (Caucasian, Mongolian, Ethiopian, American, and Malay), which separated as a result of degeneration caused by climate. As a Christian and a man of the Enlightenment, he stressed the underlying unity and continuity of racial types, although he exalted the Caucasian as the *varietas primigenia* and 'the most beautiful form'.[12]

The prevalence of environmentalism and Christian-inspired monogeneticism precluded a full-blown biological theory of race, which early thinkers saw as the result more of geography than of natural history. Not until the nineteenth century did the idea that race itself could account for human diversity begin to flourish.[13] The boom in trade with non-European countries and the debate about slavery contributed to its propagation. In the nineteenth century, the theory of a racial hierarchy went largely unopposed.[14] Perceived racial boundaries sharpened and the myth of 'Aryan' superiority over the Semites, yellows, and blacks came to rule in Britain and the West.[15]

From race to race-as-nationality

The idea of the Chinese as a 'racial' type loosely defined by nationhood grew up gradually over a couple of centuries. Early writers used colours, usually arranged in sets of four or five (black, yellow, red, white, and an optional brown), to categorise human types, with broad geographical terms as synonyms. Yellow was equated with Mongolian, Asiatic, and

Oriental. In time, the idea of an undifferentiated yellow race gave way to a new focus on Chinese as archetypal yellows or Mongoloids, except when other yellows (such as the Japanese) bobbed into political visibility and were temporarily returned to the aggregate.

In Britain, Chinese were separated from the Oriental 'racial' conglomerate in the course of political developments in China and on a global scale, including in the incipient Chinese diaspora. E. San Juan's comment that 'refinement in [racist] discrimination disaggregated the mass of "Orientals"' in the United States holds good for Britain too.[16] The racialising of the Chinese as a distinct group was the product of a string of political incidents and processes that shaped China's international relations in the nineteenth century. In the course of the construction of a Chinese racial type, older sinophobic stereotypes and prejudices were restored to currency.

In the mid-nineteenth century, literary doctrines of romantic nationalism in Europe explained national character in terms of race and primordial affinity. The construction of a separate Chinese race went hand in hand with the rise of self-regarding European nation-racialism, at a time of intensifying inter-European rivalries. Within the white race, who were the true Aryans? Campaigns by national romantics to lay a monopoly claim to Aryan status undermined 'the internationalist implications' of Aryanism.[17] Even so, white ranks otherwise at daggers drawn closed in the face of the Chinese.

The Chinese: a special case

Two features stood out in the racialising of the Chinese, its international character and its extreme intensity. These two hallmarks of sinophobia were connected, in that anti-Chinese sentiment gathered momentum as it sloshed violently around the world. British sinophobia was a complex product of British and Western perceptions of Chinese in China itself, in Chinese settlements abroad, and in Britain.

The internationalisation of sinophobia distinguished it from other forms of racial hatred. Anti-Chinese feeling at its peak at around the turn of the century was greater than that aimed at any other racial group. Jews, another widespread group with whom the Chinese were sometimes bracketed in racist discourse, also met with worldwide hostility, but anti-Semitism outside Europe rarely reached the extremes of sinophobia. Hence Vaughan Bevan's comment that 'history has singled out the Jew, internationally, and the black, in the West and the Old Commonwealth, as the most prolonged targets' of immigration laws and practices is off beam.[18] He forgets the Chinese, who in modern times have been the target of special exclusion laws in all five continents.

The worldwide dread and hatred of Chinese called forth its opposite in the form of a global grassroots Chinese politics, however sketchily constituted. Mutual-aid and self-defence societies set up by Chinese in the United States to resist persecution were exported to Britain, Australia, and other places by Chinese migrants, in the absence of a government in Beijing willing and able to protect them. The near universality of anti-Chinese prejudice was a most-favoured-nation policy in reverse, whereby each power contracting to the sinophobic treaty agreed to subject Chinese to an equal disadvantage.

Far more Chinese emigrated in the nineteenth century than other non-Europeans, including Indians (although their migrations were dwarfed by those out of Europe). In the British Empire, Indians formed 85 per cent of indentured emigrants between 1834 and 1920 (and Chinese 6 per cent),[19] but far fewer Indians than Chinese migrated on a global scale. The Chinese were not only more numerous but more widely scattered.

A comparison of British attitudes towards Chinese and Indians helps clarify sinophobia's sources and special nature. Neither Indians nor Chinese were exempt from racist animosity away from home, but the far greater spread of the Chinese rendered them specially vulnerable to worldwide abuse. The attacks were sometimes internationally orchestrated and nearly always mutually reinforcing. Political campaigns aimed at Chinese immigrants in the United States, South Africa, and Australia interacted and contributed to the shaping of British attitudes and practices, as a national variant of global sinophobia.

The global nature of sinophobia was connected not only with migration but with the special circumstances of China's encounter with imperialism. This meeting was international in scope, unlike in India, a British preserve. China's resistance to the international drive to carve it up led, in 1900, to the occupation of Beijing by an expeditionary force raised in several Western countries to crush the Boxers. These events gave rise to a worldwide China-hating outburst best captured by the sudden popularity of the Yellow Peril tag. An obvious parallel is with the Indian Mutiny of 1857–1858, which sparked a deep hatred in the British Army of the native. However, the Mutiny's repercussions were not global. Even some British saw it as a product less of 'innate sepoy brutality...than of the interference by Britain with established local customs'.[20]

Most Indians and Chinese who visited Britain in the nineteenth and early twentieth century did so as seafarers, some of whom left the sea and took up residence, temporary or permanent. A minority arrived as students, quite a few of whom remained. The number of Chinese and ethnic Chinese was far smaller than that of Indians, but their presence in the British fleet generated a deeper animosity.[21] To grasp this development, it helps to consider how Chinese and Indian migrants were differently constituted at the point of origin and arrival, in terms of their cultural, political, and legal status.[22]

English as the language of administration and education knitted together India under the Raj and won the middle classes' acceptance as a vehicle of communication and culture. Tens of thousands of Indians passed through India's universities after their founding in 1857, nearly all of them in Arts subjects. Some British observers were repelled by Indian 'decadence' and the lack of British-style progress, but others were strongly drawn to Indian culture.[23] Late eighteenth-century British historians created knowledge about India's past that acquired 'the shape of a coherent history', while imperial administrators familiarised themselves with indigenous idioms and became dependent on indigenous networks, rather than stick to 'a singular idiom or purpose'.[24]

Knowledge about India was augmented at home by the tradition of Great (later Imperial) Exhibitions staged in London and other cities between 1851 and 1938, at which India provided thousands of the exhibits, and by smaller exhibitions and lectures put on by missionaries, ethnographers, and geographical societies. The exhibitions, though racialist, self-referential, propagandistic, and triumphalist, educated visitors about artefacts and lifestyles of Indian and other colonised peoples.[25]

Aryans, the so-called *Indogermanen*, occupied top place in the racial hierarchy of race-thinkers like Comte de Gobineau, who argued that the speakers of Indo-European languages constituted a superior race. By positing a close racial tie between British and Indians, the theory of Aryanism lent itself to a patronising of northern Indians, whose complexion and features struck some British as 'almost English'. Until the eighteenth century, Chinese and Japanese had also been perceived as white by their admirers, who at first were the majority. Their detractors, on the other hand, saw them as less than white or as yellow, a view that in the end prevailed.[26] Thus the two people passed each other in opposite directions on the race ladder.

Partly because of their racial promotion, distinctive and particular features of different groups of Indians became visible to the colonisers. Studies argue the 'racial specificity' and subdivisions of coloured peoples were ignored, but this was far truer of the Chinese than of the Indians.

Whereas Chinese tended to be portrayed sketchily and lumped together, Indians were more likely to be represented as diverse.[27]

From the point of view of social composition, the Chinese lacked the multiplicity of backgrounds of Britain's early Indian residents. They gave the impression of clannishness and self-reliance, both as ship gangs and as laundry-keepers. Entrepreneurial fashions swept Chinatown as if by preconceived design and embraced nearly all residents. The Indians, on the other hand, worked in all sorts of capacities. They included servants, domestics, ayahs, pedlars, traders, merchants, businessmen, cafe-keepers, boarding-masters, oculists, doctors, lawyers, scholars, scientists, educationalists, journalists, civil servants (at India House), musicians, cricketers, and exiled princes. Some political activists melted into British politics, others struggled for colonial liberation. Although they continued to suffer discrimination and abuse, they were a complex and heterogeneous group not easily reduced to stereotype – unlike the Chinese, who came to seem unindividualised and regimented.

In the First World War, India contributed more than one million troops to the British effort. Rozina Visram shows how their performance on the battlefield helped destroy the British myth of Indian inferiority and reinforced their image as 'loyal sons of India'.[28] China sent hundreds of thousands of contract labourers to work as battlefield ancillaries, but none fought and their contribution did not arouse the same enthusiasm.

At the same time as British knowledge of India was starting to deepen and cohere, knowledge of China was on the ebb. Under the Jesuits, for many years the main source of reliable information about China, study of Chinese civilisation had prospered. In 1773, however, the Jesuit order was temporarily abolished. Most other scholars and political thinkers who took an interest in China in the eighteenth century used largely fantastical descriptions of Chinese society for little purpose other than to advance political schemes at home. Not until the early nineteenth century did sinology take off as a subject in its own right.[29] Chinese studies in Britain started decades later than in mainland Europe and did not become truly professionalised until after 1945. In 1964, a British authority described sinology as 'one of the newest sciences'.[30]

Finally, the juridical status of Indians and Chinese in Britain differed. Whereas Lascars were 'imperial citizens', only Chinese from Hong Kong and the British colonies in Southeast Asia and elsewhere held that status. Many Chinese tried to pass themselves off as British subjects to get jobs on British ships, so that practically all Chinese claiming 'Empire origin' at the height of the anti-Chinese agitation were assumed to be lying. Their 'imperial' status gave Indians juridical rights denied the Chinese.

They could appeal to the India Office and the Indian Parliament and received help from philanthropic organisations such as the League for the Protection of Lascars and the League of Coloured People, as well as from Indian unions in Britain.[31]

In the course of global cultural encounters, non-European peoples have been cast in the role of polar opposite to the West, a dichotomisation that shaped the way in which Westerners think of the world and themselves.[32] Within this polarity, 'the Chinaman and the Hindoo' were the truest others.[33] China, being less open to penetration, acted as foil to the West longer and more effectively than India. In India, missionaries and colonial writers helped break down Orientalist oppositions by moderating them with practical, first-hand knowledge.[34] There, 'colonial knowledge [was] the continuing, adaptable product of Imperial and indigenous contributions rather than a one-sided creation of British imagining and imposed conceptions'.[35] China, enigmatic and unknowable, was the country most likely to be portrayed as closed and uniform. The 'ultimate Other' of occidental imagining, it served as a screen upon which Westerners could project utopias or discontents, as part of their search for self-understanding. Whether they represented perfection (in the age of China adulation) or degradation (in the age of disillusion), the projected images said more about the West than about China.[36]

British sinophobia, from inception to (conditional) extinction

Like any racial ideology, sinophobia depends for its reproduction on events and complex social and economic interactions. Some issues nurture it: in other circumstances, it has no obvious use and does not endure.

Most of the time, even when sinophilia was out of fashion in the salons and academies, the Chinese presence in Britain was no big thing. In 1900, the Chinese were said by their Limehouse neighbours to have 'an excellent character for peacefulness and quietness' and were praised for their 'goodness and kindness to the children'.[37] In 1911, at the height of anti-Chinese agitation in other parts of Britain, 'Cockney butcherboys arm in arm with young coolies stroll into public houses' (wrote an American visitor).[38] In 1920, just a few months after attacks on Chinese in Liverpool and London, the *Daily Telegraph* reported that Chinese 'stand generally in good esteem with [with their neighbours], for in London as in the Far East, their commercial dealings are honourable and just'.[39] In 1921, claiming that Limehouse had lost much of its Chinese population as the result of actions by the local magistracy and the press, a barrister declared the remedy 'worse than the disease, for in the place of these Chinamen, who were perfectly well-conducted citizens, the houses have been taken over by people of another nationality [that is, Russians], who are very much worse than the people they replace'.[40]

But for all the routine goodwill and harmony, at times of tension locals singled the Chinese out from other foreigners for attack, despite their tiny numbers. The issue was usually jobs, yet a study on relations between British workers and Chinese in 1870–1911 concluded that 'something beyond a hostility based upon an immediate economic concern' was indicated.[41] In the following pages, the history of anti-Chinese racism in Britain is put under scrutiny, in an attempt to explain its constant resurgence and excess.

Yellow Peril

The demise of the sinophilic view coincided roughly with the start of the imperialist campaign to open up the China market. Voltaire's praise for China gave way to adverse reflections by thinkers like Jean-Jacques Rousseau and Montesquieu in France, who denounced its lack of freedom, and Adam Smith in Britain, who criticised its poverty and conservatism. In the 1820s, the German philosopher Hegel drew such criticisms together in a theory of oriental despotism that influenced Marx's view on China. These notions were compost for Yellow Peril thinking in the age of New Imperialism.

The Yellow Peril idea grew out of the perception of a deadly threat posed to the whites by yellow hordes, who had only to 'walk slowly westwards' to overwhelm Europe.[42] Politicians predicted China and Japan would kick the whites out of Asia. Trade-union leaders whipped up fears of competition from Chinese labour and cited the outcry in America and Australia. Merchants and manufacturers talked of 'unfair' competition from Japan. The Boxer Rising put the wind up China's would-be dismemberers, who gave up their plans, but it fuelled anti-Chinese hysteria. The Yellow Peril tag, allegedly invented by Kaiser Wilhelm II, spread across the world like wildfire after 1900.[43]

Hobson's choice

J. A. Hobson (1858–1940) was a British liberal campaigner whose study on imperialism deeply influenced V. I. Lenin. He had decided views on the Chinese and their place in the world – he thought they should stay at home.

Hobson believed the 'white races' could legitimately interfere in the affairs of the 'lower races' for the good of humanity. However, he excluded China and India from this liability to trusteeship, on the grounds that they were equal with the West (although different from it). China was 'a huge nest of little free village communes, self-governing, and animated by a genuine spirit of equality'. On the basis of its unexampled liberty, it had created a civilisation singular in its recognition of the dignity of labour and its reverence for things of the mind. Imperialist interference in a country so endowed with productive powers was not only unnecessary but inadvisable, for it might lead to Chinese ousting British produce from world markets and taking financial control of China's white 'quondam patrons and civilizers'. 'It is then', cautioned Hobson, 'that the real "yellow peril" will begin'. Where the Chinese were strong enough to assert their will, a flood of China goods would drive down white wages. Elsewhere, the power of the white oligarchy might be secured 'by menaces of yellow workmen or of yellow mercenary troops'.

Hobson advanced this argument as a warning rather than a prophesy, but he also took stands on more immediate 'racial' issues. In the late nineteenth century, Chinese had begun to migrate in increasing numbers to South Africa. After the Anglo-Boer War in 1902, mine owners called for the import of indentured Chinese to replenish the war-depleted workforce. Their plans met with resistance in both South Africa and in Britain, where the issue featured in the 1906 General Election. In a contribution to the debate, Hobson argued that the future of Transvaal mining depended on the presence of British colonists and opposed displacing whites by Chinese.

Hobson's curiously partitioned view of the Chinese joined sinophilia and sinophobia in a single vision. At home, they were democratic, moral, and orderly. Abroad, they were a menace, a horde 'of able-bodied males, without any women, huddled in close barracks, rigorously guarded during work and at leisure, kept continually at hard routine manual labour, deprived of all the educative influences of self-direction in a free civilized society, . . . inevitably degraded in morals by the conditions of this service'. Left alone, the Chinese had developed a rich, self-sufficient civilisation whose foreign relations were confined to 'casual intercourse'. Dragged onto the world stage, they would mutate into a Yellow Peril that destroyed white workers' livelihoods and undermined Western civilisation.[44]

Hobson's split view kicked off a century of British ambiguity about China and the Chinese. His warnings about the Chinese as competitors stuck a liberal fig-leaf on the sinophobes. How could the nervous Briton match the teeming Oriental? In the markets for business and labour, a first British reaction was to treat the Chinese as deadly rivals. In time, however, Chinese immigrants learned to cope with native intolerance by withdrawing into ethnic niches.

The Yellow Peril and the labour movement

The Yellow Peril was conceived by its originators as a threat to both capital and labour, but it was most feared by workers. Anti-foreign prejudice, endemic in parts of British cities, was triggered by economic insecurity. At around the turn of the twentieth century, workers in London and other ports expressed strong opposition to alien immigration. The xenophobic mob had high-placed leaders in the political parties. Anti-alien societies linked Chinese and Jews and speculated on the slums bringing to birth 'a slit-eyed mongrel', half Chinese and half Jewish.[45]

Some politicians, newspapers, and employers stoked up anti-Chinese feeling by arguing Chinese could be used to break strikes and praising them as docile and diligent. In 1870, the *Times* predicted 'the Chinese will become the principal workman element not only in America but in Europe', and thus 'cause discontent among our working classes,...and end by fixing itself among us like the Jews'.[46] In 1892, the Trades Union Congress pressed for restrictions on immigration; in 1898, it backed American unions' opposition to Chinese immigration in 'defence of white labour'.[47]

Labour figures subsequently feted as internationalists, including Jim Larkin, Ben Tillett, and Beatrice Webb, swelled the anti-Chinese chorus.[48] Dockers were among the most unrelenting xenophobes. Although few aliens worked the docks, the casual nature of dockers' employment created a sense of vulnerability that they blamed on immigrants. Along with seafarers, dockers carried out some of the worst attacks on Chinese.[49]

Anti-Chinese feeling was originally confined to small sectors of the British labour movement, but the importation of tens of thousands of Chinese to South Africa spread it more widely. In 1904, James Sexton, a Liverpool Irish dockers' leader, moved a resolution at the Trades Union Congress condemning the use of Chinese in South Africa. Some insisted the issue was one of opposition to indentured labour rather than to

Chinese labour as such, but in reality the main concern was to protect white workers' interests. Liberals also opposed introducing Chinese to the Transvaal, on ostensibly humanitarian grounds.[50]

The Transvaal issue blew over after the Liberal election victory, which led to an end to the issuing of licences to import Chinese into South Africa and the start of their repatriation. However, it left a residue of anti-Chinese hostility that found expression between 1906 and 1914 in various forms, including a seafarers' campaign to oust Chinese from British ships. The principal objection to Chinese crews was that they took low wages. Another was that they were forming settlements in Britain, unlike the Lascars, who signed on and off in India.[51] The campaign led to confrontations in which Chinese 'tested the quality of British muscle' and were prevented from signing on as crew in several ports.[52]

In 1911, general agitation among seafarers peaked in an international strike for union recognition, better conditions, and higher pay. Both in Britain and Europe, Chinese strike-breaking became an issue. Anti-Chinese feeling was strongest in Cardiff, where the Chinese stood out among the city's many seagoing nationalities as strike-breakers and encountered special violence. Other Chinese recruited in London were sent to help break a Dutch seafarers' strike. In both Britain and the Netherlands, the experience further soured relations between Chinese and white seafarers.

In his study on Chinese and British labour, J. P. May argued that vague threats to import Chinese as strikebreakers had no evident effect on South Wales miners in 1873 and that white seafarers in Liverpool did not oppose Chinese seafarers in prewar years as long as they stuck to the China run and kept off white routes. However, even unions not directly threatened by Chinese competition (including navvies, miners, and dockers) condemned Chinese 'slave labour' at the height of the Yellow Peril scare.

Some Labour Party leaders shamelessly milked anti-Chinese prejudice in the General Election of 1906. In Liverpool, Jim Larkin organised a procession of 'pseudo Chinamen', with yellowed faces and oakum pigtails, behind a hearse draped with the Union Flag to represent the burial of freedom.[53] That was just one of several anti-Chinese demonstrations.

Many British workers and labour leaders aimed a special venom at the Chinese and distinguished them from all other foreigners. 'Although neither absolutely nor relatively large', wrote May, 'it was nevertheless to the Chinese that objection was taken'. May describes the whites' motives as mainly economic, but adds that Chinese were associated as a result of the Transvaal episode with the Conservative Party, perceived by many workers as the enemy.[54]

In the United States, a similar distinction divided Chinese from the rest. In his account of the anti-Chinese crusade in California, Alexander Saxton pointed out that whereas non-Chinese industry was split horizontally between workers and exploiters, immigrant Chinese society 'was vertical from the indentured laborer to the importer-padrone', a transclass bloc cemented by racist pressures. Non-Chinese labour saw Chinese as a bosses' tool, a second enemy from below.[55] Saxton's point is relevant to British sinophobia. Although few Chinese entered Britain on indentures, for British workers they seemed to fit most closely the robotic, tractable stereotype of the capitalist dream, endowed 'with an extraordinary capacity of steady labour' and 'inured to a low standard of material comfort',[56] a living representation of the state to which capitalism wished to reduce the workers.

Chinese and the 1919 race riots

In 1919, British ports including Cardiff, Glasgow, Liverpool, and London were swept by racial incidents, called 'khaki riots' by association with the 'khaki election' of 1918. For a while, the spectre of revolution haunted Europe. In some countries, revolutionary movements seemed on the point of following the Bolsheviks. Even in Britain, political strikes and soldiers' mutinies created a whiff of anxiety in establishment minds.[57] However, the British crisis was more easily contained. Radicals tried to drive the unrest in revolutionary directions but it was derailed onto racist grounds, as a reactionary Anglo-Celtic counterpoint to the rise of black consciousness in the Empire.[58] Several European countries had 'khaki riots', but only Britain's degenerated into race riots.

Blacks were the rioters' main target, but Chinese also came under attack. Journalists and labour leaders in Glasgow, where the disturbances started, blamed the trouble on the employment of Chinese, even though African-descent seafarers were the most obvious 'foreign' element – a good example of the disproportionate attention paid to Chinese.[59] The accumulations of Chinese in the ports were due largely to the efforts of the National Seamen and Firemen's Union (NSFU) to stop them working. They included several hundred land workers discharged after the armistice.[60] In most ports, the disorder was triggered by non-whites trying to sign on British ships.

Blacks and Asians defended themselves where possible against the police and rioters. The Chinese were more vulnerable than other non-whites, for most could be legally repatriated. In 1919 and 1920, hundreds were deported, partly in response to agitation by British seafarers. They included some already domiciled in Britain before the war and others whose claims to imperial citizenship were ignored.[61]

The imperial reflection

If sinophobia was a cause that gained strength and momentum from its worldwide interconnections, its internationalisation was reinforced in Britain by the Empire tie, which heaped added disadvantage on the Chinese. Perceptions of a demographic threat to the British Empire by Chinese became embedded in British racial thinking, even when Chinese immigration into Britain itself was negligible. Racist measures taken in Empire countries provided a template for British legislation. James Walvin, noting this phenomenon of transfer, called the anti-Chinese prejudice 'a reflected imperial issue'.[62]

In the last two decades of the nineteenth century, British colonial authorities in various countries introduced measures to deter non-European immigration. Deterrents included a poll tax on immigrants, immigrant quotas on ships, the exclusion of 'undesirables', dictation tests, and restrictions on economic activity. In the Pacific colonies, Chinese were the principal target. Much of the initial agitation was fired up by trans-Pacific interaction between North America and Australia. For example, the passenger restriction echoed legislation passed in the United States in 1879.[63] Anti-Chinese measures migrated from one colony to the next, until they were applied almost everywhere. They included language tests, pioneered in Natal as a means of keeping out non-Europeans and then copied in other parts of South Africa and in New Zealand, Australia, and Canada.[64]

Initially, the British Government made liberal noises against such curbs, but eventually it drew on them as legislative precedents for its own controls.[65] Leaders of the British anti-alien movement declared the English 'ought not to be above learning a lesson from our Colonies'. One borrowed hurdle was the language test, introduced to placate British labour (but justified as a means of ensuring that foreign seafarers could understand orders). Other rules introduced by imperial reflection included confining immigrants to specified ports and establishing 'undesirable categories'.[66] Although not specifically aimed at Chinese, such legislation made things especially hard for them. The Lascars, being

'British', benefited from privileges and exemptions denied the Chinese. The language test, for example, did not apply to them.[67]

The imperial reflection also applied in the world of labour. Anti-alien proposals passed by the British trade unions in the 1890s followed widespread calls by labour groups in Australia in the 1880s to exclude Chinese and other coloured migrants.[68]

Imperialist anxiety and guilt

A more subtle and subconscious imperial reflection arose from the role played by opium in the early years of British trading on the China coast. Barry Milligan explains how the bad conscience of the British middle classes created 'a vague anticipation of retribution for...the Empire's controversial opium-trading practices'. This guilt-induced anxiety swelled the unease about Chinese immigration into Britain and the competition for jobs and resources it would supposedly cause. The founding of Chinatowns intimated the possibility of 'reverse colonization' by the 'vindictive Orient', envisaged as the 'Orientalization' of the English (and particularly of Englishwomen) by opium.[69]

This fear was based on magnifying China as a rival empire and serious threat, unlike the stereotypes requiring its disparagement. Together with other components of the Chinese vice cliché, it spawned a literature whose genres ranged from the polite to the lurid. Charles Dickens, who had an antipathy to Chinese, fathered the tradition's polite end. In 1869, while researching *The Mystery of Edwin Drood*, he visited a Chinese opium den. The novel opens with a description of an old and haggard woman who had 'opium-smoked herself into a strange likeness of the Chinaman', her den-companion.[70] From Dickens' story, wrote Matthew Sweet, 'textual opium dens blossomed: most subsequent journalistic and literary accounts...owe more to Dickens than [to] any genuine fieldwork'.[71] At the lurid end, formulaic articles about dens appeared in the popular press.[72] Chinatown came to be pictured as part of a global conspiracy to subvert the white race and take over the world, a charge normally associated with the Jews.

The Yellow Peril idea gave birth in Britain to the fictional Fu Manchu, described as 'the yellow peril incarnate'. A drug baron, sadist, and seducer of white womanhood, Fu Manchu was the creation of the thriller writer Sax Rohmer, whose work begat a film genre and many imitators. Rohmer never went to China but took his local colour from a superficial acquaintance with the Limehouse Chinatown. His picture of a vast Chinese vice syndicate masterminded from the East End was taken up by newspapers, which published hysterical reports about the 'Chinese Moriarty'.[73] The view of Chinatown as 'mysterious, vice-ridden and dangerous' survived in Britain into the 1970s.[74]

Sinophobia and competition

Early sociological explanations attributed racist sentiment to economic conflict, whereas contemporary studies see ideology distilled in racist images as its driving force. Our view is that labour and market rivalry have played the main role in forming British views on Chinese entrepreneurs and labour migrants, but in the context of racist discourses and the Yellow Peril ideology.

A previous chapter dealt with Chinese crews undercutting whites and, on occasions, breaking white strikes. Campaigns on this issue came and went, depending as much on political as on economic factors. At the start of the First World War, the resentment died down for a bit as the labour market tightened, but it soon flared up again. In 1916, two years into the war, local agitators renewed their assault on the Limehouse Chinatown. They were keen to clear out Chinese crews so they themselves could escape the war by joining the merchant service, at a point in the war when enlisting looked increasingly unattractive.[75] After the war, Chinese crews were again subjected to a reign of terror.

In the early years, Chinese encountered hostility from vested interests in whichever trade they entered. Police chiefs attributed part of the outcry to owners of local laundries and boarding houses.[76] The Chinese gambling craze that hit the East End around 1920 angered bookmakers by eating into their profits. After the Armistice, extensive investment in property in the East End by Chinese who had prospered in the war and the overflow of the Chinese settlement into adjacent streets incensed returning servicemen. Foreign landlords had long been a focus of resentment in the East End, where overcrowding was rife.[77] Men unable to find houses for their families wrecked lodgings let out to Chinese, torched their furniture, and beat up their white wives.[78]

The Chinese concentration in shipping and laundering alarmed workers in those industries, but the Chinese placated their competitors by keeping to marginal or inferior occupations. The campaign against Chinese hand laundries ceased when it became clear that they were unlikely to compete with the new industrial laundries. The switch to ethnic catering in the 1950s clinched this retreat into self-segregation. Sections of white labour and the NSFU subjected Chinese seafarers to persecution in the early twentieth century, until tacit lines of demarcation were drawn whereby Chinese stayed below deck and stuck to a limited number of shipping lines. Chinese 'encroachment' on the housing stock was terminated when most switched to the shophouse habit, with laundry or takeaway families living above their businesses. On every front, the Chinese abandoned the mainstream and entered ethnic niches that were invisible or engagingly exotic. In short, they rendered themselves acceptable by building a virtual 'homeland', self-sufficient and self-reliant along the lines Hobson liked to picture.

Sinophobia and sex

Against a background of racist hatred engendered by competition over jobs and houses, sexual competition can intensify 'racially' induced anxiety. Unlike the United States, Britain had no laws forbidding miscegenation, but few people countenanced sexual union between whites and non-whites until relatively late in the twentieth century. Even so, liaisons formed between Chinese men and white women and were a prime cause of the nativisation of some Chinese.

Such partnerships were inevitable given the shortage of Chinese women. The small size and the closed nature of Britain's early-Chinese community meant this miscegenation was seldom the focus of public attention. However, the children of mixed-race unions were highly visible on the dockland streets. 'In America', wrote an American visitor to Britain in 1911, 'the Chinese colony is and remains an isolated unit, but in this country it is already peculiarly and perilously involved with English life through that strongest and most persistent of human ties – a mixture of blood'.[79]

When racial tensions rose as a result of labour competition or international incidents, sexual relationships became an issue. The outcry peaked in 1906, at the height of the anti-Chinese agitation on the Transvaal question; in 1911, at the time of the international seafarers' strike; and around 1920, during the postwar economic troubles.

In 1906 and 1907, a commission appointed to inquire into Liverpool's Chinese settlement looked *inter alia* at Chinese relations with white women, which the press described as scandalous. It concluded that women married to Chinese were 'happy and contented and extremely well treated' but that the Chinese had 'frequent illicit intercourse with white women' and seduced under-age girls.[80] Liverpool's Head Constable told the Home Office of the 'strong feeling of objection to the idea of a half caste population which is resulting from the marriage of

Englishwomen to Chinese'. However, he himself blamed the ill will on commercial rivalry: 'The Chinamen have no difficulty in getting English women to marry them, and in all these relations they treat women well, they are sober, they do not beat their wives, and they pay liberally for prostitution. Unfortunately there are many women whose home surroundings are bettered by marriage or cohabitation with them.... I cannot help feeling that what is really at the bottom of most of [the resentment] is the competition of the Chinese with the laundries and boarding house keepers'.[81]

Part of the 1911 agitation centred on the Cardiff Chinese, who were accused of sexual immorality. Again, an investigation found that white women who lived with Chinese were 'content with their lot' and 'kindly treated'.[82]

The postwar outcry was more vicious and sustained than previous campaigns. Chinese who had made good in the war were said to have filled some of their newly acquired properties in the East End by importing 'degraded women into London from the slums of Cardiff and Liverpool'.[83] Others rented rooms or houses for themselves and their white consorts. 'The combination of [sex and housing] is deeply resented by the people in the English populated streets', said a report.[84] White servicemen who had returned home from the war disillusioned and embittered vented their anger on the non-whites, who had begun colonising new streets.[85] National newspapers carried a spate of articles about 'white girls and Chinamen'. London's *Evening News* ran a series on the 'lure of the yellow man', the 'hypnotisation' of white girls, and their 'vanished moral sense'. It argued that the girls were driven by unemployment and attracted by a combination of 'easy money', drugs, and the chance to gamble, though it conceded that most wives of Chinese were happy and secure. 'The girl who lives with a Chinaman', said one report, 'has money to spend, smart clothes to wear, new and fashionable shoes. She is not ill-treated'.[86]

In the war, women's economic role had changed greatly, a development with which many men were uncomfortable. The progress to female emancipation was easily joined with the racial factor by returning soldiers who resented foreigners. Opium, another issue in the agitation, contributed to the singling out of Chinese as a target and was inevitably linked to sex and race. The connection between opium smoking and the supposed degeneracy of the Chinese was a theme of the eugenicists, who feared the effects of the habit on the over-sensitive white race. 'Very many of these celestials [that is, Chinese] and Indians are mentally and physically inferior', explained a tract, 'and they go on smoking year after year and seem not very much the worse for it. It is your finer natures that suffer, deteriorate and collapse. For these, great and terrible is the ruin'.[87] It took no great leap of imagination to spot the relevance of opium-induced degradation to the postwar crisis of society and self-belief, with women as the white heel of Achilles.

Even before the war, white women taking or peddling drugs had been a feature of what Milligan calls the 'opium den narrative'.[88] Sex, gambling, and dope were three main themes of British writing about Chinatown, especially between 1916 and the mid-1920s. 'One of the most striking features of the British discourse on drugs', wrote Marek Kohn in his study on the birth of the British drugs underground,

> was its emphasis on women. Actresses, chorus girls, 'night club girls', 'bachelor girls', 'flappers', 'women of the unfortunate class'; whether they played the part of victim or harpy, the women of the drug underworld were of the uncontainable class.... Victory [in the war] had taken too long and cost too much to enhance British self-confidence.... Europe was in crisis; European values had been thrown into doubt; these instabilities had encouraged fears about the future of the race. The xenophobia of the war years persisted, and one of the ways in which it found expression was in a demonology of dope. Two individuals in particular, one Chinese and one black, were identified as 'dope kings', and invested with a highly sexualised menace.[89]

Britain's best-known Chinese 'dope king' in the early 1920s was Brilliant Chang, a West End restaurant-owner. Chang was charged in 1922 with the manslaughter of Freda Kempton, a well-known dancer, who died of a cocaine overdose.[90] The Kempton case bore similarities to another famous drugs death in 1918, that of the popular showgirl Billie Carleton, in which Chinatown suppliers were also said to have been implicated.[91] Although insufficient evidence was found to charge Chang in 1922, two years later he was gaoled and deported on new charges of possessing drugs, after being shopped by other Chinese.[92]

Journalists wrote that the Chinese used gambling games to ensnare women into opium-dealing and prostitution.[93] Together with illegal Chinese immigration, these allegations were taken as evidence of a 'vile syndicate' run from China. The *Daily Express* explained the syndicate's supposed workings:

> The headquarters of the syndicate are known to be either in Peking or Hong Kong.... Scattered throughout the world are thousands

of the agents of this secret Chinese syndicate, which promotes the pernicious opium trade, operates gambling houses, and, more important still from the national standpoint, is corrupting women and children by the fascinations of the Chinese lottery game known as puck-a-boo.... The master agent...is ostensibly a humble merchant, and he displays in the window of his shop dwelling and headquarters a few packets of tea or dried vegetables so dear to the hearts of his fellow celestials.... The police realise that there has crept into the community of the East End a 'Yellow Peril' not formed of massed battalions of saffron manned bayonets, but composed of a corruptive organised financial force backed by millions, that is undermining the morale not of the men, but of the women and children in the East End.[94]

Thus the several threads of Chinatown reporting were woven into a single fabric by journalists writing for readers fearful for the 'future of the race' and demoralised by the war.

If the Chinese coped with economic discrimination by withdrawing from disputed market-places, competition for women could not be resolved so easily. For some whites, mixed unions ceased to be a problem once familiarity began to work its magic. Others continued to ostracise white women who lived with Chinese. Even many of their own families shut them out. (Some women responded by forming sisterhoods.) Hostile whites came to terms with such relationships by portraying the women either as girls, manipulated by unscrupulous Chinese, or as 'low' women, given to promiscuity and drugs.[95] The prejudice abated over time but continued to crop up throughout the 1930s.[96] Ng Kwee Choo 吳貴竹, writing in the late 1960s, supported the view that the women suffered from 'an inferior economic position..., emotional insecurity and a background of personal rejection'.[97]

In many cases the women were themselves immigrants, mainly from Ireland. They were spirited, adaptable, and less bound by conventions than the English. Most were happy with their Chinese men, who 'were clean, treated them well, and did not beat them'. Quite a few of the men continued to support wives and children back in China, but some also took over responsibility for their white wives' children by other fathers.

They met their partners through introductions or while working in Chinese laundries or boarding houses. Some sisters specialised in Chinese husbands, with the marriages arranged by a Chinese or his white wife. (Maria Lin Wong 王林 mentions three Welsh and four Jewish sisters who married Chinese.) Some married a second and even a third or fourth Chinese husband on being widowed. That the 'Chinese wives' included large numbers of poor Irish and other non-natives tempered their 'loss' to white society in the eyes of bigots. (In Wales, they were described as 'Englishwomen of low caste'.[98]) Wives of Chinese were supposed to register as aliens, a penalty that lightened the feeling of racial betrayal with an element of gloating.[99]

The anxiety created in British establishment circles and among white men by the presence of white women in Chinatown and the attempts of middle-class do-gooders to 'rescue' them from the Chinese had parallels in the United States, where police, churchmen, and journalists called for controls on white women and girls entering Chinese-owned premises. In a study, Mary Ting Yi Lui 雷婷仪 argues such women represented in the eyes of the white middle classes the new, dangerous mobility of women and their liaisons with Chinese men symbolised immigrants' trampling of social and geographic borders. She shows that Chinatown did not grow out of some innate Chinese ethnic imperative, as people sometimes suppose, but was produced by the actions of police, evangelists, social reformers, and the press, intent on controlling the movements of Chinese men and non-Chinese women. She goes on to criticise sociologists' conceptualisation of Chinatown as a product of supposed Chinese cultural retentiveness rather than of white Orientalist discourse and processes of racial exclusion of the sort described in her book. She concludes that the emphasis on race and ethnicity at the expense of gender in the making of Chinatown effaces non-Chinese and mixed-race Chinatowners from the record and thus unwittingly realises the goal of the racial enforcers who sought to wipe out sexual mixing and maintain racial boundaries.[100]

Her point has even greater relevance to the British Chinatown, whose borders were more porous than their American equivalent. Although retrospectively pictured as a foreign world in studies and popular imagination, the early Chinatown in Britain was in reality a community whose Chinese men 'were considerably outnumbered by their white wives plus their Eurasian children'. Such is the recollection of the now elderly children, whose testimony was recently collected by Charles and Yvonne Foley, as part of their research into the deportation of the children's seafarer fathers in 1945 and 1946. The Home Office categorised the seafarers' wives as of low social class and 'of the prostitute class', thus mobilising sexism, racism, and class prejudice to justify their action.[101]

A people unsubject

There was a match and friction in the early years of Chinese settlement in Britain between European ethnocentrism and Chinese culturalism. Despite the spectre of decline that haunted the West in the early twentieth century, Anglocentric attitudes continued to form an obstacle to the mutual adaptation of English and outsiders – especially Chinese, fortified against the non-Chinese world by a similar belief in their own supremacy.[102]

In contrast to most other non-Europeans, the Chinese were neither enslaved nor colonised, except marginally. Western influence was strongest in Hong Kong, Macao, and the treaty ports, but even in Hong Kong the roots English culture struck were shallow. Unlike Indians, the Chinese had little use for English, given Mandarin's role as a national language. In the Chinese ports, pidgin English, treated with a mixture of amusement and contempt by Chinese and Westerners alike, was more likely to be heard than standard English. Full colonialism was confined to some port cities. By and large, the Chinese retained control of their own economy and society, despite China's military defeats.

After the supercession of the coolie trade, Chinese organised much of their own overseas migration. Most Chinese who went to the United States and Australia in the gold rushes and to Southeast Asia in later decades were free or sponsored migrants. Indians, by contrast, tended to be either indentured or organised by agents for the planting interest. Indentured emigration from India continued until about 1920. Even so, the main outcry in Britain against indenture was directed against the Chinese. Their singling out suggests the issue was not indenture but Chinese immigration, envisaged as Yellow Peril.

Where they were exported under indenture and other schemes, Chinese often behaved quite differently from the more stoical Indians. Hugh Tinker says the Chinese in the Creole sugar islands 'did not accept their lot, like the Indians: from the moment they came on board, they planned how they could capture the ship – or, if that was impossible – destroy the ship and themselves also.... By contrast, the protests made by Indian emigrants were isolated and insignificant'. Once abroad, Chinese tended to organise their own settlements. Unlike the less resisting Indians, 'in most cases [they] succeeded in getting away from the plantation into trading, and intermarried both with Indian and Creole women'.[103] In Australia, government officials complained that Chinese preferred to be 'their own masters', unlike the more amenable Tamils, who were moreover cheaper.[104] Less likely to truckle to their

British exploiters and more likely to run riot, their resourcefulness, rebelliousness, and self-reliance endeared them to neither bosses nor workers, who (each in their different way) saw them as a threat. Colonial perceptions coloured Britain's own Chinese residents, who were seen to cope and even thrive without patronage. Journalists imputed evil powers and a global reach to the networks, gangs, and associations that the Chinese used to get work and accommodation and guard against attack. In 1906, the *Sunday Chronicle* urged readers to remember that 'the Chinese are in close touch with one another all over the world, and when they hear from their countrymen that England is a good place where they are allowed to do as they like, they will come here in droves'.[105]

People who talked of other migrant groups as childish, lazy, temperamental, and in need of protection from their own failings saw Chinese resilience and resolution as sinister. They blamed them not only for leading whites astray but for acting 'as merchants in vice for other Asiatic or African races'.[106]

A people without the backing of a state

If early Chinese migrants' self-organisation made them seem strong, a signal weakness lay in the Qing dynasty's unwillingness to support them, at least until the 1880s, and the inability of later Chinese governments to act effectively on their behalf. It is a paradox of worldwide perceptions of Chinese that a group resented for its supposed cohesion and resilience was also despised on account of its vulnerability.

Britain's early Chinese embassies were set up as part of a campaign to protect the Chinese state and had no interest in representing emigrants. In 1866, the Chinese Foreign Ministry sent an exploratory mission to London and other European capitals. The mission was a novelty, for the Qing court had previously restricted its diplomacy to receiving delegations. It was followed in 1868 by the Burlingame Mission, China's first formal diplomatic mission to foreign powers. After an enthusiastic welcome in America, the Burlingame Mission was received coolly in London, where American intrigues were suspected.[107] Burlingame managed to persuade the United States to guarantee the Chinese right to immigrate but ignored the interests of Chinese immigrants in Britain.

China's first real embassy to Britain (and the West) was undertaken in 1876 by Guo Songtao 郭嵩焘. In his journal, Guo praised the West and railed at Chinese shortcomings, a stance that led to calls at home for his impeachment. *Punch* greeted his legation with an offensive cartoon and crude doggerel about his wife, the 'Tottering Lily of Fascin-ation'. On the streets, members of his staff were subjected to racist abuse and attacks, though on the whole they turned out to be rather popular with the English public. During his two years in London, Guo does not seem to have met other Chinese residents, except for a group of 12 naval students in 1877. He admitted the need for consular representation of Chinese, but only in California, Australia, and Hong Kong. Despite his reputation as an ethicist, he showed little interest in the problems of his lower-class compatriots. When 13 Cantonese seafarers were arrested for fighting, he refused a British request to attend their hearings. The seafarers spent a month in prison and were then deported, leading Guo to conclude that the British legal system was too lenient.[108]

The later strengthening of the Chinese embassy did not mean it auto-matically backed its nationals. In the First World War and during the postwar riots, there is no evidence of its intervening to protect Chinese workers. In the Second World War, consular officials sometimes sided with British authorities and shipping companies against the Chinese Seamen's Union. When the Home Office asked them to help restrain Chinese 'undesirables' in Liverpool in 1945, they proposed sending officers to put the seafarers under military discipline.[109]

Chinese migrants were in the same boat as migrant Jews, who also lacked diplomatic protection. Like the Chinese, Britain's Jewish immig-rants were blamed for undermining living standards, ignoring trade unions, being clannish and insanitary, and 'driving out the Englishman'. Unlike them, however, Jewish immigrants could look for support to an established community, the Anglo-Jewry. Some British Jews supported anti-alienism, but others provided humane assistance to their co-religionists. When Immigration Boards were introduced in 1906, 27 Jews were appointed to the London Board, a shield against preju-dice unavailable to the Chinese. Also unlike Chinese, most Jews were townspeople familiar with Britain's urban ways. Ultimately, they 'shared the values and heritage of Judeo-Christian civilization with the British' and differed little in appearance.[110] So the Chinese were even more isol-ated and vulnerable than the Jews, often portrayed as the least protected group.

Few Chinese could play the imperial card. British opinion-leaders were aware of the imperial tie and its implications. In the 1919 riots, the press warned against stirring up an 'imperial problem', while a seafarers' chaplain said of black victims that 'for good or bad, these dark sons of the West Indies are members of the British Empire, and to foster an antipathy towards them will not tend to cement the bonds of Empire'.[111] At higher levels, an attempt by the Australian States in 1896 to extend anti-Chinese laws to Indians was stopped on the grounds that it discriminated against a country in the Empire.[112]

British governments normally took care to avoid stirring up people protected by their country of origin. These included imperial subjects such as the Indians, who enjoyed a special civil status, and foreigners backed by a strong state in which the British had a strategic or economic interest, such as Japan.[113] The Chinese, however, had no powerful institutions to stand up for them until the 1930s, when a new perception slowly formed, and the early 1940s, when China became the West's wartime ally.

After 1949, mainland Chinese immigrants continued as if stateless for much of the rest of the century, because of Beijing's isolation and its confrontation with Taibei. Even Chinese from Hong Kong lacked effective consular protection until the late 1960s, when instability in the colony made its authorities more attentive to their subjects' (and overseas subjects') needs.

The Chinese trickster

According to a labour stereotype, the Chinese were docile and biddable, but officials found them to be devious and uncooperative. Although each view contradicted the other, the sinophobes had no difficulty in swallowing both.

Some Chinese stratagems originated in efforts to outwit British anti-immigrant measures. The 1906 language test is a case in point. The test had little effect on Chinese employment, to the fury of seafarers' leaders like the racist Captain Tupper.[114] Havelock Wilson, a Labour MP and seafarers' leader, argued that Chinese gained exemption from the test by pretending to be British subjects born in Hong Kong or Singapore and claimed (inaccurately) that their numbers on British ships were growing phenomenally as a result.[115] Other dodges included personation – 'one Chinaman, speaking English fairly well, could sign on the articles, and another man, who did not understand English at all, would go in his place'. The language test led to a boom in English classes in Chinatown. A journalist noted how 'an Englishman, who comes from the West End, visits the place daily, ... giving lessons daily to Chinese seamen at 2s. a lesson'.[116]

Chinese seafarers quickly spotted ways of circumventing inconvenient or prejudicial rules. We have seen how some increased their wages by signing on in British ports, at a higher rate than other Asians. They also quickly spotted which ports presented the fewest barriers to registering. In 1921, for example, Cardiff police told the Home Office that Chinese seafarers were taking advantage of the Welsh port's lax procedures as a way of getting registration certificates for use in England.[117]

Chinese names provided another opportunity to get one over the authorities. Officials often mistook Chinese family names (which come first in Chinese usage) for given names, and vice versa. The relatively small number of Chinese family names in common use and officials' botched efforts to transcribe them heightened the confusion and made records hard to keep.[118] In some cases, the Chinese adoption of English cognomens was a further pitfall. As a result, Chinese could run rings round the police and port authorities. Chinese naming systems continued to baffle British policemen into the new millennium. In 2000, a 'race handbook' issued by London's Metropolitan Police pointed out that the use by Chinese of a variety of naming systems should not be interpreted as an attempt to avoid immigration rules.[119]

In the early years, the Chinese gained a reputation for being anarchic and uncontrollable as a result of their high degree of self-organisation and disregard for rules. Aware of the contempt in which they were held, they showed little loyalty towards employers. Chinese working on British ships ran away if prospects ashore looked brighter than a return to sea. In the ports, some lived by their wits or worked the black market. Usually only a minority stepped outside the law, but the idea of Chinese dishonesty became a stereotype. Chinese efforts to sidestep racist rules reinforced their image as slippery and deceitful and created a vicious circle of prejudice.

The Chinese and other non-British and non-whites

Early Chinese migrants to Britain interacted not only with native whites but with other ethnic minorities. Ethnic Irish, the biggest group, formed substantial settlements in the ports. Most had few industrial skills and lived in slums. In Victorian Britain, they were the target of racist discrimination and violence by native British.[120]

Irish and their descendants were also found in large numbers in the United States and Australia, two countries of extensive Chinese immigration. In the United States, the Irish were among the poorest and least skilled, victimised by the Protestant ascendancy. They were also the most vocal opponents of Chinese immigration. Stanford M. Lyman ascribed

Irish workers' sinophobia to their 'doubtful racial identity and their Catholicism'. By displacing mainstream white society's low valuation of themselves onto the Chinese, they strove to achieve unequivocal whiteness, with its wages and perquisites.[121]

In Britain, where many English workers blamed Irish immigrants for their immiseration, anti-Irish prejudice was endemic. As in the United States, the Irish reacted by trying to shift the animosity onto newer arrivals. Large numbers of dockers were Irish, a group much given to anti-alienism.[122] By widening the social space between themselves and the Chinese, they aimed to raise their own social standing. Irish trade-union leaders in Liverpool took the lead in victimising Chinese.

In the dockland streets they shared with Africans, Jews, Scandinavians, and others, Chinese relations with their non-native neighbours were less fraught.[123] Conflicts were rarely reported, but nor was there much evidence of inter-ethnic solidarity. In 1911, a *Western Mail* reporter encountered vehement and unanimous hostility among other foreign seafarers towards the Chinese in the Cardiff docks area.[124] In June 1919, at the height of the khaki riots, black seafarers in Hull 'cleared the shipping office of Chinese seafarers so that only British – Black and White – would be employed'.[125]

Where the chance arose to form alliances with other non-white workers, the Chinese usually ignored it. In 1935, black and Indian residents countered pro-white measures by the shipping companies with a campaign to unite 'Indians, Negroes, Arabs, Somalis, Malay and Chinese' in a Colonial Seamen's Association (CSA), which remained active throughout the rest of the 1930s. The CSA had ties to British labour and the support of associations run by other 'coloured' peoples and of trade-union leaders and politicians in India, but there is no evidence of Chinese joining.[126]

The changing British view

The First World War wreaked not just physical but profound psychological damage on British society and helped erode the deep-seated belief in the supremacy of 'British values'. It also undermined Britain's position in East Asia and the world and raised a more general spectre, that of the decline of the West. For some, an immediate response to the sense of national degeneracy, realised in the riots of 1919, was to lash out at the perceived representatives in Britain of alien forces intent on subverting the British Empire.

In the longer term, the crisis gave rise to a workers' movement grounded in internationalism, which started to take a fresh look at China.

In China itself, the European war had a dramatic impact. The battle-field carnage disabused intellectuals of their trust in 'European civilisation'. Radicals sought a new way forward in Bolshevik-style revolution, while conservatives called on Chinese to discard the West's 'mechanical' philosophies and return to 'Oriental' values. The effects of this shift in perceptions also reverberated in the tiny British Chinatowns, as we saw in the previous chapter.

For several years after the war, the dominant attitude towards China and the Chinese in some British social circles remained contempt, documented by Lao She 老舍 in his *Mr. Ma & Son: A Sojourn in London*: 'For the English who've never been to China, Chinamen are unsightly, yellow-faced creatures, notoriously sinister and cunning. For the English who *have* been to China, the Chinese are a race of stinking, filthy, empty-headed slobs.... If you were to say that ordinary classes in English society detested the Chinese, then the *wealthy* classes...saw them as objects of amusement'.[127] Yet this view changed in the interwar years, as a result of a convergence in China and the West in the direction of internationalism. Labour leaders who once had no qualms about scapegoating Chinese now developed a different view of the causes of injustice. In the mid-1920s, when the killing of demonstrators by British troops in Shanghai led to a wave of strikes, anti-British boycotts, and nationalist agitation, Chinese previously reviled as scabs and cheap labour were praised at British trade-union and Labour Party meetings.[128] In early 1927, a Comintern delegation including the British trade union leader Tom Mann visited China to show their support.[129] After the Japanese invasion of 1931, the British left rallied to the Chinese cause. The new association of Chinese with courage and resistance was reinforced by the publication of a spate of sinophilic best-sellers by Pearl Buck, Edgar Snow, and others. Gradually, a positive image started to prevail.

China's heroic representation depended on the coincidence of British antifascism and the Chinese fight-back against Japan. In Britain, China's wartime status as an ally and the role played by Chinese seafarers in winning the Battle of the Atlantic reflected creditably on the Chinese image.[130] Yet the conditions for its enhancement did not last. China's Civil War of 1945–1949 and the enmeshing of London and Beijing in Cold War cancelled the advantage and created a new racist cliché, of the Chinese as yellow ants.[131]

Fighting back

The battle against racial discrimination has been conducted less intensely by Chinese than by other ethnic groups in Britain. Only a minority of activists have mounted occasional campaigns of self-defence. Some early community leaders sought to counteract the migrants' isolation by creating self-help associations and ties within the diaspora and back to China. At the start of the twentieth century, organisations like Chee Kung Tong acted as a 'people's consulate' to combat British racism.[132] Their purpose, like that of their counterparts in North America and Australia, was to 'provide a place where Chinese workers could meet without being ridiculed and humiliated by the English'.[133]

Chinese students, journalists, and diplomats have also fought back now and then against sinophobic practices. The student activists who descended on Chinatown in 1914 tried to place workers' experience of racism in an international context and raise their political awareness. For them, the central theme was 'worldwide discrimination against Chinese'.[134] In the 1910s and the 1920s, when Yellow Peril themes took off in British publishing and entertainment, racist representations of Chinese as subhuman and a threat to world health, security, and prosperity became a main target of Chinese students, who lobbied against insulting images of Chinese on stage and screen.

In 1913, a theatre company staged *Mr Wu*, a play whose eponym was a Western-dressed and educated Hong Kong Chinese, fiendishly cruel and created along classic Yellow Peril lines. Chinese students said the plot was 'un-Chinese and we were afraid that this attempt to foist it upon the British public as a specimen of modern Chinese civilisation might engender prejudices unfavourable to the Chinese in their midst'.[135] Two wrote to the Chinese Minister urging him to protest. Others campaigned to dissuade Chinese from appearing as extras. They failed to get the play banned and succeeded only in removing some particularly offensive lines. In the early 1920s, Chinese workers in the East End attacked other workers hired to act in a film scene deemed 'dishonourable'. In 1928, five plays featuring Chinese villains were staged in London, despite a complaint by the Chinese chargé d'affaires.[136]

In 1921 and again in 1928, police forces in England carried out nation-wide raids to check Chinese people's immigration status; in 1924, similar raids happened in Wales. Such actions were said to have been unprecedented in peace time. Again, some Chinese students protested, as did some newspapers in China (including *Shen bao* 申报).

Sometimes these protests and campaigns paid off, but never for long, given the community's sub-ethnic fragmentation and its lack of a strong political focus. While racism has tended to unify other oppressed ethnic and religious minorities in Britain, the Chinese have been hamstrung by their divisions and by intra-ethnic economic competition. Other ethnic groups built bases in British politics later in the twentieth century, but the Chinese were generally too dispersed and unfamiliar with democratic ideas and institutions.

Late twentieth-century anti-Chinese racism

Many of the community's strategies of avoidance were repeated by the postwar generation. Habits of self-immurement in the ethnic economy persisted among newcomers from the New Territories. Few saw competitive labour as a tolerable choice. Most stuck to enclaves of the sort carved out by the pioneers, substituting takeaways for laundries but practising the same self-reliance and self-containment. These parallels are intriguing, for the juridical and political status of the postwar immigrants was unlike that of their prewar counterparts. They enjoyed British rights and some protection by the Hong Kong Government Office in London, at least after 1969.

One explanation for the continuity in approach is that the postwar Chinese organised their own emigration, unlike most other non-white immigrants. Combined with the effects of anti-immigration legislation, the manner of their passage to Britain funnelled them into the ethnic enclave. Racism also played a role in determining their choices.

Chinese in the postwar years were way down the racists' list of targets and suffered less abuse than the pioneers. In the early twentieth century, they had stood out as the ultimate alien in an overwhelmingly white society. After the Second World War, blacks and Asians were more visible and likelier than Chinese to come up against the 'colour bar'.[137] In 1968, Chinese were spared mention in Enoch Powell's 'Rivers of Blood' speech, which led to violence against blacks and South Asians and the rise of ethnic militancy. In the 1970s and 1980s, they did not experience the same level of racist attacks as other non-white groups, which responded with political campaigns.[138] Not until 1989, when the British Nationality (Hong Kong) Act of 1990 was before parliament, were Chinese thrust (for the first time since the 1920s) to the centre of racist attention. Under the terms of the Act, 50,000 middle-class Hong Kong residents were promised British right of abode in view of the colony's retrocession to China. Resurrecting arguments previously used against blacks and South Asians, Norman Tebbit denounced the bill as a further capitulation to the idea of a 'multicultural, multiracial society'.[139] However, the campaign failed to whip up the same backlash as East African Asian immigration in the 1960s and the 1970s. Yuet Ngor Mary Pang 彭月娥 later concluded that 'while racism and attacks may have occurred on an individual level, the Chinese community as a whole escaped relatively unscathed in these volatile decades'.[140]

Even so, Chinese caterers have followed economic strategies that minimise their dealings with a society perceived as hostile. 'They have had little contact with the wider society, and have appeared to want to keep a low profile', concluded the inquiry by the British Parliament in 1983.[141] Chinese studies on Chinese employment in the United Kingdom focus on evasion of competition as a way of dealing with white racism. Irene Loh Lynn concluded that white attacks happened in the past because the Chinese were employed as seafarers, in a mainstream occupation. They 'were seen as a threat and conflict did arise. I feel this is an important point, especially when one considers the type of occupations the Chinese have been involved in since this period and up to present day times'.[142] Yuet Ngor Mary Pang argued that the Chinese escaped violence in the 1950s and the 1960s partly because they were few in number and geographically dispersed, but mostly because 'they were not recruited into positions in the wider labour market [but] went straight into the Chinese catering industry on arrival'.[143]

Chinese immigrants' self-imposed segregation and refusal to compete on the open market were therefore the main reasons for their relative exemption from racist harassment. They shaped their strategies according to a collective memory of the pioneers' experience of racism, and as a reaction to residual racism. Those who failed to stick to the ethnic niche suffered the consequences. Ethnic-Chinese refugees from mainland Southeast Asia in the 1980s are an example. To preserve a sense of community, many gathered on run-down housing estates in poor areas of big cities like London, with the result that they were subjected to racial attacks by other residents.[144]

Many members of the immigrant generation were not unhappy with the invisibility that became their hallmark. Self-containment served the interests of those who planned to return to Hong Kong or China, by confirming their status as outsiders. For people who saw a life of quiet drudgery in the takeaway as a pad from which to launch their children into the professions, a strategy of self-reliance created time and space within which to spring the scheme.

However, the takeaways were no real sanctuary. Although largely exempt from organised political campaigns by the anti-immigration lobby, the Chinese were far from immune to racist pressures. Because of their dispersal, they were exposed to harassment by local thugs and drunks. If they defended themselves, they were sometimes accused of 'taking the law into their own hands'.[145] As the new generation matured, the drawbacks of a strategy based chiefly on self-help multiplied. Its emergence from invisibility in the 1970s led to an intensification of name-calling and racist bullying – directed, now, at the schoolchildren, for whom there was no delivery from inclusion.

Just as in the interwar years, few postwar Chinese immigrants joined panethnic political organisations or paid heed to the worldwide antico-lonial movement. They shunned inter-ethnic cooperation no less than inter-ethnic competition. In more recent times, there has been little sign of immigrant or British-born Chinese subscribing to an 'Asian paneth-nicity' of the sort pioneered in the United States in the 1960s and supported by an extensive network of associations. The reason would seem to lie in the immigrants' distinct economic status, the continuing inflow of Chinese immigrants, China's increasing importance in the world, the promotion of multiculturalism by British institutions, and the South Asian connotations in Britain of the 'Asian' label – all factors that militate against subsuming the Chinese into a broader Asian group.[146]

Although the gap between Chinese and the mainstream narrowed towards the end of the twentieth century, Chinese continued to occupy a special position in the ethnic and racial hierarchy. The spectacular success of Chinese students in British education and of Chinese males in gaining equal access with whites to the class of employers and profes-sionals led to their redesignation in studies and the media as a 'model minority'. This name was imported from the United States, where it was coined in the 1960s to mean a group 'culturally programmed for economic success'.[147] Once viewed as unassimilable, stupid, cunning, and perverse, the Chinese are now held up as 'a role model for other minorities to emulate'.[148]

In the United States, criticism of the 'model minority' theory focuses on its indiscriminateness and reactionary implications. The theory portrays Asian communities as monolithic and ignores the different strategies pursued by subgroups, which are rendered invisible if they fail to come up to scratch; and it pits the 'model minority' against 'problem' minorities, notably blacks.[149] Gary Okihiro argues that the model minority stereotype reproduces the Yellow Peril image but in different form, by representing the Asian yet again as threatening, inhuman, and a legitimate focus for white resentment.[150] In Britain, the same objections hold. The approach obscures the variety of Chinese types, implies that those who do not conform to the stereotype of 'high achiever' are aberrant, and isolates the Chinese from 'undeserving' ethnic minorities.

The 'model minority' theory also obscures the persistence of racial distortions even within the salariat, where Chinese employment choices are still sometimes determined by the desire to minimise competition with whites. The strategy of avoidance has survived even into the British-born generation. On graduating, Chinese youngsters enter the technical sector and professions in which objective qualifications count more than language skills and where there are fewer white competitors. Chinese who make it into the professions tend to be held back from promotion. Research in the 1990s showed that educated Chinese are vulnerable to several types of discrimination: they need better qualifications than white colleagues to get the same job, receive less pay, are more likely to be denied promotion to senior management, and are more likely to become unemployed.[151]

In the era of the 'model minority', Chinese employment has polarised into two sectors, with few intermediate options. Those born in Britain have good jobs and prospects. Many of those born abroad, however, remain stuck at the lower end of the occupational structure and are more likely to suffer discrimination. Ineligible for the professions, they feel safest in catering, a familiar and uncontested field. Loath to enter the wider labour market, they seek shelter from unemployment in the family restaurant or takeaway.[152] Their circumstances resemble those of Chinese in the United States, who are kept out of the blue-collar sector by a 'lingering sinophobic animus'.[153]

The reason Chinese continue to be vulnerable is their lack of coherence and solidarity. Catering dictates a residential scatter rather than settlements of a sort that might allow Chinese to unite. An obvious comparison is with South Asians, who benefit from powerful ethnic and family networks perpetuated by business linkages, arranged marriages, and the unifying role of Islam and tend to form compact communities. Partly because of their fragmentation, few Chinese have replicated the political activism of other ethnic minorities, which have stronger social and religious organisations.

Although race was a burning issue in postwar British politics, Chinese were rarely involved, given their relative fewness and dispersal. The racist focus on bigger minorities and the community's own disjointedness has ruled out a united response to the low-level everyday racism catering families endure. Even private responses have been few – the House of Commons report of 1985 noted that it was rare for Chinese to complain of racial discrimination.[154]

Sometimes, however, caterers have hit back with a vehemence their tormentors cannot have bargained for. Anthony Shang reported cases in which Merseyside takeaway owners took the law into their own hands by pouring boiling fat onto assailants or installing high-voltage wires across their windows.[155] In 1963, Chinese in Britain and Hong Kong raised £10,000 to support waiters charged with manslaughter after a fight with a customer.[156]

Radical Chinese organisations have also acted to defend the community against racist attacks, organise Chinatown workers against exploitative restaurant owners, and assist illegal immigrants. Many such campaigns have been run by the London-based Chinese Information and Advice Centre (CIAC) 华人资信与咨询中心. In 1985, the CIAC criticised the House of Commons report for playing down the extent of racial abuse and failing to identify institutional racism in state agencies.[157] It has supported strikes and other actions by restaurant workers, campaigned against deportations, and helped Chinese women threatened with domestic violence.[158] In February 2000, activists in the Monitoring Group (renamed Min Quan民权 in 2002, and loosely associated with the CIAC) organised a successful protest against police failures to protect Chinese from racist aggression.[159]

Conclusions

Up until the Second World War, Chinese in Britain frequently experienced racist pressures by local whites and hostile measures by sinophobic governments, interspersed with periods of relative harmony. Whether on the labour market or in business, the threat of competition from Chinese immigrants often drew a hostile response, expressed in racist terms.

Race-thinking put a 'scientific' gloss on the notion that the Chinese were inferior and alien, an idea that gained global currency in the late-nineteenth century. However, racist practices first emerged because of the economic threat the Chinese were said to pose to whites. The Yellow Peril idea was created to visualise this threat. Widely regarded at the height of the Yellow Peril scare as subversive and ungovernable, Chinese migrants were at the same time uniquely vulnerable, given the indifference of China's foreign service. They responded with a strategy of self-help. Organisations like Chee Kung Tong, which straddled China and the diaspora, provided a refuge for victims of abuse and became a sort of consular arm.

Where they could, the early seafarers kept out of the way of British institutions, which they experienced as unfriendly. At the same time, Chinatown leaders tried to project a more positive view of the community, as hardworking, sanitary, and peaceable. Well-wishers in the British establishment and sympathetic local people shared this opinion, even at times of high anti-Chinese agitation. As always, two rival stereotypes seemed to coexist, each preparing the way for the other, as idealisation gave way to revilement and vice versa.

White British thinking has persistently essentialised Chinese identity. Certain differences between Chinese and Indians, another big migrant community in Britain, have in part lent themselves to this essentialising. The Indians, from a multiplicity of backgrounds based in class, wealth, levels of education, and colour, seldom coalesced. Early Chinese migrants, on the other hand, were primarily poor seafarers who appeared clannish and self-reliant, ostensibly the reason for the rise of Chinatowns in several British port towns. Many Chinese migrants responded to the experience of racism by concentrating in ethnic-type enterprises in the laundry and catering sectors, while the early Indians worked largely in industry, both private and public, and also established a prominent presence in the corporate sector, initially in small-scale enterprises and later among the country's leading firms.

Two unifying themes of the study of British sinophobia are its political preconditions in the world arena and its close link with economic competition. While other ethnic groups have responded to racist oppression by closing ranks, racism contributed in the Chinese case to economic competition, which led to self-segregation. The Chinese took steps to avoid overt inter-ethnic economic competition to prevent a repeat of the racist backlash against the early seafarers and laundry-owners. Instead, they sought to improve their economic situation by competing among themselves. Intra-ethnic competition is the main reason for the community's wide dispersal, a further hindrance to its capacity to unify against attacks.

Related to the theme of intra-ethnic competition is the Chinese community's historic lack of institutional support, either by the home country or by the British state. Its members have tried to overcome their vulnerability by self-organisation, but this strategy eventually breaks down – predictably, for the cohesion of the migrant cohort seldom lasts.

In most cases, especially in the laundry and catering sectors, Chinese sought to undermine their co-ethnic competitors rather than cooperate with them to deal with racial abuse and economic marginalisation. They were also unable to create ties to other non-British and non-white minorities, partly for economic reasons and partly because of the lack of a strong political leadership.

The racism Chinese have persistently experienced in Britain has been the main factor in the rise of Chinese-type institutions, embodied in the creation of Chinatowns, ethnic-type enterprises, and clan associations. The rise of these institutions might seem to substantiate arguments of the transnational theorists. However, the coming together of the Chinese was largely the product of external circumstance. The sustainability of these institutions has always been open to question, especially since the emergence of a new generation of British-born Chinese. Intra-ethnic business competition has created powerful divisions among migrants, while few British-born Chinese have shown much interest in Chinese institutions. There have been few if any signs of the emergence of an Asian panethnicity among migrant or British-born Chinese, even though they continue to experience discrimination.

It is unlikely that a new panethnic movement will emerge, led by educated middle-class members of this community, even though this cohort is still subject to discrimination. Chinese migrants continue to flow into Britain, from different places and equipped with different skills and resources. This suggests that cleavages based on place of origin and class will remain. At the same time, the better off will contribute to the debate on the need for white British to create a more inclusive society by curbing racism.

7
Ethnic Culture and Identity

This chapter looks at changes in the Chinese community resulting from adaptations and reactions to living in Britain as an ethnic minority. It deals with four main issues – Chinese ethnic identity and its transformations; the evolution of ethnic-Chinese culture; the community and the British education system; and Chinese employment patterns. Its main focus is on the second generation.

Identity

Peasants who migrate, within their countries or abroad, become aware of their cultural distinctiveness and band together to promote common interests. Where the old village boundary was geographic, the new frontier is neither fixed nor physical and entails regular contact with outsiders. In the course of that contact, migrants raise cultural contrasts to the level of social importance. Buttressed by a belief in shared descent, these contrasts mark the emergence of ethnic culture – as 'that set of elements used by a population in its own self-identification'.[1]

Until the 1960s, anthropologists treated ethnicity as a closed and static property. Today, scholars reject this approach as cultural determinism and view ethnicity as an outcome of the interplay of context and ethnic interaction. The determinists failed to see how ethnic groups reinterpret ancestral culture, subject it to selection in the light of new needs and experiences, simplify its structures, and self-consciously articulate its distinctive features. In the determinists' view, ethnic boundaries weaken over time as a result of cultural loss, leading to acculturation and assimilation. Ethnic studies reject this idea in favour of a definition of identity as the product of new circumstances and confrontations rather than as a set edifice of culture that will eventually crumble.

In some cases, ethnic markers are imposed rather than chosen. Although human interbreeding across the millennia makes nonsense of a 'biological' classification of human groups, the idea of race is strongly enough rooted for it to colour popular perceptions. 'Racial' definitions of ethnic identity are usually hostile and exclusionary. Even so, groups thus stigmatised sometimes infuse their involuntary identities with a positive content (cf. Black Pride).

Ethnic groups trapped at the bottom of the social pile have fewer choices than those at the top and are often stigmatised. Members can try to escape the stigma by passing themselves off as part of the dominant group or they can reject majoritarian norms and values and set greater store by their own identity. Ethnic groups that occupy special-ised economic niches are more likely to cohere than those whose cultural and economic boundaries fail to match.

Chain migration, where new migrants join kin in the destination country, leads to territorial or occupational concentration and reinforces ethnic cohesion. If the migrant stream is continuous, ethnic identity is stronger than if it is interrupted. Modern communications strengthen ties to the place of origin and help preserve ethnic feeling. Developments in the country of origin, including wars, revolutions, and improvements in its standing, can also affect ethnic identification.

As new generations rise, ethnic boundaries change. Immigrants' offspring may identify with the majority values of the host society or with the ancestral culture, but they may also choose to create new, liminal identities that express the ambiguities of living 'between cultures'. This view of ethnic identity as protean and multipositional is closely associated with transnational studies, which argue that ethnic communities exist simultaneously at three levels: in a state of global dispersion, in the separate national sites of settlement, and in the ances-tral homelands. 'Transnational subjects' simultaneously hold identities associated with different locations. Though influenced by local settings, such identities have a global dynamic.[2]

Transnational 'consciousness' is marked by multiple identifications and cultural fluidity. It is often represented as creolised, a reference to the construction of hybrid ethnicities from 'new' and 'old' cultural materials, in an analogy drawn from linguistics. Language creolises when a target language is screened from would-be learners by social segregation. As a result, variants form – initially as pidgins – that fill gaps in learners' knowledge of the target language by borrowing and creative innovation. The pidgin from which the creole develops is formed by mixing and adapting lexical and grammatical features of different languages. In identity studies, creolised identities are similarly constructed from heterogeneous sources.

Chinese identity and British legislation

Legislation has played a crucial role in shaping Chinese community and identity in Britain. The impact of legal and institutional frameworks and government policies is a major issue in writings on Chinese migration to the United States and the British Dominions, where laws were framed with an explicitly anti-Chinese purpose; and of work on the larger Chinese communities of Southeast Asia, where ethnicity has a strong political dimension. Studies on the Chinese in Britain have tended to ignore or underestimate the extent to which state decisions set the terms for Chinese settlement and the way in which Chinese see themselves and others.

Chinese were main targets of Britain's early immigration laws.[3] In 1813, the East India Trade Act singled out 'Asiatic' seafarers – Chinese and Lascars – for the country's first experiment with internal controls, by compelling the East India Company to take responsibility for 'Asiatic sailors' in London waiting to return home. Other legislation in 1823 and 1894 aimed at preventing them from staying in Britain. Even 'Lascars and other Asian seamen' who were British subjects were treated as aliens under the legislation.[4] According to the Merchant Shipping Act of 1894, ships' masters or owners could be fined if Asian (or African) seafarers were found destitute or convicted of vagrancy within six months of discharge in Britain. The purpose of the controls, wrote Paul Gordon, was to 'reduce the perceived social costs of immigration and, later, to protect the labour market for the indigenous white working class'.[5]

Britain's first Chinese quarter was in Shadwell in East London, a dockside area to which Chinese were in effect confined. During the Napoleonic Wars, legal restraints were imposed on alien residence in Britain. These measures were renewed, on and off, until 1836. Laws controlled internal movement by aliens and could tie residence to a given place. When tensions between France and Britain abated, the controls were lifted. Thereafter, the British authorities were, for decades, relatively tolerant of immigrants, who were too few in number to disturb the air of Victorian self-confidence and economic liberalism (until the Jewish influx towards the end of the century).[6] Even after 1836, however, the authorities discouraged Chinese dispersal. Government policy and police measures were an important factor in the formation of London's first Chinatown.

These controls strengthened the virtual walls around the East End's Chinese streets and prevented working-class Chinese from entering wider society. Some studies explain the British Chinatowns as an ethnic propensity and pay little attention to the role played by racist exclusion in restricting Chinese mobility. However, Chinese settlement in nineteenth-century London was in no small way a construct of policing. The ethnic enclave was a source of security, companionship, and solidarity, but it was also a place of confinement ruled by strongmen who exploited their compatriots and worked in league with the shipping companies and authorities.

In the early twentieth century, Chinese were subjected to legal controls within the country and at the border, this time as part of a crackdown on Jews and 'coloured aliens'. The 1905 Aliens Act, designed mainly to control Jewish refugees entering Britain from Eastern Europe and Russia, also affected Chinese. (It is even inflated by the authoritative *Encyclopaedia of Overseas and Ethnic Chinese* 华侨华人百科全书 into a measure aimed primarily at Chinese, a gauge of Chinese sensitivities on the subject.[7]) The Act restricted alien landings to 14 ports, including Cardiff, Liverpool, and London.[8] It gave immigration officers powers to refuse entry to 'undesirables' (those 'likely to become a charge on the rates or otherwise a detriment to the public') and facilitated deportations.

In the United States, discriminatory legislation in the late nineteenth century led to bans that resulted, in effect, in a near halt to immigration by Chinese women.[9] This legislation, combined with antimiscegenation laws and laws that acted as a disincentive for non-Chinese women to marry Chinese, led to decades of numerical imbalance between men and women in the Chinese community and crucially influenced its development. In Britain, no laws specifically excluding Chinese women were ever passed, but the Act of 1905 probably had the effect of excluding many, by questioning their ability to support themselves. The seafarers' community was male, but Britain's broader China-born population had always included a substantial proportion of women, some of whom arrived to join Chinese merchants and scholars who had settled in the country. In 1891, there were 126 Chinese women in London as against 176 men, and 23 women to 97 men in 1901. In 1911, however, the number of women was just 27, as against 220 men.[10] The shortage of Chinese women encouraged relationships between Chinese men and local women, which helped to distance some men from Chinatown.

Requiring immigrants to land at designated ports contributed to the persistence of Chinatowns. Once landed, a few Chinese scattered across the country and turned up far from the sea, but most remained concentrated in the usual places. From the authorities' point of view, this made the community more manageable and transpicuous. The 1905 Act did not adopt an earlier recommendation that areas of serious overcrowding be prohibited to aliens. However, the Aliens Restriction Act of 1914, rushed through parliament at the start of the First World War, required aliens to live in designated places, a hark-back to the Napoleonic years, and to register with the police. It also allowed the Home Secretary to deport people, with no right of appeal.

The provisions of the 1914 Act, which gave the government a free hand regarding aliens, became general law under the Aliens Restriction (Amendment) Act of 1919, thereafter renewed annually (until 1971). This new Act perpetuated the Executive's wartime powers regarding the deportation and exclusion of aliens. The Aliens Order 1920 required aliens to register locally and to re-register on changing residence and extended the Home Secretary's powers of deportation. It made entry into the United Kingdom for the purposes of employment conditional on possession of a work permit issued to an employer by the Ministry of Labour, a provision never assumed in the prewar climate of economic laissez-faire and free trade.[11] This permit, which authorised the holder to do a particular job for a named employer, foreshadowed the voucher system of the 1960s. During the interwar depression, labour migration was anyway reduced to a trickle, but this work-permit system made it virtually certain that those Chinese who did enter joined the ethnic enclave.[12]

The 1914 legislation was aimed ostensibly at controlling aliens, for 'foreign'-born British subjects, even non-whites, could not in law be compulsorily repatriated. In practice, however, it was used to exclude hundreds of non-white British subjects who were unable to prove their identity or whose protests were ignored. In some cases, documentation proving British nationality was destroyed.[13] In other cases, the non-white workers' nationality was arbitrarily registered as 'coloured' or even as 'seaman'.[14] Hong Kong Chinese were among those subjected to these practices, for the authorities believed many Chinese claimed falsely to have been born in Hong Kong.

In the second half of the twentieth century, changes in immigration policy and nationality law aimed primarily at ethnic minorities other than Chinese again redefined the Chinese relationship to British society and the state. These changes led to deeper transformations than the Aliens Act and its aftermath. The government took measures to control immigration: the Chinese turned them, where possible, to their own account. The laws, and the Chinese counterstrategies, affected most areas of Chinese life.

The British Nationality Act of 1948 conferred citizenship on inhabitants of the colonies and Commonwealth. A citizen 'had the right at common law to enter the United Kingdom without let or hindrance when and where he pleased and to remain here as long as he wished'.[15] For more than a decade, Chinese in Hong Kong and in Britain's colonies and former colonies in Southeast Asia enjoyed the same right to settle in the United Kingdom as other British citizens. The 1948 Act was passed at a time when the British economy was suffering acute labour shortages. By the late 1950s, the economy had absorbed as much labour as it needed for the time being and the emergence of 'racial' tensions had convinced the political establishment of the need to restrict the inflow of non-whites.[16] Blacks and South Asians were the main target of racist violence and lobbying, but Chinese did not escape the effects of legislation designed to limit 'coloured' immigration.

The Commonwealth Immigrants Act of 1962, introduced by the Conservatives, was the first in a series of measures extending statutory control of immigration from aliens to British subjects. It abolished the right of unfettered access to Britain and made entry conditional on possession of a voucher issuable to Commonwealth citizens by the Ministry of Labour. Such vouchers were available for people who had a specific job with a named employer (A vouchers), for those with 'useful' skills and qualifications (B vouchers), and for unskilled workers without named jobs (C vouchers). Between 1968 and 1971, A vouchers accounted for 87 per cent of vouchers issued to the Hong Kong-born.[17] In 1965, the C voucher was abolished and the number of A and B vouchers was severely cut. The voucher system was abolished altogether by the Immigration Act of 1971, which required non-EEC nationals to obtain a work permit, irrespective of their citizenship. (Unlike the voucher, a work permit did not confer the right to settle.)[18]

The Commonwealth Immigrants Act of 1968 stepped up the controls, primarily to keep out East African Asians with British passports. The Immigration Act of 1971 (which came into force in January 1973) concluded the process of transforming the Commonwealth immigrant into an alien and preventing further 'primary' settlement by non-whites. It introduced into law the distinction between patrial and non-patrial Commonwealth citizens and put non-patrials on the same footing as foreign workers.[19] It slashed the entry quota for Hong Kong British passport holders to 200 a year.[20]

Earlier legislation had not affected dependants, who became the main source of new non-white immigration.[21] Once primary immigration had been whittled down to a minimum, attention switched to reducing this secondary immigration. The 1968 Act introduced constraints on the entry of Commonwealth-born children. In January 1973, men not then settled in the United Kingdom could be joined by their wives and children only if they were able to support them without recourse to public funds. The British Nationality Act of 1981 (implemented in 1983) raised further barriers.[22]

Blacks and South Asians, the overwhelming majority of Britain's 'coloured' population, were the chief targets of this legislative drawbridge, whereas Chinese were not generally held to be 'troublesome'. However, Chinese were also subjected to covert controls and to complaints by vested interests. In 1959, representatives of the British catering trade complained to the Ministry of Labour about the 'steady flow' of Chinese into the United Kingdom. Officials noted that the Hong Kong Governor was already imposing restrictions on the issue of passports to British subjects 'except to people who have evidence that they have jobs and other legitimate business to come to', a practice hard to square with the law as it then was.[23] In October 1961, officials expressed alarm at the 'enormous increase' in immigration from Hong Kong and asked if it was right to 'assume that the indefinite expansion of the Chinese restaurant trade is necessary for our economic growth'.

The legislation passed between 1962 and 1981 was the single most important influence on the Chinese community in postwar Britain. The announcement in 1961 of proposals to regulate immigration led to a rush by immigrants from the West Indies and Asia (including Hong Kong) to 'beat the Bill'. In the first nine months of 1961, 1300 Hong Kong Chinese entered, compared with fewer than 500 in a normal year.[24] The voucher system introduced by the Commonwealth Immigrants Act of 1962 strengthened village and kinship migration chains by making jobs dependent on the sponsorship of an employer already in Britain and consigned all but a few new immigrants to the restaurant niche. (In 1968, 171 out of 193 vouchers were for catering jobs.[25]) In the mid-1960s, the number of wives and other dependants arriving from Hong Kong increased steadily as a response to the restrictions on primary immigration introduced in 1962 and the reduction in the number of employment vouchers in 1965.[26] The 1968 Act, which aimed at excluding anyone without a close ancestral link to the United Kingdom, also provided for the exclusion of children under the age of 16 with only one parent in the country,[27] causing a further increase in immigration by wives and in family reunions. The number of dependants reaching Britain from Hong Kong increased nearly tenfold between 1962 (when just 135 entry certificates were issued) and 1967. By 1971, more than 2000 dependants were arriving annually.[28] Not until January 1973 did the rise in the number of reunions start to slow, as a result of new restrictions.[29]

Even as late as 1971, Chinese males outnumbered females in the United Kingdom by 1.24 to 1. In 1968, however, females began to predominate among the newcomers.[30] Family reunions peaked in the 1970s, when dependants outnumbered permit-holders by four to one among new arrivals from Hong Kong. In 1980 and 1981, they outnumbered permit-holders by nine to one, but by that time the absolute inflow of dependants had slowed, to fewer than 1000 after 1977.[31] By 1987, 80 per cent of Chinese in the United Kingdom lived in families.[32]

The new laws locked Chinese latecomers into the catering economy by throwing them into the arms of relatives or fellow-villagers who needed staff. They promoted a rush of family reunions, by intimating that the door was about to shut and phasing out primary immigration. As the restrictions on admitting dependants tightened, ever fewer Chinese children stayed behind in Hong Kong.[33] Family reunion accelerated the switch to takeaways, an arrangement by which the family could live over the shop and make maximum use of its collective labour power. It also helped finish off the sojourner spirit and make settlement permanent.

Legislation was not the sole factor in shaping the Chinese community. Takeaways developed for economic and sociological reasons as well and were part of the worldwide repertory of Chinese enterprise abroad. The switch from sojourner to settler was not due solely to family formation. Events in China, and their repercussions in Hong Kong, also played a role in the emigration boom and the creation of new outlooks. The riots in Hong Kong in the late 1960s and other political changes (including the confirmation by the 1984 Sino-British Agreement of the colony's retrocession to China) raised concerns about Hong Kong's future stability. Such developments encouraged immigrants to disengage from their native places and convinced wives that the time had come to leave.[34]

Even so, the history of Chinese settlement can be understood only in the context of British immigration law. Although the Chinese have shown a hardy self-sufficiency in their relations with the British authorities and public, they were subjected throughout the twentieth century, and for part of the nineteenth, to hostile measures that helped determine their employment, geography, and demography.

Chinese identity in Britain

(a) The migrant generation

Chinese migrants to Britain brought with them their prior sub-ethnic identities – as Siyinese, Hubeinese, Cantonese Punti, Hakkas, and so on. Each sub-group formed its own associations and geographic clusters. At the start of the twentieth century, Siyinese lived in different parts of Britain from non-Siyinese, just as postwar Punti settled in different places from Hakkas. For most early migrants, homeland and intra-ethnic ties were all-important. They saw themselves as sojourners and behaved accordingly – by maintaining family connections and properties in Hong Kong, in preparation for retirement, and by sending remittances.[35]

New groups usually started by working for established groups. In the early years, Hubeinese worked for Cantonese. After the war, Siyinese and Mandarin-speaking 'northerners' recruited staff from the New Territories. Today, Fujianese and others from China work for Cantonese and Southeast Asian Chinese, and so on. However, the relationship is transient. The newcomers either take over the local market or move on and establish new markets, while at the same time trying to start up their own chains to bring in kith and kin.

Watson found that traditional antipathies persisted between Cantonese and Hakkas in the migrant phase, expressed in hostile stereotyping. However, although the dichotomy was maintained, it was less pronounced than in Hong Kong, for the two groups did not perceive each other as direct competitors. On the contrary, they downplayed their differences and were more interested in confronting their primary rivals in catering, the Bengalis and the Cypriots.[36]

In the bachelor years, Chinese society was coterminous with the restaurant and virtual Chinatown, augmented by a sketch map of routes to essential institutions of the host society. After the wave of family reunions in the 1960s and the 1970s, the social horizons of most adults shrank even further, to the takeaway. Surveys done in the 1970s and 1980s showed up to 75 per cent of the first generation had little or no English, beyond the names of menu items. Some attended English classes, but few persevered. Even Chinese who arrived as teenagers found it hard to get by in English. The immigrants' poor English restricted their access to services and made life boring.[37]

The inability to speak English persisted. A study in the late 1990s showed 57 per cent of Chinese aged 50–74 spoke no English, a far larger percentage than of Indian and Pakistani men of the same age (86 and 66 per cent of whom claimed to know the language). Older Chinese were also far less likely than Indians and Pakistanis to read English (42, 71, and 54 per cent respectively).[38]

Of the migrant generation, the Chinese seafarers and ex-seafarers in postwar Liverpool were a special case, for around 400 settled permanently in 1945, joining the working class as shoremen or mariners. The postwar community was more scattered and divided than its prewar counterpart. Part of the old Chinese quarter had been demolished in the 1930s, much of the rest was flattened by bombs.

Liverpool's longer-established Chinese divided into two main groups: businessmen and restaurateurs who had prospered in the war, married white women, and moved to the suburbs; and Chinatown shopkeepers, who tended to import Chinese wives and send their sons to China to get married. The Chinese identity of the former weakened, whereas that of the shopkeepers survived more or less intact. The seafarers, on the other hand, married working-class white or Anglo-Chinese women and stayed in the inner city, where they had white friends and in-laws. 'It would appear that the mixed marriage practice has made the Chinese in the United Kingdom more amenable to association with the local population than is the case in a number of other countries', according to one early study. Another noted their 'untroubled adjustment'. Some Chinese – including those with first wives in China – stayed in touch with their places of origin through relatives working on Blue Funnel ships. They also maintained a small Chinese community based in clubs and associations, some of which were open to whites. Celebrations such as sweeping Chinese graves in the local cemetery were carried out communally in the 1950s, but by the 1960s most such traditions were followed only by families.[39]

Studies sometimes assume that whereas the cultural and ethnic identity of the second generation is mutable, the migrant generation remains constant, a facsimile of the fashions of the place of origin. The Liverpool experience suggests otherwise. In some cases, migrants respond to new circumstances by making big changes in their cultural behaviour. They are less malleable than the children, but no wall separates the generations.

Even the routines of the more isolated immigrants – the caterers and Chinatowners – bear little resemblance to those of the sending places in China and Hong Kong. The most obvious change is the decline in family solidarity. The economics of catering results in family nuclearisation and dispersal, a process some studies rather glibly equate with 'Westernisation'. Even where elderly parents and children live under the same roof, filial care often breaks down under the pressure of work or the daughters-in-law's refusal to observe traditional roles. As a result, tensions and conflicts divide the generations and some elderly Chinese are left to fend for themselves.[40]

(b) Liverpool's second generation: the early years

The first relatively stable generation of British-raised Chinese and part-Chinese arose in Liverpool, as a result of the seafarers' settlement. More children were born to Chinese fathers in Liverpool than in any other British city until the 1970s. Liverpool's early second-generation Chinese can be divided into two groups, corresponding roughly to the 1950s and the 1960s.

Members of the first group, largely the offspring of mixed marriages, were influenced more by their mothers than by their fathers. Like their mothers, they belonged to the local parish church (Catholic or Anglican) and joined church-related youth organisations such as the Boys' Brigade and the Girls' Friendly Society. Fathers' attempts to school them in Chinese usually failed.[41] However, they switched their focus to the Chinese community on gaining adulthood. In her study on the Chinese in Liverpool, Julia O'Neill explained this transition in psychological terms. The 'mixed-race' children of the 1950s were sensitive, introverted, and insecure, and more likely than the Chinese children of the 1960s to experience racist hostility at school and on the streets.[42] Those who looked Chinese were treated as outsiders, and either went to work with the Chinese gangs at Blue Funnel or got jobs in Chinatown.[43]

Many of the second group had two Chinese parents, for in the meantime sufficient Chinese women had arrived in Liverpool. However, the youngsters' Chinese attachment was less than that of the 'mixed-race' generation. Watson concluded from his study in the late 1960s and early 1970s that exile had reinforced tradition among Chinese, who were 'by far the least assimilated of all Britain's immigrant minorities'.[44] However, he did his fieldwork among the elite Man lineage and the immigrant generation, so his findings did not necessarily apply to the wider group. Other research showed that settlement in Britain wrought big changes in the identity of long-established Chinese groups. O'Neill found three types of Chinese family in Liverpool – traditional, modern (an adaptation of tradition to new circumstances), and Anglicised (emphasising individuality). Only one in four belonged in the first, and nearly all locally born Chinese belonged in the third. Most locally born were 'generally unaware of the existence of a Chinese community and lacked contact with other Chinese people outside the family'. Few could read or write Chinese. Only a minority (five of the seventeen studied) went to work in the Chinese sector. The rest were too highly qualified or could not understand Chinese. They rarely used Chinatown's facilities and felt closer to the wider society, into which many of them married. O'Neill implied that the change was due in part to a decline in anti-Chinese feeling.[45]

(c) Chinese migrants and the second generation since the late 1960s

Laws aimed at reducing immigration, together with the effects on Hong Kong of the Cultural Revolution, led to a big increase in immigration by wives and children. This wave of reunions sealed the switch to takeaways and made settlement permanent. Takeaways (like laundries) are normally distant from one another. This has affected the way in which young Chinese see themselves and relate to other Chinese and to whites.

Chinese parents in the early years of family reunion, up to the 1970s, thought sending their children to British schools and raising them in isolation from other Chinese would lead them to forget their Chinese and acquire Western ways. That is why so many left their children behind in Hong Kong to be brought up by grandparents – speaking Chinese, acquiring desired values, and freeing their parents to work all hours in Britain. According to Watson, two-thirds of children underwent this 'granny socialisation'.[46] However, such children were at an educational disadvantage when they reached Britain. Many had been spoiled or alienated by their upbringing and they suffered extreme culture shock at school.[47] Disillusioned parents therefore abandoned the practice and instead sent their children to learn Chinese language and culture at weekend classes in Britain. Thus the first substantial British-raised generation of Chinese came into being.

The thesis that this switch from homeland socialisation led to the emergence of creolised cultures and new identities is explored in three studies, by James L. Watson (1977a,b,c), David Parker (1993), and Miri Song (1996). Other work adopts a more quantitative approach. Modood et al., in their Fourth National Survey of Ethnic Minorities, draw a map of minority cultures and identities (including Chinese) that focuses on issues such as self-description, religion, language, ties to country of origin, marriage, choice of school, and Britishness.[48] Verma et al. examine changes in Chinese adolescents' identity and aspirations and the possibility of conflict between home and school.[49] Sproston et al. look at general issues in the context of research on health and lifestyle.[50] Although these studies approach their subject from different angles, they tend towards similar conclusions.

Self-description. Modood found the Chinese self-image differed greatly from that of blacks and South Asians. Only 15 per cent found skin colour significant, compared with 60 per cent of Caribbeans and about one-third of South Asians. Just one of the 118 asked accepted the 'black' self-label, a political identity that around one-fifth of South Asians were prepared to embrace in certain contexts. Nearly half thought of themselves as British, compared with nearly two-thirds of Caribbeans and South Asians, and nearly half did not. On this point, however, the sample reflected the migrants' view, for '15 of the 16 Chinese born in Britain thought of themselves as British'.[51] Verma et al. found that 60 per cent of Chinese adolescents described themselves as 'British-Chinese', compared with 36 per cent 'Chinese' and 3 per cent 'British'. (The 'British' proportion would have been greater still but for the nature of the sample, which was drawn from students doing GCSE Chinese or attending Chinese language classes.) On the whole, the 'British' had lived longest in Britain and the 'Chinese' least long. The former were proudest of their school work, happiest, least interested in Chinese food, most at ease with English people, and most likely to prefer to live in Britain.[52]

Statistics issued by the Office for National Statistics in January 2004 suggest that by 2001–2002, the proportion of Chinese describing their national identity as British (including English, Scottish, Welsh, or Irish) had risen slightly to just under 60 per cent, compared with 80 per cent of Black Caribbeans and around three-quarters of South Asians. These figures correlate with the proportions born in the UK – around half of the Black Caribbeans and South Asians, compared with fewer than 30 per cent of Chinese.[53]

The reflections of the European-born Yu Jianzhang, in an article titled 'Chinese who don't understand Chinese', add new insights to this sketch of Chinese identity. The author has a strong sense of being European but endorses the idea of identity by lineage:

I say I'm a Chinese, but that's really just a habit. Inside me, China is unfamiliar. China is not anywhere near as close to me as Europe....

The first layer [of my identity] is natural, it's a blood relationship. I'm Chinese, I'll always be Chinese, that's something nationality, language, profession, etc. can't change. The second layer is social, an acquired option. I'm European because we were born and educated here, we received European culture. Although our ways of thinking and our values were influenced by our parents' generation, we were influenced even more by local society.[54]

But although more and more Chinese youngsters move towards the social mainstream and perceive China as alien, parts of white society continue to discriminate against them in ways that generate ambivalence and confusion. From an opposite point of view, conservative-minded members of the China or Hong Kong-born generation refer slightingly to British-born Chinese as 'bananas' – yellow on the outside, white on the inside. Some young Chinese grudgingly accept the label.[55] Others point to the influences of Chinese school and the family and argue that the terms of the equation are self-refuting when so many British view skin-colour deterministically.

Marriage and relationships. Nearly half of Modood's informants said other Chinese 'would not mind' a close relative marrying a white and 84 per cent said they themselves would not mind (compared with around half the Indians and two-fifths of the Pakistanis). However, Verma et al. imply a greater ambivalence among adolescents. Whereas around half wanted to see Chinese and English youngsters 'going out' together and less than one in six did not, a big majority (86 per cent of girls and 63 per cent of boys) thought marriages should be arranged by the family. (How far this view is carried into practice is another matter.) A study of Chinese teenagers in Glamorgan in Wales found one-quarter had only Chinese close friends, whereas 54 per cent had only white close friends and 20 per cent had both Chinese and white close friends.[56]

Other studies support the idea that mixed relationships were more common among blacks and Chinese than among South Asians at the time of the 1991 Census.[57] In the assimilation theories prevalent in the 1960s, intermarriage was seen as a final stage on the path towards the minorities' loss of ethnic distinction and their amalgamation into the larger society. Yet in her recent study on Asian (including Chinese) attitudes towards Asian-white intermarriage in the United States, Nazli Kibria suggests that second-generation Asians fear ethnic loss as a result of intermarriage and worry that future 'mixed-race' children will continue to be defined by race. Some therefore plan to marry Asians, while others aim to pass on to 'mixed-race' offspring distilled versions of their own ethnicity, particularly in the form of values, together with an understanding of the non-optional nature of racialised ethnicity. Some of the basic tensions of living in a society in which race shapes ethnicity therefore look set to survive ethnic intermarriage.[58] Intermarriage in the British context, where Chinese culture and institutions are so much thinner, will not necessarily follow the same path. However, the American experience counsels against mechanical thinking.

Social contact and support. According to cultural stereotypes, Chinese society overseas is introverted and self-reliant, resting on extensive ethnic and familial networks that cater to their members' every need, ranging from business and employment to fellowship and leisure. Laura Pitson's study on social contact and support suggests the opposite is true for many Chinese in Britain. Just over half had no relatives living in their area and more than three-quarters had no contact with Chinese Community Centres. Even in areas where there were such centres, most people did not use them. Relations with friends and neighbours were far more frequent than with relatives, especially for younger Chinese. Using a measure devised by Britain's Health and Safety Executive, Pitson concludes that 26 and 38 per cent of Chinese had 'some lack' and a 'severe lack' of social support, about three times the figure for the general population. Chinese aged 16 to 29 (32 per cent) were almost as likely as those aged 50 to 74 (36 per cent) to have a 'severe lack' of support.[59]

Language use. As a primary channel of self-expression, socialisation, and cognition, language is at the heart of identity and linguistic practices and can be a telling measure of ethnic loyalty. Modood noted a pronounced decline in competence in Chinese – far greater than in the South Asian case. Nearly a quarter of respondents could not speak Chinese or Vietnamese, and only two in five of the 16 to 34 year-olds used Chinese with family of their own age. (Four per cent of the Glamorgan sample were confident in Welsh.[60])

Chinese families in Britain invest time and effort in ensuring their children attend Chinese classes. What is the outcome of this investment? Without a comparative study, done over time, of attenders and non-attenders, it is hard to assess the classes' effect. However, several general studies confirm Modood's findings of a steep decline in Chinese-speaking. Lornita Wong 黃婉芬 concluded that many British-born pupils fail to 'express themselves clearly and fluently in Cantonese' even after years of classes. David Parker 蔣大卫 found that just 17 per cent of his informants could read and write 'more than a little in Chinese', although two-thirds had attended classes. (Most were only 'reasonably fluent' in Cantonese.) The study by Verma et al. is particularly relevant, since 86 per cent of their informants had at some point attended Chinese classes and 75 per cent were still doing so. The study found that only 5 per cent of the sample read no Chinese, whereas 11 per cent read it 'as easily as English', 56 per cent 'less well then English', and 27 per cent 'very little'.[61] Even so, seven out of ten spoke English better than Chinese and used English with friends and siblings, although only one in ten normally spoke English with his or her parents.

Many children resent Chinese classes and find them difficult. In the early 1990s, Lornita Wong estimated only one in four found them interesting, while 60 per cent were indifferent. Other studies show children drop the classes as they climb the education ladder. At the Kung Ho School in 1987–1988, for example, the infants' class had more than 90 pupils, whereas the primary class had fewer than 20 and each year of the middle school age-group fewer than ten.[62] Only Verma et al. present a more optimistic picture. Although a good half of their sample said they attended Chinese classes on parents' orders, 45 per cent denied that parental wishes played a role and 94 per cent said they went because they felt it was important to learn Chinese.

A main problem is that few teachers use modern methods of the sort children experience in their full-time schools. Much of the activity consists of parroting and rote-learning – teacher-centred activities that the children find dull. Many are less enthusiastic than their parents about classes. Given these obstacles to learning, one might expect the schools movement to be in even greater danger. Experience in other immigrant communities (including ethnic-Chinese communities elsewhere) suggests that however determined the campaign to retain it, Chinese language will not survive into the third generation in the absence of special conditions (ghettoisation, vibrant ties to the ancestral homeland, strong religious institutions, and the like) that do not obtain in Britain today, and that the purpose of Chinese education in the not too distant future will be reduced to roots-seeking.[63]

In short, Chinese children exposed to an English-language education and aware of the role of language in ensuring upward social mobility put little energy into mastering Chinese. They receive their principal education in English (whether in state or private schools). Their Chinese classes bear little resemblance to Chinese schools in parts of Southeast Asia, where the whole curriculum is taught in Chinese. Given the community's lack of cohesion, Chinese children have little chance to speak Chinese outside the home. The language movement seems destined to lose the battle to preserve even Chinese oracy, just as it is already on the point of losing that to preserve literacy. The Chinese classes' success or failure is relevant not only to language competence. It also bears centrally on the children's cultural identity, for the classes are a communal site for the transmission of Chinese morality and norms of conduct.

Hakka language. Among migrants' descendants, language-related sub-ethnic identities such as Hakka are generally subsumed into an all-embracing Chinese identity or some form of combinatory British Chinese identity, with Cantonese (or, increasingly, Mandarin) as the lingua franca. A study in the late 1990s showed the proportion of Chinese claiming to speak Hakka fell from just over 20 per cent of those older than 30 to 11 per cent of those aged 16–29, while the proportion of males claiming Hakka as their main language fell from 12 per cent of the over 50s to 2 per cent of those aged 16–29.[64] Chinese schools in Britain teach Cantonese, which is also the language of Hong Kong popular culture and the Chinese satellite media, or (in a few cases) Mandarin. Most Chinese raised in Britain are exposed to Cantonese, whatever their own sub-ethnic background. Hakka, for its part, is perceived as a lower-status language. Many of the children of Hakka-speakers have a basic grasp of the language and code-switch among themselves between Hakka and Cantonese or Mandarin. However, when they use Chinese in public settings, it is usually in its Cantonese form – including some-times in conversation with other Hakkas. Even Hakka parents sometimes speak Cantonese at home.[65]

Religion. Modood found that while more than two-thirds of South Asians mentioned religion as important, only one in four Chinese did, while more than half had no religion. Verma et al. found that more than six out of ten adolescents had no religious beliefs or were uncertain. Even so, half found ancestor worship important.[66]

On the face of it, these two findings contradict one another, but the inconsistency disappears if we distinguish between domestic memorial-ising and organised religion. Several studies comment on the salience of the domestic over the communal among British-born Chinese and the tenacity of family-based cultural practices. Verma et al. found that the Chinese family reproduces core Chinese values, especially filial respect and obedience, even though the children learn at school that authority can be questioned. The children were fully aware of the difference between domestic and school culture and able to reconcile the two worlds.[67]

Health beliefs. Ideas about health and illness are at the heart of nurturance. They are inextricable from primal beliefs about feeding and generally transmitted through the mother and grandmother. According to Verma et al., one in three adolescents say traditional Chinese medicine is better than Western medicine, compared with just one in ten Hong Kong Chinese.[68] Gervais and Jovchelovitch confirm the strong relationship between representations of health and illness and the struggle to maintain a Chinese cultural identity, based on social knowledge enacted through 'language, food and family'. They explain the coexistence of Western and Chinese biomedical beliefs in the British-born generation as an example of the 'complementarity between opposites' that underpins the Chinese world view, whereby each system compensates for the limitations of the other.[69] Another study, by Tan and Wheeler, found Chinese women in London conceptualise food and health in terms of a simplified and pragmatic version of the classical 'hot-cold' system that makes use of some English foods and develops ways of counteracting the predicted ill effect on children's health of eating English foods.[70]

Counterpoint

Studies on Chinese culture, identity, and behaviour in Britain in the closing decades of the twentieth century suggest a community mainly of families, one fragmented and atomised to a greater extent than the general population (including other ethnic minorities). Younger Chinese have acculturated more quickly than other ethnic minorities in terms of self-description, social relationships, and language use. Chinatown institutions and the government-aided Chinese Community Centres have little relevance for most Chinese, who live in isolation from one another, derive more social support from friends and neighbours than from relatives, and are likelier than the general population to be socially vulnerable and unprotected.

Small wonder that community activists and critical researchers have no time for the politicians and officials who reduce Chinese behaviour to fixed ideas about a culture of mutual aid and self-reliance. In 1986, members of the London-based Chinese Information and Advice Centre criticised the House of Commons report on the Chinese community for arguing that 'cultural characteristics' such as a tradition of 'excessive' self-help and the 'extended family' were the main reason Chinese did not make proper use of public services. They pointed out that family networks were breaking down even in urban Hong Kong and that not just the Chinese but all ethnic minorities resort to self-help solutions for their problems – not for 'cultural' reasons but because of a lack of government support and the persistence of institutional racism.[71] Wing Kwong L. Au 区荣光, writing in 1994, made a similar point about shortcomings in the state provision of Chinese elder care, which government and social service agencies excuse by pointing to a supposed Chinese culture of 'self-sufficiency', 'self-dependence', and 'self-containedness'. Instead, Au showed that Chinese self-help was a response to Chinese carers' isolation and the authorities' 'stereotypical racist approaches' and that Chinese migrant families fall far short of the 'self-sufficiency' and intergenerational support imputed to them.[72] Suk-Tak Tam 谭淑德 argued that politicians and academics use 'cultural' explanations to ignore 'structural inequalities' and 'deflate the complexity of Chinese lives into their narrowly defined categories'.[73]

Chinese creoles

The study by Verma et al. interprets the salience of core family values as a perpetuation of the Chinese cultural tradition, with its ethos of lifelong 'kinship bondage' and its Confucian ideology of fixed family roles and duties.[74] This approach is dubious and futile, for cultural tradition cannot explain cultural practice. However, the work of Parker and Song suggests explanations of Chinese youngsters' commitment to family collectivism and solidarity that avoid the circular argumentation of cultural determinism.

The studies by Watson, Parker, and Song belong together, in that each addresses similar issues. Watson sought evidence of cultural change in the immigrant generation from Hong Kong's New Territories. In the absence of a large British-educated cohort, he conducted his search among younger migrants. Parker and Song look primarily at the second generation.

Watson's essay, based on pioneering fieldwork, explored the hypothesis that members of ethnic minorities are caught 'between two cultures', that of the migrants and of wider British society. He set out to determine how much the Chinese sense of identity had changed as a result of life in Britain and undergone a 'process of ethnic redefinition – or "creolisation" to borrow a term from the Caribbean specialists'. He found the conditions for a Sino-British culture had not materialised, except in superficial ways. However, he went on to predict that the 'relative imperviousness' of the Chinese to new influences would not outlast the first generation.[75]

Parker and Song did their research in the framework of the 'new ethnicities' debate in British cultural studies. Parker argues that a static notion of culture and values underlay Watson's approach and recommends that identity be grasped 'more as a process, an ongoing construction'. Even so, his principal goal is to discover whether a British-Chinese identity of the sort Watson predicted has in fact emerged.[76] Song sets out to explore how young Chinese negotiate ethnic identity in the context of family labour.

Watson implied that the failure of Chinese to creolise was due to their recent arrival, segregation, and strong home ties. He expected them to catch up quickly in this respect with the Sikhs, Jamaicans, Italians, and other minorities, which at the time of his research were creating 'a new cultural tradition that only has meaning in the British context'.[77] However, his presumption is not confirmed by Parker's and Song's studies on the British-born and British-raised generations, which play down the extent to which young Chinese have constructed new forms of syncretic identity and creole-style 'cultures of hybridity'.

Parker's explanation for the absence of hybrid cultures draws on approaches developed in Birmingham's Centre for Contemporary Cultural Studies. On the model of Stuart Hall's analysis of the role played by cultural narratives in cementing together 'the different parts of our divided selves', he starts by examining the 'mythic narratives of unique origin' that underlie Chinese cultural identity. He concludes that the Chinese myth of origin is 'closed', that is, fixed, unitary, backward-looking, and all-encompassing, rather than open and therefore potentially pluralist. He argues the distinction between open and closed narratives is relevant to the search for 'cultures of hybridity', which he associates with the open form.[78]

In recent years, Chinese scholars have begun to question the idea of China's cultural monolithicity and to see its civilisation as comprising many cultures in dynamic interaction. Before the twentieth century, sojourners abroad identified with local and provincial Chinese culture. Only in the 1920s did national culture, represented at first by Shanghai and later by an abstract idea of China, supplant local cultures as the point of reference. In the last two decades of the twentieth century, secondary centres of culture arose in Hong Kong and Taiwan. However, they have their meaning in the framework of primary Chinese civilisation, whose deep structures they replicate. They are not marginal or subversive, like the mutually conflictive and often incompatible cultures of South Asia, but embedded within the traditional binary discourse of *nei* 內 (inner, that is, Chinese) and *wai* 外 (outer, that is, foreign).[79]

Where ethnic interaction is habitual and relentless, the 'absolutely confident' and impermeable sense of identity many outside observers attribute to Chinese[80] can change from a source of strength to one of weakness. In Parker's words, identities in a multicultural context 'are strong only to the extent that they admit of internal diversity, allow breathing space, and cede a little of themselves to others'. The 'roots' trope that pervades the sense of Chinese identity overseas hampers the emergence of 'a more exploratory and pluralistic conception of identity formation'.[81] This argument is supported by the omnipresence of 'roots' discourse in Chinese debates about identity, even where the aim is to depict it as polymorphic. Ling-chi Wang 王灵智 sets out to deconstruct the standardised and homogeneous view of ethnic-Chinese identity, but each of the expressions with which he flags his five classes of it revolves around the word *gen* 根 (root). *Luoye guigen* 落叶归根 (fallen leaves return to their roots) refers to the sojourners who remain loyal to their native places. *Zhancao chugen* 斩草除根 (to eliminate the weeds, pull up the roots) is associated with the first foreign-born generation, which tries to join the mainstream. *Luodi shenggen* 落地生根 (falling to the ground and striking root) refers to the accommodationist project and the private preservation of Chinese values. *Xungen wenzu* 寻根问祖 (searching for roots and ancestors) refers to ethnic pride. *Shigen qunzu* 失根群组 (wandering and uprooted intellectuals) refers to educated migrants who abandon their Chinese roots. To Wang's five classes the sociologist Kwok Bun Chan adds a sixth, *chonggen* 重根 (multi-rooted or re-rooted), referring to the transilient, who sinks roots in many places.[82]

Beyond his analysis of the implications of an ethnocentric and unitary cultural narrative, Parker suggests a sociological explanation for the absence of British Chinese forms of identity. He notes the tendency of British Chinese identity to polarise into compartments: a private Chinese and a public British world, their interface sealed rather than permeable. Dispersed across the country in takeaways and restaurants, young Chinese lack grounds for a strong collective self. Their lifestyles are segmented and hard to mix. Many come to hate as demeaning the catering niche that confers on them their racialised identity and offers few grounds for self-esteem. Interaction across the counter prevents the 'fluid interpenetration of cultural realms' necessary for the generation of new identities.

Chinese youth culture has also been incapable of providing grounds for inter-ethnic dialogue and mixing. Hong Kong popular culture in the form of Cantopop and Cantosoap, disseminated through videos and cable and satellite TV, provides an identity focus for some British

Chinese youth and has helped to elevate Cantonese to their lingua franca, at the expense of other 'dialects'. However, it is too private, quietist, exotic, apolitical, and commodified to influence mainstream youth culture. Cantopop lacks the broad appeal of black and South Asian music. It contributes only to the further hiding of Chinese identity and its segmentation.[83]

An exception to the pattern of cultural isolation has been the world-wide craze for East Asian martial arts and kung-fu films from Hong Kong and China. Kung fu 功夫 caught the imagination of young people of all ethnic backgrounds and opened up for Chinese young-sters in Britain the prospect of some street and playground cred. It remains popular among ethnic Chinese children around the world, who flock to China for summer courses in it. In the 1980s and the 1990s, elements of kung fu (popularised on screen by Bruce Lee 李小龙 and Jackie Chan 陈成龙) were incorporated into hip-hop, an internation-ally popular form of break dancing and rapping that originated among young African-Americans. The leading hip-hop group of the 1990s, New York's Wu-Tang Clan, took its name from the kung-fu film *Shaolin and Wu-Tang* 少林与武当, featuring China's Wudang 武当 martial-arts school, and used dialogue from the film in its debut album. But hip-hop's Chinese connections were always tenuous, while the kung-fu block-buster movies and more recent kung-fu art films like *Crouching Tiger, Hidden Dragon* 卧虎藏龙 promote an outrageous and exotic stereotype of Chineseness that is more a hindrance than a help in Chinese young people's endeavour to redefine their cultural identity.[84]

Like Parker, Miri Song finds that the identities of Chinese children in Britain are polarised between ' "Chinese" and "Western" or (white) British'. She sees this polarisation as a product of the family-work strategy pursued by Chinese immigrants. This strategy, dependent on pooling family labour and resources in the context of racist stereotyping, results in a commitment by some youngsters to family solidarity, even though they have little contact with a wider community embodying Chinese culture. In this respect, it is necessary to make a distinction between the takeaway, which 'entails a close linking of the public and private spheres' and creates a 'strong family-work configuration', and ethnic businesses in general, which tend towards competition and exploitation. British-born Chinese children are more likely than Hong Kong-born to distance themselves from the takeaway, giving rise to 'polarised ideal-typical cultural identities between siblings'. 'Good' siblings help out in the family business, 'bad' siblings rebel against doing so. Most young Chinese are ambivalent about helping out and see identity as complex and malleable, so some grounds for cultural hybridity are available. Yet even opters-out are not really free to choose their identities, for whites continue to shower them with negative and derogatory stereotypes. Under such constraints, ethnicity is not optional.[85]

These studies on Chinese ethnic culture and identity suggest that second-generation Chinese switch between Chinese and British identities rather than select from a continuum of options. Ethnic exclusion is usually part of the context of creolisation, whether linguistic or cultural. Racism expressed through stereotypes formed across the takeaway counter reinforces ethnic marginalisation. In other respects, mainstream institutions provide a pathway of upward mobility that favours the veiling or undoing of ethnic identity. The experience of racialised marginality in some contexts, particularly that of family enterprise, and of high levels of achievement and integration in others has contributed to a polarisation of young Chinese identity, rather than produce a cultural stretching of the sort that in other contexts leads to creolisation. As a result, Chinese cultural mixing is more muted than the boisterous, irreverent creations of other minorities, and British-born Chinese have creolised far less than other ethnic second generations. They lack the temper of British-born South Asians, who have a reputation for being quick to 'question, resist, challenge and repudiate'.[86]

These conclusions are supported by linguistic research by Li Wei 李嵬 on code switching by young Tyneside Chinese. According to Li Wei, Cantonese Punti have shifted in just three generations from Chinese monolingualism to English dominant bilingualism. The shift has happened at a faster rate than among British South Asians, whose children are less likely to speak English with each other and more likely to mix languages.[87] Li Wei's research provides a mirror in language for developments in the cultural identity of young Chinese in Britain.

In China, people in regular contact with Westerners often adopt English given names to supplement their Chinese ones, for the foreigners' convenience and their own amusement. Non-Chinese sometimes interpret this as a form of cultural alienation, but Chinese see it as a practical expedient. Young Chinese in Britain use anglicised names to a far greater extent than other ethnic minorities.[88] Even accepting expediency and habit as the motive, it can be argued that this practice is consistent with their readiness in other contexts to compartmentalise their identity.

This review of studies suggests that creolised, resistant Chinese culture remains stunted, though not altogether absent. The inflow of Hong Kong professionals, the growing world role of China and the Chinese economy, and other as yet unforeseeable developments may change the practices of British-born Chinese. As children, most attended Chinese-language classes, and they are likeliest of all ethnic minorities to have visited their place of 'origin'. In any case, identity construction is not mechanical and unilinear. So although British-born Chinese have assimilated to an exceptional degree to mainstream education and, increasingly, to mainstream employment, their partial re-ethnicisation cannot be ruled out.

Diaspora consciousness

Diaspora consciousness is a property attributed in migration studies to 'transnational subjects' – people who simultaneously hold identities associated with different locations. Although 'tempered by local places and people', it has a global dynamic.[89] It connotes with the idea of a 'third culture' transcending national boundaries.[90]

Diaspora consciousness is associated with a prosperous and highly educated minority jokingly designated as 'astronauts' – men (and occasionally women) who 'ride the trans-Pacific shuttles'.[91] Among such people, an attitude is said to have taken hold that Aihwa Ong 翁爱华 characterises as 'flexible citizenship'. Subjectivity, says Ong (a self-professed 'diasporan subject'), can today be transnational, in a world in which capital and individual identities are fluid and potentially global. For Ong, the multiple-passport holder 'is an apt contemporary figure; he or she embodies the split between state-imposed identity and personal identity caused by political upheavals, migration, and changing global markets'.[92]

Such ideas are not relevant to the great majority of Chinese in Britain, who have little in common with the 'astronauts'. Only a small minority – members of the wealthy, better-educated elite from urban Hong Kong and Southeast Asia – have multiple residences of the sort that yield 'spaceman' identifications. Most deplore the migrant rootlessness and 'transiliency' that some studies celebrate. Instead, they dream of negotiating stable relations in the migrant setting and achieving a secure environment for their families.

In an age in which notions of rootlessness, multiple rootedness, transilience, and related topics are high fashion in migration studies, it is interesting to note that many young British Chinese are potential globetrotters by inclination. Fewer than half of Parker's informants saw their future in Britain (47.4 per cent intended to stay, while one-quarter talked of going to Hong Kong, Canada, or the United States). Parker's findings are partly confirmed by the Glamorgan study, which found that 58 per cent of Chinese teenagers did not intend to live in Britain permanently (as opposed to 36 per cent who did and 6 per cent who were not sure). Parker suggests that the drive to cultural self-discovery and a rational assessment of career prospects are the spur. According to the Glamorgan survey, the teenagers want to 'travel around' (51.7 per cent) and 'have new experiences' (20.7 per cent) – only one mentioned racism as a reason not to stay in Britain.[93] However, this cosmopolitanism is widespread nowadays among the young of all ethnic backgrounds and cannot be explained solely as diaspora thinking.

A far smaller proportion of Chinese youngsters in Belfast in the mid-1990s said they wanted to go to Hong Kong (15.9 per cent compared with 56.8 per cent who wanted to stay in the UK), despite Northern Ireland's high unemployment. One can perhaps correlate this difference with two special features of the Chinese community in Northern Ireland: it formed later than that in Britain and it is socially and sub-ethnically less diverse. As a result, its second generation lacks the open-mindedness and self-confidence of other young Chinese, who have fewer ties to the ethnic community.[94]

Chinese art and literature in Britain

For most of the twentieth century, Chinese artists, writers, actors, film-makers, and journalists outside China explored themes of relevance to their communities. In the interwar years, topics to the fore included the experience of migration and resettlement and political questions such as the threat to China's sovereignty, as well as the limits and potential of China's artistic heritage. After 1949, for many Chinese a period of reflection in exile, issues of political and cultural freedom and artistic experimentation rose to the top of the agenda. In the late century, root-seeking, constructing a new sense of selfhood, and developing an authentic ethnic-Chinese voice (whether in Chinese or another language) were uppermost in the minds of foreign-born Chinese.[95]

Most of the better-known Chinese cultural figures outside China lived in Southeast Asia or North America. In the United States, the early community supported a lively press, joined in the 1930s by Chinese radio. In the 1920s, Chinese began to break through into the American cultural mainstream. In the 1960s and the 1970s, Chinese impresarios founded theatres in California and New York that explored Chinese-American cultural themes. In the 1970s and 1980s, Maxine

Hong Kingston 汤婷婷, Amy Tan 谭恩美, and others starting writing in English about matters at the heart of the Chinese-American experience.[96] Chinese cultural production in Britain has been puny by comparison, yet Britain's Chinese cultural scene is by no means barren and has a promising present and an interesting past.

Probably the first Chinese artist to work in Britain was the modeller Chitqua 钱呱, who produced 'striking likenesses with great expedition' in clay, at ten guineas a piece. Chitqua, said to be Cantonese, arrived in 1769 and became a minor celebrity and 'great curiosity' in London and a favourite of the King and Queen. The Royal College of Physicians has a ceramic executed by him. In 1770, when he was living in Arundell Street, he exhibited a 'portrait of a gentleman' at the Royal Academy Summer Exhibition. He appears in Zoffany's painting of 'The Academicians of the Royal Academy', owned by the present Queen. His popularity at court did not prevent him falling victim to native hostility. About to start his passage home, 'he found that the sailors looked upon him as a passenger likely to bring ill luck to the ship, and their threats so terrified the artist that he begged the carpenter, in case he was killed, to make a coffin in order that his body could be taken ashore. In his country, he said, it was not lawful to be buried in the water'.[97] A concentrated search would probably turn up more Chinese artists in Britain in the eighteenth century, when large numbers of foreign artists from many countries worked in London.[98]

In the late 1930s, a group of British-based Chinese writers attracted the attention of local audiences. At around the same time, teams of Chinese took gongs and drums onto the streets of Liverpool to publicise the anti-Japanese movement, while the Workers' Club in London raised money by staging theatre shows.[99] Other Chinese performed dragon dances on VE and VJ Day.[100] In the late 1960s, Maoist activists screened Chinese films and briefly toured the British Isles staging amateur performances of one of Jiang Qing's 江青 'model operas', perhaps the first such activity in Britain aimed exclusively at Chinese audiences. More recently, Chinese authors, artists, and performers have tried to promote 'yellow consciousness' or to play on the ambiguities of British Chinese identity.

In her wartime book on the Chinese in Britain, Barbara Whittingham-Jones dated the birth of the 1930s Chinese writers' school to the Exhibition of Chinese Art held at Burlington House in 1935 and the publication in 1934 of S. I. Hsiung's 熊式一 *Lady Precious Stream*, a Chinese folk-tale written in the form of a play, which ran for two years on the West End stage and ended up as a classroom text in British schools. The exhibition and the play 'established China as the fashion'. Even so, Chinese republicans in Britain denounced them for catering to a romantic and patronising view of 'Old Cathay', one that the critics strove to overturn in their own work. The veteran poet Chiang Yee 蒋彝, based like Hsiung at Oxford, wrote about war and nationhood in rural Yunnan. The young Cambridge-based Hsiao Ch'ien 萧乾 wrote partisan fiction and rapportage, including the influential *China but not Cathay*, and Han Suyin 韩素音 published *Destination Chungking*, a bestseller about her childhood and the war in China. Tsui Chi (Cui Ji), a historian, translated Hsieh Ping-ying's 谢冰莹 *Autobiography of a Chinese Girl*, a novel about communist women guerrillas. Some of S. I. Hsiung's later work in Britain dealt with themes of revolution and emancipation.[101]

However, these writers addressed Western readers rather than their fellow-Chinese. The biggest obstacle to the emergence of a culture relevant to Chinese in Britain lay in the nature of the community. Professionals and intellectuals were few in number and kept to their own circles. 'The two groups have very little in common and rarely identify with each other', wrote Watson in 1975.[102] Even in the 1980s, professionals made up no more than 2 or 3 per cent of Britain's Chinese population.[103] The wider Chinese community, then as in the interwar years, consisted of people with little or no formal education, many of whom led a life of drudgery. 'Culture' in the 'high' sense was foreign to them. Concerts were an unthinkable luxury.

Until the video revolution of the 1980s, late-night film shows in rented cinemas were the main form of public entertainment for the caterers. Culture as the public performance of traditional arts was, for a long time, largely absent. Chinese workers had too little free time, public space, and residential density to support performances. Unlike the more numerous British South Asians, who comprised a greater spread of classes, they had no trained dancers and just a handful of amateur musicians; they lacked the support South Asians sometimes received from Raj veterans familiar with their language; and they did not request public grants even for the New Year festival, their main cultural event. Chinese shows became more commonplace in Britain after the 1970s, but meanwhile a generation had grown to maturity with little experience of community-based culture.[104]

In the 1990s, some groups began staging regular performances of traditional Chinese culture, including Cantonese opera and lion dancing. According to Tong Soon Lee 李忠顺, an ethnomusicologist, at least 18 Cantonese opera groups are now active in Britain, among them the Liverpool Cantonese Opera Society 利物浦粤艺之家 and a unit run by the Kung Ho Association 伦敦共和协会. Grace Liu 廖丽霞, the moving spirit behind the Liverpool venture, arrived in Britain in 1974 and worked for a while in catering. Her group has between five and eight participants who meet weekly and are knowledgeable about the opera's history, styles, and repertoire. Members address each other using kinship terms, as in the old-style clan associations, and show special respect to the group's teachers and seniors. They have ties to counterparts in other British cities, mainland Europe, and China. The Kung Ho unit has also played a big role in promoting Cantonese opera and in 2005 hosted its annual European extravaganza.[105]

By the 1990s, the distance between professionals and catering workers had narrowed. Members of the educated class started providing services for the community as accountants, lawyers, and doctors, and some did voluntary work to support Chinatown's evolving institutions. These steps towards communal integration followed the emergence of a home-grown generation of professionals and activists and radical changes in the social composition of the Chinese immigrant population, which became more complex and diverse. Large numbers of mainland Chinese graduates and professionals began settling in Britain. They retained their Chinese cultural orientation and social networks, but most had a good grasp of the British way of life.[106] Although some looked down on the Hong Kong caterers, their arrival opened up new possibilities.[107] Taken together, these developments paved the way to the new British-based Chinese culture that started flourishing in the late twentieth century.

Probably the first Chinese to write about life in England from a Chinese point of view was Lao She 老舍 (1899–1966), one of modern China's greatest writers, who lived in London from 1925 until 1928. His novel *Mr. Ma & Son: A Sojourn in London* angrily attacks British racism.[108] (In 2003, his house in St James's Gardens in London was marked with an English Heritage Blue Plaque.) Many other British-based Chinese writers have written about China, but usually for non-Chinese readers. The best-known contemporary writer on British Chinese themes is the novelist Timothy Mo 毛翔青, born in Hong Kong in 1950 to a Cantonese father and an English mother and educated in Hong Kong and England. His *Sour Sweet* (1982) deals (in English) with the life of Chinese immigrants. His later work is set mainly in Asia.[109]

A new wave of creative writing by British Chinese appeared late in the twentieth century in publications such as *Dim Sum* and *Brush-strokes* 聚言集. *Dim Sum* encouraged work written 'from a distinctly British Chinese perspective' and set out to create a 'British Chinese voice'. *Brushstrokes*, funded mainly by Liverpool City Council, published

British Chinese writing and drawing and acted as a forum for Chinese 'to discuss and reflect on their life experiences' and document their history. Graham Chan 陈敬亮, its editor, talked frankly of his difficulty in attracting 'contributions of acceptable quality' and concluded that 'writing seems to be something that British-Chinese people just don't do' – because they have no interest in it or are too busy making a living.[110] Such publications therefore remain marginal, without the community-wide resonance of similar writing in some of Britain's other ethnic groups or in North America and Southeast Asia.

British Chinese artists have been more successful in gaining notice, in both the ethnic community and the British mainstream.[111] Manchester's Chinese Arts Centre, which received a £2.2 million lottery grant from the Arts Council in 2001, emphasises supporting 'British-Chinese artistic expression', although it displays work by Chinese wherever they were born. The Centre and other institutions have staged conferences and symposia on Chinese art and visual culture. British Chinese artists strive to articulate the experience of the ethnic community as well as their own personal vision. Chinese food and the takeaway are major themes. However, Diana Yeh notes that many young Chinese artists 'are moving away from direct explorations of so-called "British Chinese" issues that permeated their earlier works'. She looks to the day 'when, as in the case of "black" artists, multi-cultural labels such as "British Chinese" will have so little relevance to the art to which it refers, that they finally shed the loaded essentialising implications that burden [them] today'.[112]

The performing arts are a third arena in which British Chinese strive to produce work relevant to the ethnic and broader communities. David Yip, Britain's best-known Chinese actor (who is actually half Chinese), 'despairs at the stereotyped image that he, as an actor, was expected to perpetuate'. Several dozen British Chinese participants in a drama workshop that Yip ran in 1992 were similarly angry and frustrated.[113] Over the past few years, a lively British Chinese theatre has arisen. Mu-Lan, established in 1988 as a 'British-Oriental' theatre company, is concerned to develop opportunities for new writing, including comedy. Yellow Earth, a touring company formed by five 'British East Asian performers' in 1995, sets out to 'perform universal themes from an East Asian perspective... using traditions of east and west'. Yet like the painting, the performances lack community resonance.

The iconic and exotic clichés that have become mandatory for Chinese painters and writers striving for recognition by funders and established authorities are hot issues in British Chinese cultural circles. British Chinese authors, painters, and performers seem more concerned about racial stereotyping than their counterparts in other ethnic minorities. Resentment at media transmission of offensive images of 'orientals' – as inscrutable, exotic, cruel, mysterious, and so forth – is a recurrent theme of British Chinese writing and creative output. The close identification of Chinese with ethnic products reinforces the stereotyping. David Yip articulated this feeling in *Another Province*, a collection of work, in Chinese and English, by British Chinese writers:

> Based on the visits they make to Chinese restaurants, takeaways and other retail outlets, many people take it for granted that they have some understanding of the Chinese community in this country. But their knowledge of the Chinese population is often distorted.... Non-Chinese have written about us and typecast our image according to their own perceptions of what we should be.... Unfortunately, we have lacked a voice to express and show our diversity. However, there is an increasing groundswell of desire among the young Chinese generation to make their own representations: to explain what they want and how they want to be seen.[114]

Yet to shape the assumptions and images that others make will require great effort and exertion. The Chinese community is less compact and several times smaller than the black and South Asian groups, so it is less well-placed to fend off ignorant or hostile comment. At the same time, artists and writers in China and the big Chinese communities worldwide generate powerful images – particularly through cinema – of a robust and assertive culture to which many British Chinese have no particular tie but by which some perceive themselves to be judged and measured.[115] They are left feeling out of control of how society defines them. Small wonder that Chinese writers and artists in Britain have much to say about the racial stereotype.

Young Chinese at school and work

Immigrant and local-born Chinese children have been attending mainstream schools in Britain for around 100 years. In Britain as in North America and elsewhere outside Southeast Asia, their schooling in Chinese language and culture has been confined to evening or weekend classes, while English-medium schools have provided their regular education.

Usually singled out as the biggest influences on the school career of minority-ethnic children are the parents' educational background, goals, and expectations; the ethnic group's cultural norms and values; the families' socio-economic circumstances and material environment; teachers' expectations and behaviour; possible racist attitudes and practices at school; and the overall structure and processes of schooling. A child's age at immigration and length of stay in the new country also make a difference.

Much of the writing about Chinese children's schooling is about achievement, usually explained by Confucian culture with its emphasis on filial obedience and the value of education. Yet different generations of children and groups within generations perform differently. In 1920, the *Daily Telegraph* reported, optimistically, that 'there is...a friendly fraternising between the children, and alike in the class rooms and the playground, the Chinese youngster is treated quite as a true little Londoner'.[116] An account from the early 1950s by a Liverpool headmaster showed that Chinese children were proud and confident, expected to be treated as equals, and behaved 'as if [they] had a right to be in the school'. In a foreshadowing of the 'model minority' stereotype, they were deemed 'better adjusted than the Negro'.[117] In the 1970s, Chinese children at school were a cause for deep concern among the handful of educationalists who researched their needs. Today, the press and educational authorities portray the Chinese second generation as gifted and fulfilled, unflinchingly oriented towards success. This 'good student' stereotype is so ingrained that it is hard to believe that not long ago pedagogues held the opposite view.[118]

Immigrant parents who have little or no schooling and speak minimal English are at a disadvantage in helping their children progress through school. They may resist or fail to grasp the philosophy of British education, and they are unlikely to interact easily with teachers and school authorities or to help with homework. Seen from this angle, the children start out with a handicap. Free primary education did not become available in Hong Kong until the 1970s, and only in 1980 did nine years' schooling become compulsory. In the early 1960s, around 40 per cent of inhabitants of the New Territories never attended school. The educational level of those who emigrated to Britain was only slightly higher. In the 1990s, 33 per cent of the 50–74 age group of Chinese in Britain had no formal education.[119]

For many Chinese children in the 1970s, school was an alienating and frightening place. More were entering Britain at one point than blacks or South Asians and by the 1980s they were the third-biggest ethnic minority in schools. However, they were scattered widely and did not attract attention. Few studies were done on them, so teachers were ignorant of their needs. Only a tiny proportion of the money spent on ethnic-minority education was allotted to Chinese projects.[120] A study concluded that 'there may well be some grounds for claiming that in various degrees the educational system is guilty of covert institutional racism, through omission, with respect to pupils of Chinese origin'.[121] Another found that Chinese were shown in textbooks as 'grotesque, quaint and unreal' and were 'more subject to racial caricature than Afro-Caribbeans'.[122]

Outside the classroom, the racism took more brutal forms. Many Chinese children stayed out of the playground and off the streets to avoid the bullying and name-calling. Some – especially girls – were kept out of school altogether.[123] Observers in the 1970s and 1980s attributed their self-containment, reticence, and tendency to play truant to racial teasing and harassment.[124]

Some teachers and social workers who did concern themselves with Chinese pupils' problems took the parents to task for exploiting their children's labour and 'robbing them of their childhood'. Miri Song cites studies that argue that children's school performance was hurt by working in the takeaways, a form of labour that Song dryly notes 'does not evoke the wholesome images of children helping out on the family farm' and clashes with 'the Western idealization of childhood as a stage which should be relatively carefree, and concerned with social and creative development'. This criticism of the use of child labour, however well meant, undermined the children's sense of identity and family solidarity. Chinese youngsters had little sympathy for such judgements, which they found hostile and simplistic.[125]

Some observers in the 1970s and 1980s were deeply pessimistic about Chinese children's prospects. Teachers and educationalists drew an alarming picture of their difficulties, while a study depicted life in the takeaway as a 'socio-economic trap' that would prevent their integration into wider society.[126] Other commentators were more optimistic. The House of Commons report said in 1985 that Chinese children performed better in exams than other minorities, although it did worry about their problems with English and particularly about those who had spent their early years in Hong Kong in their grandparents' care.[127] James Watson, questioning the bleak view, noted 'the remarkable adaptability of Chinese children in Britain – given that most have come directly from the New Territories villages and that they have been in this country for only a short time'.[128]

The low levels of achievement and depressed morale of the first cohort of New Territories children appeared to bear out the pessimists.

Apart from the bullying, they were held back by poor English. Most who arrived from Hong Kong as teenagers had little knowledge of the language and no education beyond primary school. Around two-thirds of one sample said they understood less than half of classroom instructions and only one in five thought they would get to university. In London in the early 1980s, only 52 per cent of Chinese at secondary schools were fluent in English. One in four spent their time at school in 'silent misery'.[129] Probably an even greater number were 'learning in terror', the title of a Commission for Racial Equality publication in 1987.

For immigrant parents from the New Territories, excluded from the primary labour market by racism and their own lack of formal education, the takeaway was a shield against hostile pressures and an occupation that needed no special knowledge and just a smattering of English. Thanks to the takeaway, they could avoid consignment to the underclass and make the transition to independent entrepreneurship, a first step in the family journey up the social ladder. Surveys in the 1980s and the 1990s showed that most Chinese parents of all social classes, workers and entrepreneurs alike, wanted their children to do further education as a route into the professions.[130] Far from disadvantaging the children, the family enterprise provided the funds that eased their passage through school and into university.[131]

That parents of British Chinese children place an exceptionally high value on education irrespective of social class is confirmed by Becky Francis and Louise Archer, in a series of studies on British Chinese constructions of gender, education, and achievement. Francis and Archer find that British Chinese working-class children are just as likely as their middle-class counterparts to rate themselves as 'good pupils' and British Chinese girls are more likely than other girls to avoid gender-stereotypical choices. However, they also argue that British Chinese valuing of education is sometimes used by whites as 'part of a wider, pernicious discourse that positions the Chinese as diligent, conformist, and self-repressed'.[132]

By the 1990s, Chinese were twice as likely as the general population to stay on at school, four times more likely than whites to have a higher degree, and twice as likely as whites to have a first degree.[133] By 2000, a quarter of Chinese in Britain had degrees, compared with 15 per cent of whites and 17 per cent of so-called 'average ethnics'. In tests, Chinese pupils outperformed every other ethnic minority at every age.[134] The reasons for this transformation lie in changes at home and school. The end of 'granny socialisation' meant the children grew up in a British environment, fluent in English and no stranger to British education. Teachers became more enlightened about their needs and began to challenge their stereotyping, partly as a result of the authorities' efforts to cope with the arrival of thousands of Vietnamese after 1975. National conferences explored Chinese children's problems and potential. The House of Commons review helped focus attention on the second generation.[135] The community itself began to take notice of children's welfare needs and to set up institutions to meet them. All these factors combined to create circumstances in which Chinese children began to blossom and excel.

Chinese children tested in 1982 for their cognitive abilities scored best of all groups (including whites) on the non-verbal and quantitative measures but worst of all on the verbal measure, basically a test of language competence. By 2002, even this barrier had fallen, as Chinese children added English to the list of subjects in which they surpassed all groups.[136] In 2007, they outperformed every other British group in English by the age of 11 and had the best results in national curriculum tests.[137]

The Chinese community in Britain comprises people of varied provenance and social background. Statistical analysis often fails to capture this variety, so it is not always possible to pinpoint the relationship between socioeconomic status and educational achievement. Even in the early 1980s, wealthier restaurateurs bought their children an advantage by sending them to private schools.[138] In 1988 and 1995, according to research by Sean Demack et al., around 20 per cent were educated privately – a higher proportion than any other ethnic group. (In 1995, 10 per cent of Indian pupils, 8 per cent of white pupils, and less than 3 per cent of African Caribbean, Bangladeshi, or Pakistani pupils received private schooling.) The data on which Demack et al. based their findings did not reveal parents' place of origin and the sample size of Chinese was too small to take social-class factors into account, although the tables produced show clear class differences in attainment levels. Could exceptional levels of private education account for Chinese success? Apparently not, for Chinese of all social classes and at both state and private schools achieved consistently higher results than all other ethnic groups.[139]

In her study on second-generation Asian Americans, Nazli Kibria asks why Chinese families put so much emphasis on education. For her, the answer lies in the large number of skilled and educated Chinese who entered the United States after 1965. Chinese parents' response to white racism 'was essentially a private one, of individual and familial efforts'.[140] Kibria's analysis of Chinese parents' strategy holds good for their counterparts in Britain, except that most of the latter engineered their children's ascent without the advantages of a middle-class background.

The intergenerational leap in levels of schooling is reflected in an extreme polarisation in the educational profile of Chinese in Britain, who in the 1990s were more likely than most other ethnic groups to have no qualifications or to have high qualifications and more likely to have received no formal education (9 per cent compared with next to no one in the general population) or to have stayed in education after 18 (36 per cent compared with 17 per cent).[141] In 2002, when Chinese pupils were more likely to achieve high grades than any other ethnic group, 20 per cent still had no qualifications, compared with 16 per cent of whites.[142]

It is a commonplace that Chinese 'traditionally' set great store by learning and that this 'cultural value' translates overseas into high educational attainment. Studies on the Chinese in Britain tend to discount such theories and show a wide variation in attitudes. Watson argued that rural emigrant families in the New Territories were sceptical about the connection between schooling and material success. Poor parents in urban Hong Kong were less likely than rich parents to value education. According to Yuan Cheng, Chinese overseas pursue education 'more because of its function as a channel of upward mobility' than as a 'distinctive cultural value' in its own right.[143] Yuet Ngor Mary Pang 彭月娥 also found Chinese in Britain valued education as a means to social and economic advancement rather than as an end in itself, as prescribed by Confucius. In the early 1990s, Chinese students in Britain chose practical subjects that would confer marketable skills above Confucian-style humanities.[144] (Whether they will continue to do so now they have overtaken whites in English remains to be seen.)

Early comment on the career prospects of second-generation Chinese in Britain assumed a continuity from parents to children. In the jargon of the 1970s, this was known as 'class reproduction' or 'occupational inheritance', with racial discrimination compounding economic disadvantage. Social class was thought to be the main determinant of the nature and duration of children's schooling. School was 'an allocatory system, "awarding" (or not "awarding") criteria which play a significant part in determining the precise position of [migrants' children] within class relations'.[145] Later studies argued that racial exclusion affected different groups in different ways and that the British economy was 'more open and meritocratic' than sometimes assumed, although others found the 'ethnic penalty' persisted even in the better jobs.[146] The career pattern of young Chinese played a role in these discussions, for it seemed to confute the expectation of 'class reproduction'.

In considering this issue, one should distinguish between Chinese born in Hong Kong who came to Britain in their teens and those born in Britain or who arrived at an early age. In the 1980s, many Chinese under-performed at school and few entered adulthood with fluent English. Although parents dreamed of a career for their children in account-ancy, law, or medicine, the prospect facing many was unemployment or unskilled work on low pay. Most took what seemed the easy option of staying in catering, despite its disesteem and unsocial hours.[147] Noting this trend, the Home Affairs Committee said there was a danger 'that the concentration on catering, with all its attendant problems, will be perpetuated into a new generation which has not willingly chosen it'.[148] Baxter concluded that 'a childhood spent in meeting the unrelenting demands of the family shop over individual needs has left many British-born Chinese with little option but to continue to use their particular skills working in the ... ethnic economy'.[149]

By the late 1980s, however, few Chinese between the ages of 15 and 25 were prepared to countenance a career in catering. More than four out of five Liverpudlian Chinese aspired to higher education and the profes-sions, while less than one in ten looked to catering.[150] Studies in the 1990s pointed to a large outflow from catering by British-born Chinese and concluded that only Chinese with few job options continued to seek work in the sector. A survey of Chinese teenagers in Wales found that none wanted to work in a restaurant or takeaway.[151] Another found that Chinese caterers tended to be relatively old, with 56 per cent in the 45–59 age group compared with just 9 per cent of Britain's Chinese population as a whole.[152]

Young Chinese who remained in catering were more likely to have been raised in Hong Kong, speak poor English, and lack schooling. For them, the takeaway was a safety net against unemployment and discrimination in the manual-jobs market.[153] Jobs in catering were easier to find than other work, better paid, and more secure.[154] However, few parents saw this outcome as ideal and most had higher hopes. Once their children were sufficiently educated and the grounds from which to lift them out of the ethnic economy had been laid, there was no longer any pressing need to maintain the enterprise, especially if economic difficulties (including market saturation and a shortage of suitable labour) worked against them. In any case, the children were overqualified for the trade as a result of their schooling. In the early days, the takeaway had allowed immigrant families to work and live in a testing environment. The family's passage into the mainstream by way of the second generation rendered this function superfluous.

Feelings about quitting the shop were mixed. Many young Chinese had an antipathy to catering, which they experienced as oppressive and unrewarding.[155] They also found it demeaning – even more so than the laundries from which a previous second generation had recoiled, for catering entails the alienation of Chinese identity, in the sense of its sale in the form of ethnic food.[156] Quite a few, however, also had regrets about closing down, for the shop had nurtured a family solidarity.[157]

Their ascent into the salariat in the 1990s and now is well documented. The Fourth National Survey of Ethnic Minorities found Chinese were more represented than any other group, including whites, in the professions and management.[158] Second-generation Chinese became the highest earners in the 1990s.[159] These developments contradict theories that assume the perpetuation of migrants' low social class in their children and theories of ethnic economy that assume that family business culture would result in the reproduction of Chinese children as caterers.

However, discrimination continues to shape Chinese job patterns. In the era of the 'model minority', Chinese employment has polarised, with few intermediate options. In Britain as in America, native-born Chinese are in business or the professions, with foreign-born Chinese in the professions or catering. According to Stanford M. Lyman, Chinese in the United States are kept out of the blue-collar sector by a 'lingering sinophobic animus'.[160] In Britain, Chinese at the lower end of the jobs structure are more likely to see discrimination as widespread than those in the professions. Those ineligible for top jobs feel safest in catering, a familiar and uncontested space. Loath to enter the wider labour market, they seek shelter from unemployment in the family business.[161] An exceptionally high proportion of the Hong Kong-born work in catering – three out of four, according to one survey, compared with one out of three British-born.[162] In Northern Ireland, even some university graduates go into catering because they are unable to find work to match their qualifications or because they fail to achieve promotion.[163]

This bimodal pattern of employment was the focus of research by Yuet Ngor Mary Pang, who found that young Chinese adults in the 1990s were nearly four times as likely as their white counterparts to enter the professions and four times as likely to work in the service sector.[164] Such patterns are common in immigrant and ethnic minorities, whose members tend to seek out available niches rather than compete with natives.

The celebration of Chinese achievement obscures the persistence of racial distortions even within the salariat, where Chinese job choices are sometimes determined by the desire to minimise competition with whites. 'By being selective in choice of professional fields and opting for ones requiring adequate, not perfect English', writes Pang, 'the Chinese have circumvented the main obstacles which could block their entry into positions in the wider labour market.'[165] Highly qualified Chinese pay an 'ethnic penalty' in large establishments, where they are less likely than whites to be employed at higher levels.[166] In fact, Chinese have been bumping against glass ceilings ever since the 1970s, when Liverpool-born Chinese in a wide range of occupations failed to win leadership positions.[167]

Conclusions

Government policies have been critical in determining patterns of Chinese immigration, the formation of ethnic enclaves (or Chinatowns), and the use of the family in business ventures. They have also borne centrally on Chinese migrants' citizenship status and their relations with white British society. General racism was another crucial factor in the formation of Chinatowns.

The role of public policies in concentrating early Chinese migrants in just a few places raises doubts about the idea that common ethnicity unifies immigrants. Although public policies and racist practices may have forced them into enclaves, most have constantly striven to break out. The enclaves may have helped protect Chinese from racism, especially in the nineteenth century, but class differences among Chinatowners created a system of extreme exploitation.

Within the family, generational differences emerged. British-born and British-raised Chinese viewed the business sectors formed by Chinese migrants as degrading and oppressive. Chinatown meant little to the young. Their families were widely scattered and their own command of Chinese declined, especially among the better educated, who saw English as crucial for moving upwards. One study found that nearly 60 per cent of Chinese adolescents born or raised in Britain saw themselves as 'British Chinese', while other studies conclude that a 'polarised identity' – between Chinese and British – has emerged. Young Chinese switch between these two identities due to the family-work strategy adopted by the migrant cohort and their exposure to British society through education and by serving a white clientele.

For most members of the migrant generation, education was the prime means through which children could move into the professions. Family enterprise functioned principally to help children secure tertiary and professional qualifications, rather than as an avenue for migrants to acquire a greater corporate presence in the British economy. At the turn of the twenty-first century, nearly twice as many Chinese in Britain as whites had a tertiary qualification and twice as many went to private schools in 1995 as Indians and whites, an index of the value Chinese place on education. Chinese parents saw securing a higher education for their children and equipping them to join the middle class as ways of defeating the racism they faced.

Although a well-educated Chinese middle class has emerged, divisions persist between those who have moved upwards and those who stay trapped in ethnically based businesses like takeaways. While social mobility has led young Chinese to engage more intensively with British society, even the new professionals complain about discrimination and glass ceilings. This unfairness has led to the emergence of British Chinese-owned enterprises in the professional and hi-tech sectors.

Although young Chinese are still subject to discrimination, they are not widely active in community associations formed by immigrants to help counter it. There is also little evidence in the way in which young Chinese conduct business of the emergence of a transnational identity. Transformations in identity and class among young Chinese suggest that the new generations are culturally differentiated from the migrants, in spite of the racism they continue to endure. This differentiation is chiefly due to the younger generation's high level of education.

While family enterprise has played a crucial role in the development of the Chinese economy in Britain, it is most popular among migrants, who use it as a strategy to survive in an alien environment. The family business is not a Chinese cultural artefact but a mechanism adapted to cope with circumstances Chinese find hostile. As a community, they lack the distinctiveness transnational theory accords them. The cleavages that remain are based primarily on class rather than on sub-ethnicity or country of origin, the usual basis for divisions among migrants.

If a sense of 'community' appears to have emerged among the young, it is based on the idea of national belonging, as British Chinese. In spite of this emergence of a British identity, young Chinese remain subject to prejudice, rooted in the longstanding view of some whites that they do not 'belong'.

8
Conclusions

We set out in this study to write a history of the Chinese in Britain, from the angle of changes in their economic and social standing. By analysing their migration patterns, their associational structures, and the paths along which their enterprises developed, we have sought to understand processes of identity formation among members of this community – and, by extension, of ethnic minorities in general. This approach also allowed us to tackle issues raised by transnational studies concerning the organisation of capital flows, patterns of enterprise development, and the nature of identity formation in diasporic communities.

Transnational theory adopts a culturalist perspective, whereby ethnic commonalities are conceived as helping to bring about dynamic and global entrepreneurial communities. Chinese migrant communities provide a searching test of transnational theory, for Chinese have been the target of exclusion laws in all five continents. Far more Chinese emigrated in the nineteenth century than any other non-European community, including Indians. The Chinese diaspora has often suffered extreme discrimination. This discrimination is connected with the fact that proportionately far more Chinese than most other migrants have been poor.

By writing in historical perspective and focusing on the theme of generational change, we have highlighted the rise of a British identity, along with a persistent ethnic identity, among migrants' descendants, even though they continue to be subject to discrimination in various forms. Evolutionary changes in identity among such people – and even among relatively rooted migrants – bring issues of exclusion, citizenship, and rights to the fore. This volume, by means of a study of the Chinese in Britain, challenges conventional assumptions in transnational theory

361

about community organisation and economic development in diaspora. These include ideas like 'the pull of the motherland', one of several well-aired themes that have boosted an essentialist approach to identity formation among migrants and their descendants.

Transnationalism, economy, racism, and the Chinese divide

While scholars who support transnational theory hold that ethnic identity inspires mutual trust and support among diasporic groups, our history reveals a community that has always been fragmented, even when under racist siege. It shows again and again that the racism to which Chinese are subjected results from economic factors. Whether on the labour market (principally in the shipping sector) or in business (for example, laundering), the prospect of Chinese competition evoked a hostile response from native British, manifested in racist terms.

According to transnational studies, diasporic groups reinforce their communal boundaries to enable them to survive and even thrive in foreign economies, especially when they are subject to racist attacks. Yet our own study shows that the Chinese in Britain have seldom cooperated, even to protect their mutual interests. In an attempt to avoid economic competition with whites and avert a possible racist backlash, Chinese have competed among themselves to develop their businesses. Locked into ethnic niches, they are inhibited from working together against hostile state policies and actions by the white majority. In most instances, they try to undermine their co-ethnic competitors rather than band together against racial abuse and economic marginalisation. Intra-ethnic competition requires the community's geographic dispersal, further hindering attempts to cooperate even reactively to secure government protection against racist pressures. While racism often unifies oppressed ethnic and religious groups, the Chinese have been prevented from uniting by economic rivalry.

Chinese styles of enterprise development in Europe are diverse. Their variations undermine arguments about 'Chinese capitalism', a hallmark of theories that claim culture influences modes of economic activity and decision-making. Chinese in many parts of the European mainland in the interwar years were itinerant peddlers, while in Britain – and, to a lesser extent, in France – fixed businesses were the norm. The difference can be explained by the fact that while Chinese seafarers in Britain had no experience in peddling goods, the main Chinese community in mainland Europe comprised Zhejiangese with a background in itinerant trading.

The forms of livelihood pursued by Chinese migrants in Britain also differed at times from those followed in the United States, further evidence that common culture and identity do not directly determine business choices. Many Chinese in the United States were originally active in rural-based ventures and more likely to have skills they could redeploy in developing new businesses. Anti-Chinese sentiment in the United States emerged in response to the capacity of Chinese migrants to compete with local whites in agriculture. The Chinese were eventually driven into ethnic enclaves in urban areas. These enclaves resulted from the migrants' experience of racism rather than from a Chinese wish to band together in one place in ethnic solidarity. The early Chinese migrants in Britain, on the other hand, lived mainly in the ports and other cities. Void of skills that could be put to use for financial gain, they were forced into menial jobs, usually working for other Chinese who so exploited them that they could not wait to leave and establish their own enterprises. These enterprises were usually small-scale: they could be started up with next to no capital; they required minimal contact with the host population and minimal competition with native British. In both the United States and Britain, the residents of these enclaves moved on once they felt sufficiently acclimatised or had acquired the ability to function in the wider economy.

The transitions – from 'salt to soap' and 'soap to soy' – reflect some of the changes in the community. They are also evidence of the ability of Chinese in Britain to absorb ideas and techniques adopted by their counterparts in the United States – but not in mainland Europe – as a way of coping. This transatlantic exchange shows that British Chinese were influenced by the tactics developed by Chinese in the United States to survive adversity in an alien environment.

The switch from 'salt to soap' showed the growing embeddedness in British society of Chinese seafarers, who set up laundry businesses not only in the ports but in inland towns and cities, as a way of dealing with their lack of English while at the same time developing a sustainable livelihood. The trends in the laundry sector were replicated in catering as the Chinese moved from 'soap to soy', again reflecting an important transition in the community. The arrival of ethnic Chinese from different parts of Asia after the Second World War points up a further failing of transnational studies, for cooperation between new arrivals was practically inconceivable as a result of differences of class and national background. The new arrivals set themselves at odds with the 'old' Chinese by creating a niche for themselves in food catering. In the 1960s, the economic position of the old timers was threatened by migrants from the New Territories opening restaurants. The Hong Kong caterers, in their turn, met stiff competition from ethnic Chinese from Southeast Asia, who rapidly increased their share of the restaurant market in the 1980s and 1990s. The Hong Kong caterers lacked the financial and educational resources of the growing community of Southeast Asian Chinese, many of whom had initially come to study. While the Hong Kong migrants managed to corner the takeaways, Southeast Asian Chinese emerged in the 1980s as major investors in the Chinese restaurant and large-scale fast-food sector.

If transnational studies were right, one would expect that ties between ethnic-Chinese migrants and long-term residents would be spun into business networks to promote the economic interests, in catering and other enterprises, of both groups, united in a single ethnic community. Instead, the newcomers formed a serious business threat to the old hands. Many business ventures that started as immigrant partnerships in the 1960s and 1970s quickly evolved into family enterprises, a further sign of the immigrants' reluctance to engage in long-term cooperation with other Chinese in profit-sharing ventures. Partnerships were forged on grounds of expediency: once the partners had the means to source funds from British banks, the partnerships nearly always broke up. Business ties in the shape of production chains or food distribution linkages were created for mutual benefit but seldom lasted. They were situational and episodic, patterned to serve common business interests rather than to support the supposed interests of the larger Chinese community. Common ethnic identity served as a basis for business ties, but only for as long as everyone benefited: it was no longer used once it became more profitable or viable to develop business links of other sorts.

Migration, class, and the decline of associations

To support the contention that common ethnic identity unifies diasporans, transnational theorists point to mutual aid among co-ethnics to facilitate migration. However, immigrants have typically been exploited to the hilt by the co-ethnics who facilitate their entry into Britain. The number of Chinese in Britain in the nineteenth century was quite small. The community was made up primarily of seafarers who had deserted ship or been abandoned by their employers at the expiry of their contracts. In the 1880s, some Chinese who had fled the United States during the anti-Chinese campaigns and resettled in Britain started up businesses on the basis of experiences gained in America. There is no evidence that these 'double migrants' established close and lasting ties with the longer-standing community. By the middle of the twentieth century, the community was on the point of dying out, and was saved from extinction only by a big inflow of Hong Kong Chinese, starting in the 1950s. The early history of the community suggests that but for this influx, the Chinese in Britain would have melted into the larger society.

Differences in place of origin were one reason for the early immigrants' ethnic incoherence. Another was sub-ethnic difference, for example, between Siyinese and Hakkas. People's reasons for migrating also differed. Among the Siyinese, some became seafarers as a way of migrating and securing funds with which to found businesses. In China and Hong Kong, migrants from different sub-ethnic groups had already engaged in fierce competition for farmland and other scarce resources. The collective memory of conflict reinforced cleavages that emerged independently in Britain and were difficult to overcome, despite the migrants' shared experience of isolation, exploitation, and marginalisation. Class divisions among the Chinese from Hong Kong further inhibited attempts to unite around common interests.

Associations created to help migrants cope with life in Britain show that some Chinese tried to mobilise common identity as the basis for mutual help among co-ethnics. Between 1950s and the 1990s, the number of Chinese associations in Europe rocketed, from a score or so to around 520. However, this steep rise was attributable not just to the efforts of Chinese migrants to build a common front around shared economic interests but also to support and funding by Beijing and Taibei. The decline of Chinese-based associations, temporarily arrested by government action in the 'homeland' countries, was a measure of their scant relevance to diasporans in Europe.

The associations' limited and dwindling role supports the following conclusions. First, most Chinese immigrants in Britain have seldom sought help from anyone other than near relatives. The importance of the family unit, so evident in migration, is also reflected in early patterns of business formation. People frequented associations only if they were convinced by a rational calculation of the odds that it was in their interests to do so. Second, class divisions in the diaspora hindered the growth and sustainability of associations. Urban-based migrants, mainly professionals and capitalists, were wealthier and better educated than the rural and inappropriately skilled pioneers and had little desire or need to join associations. On the other hand, associations controlled by the business elite or professionals catered only marginally to poor immigrants and were even used to prevent new arrivals from entering more profitable sectors of the ethnic niche.

The history of Chinese associations in Britain shows that migrants tend to progress along a set trajectory that starts at the point of entry. Where necessary, they search out co-ethnics in the new setting. The ties thus formed seldom endure, especially among the resourceful and well-to-do. There is no evidence that British-born Chinese lead such associations, which have little to offer them. The superfluity of ethnic or clan associations from the point of view of most British-born Chinese reflects the transitions in identity across the generations.

Transnationalism, generational change, and identity formation

By the end of the twentieth century, generational change had led to developments that challenge key tenets of transnational theory. British-born Chinese or Chinese who arrived in Britain as children do not have the same view on ethnic relations as their parents. An obvious example is the way in which young Chinese view the businesses their parents founded. For migrants with limited funds and education, the family business served both as a means of livelihood and as a way of dealing with isolation and alienation. For the children, the drudgery of life in the laundry or takeaway had a strong bearing on attitudes to self and society. Their repugnance for labour-intensive ventures contributed to a decline in Chinese laundering and the flight from catering. The parents were motivated by a desire to secure educational and professional qualifications for their children and had little or no intrinsic interest in the businesses they ran. This indifference was reflected in their minimal investment of capital in such businesses. The migrants' hope for a better future for their children showed that the businesses were a way of dealing with life in Britain rather than a commitment to enterprise as such. Since few descendants have much interest in taking over from their parents, family enterprises rarely outlast the migrant generation.

Where migrants' descendants do take over, the changes they make in business strategy, organisational structure, and management style show that they are more inclined than their forebears to link up with non-Chinese business interests in inter-ethnic partnerships. These partnerships are a result chiefly of the narrowing and erasure of the educational gap between Chinese and other British children. They show that British-born Chinese are happy to work with non-Chinese. Although British Chinese are by no means exempt from discrimination, the experience of it has not reinforced intra-ethnic business cooperation to any great extent.

The proliferation of inter-ethnic business ties shows that relatively large numbers of Chinese degree-holders have joined the British middle class. Their greater integration into British society is evident in their disproportionate presence in the professions and the use of bank loans by some to create fairly large-scale enterprises. The rise of this new middle class suggests that ethnic Chinese born and bred in Britain have a national identity and are comfortable in inter-ethnic relationships.

These transitions in identity are reflected in a loss of fluency in Chinese. British-born Chinese rarely read Chinese newspapers and prefer British to Chinese TV. Identity change in the British-born generation because of class mobility and the decline in Chinese have contributed to the decay in associational life.

However, cleavages and discontents persist even in the British-born and British-raised generations. Many young Chinese who do not go to university remain confined to ethnic-type enterprises, thus creating a new intra-ethnic class divide. British Chinese who are upwardly mobile due to gaining professional and tertiary qualifications and join the middle class complain about discrimination in the workplace and instances of exclusion from higher levels of management.

Community leaders (usually members of the migrant cohort), political leaders, and transnational theorists have little to say about these transformations within Chinese society in Britain and cling to discourses based on ethnic identity. However, our study reveals the complexity of ethnic and national belonging – how it evolves over time and is reconfigured by changes in class and social standing. Transnational studies seldom capture the identity transformations that occur in the newer generations of diasporic communities. The emergence of novel forms of identification among diasporic groups and their descendants undermines the view that ethnic minorities necessarily cohere to protect vested interests.

So our social and economic history of the Chinese in Britain throws many of the principles of transnational theory into doubt. In exploring the dynamics of transnationalism, scholars have looked mainly at ways in which diasporic communities construct identity. Transnational studies are particularly preoccupied with the business activities of diasporic communities and their local and global influence. They therefore fix principally on immigrants at the point of entry and their early experience abroad and pay close attention to exercises in group solidarity, the basis on which co-ethnics are said to survive as migrants. Their thesis is that migrants form institutions and business networks that allow them to compete and thrive in relative poverty and a hostile environment by practising mutual help. Such arguments assume a sense of group solidarity forged on the basis of common identity and the collective experience of discrimination at the hands of a larger economically dominant ethnic group. But the history of the Chinese in Britain dispels such arguments by drawing attention to the class and sub-ethnic tensions that rend the community. It also highlights the complexities of cultural and national identity, not only among migrants but even more so among their descendants.

Chinese immigrants were severely exploited by co-ethnics who brought them to Britain to work as hired hands. They resented their treatment and moved away as quickly as possible. Some ended up competing with their former bosses. By setting up their own small businesses, they created a space in which they could escape exploitation by fellow Chinese and a base from which to infiltrate and hold at bay the white world. The migrants stayed in the kitchen, secluded from the customers, while their children worked at the counter. Competition was severe and led to the community's extreme dispersal, intensifying the caterers' isolation and preventing them from coming together even for cultural purposes.

The pattern of operation of Chinese-owned firms provides no evidence of a common ethnic style used to promote the economic interests of the community as a whole. The concept of 'Chinese capitalism' and the idea of tightly knit business networks connecting the community are not supported by the evidence. Competition is more likely than cooperation, even within ethnic Chinese enclaves. These enclaves, a legacy of racism, are locales that Chinese aspire to quit, if only to enlarge their business clientele beyond the ethnic community. Competition is intense, in sharp contradiction with the widely held view that the dynamism of Chinese enterprises results from intra-ethnic cooperation. If the second generation takes over, such firms usually retain little of their original form, in terms of market and organisational structure.

Although family enterprise is a prominent feature of the Chinese economy in Britain, as a style of business it has little or nothing to do with culture. Family firms came to predominate because of the problems Chinese migrants faced in securing start-up capital and hiring labour to staff new ventures. Today, generational change threatens their survival. Most descendants of the founders of these enterprises resist joining, so the firms close or are sold off. Some descendants try to recruit professional managers, who are better able to develop the business or work with non-Chinese.

This study shows that Chinese society in Britain is highly diversified and rapidly changing. However, while the Chinese seem to be moving ever forward, in the direction of a stronger national identification and a growing estrangement from the parents' and grandparents' 'homeland', white British society is insufficiently versatile in its approach to the Chinese.

Our study points up the complex and intricate interplay of ethnic and national identities in the lives of Chinese in Britain and their protean nature, negotiated and configured at points where family, lineage, community, and white society intersect. An enduring thread over the last few decades of Chinese presence has been the vigour of national identity among migrants' descendants. While British Chinese may call on transnational associations to help them promote their businesses, such alliances are rarely employed primarily to reinforce 'Chineseness'. By misinterpreting them as avowals of loyalty and belonging to the ancestral homeland, transnational studies reinforce essentialist conceptions of identity and 'cultural authenticity' in diasporic communities, and thus frustrate the promotion of ethnic co-existence and social cohesion.

Appendix: Companies Owned by British Chinese

Company (Incorporation date)	Activity	Location	Shareholders
Restaurateurs			
Singapore Sam plc (18/7/88)	Sale of Chinese Food	London	Chee L. Wong
Ching Ying Cantonese Restaurant Ltd (22/11/85)	Restaurateur	Birmingham	Siu C. Wong, Y. Y. Wong
Haythorne Ltd (29/3/89)	Restaurateur	Herts	C. S. Ng, C. Y. Ng, G. Liu, E. Liu
Lokevale Ltd (8/12/92)	Restaurateur	London	Chi L. Lai, Timothy C. Liu, Tze Lai, Yuk C. Man
Hamarus Catering Supplies Ltd (7/12/92)	Seafood caterer	London	Yuk L. Choi, Annie Choi
Colonial Catering Co Ltd (1/3/91)	Restaurateur and caterer	London	Mei-Li Tan
Ploneday Ltd (28/1/92)	Restaurateur	London	Tang Express Ltd, Wing Lai
Bayee (Village) Catering Ltd (5/7/85)	Restaurateur	London	Marco C. Yu
Special Charm Ltd (26/9/90)	Restaurateur	Manchester	Koon Y. Lee, Tak C. Keung
Steepletop Ltd (28/12/92)	Restaurateur	London	Fung Law, K. F. Law, Vi. D. Quan, K. P. Li, K. W. Wong
Singapore Garden Restaurant Ltd (19/5/87)	Restaurateur	London	Siam K. Lim, Stephen Li
Lucky Dragon (Leeds) Ltd (12/7/90)	Restaurateur	Leeds	Kam M. Mo, Ting S. Mo

Mr Kong Chinese Restaurant Ltd (20/7/87)	Restaurateur	London	K. Kong, K. C. Tang, Y. W. Lo, M. T. Lee
Kwok Man (Brothers) Restaurant Ltd (16/7/85)	Restaurateur	Manchester	Hing W. Yip, Shing C. Yip, S. Yip
Menuspeak Ltd (31/1/86)	Restaurateur	London	Sai M. Li
Wong's Enterprise Ltd (18/6/87)	Restaurateur	London	F. Y. Tsang, K. P. Wong, K. F. Wong, K. N. Wong, K. H. Wong
Signor Spumante Ltd (16/5/85)	Restaurateur	London	C. Y. Wong, T. Y. Wong
Maxon Ltd (17/9/87)	Restaurateur	London	Yung S. Peng
Samtung Co Ltd (22/2/90)	Restaurateur and property investments	Middlesex	C. T. Tang, C. M. Tang
Sam Pan Foods Ltd (10/7/79)	Restaurateur	Milton Keynes	Kam Tak Ho, Shiu Hong Yam, Sam Pan Holdings Ltd
The Lantern House Ltd (3/1/67)	Food catering	London	Albert C. Looi
New World Chinese Restaurants Ltd (8/3/84)	Restaurateur	Middlesex	E. L. K. Liu, E. H. K. Liu, T. Ng
Golden Dragon Chinese Restaurant Ltd (17/11/93)	Restaurateur	London	A. Lee, Y. W. Chan
Freddie's Chinese Restaurant Ltd (20/11/78)	Restaurateur	Newcastle	Kang Ching Mo, Sze Mai Mo
Wholesalers, supermarkets and retailers			
W. Wing Yip plc (9/12/69)	Chinese supermarket	Birmingham	W. W. Yip & Brothers (Holdings) Ltd
Wing Yip (London) Ltd (9/11/77)	Cash and carry store	London	W. W. Yip & Brothers (Holdings) Ltd

(Continued)

Company (Incorporation date)	Activity	Location	Shareholders
Wing Yip (Manchester) Ltd (31/5/77)	Cash and carry store	Manchester	W. W. Yip & Brothers (Holdings) Ltd
Seven Seas (Frozen Foods) Ltd (8/6/71)	Wholesale distributor of frozen foods	London	Eugene So, S. S. So
Seven Seas (Frozen Foods-Warwick) Ltd (14/10/75)	Wholesale distributor of frozen foods	London	Seven Seas (Frozen Foods) Ltd
Wing Fat Ltd (3/3/94)	Supermarket operator	Manchester	Fai L. Chan, Jerry Low-Chan
Hung Sung Trading Co Ltd (11/5/84)	Chinese emporium for wholesale and retail of catering supplies	Tyne & Wear	S. Y. Wu, Y. Y. Wu, S. K. Lim, Y. K. Wu, T. Wu
Hung Fat Catering Supplies Ltd	Food supplier for catering business	London	M. Y. Leung, C. H. Leung, K. H. Leung, S. M. Li, E. Y. M. Sum, S. C. Chan, C. W. Leung, C. Y. Leung
W.H. Lung Trading Ltd (25/11/88)	Chinese supermarket	Manchester	Kuen K. Chan, Wai P. Chu
Loonmoon Supermarket Ltd (14/5/70)	Retail and wholesale of food products	London	Hon T. Liu, Kau Ng
Loon Fung Ltd (16/9/83)	Chinese supermarket operator	London	James Chin
Wing's Seafood Ltd (20/11/90)	Wholesalers of seafood	Middlesex	Chi M. Chan, C. W. Liu
San Ho Ltd (5/2/81)	Distributor of Chinese food and goods	Ormskirk	n/a
Wing Lee Hong Co. Ltd (26/1/81)	Chinese food distributor	Leeds	H. Hui, C. M. Wong, J. C. Wong, D. Hui

Chan's Ltd (17/4/85)	Food wholesaler	Glasgow	Lin T. Chan, A&M Trust
Chan Brothers Ltd (30/7/91)	Wholesaler of imported and frozen food	London	Kevin W. Chan, K. S. Chan, S. W. Chan
Chi Yip Ltd (2/4/90)	Wholesale food distributor	Oldham	Jackon Liu, Stewart Yip
Dayat Foods Ltd (10/12/82)	Wholesale food distributor	Middlesex	Dayat Foods Packaging Ltd
Matahari Impex (Far East) Ltd (30/9/76)	Chinese food retailer	London	Sin K. Wong
S. W. Trading Ltd (24/1/77)	Wholesale food distributor	Middlesex	See Woo Holdings Ltd
Octopus Trading Co Ltd (22/3/88)	Wholesalers	London	Chit Y. Woo
Manning Impex Ltd (18/6/87)	Wholesaler of imported food	London	Esther E. Cheong, N. I. Cheong, M. A. Cheong
New Loon Moon Ltd (22/10/95)	Retailer of imported food	London	Esther E. Cheong, N. A. Cheong, M. Cheong, M. Wu, A. Cheong
Ling Tung Ltd (12/2/85)	Food wholesalers	London	n/a
Hang Won Hong Ltd (3/5/89)	Wholesale and retail of food	Essex	W. S. Chan
Tsang Enterprise Ltd (21/12/82)	Bakery and retail sales	Birmingham	George P. Tsang
Sun Leun Trading Co. Ltd (20/11/78)	Newspaper agent and wholesale bakery	London	Kam Tang, M. S. Lam, M. W. Yeung, S. T. Tang, S. Wong
Oriental Arts & Co. Ltd (22/3/63)	Retail of Oriental goods	Cardiff	Yew Yee Thong
Davina Fashion Shoes Ltd (8/4/86)	Shoes and fashion wear wholesale and retail	London	K. Chow, P. Chow
Imperial Cosmetics Ltd (17/7/85)	Retail chemist		Yew C. Lau, Yok C. Tan
Tsing Hing Ltd (1993)	Wholesaler and retailer of Oriental food	Tyne & Wear	J. H. Tsang, N. H. Tsang, J. S. Tsang

(Continued)

Company (Incorporation date)	Activity	Location	Shareholders
Kwok Hing (Frozen Food) Ltd (13/7/82)	Frozen food wholesaler	Birmingham	K. H. Lau, K. Y. T. Lau
Wing Hong Co. Ltd (1979)	Wholesale grocer	Newcastle	P. F. Cheng, K. K. Cheng
Chinese Medicine Centre Ltd (16/8/90)	Medicinal herbs retailer	London	Yuk T. Lam
Chung Ying Cash & Carry Ltd (15/11/84)	Food retailer	Glasgow	C. Y. Chan, C. M. Chan
Chung Wah Supermarket Ltd (17/3/88)	Food wholesaler and retailer	Liverpool	C. C. Liu, J. Liu
Walton Cheong-Leen Ltd (15/7/69)	Food retailer	London	Walton Cheong-Leen, Donald Cheong-Leen, Eula Wu
Traders (importers and exporters)			
Enta Technologies Ltd (27/7/90)	Import and sale of computers and related products	Telford	Yueh C. Tsai, Jason Tsai
Typhoon Ltd (8/6/71)	Import, export and retail of Oriental food	Swiney	Donald Cheong-Leen, Patricia Cheong-Leen
Mayron (UK) Ltd (24/9/86)	Import and distribution of audio products	Middlesex	Toon C. Ho
J. P. Metals Ltd (5/8/92)	Metal trader	London	Fuwah Yuen
Chindwell Ltd (1/9/64)	Import and export of DIY products	London	Lincoln L. Chin, P. J. Chin
Henry Yim Ltd (12/11/86)	Precious metal trading	Middlesex	Henry Yim
Exclusive Oriental Classics (UK) Ltd (1/4/87)	Import and wholesale	London	Kian H. Tay

Tronic Import Co. Ltd (23/2/87)	Merchants and importers of electrical products	Redditch	Simon Lam
W. Wing Yip (International Trading) Ltd	Import and export of food products	Birmingham	W. Wing Yip & Brothers Holdings Ltd
Manufacturing			
Way-On Foods Ltd (26/6/86)	Manufacturer of food products	Hertfordshire	See Woo Holdings Ltd
Davjon Food Ltd (20/11/75)	Manufacturer of food products	Manchester	John K. Chan, K. H. Chan
Asia Food Products Co. Ltd (25/6/71)	Manufacture and distribution of food	Essex	P. Lew, R. Lew, C. L. Tai
Hi-Tech Industries Ltd (1/9/83)	Production and retail of electrical products	Surrey	Cornel Chu, Louise Chu, Anita Fang
Hinchest Holdings plc (5/7/91)	Manufacture and distribution of pressure measurement products	Crawley	Stephen L. Ku, V. L. Chan
Cheung Kong Ltd (22/11/90)	Manufacturer of plastic products	Luton	Kong Chan, Nap Yan Chan, Hui Fong Chan
Beon Corporation Ltd (2/11/89)	Manufacturer of colour television	Edinburgh	Benson K. Wong
Shun Cheong Ltd (5/4/72)	Manufacture and retail of food products	London	Kwok Keung Wong
Chinese Food Manufacturing Cantre Ltd (1/6/95)	Food manufacturer	London	Kai Heng Tam, Lai Leon Yoke Tam, Tim Fuk Tang, Kwan Ying Tang
Winner Foods Ltd (1/7/91)	Import and manufacture of food	London	Kok L. Tan, Kwok F. Chan, Ming W. Sham
Property			
Shung Yip (UK) Co. Ltd (18/10/79)	Property	London	S. K. Chiu, F. K. Chiu, S. W. Chiu, Y. Chiu, S. Y. Chiu, E. S. Chiu

(Continued)

Company (Incorporation date)	Activity	Location	Shareholders
W. H. Lung Ltd (4/12/86)	Property	Manchester	Kuen K. Chan, Wai P. Chu
Y. P. C. Ltd (5/11/69)	Property	London	Peter Cheung, W. L. Cheung
R. J. W. Investments Ltd (14/12/84)	Property Developer	Birmingham	A. M. Wong, Siu C. Wong, S. Swindle
Reevestoke Ltd (31/7/79)	Property developer	Surrey	A. M. Ko, D. S. Ko
Man Qwan Ltd (24/3/88)	Property letting	Edinburgh	Imperial (Chinese Restaurant) Ltd
Kindgrand Ltd (20/3/85)	Property investment	London	Tak Y. Hui
Glasgow Chinatown Investments Ltd (12/2/90)	Property investment	Birmingham	Maurice Lim, Wing H. Au-Yeung
W. Wing Yip & Brothers (Properties) Ltd	Property investment	Birmingham	W. Wing Yip plc
Computer industry			
DTK Computer (UK) Ltd (7/4/92)	Sale of computers	Middlesex	L. P. Wu, Catipond Ltd
P. C. Mart (UK) Ltd (13/6/91)	Computer hardware and software dealers	London	C. Y. Chen
Moretec Electronics (UK) Ltd (23/2/90)	Software consultancy and supply	London	n/a
Phant Asia Ltd (23/9/91)	Marketing of computers	Witney	Mark Seow, Ian Seow
Ethertech Consultancy Ltd (11/12/91)	Computer consultancy	Horsham	F. S. Poon, J. H. Poon
Bellstar Computing Ltd (8/10/91)	Computer consultancy	Middlesex	A. P. Chu, Y. Chu

Investment holding companies

W. Wing Yip & Brothers (Holdings) Ltd (30/6/80)	Importers, wholesale distributors of Chinese food	Birmingham	W. W. Yip, G. Y. Yap, L. S. Yap
See Woo Holdings Ltd (7/10/88)	Investment holding	Middlesex	Tse Family
Enta (UK) Ltd (3/97)	Investment holding	Telford	Jason Tsai, Y. C. T. Tsai
Hoo Hing Holdings Ltd (6/6/78)	Importers and wholesalers of Chinese food	London	n/a
Loon Fung (London) Ltd (13/7/66)	Management consultant to supermarkets	London	James Chin
Dayat Foods Packaging Co Ltd (27/11/81)	Investment holding	Middlesex	n/a

Professional services

Upperdata Ltd (28/3/89)	Engineering consultancy	London	Ah S. Lee, Choo P. Lee
Sonas Ltd (15/6/89)	Engineering and drafting services	Inverness	Catherine A. Sim, James M. Sim
Prospect (UK) Ltd (30/3/81)	Consultant engineers	Surrey	Lois Kua, Kia Kua
Chilworth Communications Ltd (8/3/88)	Marketing consultancy	Surrey	Geraldine Wong
Winchground Ltd (6/8/84)	Commodity trading	London	Ian C. Cheong, K. P. Kwan
Tang Express Ltd (19/1/87)	Restaurateur consultant	Middlesex	Fuk Kun Tang, Tim Fuk Tang, Ping Fuk Tang, Chu Ting Tang, Chuk Ming Tang
Herkers Courtney Wong Ltd (27/2/87)	Accoutancy and secretarial services	London	Hing W. Chan, Kuk F. Chan

(Continued)

Company (Incorporation date)	Activity	Location	Shareholders
General Services			
Rical Express (UK) Ltd (4/7/79)	Freight, forwarding agents and road haulage	London	Ching W. Ha, David M. Cheung
Dimerco Express (UK) Ltd (2/4/80)	Freight and forwarding agents	London	Dionislo L. Yang, Grandrich Management Ltd
First Delivery Ltd (31/12/84)	Courier services	London	Steven S. C. Yeo
Emerald Travel Ltd (21/5/80)	Travel agency	London	Gabriel Ng Wong
L.T.S. Travel Holding Ltd (18/8/81)	Investment holding	London	Diana H. Kong
Chang Hing Farms Ltd (10/10/73)	Farming and supply of poultry	London	n/a
Associated Translators & Fotosetters Ltd (10/3/77)	Translators	London	H. Z. Zhang, Paula G. Zhang

Notes

1 Introduction

1. This transition has been noted in recent studies on ethnic minorities in Britain. See, for example, Jones 1993; Metcalf, Modood, and Virdee 1997; and Berthoud 1998.
2. See Hall 1992; Gilroy 1987, 1993; Back 1996; and Brah 1996.
3. Ethnic Chinese from Asia now own major enterprises in Britain including Laura Ashley Holdings plc, Crabtree & Evelyn Ltd, Harvey Nichols & Co Ltd, Millennium & Capthorne Hotels plc, and Port of Felixstowe plc. For a detailed account of investments in Britain economy by ethnic Chinese from China, Hong Kong, Taiwan, Singapore, and Malaysia, see Gomez 2004.
4. Massey, Alarcon, Durand, and Gonzalez 1987 and Portes and Walton 1981, in their studies on migrant communities, use this methodology to examine the peculiarities of the situation of each community.
5. See Kearney 1991 and Vertovec and Cohen 1999a,b for a discussion on transnationalism and Redding 1990 and Lever-Tracy, Ip, and Tracy 1996 for a discussion on Chinese capital flows in global perspective.
6. On Chinese and transnationalism, see Ong and Nonini 1997; Ong 1999; and Yeung and Olds, eds, 2000.
7. Portes, Guarnizo, and Landolt 1999.
8. Miyoshi 1993.
9. Castells 1993.
10. Gereffi 1994.
11. Castells 1993, pp. 177–190.
12. Basch, Glick Schiller, and Blanc-Szanton 1995, p. 7; Glick Schiller, Basch, and Blanc-Szanton 1999.
13. Vertovec 1999a.
14. Guarnizo and Smith 1998, pp. 15–20; Portes, Guarnizo, and Landolt 1999, pp. 225–227.
15. Vertovec and Cohen 1999a, p. xvi.
16. Pieke, Nyíri, Thunø, and Ceccagno 2004, pp. 11–15.
17. See, for example, Portes, Guarnizo, and Landolt 1999.
18. Vertovec 1999a, p. 447.
19. See Redding 1990; Hamilton, ed., 1996; Lever-Tracy, Ip, and Tracy 1996.
20. Pries 2001, p. 20.
21. Glick Schiller, Basch, and Blanc-Szanton 1999, pp. 26–27.
22. Portes, Guarnizo, and Landolt 1999, p. 219.
23. Vertovec and Cohen 1999a, pp. xii and xxv.
24. Redding 1990; Whitley 1992.
25. See, for example, Gomez 1999; Benton and Gomez 2001; Gomez and Hsiao, eds, 2001; Gomez and Hsiao, eds, 2004; and Gomez and Benton 2003.
26. Ong 1999, p. 7.

27. Another volume that advanced similar ideas, though not from the perspective of transnational theory, is Lever-Tracy, Ip, and Tracy 1996.
28. Ong and Nonini, eds, 1997, pp. 11 and 21.
29. Ong and Nonini, eds, 1997, pp. 323–332.
30. Redding 1990; Hamilton, ed., 1996.
31. Huntington 1996.
32. Weidenbaum and Hughes 1996.
33. Kao 1993.
34. See, for example, Redding 1990; Fukuyama 1995; Lever-Tracy, Ip, and Tracy 1996; Backman 1999; and Yeung and Olds 2000.
35. See, for example, Wong Siu-lun 1985; Redding 1990; Whitley 1992; Castells 1993; Fukuyama 1995; and Whyte 1996.
36. Chandler 1962; Penrose 1980. Among European Union countries, between 75 and 90 per cent of all firms are said to be family enterprises. One in eight of firms quoted on the London Stock Exchange is a family firm. According to an estimate by the magazine *Fortune* in 1993, nearly a third of the top 500 firms in the United States were family-owned.
37. Redding 1996.
38. See, for example, Hamilton, ed., 1996.
39. Whitley 1992; Biggart and Hamilton 1997, pp. 33–54.
40. Yeung and Olds 2000.
41. Lever-Tracy and Tracy 1999, p. 5.
42. See, for example, Gomez 1999; Gomez and Hsiao 2001; and Schak 2000.
43. Benton and Gomez 2001.
44. For a comparative study of the Chinese in Britain, Australia, and Southeast Asia, see Gomez and Benton 2003. For more information on the Chinese in Australia, see Inglis 1967 and Chin 1997. For a historical profile of the Chinese in the United States, see Hsu 2000; Zia 2000; and Chang 2003.
45. Gomez 2004.
46. Ong 1999, pp. 2 and 19.
47. See Ang 2001 for a cogent analysis of the complexity of the issue of 'Chinese identity' for migrants' offspring. For a similar perspective on the new generation of Chinese in the United States, see Louie 2004.

2   Migration and settlement

1. Wang Gungwu 1993, pp. 926–927.
2. Eriksen 1993, p. 143, calls the connection between exclusion and apparent tolerance by the ethnic majority 'the paradox of multiculturalism'.
3. The word *Huaqiao* was coined in the late nineteenth century to replace various other terms, many of them derogatory. *Hua* 华 is a literary word for China, while *qiao* 侨 means 'to sojourn, or reside temporarily away from home', a term probably used for the first time in 1858 to apply to Chinese residing abroad (but initially reserved for diplomats). *Huaqiao* heads a semantic field whose main terms are *Huayi* 华裔, a descendant of a *Huaqiao* with or without foreign nationality; *guiqiao* 归侨, an overseas Chinese who has repatriated; and *qiaojuan* 侨眷, a relative, living in China, of a *Huaqiao*.

The *qiaoxiang* 侨乡 are the regions in China of substantial overseas migration. In the late 1980s, there were thought to be one million *guiqiao* and 21 million *qiaojuan*, most of them in Guangdong and Fujian (Wang Gungwu 1991, pp. 229 and 243–244). On the coining of the word *Huaqiao*, see also Fang Xiongpu and Xie Chengjia, eds, 1993, p. 1.

4. An exception is the study by Elisseeff 1994.
5. Baker 1994, p. 292.
6. Sir E. Hertslet, quoted in Freeberne 1979, p. 27.
7. Heyndrickx 1990, pp. 121–140; Shi Kangqiang 1991, p. 104.
8. Kiernan 1978, p. 41.
9. Chan 1928, p. 175; Ch'en 1942, p. 211.
10. Heyndrickx 1990, pp. 139–140.
11. Hudson 1931, p. 326; Chan 1928, pp. 208–211.
12. Ch'en 1942, pp. 211–226.
13. Parker 1998a, p. 68.
14. Walvin 1984, p. 68.
15. The word Lascar, not considered pejorative, was incorporated into English in the seventeenth century to denote Indian seafarers; it sometimes included Chinese, just as the term Chinese could include crews of diverse colonial origin (McFarland 1991, p. 495).
16. Hu Zhiqiang 1989, pp. 19–21.
17. Ng 1968, pp. 15–18.
18. Jones 1979, p. 397. For an early description of the London rookeries and the foreign seafarers' quarter, see Beames 1850.
19. PRO, HO 45/05 5480.
20. Shang 1984, p. 8.
21. Watson 1975, p. 118.
22. Ng 1968, p. 12.
23. Jones 1979, p. 397.
24. Shang 1984, p. 9.
25. Gordon 1985, p. 7.
26. PRO, HO 45/11843, pt 1.
27. *Birkenhead and Cheshire Advertiser and Wallasey Guardian*, 7 June 1919, quoted in Murphy 1995, p. 18.
28. *East End News*, 18 January 1921.
29. *Daily Chronicle*, 15 December 1920.
30. Shang 1984, p. 10.
31. Lynn 1982, p. 10.
32. Broady 1952, pp. 8–9; Lee 1998, pp. 112–113.
33. *East End News*, 20 February 1934.
34. On the 10,000: Li and Chen, eds, 1991, p. 273.
35. Lian Guan 1981 [1978], p. 108.
36. Li and Chen, eds, 1991, p. 273.
37. Pairault 1995, pp. 25–28.
38. Xu Bin 1957, pp. 4 and 7; Chen Sanjing 1986, 33–35; Lian Guan 1981 [1978], p. 108.
39. Chen Ta 1940, ch. 9.
40. Summerskill 1982, p. 4; Baker 1994, p. 293.
41. Parker 1995, p. 56.

42. Summerskill 1982, p. 88.
43. *Evening News*, 7 October 1920; *Star* (London), 17 June 1919; Craggs 1983, p. 59; PRO, HO 45/8962 and HO 45/11843, pt 1. The story of one of the aerodromes, in Suffolk, was told in 'From the East to the Western Front: A Forgotten Army of Chinese Labourers,' BBC Radio Four, 7 March 2002.
44. Craggs and Lynn 1985.
45. PRO, HO 45/11843, pts 1 and 2.
46. Broady 1952, p. 9.
47. *Siyu* 丝语, August–September 1987.
48. Clegg 1997, pp. 144–145.
49. *Sunday Express*, 19 November 1944.
50. Collins 1957, p. 229.
51. *Liverpool Echo*, 25 March 1927, cited in Broady 1952, p. 9.
52. Broady 1952, pp. 9–10.
53. Foley and Foley 2006 includes a report on research into the Chinese seamen who were forced to leave.
54. Yi Shan 1992, p. 9; Wu Lehua, ed., 1994, p. 179; Whittingham-Jones 1982 [1944]. The *East London Advertiser* of 21 February 1942, lists fourteen 'Chinese from Pennyfields' who had died at sea; others had been killed earlier.
55. Hing 1993, p. 76, writing about Chinese miners and railroad workers in the United States.
56. PRO, HO 213/926.
57. *News Chronicle*, 19 August 1946.
58. *Liverpool Daily Post*, 14 October 1947.
59. PRO, HO 213/926.
60. Broady 1955, p. 68.
61. Craggs and Lynn 1985.
62. Shang 1984, p. 10.
63. Xu Bin 1957, pp. 63–64; Huaren jingji nianjian 1994, p. 404.
64. Ng 1968, pp. 19–20.
65. Shang 1984, p. 10.
66. House of Commons 1985, vol. 3, p. 182.
67. Ng 1968, p. 20; Shang 1984, p. 10; *Liverpool Daily Post*, 1 August 1962 (excerpted in Lynn 1982); Zhang Yunfeng et al. 1992, p. 40; Collins 1957, pp. 229–230.
68. On the Zhejiangese, see Xu Bin 1957.
69. Hood 1998; Christiansen 1998a, p. 22.
70. Chen Huaidong and Zhang Liangmin 1998, p. 73.
71. That is, Xinning 新宁 (Sunning in Cantonese).
72. Called Taishanese or Toysanese (after the Mandarin and Cantonese names of Taishan, one of the four counties).
73. Christiansen 1998a, pp. 1–11; see also the relevant entries in Pan, ed., 1998.
74. Xu Bin 1957, p. 63; Hu Zhiqiang 1989, p. 21.
75. Wubben 1986, p. 59.
76. Shang 1984, pp. 9–10; *Sing-tao* 星岛, 14 April 1987.
77. Chung 1999, p. 49.
78. Shang 1984, p. 8.
79. Chung 1999, pp. 48–61.

80. Chen Huaidong and Zhang Liangmin 1998, p. 76.
81. Baker 1994, pp. 292–293.
82. Kwok 1998b, p. 201.
83. Hu Zhiqiang 1989, p. 21; Huaren jingji nianjian 1994, p. 404.
84. Him Mark Lai 1998, p. 261.
85. Cheung 1975, p. 21.
86. Tai 1987; Christiansen 1998a, pp. 17–21.
87. Cheung 1975, pp. 22–23.
88. Benton 1983, p. 30.
89. Christiansen 1998a, pp. 7–9. Christiansen 2003 summarises the author's findings on this and other relevant issues.
90. Hu Zhiqiang 1989, p. 25.
91. House of Commons 1985, vol. 1, p. cvii; vol. 2, second pagination, p. 1; Baxter 1988, pp. 106–109; Baker 1994, pp. 293–294; Christiansen 1997b.
92. On the Man lineage, see Watson 1975.
93. Watson 1975, p. 76.
94. Baker 1994, p. 295, and 1986, p. 308.
95. Liao 1992, p. 30.
96. Baker 1994, pp. 294–295; Watson 1977b, pp. 188–192.
97. Song 1996, pp. 90–91.
98. Pang 1993, p. 123.
99. See PRO, HO 344/30, for an example from January 1960, even before the Commonwealth Immigration Act of 1962 made all but a few Commonwealth citizens subject to immigration control.
100. On the work-permit system, see Gordon 1985, pp. 11–13, and Evans 1983, pp. 153–154.
101. Watson 1977b, p. 188.
102. PRO, HO 344/30.
103. Watson 1977b, p. 188; Liao 1992, pp. 33–35.
104. London Office 1973, p. 23.
105. Cheung 1975, p. 25.
106. Shang 1984, p. 22.
107. Cheung 1975, p. 25; Evans 1983, p. 154.
108. Taylor 1987, p. 37.
109. Evans 1983, p. 157; Gordon 1985, pp. 11–12.
110. Watson 1977b, p. 188.
111. Hu Zhiqiang 1989, p. 26; Huaren jingji nianjian 1994, p. 404; Fang and Xie 1993, p. 279; Liu Hanbiao and Zhang Xinghan 1994, p. 14; Owen 1994, p. 2; Christiansen 1998a, p. 13.
112. Walton Look Lai 1998, p. 249; Willmott 1998, p. 296.
113. Oxfeld 1998, p. 345; Pineo 1998.
114. Hall 1998, p. 91.
115. Cheng 1996, pp. 167–168.
116. Bhachu 1985.
117. Merriman, ed., 1993, p. 185.
118. House of Commons 1985, vol. 2, p. 146, and vol. 3, p. 165.
119. Shang 1984, p. 60; Merriman, ed., 1993, p. 186; Cheng 1994, pp. 90, fn. 46, and 113.

120. *Record of the Seminar* 1986.
121. Shang 1984, p. 54.
122. Brah 1996, p. 34.
123. Bang and Finlay 1987, pp. 1–2.
124. Shang 1984, p. 54; House of Commons 1985, vol. 3, pp. 165–166; *Record of the Seminar* 1986; Bang and Finlay 1987, pp. 1–2.
125. Merriman, ed., 1993, p. 185; Shang 1984, p. 60; House of Commons 1985, vol. 2, p. 147, and vol. 3, pp. 165–168; *Record of the Seminar* 1986; Cheng 1994, p. 90, fn. 46.
126. Tana 1998, p. 230.
127. Merriman, ed., 1993, pp. 186–187.
128. Shang 1984, pp. 60–61; House of Commons 1985, vol. 3, pp. 165–168.
129. House of Commons 1985, vol. 3, p. 165; Cheng 1994, pp. 18 and 113; Cheng 1996, pp. 164 and 178.
130. Chinese Information and Advice Centre 1986, p. 15.
131. Bang and Finlay 1987, p. 13; Cheng 1996, p. 164.
132. Chen Huaidong and Zhang Liangmin 1998, p. 78.
133. On the Vietnamese Chinese in France, see Pairault 1995; Khoa 1994; and Live Yu-Sion 1994.
134. Li and Chen, eds, 1991, p. 277; Live Yu-Sion 1998a, p. 106.
135. Live Yu-Sion 1998b, p. 315.
136. Tyau 1920, pp. 302–304; Zhang Ningjing 1988, p. 40. Harnisch 1999, pp. 31–48 is a good introduction to overseas study in the early period.
137. Freeberne 1979, p. 29.
138. Ng 1968, p. 13.
139. Tyau 1920, pp. 305–306 and 311–317. According to Harnisch 1999, pp. 163, fn. 57, and 202, there were fewer than 70 Chinese students in Germany during the war and probably even fewer in France.
140. Ng 1968, pp. 13–14. For a list of doctoral dissertations by Chinese students in the United Kingdom between 1916 and 1961 and analyses of their distribution by institution and field of study, see Yuan 1963.
141. Harnisch 1999, pp. 268–277.
142. On the Indonesian Chinese students in the Netherlands, see Galen (1989).
143. Ng 1968, p. 14, mentions the political tradition of the Chinese Student Unions in France and the United States.
144. Levine 1985 and 1993.
145. Harnisch 1999, p. 395.
146. Galen 1989, pp. 136–137.
147. Li Minghuan 1998a, p. 14.
148. Huaqiao jingji nianjian 1996, p. 614.
149. Chen Huaidong and Zhang Liangmin 1998, p. 81.
150. Zeng 1997. According to Li Minghuan 1998a, p. 14, there were between fifty and sixty thousand mainland students and their dependants living in France and Britain in the late 1990s.
151. *Times Higher Education Supplement*, 20 April 2001, p. 1, and 1 March 2002, p. 14.
152. *Times*, 21 April 2004.
153. Zeng 1997.

154. Li Minghuan 1999b, p. 51. On the high degree of crossover from temporary to permanent status among such immigrants, see Stalker 2000 and Iredale 2000.
155. Berthoud, Modood, and Smith 1997.
156. Owen 1994, pp. 1–2; Chan and Chan 1997, pp. 125–126.
157. Cheng 1994, p. 55.
158. The Labour Force Survey is conducted every second year on the basis of a sample covering about 0.5 per cent of all households. It allows an analysis of population by country of birth, ethnic origin, and nationality, and parents' country of birth (Taylor 1987, pp. 40–41). Sampling errors and differences in response rates across the years and population groups mean that surveys of this sort are not wholly reliable. The Labour Force Survey was found in 1991 to have underestimated the size of ethnic groups by about 10 per cent. Even so, the broad outlines of its findings were confirmed. Its data provide a rough measure of the population of Chinese origin, by birthplace, in the period preceding the 1991 Census.
159. Hu Zhiqiang 1989, p. 25; Huaren jingji nianjian 1994, p. 404.
160. Cheng 1996, p. 166.
161. Chan and Chan 1997.
162. Owen 1994.
163. Li Minghuan 1998a, p. 11; Chen Huaidong and Zhang Liangmin 1998, p. 83.
164. Hu Zhiqiang 1989, p. 25; Huaren jingji nianjian 1994, p. 404.
165. Monitoring Group 2002, p. 6.
166. Chan and Chan 1997, p. 124.
167. Destexhe and Göbel 1995; Liu Hanbiao and Zhang Xinghan 1994, p. 14.
168. Howlett, ed., 1999, p. 394.
169. Gainer 1972, p. 103.
170. Evans 1983, p. 6.
171. On the trade, see Wubben 1986, pp. 119–122.
172. See the relevant chapters in Pieke and Mallee, eds, 1999.
173. Li Minghuan 1999b, p. 52.
174. John Gittings, writing in the *Guardian*, 20 June 2000, listed three routes: by train to Hungary or Poland, by air to Turkey or Greece, and by air to Moscow, from Thailand or Malaysia.
175. Hood 1998, p. 67.
176. *The Independent*, 20 June 2000.
177. Home Office 2003.
178. 'At least one third' of the 58 Chinese who died in the Dover tragedy in June 2000 were said by an ethnic-Chinese lawyer to have relatives in Britain (*Guardian*, 5 July 2000).
179. Li Minghuan 1999b, p. 52; Nyíri and van Lokven 1999.
180. This paragraph is based on Nyíri 2000.
181. Fung and Chen 1996, pp. 23–26.
182. The Fujianese pioneers do not seem to show up in the records. According to Nyíri (personal communication), this is because they used Hong Kong travel documents.
183. Pieke 2000, pp. 7–8, 12, and 27.
184. Pieke 2001, p. 3.

185. Pieke, Nyíri, Thunø, and Ceccagno 2004, p. 60.
186. Pieke, Nyíri, Thunø, and Ceccagno 2004, p. 134.
187. See Light and Bonacich 1988 for a definition of 'class resources'.
188. Interview by Gregor Benton, Jabez Lam and Bobby Chan, 20 December 2001. See also writings by Daniele Cologna on the migrants in Milan from Shenyang.
189. Pál Nyíri, report, Chinese Studies Centre, Oxford, 11 December 2001.
190. Pieke 2000, p. 23.
191. Interview by Gregor Benton, Jabez Lam, 20 December 2001.
192. Pang 1993, pp. 15–18.

3 The Chinese economy in Britian

1. Gainer 1972, p. 2.
2. Mei Weiqiang and Zhang Guoxiong, eds, 2001, p. 80.
3. Gainer 1972, p. 3.
4. Xiaojian Zhao 2002, p. 66.
5. Choi 1971, p. 111.
6. On anti-Chinese racism in the United States and Australia, see Markus 1979.
7. Lyman 1974, pp. 73–74.
8. Xinyang Wang's study of the Chinese immigrant experience in New York draws a distinction between European immigrants, many of them artisans and skilled tradesmen, and immigrants from China, mostly from a peasant background, and goes on to argue that this difference strongly shaped the subsequent evolution of the two groups. Skilled immigrants from Europe were more likely to view their settlement in the United States as permanent and to join trade unions and develop an interest in American politics. The Chinese, on the other hand, were less familiar with capitalism and its effects. However, the diversity of Chinese employment in both the United States and Australia in the early years suggests that the barrier to skilled work beyond the ethnic enclave was not insuperable and that the consignment of Chinese to the American ethnic economy in later years was the result more of racist exclusion than of Chinese unfamiliarity with wage labour. Wang's contention that only a tiny percentage of Chinese immigrants were artisans is also questionable, both because of the sources on which it rests and other evidence that suggests a range of skills beyond farming. Wang bases his idea that the number of artisans, skilled workers, and professionals was exceptionally small among Chinese immigrants to the United States on Han-sheng Chen's estimate of the ratio of tenants to wage labourers in Chinese sending areas (Han-sheng Chen 1936, pp. 115–121), which is not necessarily relevant, and on the *Annual Report of the Immigration Commission, 1901–1910*, which is not necessarily accurate (Xinyang Wang 2001, pp. 17–32).
9. Hu Tingzhen, *Zhongguo shibao, Renjian fukan*, 14 January 1983, cited in Zhang Ningjing 1988, pp. 38–40; Pratt 1943, p. 11.
10. James Ma, ed., 1961, pp. 8–9; Evans 1997, p. 258.
11. Whittingham-Jones 1944, p. 5.

12. Jones 1979, p. 397.
13. Zhang Yunfeng et al. 1992, p. 38.
14. *National Register*, 13 October 1813.
15. We owe these hunches to Mary Heidhues and Ian Welch, in personal communications. Quanzhou was transliterated as Cinceo (pronounced Chincheo) in an English translation (from the Italian) of Juan Gonsalez de Mendoza's history of China (Hudson 1931, p. 245).
16. Cited in Ng 1968, pp. 16–17.
17. Sherwood 1991, p. 242, fn. 7.
18. Lau 2002, p. 9, has a reproduction of John Anthony's Bill of Naturalisation. Another fabulously wealthy Chinese, Charles Hope, born in Macao as the illegitimate son of a British man, also applied for denization in 1848, after living and trading Britain for 30 years. See PRO, HO 45/8962.
19. *The Gentleman's Magazine*, August 1805, p. 779.
20. Jones 1979, p. 397.
21. On discriminatory measures enacted in the nineteenth century, see Kitchen 1980, pp. 178–182.
22. For the purposes of comparison, seafarers and passengers on British ships entering Glasgow between 1904 and 1913 included 3 per cent Chinese and 19 per cent 'East Indian' (McFarland 1991, pp. 495–499).
23. May 1973, pp. 34–36.
24. Gordon 1985, pp. 6–7.
25. Sherwood 1991, p. 234.
26. PRO, HO 45/11843, pt 1.
27. Maria Lin Wong 1989, pp. 25 and 96.
28. The shipping-master should not be confused with the shipmaster, the captain of a ship.
29. Craggs 1983, p. 27.
30. Strictly speaking, to crimp meant to induce a seaman to desert, but its usual definition was to find employment for him. Many non-Chinese boarding-masters were also associated with crimping – as well as with prostitution and drinking dens – but to a lesser extent than their Chinese counterparts (Daunton 1978, pp. 180–184).
31. Kitchen 1980, pp. 149–150.
32. Cited in Daunton 1978, pp. 176–177.
33. Kitchen 1980, pp. 149–155 and 548.
34. Daunton 1978, p. 192.
35. *East End News*, 15 May 1908; *The Seaman*, February 1908, p. 9.
36. *Chinese Invasion of Great Britain: A National Danger, A Call to Arms* (1909). MSS 175/3/14/2I, Modern Records Centre, University of Warwick.
37. PRO, HO 45/11843, pt 1.
38. National Archives of Singapore, oral history file A000064.
39. The role of legislation in shaping the Chinese community in Britain is discussed in Chapter 6.
40. PRO, HO 45/11843, pt 2.
41. Wubben 1986, pp. 47–56. See also Li Minghuan's brief article in Shequ minsu, p. 142. For an early account of the conditions under which Chinese seafarers lived in European ports, see van Heek 1936. On the role of the

boarding-house keeper as crew-contractor (and shopkeeper) in Britain, see Jones 1979, p. 398.

42. For a description of the boarding-houses (of which there were up to fifteen) run by Chinese in Liverpool at the start of the twentieth century, see Maria Lin Wong 1989, pp. 11–13.
43. Lane 1990, p. 174.
44. Salter 1895, p. 72.
45. *De Uitkijk*, 13 October 1911.
46. The following paragraphs are based, except where indicated, on Wubben 1986, pp. 9–34. Stoomvaart Maatschappij Oceaan was a sister company of the British Ocean Steam Ship Company.
47. Wubben 1986, pp. 42–43.
48. Jones 1979, pp. 397–398.
49. Shang 1984, pp. 9–10.
50. *Report of the Commission* 1906–1907, pp. 1749–1750.
51. *The Seaman*, June 1908, vol. 1, no. 8, p. 2.
52. Jones 1979, p. 398.
53. Maria Lin Wong 1989, p. 25 and ch. 5; McFarland 1991, p. 497.
54. *Report of the Commission* 1906–1907, pp. 1749–1750.
55. Wubben 1986, p. 59.
56. Lane 1990, pp. 23, 156, and 162–164; Broady 1952, p. 9.
57. Whittingham-Jones 1944, p. 6.
58. Craggs 1983, p. 12.
59. Clegg 1997, pp. 144–145.
60. Whittingham-Jones 1982 [1944].
61. Modern Records Centre, University of Warwick, MSS 238/IT/23/1–15.
62. Lane 1990, pp. 8–9, 23, and 162; Sherwood 1991, p. 241.
63. Gordon 1985, p. 9. A few Chinese ratings who refused to ship-out from New York were deported by the British to India, to be conscripted into a Chinese army, but the Government of India and the United States Army objected on discipline grounds so the experiment had little outcome (Lane 1990, pp. 172–173).
64. Clegg 1997, p. 144.
65. Craggs and Lynn 1985; Lane 1990, pp. 164–165 and 173; Wu Lehua, ed., 1994, p. 179.
66. See Roskill 1962, p. 32 and appx C; Lane 1990, pp. 173–174 and 178–183.
67. Lane 1990, p. 169.
68. See, for example, the report in *The Seaman*, July 1908 (no. 9, vol. 1), p. 1.
69. Xinyang Wang 2001, p. 54. After the war, however, most Chinese returned to 'ethnic' jobs once the white workers were demobilised (ibid., p. 75).
70. Bernard Wong 1982, p. 8.
71. Lane 1990, pp. 157–158, 162–172, and 177. Despite Lascar militancy in the Second World War, the gap between Lascar wages (just under £6) and Chinese wages (between £13 and £16) remained huge. Whites could earn up to £24 (Visram 2002, pp. 234–248).
72. Baxter 1988, p. 75.
73. House of Commons 1985, vol. 2, 25 April 1983, p. 13.
74. Letter from Holts, reproduced in *Brushstrokes* no. 4, November 1996, p. 4; Maria Lin Wong 1989, pp. 3–4.

75. Maria Lin Wong 1989, p. 89; Falkus 1990, p. 114. According to Evans 1997, p. 258, the Holts employed their first Chinese workers in 1893.
76. Falkus 1900, pp. 271–272.
77. James Ma 1961, pp. 47 and 54; Evans 1997, p. 260.
78. Whittingham-Jones 1944, p. 18.
79. Broady 1952, pp. 12 and 48, fn. 1; Collins 1957, pp. 234–239; Shen Guanbao and Li Ling 1998b, p. 37.
80. Letter from Holts, *Brushstrokes* no. 4, November 1996, p. 4, Evans 1997, p. 261.
81. Broady 1955, p. 66.
82. May 1973, p. 85.
83. Falkus 1990, pp. 114, 307, 271–272, and 310.
84. Broady 1952, p. 12.
85. Collins 1957, pp. 234–239; Evans 1997, p. 261; Shen Guanbao and Li Ling 1998c, p. 19.
86. PRO, HO 45/11843, pt 1.
87. PRO, HO 213/926.
88. PRO, CAB 21/4972.
89. Lane 1990, ch. 7, seems to suggest as much.
90. Live Yu-Sion 1994, pp. 26–27.
91. Maria Lin Wong 1989, pp. 37, and 90.
92. *Report of the Commission* 1906–1907, pp. 1747–1749.
93. *Report of the Commission* 1906–1907, pp. 1747–1749.
94. http://www.liverpool-about.co.uk/ch_town/history_of_chinatown.htm.
95. May 1973, pp. 74 and 128. Our deduction about the launderers' status is based on the size of the (second, reduced) Chinese claim for compensation after the Cardiff 'laundry riots' of 1911: more than £500 for loss of business and £150 for damage to laundry premises. (The initial claim was for a colossal £50,000, but this was reduced by the Chinese Legation.)
96. Gainer 1972, pp. 31–35.
97. On Zhejiangese immigration, see Chen Murong 1990; and Hood 1998.
98. Xu Bin 1957, pp. 10–11; Fang and Xie 1993, p. 282.
99. Zeng Jize 1985; Dai Hongci 1982 [1905].
100. Liang and Holzman 1989, pp. 73–74; Huaren jingji nianjian 1994, p. 405; Pairault 1995, pp. 25–26.
101. Societé rationelle des étudiants-travailleurs en France.
102. On this movement, see Marylin Levine 1993; Benton, ed. and tr., 1997, ch. 2; and Liang and Holzman 1989, p. 74. The great majority of students reached France between 1919 and 1921. However, the first hundred arrived in 1913 (Live Yu-Sion 1994, p. 13).
103. Live Yu-Sion 1994, pp. 7, 12, and 25–26, and 1998a, p. 98; Pairault 1995, pp. 25–28.
104. 'From salt to soapy water' is Shang's coinage (Shang 1984, p. 8).
105. *Daily News*, 15 September 1892.
106. Ng 1968, pp. 9–10.
107. Malcolmson 1986, p. 140.
108. Mohun 1999, p. 68.
109. According to the *Daily Express*, 18 April 1907, there were 'over a hundred laundries in Liverpool and nearly as many in outlying districts', probably an exaggeration.

110. May 1973, pp. 49 and 59; Waller 1985, p. 9; De Coughrey 1994, p. 9.
111. Maria Lin Wong 1989, p. 21.
112. May 1973, p. 59; Shang 1984, p. 10.
113. Fabian Society 1902, p. 2.
114. Cited in Fabian Society 1902, p. 2.
115. Malcolmson 1986, p. xiii. Harry Tharp, in a personal communication, thinks that mechanisation was completed earlier, in the First World War or in the interwar years.
116. Tassinari 1994, pp. 108 and 120–121; Colombo et al. 1995, p. 40.
117. Maria Lin Wong 1989, pp. 21–22 and 27–28; Hing 1993, p. 51.
118. Fabian Society 1902, pp. 3–7.
119. Gainer 1972, p. 27.
120. *Report of the Commission* 1906–1907, p. 1747.
121. Cardiff City Council 1910, p. 435.
122. Markus 1979, p. 163; Hing 1993, p. 51.
123. *Minutes of the Liverpool Trades Council for 1891*, Waller 1985, p. 9. In 1890 Jeannie Mole, the Fabian wife of a wealthy local fruit merchant, set up a Union for Laundresses and Washerwomen that lamented the rise of the Chinese laundry. It was this organisation that persuaded the Trades Council to criticise the Chinese a year later (Craggs 1983, p. 53).
124. Jones 1979, p. 399.
125. PRO, HO 45/11843, pt 2.
126. May 1973, pp. 60–66.
127. Malcolmson 1986, pp. xiii and 109.
128. Mohun 1999, p. 68.
129. Quoted in Gainer 1972, p. 29.
130. Hing 1993, pp. 51–52; Him Mark Lai 1998, p. 264.
131. Inglis 1998, pp. 274–275.
132. May 1973, pp. 59–83, 127–128, and 131–132.
133. *Report of the Commission* 1906–1907, p. 1746.
134. Craggs 1983, p. 16; Maria Lin Wong 1989, pp. 21–24.
135. Malcolmson 1986, p. 140.
136. Craggs and Lynn 1985.
137. Malcolmson 1986, pp. 12 and 156.
138. Maria Lin Wong 1989, pp. 21–23 and 90.
139. Note, however, that they had a different customer base from the power laundries, which did most of their work for hotels and other institutions.
140. On garment damage, see Joan Wang 1998. On complaints about their excessive vigour, see Evans forthcoming.
141. Malcolmson 1986, pp. 16 and 22–41; Mohun 1999, pp. 209 and 217.
142. PRO, HO 45/11843, pt 2, and 45/24683.
143. Craggs and Lynn 1985; *Daily Mail*, 9 October 1920; *South Wales News*, 8 October 1921.
144. *Report of the Commission* 1906–1907, p. 1746; *Liverpool Courier*, 15 September 1916.
145. Mohun 1999, p. 55.
146. *Daily Express*, 18 April 1907.
147. Cheung 1975, p. 21.
148. Markus 1979, p. 163; Inglis 1998, p. 277.

149. Ng 1968, p. 12.
150. Jones 1979, p. 399; Waller 1985, p. 9.
151. Fabian Society 1902, p. 4.
152. Malcolmson 1986, pp. 128 and 137.
153. Renqiu Yu 1992, pp. 9–10.
154. National Archives of Singapore, oral history file A000852.
155. Mei Weiqiang and Zhang Guoxiong, eds, 2001, p. 80.
156. Cheung 1975, pp. 41–49.
157. On London, see Jones 1979, p. 399. On Cardiff, where most of the 22 laundries listed in 1910 were owned by men called Lee, see Cardiff City Council 1910. On Liverpool, see Craggs 1983, p.17.
158. Siu 1987.
159. For France: Xu Bin 1957, pp. 10–11; Live Yu-Siou 1998b, p. 313; Zhang Ningjing 1988, p. 44; Pairault 1995, p. 28. For Belgium: Xu Bin 1957, p. 69; Li Yuan and Chen Dazhang, eds, 1991, p. 295. For Germany: Xu Bin 1957, p. 24; Gütinger 1998, pp. 197–198; Huaqiao zhi, pp. 136–137; Fang Xiongpu and Xie Chengjia, eds, 1993, p. 287. For Russia: Huaqiao jingji nianjian 1996, p. 822. For the Netherlands: Li Minghuan 1999b, p. 29. For Denmark: Thunø 1997.
160. The Chinese community in Moscow was big and stable enough to support a range of trades and businesses.
161. Malcolmson 1986, p. 159.
162. Cheung 1975, p. 22.
163. Ng 1968, p. 10; Jones 1979, p. 399.
164. Harry Tharp, personal communication.
165. Renqiu Yu 1992, p. 141.
166. Wong 1982, p. 40; Ma Mung 1993, p. 10.
167. Malcolmson 1986, p. 162.
168. Renqiu Yu 1999.
169. Harry Tharp, personal communication.
170. PRO, HO 213/235; McManners 1998.
171. Rinaldi and Gillies 1991, p. 1.
172. Milligan 1995, p. 22.
173. Berridge and Edwards 1987.
174. Sweet 2001.
175. Teff 1975, pp. 10–13; Bucknell and Ghodse 1991, pp. 1–5.
176. Jones 1979, p. 398.
177. Quoted in Clegg 1994, p. 22.
178. *East London Advertiser*, 28 December 1907; *Star*, 9 January 1919.
179. *East London Observer*, 11 January 1890, and 28 December 1907.
180. *East London Advertiser*, 28 December 1907. See also Salter (1895).
181. *East London Advertiser*, 4 July 1914.
182. *East London Advertiser*, 11 November 1909.
183. Annie Lai et al. 1986, p. 21.
184. PRO, HO 45/24683.
185. Kohn 1992, pp. 65–66.
186. *Liverpool Courier*, 16 September 1916.
187. PRO, HO 45/24683.
188. *East End News*, 20 February 1934.

189. Police reports from Liverpool in early 1945 mention opium dens and exclusions from the Seamen's Pool for drug-trafficking (PRO, HO 213/808).
190. Teff 1975, pp. 18 and 41.
191. For a journalistic account of the 'Chinese connection' in London and Europe in the 1970s, see O'Callaghan 1978.
192. PRO, HO 45/24683 and Mepo 3/469; *Star*, 9 January 1919; Wubben 1986, pp. 107–109. On the role of Dutch people in Chinese-run opium-trafficking in the Netherlands, see Wubben 1986, p. 104.
193. Annie Lai et al. 1986.
194. Ng 1968; O'Neill 1972; Lynn 1982; Shang 1984; and other studies all play down or deny Chinese crime in Britain.
195. *Report of the Commission* 1906–1907, p. 1745.
196. Wade 1900, pp. 306–307.
197. Wubben 1986, pp. 104–105.
198. *Evening News* (London), 14 October 1920.
199. Taylor 1987, p. 64.
200. Shang 1984, p. 20.
201. Fang and Xie 1993, p. 291.
202. Cheung 1975, p. 81.
203. Baker 1986, p. 308.
204. Wong 1982, p. 39; Baker 1994, p. 295.
205. Jack Goody (2000) argues that the reason Chinese food became globalised whereas African food did not can be explained by the lack of a 'hierarchically differentiated cuisine in Africa', which has to do with 'the nature of land tenure and the lack of extensive socioeconomic stratification'. So 'there was no haute cuisine, no differentiated food, no higher cooking as distinct from a lower one' – and no food globalisation. However, the chop suey case shows that the globalisation of Chinese food started off not with haute cuisine but with the humblest of dishes.
206. David Y. H. Wu 2002a, pp. 56 and 64, and 2000b.
207. 'Huaqiao Huaren baikequanshu, jingji juan' bianji weiyuanhui, eds, 2000, p. 434; Liu Hanbiao and Zhang Xinghan 1994, p. 15.
208. Ng 1968, pp. 27–28; Jones 1979, p. 400; Maria Lin Wong 1989, p. 14.
209. Whittingham-Jones 1944, p. 66.
210. Baxter 1988, pp. 87–102.
211. Baxter and Raw 1988, p. 62.
212. Baxter 1988, ch. 4.
213. Goody 2000.
214. Ng 1968, p. 28; Hu Zhiqiang 1989, p. 21; Zhang Yunfeng et al. 1992, p. 40.
215. Ng 1968, pp. 28–30.
216. Whittingham-Jones 1944, p. 65; Ng 1968, p. 29.
217. Zhang Yunfeng et al. 1992, p. 40.
218. Shang 1984, p. 10; Maria Lin Wong 1989, pp. 17 and 96.
219. Cheung 1975, p. 94; Taylor 1987, p. 64.
220. Zhang Yunfeng et al. 1992, p. 40.
221. On this point, see Pairault 1995. Pairault's study rebuts a whole series of stereotypes about the ethnic-Chinese economy. (As Pierre-Étienne Wil says in his preface to Pairault's book, 'people attribute a lot to the Chinese of Paris, principally because they don't know very much about them' [Wil

1995, p. 9].) Given that Pairault's findings are so subversive of essentialist views of Chinese ethnicity, they are worth summarising in some detail. Pairault's research focuses specifically on petty entrepreneurs rather than on big business or employees, but he prefaces his study with an occupational breakdown of the Chinese population of France. This analysis is confined to people originating in Indochina, in the absence of official data on other Chinese groups. Given that qualification, which may well affect the general picture, Pairault's findings are extraordinary, and yield a picture that shatters common preconceptions about the French Chinese community. It reveals, for example, that only 30 per cent work in the services sector (including restaurants), whereas nearly 40 per cent work in light industry (and 14 per cent in commerce); and that 57 per cent are workers (qualified or not), 19.3 per cent administrative or commercial employees, and 6.9 per cent self-employed craftsmen, shopkeepers, and heads of enterprises. In other words, the popular French view of the Chinese as a self-employed restaurateur (or a rich trader from Cholon) is stereotyped. The proportion of Chinese in France in the catering sector is lower than in other European countries, and the proportion of workers is far higher (by 87 per cent) and of self-employed craftsmen, shopkeepers, and heads of enterprises somewhat lower (by 5 per cent) than in the native French population. Pairault argues that this occupational structure is a result of the immigrants' low level of education and poor French. He also points out that only 5 per cent of Chinese from Indochina had been shopkeepers or tradespeople before becoming refugees. One might also argue that the occupational profile of the French Chinese community is as it is because the community is far more heterogeneous than its counterparts elsewhere in Europe. Chinese immigration into Britain and the Netherlands accreted along chains to a stable base, gradually and over a longer period of time. The French Chinese, in contrast, arrived in a rather sudden and compact wave, from several countries (principally Cambodia, Laos, and Vietnam) and social classes. Unlike the British and Dutch Chinese, their emigration was mostly unplanned and unprepared. Culturalist studies try to account for the prevalence of small-scale enterprise in 'overseas-Chinese' communities by reference to a supposed system of 'Asian (or Chinese) values' and the 'Confucian spirit of capitalism'. Pairault, however, argues that the Chinese who are the object of his study ended up in petty commerce chiefly because of 'linguistic difficulties and a lack of capital'. The resort to commerce was the obvious alternative to wage slavery, in a society in which professional and social mobility was blocked for Chinese immigrants by a lack of qualifications (or of recognised qualifications) and an inability to speak good French. Chinese in France went into business 'not because of a real preference … but because of a total absence of alternatives'. Even Chinese who started out in France working for their compatriots (who are in many cases kin) tended, in time, to set up their own businesses and thus to escape wage slavery and social immobility in the host economy. Chinese immigrants saw this passage through employment in the Chinese enclave as an 'obligatory phase' on the journey to self-employment, during which they accumulated the know-how, experience, connections, and capital necessary for entrepreneurship. Pairault likens it to a 'decompression chamber' that allows the immigrant to adapt and accumulate knowledge, experience, relations, and resources. Pairault adduces evidence from his own study of the Chinese in France to rebut the thesis of Gordon Redding and others that a special 'Chinese spirit of capitalism' underlies ethnic-Chinese enterprise. He concludes from his data that very few Chinese had decided before arriving in France to set up businesses and that the businesses were set up on average nine years after arrival. Although more than seven out of ten Chinese entrepreneurs in France were offspring of people who had also run their own businesses, nearly always in the place of origin, nearly nine out of ten reported that their field of business activity in France was either 'totally different' from or 'barely similar' to their parents' and only 1.6 per cent judged it 'strictly identical'. Pairault shows that Chinese enterprises in France often engage in forms of economic behaviour that cannot be defined as 'rational or entrepreneurial', and that they are no more 'enterprising' than the rest of France. For example, partnerships (which comprise around 30 per cent of small enterprises) are formed to share investment rather than risks and costs, that is, they are motivated 'more by constraint than by *desire*'. The great majority of businesses are family-based. (Enterprises based exclusively on groups of friends account for less than 10 per cent of the total.) In these family businesses, production expenses, investment, and family expenses are frequently confused, and success is signalled by conspicuous consumption. They are, in a word, profoundly anti-capitalist in nature, motivated 'by an ethos not of profit but of notability'. They are run flexibly, much like peasant farms, neither sacking nor hiring as the markets shrinks and waxes, but simply working a little less hard or a little harder. Moreover, few show much 'spirit of enterprise' in their choice of sector or territory: most stay within the protected or captive ethnic market, as if 'they had never migrated', and few establish their business in non-Asian districts. Nearly half the restaurants Pairault investigated were in Chinese rather than non-Chinese parts of Paris. Few showed much inclination to innovate in their choice of menus. Within Pairault's sample, the smaller enterprises (those with fewer than six employees) were less likely to 'leave the beaten track' and show entrepreneurial drive than the bigger ones (with six or more employees). They were also more likely to remain firmly within the ethnic niche. The employees of two-thirds of the smaller enterprises in the sample were exclusively Chinese, compared with only one-third of the bigger enterprises.

222. House of Commons 1985, vol. 1, p. xi; Huaqiao jingji nianjian 1996, p. 615; 'Huaqiao Huaren baikequanshu, jingji juan' bianji weiyuanhui, eds, 2000, p. 544.

223. Cheng 1994, p. 128; Birmingham City Council 1995, p. 12. Even so, Yuan Cheng's figures are around twice as high as those for other Asians and for the Chinese in France and three times those for British whites; even the figures based on the 1991 sample are significantly higher.

224. Yuan Cheng 1996, pp. 172 and 177–178.

225. Maria Lin Wong 1989, p. 17.

226. Watson 1977b, p. 191; Taylor 1987, p. 66; Liao 1992, pp. 120–122; De Coughrey 1994, p. 9.

227. Cited in Freeberne 1979, p. 47.

228. Liao 1992, pp. 120–122.
229. Xu Bin 1957, p. 64; Wu Shaobao 1957, p. 32; Shang 1984, p. 24; Taylor 1987, p. 59.
230. Zhang Yunfeng et al. 1992, p. 40; Xu Bin 1957, p. 64; Ng 1968, pp. 29–30.
231. Liao 1992, p. 30.
232. Watson 1977b, p. 192; Shang 1984, p. 24; Song 1996, p. 104.
233. Ng 1968, p. 31; Watson 1977b, pp. 192–194; Taylor 1987, p. 62.
234. Shang 1984, p. 24; Liao 1992, p. 129.
235. Baxter 1988, p. 139; Song 1996, p. 104.
236. Ng 1968, p. 30.
237. Watson 1977b, p. 192.
238. Cheung 1975, pp. 41–49 and 99.
239. Shang 1984, p. 22.
240. Cf. Waldinger et al. 1990.
241. Ng 1968, pp. 29–30.
242. Cheung 1975, pp. 88–92; Baxter 1988, pp. 113–118; Baxter and Raw 1988, p. 65.
243. Cheung 1975, pp. 87–88.
244. Liao 1992, p. 131. For a good ethnography of Chinese catering in Britain, see Chung Yuen Kay 1985.
245. Hong Kong Public Records Office, NT 1/2120/62c, pt I, document 197 I, Hong Kong Chinese Liaison Office, London, Half-Yearly Report, April to September 1968.
246. Shang 1984, p. 25; Baxter 1988, p. 145.
247. Interview by Gregor Benton, Jabez Lam, 20 December 2001.
248. Watson 1977b, pp. 192–193.
249. Li and Chen, eds, 1991, p. 263.
250. Watson 1975, p. 114.
251. Shang 1984, p. 60; Baker 1994, p. 304.
252. Cheung 1975, pp. 98–100.
253. Watson 1977b, p. 192.
254. Taylor 1987, p. 65.
255. Cheung 1975, p. 83.
256. Freeberne 1979, p. 62.
257. Cheung 1975, pp. 82–83; Baxter 1988, pp. 96, 129–139, and 165; Baxter and Raw 1988, pp. 67–68; Liao 1992, pp. 124–129; Huaqiao jingji nianjian 1996, p. 615.
258. Song 1995, p. 285.
259. Cheung 1975, pp. 82–83 and 96; Baxter and Raw 1988, pp. 67–68; Liao 1992 pp. 124–131; Wah et al. 1996, pp. 32–36.
260. Taylor 1987, pp. 50–54; Baxter 1988, pp. 114–118, 140, and 165; Baxter and Raw 1988, p. 67.
261. Liao 1992, pp. 123–127; Song 1996, pp. 110 and 145.
262. Baxter 1988, p. 145.
263. Hu Zhiqiang 1989, p. 24.
264. Chen Huaidong and Zhang Liangmin 1998, p. 120, estimated that there were more than one thousand British-born Chinese active in the 'senior professions', a number that was 'growing daily'. Owen 1994, p. 18, showed that the largest Chinese occupations outside catering were in the

professions: science and engineering, clerical work, and health (including nursing), 'showing that high-status white-collar occupations are also a significant source of employment for Chinese men'.

265. Chen Huaidong and Zhang Liangmin 1998, pp. 101–119.
266. Runnymede Trust, cited in Cheng 1994, p. 146.
267. Cheng 1994, ch. 5.
268. Taylor 1987, p. 64; Baxter 1988, pp. 88 and 100.
269. Jones 1979, p. 401.
270. C. W. Louise Li 1995, p. 2.
271. Freeberne 1979, p. 57.
272. Freeberne 1979, p. 48; Liao 1992, pp. 137–138 and 159–172.
273. Baker 1994, pp. 302–303.
274. Cheung 1975, p. 78.
275. Hu Zhiqiang 1989, pp. 23–24; Huaqiao jingji nianjian 1996, p. 615.
276. Baxter 1988, pp. 137–138.
277. Owen 1994, p. 17.
278. Hu Zhiqiang 1989, pp. 23–24; Huaren jingji nianjian 1994, p. 405; Huaqiao jingji nianjian 1996, p. 615; Chen Huaidong and Zhang Liangmin 1998, pp. 102–104; 'Huaqiao Huaren baikequanshu, jingji juan' bianji weiyuanhui, eds, 2000, p. 544; Monitoring Group 2002, p. 6.
279. Pieke et al. 2001.
280. Live Yu-Sion 1994; Pairault 1995.
281. *East End News*, 21 July 1916; Craggs 1983, p. 33.
282. *Daily Express*, 1 October 1920; *Evening News*, 5 October 1920.
283. Craggs and Lynn 1985; Maria Lin Wong 1989, pp. 19–21.
284. Craggs 1983, p. 26.
285. Maria Lin Wong 1989, pp. 14 and 45–46.
286. See, for example, Heek 1936; Brakenhoff 1984; Wubben 1986, pp. 145–152.
287. Ng 1968, pp. 32–33.
288. Craggs and Lynn 1985.
289. Craggs 1983, p. 26.
290. PRO, HO 45/11843, pt 1; *South Wales News*, 8 October 1921.
291. Gordon 1985, p. 11.
292. Craggs 1983, pp. 60–61; Wubben 1986, pp. 110–122; PRO, HO 45/24683 and Mepo 3/469.
293. House of Commons 1985, vol. 1, p. lxxiii; Maria Lin Wong 1989, pp. 33 and 61.
294. Annie Lai et al. 1986, pp. 18–21. See also *Daily Express*, 1 October 1920.
295. *Daily Mail*, 9 October 1920.
296. *Daily Express*, 1 October 1920.
297. See, for example, *East End News*, 29 May 1915, and 21 June 1918. The game continued to be played by Chinese in Pennyfields in later years (*East End News*, 20 December 1946).
298. *Evening News*, 6 October 1920; *East End News*, 12 October 1917.
299. Cheung 1975, pp. 120–121.
300. Ng 1968, pp. 63–66.
301. Shang 1984, pp. 31–32.
302. Baker 1994, p. 296.
303. Cheung 1975, p. 122.

304. Ng 1968, pp. 63–64; Shang 1984, pp. 31–32; House of Commons 1985, vol. 1, pp. lxxiii–lxxv; Baker 1994, p. 296.
305. Owen 1994, pp. 16–17; Modood 1997a, pp. 123–124. See also Cheng 1994, p. 124.
306. Cheng 1996, pp. 176–178.
307. Baxter and Raw 1988, p. 61.
308. Song 1996, pp. 106 and 287–289.
309. O'Neill 1972, pp. 65–66.
310. Modood 1997a, pp. 121 and 129.
311. Ward 1987.
312. Modood 1997a, p. 89. Cf. Owen 1994, p. 21, and Chan and Chan 1997, p. 129.
313. Owen 1994, pp. 20–22; Cheng 1996, pp. 175 and 178; 1994, p. 13.
314. Hu Zhiqiang 1989, p. 24; Li and Chen, eds, 1991, p. 263; Cheng 1994, pp. 127–128; Huaqiao jingji nianjian 1996, p. 619; Sally Chan 1997, p. 212; Parker 1998a, p. 307.
315. Liu Hanbiao and Zhang Xinghan 1994, p. 18.
316. Baker 1994, p. 305; Chan and Chan 1997, p. 130.
317. Chen Huaidong and Zhang Liangmin 1998, pp. 108–109.
318. For the exact proportions formed by the newer groups, see Chan and Chan 1997, pp. 125–126.
319. This argument is developed by Chen Huaidong and Zhang Liangmin 1998; see in particular pp. 181–209. Some of Chen and Zhang's points are perhaps relevant less to Britain than to mainland Europe, where foreign Chinese traders and manufacturers are more likely to experience language difficulties.
320. Huaqiao jingji nianjian 1996, pp. 615–616.
321. We viewed about 200 company files of firms owned by British Chinese; most banked with British banks.
322. However, Chen Huaidong and Zhang Liangmin 1998, p. 128, mention a Taiwanese firm that cooperated with a Hong Kong company to set up a CD factory in Belfast.
323. Chen Huaidong and Zhang Liangmin 1998, pp. 123, 176–177, and 201.
324. On Daloon, see Thunø 1998.
325. Modood 1997a, pp. 126–127.
326. For 'class resources', see Light and Bonacich 1988.
327. On this point, see Benton and Gomez 2001.
328. See, for example, Lever-Tracy, Ip, and Tracy 1996; Ong and Nonini 1997.
329. Ip 1999.
330. Watson 1997b, p. 192.
331. Pieke 1998, p. 13.
332. On this point, see Hodder 1996.
333. Pairault 1995, pp. 67 and 115–124. Where the French banking sector is unable to meet all the requirements of an entrepreneur, he or she might resort to traditional forms of indebtedness such as tontines, but as a rational choice and product of circumstance rather than a conservative or 'innate' ethnic reflex, and as a secondary rather than a primary means of finance. The tontine *à la parisienne* is, in Pairault's analysis, a survival destined for obsolescence rather than a vibrant, indispensable form of mutual aid.

He concludes that the spirit of Chinese enterprise in France is above all the spirit of adaptation and that capitalism can be born in Chinatown only on the ruins of the 'typically' Chinese values of frugality, thrift, and obstinacy.

334. Christiansen 1997b.
335. Ward 1987, p. 92, and 1991, p. 64.
336. Pairault 1995, pp. 115–124.
337. Redding 1990; Kotkin 1993; Fukuyama 1995.
338. Wong 1985.
339. Ng 1968, p. 31; Shang 1984, p. 53.

4 Institutions and divisions

1. Shetuan zhengdang 1999, pp. i–iv.
2. Castles 2000, p. 25.
3. Wong 1982; Mackie 1998, p. 83; Li Minghuan 1999b, pp. 75–76, 149–151, 213–215, and 224–226.
4. This paragraph is based on Li Minghuan 1999b, pp. 183–219.
5. Li Minghuan 1999b, p. 10; Shetuan zhengdang 1999, pp. i–ii.
6. On ethnic-Chinese associations organised at the European level, see Li Minghuan 1998b and Liang and Christiansen 1998.
7. Mackie 1998 gives an overview.
8. For example, Shetuan zhengdang 1999 and Zhou Nanjing, ed., 1993.
9. Li Minghuan 1999b.
10. Shetuan zhengdang 1999, p. iv. According to Li Minghuan 1999b, pp. 221–222, the number of Chinese associations in Europe grew by 791 per cent between 1950 and 1991, compared with 47 per cent in Asia and 380 per cent in America. In 1991, Europe had the smallest percentage of the world's ethnic-Chinese associations in 1991 – just 2 per cent.
11. Li Minghuan 1999b, pp. 53–66.
12. Live Yu-Sion 1994; Li Minghuan 1999b, pp. 68–73.
13. Mackie 1998, p. 85.
14. Live Yu-Sion 1998b, pp. 316–317; Li Minghuan 1999b, pp. 111–113.
15. Li Minghuan 1998a, p. 40.
16. Shang 1984, p. 34.
17. Jones 1979, p. 398.
18. Mackie 1998, p. 83.
19. Later renamed the Hui Tong (or Oi T'ung) Kung Sheung Wui 惠东工商会 (Ng 1968, pp. 49–51; Shang 1984, p. 33; Zhang Yunfeng et al. 1992, p. 39).
20. Wubben 1986, p. 59.
21. Shang 1984, pp. 32–33; Zhang Yunfeng et al. 1992, p. 39; Shetuan zhengdang 1999, p. 256.
22. Ng 1968, p. 19; Shang 1984, p. 34; Liu Hanbiao and Zhang Xinghan 1994, pp. 23–30; Christiansen 1998a, pp. 11–17; Shetuan zhengdang 1999, p. 651.
23. Chee Kung Tong's second to ninth presidents were Lai Qing 赖清, Li Qi 黎祺, Mei Dong 梅栋, Zhou Jiada 周加大, Liang Fu 梁福, Yu Wu 余五, Wu Zaorong 伍灶容, Tan Zan 谭赞, and Huang Chunyuan 黄春元. This information is based on a five-page manuscript obtained by Deng Lilan.

24. Murray 1994, pp. 33 and 40.
25. Collins 1957, p. 237; Shang 1984, p. 34; Li Minghuan 1995, pp. 35–36.
26. Manuscript shown to Deng Lilan by Kenny Tam.
27. Murray 1994, p. 34. The proliferation of closely related societies such as Hongmen, Tiandihui, and their various offshoots was the result of official proscription and the consequent adoption by members of new names (Murray 1994, p. 179).
28. Lai et al. 1986, pp. 18–20.
29. Cai Shaoqing 2000.
30. Collins 1957, p. 237.
31. Christiansen 1998a, p. 20.
32. Broady 1952, p. 14; Lynn 1982, p. 17; Shang 1984, p. 34; Christiansen 1998a, p. 16; Shetuan zhengdang 1999, p. 651.
33. Ng 1968, p. 19; Shang 1984, p. 34; Christiansen 1998a, pp. 11–17; Shetuan zhengdang 1999, p. 653.
34. Tianmen ren lüju haiwai shi bianzuan weiyuanhui, eds, 2001, p. 135.
35. Shang 1984, p. 33; Shetuan zhengdang 1999, p. 255.
36. Ng 1968, pp. 52–53.
37. The Siyinese group was fractured in the late 1940s when new arrivals from Haiyan (Hoy Yin in Cantonese), a cluster of villages in Siyi's Taishan county, set up their own Hoy Yin Association 旅英海宴同乡会 in Liverpool (Christiansen 1998a, p. 18; Shetuan zhengdang 1999, p. 252).
38. Xu Bin 1957, pp. 66–67.
39. Hu Zhiqiang 1989, p. 31.
40. Shang 1984, p. 34.
41. Ng 1968, pp. 49–55.
42. Clan associations may draw on lineage connections but differ from lineages in that they are not based on strict agnatic ties (Watson 1975, p. 123).
43. Watson 1977b, p. 197; Baker 1986, p. 311, and 1994, p. 302.
44. Shetuan zhengdang 1999, pp. 24–28.
45. Li Minghuan 1999b, p. 77.
46. Cheng 1996, p. 167. The Chinese residents of Paris live in concentrations scattered across the city's 9th, 10th, 11th, 13th, 18th, and 20th arrondissements (Li and Chen 1991, p. 276). According to Pairault (1995, p. 48), 60 per cent of the Chinese population live in and around Paris, of whom 24.3 per cent in the city itself, 19.7 per cent in the near suburbs, and 13.9 per cent in the outer suburbs.
47. Shang 1984, pp. 35–36; Li Minghuan 1998b, pp. 23–24; Shetuan zhengdang 1999, p. 397.
48. Ng 1968, pp. 27–28; Jones 1979, p. 400; 'Huaqiao Huaren baikequanshu, jingji juan' bianji weiyuanhui, eds, 2000, p. 434.
49. Shang 1984, p. 36; Shetuan zhengdang 1999, p. 648.
50. Its Chinese name actually means 'European Man's Clansmen Association'.
51. Watson 1975, pp. 102, 123, and 200.
52. Shang 1984, p. 36; Shetuan zhengdang 1999, p. 250. On the Man in the Netherlands, see Blom and Romeijn 1981.
53. House of Commons 1985, vol. 2; 2 February 1984, p. 179.
54. Watson 1975, p. 124; Watson 1977b, pp. 195–200; Shang 1984, p. 34.

55. Shetuan zhengdang 1999, pp. 253, 256, and 653; You Hailong, ed., 1996, pp. 169–173.
56. Interview by Gregor Benton, Kam Lee, 20 December 2001.
57. O'Neill 1972, p. 87.
58. Xu Bin 1957, p. 66.
59. PRO, HO 45/11843, pt 1. On the Lee clan's dominance of the laundry trade in London and Cardiff, see Jones 1979, p. 399, and Cardiff City Council 1910. On the rivalry among Chinese launderers in the United States, see Joan Wang 1998.
60. Ng 1968, pp. 56–60; Jones 1979, p. 400.
61. Watson 1977b, p. 199.
62. See, for example, the UK Chinese Catering Association 英国中华饮食业总商会, mentioned in Shetuan zhengdang 1999, p. 652.
63. See Shetuan zhengdang 1999, p. 418.
64. Interview by Gregor Benton, Thomas Chan, 18 December 2001.
65. Thunø 1997; Li Minghuan 1999b, pp. 69–74.
66. Liang and Holzman 1989, pp. 246–247; Pairault 1995, pp. 62–65 and 70.
67. Khoa 1994, p. 152.
68. Huaqiao jingji nianjian 1996, p. 628; Live Yu-Sion 1998a, p. 115.
69. Pairault 1995, pp. 115–124.
70. Ng 1968, pp. 54 and 60; Shetuan zhengdang 1999, p. 255.
71. Ng 1968, pp. 53–60; Shetuan zhengdang 1999, p. 255.
72. Shang 1984, p. 37; Liu Hanbiao and Zhang Xinghan 1994, p. 25; Jiaoyu keji 1999, p. 172; Shetuan zhengdang 1999, p. 254. On Sam Chen, see the following chapter.
73. Hong Kong Public Records Office, NT 1/2120/62c, pt I, document 197 I, Hong Kong Chinese Liaison Office, London, Half-Yearly Report, April–September 1968; GR 27/581/1969, pts I and II, document 16, Hong Kong Government Office – Quarterly Report, July–September 1970.
74. London Office 1974, p. 10.
75. Shang 1984, pp. 34–36; Shetuan zhengdang 1999, p. 649.
76. Cheung 1975; Watson 1977b, pp. 108 and 197–198; Taylor 1987, pp. 107–108.
77. See Appendix A (which provides a list of the firms we studied).
78. Most of these organisations are listed, alphabetically, in Shetuan zhengdang 1999. For the Lions and the Hong Kong Professionals Association, see also Shang 1984, p. 36.
79. Shang 1984, p. 60; Merriman, ed., 1993, p. 187; Shetuan zhengdang 1999, pp. 237, 256, and 418–419.
80. Hu Zhiqiang 1989, pp. 32–33; Liu Hanbiao and Zhang Xinghan 1994, pp. 23–24.
81. Hu Zhiqiang 1989, p. 31.
82. Liu Hanbiao and Zhang Xinghan 1994, p. 22.
83. Song Guanzhen 1992, p. 5.
84. Lynn 1982, p. 17; Zhang Yunfeng et al. 1992, p. 42.
85. You Hailong, ed., 1996, p. 42.
86. Shang 1984, p. 35. On the London Chinatown CCC, see Shequ minsu 2000, p. 221.
87. Lynn 1982, p. 17; Au 1994, p. 202.

88. Commission for Racial Equality 1987, p. 14.
89. House of Commons 1985, vol. 1, pp. xx–xxi.
90. Taylor 1987, p. 118.
91. Lynn 1982, p. 17.
92. *Liverpool Echo*, 12 December 1977.
93. Chung Yuen Kay 1985, pp. 14–15; Li Minghuan 1998b, pp. 46–52.
94. Pitson 1999b.
95. Shang 1984, p. 36.
96. Lakey 1997, pp. 184–188. In 1985, 51 per cent of Chinese lived in metropolitan counties, compared with 65 per cent of Indians, 71 per cent of Africans, 71 per cent of Pakistanis, 75 per cent of Bangladeshis, and 80 per cent of Caribbeans (Commission for Racial Equality 1987, p. 5).
97. Cheng 1996, p. 167.
98. Owen 1994, pp. 5–6 and 9.
99. Cheung 1975, p. 32.
100. Watson 1977b, p. 18.
101. Cheng 1996, pp. 167–168.
102. Dummett and Lo 1986, p. 7.
103. Baker 1994, p. 300.
104. Watson 1977b, p. 199.
105. Cheung 1975, p. 129.
106. Hu Zhiqiang 1989, pp. 27–28.
107. Xu Bin 1957, p. 65.
108. Watson 1977b, pp. 195 and 198.
109. Watson 1977b, p. 195.
110. Chung Yuen Kay 1985, pp. 12–15.
111. Broady 1952, p. 106.
112. Ng 1968, pp. 29 and 45–46; Shang 1984, p. 34.
113. Taylor 1987, pp. 102–103.
114. Wu Shaobao 1957, pp. 32–36.
115. On the Hakkas, see Leong 1997.
116. O'Neill 1972, p. 98; Shang 1984, p. 21.
117. Ng 1968, p. 55. According to Watson (1977b, p. 205), however, ethnic rivalry between Punti and Hakkas was rare in the 1970s.
118. Watson 1977b, pp. 185–186.
119. Shang 1984, pp. 22–24; Watson 1977b, pp. 183–188.
120. Shang 1984, pp. 54 and 60; Yuan Cheng 1994, pp. 18, 90 fn. 46, and 113.
121. House of Commons 1985, vol. III, pp. 165–168.
122. Walker and Rehman 1999, pp. 1–2. The study, based on a sample of 1022 people established through a name search of the electoral register, achieved a response rate of 70 per cent. As a sample-based study, its findings are less reliable than the Census, but they can be taken as indicative of trends, including a growth in immigration from mainland China and Hong Kong.
123. Pitson 1999a, p. 3; Chan and Chan 1997, p. 125.
124. Modood et al. 1997.
125. Cheng 1994, p. 55.
126. Hu Zhiqiang 1989, p. 26; Fang and Xie 1993, p. 279; Huaren jingji nianjian 1994, p. 404; Yuan Chen 1994, pp. 55–56.
127. Baker 1994, p. 305; Chan and Chan 1997, p. 130.

128. Watson 1977a, p. 12, and 1977b, pp. 195–196. Discussed in Suk-Tak Tam 1998, p. 83.
129. Cheung 1975, pp. 87–88. On the 'superexploitation' of the Chinese catering worker, see Chinese Information and Advice Centre 1986, p. 16.
130. Ng 1968, p. 32; Pitson 1999a.
131. Shetuan zhengdang 1999, p. ii.
132. Pan, ed., 1998, p. 74.
133. On Chinatowns round the world, see ch. 15 of Pan 1991.
134. Crissman 1967, pp. 200–203; see also Hodder 1996, pp. 154–155.
135. Wang Gungwu 1999, pp. 3–9.
136. Lyman 1974, p. 28.
137. Wong 1982, p. 13. However, Wong acknowledges that Chinatowns are the result of 'historical processes and interactions'.
138. Waller 1985, p. 9.
139. Watson 1975, pp. 116–119; Parker 1995, p. 78; Pieke 1998, p. 13.
140. Jones 1979, pp. 397–398.
141. *Liverpool Daily Post*, 1 August 1962 (excerpted in Lynn 1982); Ng 1968, p. 20; Shang 1984, p. 10; Zhang Yunfeng et al. 1992, p. 40.
142. O'Neill 1972, p. 94; Barker 1989.
143. Ng 1968, pp. 27–28; Watson 1977b, p. 196; Jones 1979, p. 400.
144. Watson 1975, p. 118; Shang 1984, p. 25.
145. Watson 1977b, pp. 196–197; Shequ minsu 2000, p. 221.
146. Watson 1975, p. 118.
147. Hu Zhiqiang 1989, p. 30.
148. Christiansen 1998b, p. 47, uses the term 'imaginary ghetto'. He develops his analysis further in Christiansen 2003.
149. Shang 1984, p. 34; Fang and Xie 1993, p. 265.
150. Christiansen 1998b, p. 49.
151. Parrott 1998.
152. Interview by Gregor Benton, Jabez Lam, 20 December 2001. On Shaftesbury plc, see for example: *Universal News Services*, 13 October 1987; *Financial Times*, 4 December 1998; Saturday Surveys RES1, 19 May 2001, p. 3; *AFX News Limited*, *AFX.COM*, 18 May 2000; *AFX News Limited*, *The Regulatory Service*, 18 May 2000, 12 December 2000, and 3 April 2001.
153. Branigan 2004.
154. Dodd and Muir 2005.
155. Interview with Judith Gordon and Barbara King, Liverpool City Council, 3 February 2000.
156. Muir 2004.
157. Said 1991, p. 103.
158. See Sarah Cheung's BA thesis on popular representations of London's Chinatown. Cheung describes Chinatown as 'a Saidian mini-Orient' (Cheung 1997, p. 5).
159. Wang Bowei 1994, p. 8; Shequ minsu 2000, p. 221.
160. Parker 1995, p. 77.
161. *Birmingham Evening Mail*, 17 December 1983; Parker 1995, p. 78; Gomez 1998.
162. Fang and Xie 1993, p. 266; Shequ minsu 2000, p. 221.
163. Cheung 1975, pp. 108–109.

164. On Manchester, see Aghedo 1994, p. 52. Information about the Liverpool Ropewalks scheme is from an interview with Judith Gordon and Barbara King, Liverpool, 3 February 2000.
165. Newell 1989, pp. 62–64.
166. Hu Zhiqiang 1989, pp. 28–29.
167. The term is also used by Song Guanzhen 1992.
168. Parker 1995, pp. 77–79, and 1998, p. 308; Christiansen 1998b, pp. 48–49.
169. *Liverpool Post*, 28 July 1944.
170. Newell 1989, p. 65.
171. Parker 1995, p. 81.
172. Jiaoyu keji, p. 4.
173. Zhuang Guotu 1998, p. 101.
174. Jiaoyu keji, pp. i–iv.
175. On these issues, see Wang Gungwu 2000.
176. By far the best study on Chinese education (including the Chinese schools movement) in Britain is Taylor 1987. For a brief survey of Chinese schools in London and Manchester, see Liu Hanbiao and Zhang Xinghan 1994, pp. 19–20.
177. Tyau 1920, pp. 311–316.
178. *Daily Telegraph*, 26 June 1920; *East London Observer*, 25 December 1920.
179. Jiaoyu keji 2000, p. 173.
180. Ng 1968, pp. 19 and 69–70; Lornita Wong 1992, pp. 63–64.
181. Collins 1957, p. 233; O'Neill 1972, p. 109.
182. Ng 1968, pp. 69–70.
183. *Liverpool Post*, 28 July 1944.
184. Zhang Yunfeng et al. 1992, p. 48.
185. Ng 1968, p. 70; Shang 1984, p. 34.
186. Lornita Wong 1992, p. 71; Hu Zhiqiang 1989, pp. 34–35; Zhang Yunfeng et al. 1992, p. 48.
187. House of Commons 1985, vol. 1, p. xxxiv.
188. Descriptions of such schools in Guangdong can be found in the oral history files of the National Archives of Singapore.
189. Cheung 1975, pp. 171–173; Taylor 1987, pp. 78–80 and 201–205.
190. Shang 1984, pp. 34–36 and 52; Hu Zhiqiang 1989, p. 35; Lornita Wong 1992, p. 79; Zhang Yunfeng et al. 1992, pp. 45–51; You Hailong, ed., 1996, pp. 46–49; Jiaoyu keji 1999, p. 173; Shetuan zhengdang 1999, p. 649.
191. Taylor 1987, pp. 184–189.
192. Fang and Xie 1993, p. 270; Li and Chen 1991, p. 263.
193. Taylor 1987, p. 191.
194. Hu Zhiqiang 1989, pp. 36–37; Jiaoyu keji 1999, p. 171.
195. Zhang Yunfeng et al. 1992, p. 49; You Hailong, ed., 1996, pp. 45–48.
196. A study in the early 1990s showed that 70 per cent of Chinese teenagers in South Glamorgan had attended classes for at least six months (Keung Fu Lee 1993, p. 45).
197. Li and Chen 1991, p. 263; Fang and Xie 1993, p. 281.
198. Fang and Xie 1993, p. 281; You Hailong, ed., 1996, p. 45; Li Minghuan 1998, p. 37. See Zhang Yunfeng et al. 1992, p. 49 for a list of the places where there were Chinese-language schools in the early 1990s.
199. Taylor 1987, pp. 185–188; Lornita Wong 1992, p. 72.

200. Most of these French Chinese classes were organised by Chinese associations. The oldest Chinese school in France was set up in 1982 in the 19th arrondissement of Paris by the Association of Chinese in France, with up to 400 pupils distributed across several classes. (See Live Yu-Sion 1994, pp. 50–51; Fang and Xie 1993, p. 283; and Li and Chen 1991, p. 279.)
201. Live Yu-Sion 1998b, p. 316.
202. Taylor 1987, p. 180.
203. Live Yu-Sion 1994, p. 50.
204. Christiansen 2003, pp. 16–17 and 124.
205. Anderson 1983; Xiaojian Zhao 2002, p. 6.
206. Xinwen chuban 1999, pp. i–v.
207. On this last point, see Carstens 1988.
208. Xinwen chuban 1999, pp. iv–v. Xiaojian Zhao 2002, ch. 5 documents the Chinese American 'press in transition'.
209. Xinwen chuban 1999, pp. xv–xvii.
210. Zhong Shuhe, ed., 1989, p. 62. Deng Lilan provided this source.
211. Huaqiao zhi bianzuan weiyuanhui, eds, 1979, p. 368, and Xinwen chuban 1999, p. 53. According to the latter, the newspaper's full English name was *California China Mail Flying Dragon* and its founder was Edward Bosqui. Berkeley's Bancroft Library has the final issue.
212. Xinwen chuban 1999, p. 316. Lyon Municipal Library has the first issue.
213. *Daily News*, 15 April 1920.
214. Xinwen chuban 1999, pp. 195–196. Beijing Library has a set.
215. Xinwen chuban 1999, pp. 162–163.
216. The Liverpool Record Office has a run of this journal from 1947 to 1949.
217. *Sunday Express*, 19 November 1944.
218. Xinwen chuban 1999, p. 244.
219. Liu Hanbiao and Zhang Xinghan 1994, p. 21; Xinwen chuban 1999, p. 159. Zhongshan Library in Guangzhou has nos 2–6 of *Jianguo zhoukan*.
220. Ng 1968, pp. 81–83; Shang 1984, p. 53.
221. Liu Hanbiao and Zhang Xinghan 1994, p. 22; Xinwen chuban 1999, pp. 301, 371, and 445–447.
222. On the Chinese press in France, see Tang Hongjin 1991, p. 131; Fang and Xie 1993, pp. 283–284; Li and Chen 1991, p. 279; Huaren jingji nianjian 1994, p. 405; Liang and Holzman 1989, pp. 182–188. On *Ouzhou ribao* and *Ouzhou shibao*, see also Xinwen chuban 1999, pp. 272–273.
223. London Office 1971, p. 10; 1972, p. 35; House of Commons 1985, vol. 1, p. xxvi.
224. Xinwen chuban 1999, p. 362.
225. *Siyu*, various issues, Liu Hanbiao and Zhang Xinghan 1994, p. 21; Xinwen chuban 1999, pp. 335–336.
226. House of Commons 1985, vol. 1, pp. lxxv–lxxvi; Yiu Man Chan 1989, p. 16.
227. Xinwen chuban 1999, pp. 201 and 327.
228. Parker 1995, pp. 144–155.
229. Him Mark Lai 1998, p. 273.
230. This paragraph draws on Everard 2000, pp. 36, 124, and 131.
231. Loong Wong 2001.
232. Hargreaves and Mahdjoub 1997; Mitchell 1997, p. 228; Guarnizo and Smith 1998; Tsagarousianou 2001.

233. This point is developed by Chau and Yu 2001, pp. 114–115.
234. You Hailong, ed., 2001, pp. 40 and 46.

5 Transnationalism

1. See Portes et al. 1999 for a survey of the field of transnational studies.
2. Milligan 1995, pp. 84–85.
3. Xu Bin 1957, pp. 4 and 7; Lian Guan 1981 [1978], p. 108; Chen Sanjing 1986, 33–35.
4. Cheung 1975, pp. 22–23.
5. Watson 1977b, p. 189.
6. Xu Bin 1957, pp. 85–86; Chen Sanjing 1986, pp. 3–4. Mette Thunø has written extensively about Qingtian and the Qingtianese.
7. Much of the information in this section was gained by Gregor Benton on a visit to Tianmen in December 2002. Sources consulted include Tianmen ren lüju haiwai shi bianzuan weiyuanhui, eds, 2001, and Liu Yan 2001. Pamela So provided some information about her Hubeinese ancestors. She has written it up in 'Annie's Story', an unpublished manuscript.
8. Xu Bin 1957, pp. 7 and 86; Hubei sheng Tianmen shi 1989.
9. This figure was given in an interview with Wang Jianming 王建鸣, Mayor of Tianmen.
10. Li and Chen 1991, p. 35.
11. Xu Bin 1957, pp. 10–11, 45, and 52–54; Huaqiao zhi 1979, p. 137; Huaren jingji nianjian 1994, p. 406; Galli 1994, p. 76; Pairault 1995, p. 28. Some sources attribute these activities in Europe to Shandongese rather than Hubeinese.
12. Activists in the European Chinatowns lament the absence of a communal memory of heroic struggles and undertakings of the sort that promotes ethnic identification in the larger Chinese settlements of Southeast Asia and North America. They see themselves as a 'people without history'. They know next to nothing about the beginnings of Chinese immigration to Europe, and their chances of learning more dwindle by the year. In this context, it is important to preserve the legend of the Hubeinese trek to Europe. It has a grounding in hard fact, despite its portrayal of endurance verging on the mythical. (An analogy is with China's other Long March, by Mao and his comrades, spun by propagandists into a focus for 'pious wonderment and burning ambition'.) Given that the Tianmenese pioneers who 'opened up' Europe are long since dead and left no known writings, the story of their journey is susceptible to exaggeration and embellishment. Officials of Tianmen's Overseas Chinese Bureau have collected migrants' letters, documents, and the oral testimony of relatives and survivors for a history of Tianmenese emigration, but the records are from the younger settlements in Asia, while the history of the European Tianmenese remains wrapped in obscurity. Meanwhile, Pam So and other descendants in Britain collect family histories and write down childhood recollections. In spite of the limitations of evidence, this endeavour to retrieve will help enrich the communal memory of early Chinese immigration.

13. Stephanie Po-yin Chung 1999, p. 49.
14. *Report of the Commission* 1906–1907, p. 12.
15. Normally, indenture is not associated with the recruitment of Chinese labour to Europe.
16. Mei Weiqiang and Zhang Guoxiong 2001, p. 141.
17. National Library of Australia, Oral History Project, TRC 2724, Arthur Lock Chang, and TRC 3662, Albert Chan.
18. McKeown 2001, pp. 69–76; Xiaojian Zhao 2002, pp. 40–47.
19. National Archives of Singapore, oral history file A000852.
20. Broady 1952, p. 105; Maria Lin Wong 1989, pp. 40 and 92.
21. Shang 1984, p. 8.
22. For Belgium, see Xu Bin 1957, p. 69; Li Yuan and Chen Dazhang, eds, 1991, p. 295. For Germany, see Yao 1988, pp. 51–52. For Scandinavia, see Xu Zhiwei 1991, pp. 38–39.
23. Craggs 1983, p. 14.
24. Interview by Gregor Benton, Frank Soo, 11 March 2002. Soo Yao raised a family in Britain, where he became a successful businessman. Part of his story was told in 'From the East to the Western Front: A Forgotten Army of Chinese Labourers', BBC Radio Four, 7 March 2002.
25. Craggs 1983, p. 26; Craggs and Lynn 1985.
26. http://www.liverpool-about.co.uk/ch_town/history_of_chinatown.htm.
27. Shen Guanbao and Li Ling 1998a, p. 21.
28. Ng 1968, p. 77.
29. Broady 1952, pp. 103–105; Shen Guanbao and Li Ling 1998a.
30. Shen Guanbao and Li Ling 1998a, p. 26.
31. National Library of Australia, Oral History Project, TRC 2724, Arthur Lock Chang.
32. Shen Guanbao and Li Ling 1998c, p. 19.
33. Sivanandan 1982, p. 102.
34. Stephanie Po-yin Cheung 1999, pp. 48–50.
35. Shen Guanbao and Li Ling 1998a,b,c.
36. Shang 1984, p. 53; Benton 1987, pp. 30–31; Christiansen 1997b.
37. In 1986, when the committee drafting the Hong Kong Basic Law was discussing the status and rights of residents of the New Territories after 1997, Hong Kong immigrants in Britain demanded that the words 'overseas Chinese' be added to the relevant clause. See 'Yingguo Huaqiao yaoqiu baozhang quanyi lieru jiben fa nei' (Overseas Chinese in Britain demand that guarantees of their rights be inserted into the Basic Law), *Dongfang ribao*, 23 August 1986, cited in Wu Qiuyu 1999, p. 199. In the legislation, 'indigenous inhabitant' was interpreted as a person who was in 1898 a resident of an established village in Hong Kong or who is descended through the male line from that person (http://www.legislation.gov.hk/eng/home.htm).
38. Watson 1977b, pp. 182–190.
39. Hong Kong Public Records Office, NT 1/2120/62c, pt I, document 179, District Commissioner, New Territories, 10 June 1968; Ng 1968, pp. 79–81; Shang 1984, p. 53. These figures exclude bank and other forms of remittances.
40. House of Commons 1985, vol. 1, pp. xi–x.

41. Ng 1968, pp. 85–86; Cheung 1975, p. 223; Shang 1984, pp. 53–55; Berthoud 1997, pp. 166–167.
42. Berthoud and Beishon 1997, p. 51; Modood 1997b, pp. 313–314.
43. Portes et al. 1999, pp. 228–229.
44. On the Chinese resort to pidgin for communication with officers, see Craggs 1983, p. 13.
45. Xiaojian Zhao (2002, ch. 7) develops a similar argument: 'the struggle between rightist and leftist factions [in the US Chinatown in the late 1940s] grew into a tense and dangerous rivalry that enabled the US government to intervene in the community's affairs' to devastating effect and the resulting pressures led to a recognition of the need to construct an American Chinese identity.
46. Watson 1977b, p. 200.
47. Romeijn 1987, p. 80.
48. You Hailong, ed., 1996, p. 159.
49. Li Minghuan 1998a.
50. On these associations, see You Hailong, ed., 1996, pp. 150–176.
51. Liang and Christiansen 1998; Li Minghuan 1998b, pp. 27–39; Shetuan zhengdang 1999, pp. i–ii.
52. Watson 1977b, pp. 183–184.
53. Shang 1984, p. 24.
54. Li Minghuan 1998b, p. 31; Shetuan zhengdang 1999, p. 394.
55. Watson 2004.
56. Shetuan zhengdang 1999, pp. 86, 172, and 530.
57. Shetuan zhengdang 1999, p. 662.
58. Christiansen 1998a, pp. 28–29.
59. Shetuan zhengdang 1999, pp. 241, 238, 252, and 239.
60. Li Minghuan 1998b, pp. 37 and 43; Nyíri 1998, pp. 358–363; Shetuan zhengdang 1999, pp. 396 and 531; Nieto 2001, p. 156.
61. Wuyi, 'five counties', is Siyi plus one county. According to Jiangmen's Overseas Office, a total of 1,775,180 Wuyi lived overseas (scattered across 91 countries) in 1989. Of these, 1,160,308 lived in the United States, 516,426 in Asia, 53,689 in Australia, 39,595 in Europe, and 3508 in Africa. The Europe-based contingent included 26,908 in Britain and 4928 in the Netherlands (Mei Weiqiang and Zhang Guoxiong, eds, 2001, pp. 74–81). These latter figures raise more questions than they answer. In the early 1950s, Taishanese sources variously put the number of Taishanese in Britain at 365 and 4250 and those in the Netherlands at 341 and 3341 (Christiansen 1998a). (Taishan is a main constituent county of Wuyi.) Why should the British population of Wuyinese have grown so much more quickly than the Dutch? Moreover, the British estimate exceeds by around 7000 the total number of China-born Chinese counted in Britain by the 1991 Census. The inclusion in the total of British-born descendants of Wuyinese and of immigrants of Wuyinese ancestry from Hong Kong and Southeast Asia may partly account for the latter discrepancy. In any case, even if we allow for some miscounting, overcounting, and confusion of categories, these statistics suggest a considerable influx of new Wuyinese migrants since the start of the 1980s.
62. S. K. Tai 1987, p. 3; Keung Fu Lee 1993, p. 10.

63. You Hailong, ed., 1996, pp. 169–173; Shetuan zhengdang 1999, pp. 253, 256, and 653;
64. Christiansen 1998a, p. 20.
65. According to O'Neill 1972, p. 86, a Hakka Association had 'recently' formed in Liverpool.
66. Liu Hanbiao and Zhang Xinghan 1994, p. 23; Fang Xiongpu and Xu Zhenli, eds, 1995, p. 338; Shetuan zhengdang 1999, pp. 170, 239, 394, 464, and 647–649.
67. Interview by Gregor Benton, Bobby Chan, 20 December 2001.
68. Fang Xiongpu and Xu Zhenli, eds, 1995, p. 111. Teresita Ang See 2001 provides a Philippines perspective on this phenomenon.
69. Information provide by Deng Lilan.
70. Liu Hanbiao and Zhang Xinghan 1994, pp. 25–27. Sam Chen died in 2004, aged 96. For an obituary, see Murray 2004.
71. Jack Chen 1976, pp. 5–7, 16–21, and 44; Lotz and Pegg 1986, p. 8.
72. 'Zhongguo liu Ying xuesheng zhi guoqing jinian' (The Chinese students in Britain celebrate National Day), *Jiaoyu zazhi*, vol. 18, no. 1.
73. *Lü Ou zazhi*, no. 19, 15 June 1917. On Zhang Shizhao, see Zou Xiaozhan 2001.
74. *Xiandai pinglun* was founded in December 1924 and ceased publication in December 1928. Its best-known contributor was the writer and philosopher Hu Shi 胡适.
75. Zhang spent his later life in the United States, whereas Luo and Chu stayed in China and were denounced as bourgeois rightists in the late 1950s.
76. Guarnizo and Smith 1998, p. 7.
77. Fang Xiongpu and Xu Zhenli, eds, 1995, pp. 123–124.
78. Li Minghuan 1995, p. 41.
79. Xu Bin 1957, pp. 66–67. For guilds with similar names and ties set up in other countries, see Manying Ip 1998, p. 288; Shetuan zhengdang 1999, p. 321.
80. Duara 1997.
81. Bergère 1998, pp. 77 and 122.
82. On the worldwide preponderance of Siyinese in Chee Kung Tong, see Hu Zhusheng 1996, p. 469.
83. Murray 1994, pp. 90–92 and 266–267, fn. 4.
84. Cai Shaoqing 2000 makes this same point about Hongmen activities in Australia at the turn of the nineteenth century.
85. Murray 1994, pp. 5 and 178–179; Pan, ed., 1998, pp. 76 and 84.
86. For a history of the Hongmen Society overseas and of the founding of Chee Kung Tong, see Qin Baoqi 2000, pp. 348–390.
87. Li Weilin, ed., 1988, pp. 44–45; Hu Zhiqiang 1989, p. 32; Fang Xiongpu and Xu Zhenli, eds, 1995, pp. 35–39.
88. Hongmen entered Australia in several waves, both directly from China and by way of Southeast Asia, starting in the mid-nineteenth century (Cai Shaoqing 2000).
89. Shetuan zhengdang 1999, pp. 19, 44, 150, 359–360, 597, and 671.
90. Qin Baoqi 2000, pp. 348–349, describes Hongmen's early activities in Southeast Asia.
91. See Broady 1952, p. 14; Chen Min, ed., 1981, pp. 1 and 9.

92. Chinben See 1988, p. 322.
93. Huang Sande 1936; Hu Zhusheng 1996, pp. 524–525. See Wang Lubin 1996 for a critique of Hang Desan's account.
94. Qiu Qianmu 1991, pp. 702–703; Zhou Yumin and Shao Yong 1993, pp. 493–494, 583–584, 600, and 747–748.
95. For documents from the period 1950–1983, see Chen Zhuyun and Chen Qicheng, eds, 1985, vol. 2, pp. 420–474.
96. Chen Min, ed., 1981, p. 11; Shetuan zhengdang 1999, p. 678.
97. Deng Lilan, interview with Kenny Tam, 3 December 2002.
98. During his visit, he was kidnapped and held captive by the Chinese legation, but he managed to send for help and gain release (Sun Yat-sen 1897; Cantlie and Jones 1912).
99. Fang Xiongpu and Xu Zhenli, eds, 1995, p. 39.
100. Ying Zhi 1980, p. 22.
101. Huaqiao zhi bianzuan weiyuanhui, eds, 1979, p. 572; Li Minghuan 1995, p. 41.
102. Information provided by Deng Lilan. Together with his fellow anarchist Li Shizeng, Wu Zhihui founded the Society for Frugal Study by Means of Labour (Societé rationelle des étudiants-travailleurs en France; Qingong jianxue 勤工俭学) that helped Chinese to enter France, find work, find a school, and use their earnings to subsidise their studies. (On this movement, see Levine 1985; Liang and Holzman 1989; Live Yu-Sion 1994; Benton, ed. and tr., 1997.)
103. Cao Yabo 1974. For details of a number of Chinese who studied in Britain in the early twentieth century, including some who joined the Revolutionary League either directly or after living in Japan, see Feng Ziyou 1981, vol. 2, pp. 51–55, 116–119, 121–125, and vol. 5, pp. 21, 34, 178, 235, and 410.
104. Chen Xiqi, ed., 1991, vol. 1, pp. 574–585; Deng Lilan 1995, pp. 88–90.
105. Liu Hanbiao and Zhang Xinghan 1994, pp. 29–30; Bergère 1998, pp. 61–67.
106. Chen Xiqi, ed., 1991, vol. 1, p. 137.
107. Kang Youwei 1980 [1904]; Ma Honglin 1988, pp. 644–648.
108. Shanghai wenwu baoguan weiyuanhui, eds, 1995.
109. Liu Hanbiao and Zhang Xinghan 1994, p. 30.
110. *The Times*, 25 November 1913.
111. Sometimes written Wong Cow. Wong was also known as Sue Capp or Samuel Capper, and his brother as Terry Capper (Craggs 1983, p. 37).
112. Craggs and Lynn 1985. In the 1920s, Wong admitted to membership of the 'Kock Mon Tong', presumably the Guomindang (Craggs 1983, p. 36).
113. Craggs 1983, p. 5.
114. Wing Chung Ng 1998, pp. 238–239.
115. Zhonghua minguo gonghui 中华民国公会 (Public association of the Chinese Republic).
116. On this point, see Wang Gungwu 2000, p. 70.
117. This paragraph is based on Deng Lilan's research.
118. Ng 1968, pp. 52–53.
119. Broady 1952, pp. 13, 44, and 89.
120. Flatau 1920.
121. Holton 1973, p. 133. Jim Larkin, a legendary hero of the early labour movement, was among the chief disparagers of Chinese seafarers before the

war, when they were denounced by trade unionists as cheap labour out to undercut white workers. (See Bower 1936, pp. 168–169.)

122. Parker 1998a, p. 74.
123. Parts of this section are based on materials supplied by Deng Lilan.
124. Tyau 1920, p. 314.
125. 'Lundun tongxin' 1922, p. 276.
126. This is an early instance of a European Chinese transnational political association. It predates the European Chinese Federation to Resist Japanese set up in 1936, which Li Minghuan identifies as the first such organisation (Li Minghuan 1998b, p. 22).
127. 'Lundun tongxin' 1922, p. 292.
128. Craggs and Lynn 1985. In the 1920s, Wong admitted to membership of the 'Kock Mon Tong' (Guomindang) (Craggs 1983, p. 36).
129. 'Lundun tongxin' 1922, pp. 276 and 299; Zhang Daofan 1962, p. 41.
130. Felber 1988, pp. 597–598; Xu Xiaosheng 1993, pp. 54–57; Levine and Chen, eds, 2000, p. 15.
131. Levine and Chen, eds, 2000, pp. 13–15 and 123.
132. Levine and Chen, eds, 2000, p. 124.
133. Fang Xiongpu and Xu Zhenli, eds, 1995, p. 124.
134. Chen Hongmin 2002.
135. Chen Chi Ziang 1943, pp. 23–24.
136. Whittingham-Jones 1944, pp. 29–31; Yang Xianyi n. d. (Yang Xianyi 1991 is an Italian translation.)
137. Xu Xiaosheng 1993, pp. 7–9.
138. Levine 1995; Pairault 1995, pp. 25–28; Benton, ed., 1997.
139. Felber 1988, pp. 596–597; Felber and Hübner 1988a, p. 154; Benton, ed., 1997; Benton 2007.
140. The France-based Communist Youth Party, formed by Chinese work-study students in June 1922, adopted the name 'European Branch of the Chinese Communist Youth League' in the same year, on the instructions of the China-based party. Those who had already joined the party itself organised the European Branch of the Chinese Communist Party. See Hu Hua 1980, p. 93.
141. Tianjin shi renmin tushuguan, ed., 1979, p. 227; Benton, ed., 1997, pp. 27–29.
142. Lao She 1991 [1935], pp. 361–362.
143. Felber and Hübner 1988a, pp. 153–155; Benton, ed., 1997, pp. 42–43.
144. Felber and Hübner 1988b.
145. Wang Yongxiang, Kong Fanfeng, and Liu Pinqing 1985, p. 184.
146. Fang Xiongpu and Xu Zhenli, eds, 1995, p. 84.
147. Lo Wen Kan et al. 1925.
148. Fang Xiongpu and Xu Zhenli, eds, 1995, pp. 86–87.
149. These paragraphs are based on Xu Xiaosheng 1987 and 1993, except where otherwise indicated.
150. This journal was edited in Moscow under the general direction of Wang Ming, Mao Zedong's rival for the CCP leadership in the late 1930s.
151. Shum Kui-Kwong 1988, pp. 30–37.
152. Hu Qiuyuan returned to China from Japan in the early 1930s and wrote a book on Plekhanov's theory of art as well as other studies on Marxism (Leo Ou-Fan Lee 1983, p. 434).

153. Li Minghuan 1998b, pp. 22–23; Shetuan zhengdang 1999, p. 417.
154. Liu Xiaoqin 2002.
155. Huaqiao zhi bianzuan weiyuanhui, eds, 1979, p. 582.
156. Felber and Hübner 1988b.
157. Cantonese Tang Fat, anglicised as Fat Tang.
158. On Deng Fa in the UK, see He Jinzhou, Huang Daxun, and Liu Hansheng 1994, pp. 130–133; Yingguo gonghe xiehui, eds, 1997, p. 52; Li Pei 2002 [1984]; Zhu Xuefan 2002 [1979].
159. Yang Xianyi n. d., on which most of the following is based.
160. Clegg 1997, p. 23.
161. 'Qiao kanghui erdaihui yijuean gangyao' (Outline of resolution passed at the second representative meeting of the overseas anti-enemy association), *Taishan Huaqiao zazhi* (Taishan overseas Chinese journal), 30 September 1938.
162. Whittingham-Jones 1944, pp. 44–45.
163. Collins 1957, pp. 228–229.
164. Whittingham-Jones 1944, pp. 40–47.
165. Collins 1957, p. 237; Broady 1952, p. 13; Whittingham-Jones 1944, p. 15.
166. Huang Wenzhong 1986, p. 29.
167. Whittingham-Jones 1944, p. 47.
168. Examples include 'Fang Ouzhou Huaqiao liwei Liu Ruxin' (A visit to the overseas Chinese committee member Liu Ruxin), *Chung Hwa Chou Pao*, no. 199, 27 May 1948, and Yi Jia'ou 1946.
169. O'Neill 1972, p. 86.
170. Hu Zhiqiang 1989, p. 32.
171. Ng 1969, p. 53.
172. Whittingham-Jones 1982 [1944].
173. Shetuan zhengdang 1999, pp. 252–253.
174. Xu Xiaosheng 1987.
175. Yang Xianyi n. d.
176. Xinwen chuban 1999, p. 244.
177. Li Minghuan 1995, p. 64.
178. 'Xin nian' (New year), *Chung Hwa Chou Pao*, no. 178, January 1948.
179. 'Duan ping' (Short comment), *Chung Hwa Chou Pao*, no. 216, 7 October 1948.
180. 'Qiaobao yaoqiu jiejue de shi' (Solving the demands of the overseas Chinese), *Chung Hwa Chou Pao*, no. 227, 6 January 1949.
181. Liu Jingquan 1996, pp. 274–275.
182. Li Enguo 2000b, p. 339.
183. 'Guoda daibiao ji lifa weiyuan xuanju (zhuan fang) (Special report on the election of national representatives and legislative representatives)', *Chung Hwa Chou Pao*, 27 May 1948, no. 199; *Chung Hwa Chou Pao*, 1948,10,7, no. 216.
184. 'Lü Ying qiaobao wei lao Liu daibiao fanying' (British overseas Chinese celebrate the return of Representative Liu), *Chung Hwa Chou Pao*, no. 153, 3 July 1947.
185. See Li Enguo 2000c, p. 350, for an account of British Chinese efforts to support these policies.
186. Ng 1968, pp. 71–72; Li Minghuan 1998a, pp. 54–55.
187. Xu Bin 1957, p. 66.

188. O'Neill 1972, pp. 89–90.
189. Yingguo gonghe xiehui, eds, 1997; Wen Liangsheng 2001.
190. O'Neill 1972, pp. 89–90.
191. Wah-Shing still exists in Liverpool, though informants are unable to say whether the Tai Ping Club has survived.
192. Ng 1968, pp. 55–60.
193. Yingguo gonghe xiehui, eds, 1997.
194. Deng Lilan, interview with Wen Liangsheng, 22 January 2003.
195. Yingguo Lundun Huaqiao huzhu gongtuan, eds, 2001.
196. Liang Xiujing 2001, pp. 94–97 and 233–243.
197. Ng 1968, pp. 71–74.
198. Deng Lilan, interview with Kenny Tam, 3 December 2002.
199. Deng Lilan, interview with Mr Jiang, 13 January 2003.
200. Li Minghuan 1998b, p. 54.
201. An exception is the London-based Chinese Information and Advice Centre, which takes radical stands on community issues.
202. We would like to thank Chau Yick (Hong Kong) for his comments and advice regarding the relationship between Chinatown and the HKGO.
203. Director of the Hong Kong Government Office 1953, p. 1.
204. *The Star* (Hong Kong), 28 April 1972; London Office 1974, p. 9; *Lords Hansard*, 25 November 1996.
205. Benton 1983, pp. 14–30, a description based mainly on the oral recollections of Wang Fanxi. For an eye-witness account, see Zhou Yi 2002. This best-selling memoir of Hong Kong leftism by a veteran of the workers' movement and a journalist and photographer for *Wenhui bao* went through three editions within months of its publication. In 2004, Zhou Yi published a volume of memoirs and other documents relating to the Hong Kong-Kowloon battalion of the Dongjiang Column.
206. Degolyer n. d.
207. London Office 1971, pp. 4 and 23–31.
208. Hong Kong Public Records Office, CR 9/5215/56, pt IV, document 27, A Report by Mr W. V. Dickinson, September 1968.
209. Yingguo gonghe xiehui, eds, 1997, p. 43.
210. Zheng Zhuying 2001, p. 39.
211. Ling Wengcheng 2001, p. 38.
212. On the East River Detachment, see Benton 1999 and www.sen. parl.gc.ca/vpoy/english/Special_Interests/speeches/Speech%20%20HK%20-Stamp%20Society.htm.
213. Deng Lilan, interview with Li Zhizhang, January 12, 2003.
214. Wen Hongzhong 1997, p. 41.
215. Usually shortened to Zhongzhi gonghui 种植总公会.
216. Zhou Yi 2002, pp. 158–167 and 336–338.
217. Hong Kong Public Records Office, CR 9/5215/56, pt IV, document 27, A Report by Mr W. V. Dickinson, September 1968; NT 1/2120/62c, pt I, document 188, Minutes of a Meeting of the District Commissioner, New Territories, with Representatives of the Kuk, 25 July 1968; ibid., document 152, Hong Kong Chinese Liaison Office Half-Yearly Report, 9 October 1967; ibid., document 148, Hong Kong Chinese Overseas, 9 September 1967. Zhou Yi

2002, p. 287, mentions an 'overseas Chinese' among those arrested in Hong Kong in August 1967.

218. Chau Yick, personal communication, 2 September 2003.

219. For the Siyinese viewpoint, see Siyi zonghuiguan, eds, 1986. Kenny Tam, president of the See Yip Association, gives an example of the persecution to which some migrants' relatives were subjected. His grandfather, a labourer in Liverpool, bought land in Taishan with his foreign earnings. As a result, his wife was classed as a landlord in 1952 and killed (Deng Lilan, interview with Kenny Tam, 3 December 2002).

220. In other places, the Cultural Revolution had a different impact. In the United States, where the Chinese community was older and more diverse, the events in China influenced the founding in San Francisco of a Red Guard Party and a revolutionary organisation called I Wor Kuen 义和拳 (Boxers). The Red Guards, nearly all American-born, were part of a wider movement for Yellow Power that strove to unify Asian American ethnic groups and allied itself with the Black Panthers. Their thinking was shaped by the antiwar and anti-colonial movement. Although they borrowed slogans and propaganda from China and advocated pro-Beijing patriotism, they campaigned on Chinatown issues such as unemployment, bad housing, racism, and police harassment. Under the influence of the new left, they championed Regis Debray's fashionable *foco* theory of armed struggle and campaigned for Asian American studies at the universities. Their actions met with vehement opposition from Chinese anti-communists. (For a recent history of the Red Guard Party and I Wor Kuen written by onetime members, see *Asian American Revolutionary Movement Ezine*, an internet publication.) In many respects, their movement differed from that in Britain, where homeland issues held sway and most campaigners were rural immigrants.

221. Hong Kong Public Records Office, NT 1/2120/62c, pt I, document 161 I, Minutes of a Meeting, 27 November 1967.

222. Wen Hongzhong 1997, p. 41.

223. Hong Kong Public Records Office, CR 9/5215/56, pt III, document 252, Memorandum, 19 April 1968; ibid., NT 1/2120/62c, pt I, document 179, District Commissioner, New Territories, 10 June 1968.

224. *South China Morning Post*, 22 October 1968.

225. Hong Kong Public Records Office, CR 9/5215/56, pt IV, document 27, A Report by Mr W. V. Dickinson, September 1968; and document 14, appendix D, The Future Organization of the Hong Kong Government's Agencies in London, 10 September 1968.

226. Liverpool Maritime Museum archives, 6E-2579, 'Chinese Crews.' On the seafarers' movement in Hong Kong in those years, see Zhou Yi 2002, pp. 216–218.

227. London Office 1972, p. 25.

228. See, for example, the restrictions on the issue of passports mentioned in file HO 344/30 in the Public Records Office in London.

229. London Office 1971, p. 10.

230. Hong Kong Public Records Office, NT 1/2120/62c, pt I, document 148, Hong Kong Chinese Overseas, 9 September 1967.

231. London Office 1971, pp. 10 and 25, and 1972, p. 35; House of Commons 1985, vol. 1, p. xxvi; Hong Kong Public Records Office, CR 9/5215/56, pt III, document 239, A Note on the Activities of the London Office, 26 January 1968.

232. Hong Kong Public Records Office, NT 1/2120/62c, pt I, document 148, Hong Kong Chinese Overseas, 9 September 1967, and document 194 II; London Office 1971, p. 31. In the United Kingdom, the communists did their best to block their opponents' films, while in Hong Kong the colonial authorities banned the communists' films – an irony that escaped the HKGO. Zhou Yi 2002, pp. 185–188, describes the bannings.

233. Hong Kong Public Records Office, CR 9/5215/56, pt IV, document 27, A Report by Mr W. V. Dickinson, September 1968; ibid., GR 27/581/1969, pts I and II, document 19, London Office Quarterly Report, October to December 1970, 12 January 1971; London Office 1971, pp. 26–27, and 1973, p. 21.

234. Hong Kong Public Records Office, GR 27/581/1969, pts I and II, document 14, Hong Kong Government Office Quarterly Report, April to June 1970; ibid., CR 9/5215/56, pt IV, document 31D, Letter from Secretary of State to Governor of Hong Kong, 1 February 1969.

235. Ng 1968, p. 33 and 56–60; Cheung 1975, pp. 106 and 194–203; Jones 1979, p. 400; You Hailong, ed., 1996, p. 42.

236. House of Commons 1985, vol. 1, p. xxvi.

237. Benton 1983, p. 18.

238. Liang Xiujing 2001, p. 252.

239. *South China Morning Post*, 31 October 1990; *Dateline Hong Kong*, no. 3, 1991.

240. You Hailong, ed., 1996, p. 42.

241. Howlett, ed., 1999, pp. 108–109.

242. Degolyer n. d. For an explanation of the withdrawal of recognition, see Zhou Yi 2002, pp. 166–167.

243. Hong Kong Legislative Council, Report Of Proceedings, 9 December 1959, Heung Yee Kuk Bill, 1959.

244. Hong Kong Public Records Office, NT 1/2120/62c, pt I, document 179, District Commissioner, New Territories, 10 June 1968.

245. Hong Kong Public Records Office, NT 1/2120/62c, pt I, document 153, District Commissioner, New Territories, 31 October 1967; document 179, District Commissioner, New Territories, 10 October 1969; document 148, Hong Kong Chinese Overseas, 9 September 1967; document 183, Liaison with Chinese People Living in Britain; document 188, Minutes of a Meeting of the District Commissioner, New Territories, with Representatives of the Kuk, 25 July 1968; document 192, District Commissioner, New Territories; document 198, District Commissioner, New Territories, 28 October 1968.

246. London Office 1972, p. 29, and 1974, pp. 11–13.

247. *South China Morning Post*, 29 October and 3 November 1990.

248. A well-known example of the former is described in Watson 1975.

249. Wickberg 1998, p. 117.

250. Shetuan zhengdang 1999, pp. 27–28 and 648–650; Fang and Xie 1993, p. 281; Chang Kai 1992; Liu Hanbiao and Zhang Xinghan 1994, p. 23.

251. Interview with Wilfred Sng, 17 December 1999.

252. On these two organisations, see Li Minghuan 1998b, Shetuan zhengdang 1999, pp. 249 and 394, and Liang and Christiansen 1998.

253. The Nationalists also use this term, but to describe the 'diplomatic' role of their ethnic and overseas Chinese supporters.
254. British Library, Manuscripts, *Cecil Papers*, add. 51101–51193. Research on the Cecil Papers was done by Deng Lilan.
255. British Library Manuscripts, *Cecil Papers*, add. 51180, f119.
256. British Library, Manuscripts, *Cecil Papers*, add. 51183, f1 39–141.
257. Wang Ching-Chun 1941.
258. See the National Museum of Labour History, Manchester, CP/ORG/MISC/2/14.
259. 'Aims of the China Campaign', *China Bulletin*, no. 5, 1 February 1938.
260. 'What the Dockers Did in Southampton', *China Bulletin*, no. 3, 15 December 1937.
261. Whittingham-Jones 1944, pp. 58–59; Liu Hanbiao and Zhang Xinghan 1994, p. 25.
262. Arthur Clegg 1997 and Jenny Clegg 1999, the main sources for our discussion of these campaigns. (Jenny Clegg is Arthur's daughter.)
263. 'Activities of the China Campaign Committee', *China Bulletin*, no. 2, 30 November 1937.
264. 'Aid China Committee in Holland, Belgium and South Africa', *China Bulletin*, no. 4, 8 January 1938.
265. 'Famous Intellectuals Support Boycott and Embargo', *China Bulletin*, no. 4, 8 January 1938.
266. See the National Museum of Labour History, Manchester, CP/IND/HANN/11/08 and CP/CENT/ORG/20/01.
267. Tie Zhuwei 1998, pp. 97–98.
268. Tie Zhuwei 1998; Fang Xiongpu and Xu Zhenli, eds, 1995, pp. 2–3.
269. *Liverpool Courier*, 27 November 1906; Broady 1955, p. 68.
270. Ma Chaojun 1959, vol. 1, pp. 47–50 and 61; Li Yuan and Chen Dazhang, eds, 1991, p. 40.
271. *East London Advertiser*, 4 May 1912. 'White Lily' is perhaps a mistranslation for White Lotus, the name of a millenary folk-Buddhist cult that together with its offshoots was popular throughout China in the late Qing and under the Republic.
272. Lowe Chuan-hua 1933, quoted in Wales 1945, p. 202.
273. PRO, HO 45 24683.
274. PRO, HO 45/11843, pts 1 and 2; *East End News*, 9, 13, and 16 March and 4 May 1917.
275. Wales 1945, pp. 22–24 and 202.
276. Craggs 1983, p. 54.
277. Li and Chen 1991, p. 288; Fang and Xie 1993, p. 294; Wusijiluofu 1997; Larin 1998, pp. 281–285 and 297.
278. Ma Chaojun 1959, vol. 1, pp. 150–151 and 166–167.
279. Other dates are also given for its founding (see Wales 1945, p. 203).
280. Wales 1945, p. 204.
281. Song Chao et al. 1985, p. 78.
282. Song Chao et al. 1985, pp. 92–105; Liao Chengzhi 1991, p. 341; Min Yifan 1991, pp. 351–354; 'Shanghai haiyuan', eds, 1991, pp. 117–120, 316, and 323. Hardy 1956, pp. 212–228, is a British communist memoir of the Seamen's International.

283. Fang Xiongpu and Xu Zhenli, eds, 1995, p. 2; Felber and Hübner 1988b, pp. 164, fn. 57.
284. Song Chao et al. 1985, pp. 94–95; Wubben 1986, pp. 137–144; Tie Zhuwei 1998, pp. 92–106; Benton 2007.
285. Haiyuan gonghui. See Song Chao et al. 1985, pp. 94–95.
286. On Chu Hsueh-fan's career, see Wales 1945, p. 122. Sam Chen was expelled from the CPGB in 1963, when he sided with China during the Sino-Soviet split. Later, he is said to have joined the CCP (Murray 2004).
287. Clegg 1997; and his daughter Jenny Clegg (in a personal communication). Another ethnic Chinese in the CPGB leadership was H. B. Lim, a Malayan. (See the CPGB archive at Manchester's National Museum of Labour History, CP/CENT/INT/36/04.)
288. Whittingham-Jones 1944, pp. 18–27; Craggs 1983, p. 54.
289. National Library of Australia, Oral History Project, TRC 2724, Arthur Lock Chang.
290. Benton 2007.
291. PRO, CAB 21/4972.
292. Evans 1997, p. 263.
293. Benton and Gomez 2001.
294. Carchedi 1994, pp. 49–50, 65, and 70; Galli 1994, p. 79. The freezing of the agreement after the Tian'anmen Square Incident of June 1989 created problems for Chinese entrepreneurs in Italy. (See Carchedi and Ferri 1994, p. 271.)
295. House of Commons 1985, vol. 1, January 17, pp. vii–viii.
296. O'Neill 1972, p. 109.
297. Sivanandan 1982 tells the story of Black organisation in Britain.
298. Ng 1968, pp. 47–49; Shang 1984, p. 37.
299. Gomez 1998.
300. Yang Qingyun 1996; Chen Huaidong and Zhang Liangmin 1998, pp. iv–v and 195; Li Minghuan 1998b, pp. 27–39; Christiansen 2003.
301. Li Minghuan 1998a, p. 59, 1999a, and 1999b, pp. 142–147 and 224; Liang Xiujing 2001, pp. 225–251. However, Liang argues that a 'pan-European overseas Chinese community exists', on the grounds that 'Chinese association leaders from all parts of Europe interact with each other across European borders' (ibid., p. 292).
302. Modood 1997b, pp. 298–300. Of majority whites, 31 per cent have no religious affiliation; percentages among Irish, Caribbean, Indian, African Asian, Pakistani, and Bangladeshi are 14, 28, 5, 2, 2, and 1.
303. Howlett, ed., 1999, pp. 313–314. We have no up-to-date estimate of the number of ethnic-Chinese Christians in Malaysia. In the late 1970s, however, 2.5 per cent of the Malaysian population were Christians, and most of that 2.5 per cent were ethnic Chinese and Indians. (Luo Manhua, ed., 1981, p. 184.)
304. Luo Manhua, ed., 1981, p. 422.
305. Szeming Sze 1931, p.10.
306. Tyau 1920, p. 308.
307. Tyau 1920, pp. 315–316.
308. 'Lundun gongshang gonghui laishu' (A letter from the London Workers and Merchants' Union), *Lü Ou Zazhi*, no. 19, June 1917.

309. Luo Manhua, ed., 1981, p. 406.
310. Chinese Church in London, Lundun Zhonghua Jidu jiaohui 2000.
311. Ng 1968, pp. 68–69; O'Neill 1972, p. 105.
312. Galli 1994, pp. 85–87; Li Minghuan 1998a, p. 54.
313. Interview with Father Matteo Luo, Dodici Apostoli church, Piazza Venezia, Rome. See also Xu Bin 1957, pp. 59–60; Li and Chen 1991, p. 297.
314. You Hailong, ed., 2001, p. 204.
315. Li Minghuan 1998a, p. 54.
316. Shang 1984, p. 46.
317. Wah et al. 1996, p. 68; You Hailong, ed., 2001, p. 204.
318. http://www.letusreason.organisation/Cults3.htm;   http://www.tjc-ukga.ndirect.co.uk.
319. Li Wei 1995; Li Wei, talk at the Institute for Linguistics, Aarhus University, 24 November 1999.
320. Garland Liu 1992 and 1998.
321. Tan Chee-Beng 2000a.
322. Li Minghuan 1998a, p. 53.
323. Baker 1986, p. 312.
324. On the Mazu cult in Scotland, see 'Dapeng mingzhu – Ji'ao' choubei weiyuanhui, eds, 2001, p. 86.
325. On the transnational nature of the Mazu cult, see Fang Xiongpu and Xu Zhenli, eds, 1995, pp. 219–223; Li Minghuan 1998a; Tan Chee-Beng 2000.
326. The Chinese name is somewhat different in meaning from the English one. It means European Kut O Fishermen's Federation.
327. 'Dapeng mingzhu – Ji'ao' choubei weiyuanhui, eds, 2001, pp. 86 and 99.
328. Portes et al. 1999, p. 221.
329. Collins 1957, p. 237; Shang 1984, p. 37.
330. Siu and Faure 1995, p. 221.
331. You Hailong, ed., 1996, p. 38.
332. Li Minghuan 1998a, p. 38.
333. Watson's early comment (1977b, p. 200) on the underdevelopment of the status hierarchy of the ethnic-Chinese political leadership in Britain is pertinent.
334. Portes et al. 1999, p. 224.
335. Cohen 1997, 27.

6 British Racism and the Shaping of the Chinese community

1. On early racial theory, see Banton 1977 and the introduction to Augstein 1996.
2. Yarwood and Knowling 1982, p. 177.
3. Banton 1977, pp. 54 and 96.
4. Barkan 1992.
5. Miles 1982, p. 111.
6. Banton 1977, p. 69; Augstein 1996, p. xiv.
7. Miles 1982, pp. 109–119.
8. This section is based unless otherwise indicated on Chan 1928.

9. Chan 1928, pp. 13 and 208; Zhang Longxi 1988, pp. 119–122; Ch'en 1942, pp. 208–209.
10. Milligan 1995, pp. 17–20.
11. Augstein 1996, p. xii.
12. Baker 1974, pp. 24–27.
13. Augstein 1996, pp. xix–xxxi.
14. Montagu 1997, pp. 72–80.
15. Barkan 1992, pp. 19–25.
16. San Juan 1999, pp. 36–37.
17. Bolt 1984, p. 130.
18. Bevan 1986, p. vii.
19. Northrup 1999, pp. 88–89.
20. Bolt 1984, pp. 138–141.
21. On students, see Visram 2002, p. 255.
22. This point echoes Avtar Brah's discussion of diaspora (Brah 1996, pp. 182–183).
23. Moore 1999, p. 431; Bolt 1984, p. 138.
24. Majeed 1992, pp. 36 and 194–197.
25. MacKenzie 1999, pp. 282–290.
26. Mungello 1999, pp. 92–94, quoting research by Walter Demel.
27. Barkan 1992, p. 23; Bolt 1984, pp. 136–138.
28. Visram 2002.
29. Mungello 1999.
30. Dawson 1964a, pp. 1–2.
31. Sherwood 1991, pp. 232–235. However, special legislation often deprived Lascars of their technical status as British subjects from the point of view of employment rights, except in certain specified parts of the world. In seafarers' eyes, Lascars and Chinese were lumped together as 'Asiatic' (Visram 2002, p. 58).
32. Dawson 1964a, p. 22, cited in Zhang Longxi 1988, p. 127.
33. Inden 1990, p. 54.
34. Bolt 1984, p. 139; Teltscher 1995, p. 8.
35. Burroughs 1999, p. 184.
36. This is a thesis of Zhang Longxi 1988, building on Edward Said's theory of Orientalism.
37. Wade 1900, p. 304.
38. Scheffauer 1911, p. 645.
39. *Daily Telegraph*, 26 June 1920.
40. *East End News*, 18 January 1921.
41. May 1973, p. 132.
42. Admiral Lord Fisher, quoted in Waller 1985, p. 14.
43. Gollwitzer 1962, pp. 20–42. See also *Le péril jaune* (Paris: Félix Juven), published by Edmond Théry in 1901. According to Jeffrey Richards, speaking at a workshop at the Centre for the Study of Colonial and Postcolonial Societies held at Bristol University on 4 May 2005, the Yellow Peril theme was first depicted in 1895, in a painting inspired by Kaiser Wilhelm.
44. Hobson 1988 [1902], pp. 276–321; Gainer 1972, pp. 84–85.
45. Gainer 1972, pp. 112 and 166.
46. Quoted in May 1973, p. 1.

47. Gainer 1972, p. 96; Clegg 1994, p. 26.
48. On these labour 'heroes', see *inter alia* Gainer 1972; May 1973, p. 124; Jenkinson 1986, p. 185.
49. For labour opposition to the Yellow Peril idea, see Kirk 2003, pp. 164–165 and 180–196.
50. May 1973, pp. 13–28.
51. *The Seaman*, June 1908, p. 4.
52. *East End News*, 5 and 12 May 1908.
53. Bower 1936, pp. 168–169.
54. May 1973, pp. 22–23, 38–59, and 122–134; May 1978, pp. 115–121; Wubben 1986, pp. 9–19.
55. Saxton 1971, p. 258.
56. Hobson 1988 [1902], pp. 305–308 and 316.
57. Hinton 1983, p.109.
58. May and Cohen 1974. On the race riots, see Fryer 1984, pp. 298–316.
59. Jenkinson 1986, pp. 184–185. See also Visram 2002, p. 199, on the special vehemence of white working-class hostility towards Indians and Chinese in Scotland in this period.
60. HO 45/11843, pt 1.
61. HO 45/11843, pt 1; Murphy 1995, pp. 18–19 and 62.
62. Walvin 1984, p. 71.
63. Walvin 1984, p. 71.
64. Yarwood and Knowling 1982, p. 9; Constantine 1999, pp. 183–184.
65. Bevan 1986, p. 66.
66. Gainer 1972, pp. 112 and 199–207. On the changing public mood, see Yarwood 1967, p. 154.
67. Visram 2002, p. 57.
68. Yarwood and Knowling 1982, p. 185.
69. Milligan 1995, pp. 32–42 and 84–102.
70. Ackroyd 1990, pp. 838 and 1046–1050.
71. Sweet 2001.
72. Milligan 1995, p. 85.
73. See, for example, the *Daily Express*, 11 October 1920.
74. O'Neill 1972, pp. 53–54. On the Fu Manchu tradition, see Clegg 1994.
75. PRO, HO 45/11843, pt 2.
76. PRO, HO 45/11843, pt 2.
77. *Evening News*, 7 October 1920; Gainer 1972, pp. 36–49.
78. *Star*, 17 June 1919; *Daily Mail*, 9 October 1920; *Daily News*, 15 April 1920; Tyau 1920, p. 317.
79. Scheffauer 1911, p. 466.
80. *Report of the Commission* 1906–1907.
81. PRO, HO 45/11843, pt 2; Law 1981, p. 24.
82. Cayford 1991, p. 45.
83. *Daily Mail*, 9 October 1920.
84. *Star*, 17 June 1919.
85. Tyau 1920, p. 317; *Daily Telegraph*, 17 June 1919.
86. *Evening News*, 4–14 October 1920.
87. Cited in Clegg 1994, p. 22.
88. Milligan 1995, p. 86.

89. Kohn 1992, pp. 5–7.
90. PRO, Mepo 3/469; Annie Lai et al. 1986, p. 23; Sarah Cheung 1997, p. 32.
91. Clegg 1994, p. 30; Sarah Cheung 1997, p. 23.
92. *East End News*, 15 April 1924; Annie Lai et al. 1986, p. 23; Kohn 1992, p. 128.
93. The main game was pakapoo or puck-a-boo 白鴿票, a game resembling lotto.
94. *Daily Express*, 1 October 1920.
95. *Evening News*, 4 and 7 October 1920.
96. Lee 1996, pp. 212–216.
97. Ng 1968, p. 76.
98. *South Wales Graphic*, 20 September 1906, p. 9.
99. *Evening News*, 14 October 1920; Collins 1957, p. 232; Maria Lin Wong 1989, pp. 66–73; Lynn 1982, p. 12; Craggs and Lynn 1985; Broady 1955, pp. 72–73.
100. Mary Ting Yi Lui 2005.
101. Foley and Foley 2006.
102. Wu Qiuyu 1999, p. 198.
103. Tinker 1974, pp. 168 and 218.
104. Herbert Parsons, 'The Truth about the Northern Territory,' Adelaide 1907, p. 58, quoted in Martínez 1999, p. 64.
105. *Sunday Chronicle*, 2 December 1906, quoted in Clegg 1994, p. 9.
106. *Evening News*, 5 October 1920.
107. Williams 1912, pp. 170–173; Wolski 1994.
108. Frodsham 1974, pp. xli–xliii and 93–94; Guo Songtao et al. 1998, pp. 156–157 and 161.
109. PRO, HO 213/808.
110. Gainer 1972, pp. 19–24, 55–56, 148–149, 201, and 214.
111. *Daily Express*, 17 June 1919; May and Cohen 1974, pp. 121–122.
112. Bevan 1986, p. 67.
113. Yarwood 1967 documents British attitudes to these two groups.
114. Tupper 1938, pp. 142–143.
115. MSS 175/3/14/2, Modern Records centre, University of Warwick, *Chinese Invasion of Great Britain: A National Danger, a Call to Arms* (1909); *The Seaman*, February 1908; May 1973, pp. 28–38.
116. *East London Observer*, 10 April 1909.
117. PRO, HO 45/11843, pt 1.
118. PRO, Mepo 2/1692, and HO 45/15592.
119. The booklet, titled *Policing Diversity: The Metropolitan Police Service Handbook on London's Religions, Cultures and Communities*, is by Constable Jonathan Wilson.
120. Miles 1982, ch. 6.
121. Saxton 1971, pp. 28–30; Lyman 2000a,b.
122. Gainer 1972, pp. 22–23 and 57–58.
123. Broady 1952, p. 5.
124. Cayford 1991, p. 47.
125. *Marine Caterer*, June 1919, quoted in Jenkinson 1986, p. 204.
126. Visram 2002, p. 219.
127. Lao She 1991 [1935], pp. 211 and 285.

128. Clegg 1994, pp. 34–35.
129. Isaacs 1961 [1938], p. 109.
130. Collins 1957, p. 228.
131. This stereotype did not usually attach to Chinese in postwar Britain, who were mostly from Hong Kong.
132. The term is Cai Shaoqing's (Cai Shaoqing 2000).
133. Shang 1984, p. 33.
134. Tyau 1920, pp. 315–316.
135. Bickers 1999, p. 46.
136. Tyau 1920; Lao She 1991 [1935], p. 361.
137. Watson 1977b, p. 206.
138. Brah 1996, pp. 21–48.
139. Parker 1995, pp. 74–75.
140. Yuet Ngor Mary Pang 1993, p. 208.
141. House of Commons 1985, vol. 1, January 17, p. vii.
142. Lynn 1982, p. 13.
143. Yuet Ngor Mary Pang 1993, pp. 208–256.
144. Shang 1984, p. 60.
145. Shang 1984, p. 27.
146. Kibria 2002, pp. 14–17, discusses the Asian American phenomenon.
147. Kibria 2002, p. 11.
148. Leung-Clifford 1989, p. 93; Yuan Cheng 1994, p. 251.
149. San Juan 1999, p. 49; Pimentel 2001.
150. Okihiro 1994, p. 142, quoted in Kibria 2002, pp. 132–133.
151. Yuet Ngor Mary Pang 1993, pp. 208–256; Owen 1994, pp. 21 and 24.
152. Yuet Ngor Mary Pang 1993, pp. 201–215; Alfred Chan 1986, p. 11; Yuan Cheng 1996, p. 175.
153. Lyman 2000b.
154. Dummett and Lo 1986, p. 3.
155. Shang 1984, p. 27.
156. O'Neill 1972, pp. 125–126.
157. Chinese Information and Advice Centre 1986, pp. 17–19.
158. Parker 1998d, p. 308.
159. See Monitoring Group 2000 and 2002.

7 Ethnic culture and identity

1. Friedman 1994, pp. 87–89.
2. Mitchell 1997, p. 228; Guarnizo and Smith 1998.
3. In the United States, too, their presence led to the first federal immigration law (Hing 1993, p. 19)
4. McFarland 1991, p. 497; Sherwood 1991, pp. 229–230.
5. Gordon 1985, pp. 8 and 107.
6. Bevan 1986, pp. 58–67.
7. 'Huaqiao Huaren baikequanshu, falü tiaolie juan' bianji weiyuanhui, eds, 2000, p. 542.
8. Gainer 1972, p. 199.
9. Hing 1993, pp. 24–36.

10. Ng 1968, p. 11.
11. Gainer 1972, pp. 207–208; Evans 1983, pp. 7 and 10–12; Gordon 1985, pp. 7–10; Bevan 1986, p. 73.
12. In the 1960s, however, Commonwealth citizens with vouchers had a statutory right to enter Britain and remain unconditionally, a right not granted to alien work-permit holders.
13. Little 1947, pp. 63–66; Gordon 1985, pp. 6–7.
14. Sherwood 1991, pp. 235–236.
15. Evans 1983, pp. 34–35 and 57–58.
16. Sivanandan 1982, pp. 101–108.
17. Taylor 1987, p. 37.
18. Evans 1983, p. 154.
19. Sivanandan 1982, pp. 110–111; Bevan 1986, pp. 83–84. A patrial is a person born in the UK or one of whose parents or grandparents was a naturalised citizen or a former Commonwealth citizen resident in Britain in 1971.
20. London Office 1973, p. 22.
21. Gordon 1985, pp. 15–17.
22. Evans 1983, pp. 19 and 72–74; Bevan 1986, pp. 78–86.
23. PRO, HO 344/30.
24. PRO, HO 344/154; Bevan 1986, p. 78.
25. Lynn 1982, p. 16.
26. Shang 1984, p. 20; Baker 1994, p. 298.
27. Bevan 1986, pp. 80–83.
28. Baker 1986, pp. 309–310.
29. Evans 1983, p. 19.
30. Cheung 1975, p. 37.
31. Baker 1986, p. 310, and 1994, p. 298; Liao 1992, p. 34.
32. Li Minghuan 1998, p. 15.
33. Wong 1992, p. 30.
34. Nine out of the 13 Chinese interviewed gave Hong Kong's political instability as a reason for not wanting to return there (Lornita Wong 1992, p. 30).
35. Watson 1975; House of Commons 1985, vol. II, first pagination, p. 3.
36. Watson 1977b, p. 205.
37. Ng 1968, p. 70; Cheung 1975, p. 166; House of Commons 1985, vol. I, p. xii. Cheung 1975, p. 55, found that only five of his sample of 75 informants could converse in complete sentences in English, and that half had hardly any English. Watson 1975 estimated that fewer than 10 per cent could speak English and Baker 1986, p. 313, thought less than half could. On gambling in the 1960s, see Ng 1968, pp. 63–66.
38. Pitson and Whitfield 1999.
39. Broady 1952, pp. 9–11, 48, and 111 and 1955, pp. 70–74; Collins 1957, pp. 232–239; O'Neill 1972, pp. 94–96. Broady, notes other ways in which Liverpool's settled Chinese adapted their behaviour to local norms, although he concluded that they 'cannot be said to be assimilated'.
40. Lynn 1982, pp. 46–59; Ye 1989; Au 1994, pp. 191–197, 206, and 379; Au and Au 1994, p. 7.
41. Broady 1952, p. 13; Collins 1957, pp. 233–238.
42. O'Neill 1972, pp. 256–257.

43. Collins 1957, p. 234.
44. Watson 1977b, pp. 193 and 205–206. Chung Yuen Kay 1985 also questions Watson's findings and even questions the application of the concept of 'community' to the Chinese.
45. O'Neill 1972, pp. 130, 206–208, and 224–258.
46. Watson 1977b, p. 201.
47. Cheung 1975, pp. 170–177; Lynn 1982, pp. 22–30; House of Commons 1985, vol. I, p. xxxiv; Alfred Chan 1986.
48. Modood 1997b. Modood and his colleagues achieved a sample of 214 Chinese with a response rate of 66 per cent (Berthoud, Modood, and Smith 1997, p. 11).
49. Verma et al. 1999. This study is based on a sample of 362 'British-Chinese', 65 per cent of whom were born in Britain and 77 per cent of whom had lived in Britain for more than ten years.
50. Sproston et al. 1999.
51. Modood 1997b.
52. Verma et al. 1999.
53. National Statistics Online 2004.
54. Yu Jianzhang 1991; Wu Qiuyu 1999, pp. 201–202.
55. Gervais and Jovchelovitch 1998, pp. 26–28.
56. Keung Fu Lee 1993, p. 55.
57. Owen 2001, p. 150. An analysis of the 1991 Census shows that nearly a quarter of Chinese women and 13 per cent of Chinese men have non-Chinese partners (Parker 1998d, p. 307).
58. Kibria 2002, pp. 159–196.
59. Pitson 1999b. Even so, Chinese were more likely to live in large households and slightly less likely to live alone than the general population (Pitson 1999a).
60. Keung-fu Lee 1993, p. 38.
61. Lornita Wong 1992, pp. 76–77.
62. 'Yingguo Huaqiao qingnian yidai, duoshu buyuan xuexi Zhongwen' (Most overseas Chinese youth in Britain don't want to study Chinese), *Huaqiao ribao*, 19 January 1988, cited in Wu Qiuyu 1999, pp. 202–203. On attitudes towards Chinese schools, see also Collins 1957, p. 233, for the 1950s, and Au 1994, p. 188, for the early 1990s.
63. Taylor 1987, pp. 185–197; Lornita Wong 1992, pp. 72–80; Au 1994, p. 188; Parker 1995, pp. 146 and 154; Verma et al. 1999, pp. 77–80.
64. Pitson and Whitfield 1999.
65. Personal communication, Dylan Sung, 9 December 2003.
66. On religious observance at the household level, see Wah et al. 1996, pp. 67–78.
67. Verma et al. 1999, p. 185.
68. Verma et al. 1999, pp. 104–105. In both groups, half were uncertain.
69. Gervais and Jovchelovitch 1998, pp. 65–67.
70. Tan and Wheeler 1983. Sproston 1999c notes that Chinese use the national health service less than whites and other ethnic minorities in part because of their reliance on traditional Chinese medicine. Others, however, blame this underuse on the lack of official support systems, especially interpreting (for example, Lynn 1982, pp. 39–44; Suk-Tak Tam 1998, p. 85). Gervais and

Jovchelovitch 1998 treat the issue from various angles, both cultural and administrative. Owen 1994, pp. 11–13, examines ethnic health differentials on the basis of the 1991 Census. In 1997–1998, Oxford University's Institute of Health Sciences found that nearly all Chinese living in rural parts of Oxfordshire were over 50 years of age and that one in five had not registered with a GP because of lack of information and language problems (Michael Chan 1999, p. 9).

71. House of Commons 1985, vol. I, p. xiii; Chinese Information and Advice Centre 1986.
72. Au 1994, pp. 378–382.
73. Suk-Tak Tam 1998, pp. 86–88.
74. Verma et al. 1999, p. 159.
75. Watson 1977a, p. 3, and 1977b, pp. 205–206.
76. Parker 1995, pp. 10–14.
77. Watson 1977a, p. 3.
78. Parker 1995, pp. 32–37.
79. Wang Gungwu 2004.
80. An example is Dummett and Lo 1986, p. 1.
81. Parker 1995, p. 237.
82. L. Ling-chi Wang 1994, pp. 185–212; Kwok Bun Chan 1997, pp. 207–209.
83. Parker 1994a and 1995.
84. Coonan 2006 describes the current state of martial arts in China and their international marketing. On the Wu-Tang Clan, see the work of Greg Tate, essayist and journalist for the *Village Voice*.
85. Song 1995, pp. 288–289, and 1996, pp. 306–310, and 1997. On the exploitation of Chinese women and children in big restaurants in the early years of postwar immigration, see Baxter 1988, p. 118.
86. Brah 1996, p. 65. The patterns of residence of Chinese and South Asians in Britain – dispersed in the Chinese case, concentrated in the South Asian – are reversed in Toronto. There, Indians are the more assimilated, thus inverting the British order. The South Asians in Toronto are not only highly diverse but scattered, whereas the Chinese close ranks in an ethnic enclave, a divergence said to explain the two populations' relative positions on Toronto's 'index of dissimilarity' (Marger 1990, p. 556).
87. Li Wei 1995; Li Wei, talk at the Institute for Linguistics, Aarhus University, 24 November 1999.
88. Prior et al. 1997, pp. 84–85.
89. Mitchell 1997, p. 228; Guarnizo and Smith 1998.
90. In the context of this study, we find it helps to distinguish between ethnic consciousness that preserves distinct cultures across continents and creolisation, which emphasises localised accommodation of cultures.
91. Ong and Nonini, eds, 1997, p. 169.
92. Ong 1999, pp. 2 and 19.
93. Keung Fu Lee 1993, pp. 66–67; Parker 1995, p. 200.
94. These comments and statistics are drawn from Pang 1996.
95. See the essays by Lee Seok Chee, Scarlet Cheng, and John Cayley in Pan, ed., 1998, pp. 128–135.
96. Him Mark Lai 1998, p. 273.

97. Whitley 1928, pp. 268–272. Chitqua (also known as Shykinqua) is wrongly reported to have been a Royal Academician (see Kiernan 1978, p. 41, where the artist's name is transliterated as Tan-chet Gua). The name Chitqua has an interesting etymology. The names of nearly all early China-coast artists recorded in the West end with *qua* (for example, Lam Qua, Hing Qua, Foeiqua, and Chinqua). This usage originated in southern Fujian, where it was the custom to address people of high status as *qua*, as part of the local Hokkien naming system. The custom spread to Guangzhou and other ports in South China and Southeast Asia. Western merchants used the suffix less discriminatingly, to avoid causing possible offence. Its application to the Guangzhou-based artists (some of whom were Hokkien) probably had nothing to do with status. This footnote is compounded from personal communications by James Chin, Rubin Lien (Christies, citing Patrick Conner, *The China Trade*, catalogue of the exhibition in Brighton Pavilion in 1986, p. 49, no. 58), Andrew Potter (Royal Academy Library), Bill Shang, and Geoff Wade.

98. Kiernan 1978, p. 41, found a third and more foreign names in random lists of artists.

99. Ng 1968, p. 53; Hu Zhiqiang 1989, p. 32.

100. Huang Wenzhong 1986, p. 29; Li Minghuan 1995, p. 64.

101. Whittingham-Jones 1944, pp. 47–55.

102. Watson 1975, pp. 53 and 57, quoted in Simsova and Chin 1985 [1982], p. 32.

103. House of Commons 1985, vol. I, p. xi.

104. On the Chinese arts in Britain up to 1978, see Khan 1978, ch. 3. According to Verma et al. 1999, pp. 81–82, only 4 per cent of Chinese youngsters in the late 1990s attended Chinese cultural activities often, whereas 41 per cent never did and 37 per cent rarely did. However, surveys conducted in the 1970s and 1980s revealed a strong interest in listening privately to commercial recordings of Chinese music (Taylor 1987, pp. 109–110).

105. Tong Soon Lee forthcoming. This paragraph also draws on personal correspondence from Tong Soon Lee, dated 28 July 2006.

106. Amy D. Y. Lai discusses these issues in her 1995 thesis.

107. House of Commons 1985, vol. II, first pagination, p. 4; Simsova and Chin 1985 [1982], p. 32.

108. Lao She 1991 [1935].

109. For a bibliography of Chinese creative writers who were born or have lived for a long time in Britain or North America and write predominantly in English, see Graham Chan's website at http://www.staff.livjm.ac.uk/leagchan/.

110. For the passages quoted, see Graham Chan's website.

111. For introductions to some of these artists, see Leung Win 2001 and Barraclough et al. 2002.

112. Diana Yeh 2001.

113. Amy Lai 1995, p. 80.

114. Lim and Yan 1994, p. v.

115. The need felt by the second generation for 'disidentification' – the establishment of difference – from the Chinese foreigner and the foreign-born immigrant, a related phenomenon, is discussed in Kibria 2002, pp. 84–92.

116. *Daily Telegraph*, 26 June 1920.
117. Broady 1952, p. 3.
118. The debate about Chinese education in the United States deals with similar issues but at a more advanced stage, given the greater maturity and influence of the American Chinese community. According to Hing 1993, pp. 140–152, Asian Americans at school are now stereotyped as 'whiz kids, especially in math, science, and other technical fields'. Their success is 'routinely attributed to a culturally grounded "achievement syndrome"' and the Chinese devotion to education. However, these images mask big differences of ethnicity, gender, class, and generation and a growing problem of indiscipline and dropping out. Hing's thesis is supported by a study published by the American Council on Higher Education (Hune and Chan 1997), which found big differences in the educational achievement of Asian Pacific Americans – although more went to college than in the general population and other minority groups, more also had only an eighth-grade education or below compared with the total population and all whites. In other words, the community is polarised and diverse, a situation the model-minority myth conceals (Alethea Yip 1997).
119. Cheung 1975, pp. 17–18 and 53; Benton 1983, pp. 25–26; Yuan Cheng 1994, pp. 101–105; Pang 1996, p. 80; Pitson 1999a, p. 11.
120. House of Commons 1985, vol. II, second pagination, p. 240; Dummett and Lo 1986, pp. 8–9; Lornita Yuen-Fan Wong 1992, p. 32. The first guide to Chinese children's needs was published by the Nuffield Foundation in 1981.
121. Taylor 1987, p. 313.
122. Leung-Clifford 1989, pp. 12–13.
123. Jackson and Garvey 1974; Shang 1984, p. 68.
124. House of Commons 1985, vol. II, second pagination, p. 241; Amy D. Y. Lai 1995, p. 69, quoting *The Guardian*, 3 May 1977.
125. Song 1996, pp. 13–15, 39, and 312.
126. Jackson and Garvey 1974; Baxter 1988, p. 165.
127. House of Commons 1985, vol. I, p. xxxiv.
128. Watson 1977b, p. 202.
129. Alfred Chan 1986, pp. 6–14; Dummett and Lo 1986, pp. 8–9; Lornita Yuen-Fan Wong 1992, pp. 56–57; Pang 1996, pp. 83–84.
130. Yuet Ngor Mary Pang 1993, pp. 112–113, 137–150, and 171–172; Pang 1996, pp. 118–123.
131. These arguments draw on Yuet Ngor Mary Pang 1993 and C. W. Louise Li 1995, pp. 79–80.
132. Francis and Archer 2005a,b,c.
133. Owen 1994, pp. 23–24; Planning Studies Group 1994, p. 4; Birmingham City Council 1995, p. 13; O'Leary and Betts 1999; Pitson 1999a, p. 11. These figures mask differences among Chinese from different parts of the world. Even so, the ethnic advantage applies to most Chinese groups (Yuan Cheng 1996, pp. 170–171).
134. *Times Higher Education Supplement*, 23 November 2001; National Office of Statistics, 8 January 2004.
135. Taylor 1987, pp. 1–2.
136. Figueroa 1991, pp. 166–167; Garner 2004.

137. Garner 2007.
138. Shang 1984, p. 62.
139. Demack et al. 2000; Gillborn and Mirza 2000; Sean Demack, personal communication.
140. Kibria 2002, pp. 53 and 65.
141. Yuan Cheng 1994, ch. 4, and 1996; Pitson 1999a.
142. National Office of Statistics, 8 January 2004.
143. Yuan Cheng 1994, ch. 4; Watson 1975.
144. Yuet Ngor Mary Pang 1993, pp. 168–169. However, Pang (1993, pp. 142–155), citing Boissevain and Grotenbreg, accepts that where 'structure' reinforces the transmission of 'culture', appropriate cultural traits can be transmitted across the generations. According to Boissevain and Grotenbreg (1987, pp. 120–121), cultural attributes such as sobriety, diligence, discipline, saving, and patriarchy 'change but slowly ... [and] are important resources for a successful small enterprise .... Values generated in the workplace thus become part of the family culture and are transmitted from one generation to the next. In this way the production and reproduction of culture takes place'. In the British case, Pang argues that filial piety and the work ethic ensure educational and occupational attainment while at the same time preserving family unity.
145. Miles 1982, pp. 179–180. Yuet Ngor Mary Pang 1993, pp. 30–32 and 155, discusses these theories.
146. Modood 1997a, p. 84.
147. Shang 1984, p. 62; Alfred Chan 1986, pp. 6–14; Pang 1996, p. 84.
148. House of Commons 1985, vol. 1, pp. xlv–xlvi.
149. Baxter 1988, p. 152.
150. *The Guardian*, 8 June 1987.
151. Keung Fu Lee 1993.
152. Yi Liao 1992, pp. 108–109.
153. Song 1996, pp. 299 and 314–315.
154. C. W. Louise Li 1995, pp. 65–83.
155. Yi Liao 1992, pp. 108–109. According to Yuet Ngor Mary Pang 1993, pp. 96–114, young adults' reasons for not entering catering included bad conditions (57 per cent), poor rewards (36 per cent), their overqualification or lack of relevant qualifications (14 per cent), family considerations (12 per cent), and off-putting childhood experiences (24 per cent). The main reason was the poor quality of life and an unwillingness to endure the same hardship as their parents. Even so, 27 per cent had not eliminated catering as an option. See also Sally Chan 1997, p. 215.
156. On catering as ethnic self-alienation, see Parker 1994a, pp. 624–627.
157. This is the argument of Miri Song (1996, p. 300).
158. Modood 1997a.
159. Hugill 1997.
160. Lyman 2000b.
161. Alfred Chan 1986, p. 11; Yuet Ngor Mary Pang 1993, pp. 201–215; Yuan Cheng 1996, pp. 175–178; Prior et al. 1997, p. 17.
162. C. W. Louise Li 1995, p. 70. However, according to Yuet Ngor Mary Pang 1993, p. 83, only one in five young Chinese adults works in the ethnic niche.

163. Pang 1996, pp. 119 and 160.
164. Yuet Ngor Mary Pang 1993, pp. 87–90.
165. Yuet Ngor Mary Pang 1993, p. 223.
166. Modood 1997a.
167. Taylor 1987, p. 278.

Bibliography

Ackroyd, Peter. 1990. *Dickens*. London: QPD.

Aghedo, Nayaba. 1994. 'Chinatown.' *City Life*, no. 246 (January–February), pp. 52–53.

Anderson, Benedict. 1983. *Imagined Communities: Reflections on the Origin and Spread of Nationalism*. London: Verso.

Ang, Ien. 2001. *On Not Speaking Chinese: Living Between Asia and the West*. London: Routledge.

Ang See, Teresita, ed. 2000. *Intercultural Relations, Cultural Transformations, and Identity: The Ethnic Chinese. Selected Papers Presented at the 1998 ISSCO Conference*. Manila: Kaisa Para Sa Kaunlaran, Inc.

Ang See, Teresita. 2001. 'Globalisation and the Ethnic Chinese: The Philippines Perspective.' Paper presented at the conference *Chinese Community Organisations and Globalisation: Comparative International Perspectives*, Singapore, March 9–10, 2001.

Archaimbault, Charles. 1987. 'Boeren en Landlopers: Migranten uit Oost-China.' In Benton and Vermeulen, eds, pp. 22–26.

Au, Wing Kwong L. 1994. *Elder Care and the Chinese Community Carers in Liverpool*. PhD thesis. University of Liverpool.

Au, Wing Kwong L., and Kerrie P. K. Lin Au. 1994. *Care in the Chinese Community: The Way Ahead*. Liverpool: Merseyside Chinese Community Development Association.

Augstein, Hannah Franziska. 1996. *Race: The Origins of an Idea, 1760–1850*. Bristol: Thoemmes.

Back, Les. 1996. *New Ethnicities and Urban Youth Cultures*. London: UCL Press.

Backman, Michael. 1999. *Asian Eclipse: Exposing the Dark Side of Business in Asia*. Singapore: John Wiley and Sons (Asia).

Baker, Hugh D. R. 1986. 'Nor Good Red Herring: The Chinese in Britain.' In Yu-ming Shaw, ed., *China and Europe in the Twentieth Century*, Taipei: Institute of International Relations, National Chengchi University, pp. 306–315.

Baker, Hugh D. R. 1994. 'Branches All Over: The Hong Kong Chinese in the United Kingdom.' In Skeldon, ed., pp. 291–307.

Baker, John R. 1974. *Race*. London: Oxford University Press.

Bang, Suzanne, and Rosalind Finlay. 1987. *Working to Support Refugees: A Report of a Training Project to Prepare Vietnamese and Chinese Field Staff to Work with People from Vietnam Resettled in the U.K.* Derby: Refugee Action.

Banton, Michael. 1967. *Race Relations*. London: Tavistock.

Banton, Michael. 1977. *The Idea of Race*. London: Tavistock.

Banton, Michael. 1979. 'It's Our Country.' In Robert Miles and Annie Phizacklea, eds, *Racism and Political Action in Britain*, London: Routledge, pp. 223–246.

Banton, Michael. 1982. 'The Direction and Speed of Ethnic Change.' In Charles F. Keyes, ed., *Ethnic Change*, Seattle: University of Washington Press, pp. 31–52.

Barkan, Elazar. 1992. *The Retreat of Scientific Racism: Changing Concepts of Race in Britain and the United States Between the World Wars*. Cambridge: Cambridge University Press.

Barker, Paul. 1989. 'Sunday Best.' *The Independent*, August 7.

Barraclough, Jon, Deborah Chan, and Wing-Fai Leung. 2002. *Ten Thousand Li: Chinese Infusion in Contemporary British Culture*. Liverpool: Liverpool School of Art and Design.

Basch, Linda, Nina Glick Schiller, and Cristina Blanc-Szanton. 1995. *Nations Unbound: Transnational Projects, Postcolonial Predicaments and Deterritorialized Nation-States*. Basle: Gordon and Breach.

Baxter, Sue, and Geoff Raw. 1988. 'Fast Food, Fettered Work: Chinese Women in the Ethnic Catering Industry.' In Sallie Westwood and Parminder Bhachu, eds, *Enterprising Women: Ethnicity, Economy and Gender Relations*, London: Routledge, pp. 58–75.

Baxter, Susan Chui Chi. 1988. *A Political Economy of the Ethnic Chinese Catering Industry*. PhD thesis. Aston University.

Beames, Thomas. 1850. *The Rookeries of London: Past, Present, and Prospective*. London: Bosworth.

Bean, R. 1973. 'Aspects of "New" Unionism in Liverpool, 1889–1891.' In Hikins, ed., pp. 97–118.

Benton, Gregor. 1983. *The Hongkong Crisis*. London: Pluto.

Benton, Gregor. 1987. 'San Tin: Lineage en Emigratie in Hongkong.' In Benton and Vermeulen, eds, pp. 27–33.

Benton, Gregor. 1992. *Mountain Fires: The Red Army's Three-Year War in South China, 1934–1938*. Berkeley: University of California Press.

Benton, Gregor, ed. and tr. 1997. *An Oppositionist for Life: Memoirs of the Chinese Revolutionary Zheng Chaolin*. Atlantic Highlands, New Jersey: Humanities Press.

Benton, Gregor. 1999. *New Fourth Army: Communist Resistance Along the Yangtze and the Huai, 1938–1941*. Berkeley: University of California Press.

Benton, Gregor. 2003. 'Chinese Transnationalism in Britain: A Longer History.' *Identities: Global Studies in Culture and Power*, no. 10, pp. 347–375.

Benton, Gregor. 2007. *Chinese Migants and Internationalism: Forgotten Stories, 1917–1945*. London: Routledge.

Benton, Gregor, and Edmund Terence Gomez. 2001. *Transnationalism and Chinatown: Ethnic Chinese in Europe and Southeast Asia*. Canberra: Centre for the Study of the Chinese Southern Diaspora, Australian National University.

Benton, Gregor, and Frank Pieke, eds. 1998. *The Chinese in Europe*. Basingstoke: Macmillan.

Benton, Gregor, and Hans Vermeulen, eds. 1987. *De Chinezen: Migranten in de Nederlandse Samenleving*. Muiderberg: Coutinho.

Benton, Gregor, and Liu Hong, eds. 2004. *Diasporic Chinese Ventures: The Life and Work of Wang Gungwu*. London: Curzon-Routledge.

Bergère, Marie-Claire. 1998. *Sun Yat-sen*. Translated by Janet Lloyd. Stanford: Stanford University Press.

Berridge, Victoria, and Griffith Edwards. 1987. *Opium and the People: Opiate Use in Nineteenth Century England*. London: Yale University Press.

Berthoud, Richard. 1997. 'Income and Standards of Living.' In Modood et al., pp. 150–183.

Berthoud, Richard. 1998. *The Incomes of Ethnic Minorities* (ISER Report 98–1). Colchester: Institute for Social and Economic Research: University of Essex.

Berthoud, Richard, and Sharon Beishon. 1997. 'People, Families and Households.' In Modood et al., pp. 18–59.

Berthoud, Richard, Tariq Modood, and Patten Smith. 1997. 'Introduction.' In Modood et al., pp. 1–17.

Bevan, Vaughan. 1986. *The Development of British Immigration Law*. London: Croom Helm.

Bhachu, Parminder K. 1985. *Twice Migrants: East African Sikh Settlers in Britain*. London: Tavistock.

Bickers, Robert. 1999. *Britain in China: Community, Culture and Colonialism, 1900–1949*, Manchester: Manchester University Press.

Biggart, Nicole W., and Gary G. Hamilton. 1997. 'On the Limits of a Firm-Based Theory to Explain Business Networks'. In Marco Orrù, Nicole Woolsey Biggart, and Gary G. Hamilton, eds, *The Economic Organization of East Asian Capitalism*, Thousand Oaks, CA: Sage Publications, pp. 33–54.

Birmingham City Council. 1995. *Community Profiles: Chinese*. Birmingham: Birmingham City Council.

Blom, Elsbeth, and Tina Romeijn. 1981. 'De Kracht van Traditie: Hoe Chinezen Succesvol Opereren in het Restaurantwezen' (The Power of Tradition: How Chinese Operate Successfully in the Restaurant World). *Sociologische Gids*, 28, pp. 228–238.

Bloom, Leonard. 1972. 'Introduction.' In Little, ed. pp. 1–45.

Boissevain, Jeremy, and Hanneke Grotenberg. 1987. 'Ethnic Enterprise in the Netherlands: The Surinamese of Amsterdam.' In Goffee and Scase, eds, pp. 105–130.

Bolt, Christine. 1984. 'Race and the Victorians.' In Eldridge, ed., pp. 126–147.

Bower, Fred. 1936. *Rolling Stonemason: An Autobiography*. London: Cape.

Brah, Avtar. 1996. *Cartographies of Diaspora: Contesting Identities*. London: Routledge.

Brakenhoff, Ciska. 1984. *Tussen Wal en Schip: Chinese Zeelieden en Pindaventers in Nederland (1920–1940)* (The Predicament of Chinese Seafarers and Peanut-Candy Peddlers in the Netherlands [1920–1940]). Amsterdam: ZZOA Working Paper.

Branigan, Tania. 2004. 'Development Casts Shadow on Chinatown.' *The Guardian*, November 22.

Broady, Maurice. 1952. *The Chinese Family in Liverpool*. BA thesis. University of Liverpool.

Broady, Maurice. 1955. 'The Social Adjustment of Chinese Immigrants in Liverpool.' *Sociological Review*, vol. 3, no. 1, pp. 65–75.

Brown, Judith M., and Wm. Roger Louis, eds. 1999. *The Oxford History of the British Empire*, vol. IV, *The Twentieth Century*. Oxford: Oxford University Press.

Bucknell, Patrick, and Hamid Ghodse. 1991. *Misuse of Drugs*. Second edition. London: Waterlow.

Burroughs, Peter. 1999. 'Imperial Institutions and the Government of Empire.' In Porter, ed., pp. 170–197.

Cai Shaoqing. 2000. Analysing Chinese Secret Societies in Australia. Unpublished paper.

Campani, Giovanna, Francesco Carchedi, and Alberto Tassinari, eds. 1994. *L'immigrazione silenziosa: Le comunità cinesi in Italia*. Torino: Fondazione Giovanni Agnelli.

Cantlie, James, and C. Sheridan Jones. 1912. *Sun Yat-sen and the Awakening of China*. New York: Fleming H. Revell.

Cao Yabo 曹亚伯. 1974. 'Yang Dusheng dao hai' (Yang Dusheng Drowns in the Sea). *Geming wenxian*, no. 66, pp. 408–414.

Carchedi, Francesco. 1994. 'La presenza cinese in Italia: Direzionalità dei flussi, dimensioni del fenomeno e caratteristiche strutturali.' In Campani et al., eds, pp. 41–74.

Carchedi, Francesco, and Marica Ferri. 1998. 'The Chinese Presence in Italy: Dimensions and Structural Characteristics.' In Benton and Pieke, eds, pp. 261–277.

Cardiff City Council. 1910. *Reports of Council and Committees. Health and Port Sanitary Committee*. September 20.

Carstens, Sharon A. 1988. 'Chinese Publications and the Transformation of Chinese Culture in Singapore and Malaysia.' In Cushman and Wang, eds, pp. 75–95.

Castells, Manuel. 1993. *The Information Age I: The Rise of the Network Society*. Oxford: Blackwell.

Castles, Stephen. 2000. *Ethnicity and Globalization: From Migrant Worker to Transnational Citizen*. London: Sage.

Cayford, Joanne M. 1991. 'In Search of "John Chinaman": Press Representations of the Chinese in Cardiff, 1906–1911.' *Llafur: Cylchgrawn Hanes Llafur Cymru*, vol. 5, no. 4, pp. 37–50.

Chan, Alfred. 1986. *Employment Prospects of Chinese Youth in Britain: A Research Report*. London: Commission for Racial Equality.

Chan, C. P. 1979. *The Chinese in Birmingham: A Study of the Chinese Community in Birmingham and Its Pattern of Life*. MSc thesis. University of Birmingham.

Chan, Kwok Bun. 1997. 'A Family Affair: Migration, Dispersal, and the Emergent Identity of the Chinese Cosmopolitan.' *Diaspora*, vol. 6, no. 2, pp. 195–214.

Chan, Michael. 1999. 'Beyond the Take-Away.' *Connections*, spring issue, pp. 8–9.

Chan, Sally. 1997. 'Migration, Cultural Identity and Assimilation Effects on Entrepreneurship for the Overseas Chinese in Britain.' *Asia Pacific Business Review*, vol. 3, no. 4, pp. 211–222.

Chan, Shau Yi [Ch'en Shou-i]. 1928. *The Influence of China on English Culture During the Eighteenth Century*. PhD thesis. University of Chicago.

Chan, Yiu Man. 1989. *Development of Local Radio for the Chinese Community in England*. MEd thesis. University of Manchester.

Chan, Yiu Man, and Christine Chan. 1997. 'The Chinese in Britain.' *New Community*, vol. 23, no. 1, pp. 123–131.

Chandler, Alfred D. Jr. 1962. *Strategy and Structure: Chapters in the History of the American Industrial Enterprise*. Cambridge, MA: MIT Press.

Chang, Iris. 2003. *The Chinese in America: A Narrative History*. New York: Penguin.

Chang Kai 常恺. 1992. 'Wei quan Ying Huaren de gongtong liyi' (For the Common Interests of the Chinese of the Whole of England). *Ouhua*, no. 6 (August), p. 3.

Chang Lin. 1991. 'Zhongguo canguanye de xianzhuang yu sikao' (The Present Situation of Chinese Catering, and Some Reflections). *Ouhua*, trial issue (August 25), pp. 3–4.

Chau, Ruby C. M., and Sam W. K. Yu. 2001. 'Social Exclusion of Chinese People in Britain.' *Critical Social Policy*, vol. 21, no. 1, pp. 103–125.

Chen Chi Ziang. 1943. *A Chinese Embassy in London*. Thesis report. University of Liverpool.

Chen, Han-sheng. 1936. *Landlord and Peasant in China: A Study of the Agrarian Crisis in South China*. New York: International Publishers.

Chen Hongmin 陈红民. 2002. ' "Xin Guomindang" zai haiwai de huodong' (The 'new Guomindang's' Overseas Activities). *Minguo dang'an*, no. 1.

Chen Huaidong 陈怀东 and Zhang Liangmin 张良民. 1998. *Ouzhou Huaren jingji xiankuang yu zhanwang* (The Present Economic Situation and Prospects of the Chinese in Europe). Taibei: Shihua jingji chubanshe.

Chen, Jack. 1976. *Inside the Cultural Revolution*. London: Sheldon Press.

Chen Min 陈民, ed. 1981. *Zhongguo zhigong dang* (The China Chee Kung Party). Beijing: Wenshi ziliao chubanshe.

Chen Murong 陈慕容. 1990. *Qingtian xianzhi* (Qingtian Gazetteer). Hangzhou: Zhejiang renmin chubanshe.

Chen Sanjing 陈三井. 1986. *Huagong yu Ou zhan* (The Chinese Labour Force in the First World War). Taibei: Institute of Modern History, Academia Sinica.

Chen Ta. 1940. *Emigrant Communities in South China: A Study of Overseas Migration and its Influence on Standards of Living and Social Change*. New York: Institute of Pacific Relations.

Chen Xiqi 晨锡祺, ed. 1991. *Sun Zhongshan nianpu changbian* (An Extended Biographical Chronology of Sun Yat-sen). Beijing: Zhonghua shuju.

Chen Zhuyun 陈竹筠 and Chen Qicheng 陈起城, eds. 1985. *Zhongguo minzhu dangpai lishi ziliao xuanbian* (Edited Selections of Historical Materials Relating to China's Democratic Parties). 2 vols. Shanghai: Huadong shifan daxue chubanshe.

Ch'en, Jerome. 1979. *China and the West: Society and Culture, 1815–1937*. London: Hutchinson.

Ch'en, Kenneth. 1942. 'Hai-lu, Forerunner of Chinese Travel Accounts of Western Countries.' *Monumenta Serica*, no. 7, pp. 208–226.

Cheng, Yuan. 1994. *Education and Class: Chinese in Britain and the US*. Aldershot: Avebury.

Cheng, Yuan. 1996. 'The Chinese: Upwardly Mobile.' In Peach, ed., pp. 161–180.

Cheung, Cheun-hing William. 1975. *The Chinese Way: A Social Study of the Hong Kong Chinese in a Yorkshire City*. MPhil thesis. University of York.

Cheung, Sarah. 1997. *The Dark Night of Chinatown: Popular Representations of the London Chinese in Fiction, 1914–1934*. BA thesis. History of Design, University of Brighton.

Chin, Kwet-Hon. 1997. *Intra-ethnic Conflict Among the Chinese in Sydney*. PhD thesis. Australian National University.

Chinese Church in London, Lundun Zhonghua Jidu jiaohui 伦敦中华基督教会. 2000. *Fifty Years of Growth, Wushi nian de chengzhang*. London: Chinese Church in London. Bilingual publication.

Chinese Information and Advice Centre. 1986. 'A Response.' In Dummett and Lo, pp. 14–20.

Choi Ching Yan. 1971. *Chinese Migration and Settlement in Australia with Special Reference to the Chinese in Melbourne*. PhD thesis. Australian National University.

Christiansen, Flemming. 1997a. *Overseas Chinese in Europe: An Imagined Community?* Leeds East Asia Paper No. 48.

Christiansen, Flemming. 1997b. *Overseas Chinese, Ancestral Rights and the New Territories*. Leeds East Asia Paper No. 49.

Christiansen, Flemming. 1997c. *Understanding Chinese Communities in Europe: Between Primordialism and Instrumentalism*. Leeds East Asia Paper No. 51.

Christiansen, Flemming. 1998a. *Sub-Ethnic Identities: The Chinese from Siyi and Qingtian*. Leeds East Asia Papers No. 54.

Christiansen, Flemming. 1998b. 'Chinese Identity in Europe.' In Benton and Pieke, eds, pp. 42–63.

Christiansen, Flemming. 2003. *Chinatown, Europe: An Exploration of Overseas Chinese Identity in the 1990s*. London: RoutledgeCurzon.

Chung, Stephanie Po-yin. 1999. 'Mobilization Politics: The Case of Siyi Businessmen in Hong Kong, 1890–1928.' In Douw et al., eds, pp. 45–66.

Chung Yuen Kay. 1985. 'At the Palace: Work, Ethnicity and Gender in a Chinese Restaurant.' *Studies in Sexual Politics*, no. 3, Department of Sociology, University of Manchester.

Clegg, Arthur. 1997. *Aid China, 1937–1949: A Memoir of a Forgotten Campaign*. Revised edition. Beijing: New World Press.

Clegg, Jenny. 1994. *Fu Manchu and the 'Yellow Peril': The Making of a Racist Myth*. Oakhill: Trentham Books.

Clegg, Jenny. 1999. 'People to People.' *China in Focus*, no. 7, pp. 17–19.

Cohen, Robin. 1997. *Global Diasporas: An Introduction*. London: UCL Press.

Collins, Sydney. 1957. *Coloured Minorities in Britain: Studies in British Race Relations Based on African, West Indian and Asiatic Immigrants*. London: Lutterworth.

Colombo, Massimo, Corrado Marcetti, Maria Omodeo, and Nicola Solimano. 1995. *Wenzhou-Firenze: Identità, imprese e modalità di insediamento dei cinesi in Toscana*. Florence: Angelo Pontecorboli Editore.

Commission for Racial Equality. 1979. *The Chinese in the UK*. London: The Group.

Commission for Racial Equality. 1987. *The Needs of the Chinese in the North West*. N. p.: N. p.

Constantine, Stephen. 1999. 'Migrants and Settlers.' In Brown and Louis, eds, pp. 163–187.

Coonan, Clifford. 2006. 'Everybody is Kung Fu Fighting.' *The Independent*. August 11.

Craggs, Susan. 1983. *The Chinese Community in Merseyside: A Historical Study of Its Development*. Dissertation, Local History Studies, Liverpool University.

Craggs, Susan, and I. Loh Lynn. 1985. *A History of the Chinese Community*. Liverpool: Merseyside Community Relations Council.

Crissman, Lawrence W. 1967. 'The Segmentary Structure of Urban Chinese Communities.' *Man*, vol. 2 (new series), pp. 185–204.

Curran, James, and Robert A. Blackburn. 1991. *Paths of Enterprise: The Future of the Small Business*. London: Routledge.

Cushman, Jennifer, and Wang Gungwu, eds. 1988. *Changing Identities of the Southeast Asian Chinese since World War II*. Hongkong: Hong Kong University Press.

Dai Hongci 戴鸿慈. 1982 [1905]. *Chu shi jiu guo riji* (Diary of a Visit to Nine Countries). Changsha: Hunan renmin chubanshe.

'Dapeng mingzhu – Ji'ao' choubei weiyuanhui 大鹏明珠- 吉澳筹备委员会, eds. 2001. *Dapeng mingzhu Ji'ao: Cang hai yizhu sanbai nian* (Kut O Island, Pearl of Tai Pang Bay: Three Hundred Years of the Creation of a Pearl in the Vast Sea). Hong Kong: Ji'ao cun gongsuo zhilihui, Lü Ou Ji'ao tongxianghui, Lü Ou Ji'ao yu lianhui.

Daunton, M. J. 1978. 'Jack Ashore: Seamen in Cardiff Before 1917.' *Welsh History Review*, vol. 9, pp. 176–203.

Dawson, Raymond. 1964a. 'Introduction.' In Dawson, ed., pp. 1–27.

Dawson, Raymond, ed. 1964b. *The Legacy of China*. London: Oxford University Press.

De Coughrey. 1994. 'Chinatown: The Chinese Centre of the North West.' *Northern Life*, no. 1, pp. 8–10.

Degolyer, Michael. N. d. 'Role Of Civil Society (Ngos, Media, Etc).' Unpublished paper.

Demack, S., D. Drew, and M. Grimsley. 2000. 'Minding the Gap: Ethnic, Gender and Social Class Differences in Attainment at 16, 1988–95.' *Race, Ethnicity and Education*, vol. 3, no. 2, pp. 117–143.

'Deng Fa jinian wenji' bianji bu "邓发纪念文集" 编辑部, eds. 2002. *Deng Fa jinian wenji* (Collection of essays about Deng Fa). Beijing: Zhonggong dangshi chubanshe.

Deng Lilan 邓丽兰. 1995. *Linshi da zongtong he tade zhichizhe: Sun Zhong-shan Yingwen zangdang toushi* (The Provisional President and his Supporters: Perspectives on English-Language Archives on Sun Yat-sen). Beijing: Zhongguo wenshi chubanshe.

Deschamps Chapeaux, Pedro, and Juan Pérez de la Riva. 1974. *Contribución a la historia de la gente sin historia*. Havana: Editorial de Ciencias Sociales.

Destexhe, Jean-François, and Derek Göbel. 1995. 'The Effects of the Impending Transfer of Power on the Economy and People of Hong Kong.' In Menski, ed., pp. 121–158.

Dim Sum (Little Pieces of Heart: British Chinese Short Stories). 1997. Manchester: Crocus.

Director of the Hong Kong Government Office in London. 1953. *Annual Departmental Report, 1952–53*. Hong Kong: Government Printer.

Dirlik, Arif, ed. 2001. *Chinese on the American Frontier*. Lanham: Rowman and Littlefield.

Dodd, Vikram, and Hugh Muir. 2005. 'New Year, New Challenge for London's Chinatown.' *The Guardian*. February 14.

Douw, Leo, Cen Huang, and Michael R. Godley, eds. 1999. *Qiaoxiang Ties: Interdisciplinary Approaches to 'Cultural Capitalism' in South China*. London: Kegan Paul.

Duara, Prasenjit. 1997. 'Nationalists among Transnationals: Overseas Chinese and the Idea of China, 1900–1911.' In Ong and Nonini, eds, pp. 39–60.

Dummett, Ann, and Jenny Lo. 1986. *The Chinese Community in Britain: The Home Affairs Committee Report in Context*. London: The Runnymede Trust.

Eldridge, C. C., ed. 1984. *British Imperialism in the Nineteenth Century*. London: Macmillan.

Elisseeff, Danielle. 1994. *Moi, Arcade: Interprète Chinois du Roi-Soleil*. Paris: Éditions Arthaud.

Eriksen, Thomas Hylland. 1993. *Ethnicity and Nationalism: Anthropological Perspectives*. London: Pluto.

Evans, Bob. 1997. *Mersey Mariners*. Birkenhead: Countyvise.

Evans, J. M. 1983. *Immigration Law*. London: Sweet and Maxwell.

Evans, Neil. Forthcoming. *Darker Cardiff*. Cardiff: University of Wales Press.

Everard, Jerry. 2000. *Virtual States: The Internet and the Boundaries of the Nation-State*. London: Routledge.

Fabian Society. 1902. *Life in the Laundry*. Fabian Tract no. 112. London: The Fabian Society.

Falkus, Malcolm. 1990. *The Blue Funnel Legend: A History of the Ocean Steam Ship Company, 1865–1973*. Basingstoke: Macmillan.

Fang Xiongpu 方雄普 and Xie Chengjia 谢成佳, eds. 1993. *Huaqiao Huaren gaikuang* (The General Situation of Overseas Chinese and Ethnic Chinese). Beijing: Zhongguo Huaqiao chubanshe.

Fang Xiongpu 方雄普 and Xu Zhenli 许振礼, eds. 1995. *Haiwai qiaotuan xunzong* (In Search of Overseas Chinese Associations). Beijing: Zhongguo Huaqiao chubanshe.

Faure, David, and Helen F. Siu, eds. 1995. *Down to Earth: The Territorial Bond in South China*. Stanford: Stanford University Press.

Felber, Roland. 1988. 'Der Grosse Oktober und die Entstehung erster Organisationen chinesischer Kommunisten Anfang der zwanziger Jahre in Europa.' *Beiträge zur Geschichte der Arbeiterbewegung*, vol. 30, no. 5, pp. 592–605.

Felber, Roland, and Ralf Hübner. 1988a. 'Chinesische Demokraten und Revolutionäre in Berlin (1900–1924).' *Wissenschaftliche Zeitschrift der Humboldt-Universität zu Berlin, Reihe Gesellschaftswissenschaften*, vol. 37, no. 2, pp. 148–156.

Felber, Roland, and Ralf Hübner. 1988b. 'Chinesische Demokraten und Revolutionäre in Berlin (1925–1933).' *Wissenschaftliche Zeitschrift der Humboldt-Universität zu Berlin, Reihe Gesellschaftswissenschaften*, vol. 37, no. 2, pp. 157–172.

Feng Ziyou 冯自由. 1981. *Geming yishi* (Revolutionary Lost Histories). 6 vols. Beijing: Zhonghua shudian.

Figueroa, Peter. 1991. *Education and the Social Construction of 'Race'*. London: Routledge.

Fitchett, Norman. 1976. *Chinese Children in Derby*. Derby: Bishop Lonsdale College of Education.

Flatau, Dorota. 1920. 'Chinatown as I Know it: Glimpses into the Life of Yellow Men's Wives.' *Evening News*. October 7.

Foley, Charles, and Yvonne Foley. 2006. Liverpool's Chinese Community and the Dragons – 'Children of the Disappeared.' Unpublished paper.

Francis, Becky, and Louise Archer. 2005a. ' "British Chinese Pupils" and Parents' Constructions on the Value of Education.' *British Educational Research Journal*, vol. 31, no. 1, pp. 89–108.

Francis, Becky, and Louise Archer. 2005b. 'British Chinese Pupils' Constructions of Gender and Learning.' *Oxford Review of Education*, vol. 31, no. 4, pp. 491–515.

Francis, Becky, and Louise Archer. 2005c. ' "They Never Go off the Rails Like Other Ethnic Groups": Teachers' Constructions of British Chinese Pupils' Gender Identities and Approaches to Learning.' *British Journal of Sociology of Education*, vol. 26, no. 2, pp. 165–182.

Freeberne, John Derek Michael. 1979. *The Chinese Community in Britain: With Special Reference to Housing and Education*. PhD thesis. London University.

Friedman, Jonathan. 1994. *Cultural Identity and Global Process*. London: Sage.

Frodsham, J. D., translator and annotator. 1974. *The First Chinese Embassy to the West: The Journals of Kuo Sung-t'ao, Liu Hsi-hung and Chang Te-yi*. Oxford: Clarendon.

Fryer, Peter. 1984. *Staying Power: Black People in Britain Since 1504*. London: Pluto.

Fukuyama, Francis. 1995. *Trust: The Social Virtues and the Creation of Prosperity*. New York: Random House.

Fung, Edmund S. K., and Chen Jie. 1996. *Changing Perceptions: The Attitudes of the PRC Chinese Towards Australia and China, 1989–1996*. Centre for the Study of Australia-Asia Relations. Australia-Asia Paper No. 78. Faculty of Asian and International Studies: Griffith University.

Gainer, Bernard. 1972. *The Alien Invasion: The Origins of the Aliens Act of 1905.* London: Heinemann.

Galen, Kees van. 1989. 'Dorp Zonder Naam: De Chinezen uit Indonesië.' In Benton and Vermeulen, eds, pp. 132–146.

Galli, Susanna. 1994. 'Le comunità cinesi in Italia: Caratteristiche organizzative e culturali.' In Campani et al., eds, pp. 75–104.

Garner, Richard. 2007. 'Chinese Perform Better in English than White Children.' *The Independent*, February 25, pp. 4–5.

Garvey, A., and B. Jackson. 1975. *Chinese Children*. Cambridge: National Educational Research and Development Trust.

Gereffi, Gary. 1994. 'Capitalism, Development and Global Commodity Chains.' In Leslie Sklair, ed., *Capitalism and Development*, London: Routledge, pp. 211–231.

Gervais, Marie-Claude, and Sandra Jovchelovitch. 1998. *The Health Beliefs of the Chinese Community in England: A Qualitative Research Study*. London: Health Education Authority.

Gillborn, David, and Heidi Safia Mirza. 2000. *Educational Inequality: Mapping Race, Class and Gender, A Synthesis of Research Evidence*. London: Office for Standards in Education.

Gilroy, Paul. 1987. *There Ain't No Black in the Union Jack*. London: Hutchinson.

Gilroy, Paul. 1993. *The Black Atlantic*. London: Verso.

Glick Schiller, Nina, Linda Basch, and Cristina Blanc-Szanton. 1999. 'Transnationalism: A New Analytic Framework for Understanding Migration.' In Vertovec and Cohen, eds, pp. 26–49.

Goffee, Robert, and Richard Scase, eds. 1987. *Entrepreneurship in Europe: The Social Processes*. London: Croom Helm.

Gollwitzer, Heinz. 1962. *Die Gelbe Gefahr: Geschichte eines Schlagworts – Studien zum imperialistischen Denken*. Göttingen: Vandenhoeck and Ruprecht.

Gomez, Edmund Terence. 1998. Chinese Business in Britain. Unpublished manuscript.

Gomez, Edmund Terence. 1999. *Chinese Business in Malaysia: Accumulation, Ascendance, Accommodation*. Richmond: Curzon.

Gomez, Edmund Terence. 2004. 'Intra-Ethnic Cooperation in Transnational Perspective: Malaysian Chinese Investments in the United Kingdom.' In Gomez and Hsiao, eds, pp. 109–148.

Gomez, Edmund Terence, and Gregor Benton. 2003. 'Transnationalism and the Essentializing of Capitalism: Chinese Enterprise, the State, and Identity in Britain, Australia, and Southeast Asia.' *East Asia: An International Quarterly*, vol. 20. no. 4, pp. 3–28.

Gomez, Edmund Terence, and Jomo K. S. 1999. *Malaysia's Political Economy: Politics, Patronage and Profits*. Cambridge: Cambridge University Press.

Gomez, Edmund Terence, and Michael H. H. Hsiao, eds. 2001. *Chinese Business in Southeast Asia: Contesting Essentialism, Understanding Entrepreneurship*. London: Curzon.

Gomez, Edmund Terence, and Michael H. H. Hsiao, eds. 2004. *Chinese Enterprise, Transnationalism and Identity*. London: RoutledgeCurzon.

Goody, Jack. 2000. Chinese Food. LBO-Talk Archive.

Gordon, Paul. 1985. *Policing Immigration: Britain's Internal Controls*. London: Pluto.

Greenberger, Allen J. 1969. *The British Image of India: A Study in the Literature of Imperialism, 1880–1960*. London: Oxford University Press.

Grossholtforth, Petra. 1985. *Chinesen in London: Lao She's Roman Er Ma*. Bochum: Chinathemen.

Guarnizo, Luis Eduardo, and Michael Peter Smith. 1998. 'The Locations of Transnationalism.' In Smith and Guarnizo, eds, pp. 3–34.

Guo Songtao 郭嵩焘 et al. 1998. *Guo Songtao deng shi xiji liuzhong* (A Collection of Six Books by Guo Songtao et al. on Their Travels in the Western World). Shanghai: Shenghuo dushu xinzhi sanlian shudian.

Gütinger, Erich. 1998. 'A Sketch of the Chinese Community in Germany: Past and Present.' In Benton and Pieke, eds, pp. 197–208.

Gyory, Andrew. 1998. *Closing the Gate: Race, Politics, and the Chinese Exclusion Act*. Chapel Hill: University of North California Press.

Hall, Laura. 1998. 'The Arrival and Settlement of the Chinese in 19th Century British Guiana.' In Wang Ling-chi and Wang Gungwu, eds, pp. 86–111.

Hall, Stuart. 1992. 'New Ethnicities'. In James Donald and Ali Rattansi, eds, *'Race', Culture and Difference*, London: Sage.

Hamilton, Gary G., ed. 1996. *Asian Business Networks*. Berlin: W. de Gruyter.

Hardy, George. 1956. *Those Stormy Years: Memories of the Fight for Freedom on Five Continents*. London: Lawrence and Wishart.

Hargreaves, Alec G., and D. Mahdjoub 1997. 'Satellite Television Viewing Among Ethnic Minorities in France.' *European Journal of Communication* vol. 12, no. 4, pp. 459–477.

Harnisch, Thomas. 1999. *Chinesische Studenten in Deutschland: Geschichte und Wirkung ihrer Studienaufenthalte in den Jahren von 1860 bis 1945*. Mitteilungen des Instituts für Asienkunde no. 300. Hamburg: Institut für Asienkunde.

He Jinzhou, Huang Daxun, and Liu Hansheng. 1994. *Deng Fa zhuan* (A Biography of Deng Fa). Beijing: Jingji ribao chubanshe.

Heek, Frederik van. 1936. *Chineesche Immigranten in Nederland*. Amsterdam: Emmering.

Heyndrickx, Jerome. 1990. *Philippe Couplet, S.J. (1623–1693): The Man Who Brought China to Europe*. Monumenta Serica Monograph Series XXII. Nettetal: Steyler Verlag.

Hikins, Harold R., ed. 1973. *Building the Union: Studies in the Growth of the Workers' Movement: Merseyside, 1756–1967*. Liverpool: Toulouse Press.

Hing, Bill Ong. 1993. *Making and Remaking Asian American Identity Through Immigration Policy, 1850–1990*. Stanford: Stanford University Press.

Hinton, James. 1983. *Labour and Socialism: A History of the British Labour Movement, 1867–1974*. Brighton: Wheatsheaf.

Hobson, J. A. 1988 [1902]. *Imperialism: A Study*. With an Introduction by J. Townshend. London: Unwin Hyman.

Hodder, Rupert. 1996. *Merchant Princes of the East: Cultural Delusions, Economic Success and the Overseas Chinese in Southeast Asia*. Chichester: John Wiley and Sons.

Holmes, Colin. 1978a. 'Introduction: Immigrants and Minorities in Britain.' In Holmes, ed., pp. 13–22.

Holmes, Colin, ed. 1978b. *Immigrants and Minorities in British Society*. London: Allen and Unwin.

Holton, Bob. 1973. 'Syndicalism and Labour on Merseyside, 1906–14.' In Hikins, ed., pp. 121–150.

Home Office. 2003. *Control of Immigration: Statistics United Kingdom 2002*. London: Stationery Office.

Hood, Marlowe. 1998. 'Emigrant Communities in Zhejiang' and 'Clandestine Migration.' In Pan, ed., pp. 39–42 and 63–67.

House of Commons. 1985. *Second Report from the Home Affairs Committee, Session 1984–1985. Chinese Community in Britain*. 3 vols. London: Her Majesty's Stationery Office.

Howlett, Bob, ed. 1999. *Hong Kong 1998*. Hong Kong: Information Services Department.

Hsu, Madeline Y. 2000. *Dreaming of Gold, Dreaming of Home: Transnationalism and Migration Between the United States and South China, 1882–1943*. Stanford: Stanford University Press.

Hu Hua. 1980. *The Early Life of Zhou Enlai*. Translated by Chen Xiaoying. Beijing: Foreign Languages Press.

Hu Lanqi 胡兰畦. 1985. *Huiyilu (1901–1936)*. Chengdu: Sichuan renmin chubanshe.

Hu Zhiqiang 胡志强. 1989. *Yingguo Huaqiao gaikuang* (The General Situation of the Overseas Chinese in Britain). Haiwai Huaren qingshaonian congshu. Taibei: Zhengzhong shudian.

Hu Zhusheng 胡珠生. 1996. *Qingdai Hongmen shi* (A History of the Hongmen in the Qing era). Shenyang: Renmin chubanshe.

Huang Jianda 黄建大. 1999. *Zheng Jiale zhuan* (A Biography of Arthur Lock Chang). Shijiazhuang: Huashan wenyi chubanshe.

Huang Sande 黄三德. 1936. *Hongmen geming shi* (The Revolutionary History of the Hongmen). Los Angeles: N. p.

Huang Wenzhong 黄文忠. 1986. 'Ying Lun Siyi zonghuiguan shilüe' (A Brief History of the See Yip Association in England). In Siyi zonghuiguan, eds, pp. 28–29.

'Huaqiao Huaren baikequanshu, falü tiaoli juan' bianji weiyuanhui "华侨华人百科全书，法律条例卷" 编辑委员会, eds. 2000. *Huaqiao Huaren baikequanshu, falü tiaolie juan* (Encyclopaedia of Overseas Chinese and Ethnic Chinese: Laws and Regulations Volume). Beijing: Zhongguo Huaqiao chubanshe.

'Huaqiao Huaren baikequanshu, jiaoyu keji juan' bianji weiyuanhui "华侨华人百科全书，教育科技卷" 编辑委员会, eds. 1999. *Huaqiao Huaren baikequanshu, jiaoyu keji juan* (Encyclopaedia of Overseas Chinese and Ethnic Chinese: Education, Science, and Technology Volume). Beijing: Zhongguo Huaqiao chubanshe.

'Huaqiao Huaren baikequanshu, jingji juan' bianji weiyuanhui "华侨华人百科全书，经济卷"编辑委员会, eds. 2000. *Huaqiao Huaren baikequanshu, jingji juan* (Encyclopaedia of Overseas Chinese and Ethnic Chinese: Economics Volume). Beijing: Zhongguo Huaqiao chubanshe.

'Huaqiao Huaren baikequanshu, jingji juan' bianji weiyuanhui "华侨华人百科全书，经济卷"编辑委员会, eds. 2000. *Huaqiao Huaren baikequanshu, jingji juan* (Encyclopaedia of Overseas Chinese and Ethnic Chinese: Economics Volume). Beijing: Zhongguo Huaqiao chubanshe.

'Huaqiao Huaren baikequanshu, renwu juan' bianji weiyuanhui "华侨华人百科全书，人物卷"编辑委员会, eds. 2001. *Huaqiao Huaren baikequanshu, renwu juan* (Encyclopaedia of Overseas Chinese and Ethnic Chinese: Who's Who Volume). Beijing: Zhongguo Huaqiao chubanshe.

'Huaqiao Huaren baikequanshu, shequ minsu juan' bianji weiyuanhui "华侨华人百科全书, 社区民俗卷" 编辑委员会, eds. 2000. *Huaqiao Huaren baikequanshu, shequ minsu juan* (Encyclopaedia of Overseas Chinese and Ethnic Chinese: Communities and Customs volume). Beijing: Zhongguo Huaqiao chubanshe.

'Huaqiao Huaren baikequanshu, shetuan zhengdang juan' bianji weiyuanhui "华侨华人百科全书, 社团政党卷" 编辑委员会, eds. 1999. *Huaqiao Huaren baikequanshu, shetuan zhengdang juan* (Encyclopaedia of Overseas Chinese and Ethnic Chinese: Associations and Political Parties Volume). Beijing: Zhongguo Huaqiao chubanshe.

'Huaqiao Huaren baikequanshu, wenxue yishu juan' bianji weiyuanhui "华侨华人百科全书, 文学艺术卷" 编辑委员会, eds. 2000. *Huaqiao Huaren baikequanshu, wenxue yishu juan* (Encyclopaedia of Overseas Chinese and Ethnic Chinese: Literature and Art Volume). Beijing: Zhongguo Huaqiao chubanshe.

'Huaqiao Huaren baikequanshu, xinwen chuban juan' bianji weiyuanhui "华侨华人百科全书, 新闻出版卷" 编辑委员会, eds. 1999. *Huaqiao Huaren baikequanshu, xinwen chuban juan* (Encyclopaedia of Overseas Chinese and ethnic Chinese: Media and Publications Volume). Beijing: Zhongguo Huaqiao chubanshe.

Huaqiao jingji nianjian bianji weiyuanhui 华侨经济年鉴编辑委员会, eds. 1996. *Huaqiao jingji nianjian* (Overseas Chinese Economic Yearbook). Taibei: Qiaowu weiyuanhui.

Huaqiao zhi bianzuan weiyuanhui 华侨志编纂委员会, eds. 1979. *Huaqiao zhi (zong zhi)* (Annals of the Overseas China [General Section]). Taibei: Huaqiao zhi bianzuan weiyuanhui.

Huaren jingji nianjian bianji weiyuanhui 华人经济年鉴编辑委员会, eds. 1994. *Huaren jingji nianjian* (Yearbook of the Huaren Economy). Beijing: Zhongguo shehui kexue chubanshe.

Hubei sheng Tianmen shi difang zhi bianzuan weiyuanhui 湖北省天门市地方志编纂委员会, eds. 1989. *Tianmen xianzhi* (Tianmen gazetteer). Hubei renmin chubanshe.

Hudson, G. F. 1931. *Europe and China: A Survey of Their Relations from the Earliest Times to 1800*. London: Edward Arnold.

Hugill, Barry. 1997. 'Chinese Top UK Earnings.' *The Observer*, March 30.

Hune, Shirley, and Kenyon S. Chan. 1997. 'Special Focus: Asian Pacific American Demographic and Educational Trends.' In Deborah Carter and Reginald Wilson, eds, *Minorities in Higher Education*, Washington: American Council on Higher Education.

Huntington, Samuel P. 1996. *The Clash of Civilizations and the Remaking of World Order*. New York: Simon and Schuster.

Ibrahim, Abdul Latif Haji. 1981. *Hou Wang Miau: A Study of the Material Culture of the Chinese Temple, Atherton*. Graduate Diploma, Material Culture Unit, James Cook University of Northern Queensland.

Inden, Ronald. 1990. *Imagining India*. Oxford: Blackwell.

Inglis, Christine. 1967. *The Darwin Chinese: A Study in Assimilation*. MA thesis. Department of Sociology, Australian National University.

Inglis, Christine. 1998. 'Australia.' In Pan, ed., pp. 274–285.

Ip, David. 1999. 'The Asian Financial Crisis: Responses of Chinese Diaspora Capitalism.' *IIAS Newsletter*, no. 19 (June), p. 29.

Ip, Manying. 1998. 'New Zealand.' In Pan, ed., pp. 286–291.

Iredale, Robyn. 2000. *The Validity of Using Different Approaches to Assess the Training and Skills of Permanent and Temporary Professional Migrants*. Paper presented at the International Conference on Immigrant Societies and Modern Education, Singapore, August 31–September 3.

Isaacs, Harold R. 1961 [1938]. *The Tragedy of the Chinese Revolution*. Second revised edition. Stanford: Stanford University Press.

Jackson, Brian, and Anne Garvey. 1974. 'Chinese Children of Britain.' *New Society*, October 3.

Jenkinson, Jacqueline. 1986. 'The 1919 Race Riots in Britain: A Survey.' In Lotz and Pegg, eds, pp. 182–207.

Jiaoyu keji 教育科技. *See* 'Huaqiao Huaren baikequanshu, jiaoyu keji juan' bianji weiyuanhui, eds, 1999.

Jones, Douglas. 1979. 'The Chinese in Britain: Origins and Development of a Community.' *New Community*, vol. 7, no. 3, pp. 317–402.

Jones, D. 1987. 'The Chinese in Britain.' *New Community*, vol. 14, nos. 1–2, pp. 245–247.

Jones, James A. 1931. 'The Life of London's 190,000 Foreigners.' *Evening News*, April 11.

Jones, Trevor. 1993. *Britain's Ethnic Minorities: An Analysis of the Labour Force Survey*. London: Policy Studies Institute.

Kang Youwei 康有为. 1980 [1904]. *Ouzhou shiyi guo youji* (A Diary of Visits to Eleven European Countries). Changsha: Hunan renmin chubanshe.

Kao, John. 1993. 'The Worldwide Web of Chinese Business.' *Harvard Business Review*, March–April.

Kearney, Michael. 1991. 'Borders and Boundaries of State and Self at the End of Empire.' *Journal of Historical Sociology*, vol. 4, no. 1, pp. 52–74.

Kelso, Paul. 2000. 'Rise in Violence Aimed at Chinese Community.' *The Guardian*, April 12.

Khan, Naseem. 1978. *The Arts Britain Ignores: The Arts of Ethnic Minorities in Britain*. Second edition. London: Commission for Racial Equality.

Khoa, Le Huu. 1994. 'La presenza cinese a Parigi: Struttura comunitaria e reti di affinità.' In Campani et al., eds, pp. 149–182.

Kibria, Nazli. 2002. *Becoming Asian American: Second-Generation Chinese and Korean American Identities*. Baltimore: The Johns Hopkins University Press.

Kiernan, V. G. 1978. 'Britons Old and New.' In Holmes, ed., pp. 23–59.

King, Russell, and Nancy Wood, eds. 2001. *Media and Migration: Constructions of Mobility and Difference*. London: Routledge.

Kirk, Neville. 2003. *Comrades and Cousins: Globalization, Workers and Labour Movements in Britain, the USA and Australia from the 1880s to 1914*. London: Merlin.

Kitchen, Jonathan S. 1980. *The Employment of Merchant Seamen*. London: Croom Helm.

Kivisto, Peter. 2001. 'Theorizing Transnational Immigration: A Critical Review of Current Efforts.' *Ethnic and Racial Studies*, vol. 24, no. 4, pp. 549–577.

Kohn, Marek. 1992. *Dope Girls: The Birth of the British Drug Underground*. London: Lawrence and Wishart.

Kotkin, Joel. 1993. *Tribes: How Race, Religion, and Identity Determine Success in the New Global Economy*. New York: Random House.

Kwok Kian Woon. 1998b. 'Singapore.' In Pan, ed., pp. 200–217.

Lai, Amy D. Y. 1995. *Patterns of Chinese Immigration into Britain*. M.Phil. Faculty of Education, Manchester University.

Lai, Annie, Bob Little, and Pippa Little. 1986. 'Chinatown Annie: The East End Opium Trade 1920–35: The Story of a Woman Opium Dealer.' *Oral History Journal*, vol. 14, no. 1, pp. 18–30.

Lai, Him Mark. 1998. 'The United States.' In Pan, ed., pp. 261–273.

Lai, Walton Look. 1998. 'The Caribbean.' In Pan, ed., pp. 248–253.

Lakey, Jane. 1997. 'Neighbourhoods and Housing.' In Modood et al., pp. 184–223.

Lane, Tony. 1990. *The Merchant Seamen's War*. Manchester: Manchester University Press.

Lao She. 1991 [1935]. *Mr. Ma & Son: A Sojourn in London*. Translated by Julie Jimmerson. Beijing: Phoenix Books.

Larin, Alexander G. 1998. 'Chinese in Russia: An Historical Perspective.' In Benton and Pieke, eds, pp. 281–300.

Lau, Steve. 2002. *Chinatown Britain*. N. p.: Chinatown Online.

Law, Ian. 1981. *A History of Race and Racism in Liverpool, 1660–1950*. Liverpool: Merseyside Community Relations Council.

Lee, Gregory Barry. 1996. *Troubadours, Trumpeters, Troubled Makers: Lyricism, Nationalism and Hybridity in China and its Others*. London: Hurst.

Lee, Gregory Barry. 1998. 'Paddy's Chinatown: A Short (Hi)story of a Liverpool Hybridity.' *Interventions*, vol. 1 (1), pp. 97–124.

Lee, Keung Fu. 1993. *A Study on the Problems and Needs of the Chinese Teenagers in South Glamorgan*. MSc thesis. University of Wales, College of Cardiff.

Lee, Leo Ou-Fan. 1983. 'Literary Trends: The Road to Revolution, 1927–1949.' In John K. Fairbank and Albert Feuerwerker, eds, *The Cambridge History of China*, vol. 13, *Republican China, 1912–1949*, part 2, Cambridge: Cambridge University Press, pp. 452–504.

Lee, Tong Soon. Forthcoming. 'Cantonese Opera and the Chinese Diaspora in England.' In Helen Rees, ed., *Lives in Chinese Music*, Urbana: University of Illinois Press.

Leong Sow-Theng. 1997. *Migration and Ethnicity in Chinese History: Hakkas, Pengmin, and their Neighbors*. Stanford: Stanford University Press.

Leung Win. 2001. 'Ten Thousand Li.' *Point: Art and Design Research Journal*, autumn–winter, pp. 28–36.

Leung-Clifford, Dominique. 1989. *Expectation and Reality: An Investigation into the Educational Experience of Chinese Children in Liverpool in the 1980's*. MEd thesis. University of Liverpool.

Lever-Tracy, Constance, and Noel Tracy. 1999. 'The Three Faces of Capitalism and the Asian Crisis.' *Bulletin of Concerned Asian Scholars*, vol. 31, no. 3, pp. 3–16.

Lever-Tracy, Constance, David Ip, and Noel Tracy. 1996. *The Chinese Diaspora and Mainland China: An Emerging Economic Synergy*. London: Macmillan.

Levine, Marylin A. 1995. *The Found Generation: Chinese Communism in Europe, 1919–1925*. PhD thesis. University of Chicago.

Levine, Marilyn A. 1993. *The Found Generation: Chinese Communists in Europe During the Twenties*. Seattle: University of Washington Press.

Levine, Marilyn A., and Chen San-ching, eds. 2000. *The Guomindang in Europe: A Sourcebook of Documents*. Berkeley, University of California.

Li Changfu 李长傅. 1981 [1936]. *Zhongguo zhimin shi* (A History of Chinese Colonisation). Shanghai, 1936. Excerpted in Chen Hansheng, ed., pp. 111–143.

Li Enguo 李恩国. 2000a. *Li Enguo wen ji* (Li Enguo's Collected Papers). Taibei: Lü Ying zhonghuo xueshu jizhuan yexiehui.

Li Enguo 李恩国. 2000b. 'Zhonghua minguo xianfa yu Huaqiao canzhengquan (The Constitution of the Republic of China and the Right of Overseas Chinese to Participate). In Li Enguo 2000a, p. 339.

Li Enguo 李恩国. 2000c. 'Shang qiao weihui weiyuanzhang Mao Songnian shu' (A Letter to President of Overseas Committee Mao Songnian). In Li Enguo 2000a, p. 350.

Li, C. W. Louise. 1995. *Occupational Mobility/Diversity of Second Generation Chinese in Britain*. MSc thesis. University of Wales, College of Cardiff.

Li Minghuan 李明欢. 1995. *Dangdai haiwai Huaren shetuan yanjiu* (Studies in Contemporary Ethnic Chinese Associations Overseas). Xiamen: Xiamen daxue chubanshe.

Li Minghuan 李明欢. 1998a. Ouzhou Huaqiao Huaren gaikuang diaocha baogao (Report of an Investigation into the Situation of Overseas Chinese and Ethnic Chinese in Europe). Unpublished manuscript. Amsterdam.

Li Minghuan. 1998b. 'Transnational Links Among the Chinese in Europe: European-wide Chinese Voluntary Associations.' In Benton and Pieke, eds, pp. 21–41.

Li Minghuan. 1999a. *The Chinese Community in Europe*. Amsterdam: European Federation of Chinese Organisations.

Li Minghuan. 1999b. *'We Need Two Worlds': Chinese Immigrant Associations in a Western Society*. Amsterdam: Amsterdam University Press.

Li Pei 李佩. 2002 [1984]. 'Huainian Deng Fa tongzhi' (In Commemoration of Comrade Deng Fa). In 'Deng Fa jinian wenji' bianji bu, eds, pp. 116–118.

Li, Tana. 1998. 'Vietnam.' In Pan, ed., pp. 228–233.

Li Wei. 1993. 'Mother Tongue Maintenance in a Chinese Community School in Newcastle upon Tyne.' *Language and Education*, vol. 7, no. 3, pp. 199–215.

Li Wei. 1994. *Three Generations, Two Languages, One Family: Language Choice and Language Shift in a Chinese Community in Britain*. Clevedon: Multilingual Matters.

Li Wei. 1995. 'Variations in Patterns of Language Choice and Code-Switching by Three Groups of Chinese/English Speakers in Newcastle upon Tyne.' *Multilingua*, vol. 14, no. 3, pp. 297–323.

Li Weilin 李为麟, ed. 1988. *Huaqiao geming shi* (A Revolutionary History of the Overseas Chinese). Taibei: Zhengzhong shuju.

Li Yuan 李原 and Chen Dazhang 陈大璋, eds. 1991. *Haiwai Huaren jiqi juzhudi gaikuang.* (A General Account of Chinese Overseas and their Places of Residence). Beijing: Zhongguo Huaqiao chuban gongsi.

Lian Guan 连贯. 1981 [1978]. 'Huaqiao de lishi ji qi guangrong chuantong' (The History of the Overseas Chinese and their Glorious Tradition). *Renmin ribao*, April 13, 1978. Reprinted in Chen Hansheng, ed., *Huagong chu guo shiliao* (Historical Materials on the Emigration of Chinese Labourers), Beijing: Zhonghua shuju, 1981, vol. 4, pp. 108–110.

Liang, Tsong-heng, and Marie Holzman. 1989. *Chinois de Paris*. Paris: Éditions Seghers.

Liang Xiujing. 2001. *Exploring the Ethnic Identity of Overseas Chinese Community Leaders in Europe*. PhD thesis. Aalborg University.

Liang Xiujing and Flemming Christiansen. 1998. 'Chinese Pan-European Organizations.' In Pan, ed., pp. 88–89.

Liao Chengzhi 廖承志. 1991. 'Wo zai Ouzhou lingdao Zhongguo haiyuan jinxing zhengzhi douzheng' (My Leadership of the Chinese Seafarers' Political Struggle in Europe). In 'Shanghai haiyuan', eds, pp. 341–342.

Liao, Yi. 1992. *The Chinese Community in Greater Manchester*. MPhil thesis. University of Manchester.

Light, Ivan, and Edna Bonacich. 1988. *Immigrant Entrepreneurs: Koreans in Los Angeles, 1965–1982*. Berkeley: University of California Press.

Lim, Jessie, and Li Yan. 1994. *Another Province: New Chinese Writing from London. Tianwai you tian: Lundun Huaren xin xiezuo xuan*. London: Lambeth Chinese Community Association and *Siyu Chinese Times*.

Ling Wencheng 凌文城. 2001. 'Huiqing suixiang' (Thoughts About the Association Celebrations). In Yingguo Lundun Huaqiao huzhu gongtuan, eds, p. 38.

Little, Kenneth. L. 1947. *Negroes in Britain: A Study of Racial Relations in English Society*. London: Kegan Paul.

Little, Kenneth L. 1972. *Negroes in Britain: A Study of Racial Relations in English Society*. Second Revised edition. London: Routledge and Kegan Paul.

Liu, Garland. 1998. 'The Role of the True Jesus Church in the Communal Development of the Chinese People in Elgin, Scotland.' In Sinn, ed., pp. 425–446.

Liu, Garland Ching-Mui. 1992. *A Sociological Study of the Chinese People in Aberdeen and Elgin, With Special Reference to the Catering Business*. PhD thesis. Aberdeen University.

Liu Hanbiao 刘汉标, and Zhang Xinghan 张兴汉. 1994. *Shijie Huaqiao Huaren gaikuang (Ouzhou, Meizhou juan)* (The General Situation of Overseas Chinese and Ethnic Chinese Throughout the World [Europe and America Volume]). Guangzhou: Jinan daxue chubanshe.

Liu Jingquan 刘景泉. 1996. *Beijing minguo zhengfu de yihui zhengzhi* (The Parliamentary Politics of the Beijing Republican Government). Tianjin: Guji chubanshe.

Liu Weisen 刘伟森. 1999. *Sun Zhongshan yu Mei Jia Huaqiao* (Sun Yat-sen and the Overseas Chinese of North America). Taibei: Jindai Zhongguo chubanshe.

Liu Xiaoqin 刘晓琴. 2002. *Zhongguo jindai liu Ying jiaoyu yanjiu* (Research into the Education of Chinese Students in Britain in the Modern Period). PhD thesis. Nankai University.

Liu Yan 刘彦. 2001. *Hubei Tianmen ren yiju Nanyang shi* (A History of Tianmenese Migration to Southeast Asia). Kuala Lumpur: Malaixiya Hubei tongxianghui, Xinjiapo Nanyang Hubei Tianmen huiguan.

Live Yu-Sion. 1991. 'Immigration chinoise en France (1911–1975).' In Ng Yok-Soon, ed., pp. 107–111.

Live Yu-Sion. 1992. 'Les Chinois de Paris depuis le début du siècle: Présence urbaine et activités économiques.' *Revue Européenne des Migrations Internationales*, vol. 8, no. 3, pp. 155–173.

Live Yu-Sion. 1994. *Chinois de France: Un siècle de présences de 1900 à nos jours*. Paris: Éditions Mémoire Collective.

Live Yu-Sion. 1998a. 'The Chinese Community in France: Immigration, Economic Activity, Cultural Organization and Representations.' In Benton and Pieke, eds, pp. 96–124.

Live Yu-Sion. 1998b. 'France.' In Pan, ed., pp. 311–317.

Lo Wen Kan et al. 1925. *China's Case*. London: The Union of Chinese Associations.

London Office. 1971. *Annual Departmental Report, 1970–71*. Hong Kong: Government Printer.

London Office. 1972. *Annual Departmental Report, 1971–72*. Hong Kong: Government Printer.

London Office. 1973. *Annual Departmental Report, 1972–73*. Hong Kong: Government Printer.

London Office. 1974. *Annual Departmental Report, 1973–74*. Hong Kong: Government Printer.

Lotz, Rainer, and Ian Pegg. 1986a. 'Introduction.' In Lotz and Pegg, pp. 1–13.

Lotz, Rainer, and Ian Pegg, eds. 1986b. *Under the Imperial Carpet: Essays in Black History, 1780–1950*. Crawley: Rabbit Press.

Louie, Andrea. 2004. *Chineseness Across Borders: Negotiating Chinese Identities in China and the United States*. Durham: Duke University Press.

Lowe Chuan-hua. 1933. *Facing Labor Issues in China*. Shanghai: China Institute of Pacific Relations.

Lui, Mary Ting Yi. 2005. *The Chinatown Trunk Mystery: Murder, Miscegenation, and Other Dangerous Encounters in Turn-of-the-Century New York*. Princeton: Princeton University Press.

'Lundun tongxin, Ying Lun Huaqiao rexin guoshi zhi jingguo' 伦敦通信, 英伦华侨热心国事之经过 (London Bulletin, Overseas Chinese in London are Enthusiastic About National Affairs). 1922. *Shen bao*, vol. 177, January 16.

Luo Manhua 罗曼华, ed., 1981. *Huaren jiaohui shouce* (Chinese Churches Handbook). Hong Kong: Shijie Huaren fuyin shigong lianluo zhongxin.

Lyman, Stanford M. 1974. *Chinese Americans*. New York: Random House.

Lyman, Stanford M. 2000a. 'The "Chinese Question" and American Labor Historians.' *New Politics*, vol. 7, no. 4 (new series), whole no. 28.

Lyman, Stanford M. 2000b. 'Engels was Right! Organized Labor's Opposition to Chinese in America: A Rejoinder to Andrew Gyory.' *New Politics*, vol. 8, no. 1 (new series), whole no. 29.

Lynn, Irene Loh. 1982. *The Chinese Community in Liverpool: Their Unmet Needs with Respect to Education, Social Welfare and Housing*. Merseyside Area Profile Group, Department of Sociology, University of Liverpool.

Ma Chaojun 马超俊. 1959. Zhongguo laogong yundong shi (A History of the Chinese Labour Movement). 5 vols. Taibei: Zhongguo laogong fuli chubanshe.

Ma Honglin 马洪林. 1988. *Kang Youwei da zhuan* (Biography of Kang Youwei). Shenyang: Liaoning renmin chubanshe.

Ma, James. 1961. *Look Back in Hope*. Liverpool: Light and Salt Editorial Committees.

Ma, James, ed. 1961. *The Opening of the Chinese Seamen's Centre*. Liverpool: Chinese Seamen's Centre.

Ma Mung, Emmanuel. 1993. *The Chinese Entrepreneurship in France*. Paper presented at the International Symposium on Ethnic Chinese Economy, Shantou University, November 27–December 2.

Mackie, J. A. C. 1998. 'Overseas Chinese Organizations.' In Pan, ed., pp. 83–93.

MacKenzie, John M. 1999. 'Empire and Metropolitan Cultures.' In Porter, ed., pp. 270–293.

Majeed, Javed. 1992. *Ungoverned Imaginings: James Mill's The History of British India and Orientalism*. Oxford: Clarendon Press.

Malcolmson, Patricia E. 1986. *English Laundresses: A Social History, 1850–1930*. Urbana: University of Illinois Press.

Marger, Martin N. 1989. 'Asians in the Northern Ireland Economy.' *New Community*, vol. 15, no. 2, pp. 203–210.

Marger, Martin N. 1990. 'East Indians in Small Business: Middleman Minority or Ethnic Enclave?' *New Community*, vol. 16, no. 4, pp. 551–559.

Markus, Andrew. 1979. *Fear and Hatred: Purifying Australia and California, 1850–1901*. Sydney: Hale and Iremonger.

Martínez, Julia. 1999. *Plural Australia: Aboriginal and Asian Labour in Tropical White Australia, Darwin, 1911–1940*. PhD thesis. University of Wollongong.

Massey, Douglas, Rafael Alarcon, Jorge Durand, Humberto Gonzalez. 1987. *Return to Aztlan: The Social Process of International Migration from Western Mexico*. Berkeley: University of California Press.

May, J. P. 1973. *The British Working-Class and the Chinese, 1870–1911, with Particular Reference to the Seamen's Strike of 1911*. MA thesis. University of Warwick.

May, J. P. 1978. 'The Chinese in Britain, 1860–1914.' In Holmes, ed., pp. 111–124.

May, Roy, and Robin Cohen. 1974. 'The Interaction Between Race and Colonialism: A Case Study of the Liverpool race Riots of 1919.' *Race and Class*, vol. 16, no. 2, pp. 111–126.

McFarland, E. W. 1991. 'Clyde Opinion on an Old Controversy: Indian and Chinese Seafarers in Glasgow.' *Ethnic and Racial Studies*, vol. 14, no. 4 (October), pp. 493–515.

McKeown, Adam. 2001. *Chinese Migrant Networks and Cultural Change: Peru, Chicago, Hawaii, 1900–1936*. Chicago: Chicago University Press.

McManners, Hugh. 1998. 'Navy to Scrub its Chinese Laundries.' *The Sunday Times*, February 8.

Mei Weiqiang 梅伟强, and Zhang Guoxiong 张过雄, eds. 2001. *Wuyi Huaqiao Huaren shi* (A History of Overseas Chinese and Ethnic Chinese from Wuyi). Guangzhou: Guangdong gaodeng jiaoyu chubanshe.

Menski, Werner, ed. 1995. *Coping With 1997: The Reaction of the Hong Kong People to the Transfer of Power*. GEMS no. 2. Oakhill: Trentham.

Merriman, Nick, ed. 1993. *The Peopling of London: Fifteen Thousand Years of Settlement from Overseas*. London: Museum of London.

Metcalf, Hilary, Tariq Modood, and Satnam Virdee. 1997. *Asian Self-Employment: The Interaction of Culture and Economics in England*. London: Policy Studies Institute.

Miles, Robert. 1982. *Racism and Migrant Labour*. London: Routledge and Kegan Paul.

Milligan, Barry. 1995. *Pleasures and Pains: Opium and the Orient in Nineteenth-Century British Culture*. Charlottesville: University Press of Virginia.

Min Yifan 闵一帆. 1991. 'Wo zai haiyuan guoji ji Shanghai congshi haiyuan gongyun de huiyi' (Memoirs of Serving the Seafarers' Movement in the Seafarers' International and Shanghai). In 'Shanghai haiyuan', eds, pp. 351–362.

Mitchell, Katheryne. 1997. 'Transnational Subjects: Constituting the Cultural Citizen in the Era of Pacific Rim Capital.' In Ong and Nonini, eds, pp. 228–256.

Miyoshi, Masao. 1993. 'A Borderless World? From Colonialism to Transnationalism and the Decline of the Nation-State.' *Critical Inquiry*, vol. 19, no. 4, pp. 726–751.

Modood, Tariq. 1997a. 'Employment.' In Modood et al., pp. 83–149.

Modood, Tariq. 1997b. 'Culture and Identity.' In Modood et al., pp. 290–338.

Modood, Tariq. 1997c. ' "Difference", Cultural Racism and Anti-Racism.' In Werbner and Modood, eds, pp. 154–172.

Modood, Tariq, et al. 1997. *Ethnic Minorities in Britain: Diversity and Disadvantage.* London: Policy Studies Institute.

Mohun, Arwen P. 1999. *Steam Laundries: Gender, Technology, and Work in the United States and Great Britain, 1880–1940.* Baltimore: John Hopkins University Press.

Monitoring Group. 2000. *Baowei shequ, ziwei wuzui* (Defend the Community, Self-Defence is No Offence). February 6. London: N. p.

Monitoring Group. 2002. *The Launch of Min Quan and the First Annual Report.* April. London: N. p.

Montagu, Ashley. 1997. *Man's Most Dangerous Myth: The Fallacy of Race.* Sixth edition. Abridged student edition. Walnut Creek: AltaMira Press.

Moore, Robin J. 1999. 'Imperial India, 1858–1914.' In Porter, ed., pp. 422–446.

Muir, Hugh. 2004. 'Livingstone Looks East for New Chinatown.' *The Guardian,* May 1.

Mungello, D. E. 1999. *The Great Encounter of China and the West, 1500–1800.* Lanham: Rowman and Littlefield.

Murphy, Andrea. 1995. *From the Empire to the Rialto: Racism and Reaction in Liverpool, 1918–1948.* Birkenhead: Liver Press.

Murray, Charles Shaar. 2004. 'Samuel Chinque.' *The Guardian,* December 17.

Murray, Dian H. 1994. *The Origins of the Tiandihui: The Chinese Triads in Legend and History.* Stanford: Stanford University Press.

National Statistics Online. 2004. *Ethnicity and Identity.* January 8.

Newell, Venetia. 1989. 'A Note on the Chinese New Year Celebration in London and Its Socio-Economic Background.' *Western Folklore,* no. 48 (January), pp. 61–66.

Ng Kwee Choo. 1968. *The Chinese in London.* London: Oxford University Press.

Ng, Wing Chung. 1998. 'Canada.' In Pan, ed., pp. 234–247.

Ng Yok-Soon, ed. 1991. *Guide de la Communauté Chinoise en France (1991–1992).* Paris: Éditions les Cent Fleurs.

Nieto, Gladys. 2001. *Las asociaciones chino-españolas en la construcción de una comunidad imaginada.* PhD thesis. Universidad Autónoma de Madrid, Departamento de Antropología Social y Pensamiento Filosófico Español.

Nonini, Donald, and Aihwa Ong. 1997. 'Chinese Transnationalism as an Alternative Modernity.' In Ong and Nonini, eds, pp. 3–33.

Northrup, David. 1999. 'Migration from Africa, Asia, and the South Pacific.' In Porter, ed., pp. 88–100.

Nuffield Foundation. 1981. *Teaching Chinese Children: A Teacher's Guide.* London: Nuffield Foundation.

Nyíri, Pál. 1998. 'New Migrants, New Community: The Chinese in Hungary, 1989–1995.' In Benton and Pieke, eds, pp. 350–379.

Nyíri, Pál. 1999. *New Chinese Migrants in Europe: The Case of the Chinese Community in Hungary.* Aldershot: Ashgate.

Nyíri, Pál. 2000. From Class Enemies to Patriots: Overseas Chinese and Emigration Policy and Discourse in the People's Republic of China. Unpublished manuscript.

Nyíri, Pál, and Edgar van Lokven. 1999. 'The Chinese and the Problem of Organized Crime.' In European Federation of Chinese Organizations, ed., *The Chinese Community in Europe,* Amsterdam: EFCO, pp. 76–83.

O'Callaghan, Sean. 1978. *The Triads: The Mafia of the Far East*. London: Universal.

Okihiro, Gary. 1994. *Margins and Mainstreams: Asians in American History and Culture*. Seattle: University of Washington Press.

O'Leary, John, and Hannah Betts. 1999. 'Inspectors Accuse Schools of Racism.' *The Times*, March 11.

O'Neill, Julia A. 1972. *The Role of Family and Community in the Social Adjustment of the Chinese in Liverpool*. MA thesis. University of Liverpool.

Ong, Aihwa. 1997. 'Chinese Modernities: Narratives of Nation and Capitalism.' In Ong and Nonini, eds, pp. 171–202.

Ong, Aihwa. 1999. *Flexible Citizenship: The Cultural Logics of Transnationality*. Durham: Duke University Press.

Ong, Aihwa, and Donald M. Nonini. 1997a. 'Toward a Cultural Politics of Diaspora and Transnationalism.' In Ong and Nonini, eds, pp. 323–332.

Ong, Aihwa, and Donald M. Nonini, eds. 1997b. *Ungrounded Empires: The Cultural Politics of Modern Chinese Transnationalism*. London: Routledge.

Owen, Charlie. 2001. ' "Mixed Race" in Official Statistics.' In Parker and Song, eds, pp. 134–153.

Owen, David. 1994. *Chinese People and 'Other' Ethnic Minorities in Great Britain: Social and Economic Circumstances. 1991 Census Statistical Paper* no. 8. Coventry: Centre for Research in Ethnic Relations, University of Warwick.

Oxfeld, Ellen. 1998. 'India.' In Pan, ed., pp. 344–346.

Pairault, Thierry. 1995. *L'intégration silencieuse: La petite entreprise chinoise en France*. Paris: Éditions L'Harmattan.

Pan, Lynn. 1991. *Sons of the Yellow Emperor: The Story of the Overseas Chinese*. London: Mandarin.

Pan, Lynn, ed. 1998. *The Encyclopedia of the Chinese Overseas*. Singapore: Archipelago Press.

Panayi, Panikos. 1994. *Immigration, Ethnicity and Racism in Britain, 1815–1945*. Manchester: Manchester University Press.

Pang, Yuet Ngor Mary. 1993. *Catering to Employment Needs: The Occupations of Young Chinese Adults in Britain*. PhD thesis. University of Warwick.

Pang, Lai Chun. 1996. *An Investigation into the Social Structure of the Chinese Community in Belfast*. MPhil thesis. Department of Sociology and Social Policy, Queen's University, Belfast.

Parker, David. 1993. *The Cultural Identities of Young People of Chinese Origin in Britain*. PhD thesis. University of Birmingham.

Parker, David. 1994a. 'Encounters Across the Counter: Young Chinese People in Britain.' *New Community*, vol. 20, no. 4, pp. 621–634.

Parker, David. 1994b. *The Chinese in Britain: Annotated Bibliography and Research Resources. Bibliography in Ethnic Studies*, no. 12. Centre for Research in Ethnic Relations, University of Warwick.

Parker, David. 1995. *Through Different Eyes: The Cultural Identities of Young Chinese People in Britain*. Aldershot: Avebury.

Parker, David. 1998a. 'Chinese People in Britain: Histories, Futures and Identities.' In Benton and Pieke, eds, pp. 67–95.

Parker, David. 1998b. 'Emerging British Chinese Identities: Issues and Problems.' In Sinn, ed., pp. 91–114.

Parker, David. 1998c. 'Britain.' In Pan, ed., pp. 304–309.

Parker, David, and Miri Song, eds. 2001. *Rethinking 'Mixed Race'*. London: Pluto.

Parrott, Stuart. 1998. 'Facing a Chill Wind in the World's "Coolest City"'. *Asia Inc.*, November.

Peach, Ceri, ed. 1996. *Ethnicity in the 1991 Census*. Vol. 2. *The Ethnic Minority Populations of Great Britain*. London: HMSO.

Penrose, Edith T. 1980. *The Theory of the Growth of the Firm*. Oxford: Basil Blackwell.

Pieke, Frank N. 1987. 'De politiek van China ten aanzien van de Overzeese Chinezen.' In Benton and Vermeulen, eds, pp. 34–39.

Pieke, Frank N. 1998. 'Introduction.' In Benton and Pieke, eds, pp. 1–17.

Pieke, Frank N. 2000. Recent Trends in Chinese Migration to Europe: Fujianese Migration in Perspective. Unpublished paper.

Pieke, Frank N. 2001. Preliminary Findings and Policy Recommendations. ESRC Research project 'At the Margin of the Chinese World System: The Fuzhou Diaspora in Europe.' Unpublished paper.

Pieke, Frank N., and Hein Mallee. 1999. *Internal and International Migration: Chinese Perspectives*. London: Curzon.

Pieke, Frank N., Pál Nyíri, Mette Thunø, and Antonella Ceccagno. 2001. 'At the Margins of the Chinese World System: The Fuzhou Diaspora in Europe.' *Transnational Communities, Research Briefing* no. 4.

Pieke, Frank N., Pál Nyíri, Mette Thunø, and Antonella Ceccagno. 2004. *Transnational Chinese: Fujianese Migrants in Europe*. Stanford: Stanford University Press.

Pimentel, Benjamin. 2001. 'Model Minority Image is a Hurdle: Asian Americans Feel Left out of Mainstream.' *San Francisco Chronicle*. August 5.

Pineo, Huguette Ly-Tio-Fane. 1998. 'Mauritius.' In Pan, ed., pp. 351–355.

Pitson, Laura. 1999a. 'Characteristics of the Chinese Population in England.' In Sproston et al., pp. 3–24.

Pitson, Laura. 1999b. 'Social Contact and Social Support.' In Sproston et al., pp. 159–175.

Pitson, Laura. 1999c. 'Racial Harassment.' In Sproston et al., pp. 176–193.

Pitson, Laura, and Grahame Whitfield. 1999. 'Language.' In Sproston et al., pp. 25–44.

Planning Studies Group. 1994. *Ethnic Groups in Manchester*. Manchester: Manchester City Council.

Porter, Andrew, ed. 1999. *The Oxford History of the British Empire*, vol. III, *The Nineteenth Century*. Oxford: Oxford University Press.

Portes, Alejandro, and John Walton. 1981. *Labour, Class and the International System*. New York: Academic Press.

Portes, Alejandro, Luis E. Guarnizo, and Patricia Landolt. 1999. 'Introduction: Pitfalls and Promise of an Emergent Field.' *Ethnic and Racial Studies*, special issue, vol. 22, no. 2 (March), *Transnational Communities*, pp. 217–237.

Pratt, Sir John T. 1943. *China and Britain*. London: Collins.

Pries, Ludger. 2001. 'The Approach of Transnational Social Spaces: Responding to New Configurations of the Social and the Spatial.' In Ludger Pries, ed., *New Transnational Social Spaces*, London: Routledge, pp. 3–33.

Prior, Lindsay, See Beng Huat, Pang Lai Chun, and Michael Bloor. 1997. *The Health Needs and Health Promotion Issues Relevant to the Chinese Community in England*. Cardiff: School of Social and Administrative Studies, University of Wales, Cardiff.

Qin Baoqi 秦宝琦. 2000. *Hongmen zhenshi* (The True History of the Hongmen). Fuzhou: Fujian renmin chubanshe.

Qiu Qianmu 丘钱牧, ed. 1991. *Zhongguo zhengdang shi (1894–1949)* (A History of China's Political Parties [1894–1949]). Taiyuan: Shanxi renmin chubanshe.

Record of the Seminar Held Jointly Between Vietnamese Settlers and the Local Authorities. 1986. N. p.: N. p.

Redding, S. Gordon. 1990. *The Spirit of Chinese Capitalism.* Berlin: De Gruyter.

Redding, S. Gordon. 1996. 'Weak Organizations and Strong Linkages: Managerial Ideology and Chinese Family Business Networks.' In Hamilton, ed., pp. 27–40.

Report of the Commission Appointed by the City Council to Inquire into Chinese Settlements in Liverpool. 1906–1907. *Proceedings of the Council*, pp. 1739–1753.

Rinaldi, Fiori, and Peter Gillies. 1991. *Narcotic Offences.* Sydney: The Law Book Company.

Romeijn, Tina. 1987. 'De Man-lineage.' In Benton and Vermeulen, eds, pp. 77–83.

Roskill, S. W. 1962. *A Merchant Fleet in War: Alfred Holt & Co, 1939–1945.* London: Collins.

Said, Edward W. 1991. *Orientalism: Western Conceptions of the Orient.* Harmondsworth: Penguin.

Salter, J. 1895. *The East in the West or Work Among the Asiatics and Africans in London.* London: Partridge.

San Juan, E. 1999. 'From the Immigrant Paradigm to Transformative Critique: Asians in the Late Capitalist United States.' In Paul Wong, ed., pp. 34–54.

Saxton, Alexander. 1971. *The Indispensable Enemy: Labor and the Anti-Chinese Movement in California.* Berkeley: University of California Press.

Schak, David C. 2000. 'Networks and Their Uses in Taiwanese Society'. In Chan Kwok Bun, ed., *Chinese Business Networks: State, Economy and Culture*, Singapore: Prentice-Hall, pp. 112–128.

Scheffauer, Herman. 1911. 'The Chinese in England: A Growing National Problem.' *The London Magazine*, June, pp. 465–480, and July, pp. 644–657.

See, Chinben. 1988. 'Chinese Organizations and Ethnic Identity in the Philippines.' In Cushman and Wang, eds, pp. 319–334.

Shang, Anthony. 1984. *The Chinese in Britain.* Communities in Britain Series. London: Batsford Academic and Educational.

'Shanghai haiyuan gongren yundong shi' bianjibu "上海海员工人运动史" 编辑部, eds. 1991. *Shanghai haiyuan gongren yundong shi* (A History of the Shanghai Seafarers' Workers' Movement). Beijing: Zhonggong dangshi chubanshe.

Shanghai wenwu baoguan weiyuanhui 上海文物保管委员会, eds. 1995. *Lie guo youji: Kang Youwei yigao* (Diary of Travel in Various Countries: Draft Writings Left Behind by Kang Youwei). Shanghai: Shanghai renmin chubanshe.

Shen Guanbao 沈关宝, and Li Ling 李聆. 1998a. 'Yi sheng liuli, yisheng chou' (A Life on the Move, A Life of Anxiety). *Shehui*, no. 6, pp. 25–26, and no. 7, pp. 20–22.

Shen Guanbao 沈关宝, and Li Ling 李聆. 1998b. 'Wugen de piaobo' (A Rootless Wandering Life). *Shehui*, no. 8, pp. 36–38.

Shen Guanbao 沈关宝 and Li Ling 李聆. 1998c. 'Shengming shi yizhong yuan' (Is Life Predestined?) *Shehui*, no. 9, pp. 18–20.

Shequ minsu 社区民俗. *See* 'Huaqiao Huaren baikequanshu, shequ minsu juan' bianji weiyuanhui, eds, 2000.

Sherwood, Marika. 1991. 'Race, Nationality and Employment Among Lascar Seamen, 1660 to 1945.' *New Community*, vol. 17, no. 2, pp. 229–244.

Shetuan zhengdang 社团政党. *See* 'Huaqiao Huaren baikequanshu, shetuan zhengdang juan' bianji weiyuanhui, eds, 1999.

Shi Kangqiang 施康强. 1991. 'Zui zao da Faguode Zhongguoren' (The Earliest Chinese to Reach France). In Ng Yok-Soon, ed., p. 104.

Shum Kui-Kwong 1988. *The Chinese Communists' Road to Power: The Anti-Japanese National United Front, 1935–1945*. Hong Kong: Oxford University Press.

Simsova, Sylva, and Wey Tze Chin. 1985 [1982]. *Library Needs of Chinese in London*. School of Librarianship and Information Studies, Polytechnic of North London, Research report No. 9.

Sinn, Elizabeth, ed. 1998. *The Last Half Century of Chinese Overseas*. Hong Kong: Hong Kong University Press.

Siu, Helen F., and David Faure. 1995. 'Conclusion: History and Anthropology.' In Faure and Siu, eds, pp. 209–222.

Siu, Paul C. P. 1987. *The Chinese Laundryman: A Study of Social Isolation*. New York: New York University Press.

Sivanandan, A. 1982. *A Different Hunger: Writings on Black Resistance*. London: Pluto.

Siyi zonghuiguan 四邑总会馆, eds. 1986. *Siyi zonghuiguan bashi zhou nian jinian tekan, 1906–1986* (Special Publication on the Eightieth Anniversary of the Siyi Association, 1906–1986). Hong Kong: Ying Lun Siyi zonghuiguan.

Skeldon, Ronald, ed. 1994. *Reluctant Exiles? Migration from Hong Kong and the New Overseas Chinese*. Armonk: M. E. Sharpe.

Skeldon, Ronald. 1995a. 'Emigration from Hong Kong, 1945–1994: The Demographic Lead-up to 1997.' In Skeldon, ed., pp. 51–77.

Skeldon, Ronald, ed. 1995b. *Emigration from Hong Kong: Tendencies and Impacts*. Hongkong: The Chinese University Press.

Smith, Michael Peter, and Luis Eduardo Guarnizo, eds. 1998. *Comparative Urban and Community Research*, vol. 6, *Transnationalism from Below*. New Brunswick, NJ: Transaction Publishers.

Smith, Michael Peter, and Luis Eduardo Guarnizo, eds. 1999. *Transnationalism From Below*. New Brunswick, NJ: Transaction Publishers.

Song Chao 宋超, Shao Mingxi 邵名喜, and Tian Xiangdong 宋冠珍. 1985. *Zhongguo haiyuan yundong shihua* (A Narrative History of the Chinese Seafarers' Movement). Beijing: Renmin jiaotong chubanshe.

Song, Angela Miri. 1996. *Family, Work, and Cultural Identity: Children's Labor in Chinese Take-away Businesses in Britain*. PhD thesis. London School of Economics.

Song Guanzhen 宋冠珍. 1992. 'Huaren shetuan fazhan de sange qushi' (Three Trends in the Development of Chinese Associations). *Ouhua*, no. 6 (August), p. 5.

Song, Miri. 1995. 'Between the Front and the Back: Chinese Women's Work in Family Business.' *Women's Studies International Forum*, vol. 18, no. 3, pp. 285–298.

Song, Miri. 1997. ' "You're Becoming More and More English": Investigating Chinese Siblings' Cultural Identities.' *New Community*, vol. 23, no. 3, pp. 343–362.

Song, Miri. N. d. Belonging in Britain: The Second Generation Chinese in Britain. Unpublished paper.

Sproston, Kerry. 1999a. 'Health Status.' In Sproston et al., pp. 45–59.

Sproston, Kerry. 1999b. 'Heath Beliefs.' In Sproston et al., pp. 60–71.

Sproston, Kerry. 1999c. 'Use of Health Service.' In Sproston et al., pp. 72–98.

Sproston, Kerry. 1999d. 'Use of Traditional Chinese Medicine.' In Sproston et al., pp. 99–116.

Sproston, Kerry. 1999e. 'Physical Activity.' In Sproston et al., pp. 142–158.

Sproston, Kerry, Laura Pitson, Grahame Whitfield, and Errol Walker. 1999. *Health and Lifestyles of the Chinese Population in England*. London: Health Education Authority.

Stalker, Peter. 2000. *Workers Without Frontiers: The Impact of Globalization on International Migration*. London and Boulder, CO: Lynne Rienner.

Summerskill, Michael. 1982. *China on the Western Front: Britain's Chinese Work Force in the First World War*. London: Michael Summerskill.

Sun Yat-sen. 1897. *Kidnapped in London*. Bristol: Arrowsmith.

Sweet, Matthew. 2001. 'Victorian Values.' *Independent on Sunday*, October 21.

Sze, Szeming. 1931. *Chinese Students in Great Britain: A Lecture Before the China Society, London, November 21, 1930*. N. p.: The China Society, 1931, p. 10.

Tai, S. K. 1987. *Handbook of Chinese Organisations in South Glamorgan*. Cardiff: Cardiff Chinese Community Service Association.

Tam, Suk-Tak. 1998. 'Representations of "the Chinese" and "Ethnicity" in British Racial Discourse.' In Sinn, ed., pp. 81–90.

Tan Chee-Beng. 2000. 'Localization, Transnational Relations, and Chinese Religious Traditions.' In Ang See, ed., pp. 284–300.

Tan, Swee Poh, and Erica Wheeler. 1983. 'Concepts Relating to health and Food held by Chinese Women in London.' *Ecology of Food and Nutrition*, vol. 13, pp. 37–49.

Tang Hongjin. 1991. 'Aperçu sur la presse écrite en chinois dans les années 80 en France.' In Ng Yok-Soon, ed., pp. 130–132.

Tassinari, Alberto. 1994. 'L'immigrazione cinese in Toscana.' In Campani et al., eds, pp. 105–126.

Taylor, Monica J. 1987. *Chinese Pupils in Britain: A Review of Research into the Education of Pupils of Chinese Origin*. Windsor: NFER-NELSON.

Teff, Harvey. 1975. *Drugs, Society and the Law*. Farnborough: Saxon House.

Teltscher, Kate. 1995. *India Inscribed: European and British Writing on India, 1600–1800*. New Delhi: Oxford University Press.

Thunø, Mette. 1996. 'Chinese Emigration to Europe: Combining European and Chinese Sources.' *Revue Européenne des Migrations Internationales*, vol. 13, no. 2, pp. 63–79.

Thunø, Mette. 1997. *Chinese Migration to Denmark: Catering and Ethnicity*. PhD thesis. University of Copenhagen.

Thunø, Mette. 1998. 'Chinese in Denmark.' In Benton and Pieke, eds, pp. 168–196.

Tianjin shi renmin tushuguan 天津市人民图书馆, eds 1979. *Zhou Enlai tongzhi lü Ou wenji* (Comrade Zhou Enlai's European Articles). Beijing: Wenwu chubanshe.

Tianmen ren lüju haiwai shi bianzuan weiyuanhui 天门人旅居海外史编纂委员会, eds. 2001. *Tianmen ren lüju haiwai shi* (A History of Tianmenese Residing Overseas). Tianmen: Hubei sheng xinhua yinwu youxian gongsi.

Tie Zhuwei 铁竹伟. 1998. *Liao Chengzhi zhuan* (Biography of Liao Chengzhi). Beijing: Renmin chubanshe.

Tinker, Hugh. 1974. *A New System of Slavery: The Export of Indian Labour Overseas, 1830–1920*. London: Oxford University Press.

Tsagarousianou, Rosa. 2001. '"A Space Where One Feels at Home": Media Consumption Practices Among London's South Asian and Greek Cypriot Communities.' In King and Wood, eds, pp. 158–172.

Tu Wei-ming, ed. 1994. *The Living Tree: The Changing Meaning of Being Chinese Today*. Stanford: Stanford University Press.

Tupper, Edward. 1938. *Seamen's Torch: The Life Story of Captain Edward Tupper, National Union of Seamen*. London: Hutchinson.

Tyau, Min-ch'ien T. Z. 1920. *London through Chinese Eyes, or My Seven and a Half Years in London*. London: Swarthmore Press.

Verma, Gajendra, Yiu Man Chan, Christopher Bagley, Sylvia Sham, Douglas Darby, Derek Woodrow, and George Skinner. 1999. *Chinese Adolescents in Britain and Hong Kong: Identity and Aspirations*. Aldershot: Ashgate.

Vertovec, Steven. 1999a. 'Conceiving and Researching Transnationalism.' *Ethnic and Racial Studies*, special issue, vol. 22, no. 2 (March), *Transnational Communities*, pp. 447–462.

Vertovec, Steven. 1999b. 'Three Meanings of "Diaspora", Exemplified Among South Asian Religions.' *Diaspora*, vol. 6, no. 3, pp. 277–299.

Vertovec, Steven, and Robin Cohen. 1999a. 'Introduction.' In Vertovec and Cohen, eds, pp. xiii–xxviii.

Vertovec, Steven, and Robin Cohen, eds. 1999b. *Migration, Diasporas and Transnationalism*. Cheltenham: Elgar.

Virdee, Satnam. 1997. 'Racial Harassment.' In Modood et al., pp. 259–289.

Visram, Rozina. 2002. *Asians in Britain: 400 Years of History*. London: Pluto.

Wade, George A. 1900. 'The Cockney John Chinaman.' *The English Illustrated Magazine*, vol. 23, no. 202 (July), pp. 301–307.

Wah, Yung Yung, et al. 1996. *British Soil, Chinese Roots: Chinese Life in Britain*. Liverpool: Countywise.

Waldinger, Roger David, Howard Aldrich, Robin H. Ward, and associates. 1990. *Ethnic Entrepreneurs: Immigrant Business in Industrial Societies*. Newbury Park, CA: Sage.

Wales, Nym. 1945. *The Chinese Labor Movement*. New York: John Day.

Walker, Errol, and Hamid Rehman. 1999. 'Introduction.' In Sproston et al., pp. 1–2.

Waller, P. J. 1985. 'Immigration to Britain: The Chinese.' *History Today*, September, pp. 8–14.

Walvin, James. 1984. *Passage to Britain: Immigration in British History and Politics*. Harmondsworth: Penguin.

Wang Bowei 汪伯微. 1994. 'Lundun Zhongguocheng de da guanjia' (The Great Steward of London's Chinatown). *Ouhua*, no. 19 (August), pp. 8–9.

Wang Ching-Chun. 1941. *Japan's Continental Adventure*. With a preface by Lord Robert Cecil. New York: Macmillan.

Wang Gungwu. 1991. *China and the Overseas Chinese*. Singapore: Times Academic Press.

Wang Gungwu. 1994. 'Among Non-Chinese.' In Tu Wei-ming, ed., pp. 127–146.

Wang Gungwu. 1993. 'Greater China and the Chinese Overseas.' *The China Quarterly*, no. 136, December 1993, pp. 926–948.

Wang Gungwu. 1999. 'A Single Chinese Diaspora? Some Historical Reflections.' In Wang Gungwu and Annette Shun Wah, *Imagining the Chinese Diaspora: Two Australian Perspectives*. Canberra: Centre for the Study of the Chinese Southern Diaspora, pp. 1–17.

Wang Gungwu. 2000. *The Chinese Overseas: From Earthbound China to the Quest for Autonomy*. Cambridge, Mass.: Harvard University Press.

Wang Gungwu. 2004. 'Cultural Centres for the Chinese Overseas.' In Gregor Benton and Hong Liu, eds, *Diasporic Chinese Ventures: The Life and Work of Wang Gungwu*, London: Routledge, pp. 210–226.

Wang, Joan S.H. 1998. The Characteristics of Chinese Laundries in the Eastern United States, 1882–1943. Paper presented at the International Conference on the Ethnic Chinese, Manila, Philippines, November 22–28.

Wang, L. Ling-chi. 1994. 'Roots and the Changing Identity of the Chinese in the United States.' In Tu Wei-ming, ed., pp. 185–212.

Wang Ling-chi and Wang Gungwu, eds. 1998. *The Chinese Diaspora: Selected Essays*. 2 vols. Singapore: Times Academic.

Wang Lubin 王禄斌. 1996. 'Sun Zhongshan yu Huang Sande: Jianping Huang zhuan "Hongmen geming shi"' (Sun Yat-sen and Huang Sande: Including a Criticism of Huang's 'Revolutionary History of the Hongmen'). In Zhongshan daxue Sun Zhongshan yanjiu suo, eds, pp. 332–354.

Wang Qisheng 王奇生. 1995. *Liuxue yu jiuguo: Kangzhan shiqi haiwai xueren qunxiang* (Studying Abroad and Saving the Country: A Composite Image of Chinese Scholars Overseas During the Japanese War). Guilin: Guangxi shifan daxue chubanshe.

Wang, Xinyang. 2001. *Surviving the City: The Chinese Immigrant Experience in New York City, 1890–1970*. Lanham: Rowman and Littlefield.

Wang Yongxiang 王永祥, Kong Fanfeng 孔繁丰, and Liu Pinqing 刘品青. 1985. *Zhongguo gongchandang lü Ou zhibu shihua* (History of the European Branch of the Chinese Communist Party). Beijing: Zhongguo qingnian chubanshe.

Ward, Robin. 1987. 'Ethnic Entrepreneurs in Britain and Europe.' In Goffee and Scase, eds, pp. 83–103.

Ward, Robin. 1991. 'Economic Development and Ethnic Business.' In Curran and Blackburn, eds, pp. 51–67.

Ward, Robin, and Richard Jenkins, eds. 1984. *Ethnic Communities in Business: Strategies for Economic Survival*. Cambridge: Cambridge University Press.

Watson, James L. 1974. 'Restaurants and Remittances: Chinese Emigrant Workers in London.' In George M. Foster and Robert V. Kemper, eds, *Anthropologists in Cities*, Boston: Little, Brown and Company, pp. 201–222.

Watson, James L. 1975. *Emigration and the Chinese Lineage: The Mans in Hong Kong and London*. Berkeley: University of California Press.

Watson, James L. 1977a. 'Introduction: Immigration, Ethnicity, and Class in Britain.' In Watson, ed., pp. 1–19.

Watson, James L. 1977b. 'The Chinese: Hong Kong Villagers in the British Catering Trade.' In Watson, ed., pp. 181–213.

Watson, James L., ed. 1977c. *Between Two Cultures: Migrants and Minorities in Britain*. Oxford: Blackwell.

Watson, James L. 2004. 'Presidential Address: Virtual Kinship, Real Estate, and Diaspora Formation – the Man Lineage Revisited.' *Journal of Asian Studies*, vol. 63, no. 4, pp. 893–910.

Weidenbaum, Murray, and Samuel Hughes. 1996. *The Bamboo Network*. New York: The Free Press.

Wen Hongzhong. 温宏忠. 1997. 'Yuanlao xinsheng' (A Veteran's Column). In Yingguo gonghe xiehui, eds, p. 41.

Wen Liangsheng 文良生. 2001. 'Pijing zhanji, yi wang zhi qian' (Hacking One's Way Through Difficulties, Always Onwards). In Yingguo Lundun Huaqiao huzhu gongtuan, eds, p. 41.

Werbner, Pnina. 1997. 'Introduction: The Dialectics of Cultural Hybridity.' In Werbner and Modood, eds, pp. 1–26.

Werbner, Pnina, and Tariq Modood, eds. 1997. *Debating Cultural Hybridity: Multi-Cultural Identities and the Politics of Anti-Racism.* London: Zed Books.

Whitley, Richard. 1992. *Business Systems in East Asia: Firms, Markets and Societies.* London: Sage.

Whitley, William T. 1928. *Artists and Their Friends in England, 1700–1800.* 2 vols. New York: Benjamin Blom.

Whittingham-Jones, Barbara. 1944. *China Fights in Britain: A Factual Survey of a Fascinating Colony in Our Midst.* London: Allen and Co.

Whittingham-Jones, Barbara. 1982 [1944]. 'Influx of Chinese Seamen and University Students into Liverpool Creates a New Chinatown.' *Illustrated*, April 17. Reproduced in Lynn, pp. 85–87.

Whyte, Martin King. 1996. 'The Chinese Family and Economic Development: Obstacle or Engine?' *Economic Development and Cultural Change*, vol. 45, no. 1, pp. 1–30.

Wickberg, Edgar. 1998. 'Relations with Non-Chinese.' In Pan, ed., pp. 114–121.

Wil, Pierre-Étienne. 1995. 'Préface.' In Pairault, pp. 9–13.

Williams, Frederick Wells. 1912. *Anson Burlingame and the First Chinese Mission to Foreign Powers.* New York: Charles Scribner's Sons.

Willmott, W. E. 1998. 'The South Pacific.' In Pan, ed., pp. 292–296 and 299–302.

Wolski, Claudia. 1994. *Amerikanische Politik in China, 1861–1870: Anson Burlingame und die erste chinesische Gesandschaft in den Westen, unter Berücksichtigung ihres Aufenthalts in Berlin. Chinathemen* vol. 79. Bochum: Universitätsverlag.

Wong, Bernard P. 1982. *Chinatown: Economic Adaptation and Ethnic Identity of the Chinese.* Fort Worth: Holt, Rinehart and Winston.

Wong, Brenda. 1992. *'The Silent Minority': A Study of the Chinese Community and Culture Dynamics in Britain.* N. p.: N. p.

Wong, Loong. 2001. 'Who am I?': The Chinese, Diaspora and the Internet. Paper presented at the International Conference on Migrating Identities, Australian National University, September 26–28.

Wong, Lornita Yuen-Fan. 1992. *Education of Chinese Children in Britain: A Comparative Study with the USA.* Clevedon: Multilingual Matters.

Wong, Maria Lin. 1989. *Chinese Liverpudlians: A History of the Chinese Community in Liverpool.* Birkenhead: Liver Press.

Wong, Paul, ed. 1999. *Race, Ethnicity, and Nationality in the United States: Toward the Twenty-First Century.* Boulder: Westview.

Wong Siu-lun. 1985. 'The Chinese Family Firm: A Model.' *British Journal of Sociology*, vol. 36, no. 1, pp. 58–72.

Wu, David Y. H. 2002a. 'Improvising Chinese Food Overseas.' In Wu and Cheung, eds, pp. 56–66.

Wu, David Y. H. 2002b. 'Cantonese Cuisine (*Yue-cai*) in Taiwan and Taiwanese Cuisine (*Tai-cai*) in Hong Kong.' In Wu and Cheung, eds, pp. 86–99.

Wu, David Y. H., and Sidney C. H. Cheung, eds. 2002. *The Globalization of Chinese Food.* Richmond: Curzon.

Wu Lehua 巫乐华, ed. 1994. *Huaqiao shi gaiyao* (A General History of the Overseas Chinese). Beijing: Zhongguo Huaqiao chubanshe.

Wu Ming 吴名. 1994. 'Yingguo gaikuang' (The General Situation in England). *Ouhua*, no. 19 (August), p. 13.

Wu Qiuyu 巫秋玉. 1999. 'Ronghe yihuo youli: Ju Ying Xianggang Huaren de wenhua shiying' (Assimilation or Dissociation: The Cultural Adaptation of Hong Kong Ethnic Chinese Residing in the United Kingdom). In Zhong Hanbo and Zhang Yinglong, eds, pp. 188–208.

Wu Shaobao. 1957. *Ouyou hongzhao* (Travels in Europe). Singapore: Nanyang shangbao she.

Wubben, Henk J. J. 1986. *'Chineezen en Ander Aziatisch Ongedierte': Lotgevallen van Chinese Immigranten in Nederland, 1911–1940* ('Chinese and Other Asian Vermin': The Vicissitudes of Chinese Immigrants in the Netherlands, 1911–1940). Zutphen: De Walburg.

Wusijiluofu [V. M. Ustinov] 乌斯季洛夫. 1997. 'Zai Suweiai Eguo de Huaren gongchan zhuyi zuzhi' (Chinese Communist Organisation in Soviet Russia). In Zhonggong zhongyang dangshi yanjiushi diyi yanjiubu, eds, pp. 28–39.

Xinwen chuban 新闻出版. *See* 'Huaqiao Huaren baikequanshu, xinwen chuban juan' bianji weiyuanhui, eds, 1999.

Xu Bin 徐斌. 1957. *Ouzhou Huaqiao jingji* (The Overseas Chinese Economy in Europe). Second edition. Taibei: Haiwai chubanshe.

Xu Xiaosheng 许肖生. 1987. 'Ouzhou Huaqiao kang Ri jiuguo zuzhi he quan Ou Huaqiao kang Ri jiu guo lianhe hui' (The European Overseas Chinese' Organisation and Their Pan-European anti-Japanese National-Salvation Joint Conferences). *Qiaoshi ziliao* no. 3, pp. 8–12.

Xu Xiaosheng 许肖生. 1993. *Huaqiao yu diyici guogong hezuo* (The Overseas Chinese and the First United Front). Guangzhou: Jinan daxue chubanshe.

Xu Zhiwei 許智偉. 1991. *Danmai, Nuowei, Ruidian Huaqiao gaikuang* (A General survey of the Overseas Chinese in Denmark, Norway, and Sweden).Taibei: Zhengzhong shudian.

Yang Qingyun 杨青云. 1996. 'Lü Ying Huaren kan "Ou meng" ' (The 'European Union' in the Eyes of Britain's Ethnic Chinese). In You Hailong, ed., pp. 36–38.

Yang Xianyi. N. d. Memoirs. Unpublished manuscript.

Yang Xianyi. 1991. *Da mandarino a compagno* (From Mandarin to Comrade). Tr. Paola Fiore. Turin: Nuova Eri.

Yao Shun 姚舜. 1988. *Xi De, Aodili, Ruishi Huaqiao gaikuang* (The General Situation of the Overseas Chinese in West Germany, Austria, and Switzerland). Haiwai Huaren qingshaonian congshu. Taibei: Zhengzhong shudian.

Yarwood, Alexander T. 1967. *Asian Migration to Australia*. Second edition. Melbourne: Melbourne University Press.

Yarwood, Alexander T., and Michael J. Knowling. 1982. *Race Relations in Australia: A History*. North Ryde: Methuen Australia.

Ye, Marie. 1989. *Chinese Elderly in Westminster*. N. p.: N. p.

Yeh, Diana. 2001. 'A Number Six, Please.' *Eastern Art Report on Line: The International Magazine of the Visual Arts*.

Yeung, Henry W. C., and Kris Olds, eds. 2000. *Globalization of Chinese Business Firms*. Basingstoke: Macmillan.

Yi Jia'ou. 1946. 'Gei yiwei Yingguoji Zhongguo nülang de xin' (Letter to a Chinese Girl with British Citizenship). *Chung Hwa Chou Pao*, no. 115, September 19.

Yi Shan 伊山. 1992. 'Yingguo Huabu lüeying' (A Brief Sketch of England's Chinatown). *Ouhua*, no. 6 (August), pp. 6–9.

Ying Zhi 颖之. 1980. *Zhongguo jindai liuxue jianshi* (A Brief History of Chinese Studying Abroad). Shanghai: Shanghai jiaoyu chubanshe.

Yingguo gonghe xiehui 英国共和协会, eds, 1997. *Yingguo gonghe xiehui wushi zhounian jinian tekan* (Special Publication on the 50th Anniversary of the UK Kung Ho Association). London: Yingguo gonghe xiehui.

Yingguo Lundun Huaqiao huzhu gongtuan 英国伦敦华侨互助工团, eds, 2001. *Yingguo Lundun Huaqiao huzhu gongtuan chengli bashiwu zhounian jinian tekan* (Special Publication on the 85th Anniversary of the Establishment of the UK London Overseas Chinese Mutual Aid Workers' Club). London: N. p.

Yip, Alethea. 1997. 'All Things Being Equal….' *AsianWeek*. September 5–11.

You Hailong 游海龙, ed. 1996. *Yingguo Huaqiao shouce* (The Overseas Chinese in Britain: A Handbook). London: Xingdao Zhongguo shiye (Yingguo) youxian gongsi.

You Hailong 游海龙, ed. 2001. *Yingguo Huaren zonglan, xin jiyuan* (The Ethnic Chinese in Britain, New Era). London: Ya Mei qiye youxian gongsi.

Yu Jianzhang. 1991. 'Bu dong Zhongwen de Zhongguoren?' (Chinese Who Don't Understand Chinese?). *Ouhua*, trial issue (August 25), pp. 5–7.

Yu, Renqiu. 1992. *To Save China, To Save Ourselves: The Chinese Hand Laundry Alliance of New York*. Philadelphia: Temple University Press.

Yuan, Tung-li. 1963. 'Doctoral Dissertations by Chinese Students in Great Britain and Northern Ireland, 1916–1961.' *Chinese Culture*, vol. 4, no. 4 (March).

Zeng, J. 1997. 'When East meets West: Mainland Chinese Students and Scholars in UK Higher Education Institutions.' *Journal of International Education*, vol. 7, no. 3.

Zeng Jize 曾纪泽. 1985. *Shi xi riji* (Diary of an Embassy to the West). Changsha: Hunan renmin chubanshe.

Zeng Ruiyan 曾瑞炎. 1988. *Huaqiao yu kang Ri zhanzheng*. Chengdu: Sichuan daxue chubanshe.

Zhang Daofan 张道藩. 1962. 'Suantian kula de huiwei' (Remembering Life's Joys and Sorrows). *Zhuanji wenxue*, Taibei, vol. 1, no. 6, p. 41.

Zhang Longxi. 1988. 'The Myth of the Other: China in the Eyes of the West.' *Critical Inquiry*, no. 15, pp. 108–131.

Zhang Ningjing 张宁静. 1988. *Faguo Huaqiao gaikuang* (The General Situation of the Overseas Chinese in France). Haiwai Huaren qingshaonian congshu. Taibei: Zhengzhong shuju.

Zhang Yunfeng 张云枫 et al. 1992. *Yingguo Huaqiao Huaren shenghuo shouce* (The Life of Overseas Chinese and Ethnic Chinese in Britain: A Handbook). Hongkong: Wenhui bao.

Zhao, Xiaojian. 2002. *Remaking Chinese America: Immigration, Family, and Community, 1940–1965*. New Brunswick, New Jersey: Rutgers University Press.

Zheng Zhuying 郑珠樱. 2001. 'Huiyi' (Memoir). In Yingguo Lundun Huaqiao huzhu gongtuan, eds, p. 39.

Zhong Hanbo 钟汉波 and Zhang Yinglong 张应龙, eds. 1999. *Guangdong qiaoshi luncong* (Collection of Articles on the History of Overseas Chinese from Guangdong). vol. 1. Hong Kong: Rongyu chuban youxian gongsi.

Zhong Shuhe 钟叔河, ed. 1989. *Cong dongfang dao xifang: Zou xiang shijie congshu xulun ji* (From East to West: Reviewing a Series of Books About the World). Shanghai: Shanghai renmin chubanshe.

Zhongshan daxue Sun Zhongshan yanjiusuo 中山大学孙中山研究所, eds. 1996. *Sun Zhongshan yu Huaqiao: 'Sun Zhongshan yu Huaqiao' xueshu taolunhui wenji* (Sun Yat-sen and the overseas Chinese: Collected papers of the 'Sun Yat-sen and the Overseas Chinese' Academic Conference). *Sun Zhongshan yanjiu luncong* (Sun Yat-sen Research Series) no. 13. Guangzhou: Zhongshan daxue chubanshe.

Zhou Nanjing 周南京, ed. 1993. *Shijie Huaren Huaqiao cidian* (World Dictionary of Overseas Chinese). Beijing: Beijing daxue chubanshe.

Zhou Yi 周弈. 2002. *Xianggang zuopai douzheng shi* (A History of the Struggle of the Hong Kong Leftists). Third (revised) edition. Hong Kong: Liwen chubanshe.

Zhou Yi 周弈, ed. 2004. *Xianggang yingxiong ernü: Dongjiang zongdui Gang Jiu dadui kang Ri zhanshi* (Hong Kong's Heroic Sons and Daughters: A Military History of the Resistance to Japan by the Hong Kong-Kowloon Battalion of the Dongjiang Column). Hong Kong: Liwen chubanshe.

Zhou Yumin 周育民, and Shao Yong 邵雍. 1993. *Zhongguo banghui shi* (A History of China's Secret Societies). Shanghai: Renmin chubanshe.

Zhu Xuefan 朱学范. 2002 [1979]. 'Deng Fa tongzhi he wo cong Bali dao Shanghai' (How Comrade Deng Fa and I Went from Paris to Shanghai). In 'Deng Fa jinian wenji' bianji bu, eds, pp. 107–115.

Zhuang Guotu. 1998. 'Relations with China.' In Pan, ed., pp. 98–103.

Zia, Helen. 2000. *Asian American Dreams: The Emergence of an American People.* New York: Farrar, Straus, and Giroux.

Zou Xiaozhan 邹小站. 2001. *Zhang Shizhao shehui zhengzhi sixiang yanjiu, 1903–1927* (Researches into Zhang Shizhao's Social and Political Thought, 1903–1927). Changsha: Hunan jiaoyu chubanshe.

Index

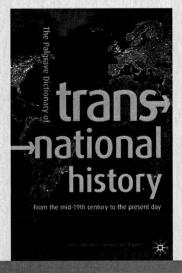

Plate 1 Portrait of Shen Fuzong (1687), probably Britain's first Chinese visitor by Sir Godfrey Kneller (1646–1723). The Royal Photograph Collection.

Plate 2 Chitqua (fifth from left) in a portrait by Zoffany, late eighteenth century. The Royal Photograph Collection.

Plate 3 Limehouse Chinatown, early twentieth century. From Anthony Shang, *Chinese in Britain* (London: B.T. Batsford Ltd, 1982).

Plate 4 A Hubeinese family in Europe, bound for the United States at around the turn of the twentieth century. Reproduced with permission of Pam So.

Plate 5 A Chinese immigrant family from Tianmen, Hubei, 1915. Reproduced with permission of Pam So.

Plate 6 Chee Kung Tong in Limehouse, 1926–1928.

Plate 7 Current Headquarters of the Chee Kung Tong or Chinese Freemasons, Liverpool. Photograph by Song Yingxian, reproduced with permission.

Plate 8 Philip Noel Baker, MP, and Mrs Atlee, wife of the Labour leader, in a poster parade, February 1938. From Arthur Clegg, *Aid China: A Memoir of a Forgotten Campaign* (Beijing: Foreign Languages Press, 1992).

Plate 9 Chinese children in Leicester support an anti-Japanese demonstration, July 1939. From Clegg, *Aid China*.

Plate 10 Ai-leen Tai, dancing for the China Campaign Committee, 1938. From Clegg, *Aid China*.

Plate 11 Sam Chen, wartime seafarers' leader, and his daughter Anna Chen, a British Chinese artist and performer. Reproduced with permission of Anna Chen.

Plate 12 (Left to right) Deng Fa (CCP emissary to the Chinese seafarers), Chen Jiahang, and Sam Chen (Liverpool Chinese seafarers' leader), 23 November 1945. Reproduced with permission of Anna Chen.

Plate 13 Deng Fa, 'mentor' of the Liverpool Chinese seafarers, in his Yan'an days, when he was Mao's chief security officer. From Edgar Snow, *Red Star Over China*, reproduced with permission from Lois Wheeler Snow.

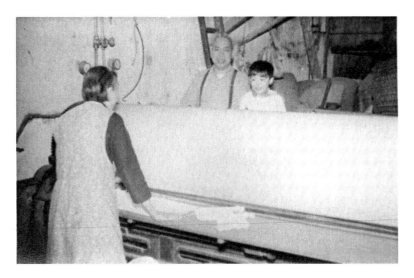

Plate 14 Chinese laundry, 1949. Courtesy of Frank Soo.

Plate 15 Frank Soo and a school friend outside the family laundry, 1949. Courtesy of Frank Soo.

Plate 16 A Chinese family outside a restaurant, 1952.

Plate 17 First Chinese restaurant in Cheltenham, 1957. Courtesy of Frank Soo.

Plate 18 Opera performers, Camden (London), Chinese Community Centre, 1983. From Shang, *Chinese in Britain*.

Plate 19 Current Headquarters of Liverpool's Say Yap Association. Photograph by Song Yingxian, reproduced with permission.

Plate 20 Chinese takeaway, Castell Newydd Emlyn, Ceredigion, 2007. Photograph by Jane Evans, reproduced with permission.

Plate 21 Newport Street in London's Chinatown. Photograph by Tom Ying-Leung Cheung, reproduced with permission.

Plate 22 Liverpool's Chinatown arch. Photograph by Song Yingxian, reproduced with permission.

Plate 23 The 'Aroma' Restaurant, Chinatown, London. Photograph by Tom Ying-Leung Cheung, reproduced with permission.

Plate 24 A medical centre in London's Chinatown. Photograph by Tom Ying-Leung Cheung, reproduced with permission.